Commentary on the Pentateuch

Henry Downing, Otto von Gerlach

BIBLIOLIFE

Copyright © BiblioLife, LLC

This historical reproduction is part of a unique project that provides opportunities for readers, educators and researchers by bringing hard-to-find original publications back into print at reasonable prices. Because this and other works are culturally important, we have made them available as part of our commitment to protecting, preserving and promoting the world's literature. These books are in the "public domain" and were digitized and made available in cooperation with libraries, archives, and open source initiatives around the world dedicated to this important mission.

We believe that when we undertake the difficult task of re-creating these works as attractive, readable and affordable books, we further the goal of sharing these works with a global audience, and preserving a vanishing wealth of human knowledge.

Many historical books were originally published in small fonts, which can make them very difficult to read. Accordingly, in order to improve the reading experience of these books, we have created "enlarged print" versions of our books. Because of font size variation in the original books, some of these may not technically qualify as "large print" books, as that term is generally defined; however, we believe these versions provide an overall improved reading experience for many.

COMMENTARY

ON

THE PENTATEUCH.

Translated from the German of

OTTO VON GERLACH.

BY

REV. HENRY DOWNING,
INCUMBENT OF ST. MARY'S, KINGSWINFORD.

PHILADELPHIA:
SMITH, ENGLISH & CO.
EDINBURGH. T. & T. CLARK
1860.

PREFACE.

The life of the author of the following "Bible work," as it is called, or explanation of the Bible, offers very little that will be interesting to the general reader. It was not, in the usual sense of the word, at all an eventful life, being that of a studious hardworking German Pastor in Berlin.

Otto Von Gerlach was born in that capital in 1801. His mother belonged to the family of Von Raumer. His father's family originally came from Pomerania. For three generations his ancestors had held offices under government. Otto was the youngest of four. He studied at the Universities of Berlin, Heidelberg, and Gottingen, as it is usual in Germany for students to attend more than one university. For some time the study of jurisprudence engaged Von Gerlach's attention; but, after a while, he devoted himself entirely to theology. He attended the lectures of Schleiermacher, then in the zenith of his influence, and also of Neander, Marheineke, and Hengstenberg. After the completion of his university studies, he hesitated whether he should follow the vocation of a professor, or that of a parochial clergyman. He determined on the latter, though he delivered some lectures in Berlin on ecclesiastical law and history, and on the interpretation of Scripture. His publication in Germany of a translation of Baxter's "Saints' Rest" and "Reformed Pastor," had attracted to him the attention of the King. He was ordained in 1835, and appointed to the lately consecrated Elizabeth Church. In this post he remained, devoting himself indefatigably to his pastoral duties and to study, until 1847, when he was nominated Preacher at the Dom (Cathedral). In 1849 the third portion of his work on the Holy Scriptures appeared. He had devoted great part of his life to its preparation; but he did not survive to complete it. He died in the October of the same year.

This Scripture Commentary bears a high character in its own country. It has passed through several editions, and is regarded as a standard work of its kind. The notes of Von Gerlach cannot be called learned. They do not make pretension to such a character. The work is rather of a popular than a scientific caste. It is intended to help towards the profitable devout reading of Holy Scripture; and the author of the annotations never loses sight of the practical application of the text, and yet the notes will be found to condense a great amount of Scriptural knowledge, as a patient reader who will examine them carefully is sure to find. The general meaning and bearing of different passages are usually explained with sufficient fulness.

The portion of the work chosen for translation is the Pentateuch, which has been selected chiefly because commentaries in English on this part of Scripture are less accessible than on other books of the Bible. Should the present translation of the notes on the Book of Moses be considered useful, a version of those on the Minor Prophets will next appear. These latter deal rather more in explanation than those on the Pentateuch; but, it is believed, few will use the notes of Von Gerlach in their study of the Bible, without finding their knowledge of God's word enlarged.

The Translator may be allowed to add, as some proof of the estimation in which the work is held by Germans themselves, that Professor Ranke recommended it to him as a Bible commentary which deserved to be better known by all educated Englishmen.

December 1859.

INTRODUCTION

TO THE

SCRIPTURES OF THE OLD TESTAMENT,

MORE PARTICULARLY TO

THE BOOKS OF MOSES.

The belief in a redemption of mankind, which is the soul and support of the Christian Church, must have its essential origin in a revelation of the Divine love and wisdom. The invisible existence of God, "His eternal power and godhead," so far as man can have a conception thereof, may indeed be seen from His works; but the mirror of the Divine image in the human soul, which had been marred by sin, had not the power of reflecting with clearness the illumination which had been received from thence. As the Divine life is the light of His creatures, so was there needed some working on God's part, which should renew, awaken, strengthen, as well as enlighten the whole man, in order to lead him back to his sublimely exalted destiny. This work on God's part is Revelation,—a history of God's doings for man's redemption from the very beginning of the human race to its completion,—a history which, the farther it proceeds, shall in the same proportion explain itself by the Word which accompanies it. It shows us how the condescension of God vouchsafed, from the very beginning, to deal with man after a manner intelligible to man; to speak to him after a human fashion; and, while it appeared to single out some individuals for preference, and to be completely occupied in some particular portion above the rest, nevertheless kept in view the grand connection by which each portion was united in one majestic whole.

But what God had done for man, and spoken to him, needed abiding record in *Scripture* in order to be retained by man. Had God's almighty power redeemed a people from the darkness and bondage of Egyptian heathenism, and then by His law united that people into one community,—had Christ enlightened His disciples, and sent them out into the world to preach His Gospel, and to found His Church, without affording the written witness of His will and love in a Law and a Gospel—then, indeed, must God's people and kingdom on earth have been deprived of His immediate guidance. The Church might be established without the written Word; but it could not continue in existence without the ever pure and fresh life-giving stream of that Word.

Accordingly, the Lord Himself wrote the Ten Commandments on tables of stone, and Moses collected all the memorable events and laws in a Book, which was laid up " in the side of the ark of the covenant of the Lord" (*vide* Deut. xxxi. 26). We find, at a later period, that Joshua added the history of his own life to the Book of the Law (*vide* Joshua xxiv. 26); that Samuel laid up " before the Lord," for preservation, a description of the privileges of the kingdom (1 Sam. x. 25); that one of the greatest of the prophets, Isaiah (chap. xxxiv. 16), even laid an injunction on his descendants, that they should read in the " Book of the Lord" his own prophecies. We find that, after a long period of national degradation under kings and priests, the Book of the Covenant was discovered in the House of the Lord, in the days of Josiah, 2 Kings xxiii. 2. Thus were the laws, the histories, and the prophecies, that had been divinely attested, already in ancient times laid up for preservation in the Sanctuary, where, indeed, they often remained closed, an unvalued treasure; still they had from time to time a reviving and renovating effect on the Church of God. When the people returned from the Babylonish captivity, and in mournful days set to work to re-establish themselves in their own land, at the outset the prophets of the Old Covenant were still at hand to urge on these tardy Israelites to rebuild the Temple, and to restore the ordinances and statutes of the Lord, to restrain them from contamination with heathen corruptions. But in the Sanctuary the "ark of the covenant" was no longer; the High Priest was deprived of the "light and righteousness" from the Lord. During the Captivity the great body of the people had exchanged the Hebrew language for the Chaldee. They could not understand their own Scriptures without interpretation, and the Spirit of prophecy soon vanished from among them. In this period were the men of God, who built up again the fallen Zion, anxiously occupied in collecting the Sacred Writings, and establishing their hold on the people. In the days of Ezra and Nehemiah was the collection of the writings of the Old Testament made, under the direction of a body of pious scribes, or men learned in Scripture, to whom Jewish tradition of a later period gave the name of "the Great Synagogue." About that time gradually were established in all the greater, and even smaller places, schools, or synagogues, for the purpose of keeping alive among the people a knowledge of the law; so that, since that time, "Moses had in every city them that preached him, being read in the synagogues every Sabbath day:" Acts xv. 21. At first the Law, afterwards the Prophets also to the end, were divided into separate portions. A variety of Chaldee translations and paraphrases made the Jews who lived in Palestine acquainted with the Word of God in their own tongue: and the same benefit was conferred on the Greek-speaking Jews, by means of the Greek translation of the Seventy, which was gradually completed, under the Ptolemies in Egypt, about the third century before Christ. This was the time, too, when a clear definite conception of the meaning of the Old Covenant taught the distinction to be drawn between the Word which was really given by the Lord Himself, and that which, though written with a good religious purpose, was still the word of man. We gather from the history of the time of the Maccabees, that the people, under the guidance of gifted, pious men, were animated to marvellous deeds of heroism in defence of their law—restored the Sanctuary and the ordinances of God's Word with carefulness; but we meet in these times with the clearest proofs that then no prophet existed in Israel, as for a long time none had arisen (1 Macc. iv. 46, ch. ix. 27, ch. xiv. 4). The grandson of Jesus Sirach, who lived before this period, and who translated into Greek his grandfather's book, speaks in the preface to it of the Holy Scriptures, as of a collection already concluded. He is acquainted with the customary division into " the Law, the Prophets, and the other Writings," which still exists among the Jews. The collection of the books of the Old Testament was, accordingly, distinctly separated from everything which emanated from the reviving Jewish literature, whether consisting of histories of the period (as the Books of the Maccabees), or of allegories (Judith and Tobit), or of other instructive writings, which either followed the pattern of the Old Testament (as Ecclesiasticus), or copied the manner of the Hellenist Jews, as in the Book of Wisdom.

The original division, therefore, of the collected writings of the Old Testament, as it existed in the time of Christ and the apostles, viz., into the Law, the Prophets, and the other Scriptures, is still the customary one among the Jews of this day, and is found in our Hebrew Bibles. The name " the Law" (Thorah, *i. e.*, instruction, teaching) comprises often the whole of the Old Revelation, but in the more precise division signifies only the five Books of Moses. These books, in the time of the Old Covenant, were esteemed the more especial foundation of the whole Divine revelation; and all the posterior histories and prophecies were either built upon them, or had immediate relation to them. The second division of the Prophets (Nebiim) is subdivided into the " Earlier and Later Prophets." To the first of these subdivisions belong the historical books, Joshua, Judges, Samuel, Kings; to the latter, the first three prophets, Isaiah, Jeremiah, Ezekiel, and the twelve minor prophets. The historical books are reckoned among the " Prophets," for this reason, that their authors, according to the generally received opinion, were esteemed prophets by virtue of their office and position among God's people. The third division of the Scriptures (Kethubim) comprises all the remaining sacred books, whose authors either were not, strictly speaking, " prophets" (however high they stood as servants of God, and however much they were under the guidance of His Holy Spirit), or writings which, by reason of the nature of their contents, were properly classed under other heads of these last divisions; as, for example, the

Lamentations of Jeremiah were classed under the same head with the Psalms. The old order of the writings of this division is as follows: Psalms, Proverbs, Job, the Song of Solomon, Ruth, Lamentations, Ecclesiastes, Esther, Daniel, Ezra, Nehemiah, Chronicles. This is the order of the sacred writings as it existed in the time of Christ and His apostles. All the books of the first two divisions are written in Hebrew, but a part of Daniel and of Ezra is in Chaldee. Not one of these writings was wanting in the collection in the time of Christ. They are all regarded as sacred by the Jews. Christ Himself both quoted them as the Word of God, and expounded them to His disciples. They have therefore a claim on all Christians to be received as sacred and inspired; and, in respect to their origin, stand on the same footing with the books of the New Testament; at the same time, as regards the character of their contents, they are composed with reference to the times of nonage, for which they were especially written, and were preparatory to the time of fulfilment of all which God hath spoken.

"The law was given by Moses, but grace and truth came by Jesus Christ:" John i. 17. These simple words of the evangelist point out to us not only the difference of the Old and New Testaments, but they declare the perpetual importance of the Old Testament to Christians. While the mass of the nations of the ancient world had wandered away from that original revelation of the holy, beneficent, personal Deity, which had been given to them, and which leaves an irrepressible yearning in the soul of every man, and had adopted a worship of nature, or made vain imperfect attempts to rise above it, there stood out one people from among the mass, altogether peculiar in character, which has preserved in its holy writings the historical revelations of the Deity, who is at the same time immeasurably raised above creation, yet intimately united with it, whose hand created all things, whose breath animates all things. In these writings we have the narrative of the creation: man is elevated above the order of the natural world as God's image; his fall, and its necessary consequence, punishment, are the beginnings of his history, in which God's wisdom and love in a wonderful manner lead him on to redemption. The law witnesses against sin, since God, by giving therein a pattern and rule of holiness of life, with which no man perfectly conforms, awakens a presage of the accomplishment and fulfilment of the will of God, and is itself the greatest of all predictions. While all heathen nations, from the earliest times even to our own days, after a short season of prosperity, have languished and perished, without hope of revival, among the people of God's covenant, in the time of deepest misery, the Spirit of prophecy has been awakened most powerfully, and has pointed to times when God's people shall receive twofold for all their sins, when the kingdom of God shall embrace the whole world, and be raised to a height of glory never before experienced. The times of the fulfilment in Christ have a twofold relation to the Old Covenant: Christ and His apostles build on the Old Testament revelation concerning the creation, the fall of man, and the law, which witnesses against sin, all their doctrines, which are only developments of the earlier truths on these subjects; and likewise they explain and determine more accurately what of ancient prophecy has been already fulfilled, and what is in course of fulfilment in Christian times. The grace and the truth of the Gospel are therefore unintelligible without the law; for how can we understand the gift of grace without the fact of sin to be forgiven? or how can we understand the power of truth unless we are acquainted with the shadows which have gone before? Where the indissoluble connection of the Old and New Testament is lost sight of, there inevitably will their contents be misunderstood, and perverted at pleasure. "The law" contained in the five Books of Moses forms the foundation-stone of the revelations of the Old Covenant. Of these Moses clearly gives himself out as the author, although he speaks of himself in the third person. It was a deep feeling of the intense sublimity and dignity of the sacred history which moved the men of God to treat their own individuality, wherever it was mixed up with the events they related, as something foreign to themselves, and merely as part of the narrative. In this way the evangelists wrote, and Matthew and John speak of themselves in their own writings as if they were strangers. The first Book of Moses, Genesis, though it begins with the creation, by no means consists of fragments loosely tacked together, partly agreeing with, partly contradicting, each other, which is the notion of a superficial scepticism. Even the conjecture of an original writing, worked out by a later hand, is utterly untenable without the most violent expedients; such as the supposition of interpolations, wherever the text itself contradicts the presupposed idea. There runs throughout this book, from beginning to end, a carefully conceived plan, which is never lost sight of, and at the same time a constant reference to the contents of the other books. It is much less conceivable that the history of the primeval period, and of the patriarchs, in Genesis, could have been compiled from fragmentary writings, even than that Homer's Iliad and Odyssey, which are arranged with so much art, and contain references of the later parts to the earlier, could have sprung into existence out of the rhapsodies of wandering bards. At the very commencement we meet with a connected history of the creation in seven days, in which God is revealed only as the Creator. No repetition of this account is given; but there follows a more minute description of the creation of man as preparatory to the history of his fall, and the first historical revelation of God in man's original condition, and after the fall. A string of genealogies is drawn from thence through the whole book up to Jacob, which often seems dropped, but is again resumed with marked completeness and purpose. In these tables of genealogy, in the history of the flood and of the patriarchs, there are abundant references to the history of the creation and of the fall (see, *e. g.*, ch. v. 29, vi. 3, ix. 2, xiv. 22, xviii. 25). And in almost every narrative may the reason clearly be perceived why it is told in this particular place, and could not stand anywhere else (see, *e. g.*, ch. xxxviii.). Moreover the law is not intelligible without sin, of which it witnesses; the passage out of Egypt presupposes the promises made to the patriarchs; the establishment of the ordinance of marriage forms the groundwork of all precepts about the relation of the sexes; the particular regulations about the hallowing of the ground and of the trees (Lev. xix. 25), point back to the curse pronounced on the ground; the unblessedness in Jacob's double marriage is certainly not mentioned without an eye to the forbidding of such unions with two sisters (Lev. xviii. 18). In the prophecy about Canaan, in the histories of Moab and Ammon, and of Edom, may we perceive plain references to the events relating to their descendants which are mentioned in the following books; and so in other cases. That the following books were written by Moses is told us repeatedly in them. At the first triumph of Israel over Amalek (Exod. xvii.), it is expressly commanded that the account of this event should be recorded in "*the Book*"—plainly, *i. e.*, a known, then existing book. The laws which follow immediately after the Ten Commandments were written in "the Book of the Covenant" (Exod. xxiv. 4–7), which was read in the ears of the people at the solemn conclusion of the covenant. In the last days of his life, in the field of Moab, Moses arranged together all the particular histories and laws, and made some additional observations, as, for instance, Exod. xvi. 35. How far Moses wrote and arranged the books is told us plainly in Deut. xxxi. 24. The song which follows (ch. xxxii.), and the blessing, was written or dictated by him, although after he had concluded the book, and handed it over to another. This other carried on the narrative from thence (as the words in the place above quoted show), and concluded with the death and burial of Moses. This person probably was Joshua, since both his position towards Moses, and also the evidence that he wrote the history of his life in the Book of the Law of God (see Joshua xxiv. 26), point out to him as the author.

In even a higher sense than he intended, has the opinion of a learned man of the last century (J. D. Michaelis) been verified in our days. "The more one pays attention to little points in the Books of Moses, and carefully investigates them, the more will a man be convinced of their antiquity and authenticity;" note on Gen. xliv. 2. It was supposed, in the last century, that the chronology among the people of Eastern Asia, the Hindoos, the Chinese, the Japanese, pointed to a much earlier date for the creation than the scriptural chronology could allow of; when, lo! the more accurate inquiry of our age has shown that the authentic history of these people did not extend, at most, farther back than 800 years B. C., somewhat about the time of Isaiah, and all before that is uncertain or fabulous! It has again been supposed that the intellectual horizon in the time of Moses was far too circumscribed to allow of the extensive view of the relation of the different people, such as we meet with in the 10th of Genesis; and yet recent investigation has shown that long before the time of Moses the whole of Asia Minor was subject to the Egyptians, and with this country (as the Egyptian remains prove) the most constant intercourse on the part of the people of those countries was carried on. It has been doubted whether the whole world could ever have had "one speech and one language." At the same time the notion was received with much favour, that men were a kind of natural product of the particular countries they inhabited, and were not derived from a single pair; and yet later inquiry has most satisfactorily proved that all the languages on the face of the globe have an original connection. People have found in the Books of Moses intimations of a knowledge of Egypt which appeared not to agree with what was known from other sources of the state of culture in that country. About half a century ago the French were prompted by motives of avarice to invade Egypt. They contended with the English for the mastery over those countries which were the scene of the most ancient history of the Bible. Vast changes in the world's politics seemed likely to arise from thence. These, however, lasted but a short time, and matters returned to their former state, in which they now continue, and the great political commotion appeared to have taken place to no purpose. But the French had brought one thing out of Egypt,—a small, black, much damaged basalt stone, with a surface not quite four feet square: on this stone stood the remarkable inscription from Rosette, in three characters, which became the key to all the subsequent discoveries in the inscriptions of Egyptian monuments, and though much that is uncertain may still remain, it has been the means of discovering to us some very remarkable facts. The notion used to be, that, in the time of Moses, the art of writing, if discovered, as might be the case, was still not yet in such general use, as to render it probable that a work of the compass of the Pentateuch could have been composed in the wilderness. But these witnesses of former ages, newly brought to light, show us, that in old Egypt the art of writing was in use in all relations of life, and especially that there was in the priest-caste a class of "holy scribes," who kept the books which contained their higher knowledge. In accordance with the origin of the people of Israel from a patriarchal family, the oldest Israelitish officers are scribes[1] (see Exod. v. 6), who probably carried on the genealogical tables, with the composition of which the art of writing had begun among them. Everywhere in the Books of Moses we see references to Egyptian customs and regulations, which prove at the same time an acquaint-

---

[1] The word rendered in the Engl. version "officers" means properly "scribes," Heb "Schoterim"—See note *in loc*.

ance with them, and yet witness against their spirit. Modern geographical science has removed, in the most easy and obvious way, a number of apparent contradictions; and if at present every difficulty is not solved—if all the discoveries of modern science are not in all points agreeing with revelation—still must our age thankfully acknowledge that it entertains a lively hope of its perfect triumph over unbelief from the progress made in modern scriptural research, which a short time ago was so unlooked for. Truly these Books of Moses display to us a wonderful richness and harmony in their revelation of the Divine wisdom and knowledge, though for some time their important and prophetic histories were treated as mere fables, and their momentous precepts regarded as the arbitrary unmeaning fancies of a bygone age, not worth remembering. While we consider Moses to be an eye-witness and an actor in most of the events of the four last books, yet he must, in the composition of the first book, have made use of the ancient traditions, which, together with the genealogical tables, were in existence. Some short and now scarcely intelligible notifications (*e. g.*, ch. v. 24, vi. 4, x. 12) in these ancient memorials show how much was inserted in them which appeared to the contemporaries of more consequence than to posterity, and at the same time offer a proof of their great antiquity. The perfect resemblance of the style, the purpose shown in the arrangement of events, and the reference to the law (which was mentioned above), all this proves that Moses independently worked out the whole which came into his hands. The account of the creation and of the flood form in the narrative an entire connected history, and point back to an original revelation which existed before the flood, and was handed down, by means of an unbroken tradition, as a precious legacy in the family of God's children. But that these narratives were only the concealed figurative representations of some general truth which the history contained, cannot be admitted, since in such very ancient times the conscious clothing of a history in the garb of allegory is altogether inconceivable. In compiling these old narratives into a continuous history of the kingdom of God, one and the same Spirit of God inspired Moses; which Spirit he had received in a greater measure than all his brethren, since he was *the* servant to whom was intrusted the administration of the whole house of God. (Num. xii. 7.)

The first book may be divided into the following principal sections:—

I. The history of mankind before the flood: (1.) The creation, ch. i.–ii. 4. (2.) Paradise, the institution of marriage, the fall and its punishment, ch. ii. 5–ch. iii. (3.) Cain and Abel, the genealogy of Cain's descendants; Seth and Enos, ch. iv. (4.) The genealogy of the patriarchs to Noah, ch. v.—II. The flood and the dispersion of the nations: (1.) Cause, prediction, coming, and course of the flood, ch. vi.–ix. 17. (2.) Shem, Ham, and Japhet, ch. ix. (3.) The list of the nations, ch. x. (4.) The dispersion. (5.) The descendants of Shem up to Noah.—III. The history of Abraham: (1.) His call and journey to Canaan, ch. xii. 1–9. (2.) His journey into Egypt, ch. xii. 10 to end. (3.) His separation from Lot, ch. xiii. (4.) The war of the kings, and the blessing of Melchisedec, ch. xiv. (5.) The covenant of God with Abraham, ch. xv. (6.) Hagar's flight and the birth of Ishmael, ch. xvi. (7.) The sign of the covenant, the institution of circumcision, ch. xvii. (8.) The promise of Isaac, and the destruction of Sodom, ch. xviii. 19–29. (9.) The origin of the children of Moab and Ammon, ch. xix. 30–38. (10.) Sarah in the house of Abimelech, ch. xx. (11.) The birth of Isaac, and the expulsion of Hagar, ch. xxi. 1–21. (12.) Abraham in the land of the Philistines, ch. xxi. 22–34. (13.) The offering up of Isaac, ch. xxii. (14.) Sarah's death and burial, ch. xxiii. (15.) Rebecca sought in marriage, ch. xxiv. (16.) Death of Abraham, ch. xxv. 1–11. (17.) The descendants of Ishmael, ch. xxv. 12–18.—IV. The history of Isaac and Jacob: (1.) Birth of the twins, sale of the birthright, ch. xxv. 19–34. (2.) Isaac in the land of the Philistines, ch. xxvi. (3.) Blessing upon Jacob and Esau, ch. xxvii. (4.) Jacob's flight; his sojourning with Laban, marriages, children, return, ch. xxviii.–xxxiii. (5.) Dinah's shame, ch. xxxiv. (6.) Jacob in Canaan; Isaac's death, ch. xxxv. (7.) Esau's descendants, ch. xxxvi.—V. The history of Joseph: (1.) His dreams, and his being sold, ch. xxxvii. (2.) The children of Judah, ch. xxxviii. (3.) Joseph in the house of Potiphar, and his imprisonment, ch. xxxix. xl. (4.) His interpretation of Pharaoh's dream, ch. xli. (5.) Joseph and his brethren, ch. xlii.–xlv. (6.) Jacob comes down into Egypt; the genealogy of the descendants of his sons, ch. xlvi. (7.) Jacob in Egypt, ch. xlvii. (8.) The blessing of Jacob on Ephraim and Manasseh, ch. xlviii. (9.) Jacob's blessing on his sons, and his death, ch. xlix. (10.) The entombment of Jacob and Joseph, ch. l.—In order to understand the plan and arrangement of the narrative, it is important to follow the continuous order of the genealogical tables: they are found, ch. v.; ch. vi. 9–10; ch. x.; ch. xi. 10–27 (interposed are, ch. xxii. 20–24; ch. xxv. 1–4, 12–15); ch. xxv. 19, 20; ch. xxv. 22, 26 (interposed ch. xxxvi. 9–19); ch. xxxvii. 2; ch. xxxviii.; ch. xlvi. 8–26.

The principal contents of the second book, Exodus, are as follows:—I. (1.) The oppression of Israel, ch. i. (2.) Birth and education of Moses, the killing of the Egyptian, the flight of Moses, ch. ii. (3.) His call and return, ch. iii. (4.) The first nine plagues, v.–x. (5.) The last plague, the institution of the Passover, the passage out of Egypt, the preservation, ch. xi.–xiv.—II. The march to Mount Sinai, and the delivery of the law: (1.) Events in the wilderness up to the arrival at Mount Sinai, ch. xv.–xviii. (2.) The delivery of the Ten Commandments, ch. xix. 20, 21. (3.) Further explanations of their meaning: the Book of the Covenant, ch. xxiv. (4.) Conclusion of the covenant, ch. xxiv. (5.) Regulations with respect to the Tabernacle, ch. xxv.–xxxi. (6.) Idolatry of the people, renewal of the covenant, ch. xxxii.–xxxv. (7.) Making, etc., of the Tabernacle, its dedication, ch. xxxvi.–xl.

The third book, Leviticus, concludes the giving of the law on Mount Sinai, with the order of sacrifices and of the priests, and the laws of purification. (1.) The general order of the sacrifices, ch. i.–vii. (2.) Consecration of the priests, and the circumstances accompanying it, ch. viii.–x. (3.) The laws of purification, ch. xi.–xv. (4.) The day of atonement, ch. xvi. (5.) Eating of blood and of the fat forbidden, ch. xvii. (6.) Unlawful marriages forbidden, ch. xviii. (7.) Sundry laws, ch. xix. (8.) Penalties for certain offences, ch. xx. (9.) Description of the character of the priests and of the sacrifices, ch. xxi. xxii. (10.) Appointment of the feasts, ch. xxiii. (11.) Preparation of the oil and of the shew-bread, ch. xxiv. 1–9. (12.) Laws concerning blasphemy, ch. xxiv. 10–xxv. (13.) The year of rest and of jubilee, ch. xxv. (14.) Conclusion of the law-giving on Mount Sinai, with promises and threatenings, ch. xxvi. (15.) Supplemental laws respecting vows and tithes, ch. xxvii.

The fourth book, Numbers, contains—I. (1.) The number of the men of war, the order of the camp, the number of the Levites and firstborn, the qualifications of the different families of the Levites, ch. i.-iv. Here is inserted (2.) The command concerning the purification of the camp, the trial of jealousy, the law of the Nazarite, ch. v.-vi. 21. (3.) The form of blessing, ch. vi. 22-27. (4.) Sacrifices and gifts to the Tabernacle, dedication of the Levites, ch. vii. viii. (5.) The first Passover ordained, and an after Passover for those who were defiled, ch. ix. 1-14. (6.) Signs for encamping and marching, ch. ix. 15-23. (7.) The trumpets, the departure.—II. The march through the wilderness to the borders of Canaan: (1.) The graves of lust, ch. xi. (2.) Miriam's and Aaron's opposition, ch. xii. (3.) The spies, ch. xiii. xiv. (4.) Law of meat and drink offerings, ch. xv. 1-31. (5.) Punishment of the Sabbath-breaker, ch. xv. 32-41. (6.) Korah's rebellion, ch. xvi. (7.) Confirmation of the priesthood by means of Aaron's rod, ch. xvii. (8.) The portion of the priests and Levites, ch. xviii. (9.) The water of separation, ch. xix. (10.) Water out of the rock at Kadesh; Aaron's death, ch. xx. (11.) The fiery serpents; Arad, Sihon, and Og overcome, ch. xxi. (12.) The prophecies of Balaam, ch. xxii.-xxiv. (13.) Seduction by the Midianites, ch. xxv. (14.) Fresh numbering of the people, ch. xxvi. (15.) The law of inheritances, ch. xxvii. 1-11. (16.) The death of Moses announced; Joshua his successor, ch. xxvii. 12-23. (17.) Regulations concerning different sacrifices, ch. xxviii. xxix. (18.) The binding of vows, ch. xxx. (19.) Defeat of the Midianites, ch. xxxi. (20.) Division of the land east of Jordan, ch. xxxii. (21.) Specification of the journeys of the Israelites, ch. xxxiii. (22.) Borders and division of Canaan, ch. xxxiv. (23.) The cities of the Levites, and the cities of refuge. (24.) Law concerning heiresses, ch. xxxvi.

The fifth book, Deuteronomy, contains—I. The farewell words of Moses to the people: (1.) The first address, ch. i.-iv. 40. (2.) Separation of three cities of refuge on the east side Jordan, ch. iv. 41-43. (3.) The second address; recapitulation of the Ten Commandments, with exhortations, ch. v.-xi. The service of God's worship to be in one place, ch. xii. Punishment of idolatry, of the seducer and seduced, ch. xiii. Regulations concerning mourning, meats, tithes, ch. xiv. The year of release; concerning the firstborn, ch. xv. The feasts, ch. xvi. Of judges and kings, ch. xvii. Of priests and prophets, ch. xviii. The cities of refuge, false witnesses, ch. xix. Laws of war, ch. xx. Sundry laws, ch. xxi.–xxvi.—II. Events to the death of Moses: (1.) Appointing of the stones of memorial, of blessing and cursing, promises and threatenings, ch. xxvii. xxviii. (2.) Renewal of the covenant, ch. xxix. xxx. (3.) Moses delivers up his office to Joshua, the Book of the Law to the priests, ch. xxxi. (4.) The song of Moses, ch. xxxii. (5.) The blessing of Moses, ch. xxxiii. (6.) The death of Moses, ch. xxxiv.

THE FIRST BOOK OF MOSES,

(CALLED GENESIS, *i. e*, CREATION).

CHAPTER I.

GOD, the eternal, self-existent, personal source of all life,—He who was before all things, and in whom all things subsist, has created heaven and earth, and all that therein is, visible and invisible, by means of His Word, the utterance of His will. With this one declaration at its commencement does the Book of all books distinguish itself from everything which heathen tradition or human wisdom has ever taught of the origin of things. The world is not God,—not an effluence from God, a part of His being; but it has been created by His will, to be a glorious manifestation of His eternal might, wisdom, and love. (*Vide* Ps. xxxiii. 6, 9; Isa. xlii. 5; Neh. ix. 6.) Of this His great work has God given to His children the history in Holy Scripture, which is designed to prove a word of instruction and wisdom for life in Him, in order that He may instruct man, created after His own image, and who is His fellow-worker, after the example of his Creator, to tend the little field of labour which is intrusted to his care; to bring it out of disorder and wildness, and to make it more and more subject to His Spirit. By means of this Word has He taught him to strive after rest through labour, and at the end of every week to place a landmark on his journey, from whence he may look back on what is done, observe what is wanting, and gather up strength for the coming days' labour. By means of this same rest has He given to man, pressed down under the burden of sin, and labouring in his work of the new creation (viz., sanctification), a type of the eternal rest, in which God has called His people to participate.

The works of the first three days and the last three correspond with one another. On the first day is light created; on the fourth day, the lights in heaven: on the second, the visible heaven with the waters; on the fifth, the fishes of the sea and the fowls of the air: on the third, the dry land, with its clothing of vegetation; on the sixth, the land animals and man—on the first three days the inanimate substances, on the last three the living inhabitants, are produced. In the vegetable world the dry land attains its destined purpose, as the animal world, and indeed the whole creation, attains its end in man. All the following history is written only for *man*; and therefore the sun, moon, and stars, and the whole host of heaven, appear only as lights in the firmament of heaven. Of the inhabitants of heaven nothing is told us. Still in this book angels are frequently spoken of, and the fall of some is presupposed (ch. iii.). In the book of Job (ch. xxxviii. 7), it is intimated that the angels were spectators of the six days' work of creation.

CHAPTER I.

Ver. 1. *In the beginning*; *i.e.*, of all things, since all things have had a beginning, and are not eternal as God is. All creation is temporal, and time was created with it. But in the beginning, when all things came into existence, there *existed* already the Word (St John i. 1). It never was created, had no beginning in time; and through the Word was everything in the beginning created.

Created.—" To create," in Scripture language, always means, to call forth something into real existence. Heaven and earth are *created*, and not, as the heathens imagined, merely *formed* out of matter already existing. This teaching raises the revelation of Holy Scripture above the whole heathen wisdom, which never could soar beyond the notion of opposition between God and the world, Spirit and nature. And still is the doctrine of the creation the boundary-line betwixt Christianity and the speculations of philosophy.

God.—Where in the Old Testament, in our translation, the word "God" stands, there in the Hebrew is the word "Elohim" (which signifies strictly, "the One to be feared, to be reverenced"). Where the word "Lord" occurs, it is commonly in Heb. "Jehovah." Elohim is properly a plural, "the Beings to be feared;" it has, however, the verb in the singular. Elohim is the more general name, answering somewhat to our word "Deities," and is therefore used also of the gods of the heathen. The Plural "Deities" expresses the comprehensiveness of all Divine attributes. This more general word "God" describes the Almighty in His relation as Creator and Lord of the world, whose "eternal power and godhead" might be known by the heathen, as declared in the works of creation (Rom. i. 19, 20). The word "Jehovah," properly expressed "Jahaveh" (the Jews, out of superstitious fear of uttering this word, placed the vowels of "Adonaj" [Lord] under "Jahaveh," and read this word instead of "Jahaveh"), means Him "who is;" *i. e.*, the true, only, eternal Self-existent. This word represents always the living, personal God, *in His revealed character, in His covenanted relations to man* (see Exod. iii. 14). Where the true God appears in His character as the "Creator" (as here), where the serpent (ch. iii. 2), where the heathen (ch. xx. 4) use His name; again, in the description of the flood (ch. vi. 11), of the dispersion of mankind (ch. ix. 10),—in all these cases the word God, Elohim, occurs: but where, in the revelation of Himself in the prayers and sacrifices of men, the covenanted relation between the personal God and mankind is prominently represented (*e. g.*, ch. iv. 3, 26; ch. v. 29; ch. vii. 1; ch. xii. 1), there the word Jehovah is especially employed (though, indeed, sometimes the words are used indiscriminately). There are some passages (as ch. xvii. 18, 22), in which first "God" (Elohim), then "Lord" (Jahaveh), stands, in order to point out how by a new revelation the "Most Highest" would declare Himself as the true living God of covenant. Both words stand together ("Jehovah Elohim," "God the Lord") in the section which follows this present one (viz. in ch. ii. 5, and iii. 24). And very significantly. The words are there used in order to impress on us, that He who has revealed Himself to mankind—who by command, by threats, by punishment, by promise, declares Himself as the per-

B

sonal Jehovah, the ruler of their destiny, is the same God and Creator of all things whose great work has just been narrated.

And the earth.—The original meaning of heaven and earth is, the high and the lower place. What the eye beholds as the visible emblem of heaven—the firmament, with sun, moon, and stars—is calculated to fill the mind with anticipations of the higher invisible world, which is emphatically called in Scripture "heaven," the place which the holy beings inhabit who are not separated from God by sin, and where therefore He Himself can reveal His majesty more fully. But, independently of the division which sin has made in God's creation, He did not "in the beginning" create the heaven and earth as one, but separated them from each other. The world is destined to develop itself in the distinction of heaven and earth, which is repeated again on earth in a smaller degree by the distinction of spirit and nature, flesh and spirit,—distinctions, which will abide even when sin is taken away (Rev. xxi. 1), yet in such a manner, that the earth will become heavenly, as the body will become "spiritual:" so do the very first words of Scripture point at a mighty mystery, which in the course of revelation is ever more and more unveiled to our view. At the same time these words have a very important bearing on what presently follows in ch. iii., the history of the origin of sin. God is the Creator of all that exists: the origin of evil, therefore, is not to be sought for in the world which He made,—in the natural preponderance, so to speak, of the coarser matter, *i. e.*, the flesh, over spirit, as the heathens and heathenish-minded Christians have taught, but in the perverseness of the being who was created with free-will. This first verse is not to be understood as the mere preface to the history of the creation which follows, much less as that of the history of a creation before that of the six days; but as if it stood thus: "When in the beginning God created the heaven and earth, then was the earth without form and void." [Nevertheless the supposition of the existence of the earth in a chaotic state, before it was prepared for man's use (possibly the wreck of another world), is not contradictory to Scripture, and is most in accordance with the discoveries of geology.—*Trans.*]

Ver. 2. *Without form and void.* Lit. "Wasteness and emptiness," a mass without form or light.—This is said of the *earth* alone, not of *the heaven and earth,* as beyond the visible, material heaven, lies another kingdom not "without form and void,' but glorious and beautiful, of which this material heaven is the emblem. Of the creation of this invisible world nothing is told us, since the Word of God speaks from the commencement to man, and in accordance with man's necessities. "Why has God created the heaven all glorious and perfectly formed, but the earth 'without form?' He has not done this without design, but in order that in the more glorious part of creation we might perceive His creative power, and not suppose that through 'failure in might He has made the earth as He did,' viz., without form.'—St Chrysostom.

The deep; i.e., the floods which covered the earth.—Without form, void, and dark, came forth the earth at the commencement from God's hand; and in this gradual formation and development of the rude mass was it God's will to resemble a human worker, that man might for his part be like God. In its *becoming* perfect, and not being so at once, lies the essential character of everything created. In God there is none of the impatient longing for the end which is characteristic of sinful man with his narrow views.

Moved.—This word "brooded" is used (Deut. xxxii. 11) of the eagle who sits on its young, warms and defends them (in English translation, "fluttereth"). Hence we gain the notion of the Spirit of God brooding over the mass which contained the germ of all life. "This appears to me to point out the truth that a vital power resided in the water; that it was no unmoveable and standing water, but full of motion and the power of life."—St Chrysostom. By "the Word" God creates, by the Spirit He gives life and sustains all creation: yea, He Himself lives in the created, He "the God of the spirits of all flesh." "Wind" and "Spirit" are the same word in Hebrew. The wind is the breath of the universe. In this breath of life is the life-giving and life-sustaining Spirit of God Himself: Ps. civ. 30.

Ver. 3. *Light.*—"Here, it is to be observed, that these are the words not of Moses, but of God, *i.e.*, realities, things, existences. God calls to that which is not, that it may exist, and He utters not words but things; so that what with us is a sound, with God is a thing. God says, 'Let the sun shine,' and the sun is there and shines. Here must we make a difference between the uncreated and the created Word. Since what is the universe but God's spoken Word? The uncreated Word is the Divine thought, the inward command which abides in God, and is one with God, and yet a distinct Person."—Luther. Light is created before everything else; since without light, which discloses all things, and is an effluence from the Eternal Source of light, everything is buried in death (St John i. 4). Light is the most spiritual of all material things. Light, we find here, does not proceed from the sun (*vide* ver. 14), and yet the day is divided into the regular alternations of light and darkness. The sun has not light in itself (not even in a physical sense, since we now know that the sun is an opaque body, with an illuminating atmosphere). Light is an effluence of the life which God breathed into the universe; and only when everything is in due order distinguished, is light apportioned to the sun to rule and to adorn the earth. On the first day was nothing but light created; we may therefore infer with probability that the creation of it was not the work of a moment.

Ver. 4. *Good.*—On every glorious work, as it is completed, the eye of Divine love rests, full of joy. To impart His glory, to fill all things with His sanctifying, blessing love,—this is the object of His creation. Every created work is to us an evidence of God's mercy and wisdom; to Himself, a source of fresh joy. The expression which is so constantly repeated, "God saw that it was good," declares to us this truth, that God is the holy Source of all good, and that in this world there lies no incentive to sin, but sin is the fault of man.

Darkness.—The words, "God divided the light from the darkness," is so to be understood that this necessarily took place through the creation of light, since light is one thing, the absence of light, which God had *ordained* in the darkness opposed to light, another. It is not said, God *made* the darkness (as also it is not said, God saw the night that it was good, since only in its relation to the day is it good). God creates only entities, and the darkness belongs to the nonentity out of which God created everything. Still God appointed the cessation or suspension of the existence, so that also the non-existence is ordained by God's all-directing guidance.—St Augustine.

Ver. 5. *Night.*—" Every light is not day, nor every darkness night; but light and darkness, following each other according to a regular order and succession, are called Day and Night.—St

Augustine. The "calling" is the same as "determining anything in accordance with its nature and appearance;" thereby is signified the might of God, which determines and wills all.

Day.—The darkness out of God was the original condition, the beginning of creation, insomuch as God had not penetrated the whole of created matter with His life. God called the light to shine out of darkness (2 Cor. iv. 6): therefore the day begins with the evening; and the Israelites, who closely adhered to the history of the creation, continued this mode of reckoning. When the darkness succeeded to the light after its ordained continuance, the first day (lit. a day) closed. As the light had come out of darkness, and was appointed continually so to do, and as the darkness was no longer simply darkness, but a state which introduces day, therefore the two together are called "Day." Darkness had its existence only for the sake of the day.

Ver. 6. *Firmament.*—Heb., Expansion, like a tent-cover, to which it is often compared.

Ver. 7. *From the waters,* which drop from the clouds: Ps. cxlviii. 4.

Ver. 8. *Heaven.*—The upper vault from which light, and warmth, and fructifying moisture come down to bless the earth, which, with its moving and its stationary lights, has always aroused the attention even of the rudest of mankind, and carried up their aspirations to dwell on a higher power than the earthly, and which is the visible pledge, yea, perhaps, the distant glimpse of a world of light. It therefore bears the same name with that kingdom where "our Father in heaven" manifests Himself.

Ver. 9. *Dry land.*—The land was originally mixed up with the water, and covered by it. It was raised out of the water probably by means of fire. See Ps. civ. 5. As originally all was sea, so on "the new earth" shall there be "no more sea:" Rev. xxi. 1. On the second day, it is not said that God "saw that it was good," probably for this reason, that the second day's work receives its completion on the third day, with the covering of the earth, its plants and vegetation, which is to the ground what man is to the whole earth, viz., its crown and perfection.

Ver. 11. *Kind.*—A higher order of trees and plants than had existed before now sprung out of the earth, which was watered from above. The vegetable kingdom is in its nature perishable: but by "the herb yielding seed," a provision is made for its constant renewal. It would be a mistake to imagine, because *fruit-bearing* trees are here spoken of, that others, as thorns and thistles, came into being only after the fall. Who can determine what utility the even apparently useless may afford to man? Even of thorns and thistles St Augustine says, "It is not probable that these were called into existence after the fall, since, perhaps, because even in this kind of plant there is much utility, they at the beginning had their place assigned without injury or punishment to man; but the point of his punishment consisted in this, that these things grew in the fields from which, with much labour, he had to gain his nourishment."

Ver. 14. *Years.*—The "signs" are the prognostics, *e. g.*, of the weather; the "seasons," the periods appointed for festivals, etc., to which especially the new moons belonged. As the months are reckoned by the moon and the years by the sun, and both must be brought into agreement, in very early times the years were reckoned by the sun and moon conjointly, not, as with us, by the sun alone.

Ver. 18. *Darkness.*—It is remarkable that the sun, moon, and stars were created only on the fourth day. These heavenly lights were then only placed in the firmament; and since already light had been created, and the successions of day and night taken place, these bodies were rather serviceable for the order and adornment of the earth than absolutely necessary. Moreover they appear here not for their own sakes, but for the service of man and of the earth in ruling day and night. In both these points is Scripture opposed to the notions of the old heathens. In most of the heathen religions the worship of the sun, moon, and five principal planets (from which we derive the names of the days of the week), viz., Mars, Mercury, Jupiter, Venus, Saturn, formed a main article of all religions. See Jer. xix. 13; Zeph. i 5; Acts vii. 42.

Ver. 20. *Fly.*—Heb, "Let the fowl fly on the earth under the firmament of heaven." The Scripture does not say that the fowl were produced from the water.

Ver. 22. *Multiply.*—As a higher species of being than all the former, these are honoured with an especial blessing. It is remarkable that land animals, which stand nearer to man than the foregoing, follow after the heavenly bodies: the animals, as endowed with a certain intelligence and will—with a soul, if not a spirit—stand above all inanimate creation. Such a gradation of created things is one which Holy Scripture alone recognises, and is unknown to heathenism.

Ver. 25. *Kind.*—The higher kinds of animals were from the first designed for man's use. The position of the creatures in their order, as here pointed out, so entirely rests on the original creation, that man has never attained to tame any fresh kind of animal. All the domestic animals have come down to us from the first times, and most probably were never wild; but only similar species, and degenerate branches of the same species, have been so; just as corn has never been a wild plant, and man has never been able to discover any kind of vegetable which he could cultivate and use in the same way.

Ver. 26. *Make.*—God takes counsel with Himself that He may create the most perfect of all earthly creatures. We are to understand by this mode of expression that with man a new, and indeed the highest, order of creatures begins. By God saying, "Let *us*," etc. (cf. ch. iii. 22, *One* of us), undoubtedly allusion is intended to a plurality in the Godhead, to which, in a later chapter, the "Angel of the Lord," who is different from God the Lord, and yet One with Him, even more clearly points. Before the creation of the world, and independently of it, God was love; and in order to love, must He have an object of knowledge and love, as well as an eternal personal bond which united Him with the object of His eternal love. Therefore the greatest work of His eternal love—the creation of man, whom He can love, and who shall be able both to know and love Him—this is a fitting subject of consultation between the Father and the Son.

Image.—" After God had said, 'Let us make,' etc., He immediately adds, 'Let them have dominion,' etc., in order that we may understand man's resemblance to the Divine image to consist in that particular in which he is superior to the irrational brutes, and that is—in reason, or knowledge, or mind, or whatever else we may most properly call it. And so the Apostle (Col. iii. 10) says, 'Be ye renewed in the spirit of your minds, and put on the new man, which is renewed in knowledge of God, after the image of Him who created him:' and thereby he declares to us very clearly by this how far man is created after the image of God, viz., not in respect to the bodily lineaments, but in respect to the invisible form of the enlightened soul."—St Augustine. Holy Scripture speaks of God's image in man in two senses. On the one hand, we understand the spiritual, moral, intellectual part of his being, which man cannot lose (ch. v. 1; ch. ix. 6; cf. St Matt. xxii. 21). The capacity to know God, and to love Him when known, and through the knowledge and love of God to become partaker of the highest blessedness,—this makes the soul of man a mirror of the Deity, and distinguishes him from the brutes. Hence follows his capacity of acting not simply in obedience to what is pleasant or unpleasant to the senses,—his capacity of acting in obedience to the Divine law, his free-will, and his accountableness should he not so act; hence follows the capacity of improvement and advance, both as regards the human race as a whole, and the individual man. By means of reason, which is one with freedom, and capable of an ever-progressive advance, man is lord of nature; and "the highest aim," says St Anselm, "of rational beings is this—to *express*, by act of the will, that image which the Creator has *impressed* on them by the gift of this faculty of obedience." This image of God in man (*i.e.*, this faculty of knowing and loving God, and of free-will) "cannot be destroyed even in hell; it can burn, but cannot be consumed—it can be tormented, but not destroyed," says St Bernard. If it could cease, then would cease also the feeling of sin and its punishment, and thus the very punishment of the lost. But Holy Scripture speaks also of an image of God which man has lost by sin, and to which he is renewed through Christ (see Eph. iv. 24; Col. iii. 10; cf. Eccles. vii. 29); and therefore this renewal is also called "a new creature." God has not merely created man with the *power* to know and love Him, and free to choose His laws; but He has likewise in the beginning *actually revealed* Himself to his knowledge and love, and *given* his will an inclination toward His law (cf. ch. iii. 3). He has created him good and happy. Man was also the image of God in this respect: that as God possesses self-consciousness, knows and loves Himself, and in this knowledge and love enjoys the highest bliss, so also man, by means of his freedom and self-consciousness, knew and loved God, and so was happy. *This* image of God in man is altogether lost by sin, and is only restored by the preventing, renewing, grace of God. But between the image of God in man's nature which cannot be erased, and the image which has been lost by sin, there is a close connection, since, by man's alienation from God, he has become carnal, brutalised, and is in danger of losing the power of knowing and loving God, if not entirely, yet in a very great degree, as is the case with mankind everywhere, and was more entirely the case with the heathen world. This is eternal decay and perishableness—eternal death, which is the penalty of sin.

Creepeth.—Even irrational nature praises their Creator, if rational man knows that it is well and beautifully ordained. As long as man, in obedience to God, understood the Divine purpose which had produced nature, he made the irrational creatures of service to himself, for whose use they were created.

Ver. 27. *In the image.*—This great truth—the summit of all revelation—is repeated, as if it were a matter to excite our wonder and admiration.

Female.—As is frequently the case in the book before us, that is only now briefly alluded to which, in the following chapter, is more fully discussed. In this history it is the chief object to represent prominently the completion of the whole creation. The history of the oldest covenant of God with man is not yet touched on. The reader will carefully keep clear of the Jewish fable (which has even found admittance among Christians), viz., that man was first created man and woman in one, and afterwards both sexes were separated. In refutation of so ridiculous a notion, it is sufficient to observe that the sacred writer says, " He created *the* man, Adam, after His image, man and woman created He *them.*"

Ver. 28. *Subdue it.*—These words show it was intended that man should *gradually make nature subject to himself*, and that it was not all at once subjected to him. Man obtains this dominion over the earth by means of a more perfect knowledge of the order, laws, and powers of nature. Thus he learns to make nature subserve his wants; but he will never attain to a perfect control over it, until he has returned himself to the service of God. It is altogether a false notion to suppose that our first parents possessed a perfect insight into nature and its powers, and that nature in some magical manner rendered obedience to this, and so the necessity for work of every kind was removed. The first of mankind were rather children in understanding;

and were intended to arrive at maturity of mind, especially through labour in the field of nature.

Ver. 30. *Meat.*—As yet flesh was not eaten (cf. ch. ix. 1), although the permission to eat flesh when it was necessary was included in the gift granted to man of dominion over the beasts. The first age up to the flood was the childhood of the human race, in which man partook of the food of children. The beasts were supported by the same kind of nourishment; and therefore at the beginning the eating of flesh had not begun with them, and shall likewise at some time discontinue. Is. xi. 7.

Ver. 31. *Very good.*—God had pronounced His approval of the portions of creation singly, and now in even a higher degree He pronounces that He is well pleased with the whole.

CHAPTER II.

Ver. 1. *Host.*—The stars of heaven figuratively, and the angels properly, are often called "the host of heaven" (Is. xl. 26; Jer. xix. 13; Zeph. i. 5; St Luke ii. 13). God is therefore "the Lord of hosts," "Jehovah Sabaoth." All creatures, especially the highest, stand ready to "do Him service," to perform His commands, and to contend on His behalf.

Ver. 2. *Ended.*—The works are said only to be finished when the creation of them as a whole is ended, and they begin by means of their inherent power to live, to grow, and to act on each other.

God rested, inasmuch as He now ceased to create, although He continues unceasingly to work in the preservation and renewal of His works. Perfect rest and perfect activity are one and the same in Him: cf. St John v. 17. But observe, "God rested" does not *merely* mean, He ceased to create, as Exod. xxxi. 17 shows. "He refreshed Himself:" cf. Exod. xxiii 12. This strong human expression is, of course, not applicable in the sense of His having become weary (cf. Isa. xl. 28), but it may be well applied in the sense of His receiving divine satisfaction in the contemplation of His glorious and blessed work; and so, after the manner of an earnest, skilful human workman, He may be said to "rest" after the completion of His work. God, after the creation of the world, which develops itself in time, lives also with it in time, without detraction from His immutability. By means of His love, He imparts happiness to His creatures; and from every development of the glory which He has bestowed on them arises a heavenly song of praise. The Holy Scripture knows nothing of a God who, in eternal, immovable unchangeableness, views all things, past, present, and future, just in the same way, but One who, after creating the world, with man, its king, partakes by means of His love in the joy and pain of His creation, yet without diminution of His eternal blessedness. At length He suffered in the flesh, with and for His creature, and through suffering again returns to glory. "Christ also rested in the grave on the Sabbath day, and passed the whole of it in sacred quiet, after He had finished all His works on the sixth day, since all which was written of Him was fulfilled on the cross, and He cried, 'It is finished.'"—St Augustine.

Ver. 3. *Sanctified; i. e.*, He separated it from the other days for Himself, the Holy One, so that everything which, in accordance with the Divine intention, was done on this day might bring with it an especial sanctification for man, since "the Sabbath is for man, not man for the Sabbath." This day was sanctified for man's use, in order that on this rest-day of the creation of the world he might be reminded of the blessed rest of God from His work, and carry on his thoughts to that rest which awaits himself when the daywork of this world shall be completed. Even from this we may infer that the Sabbath celebration is not an unconditional one; that the command of love towards God and our neighbour is before it; and the observance of the Sabbath ought to lead to these duties, and to be regulated by them (see St Matt. xii. 7, 8; St Mark ii. 27, 28). In the New Testament the outward shell of this commandment is taken away, and the kernel remains. It is God's eternal will that we in the communion of the Church should celebrate holy days and seasons, for the purpose for which they have been ordained—to draw off the soul from the business of this world, and to raise it up to the calm contemplation of our heavenly calling. With this object in view, rest from labour is with Christians by no means a matter of choice, but it is the Divine command of Him who came not to destroy, but to fulfil the law. Still, the Church has shown her freedom from subjection to mere outward ordinances, partly by the significant change of the day of rest from the last day of the week to the first, which has been blessed and sanctified by Christ's resurrection, who has entered into His eternal rest, that He might prepare places for us in His Father's house,—partly by the setting apart of this day for assembling together in divine worship,—partly by the appointment of other festivals besides this, and, lastly, by the release of Christians from the obligation of many external observances, as, *e. g.*, Exod. xxxv. 3. Whether the celebration of the seventh day was ordained at the same time with the revelation of the history of the creation, or whether it was first given to the people of Israel together with the other commandments of the law, is involved in much uncertainty, though the latter supposition is the more probable one. At all events, we discover no trace of the celebration of the Sabbath in the Book of Genesis, still less among any heathen nations. The division of time into weeks, which we find among some of them, might be a regulation according to the quarters of the moon.

Ver. 5. *Grew.*—This verse should rather be translated, "And every plant was not yet in the field, and every herb had not yet grown in the field," and ought not to be considered as belonging to the preceding verse, as a new paragraph begins here—the history of the earth and of man. It does not mean to say that plants and herbs did not yet exist, since the creation of the vegetable kingdom has already been narrated, ch. i. 11; but—the beginnings only of all things, and of the vegetable kingdom especially, existed because there was no man to till the ground; then God created man, etc. In this verse, in which man is represented, not, as in the preceding chapter, merely as a portion of the creation, but in his personal covenant relation to God, the destination of all earthly things for man's use, and of man himself to be the workman on the earth, is very clearly pointed out. The planting of the garden (ver. 8) first takes place.

Ver. 6. *Ground.*—It appears that at that time it had not rained, but that all moisture for the nourishment of plants and herbs was supplied by means of dew. The choice of the rainbow, as a sign of the covenant with Noah (ch. viii.), agrees with this description. Primeval nature, as compared with what she afterwards became, appears to have been of a more tender and delicate character. We perceive from what is here said that the plants and herbs did not suddenly shoot forth into maturity; but that the fruit-bearing seeds which were laid in the earth were brought to perfection by rain and by cultivation.

Dust of the ground.—In the Hebrew the first man is simply called "Adam," *i. e.*, the man, since Adam is both the word for the human race, and for the first man. In him was the whole race continued, which is therefore styled "the children of Adam," or merely "Adam," in the same way as the Israelites were called either "the children of Israel," or simply "Israel." The word "Adam" has the same root and signification with "Adama," earth. Both words mean "red;" and by the connection of the two words it is clearly intimated that "the man" was "earthy," made out of the earth. There is a deep truth contained in the declaration that God made man out of the dust of the earth; for it expressly represents to us, that at the outset he was a portion of the creatures which belong to this earth, and in his body was himself of an earthly kind. It was ordained that nature should be governed by one of a like, yet, at the same time, of a higher order than itself, in the same manner as it is appointed that mankind should be ruled by a God-man (cf. Rom. viii. 22). "The first man was of the earth, earthy," 1 Cor. xv. 47; and, therefore, could only become, according to God's purpose, heavenly, spiritual, through "the second Man, the Lord from heaven." It is moreover to be observed, that God creates the body only out of the earth, while the soul is breathed into it, which exactly takes place at the birth of every one of us. The soul is not that which has formed the body for itself; but body and soul are both called into existence by God's creative will and purpose.

Ver. 7. *Breath of life.*—Breath, on which depends the life of the body, is an emblem of the Divine life which was breathed into man. Indeed, it is the breath of God by means of which everything is preserved in life (Ps. civ. 30). Yet this especial breathing of breath into man points out that the personal life of man proceeds from God, and is related to God.

A *living soul*—a living, spiritual being. As in the beginning the heaven and the earth were created in contrast one with the other, and yet with the purpose of mutually acting on each other, so in the case of man the body was created out of the dust, the spirit was given by God. Both were God's creation, so there could be no hostile opposition between the two; still, from the very first, the duty was imposed on man, to bring into subjection the world without him, and to subjugate his own flesh more and more to the spirit—to rule, to sanctify, to glorify it through the spirit. Man was to have not merely "a living soul," but a "life-giving spirit," as Christ the second Adam had, and as all believers have received from Christ (cf. 1 Cor. xv. 47). By means of "the dust," out of which he was created, man belonged to the earth, and so was partaker of the perishable: he carried with him a natural life, as the other animals do, which as distinct beings, perish—as races, are continued; therefore *he had a capability of dying.* But through the spirit, derived from God, he possessed an unperishing personality, and so he was endowed with a *capability* of immortality. The dust, out of which he was created, as well as the earth itself, was made for a higher life of glory. Life and death were placed before him, and he chose death.

Ver. 8. *Eden* means "pleasantness," "loveliness."—Towards the east, in this delightsome region, lay the garden. We are accustomed to call it "Paradise" (after a word probably of Armenian origin), as it is called in the old Greek and Latin translations.

Put the man.—The labour in a garden in a mild climate is the easiest possible, and the most suitable to the childhood of man's race. Here his powers could prepare themselves for severer labours. The oldest known fruit-trees, the domestic animals, corn, were legacies from this primeval period.

Ver. 9. *Tree of life.*—Man was created not subject to death, but capable of dying. The tree of life, which before the fall he was permitted to taste, was meant for his sustenance. Man, in his infant condition, required some sensible corporeal assurance of immortality, and the tree of life afforded him immortality, if not by its own immediate power, yet by virtue of the promise imparted to it. But man could only continue to taste of this tree of life, so long as he, by the obedience of faith, remained in communion with God.

Tree of knowledge of good and evil.—In order to understand the whole account, it is of great importance that we should rightly comprehend what "the knowledge of good and evil" here, and ch. iii. 5, 22, means. Not to know what is good and evil, elsewhere (Deut. i. 39) signifies a state of childhood—the opposite to the wisdom of angels (2 Sam. xiv. 17), and of God Himself (ch. iii. 5, 22). In the first place, then, this knowing or understanding, in its full scriptural sense, includes " choice," will, and action (cf. Is. vii. 16, " to refuse the evil and choose the good") : 1 Cor. viii. 3. Knowledge of good and evil is therefore the conscious freedom of the will. Now, it certainly was not God's will that man should remain excluded from this. Nay, the contrary is clear, from the very fact that God had created man after His own image,—had committed to his charge the earth, to " subdue it," and to become in that respect "as God :" that he, with clear knowledge of the Divine law, and with firm decision of his own will, should know the evil and reject it— should know the good and choose it ; and thus should emerge from the condition of infantine innocence into the state of angelic innocence. For the working out of this transition, it was necessary that he should possess the power to will otherwise than God's will. The command to abstain from one tree in the garden afforded this possibility. Two ways offered themselves to man's choice, in order to attain to this conscious freedom of will. The right way was, by means of this command, to become acquainted with the temptation to evil, and to overcome it. Thereby would man, without experiencing either sin or death, have passed into that condition in which the possibility of sinning was as far removed from him as from the angels—nay, from God Himself. So, subsequently, Christ the second Adam, by overcoming all incentives to evil, passed out of the condition of temptation (the possibility of sinning) into the condition of Divine perfection. Besides this right way, there was presented before Adam a wrong way, ver. 3 : that he should exchange the true freedom of guiding himself in accordance with God's law without enticement to evil, for the false freedom of regulating himself according to his own changeable inclination. He was not tempted by the want of anything to transgress the law, since he lived in the enjoyment of the rich abundance of God's gifts ; he was not tempted by fleshly passions, since these did not exist before the fall : but simply was he tempted by the desire of self-exaltation, and the endeavour to attain a false independence. So soon as he acquired the knowledge of good and evil, his innocence was lost. He became acquainted with evil from his own experience. He became in a certain sense his own master, and was in this respect "as God;" yet at the same time he became a slave to sin and the flesh, and subject to temporal and eternal death. The tree of the knowledge of good and evil gave therefore to man what its name imports, yet to his great hurt, until, by God's interposition in the work of redemption, this hurt was changed into a great gain. The tree of knowledge was placed by God in the midst of the garden, in some conspicuous place, by the side of the tree of life. So might man, in the very place where he received the greatest of all God's favours—immortality, practise the duty of obedience. We must not for a moment suppose that the tree of good and evil was in itself injurious or brought out of the kingdom of the devil.

Ver. 10. *Thence;* i. e., in Eden there was one stream; but on its exit from the garden on the land, it was divided.

Ver. 14. *Euphrates.*—In order to know the situation of "the garden," which is here described to us from names and facts which were familiar to the ancients, we must begin from those that are known to us. The fourth river, called in Hebrew "Phrath," is that which often occurs in the Old Testament, and which we call Euphrates. The Hiddekel is the Tigris. It occurs under this name in Dan. x. 4, and is still called, with a slight variation of its original name, in Aramaic "Diglat," in Arabic "Didschlat;" it flows to the east of Assyria, under which name is to be understood the northern part of Mesopotamia, which belongs to Assyria. The Pison (Phischon) is more closely described by the name of the land of gold and precious stone, Chavila, round which it flows. It seems to have been the Phasis of the ancients, which rises in the mountains of Armenia (the Moschick), and flows out of Cholchis (which may easily be the same with Chavila), and empties itself into the Black Sea. It is still called Reou, or Phasch, by the Turks, as the fortress at its mouth is called Poti or Phasch. This river was renowned among the ancients as abounding in gold, and from thence, according to the Greek fable, the Argonauts brought the golden fleece. The land was distant, and not well known; for that reason it is here more circumstantially described. The Hebrew word Bedolach, Greek Bdellium, describes apparently a kind of sweet-smelling resin, in berries like the manna (Num. xi. 7).

For "onyx" the Hebrew word is Schoham, "a precious stone" — either that or the emerald.—The second river, "Gihon," or Gichon, is the most difficult to decide on, as there were and still are many rivers which bear this name, "the breaking forth." The Arabians still call by this name a large river, which descends from the Tibetanian high mountains, and towards its source is designated Kolscha; lower down, Amu. The ancients named it the Oxus; but the Aras also, which flows from the Armenian mountains into the Caspian Sea, and which was called by the ancients Araxes, is now the Dschihun-Ras. In the case of both of these rivers, it is difficult to explain how either could encompass the whole land of Kusch, *i. e.*, Ethiopia, as this points out to a country which lay to the south, even if it does necessarily imply Africa. The far East must likewise be included in this description. In any case, we must suppose Eden to be a district in which the Euphrates, Tigris, Phasis, and (perhaps) Araxes, could rise from one source before the nature of the countries was changed by the great flood. This district can only be the western highland of Asia, Armenia. Here, where after the flood Noah left the ark, was, according to Holy Scripture, situated Eden, the cradle of the human race.

Ver. 15. *To keep it.*—From the beginning God created man for labour, and for such a labour as might gradually subdue the earth, at the same time that man learnt to know his powers. The first labour was the peaceful, ennobling, improving one of garden work. We see from the fact, that man was appointed "to dress it and keep it," that the resistance of nature was to be overcome by man, and all its powers of injury to be subjugated in order that it might become useful and beneficial. This opposition of nature to man existed at the first; only it did offer then, as it frequently does now, an irresistible obstacle to his efforts.

Ver. 17. *Die,*—*i. e.*, thou shalt surely become subject to death, shalt become mortal, as the following history shows. When God had spoken the irreversible judgment, it stood before Him as already accomplished. "Death" signifies here, as ch. iii 19 shows, primarily, the death of the body. But even in the Old Testament (though more clearly in the New Testament) is the term "destruction," "misery," applied to the soul, and therefore signifies eternal as well as temporal death, in the same way that "life" betokens eternal blessedness (Prov. ii. 18; ch.

xi. 19; ch. xiv. 12; cf. especially the figurative expression, Prov. iii. 18, "the tree of life"); and so, as the view was more directed to the life beyond the grave, death appeared also as "condemnation" (Eccles. xi. 9; Dan. xii. 2). "If the question is asked, What kind of death God here means, we must gather the explanation from the contrary—viz., what was the kind of life forfeited. It was in every respect a happy one: the life embraced equally body and soul. In man's soul prevailed right knowledge, and a proper moderation of all desires; his bodily powers were perfect, and so he was entirely free from death. His life on earth, indeed, would only have been a temporal one; but he would have passed on to heaven without pain or dying. But he dreads death; because, in the first place, it is a kind of annihilation of the body; next, because the soul feels the curse of God; and, lastly, because the judgment of death is alienation from God. Hence it is that, under the word death, is comprehended all that is miserable; and to this Adam by his fall became subject. As soon, too, as he fell away from God, who is the source of life, he lost his former position, and was made to feel that life apart from God is only misery, the prey of corruption, and so as bad as death itself. Accordingly, man's situation after the fall was rightly called death. The wretchedness of soul and body during the life on earth is, as it were, the vestibule of death, until death comes and follows it up. As soon as the judgment was pronounced on him, Adam came under the dominion of death, until grace, which followed thereon, brought the means of salvation."—Calvin.

Ver. 18. *Not good.*—Above, it is said, "God saw all that He had made, and, behold, it was very good:" here it is not good, for no other reason than because all was not yet completed. The narrative here goes back to the sixth day of creation.

Meet for him.—This consultation of God with Himself is similar to that of ch. i. 26. The importance of the new creation is enhanced by this mode of speech. Marriage, as a manner of union altogether different from that which prevailed in the lower creation, was entirely a fresh ordinance of God, and had not any existence among the rest of God's creatures. The man is first created; then the woman, to be his helper, in order to show that not the man and woman combined constitute one perfect human being, but the position of the man was an independent one, that of the woman for the sake of man. In the ordinance of marriage is typified the relation of God to His reasonable creatures.

Ver. 20. *Help meet.*—From seeing all the beasts after their manner in the enjoyment of fellowship, man was made to feel the want of communion with his equal; and by the fact that he perceived this need so keenly, is it made evident to him that no mere transient carnal union could satisfy his longings. This verse points out to us the origin of language. The animals are capable of receiving from the surrounding objects only the impressions of pleasure or pain, and of expressing these merely by unmeaning sounds; man, on the contrary, from his being created in the likeness of God, feels the desire to understand the Divine idea which is impressed on His creatures, and to designate them in accordance with his comprehension of their design. Thus, then, when God brought the beasts before Adam, out of the conception in his mind arose of itself—words, speech. This narrative proves, in a striking manner, that language did not first arise as a means of intercommunion of thought, but was the necessary embodying of the ideas which existed in the human soul. Still we are not to suppose that Adam's insight into the character of the animals was a perfect comprehension of the secrets of nature; but it is rather to be regarded as the pure, simple, lively view of an innocent child full of undeveloped depth of mind. That the beasts, all of them, come to Adam, is a sign that their present natural wildness did not then exist; but their nature was like that described, Isa. xi. 6, as their future condition on the glorified earth. The same is seen from the colloquy of the serpent with the woman.

Ver. 21. *Deep sleep.*—"What happened to him at this time was neither a mere trance nor an ordinary sleep; but, as the wise and skilful Creator of our nature designed to take from him a rib, He caused a deep sleep, like a trance, to fall upon him, and as by a weight to keep him down, in order that he might not feel pain, and on that account entertain a dislike towards her who was formed out of his side."—St Chrysostom. Although this sleep was something of an unusual kind, yet we must not imagine that sleep itself was a consequence of sin. Certainly it is a curtailment of the natural life, but was, with the alternations of day and night, ordained for the whole creation, and by no means contemporary with the fall. The Jewish fable, that Adam, before the fall, had conceived a carnal appetite (from his observation of the conduct of the animals), and that this sleep arose from a sort of sensual intoxication, and that God, to ward off a greater evil, separated the man from the woman—destroys the whole meaning and coherence of this most incomparable narrative, is directly opposed to Scripture (1 Tim. ii. 14), and ought, therefore, never to have been repeated by Christians.

Ver. 22. *Brought her.*—" With the sleep, a trance likewise fell upon him, so that he did not feel what had taken place. When we hear, then, that he, on sight of the woman, clearly declares what has happened, we must be convinced that he utters these words from a prophetic gift, and had been taught by the Holy Ghost."—St Chrysostom. What is here narrated of the creation of the woman points out the peculiarity which exists in the union of man and woman. In the case of the animals, both sexes could be created side by side; in the case of man, however, where marriage is intended to be a communion of soul in the service of God, an union of authority and obedience on the one side, and of all-compensating love on the other—where the education and training of the fruits of marriage for God's service and kingdom, the ordering and governance of the house and of the earth, formed a main part of the task imposed—there must the origin of the woman point to the indissoluble union by which two persons become one until their life's end. The woman was taken out of the man (and out of that part of him which lay nearest to his heart), in order to show that this union of soul in love extended to the unity of the flesh likewise—embraced all, both within and without, and, as a Divine ordinance, was indissoluble. The coarse, animal-like man regards his children only as his flesh and blood, and considers his connection with them closer than with his wife; but the Word of God teaches him that his wife is his own flesh and blood, and that God's appointment has made her so entirely one with himself, that if he hates his wife he hates his own flesh: Eph. v. 25. Here, then, we find in the beginning of Scripture a doctrine taught concerning marriage (less, indeed, by word than by a Divine action, as was most suitable to the infant age of the world), which, on account of the hardness of men's hearts, was afterwards withdrawn for a time, and only again restored in its fulness by Christ: St Matt. xix.

Ver. 23. *Woman.*—In Heb. the man "Isch," the woman "Ischa."

Ver. 24. *Leave father and mother.*—These are the words of Moses, and also of God; but not Adam's. They would be more correctly expressed,—" Therefore may a man leave his father and mother, but he shall cleave to his wife, and they shall be one flesh." There will be times and circumstances when a man is permitted, nay, is commanded, to leave his father and mother; but his wife is he never permitted to leave—they both shall be one. This is not said of the woman, because she already by her marriage has left father and mother, and become subject to her husband. Here it is not spoken of leaving father and mother for the sake of marrying, but of a leaving after marriage.

Ver. 25. *Not ashamed.*—So long as man keeps his body in perfect obedience to the spirit, and is therefore free from all inordinate concupiscence, no lust can arise, which makes a hiding of himself necessary, and so no shame. At the same time, this circumstance plainly shows that the marriage relation is in itself perfectly pure, and that the abstinence from it is by no means a higher and more sinless state; still, the full restoration of this original purity is not to be looked for so long as sin reigns in our mortal members and human sinfulness continues.

CHAPTER III.

The history of the fall stands in close connection with what precedes it, and is to be understood literally, as all the foregoing account. The exact designation of the situation of the garden of Eden, the appointment of man to keep it, both show us that we have to do with earthly relations, and are transported to the childhood of the human race. With childlike inexperience, our first parents believe that in the serpent they see only an animal to whom the gift of speech is granted. Verses 1 and 15 prove that in the narrative a real animal is intended. We are, likewise, not to be surprised at finding that (as in the preceding chapter) God walks in the garden in human form, and converses with Adam and Eve. We find throughout the whole of Holy Scripture that God has ever condescended to human wants, and ordered the revelations in accordance with them. But in later periods the visible manifestations in human shape become less frequent and altogether cease, while miracles take their place, which, at first, are addressed nakedly to the outward senses, until, in the New Testament, these also become of a more hidden character. The sensible and the visible decrease, the inner perception increases. Man is put to the test whether he will out of free love obey God and depend on Him, and overcome evil. Thus would he rise to a higher condition. But the desire tempts him to know and decide for himself what is good and what evil, instead of renouncing his own will from the love of God. The temptation assails him to be as God, *i.e.*, independent—his own master. In this consists, according to the Scripture narrative, the essence, the real character of the first sin, the origin of all after sin of mankind. The desire to eat of the forbidden fruit follows on the inward alienation from God; and so, while the sin was in its real character and origin so great and fearful, its outward form, the act of eating of the forbidden fruit, has the character of a childlike disobedience—in accordance with man's condition—though even then we must not attempt to extenuate the nature of the sin. The immediate consequence of his fall was to awaken the feeling of shame—*i.e.*, the consciousness that now his soul, alienated from God, has lost its control over the flesh. This feeling of shame arouses consciousness of guilt, fear of appearing in the presence of God. The serpent, as a creature of God, has in itself nothing devilish; still it was an animal capable of becoming the type and instrument of temptation. The real tempter, of course, could not be an animal, but only a higher evil spirit, the devil, who made use of the animal as his instrument. There is no mention in Scripture of any personal bodily manifestation of this evil spirit, and it is altogether impossible. Accordingly, he was obliged to speak through the medium of the serpent. God leaves man in the notion that he has to do with an animal only, punishes the serpent in an emblematic manner by a bodily infliction, and the deep loathing of it which is implanted in man's nature. He promises grace to mankind in the judgment pronounced on the tempter. The New Testament fully explains the meaning of this history. St John viii. 44; Rom. xvi. 20; 2 Cor. xi. 3; Rev. xii. 9.

Ver. 1. *Subtle.*—The subtlety of the serpent became proverbial (see St Matt. x. 16; 2 Cor. xi. 3, 11). Adam and Eve had observed this characteristic of the serpent; from which circumstance, and from their infantine inexperience, we must explain the fact, that the speaking of the serpent did not surprise them. It appears, also, that they supposed they had to deal only with an intelligent beast: hence was their guilt the greater, inasmuch as they believed an animal, which was placed under their authority, rather than their Creator. The word "subtle" does not bear here the bad sense of "craft," "cunning:" it stands in a good sense, Prov. i. 4; ch. viii. 5.

Hath God said?—The tempter first seeks to instil into the woman doubt as to the Divine command by showing it to be unjust, and therefore that it could not proceed from God. "What good is life in paradise if one may not enjoy the things which are found therein, but only feels the more pain by seeing them before one's eyes, while one is forbidden to take and eat of them?"—St Chrysostom. The enticement of acquisitiveness—of obtaining that which is forbidden, the want of which makes a man feel himself only the poorer,—this feeling could not yet be a temptation to pure and sinless beings: another and a stronger allurement must be added.

Ver. 3. *Lest ye die.*—This answer shows that the first of our race sinned against a clear, known command (cf. Rom. v. 13). The temptation as yet meets with no response; but the woman's engaging in a discussion upon the subject is a proof of her weakness.

Ver. 5. *Good and evil.*—The serpent represents God as envious, as He has ever appeared to unbelief to be. (Every deity is envious, says Herod: cf. St Luke xix. 21.) The serpent makes use of man's consciousness (which had been imparted to him by God) that he was destined for a higher resemblance to the Divine nature, by means of which he should acquire full freedom from every temptation; and blinds him with a deceitful resemblance, by leading him to suppose this likeness to God lies in freedom of choice merely. Instead of striving after true freedom, which consists in the mastery over incentives to evil, man sought by a wrong road the mere shadow of freedom, the right of being independent to choose good and evil—to be his own master—by his own experience to know the evil as well as the good—to be independent of God, to make a choice without considering that it was through the power and love of God that he was free from the power of sense, and so lord of himself and the earth. This was the first sin; and it is now the main source and origin, of which other sins are but the particular forms, or the consequences and fruits. The origin, too, of sin lies (as this history shows), not in sense, but in the striving after independence of God—a false *self-dependence*. But since man's true and eternal *self* has its *existence* only in God, this self-seeking caused immediately the fall into the power of sense,—man now cares only for his temporal material self. Therefore is sin and the temptation and power of sense to be distinguished, not only as cause and effect, but as soul and body. The *form* which man's sin assumes—nay, every object of the inward evil desire—is always belonging to the *flesh* or the *world*; but its *soul*, even in its coarsest form of sensuality, is always—*self-exaltation*.

Ver. 6. *Make one wise.*—Lit.: "That it was a good tree to eat thereof, that it was a desire (well-pleasing) for the eyes, and that the tree was lovely to look on." This threefold description of the same thought is intended to represent the temptation to the senses which was aroused in the woman, so soon as the thought of being equal with God had gained possession of her soul.

He did eat.—The temptation first overcame the weaker sex, which should always bear in mind the origin of sin, since the same liability to fall under temptation still remains: 1 Tim. ii. 14; 2 Cor. xi. 3.

Ver. 7. *Aprons.*—Their eyes were truly opened, as the serpent had promised them; but only to see that, in the moment when they departed from God, they became slaves of the flesh— that the free-will of independence of God, and knowing the good and the evil, delivers them up to the power of evil. Man, who had his glorious destiny before him, of becoming, by means of the knowledge and love of God, and by obedience, the free lord of the world, ceases, by disobedience, to be master of himself. He can no longer govern that which is a part of himself—his own flesh; much less can he rule outward nature. So long as his will was governed by God's law only, he felt not sensual lust, or any need of withdrawing from its influence (ch. ii. 25), but, so soon as he is left to himself, he perceives that he has no longer control over his fleshly appetites, and especially the most powerful of all of them, and that he can keep himself unharmed amidst the storm of desires, only by keeping out of sight the external incentives thereto. This is the origin of that feeling of shame which is a continual remembrancer of our fallen condition, as it shows us we are the slaves of the flesh, through sin. But shame is likewise the embodiment of conscience—the unconscious defence against subjugation to the flesh, the first resistance to the power of the evil one, which induces a man, when he cannot overcome, at least to flee from, sin. Therefore does God afterwards confirm and implant in man this feeling of shame, ver. 21. "After they (our first parents) had fallen from their glorious condition, and their body had felt the desires of the flesh, the promoters of disease and death, still did the reasonable soul, in the very midst of her punishment, afford a proof of her noble origin, and felt shame on account of the animal desires, not merely because she suddenly became aware of their presence, but because the evil emotion had its origin in the breaking of the commandment. Then did they feel with what grace they were clothed when, though naked, they were the slaves of no unseemly desires. In their hastening to make an apron of fig-leaves, they appear to have been moved by some mysterious impulse, and to have adopted unwittingly this sign of their punishment—a conviction of sinfulness to themselves, and still a memento of the same to every one who yet reads the narrative."—August.

Ver. 8. *Cool of the day.*—Lit.: "Wind of the day." Perhaps we may infer from this passage, that usually, in the cool of the evening—that time so especially delightful in an eastern climate—God had walked in the garden in the likeness of man, and held intercourse with him. At the time, therefore, when it had happened so often before, they heard His voice—*i.e.*, perceived some sound which was a token of His presence.

Ver. 10. *Hid myself.*—This need not be considered as a mere pretext: nakedness was to him painful, now when "he perceived another law in his members warring against the law of his mind, and bringing him into captivity to the law of sin which was in his members." The feeling of shame was a perpetual reproach of conscience. Still, clearly Adam tried, under this feeling of shame, to hide the sin of disobedience.

Ver. 11. *Not eat.*—Where is the innocence which clothed thee, so that thou didst not require any covering? Hast thou not acquired the knowledge of good and evil by eating of the tree, and thereby art become evil?

Ver. 12. *She gave me.*—The first sin at once shows itself as the mother of another. Instead of confessing his sin, the man immediately throws the weight of it on the woman—nay, through the words, "whom *Thou* gavest me," on God Himself; just as now sinners try to lay the fault on the temptations of others, and then on the circumstances of life, which were ordained by God.

Ver. 13. *Beguiled me.*—The woman follows the same course of sinful self-excuse. God condescends to enter into these reasons, since, of course, there was a truth mingled with the lie, yet without freeing them from the punishment.

Ver. 14. *Dust shalt thou eat.*—The words are directed to the actual serpent, and announce his forthcoming punishment—since a curse, which with a man is a mere wish, with God is an act. The serpent, more than any other animal, excites in man an involuntary loathing. "A beast which is like to an embodied flash of lightning, variegated as though fire-streaked, or black and dark as night, eyes like sparks, a forked black tongue like a flame, its throat an abyss, its teeth poison-fountains, its noise a hiss: add thereto its motion—an effort to quiver like lightning, or fly aloft like an arrow, did not its bodily form hinder its doing so." The "going on its belly" shows that in the beginning the serpent had an erect form. The "eating dust" is not to be understood of the nourishment of the serpent, but expresses its grovelling way of life, and that the earth must be mingled in its food. The punishment is significant—how a like punishment should be inflicted, according to the law, on every beast which injured man (ch. ix. 6; Exod. xxi. 28; Lev. xx. 15, 16). This emblematic punishment of the serpent—"dust shalt thou eat" —continues after the restoration of nature, when its power to injure shall be taken away: Isa lxv. 25. Inasmuch as God addresses the tempter in the serpent, the punishment of a deeper degradation is hereby declared against him. "As a loving father punishes him who has slain his son, breaks likewise in pieces the weapon—sword or poignard—by which the death has been brought about, so does the merciful God inflict on the beast whose subtlety had served as a weapon to the devil a lasting punishment, that we, from the sensible and visible, might understand how He has also disgraced him."—St Chrysostom.

Ver. 15. *Bruise his heel.*—These words are especially addressed to the serpent. Henceforth shall there be enmity between the human race and that of the serpents. This is the first breach among the creatures of earth, which has ever since widened. Many other beasts are now emblems of human vices, and therefore objects of abhorrence to man: the craft, the lust, the rapacity, the pride of many animals, are proverbial among us; they point out to a mysterious connection of man with nature, and continually remind him of sin and the fall, since originally nothing which was created could inspire man with dread or loathing. The man "shall bruise the serpent's head," and it shall bruise his heel; *i.e.*, man shall in open fight inflict deadly wounds on the serpent (which can be wounded fatally only in the head), while it shall often, by cunning, wound man in a painful, dangerous, and even fatal manner. As God pronounces here His sentence on the *serpent*, He must also foretell, in this enmity that is betwixt man and it, the final triumph of man. If this judgment is applied to the spiritual tempter (as in N. T. St Luke x. 19; Rom. xvi. 20), then the word "seed," descendants, acquires necessarily a spiritual meaning. (Seed can in Hebrew never mean an individual, but only an aggregate of persons.) Man has been overcome by the devil, but the hope of preservation has not yet been destroyed. The "seed of the woman" are, therefore (in opposition to "the children of the devil"), all who are true to their original destiny, who cleave to God and serve Him. The "seed of the serpent" are all bad men and evil spirits, who are adherents of Satan (St Matt. xxiii. 33; 1 John iii. 8). The descendants of the woman—mankind—shall, on some future day, obtain an entire triumph over the devil, and bring to nought the power of the evil one. It is to be observed that the triumph is promised to the *woman's* seed; and there appears in this a manifest reference to Him whose mother "knew not a man," and through Him to His spiritual descendants. This is the first dark prediction of a future redemption of mankind—a victory over the tempter, and thereby over temptation, with all its consequences. A personal Saviour is not here expressly promised—

only alluded to. It is said, the "woman's seed," not Christ; but in Him only has the prophecy attained its completion, which at first was obscure, and afterwards became more and more clear. He, and they who believe on Him, before and after His appearing, these are they who tread on the serpent's head ("the seed of Abraham, and heirs according to the promise:" Gal. iii. 29). The fulfilment is not, therefore, granted once for all, but attains accomplishment only at that time when "all enemies shall be put under His feet."

Ver. 16. *Bring forth children.*—The woman first receives the punishment which was her peculiar share. That which is afterwards adjudged to the man affects her together with him. Childbirth, with all that precedes and follows, is the especial portion of the female sex; and the most healthy women suffer pain, and even death, in a very great measure from this cause.

Thy desire;—i. e., Notwithstanding the pangs of pregnancy and childbirth, thy desire shall still remain towards him who hath made thee subject to himself.

Rule over thee.—From the beginning the woman was for "the sake of the man," as his helper, and therefore was she dependent on him. But the severe relationship of master and subject was from henceforth to be the prevailing one in marriage. Among most heathen nations the women lived, and still live, in a hard and oppressive state of subjection; and it is one of the fruits of Christianity to have removed the original curse, and so altered woman's position, so that (more particularly with regard to the inner life) it may be said, "Here is neither male nor female, but ye are all one in Christ:" Gal. iii. 28. Nevertheless, as sin still remains even in believers, the subjection must continue, only it is mitigated by affection.

Ver. 19. *Unto dust shalt thou return.*—A twofold punishment is here inflicted on Adam—the cursing of the earth, and death. Both affect the woman at the same time, who, over and above these, has her own especial punishment by reason of her guilt in tempting her husband. In the place of the easy "keeping of the garden," is appointed for man the tilling of the ground, which at the beginning was attended with peculiar difficulties: instead of the fruits of all the trees of the garden, man must "eat the herb of the field." And moreover a curse is laid on the ground itself, that, in spite of all man's efforts, his work shall not be altogether successful. The labour of the field is but a single example of man's outward condition on earth. On every state, every position, every business on earth, is the curse laid— that much pain, and labour, and carefulness, and wearisome toil is every man's lot in his calling. This is the punishment of sin. By reason of this curse, the earth is become a valley of tears, so that everything under the sun is vanity (Eccles. i. 2, 3, 14), and man is induced to strive more earnestly after his "inheritance incorruptible and undefiled in heaven :" St Pet. i. 4. It is clear that this is but one side of the picture, and that man, under the dispensation of grace, and by means of it, can, when converted to God, change into a wholesome means of discipline and a precious medicine that chastisement which is only a punishment to man as long as he continues in sin, and a foretaste of a more fearful, an eternal punishment. Since this time a great change has taken place in nature. She opposes man's rule over her; and it is only by means of much wisdom and skill that this opposition is in a small degree overcome; and it is only there abidingly overcome where the blessings of redemption have been extended over people and lands. The second punishment is death, with all that precedes it (sickness and the necessities connected therewith), and that which follows after, viz., the eternal destruction of the soul. Bodily death is the visible image and forerunner of eternal death,—the dark curtain before that unseen world which conceals behind it nothing but hopeless misery for the unrepentant sinner.

Ver. 20. *Mother of all living.*—It seems as though, in this name which Adam gave to his wife, he would express his belief in the promise (given ver. 15) of a future restoration of the human race through the seed of the woman. " Though condemned to death, yet will not the human race perish, but will triumph through the woman over the tempter to sin and death." (Heva, properly Chawwah, signifies life; therefore the Greek name is Zoe).

Ver. 21. *Coats of skins.*—This presupposes the killing of animals, and permission given by God to do so, which laid the foundation of bloody sacrifices. What had been done by themselves under the first impulse of shame after the fall, this God now does for them after a more perfect manner. He sanctions the feeling of shame, and the sense of decency and propriety which arises therefrom. This is the beginning of the domestic life, by the appointment of which the incentive to sin is diminished; an external acknowledgment of God's will is enforced among men, and a consciousness of sin awakened, though by means of these outward ordinances the inward subjugation of sin was not possible. It was designed by this training to lead on to the full triumph over sin, and the perfect fulfilment of the law, in Jesus Christ.

Ver. 22. *Good and evil.*—Had the tempter, then, not lied, as God here confirms what he said? The explanation will not be difficult for any one who has understood the history of the temptation and the fall. Man strove to attain the higher condition of life for which God had destined him by self-exaltation, by becoming independent of God. He wished to be his own master: this was certainly possible by sin, yet at the cost of his own destruction. He is free from God: he is by nature no longer under the guidance of God: he knows himself he can discern good and evil. But as there is but one God—as the creature cannot become the Creator, but must depend on the Creator or else perish—so is temporal and eternal death the immediate result of this presumption to be like God, this empty freedom. Perfect freedom, without any desire to act otherwise than in obedience to God's law—this was the end which man by obedience would have attained: freedom from law, self-will—this was the object towards which he was tempted by the devil, and which he by disobedience really attained.

Tree of life.—Had man now further eaten of the tree of life, and lived for ever, then would he have been independent of God, a self-dependent creature, and sin would have been perpetuated. This, in itself, impossible, God hindered by His punishment. The exclusion from the way to the tree of life is the fulfilment of the threat of death in ch. ii. 15, and is explained therefore by that. Since man was not forbidden at first to eat of the tree of life, we may conclude that only the continual partaking of it would have procured for him immortality.

Ver. 23. *From the garden of Eden.*—The narrative proceeds, in order to avoid repetition, from the word of God to the act of God. The "Cherubim" are frequently mentioned both in the Old and New Testament. They were fashioned of gold on the ark of the covenant, and bore there, emblematically, the throne of the invisible God. They are mentioned as the chariot on which God rides (Ps. xviii. 11). They are the four living beasts which, in the Revelation of St John, stand round about the throne (ch. iv. 6). In their fourfold resemblance—to a man, a lion, an ox, and an eagle—they represent the idea of what is highest in creation: the thinking man, the strong lion, the beneficial ox (the image of the productive power in nature), and the soaring, sharp-sighted eagle. In what form we are here to imagine them is not told us. As the highest beings in creation, they guard the entrance to its highest treasure—the earthly paradise—until it was swept away from the world. But, without passing from the proper explanation of the history into an allegorical interpretation, we may, in the flaming sword which turned every way, perceive the image of the natural phenomena of storms and tempests, which, in the Old Testament, are often referred to the angels as God's instruments which minister thereto. The cherubim are purposely mentioned as the authors of these natural events, in order so much the more clearly to represent them as Divine judgments. The reason why man was driven out of the garden, and the way to the tree of life closed against him, rather than the tree deprived of its imparted virtue, and the garden made to vanish from Adam's eyes, was this: that thereby he should ever be reminded he once really had been in the garden of Eden—had once really, by eating of the tree of life, been gifted with the certainty of life, but by the eating of the forbidden fruit had forfeited it, and become subject to death, etc. The whole narrative partakes of that character of addressing the senses as in speaking to children, whereby God was pleased to communicate with our first parents. The simple historical sense of this narrative nowhere presents essential difficulty—nay, the depths which are disclosed to us by the natural, unforced interpretation, are far greater than any which can be attained by a (pretended) more dignified and more deep allegorical explanation.

CHAPTER IV.

So great is now the inherent power of sin, so completely is the state of innocence lost, that an act of murder is committed by one of Adam's sons. In this instance likewise the progress of the sin, from its deep inward source to the fearful outward act, is remarkably evident. This great act of wickedness, like Adam's first sin, has its origin not in any allurement of the senses, or in any momentary temptation of circumstances, but in the state of the heart. This shows itself on the occasion of the first outward service paid to God by sacrifice. Man, alienated from God, but feeling his need of Him, would deserve His favour by an act of worship. God values such a work only as the outward expression of an inward devotion of the heart. God's warning points out the lurking germ of sin, that man may repress it before it springs up, and proceeds to outward deed. As this is not done, outward and inward condemnation is the consequence, though even then not without evident signs of Divine mercy.

Ver. 1. *Cain* signifies "possession." The exclamation and the name betoken the great joy of the mother at the sight of a possession, which has no equal.

Ver. 2. *Abel* signifies "perishableness" (breath, vapour). After the joy in the first-born, there glances forth, in this name of the second son, the feeling of the transitory nature of life, perhaps a prophetic foreboding of his early death. The curse, "To dust shalt thou return," does not permit the continuance of joy in any earthly possession.

Tiller of the ground.—In their earliest condition, men tended the domestic animals, and cultivated corn. Sheep cannot live without man's care and protection; and corn is nowhere on the earth found in a wild state, and without cultivation it at once degenerates. The choice of the more simple life of tending the flocks, and of the more artificial employment of husbandry, with its greater demands on the attention, betokens here the different characters of the two brothers. We meet with the same among Cain's descendants.

Ver. 4. *Firstlings.*—As the eating of flesh is not mentioned until after the flood, so probably Abel kept his flocks to procure food from the milk, and clothing from the skins; possibly also the sacrifice itself might be an unbloody one—of the wool and the milk of the herd. Sacrifice is the emblematic expression of the thankful offering of the heart to God, since man, in an acceptable offering made to God, presents, as it were, his heart therewith. In bringing each of the produce of his labour and calling—Cain of the fruits of the earth, Abel of the flock—the use and the enjoyment of the rest, and the daily labour itself,—all were to be sanctified to God. There is no mention made of an express Divine appointment of sacrifices. They appear to have originated from the direct feeling of man's heart, from whom the visible intercourse of God was not yet withdrawn; and in that intercourse of God with man, sacrifice received its ratification. Sacrifices belong to the number of those Divine gifts which remain to us from man's original state of innocency, and which, like speech, marriage, the practice of agriculture, and the tending of flocks, are to be found among all people on earth which are not sunk in the deepest barbarism. Sacrifice presupposes a living, personal relationship of man to God, Himself a Person.

Ver. 5. *Had not respect.*—We are not told in what manner the Lord manifested His pleasure or displeasure. Some have supposed the acceptance was made known by means of the consuming of the one sacrifice by lightning from heaven, as took place in after times (Lev. ix. 24; Judges vi. 21; 1 Kings xviii. 38), and the displeasure by withholding it in the other case; others, by the ascending or descending of the smoke of the offering; others (which is very unlikely), from the blessing on the cattle or fruits which followed. But in all these suppositions persons have had in view the manner of the sacrifices of later times. In the early condition of man, we must rather regard the sacrifice as a personal gift offered to a visible God, who, in compassion to the weakness of His children, held direct intercourse with them in a fatherly manner; and therefore the sign given by means of this nearer intercourse of God with His creatures would be some more direct one, and accordingly is not mentioned. The ground of the acceptableness or non-acceptableness lay in the believing temper of Abel, who brought his sacrifice in a childlike spirit, as a thank-offering to the gracious God; on the other hand, in the unbelieving temper of Cain, who, inwardly alienated from God, thought by a gift, as if meritorious in itself, to acquire the favour of God. Such hypocrisy is an abomination in God's sight; since He desires above all things the offering up of ourselves, and then our works, as the marks of our obedience.

Ver. 7. *If thou doest well.*—Heb. "If thou art good (properly, "makest thy way good"), there is a lifting up;" *i.e.*, in opposition to the falling of the countenance, then thou canst cheerfully lift up thy countenance—needest not cast gloomy looks down on the ground. God would graciously persuade Cain, who sought for the cause of his dissatisfaction in what was without, to look into his own heart. This, and the following colloquies of God with Cain, we are not to look on as what took place inwardly in his heart and conscience; but God as yet continued to communicate in human form with the primeval men.

Sin lieth at the door;—*i.e.*, "It lies in ambush, like a wild beast, at the door of thy dwelling, that it may spring upon thee when thou goest forth." When the inward declension from God has taken place, an opportunity only is required in order that "lust, after it has conceived, may bring forth sin;" and so the sinful desire may break forth into the sinful deed. This image clearly alludes to the serpent; as the exhortation which is attached thereto, reminds us of the promise of triumph over it, and encourages to undertake the struggle.

Rule over him.—God offers to the tempted the whole help of His almighty grace to withstand sin. His will is that he should not suffer sin one moment. If man unites himself in covenant with this Divine will, then can nothing overcome him, as he has Almighty Power on his side, which has given him the promise that he both can and shall "bruise the serpent's head." [Luther's translation is here different from our own;—it is, "Do not give to sin its will, but rule over it." Our version understands the Hebrew as referring to Abel, and giving a promise to Cain that he should rule over him as being the younger, and this view has the sanction of St Chrysostom; but the other translation is the preferable one.—*Transl.*]

Ver. 8. *Cain talked.*—Some old translations have here the words, "Let us go out into the field." Indeed, something appears to be omitted; though the words even of themselves would signify, Cain talked with his brother, in order to make him confident and allure him out. The last warning made to Cain had only hardened him.

Ver. 9. *Brother's keeper.*—As Adam before him, so now Cain imagines he can conceal himself from the Omniscient. The idea of the Divine omniscience does not seem to have been as yet developed in man's understanding; therefore, as soon as they had in their hearts departed from God, they believed at once that they could hide themselves from His punishment. The mental blindness is not greater than if, in our time, a servant of sin, in order to bring ease to his conscience, should make to himself a god who leaves sin unpunished. We see here, in the sin and in the defiant, hardened state after its completion, as in comparison with Adam's, the progress of corruption. The same may be observed in the punishment and the despair of Cain.

Ver. 10. *Thy brother's blood.*—Or, literally, "It is a voice (or, I hear a voice) of the blood of thy brother, that cries to Me from the earth." The blood of Abel cried to the heavenly Avenger of blood for vengeance, since Abel was by faith the child of God. By the act of sin has the will of the creature put itself in the place of that of the Creator; therefore, the consequences of such a deed cry to the Creator, that He, by retribution, should restore the order which had been broken.

Ver. 11. *Cursed from the earth.*—Cursed away from it,—driven from off it by the curse, so that it shall no more afford thee a secure resting-place.

Ver. 12. *Yield unto thee.*—The first curse after the fall consisted only in this, that the field should be cultivated with pain and labour: but Cain must depart into lands where the earth, though cultivated with care, should yield him no return.

A vagabond; i.e., banished from the land of his family—homeless; but he is not forbidden to found for himself a new home.

Ver. 13. *Can bear.*—Cain felt no real repentance; but he feared the retribution with a feeling of despair.

Ver. 14. *Shall slay me.*—The land out of which he was driven was the place where God reveals Himself, and is the Guide of His people. Driven from this spot, he believes he shall be exposed to all that is dreadful. He does not indeed suppose that he shall be out of the kingdom of God's power; he had already experienced the presence of that power too much to think this: but he shall be driven away from the visible manifestations of His grace. He fears the vengeance of blood from his nearest kin, when Adam's descendants increase. Bloodshed, Cain feels, demands the shedding of blood.

Ver. 15. *Sevenfold.*—Heb. " And the Lord said to him, Therefore shall every one who slayeth Cain have vengeance on him sevenfold,"—*i.e.*, in order that it may not take place. From the beginning God takes punishment into His own hand, or commits it to His vicegerents on earth—the magistrates. If the punishment of blood were allowed to every one, then would the human race fall into the depths of barbarism. Vengeance would not stop with the just retribution, but sin would be heaped on sin. At the same time, God threatens a fresh murder with the extremity of punishment. The order of the world has been fearfully overturned. What would take place, in the increasing wickedness and sin of mankind, if, by God's power, a bridle were not put on their fury! The Lord declares also, that if any one should follow Cain's example, he shall not be without punishment on account of his example, but rather shall incur a heavier penalty, as he ought to have been taught by him how horrible the crime was in God's sight.

Set a mark: *i.e., not,* He put a mark on him, whereby he might be known; but, He gave him a sign as a pledge of His promise, by means of which Cain gained confidence, and felt himself secure notwithstanding his banishment.

Ver. 16. *Nod* signifies banishment, exile. He gave the name himself. Some have wished to find intimation of the name *Hind,* India.

Ver. 17. *Enoch* sign. "instructed," or consecrated, dedicated: the beginning of the arts of life may be here represented. Cain and his descendants leave the pastoral life, and begin to live in cities. We now meet with the first genealogical table—that of the descendants of Cain. Banished from the land of God's immediate revelation, settled in an unfruitful region, prone to sensual pleasures, this family applies their whole powers to the cultivation of manual skill. Thus, in their way, are they made to serve to the kingdom of God. In the line of Seth, which succeeded in the place of Abel, a barrier was put to the further increase of irreligion, by more direct communion in the worship of God. It has been no uncommon phenomenon in the history of fallen man, to find that an increase of sin has led to a development of man's lower powers. Prudence, cleverness, invention, have existed among a people sunk in vice, who in the arts of life have at first excelled the better and more religious nations; but, in the end, the more calm and deep ripening of all their powers in the children of God, has given them a lasting superiority, if they have only continued to hold fast to their principles.

Ver. 18. *Irad*, *i.e.*, towns; *Mehujael* = destroyed or smitten by God; *Methusael* = man of God; *Lamech* = a powerful man.

Ver. 19. *Zilla*.—The progress of the corruption of sin perceptible in the first polygamy.

Ver. 22. *Artificer*.—The invention of the chief arts and sciences of life took place among the sons of Lamech, who was inflated with pride on account of his remarkable strength. Jubal is the founder of the nomadic pastoral life, in a way which had not existed before. This is the kind of life which afterwards the patriarchs led, as do the most of the Arabs at the present day: a life in which the head of a family, with his children and servants, pitches his tent on a fruitful spot, which is the particular property of no one; and, when this is grazed, moves onwards. Hitherto it would seem that the agricultural and pastoral life, in a state of greater simplicity, were united; but here begins the separation of work and calling.—In the names, Jubal and Tubal-Cain, early traces of the heathen gods Apollo (who is also called Abellos) and of Vulcan have been found.

Ver. 24. *Seventy and sevenfold*.—This appears to be an old poem or song (see Lowth, edit. 1821, p. 39), which was handed down from Lamech, and expresses the self-confidence with which he was filled on account of the inventions of his family, and especially those of his youngest son. "Hear my voice, ye wives of Lamech, and give ear to my speech: Since I have slain a man to my wounding, a young man to my hurt, if Cain is revenged seven times, Lamech shall be seventy times sevenfold." It would appear from this that he had committed a murder in spite of God's command on the subject, and would by his own power wrest a like immunity from punishment with Cain. Yet it may be so understood, "If I had slain a man to a wound (*i.e.*, who had wounded me), then, if Cain seven times, Lamech seven and seventy times, would be revenged." The increasing wildness and lawlessness of men which brought on the flood is here already apparent. In this genealogical table there appear some members to be left out, or the list does not extend to the flood, as the number of generations is only seven.

Ver. 25. *Seth;* i.e., compensation.

Ver. 26. *Enos* signifies "man," yet with the notion attached of helplessness.

Name of the Lord; i.e., to offer up solemn prayers to His name. This was the beginning of a regular worship, which did not consist in preaching or teaching (as this did not exist among any people of the old world), but in prayers and hymns, to which afterwards were added regular sacrifices. Hitherto ther had been among men no solemn ordinances of this kind. It is a sign, on the one hand, of increasing corruption among men, which made such appointments necessary; on the other hand, a proof of the gradual progress of the work of salvation among men.

CHAPTER V.

Here commences the series of genealogical tables, which, though interrupted by the narrative, is continued throughout this book in such a manner as to make up a regularly connected chain. These genealogical tables form, as it were, the outward framework on which the history is built, and which consists for the most part of mere names, during a period of more than 1500 years. This is all, together with a few fragmentary notices, which remains to us of the history before the flood,—just as, in our life, the comparatively long period of childhood is lost in oblivion. We have here the genealogical table of the family in which was preserved the pure knowledge of God. We see from ver. 29, that these patriarchs felt themselves forlorn on the now corrupt earth, and looked for better times; from ver. 22, that they had a good hope of an eternal life. The length of days of the patriarchs before the flood, and its gradual diminution afterwards, shows by what slow degrees the effects of the paradisaical state wore out. This circumstance should serve to remind us, that at the beginning man was destined for immortality, while at the same time the long life at first allowed was (as ver. 24, 29 seem to indicate) not felt to be a blessing. However, the great age attained by the first inhabitants of the earth enabled them more readily to keep up the traditions of early times. Noah, who was born A.M. 1056, had known Adam's grandson, Enos, who died in the year 1140; and Lamech, Noah's father, had known Adam himself.

Ver. 1. *Likeness of God.*—God Himself stands at the head of the table of man's descendants; not merely as the Creator, since He was also the Creator of all things living, but as the Father of men: St Luke iii. 38. Not without an object, therefore, is the Divine origin of the human race mentioned at the beginning of this list of genealogy, since it contains the names of those patriarchs who remained faithful to God, and therefore were justly called "the sons of God" (ch. vi. 2).

Ver. 3. *After his image.*—This expression does not contain a reference to the fall, but rather signifies the continuance of the Divine image, which was man's original condition. As Adam was created in the image of God, so was he able to beget sons after his image. The prevalence and continuance of original inherited sin is taken for granted throughout the whole history.

Ver. 6. *Enos*, which signifies "man," with the notion of weakness, mortality added thereto. (Enosch—man, from "anasch," to be sick, weak.)

Ver. 9. *Cainan*, or *Kenan*, signifies "possession," like Cain.

Ver. 12. *Mahalaleel* = "the praise of God."

Ver. 15. *Jared* = condescension.

Ver. 18. *Enoch* = "consecrated." We may infer from this name that he was from childhood, and in a peculiar sense, given up to God's service.

Ver. 21. *Methuselah* = the man of sending: it afterwards acquired the meaning of a missile, which does not seem to suit here.

Ver. 22. *Walked with God*; so ver. 24. He lived a life in the closest communion with God, as afterwards Noah did (ch. vi. 9). The expression is stronger than *before* God (ch. xvii. 1), before His countenance, or after God. To walk after God is to obey Him, to follow Him: Deut. viii. 19. We have here an example of a man, of the most ancient times, who, in faith on the revelations and promises of God which had been made to our first parents, and repeated to their descendants, was able to overcome the prevailing moral corruption so completely, that while on earth he walked in communion with God. It has been regarded as a Divine sanction of the marriage-state, that Enoch, even in such a life as this, begat sons and daughters.

Ver. 24. *Was not*—an expression that often elsewhere occurs of sudden disappearances which cannot further be explained (ch. xlii. 13, 36; Job vii. 8, etc.). The expression certainly signifies that Enoch was suddenly removed by God out of the world without seeing death, which expression is confirmed by Heb. xi. 5. All other questions upon this translation, as well as upon that of Elias—such as, whither they were carried? where they are now? what change took place on the passage?—Scripture answers not; but it places before us Enoch as an example of a blessed, eternal life, even among the first generations of the world. While in later times all hopes and prospects even among the people of God under the Old Testament were directed to this world, and long life was regarded as a sign of God's favour, early death a mark of His displeasure, there stands forth in the very oldest time one who, after a short life—short, that is, for the time in which he lived—was taken away because he was well-pleasing to God. It has been observed, that the duration of his life bears the same relation to the extreme length of man's life before the flood, as the duration of the earthly life of Christ does to the extreme length of man's life in that age.

Ver. 28. *Comfort us.*—Noah signifies peace, which word in the Hebrew bears a relation to "comforting." With prophetic glance he saw in Noah a just man of the very rarest kind, and hoped from him consolation under the weight of sorrow on the earth, which was then more than ever full of iniquity. This was a look of hope cast towards the future, which had been awakened by the promise given to our first parents, ch. iii. 15.

Ver. 32. *Shem.* — Schem signifies "name."—He it was in whose descendants the name of God, the knowledge of His revealed will, should be preserved.—*Ham*, "Cham," signifies "heat,"—the forefather of the inhabitants of the hottest countries, among whom particularly are the Cushites, the negroes.—*Japhet* signifies "spreading abroad,"—the son who should have by far the greatest number of descendants. It is possible that these names were given at the very time when Noah received the prophetic insight into their future destiny, which we read in ch. ix. 15-27.

CHAPTER VI.

MEN, now deeply sunk in corruption, depart more and more from God. The earth is full of violence, and God must warn of punishment to come. Yet in wrath He shows mercy, by granting so long a time for repentance, and by saving one whole family from the destruction.

The fact of a flood having once covered our highest mountains, and overwhelmed the former earth, is attested by nature itself. The traditions of different nations likewise afford a testimony independently of what Scripture tells us. On the highest mountains are found petrifactions of muscles, snails, fish, also the remains of innumerable genera of animals now no longer existing. The old world shows in its remains the forms of rude, uncouth animals and plants; the more delicate and refined kinds of both seem to have been developed after the flood. The race of primeval men would appear to have been of the like character (though no remains of them have been discovered, probably for the reason that they did not live in those countries where search has been made). The mention of giants is an intimation of this their character. Moreover the world before the flood must have had a very different climate from the present, since the remains of animals of hot countries are found in regions of perpetual ice. This fact, which nature reveals without any explanation, Scripture tells us was a punishment inflicted by God. We see in the flood a foreshadowing of other similar judgments in after ages, and of God's compassion at the same time. The flood was both the tomb of the old world and the womb of the new. The death of men and of all living creatures is a type of our death and resurrection in baptism. As Noah was saved by faith, and the flood was the entrance into covenant with God, so do we die and are buried with Christ in baptism, through which we rise to the life of the new man, as likewise the Israelites were baptized unto Moses in the cloud, and in the sea (cf. 1 Pet. iii. 18–20; 1 Cor. x. 1). "Since as the flood and the Red Sea were instruments for the preservation of Noah and Israel, and conduct them to life, even so to us is death, if we abide in faith, the way to life."—Luther.

[It may be remarked, that what V. Gerlach says of the flood and its remains is scarcely in agreement with the present notions of scientific men on the subject. It is thought that the remains of which V. Gerlach speaks are those of the animal and vegetable kingdoms of this earth, *before* it was prepared for man's use, and consequently before the Mosaic account, and that the flood extended over but a comparatively small part of the globe.—*Trans.*]

Ver. 2. *Sons of God* are here the descendants of Seth, who called on the name of the Lord, and were named therefore after Him (see ch. iv. 25). God is placed at the head of this race who now bear His name, as afterwards the Israelites were called the children of Jehovah, because they, beyond all mankind, were sanctified to Him. As men multiplied on the earth, they forgot their holy calling, and their separation from the rest of the world as the sons of God, and, like the God-forgetting Israelites in later times (to whom they are here held up as a warning example: cf. ch. xxvii. 46; ch. xxviii. 1; Exod. xxxiv. 15, 16; Deut. vii. 3, 4; Num. xxv. 1; 1 Kings xi. 1, 2), they look only at bodily beauty, and not at the knowledge and service of the true God. The older Jewish writers, and some fathers of the Church, falsely explain "the sons of God" by "the angels," and understand their fall to have taken place then. But Holy Scripture knows nothing of a fleshly intercourse of angels and men (cf. St Luke xx. 35); and "if the saints who had been made partakers of the Holy Ghost could not bear the sight of the angels, and Daniel himself, the 'man greatly beloved,' lay also lifeless by reason of such visitation (Dan. x. 11), who would be so irrational as blasphemously and foolishly to suppose that the immaterial and spiritual natures could ally themselves with the fleshly?"—St Chrysostom. Besides, such an interpretation does not agree with the context, as, according to it, the sin would have originated with the angels; whereas the narrative speaks of sin introduced by man, and men, not angels, are punished for it.

Ver. 3. *A hundred and twenty years.*—The most probable translation of this difficult place is (after the ancients), "My Spirit shall not always rule in man in their aberrations: they are flesh; their days shall be 120 years." Then the sense is, "My Spirit, which was breathed into man at the creation—the breath of life, shall not always, in their state of great corruption, rule—dwell, abide in them: their punishment have I in My own hand, as they are powerless, mortal beings; after 120 years will I destroy them." (The opposition of "spirit" and "flesh" in a moral sense, as in St Paul's Epistles, does not occur in the Old Testament.) Probably we are to consider these words as a prophecy uttered by God to those among the corrupt race who acknowledged Him. Now, when the salt had lost its savour, when in the dark world the light began to be extinguished, was the time come that God's judgments should fall. The carcase was there, ready for the gathering together of the eagles. None of God's greater judgments has ever taken place without a time for repentance after the threatening of it;—so the death incurred by Adam took place after a long life; the destruction of the Amorites after 400 years (ch. xv. 16). So He gave to the Ninevites forty days', to Nebuchadnezzar a year's respite; to the Jews, after their rejection of Christ, forty years. From this announcement was Noah sure that the flood would be brought on the world. He was at the time four hundred and eighty years old.

Ver. 4. *Giants.*—It is not here said that the giants were born from the marriages of the sons of God and daughters of men. By this name we understand men of great size, but, still more, men of violence (the word signifies, according to its derivation, " breakers in," *i. e.*, robbers). Such a race existed on the earth before this time, but it acquired still more by these dangerous marriages the upper hand. Moses first relates that at that time giants existed; then he goes on to say that some of them sprung from those mixed marriages. It would have been no wonder if among Cain's descendants such violence had prevailed; but how general the corruption was is seen more clearly from this circumstance, that even the holy race was infected with the same evil. The pestilence was so prevailing a one, that it had even seized on the few families who ought to be temples of God. The words of Moses allude to old sayings and traditions which Scripture does not communicate; since of these " men of renown" we know nothing. Perhaps many of these legends have passed over into the heathen mythology, for which cause Scripture buries them in silence.

Ver. 6. *Repented the Lord.*—The opposite feeling which Scripture often expresses—that God repenteth of anything, and that God is not a man that He should repent (both expressions occur in one chapter, 1 Sam. xv. 11, 29)—this requires some fuller discussion on our parts. God is, according to His own nature, unchangeable; nothing can happen without Him; His counsels are eternal (Num. xxiii. 19; Hosea xi. 19; Acts xv. 18; Rom. xi. 29; James i. 17); yet has He, since He created man, whose whole existence in time, after His own image, vouchsafed to have a life in time and finiteness, while still He continues to be the Unchangeable and the Eternal. As, therefore, man is capable of loving God, yet capable also of turning away from Him, so God feels love or anger towards him as he loves or contemns God. Of His infinite love, He has created and redeemed. He sustains and bears with man, and feels the deepest sympathy in all that concerns him; yet His holy anger burns against every sinner, and, when obstinately hardened, delivers him over to eternal punishment. As Christ, although the Son of God, perfectly sympathised in all the sorrows of fallen man, so God, by His Holy Spirit, is so fully, so inwardly joined with man, that He is troubled by his sins, and in him sighs and strives after the restoration and fulfilment of His image in him (Rom. viii. 26, 27; Eph. iv. 30). Even before Christ's incarnation the relation of God to man existed. By His incarnation has it attained its perfection. If we keep in mind this doctrine of Scripture, we perceive clearly what this strong expression, "It repented and it grieved God," means. As in the garden of Gethsemane Christ's human feeling is displayed when He prays that the cup might pass from Him, and yet at the same time is brought into perfect obedience to God's will, in order to show how He was a partaker in all our infirmities, yet without sin,—so also in these expressions, "repenting" and "grieving," that human feeling is distinctly and purposely mentioned which (independently of punishment and redemption) the sight of the deeply corrupted world was calculated to awaken in God. The personal loving God cannot feel indifferent as to man's degradation. To allow a world to perish, though His just punishment, in cold indifference—this had been the work of iron fate, not of a personal living God. Much more does the fall of man grieve Him: His work is corrupted, His labours lost. This is the first feeling which is represented in Scripture as belonging to God, who vouchsafes to experience the human feeling of love. But the Almighty, Holy, All-wise God triumphs over everything that opposes Him, and the very opposition serves all the more to bring to light the majesty of His redeeming love and might (Rom. iii. iv. v. vii.). This latter attribute is ever present with God; and therefore His "grieving" can never resemble the short-sighted, changeable sorrow of man, but is ever overpowered by His omnipotent love. But to the end that we may never forget what an offence sin is in God's sight, as He could never have created us in sin, and cannot away with sin, Holy Scripture, in several places, represents after a human fashion the feelings which sin excites in the Divine mind. The human side of this expression has its perfect truth, and can mislead us to form incorrect ideas of God, only when we sever it from the declarations concerning God's nature which are of a contrary character, but do not really contradict this. We may learn from these words that God does not recognise man in his deeply corrupted state for His own creation, as if He should say, "This is not My work; this is not the being made after My image and endowed with such noble gifts; this apostate creature I disdain to acknowledge as Mine." So much as regards His "repentance." Of a similar kind is the "grieving"—namely, that through man's horrible sins God is not less injured than as if His mind had been wounded by a deadly pain. Here is expressed the difference between the original nature as created by God, and the present human nature as corrupted by man. Would we not therefore defy and grieve God, we must both abhor and flee from sin. Yea, His fatherly goodness and patience would draw us from sinful desires, since God Himself, the more to win our hearts, has Himself taken our feelings (Calvin). We may add to this Luther's explanation. He understands "'the repenting' and the 'grieving' as belonging to God's true children. Noah and the patriarchs were moved with the most lively grief, when the Spirit revealed to them this wrath of God." These sighings, therefore, were ascribed to God Himself, because they proceeded from His Spirit. We see in after times an example in Abraham of the same thing, as he placed himself like a wall before Sodom, and would not cease from pleading for its preservation until he had reached the number of the five just persons. With what endless sighs does the Holy Spirit fill the breast of Abraham in his vain efforts to help the wretched Sodomites! In like manner, what will not Samuel do for Saul? God even saith to him, "How long wilt thou grieve for Saul, whom I have rejected?" So does Christ also weep over Jerusalem.

Ver. 7. *Have made them.*—"But why, some one may say, if man inclines to evil, are the irrational creatures subjected to the same punishment? Altogether naturally; since they were created for man's sake, and for man's sake are they destroyed. They are made partakers of our chastisement, that the exceeding greatness of the Divine wrath may be seen. As by the sin of the first man the earth was cursed, so do they share his destruction in the flood; in like manner, when man is restored to God's favour, the animals also will be partakers of his blessedness—since the creation, as St Paul says, will be freed from the bondage of corruption into the glorious liberty of the sons of God."—St Chrysostom.

Ver. 8. *Noah found grace.*—God revealed His holy anger and the approaching judgment to Noah, who walked before Him with a childlike believing mind. To the time before the flood 1 Pet. iii. 18–20 contains some weighty allusions; and Christ also warns us of the security of the men of that time, and represents it as a type of what will take place before the last day: St Matt. xxiv. 37–39.

Ver. 9. *Perfect.*—*i.e.*, Noah stood at that time altogether alone, or at least in some special near relationship to God. The word "walked" is the same as that used ch. v. 24 of Enoch.

Ver. 10. *Begat three sons.*—Here the genealogical table is continued from ch. v. 29; and Noah's family is again mentioned, because from henceforth their history will form the subject of the narrative.

Ver. 11. *Before God.*—This expression implies that man's corruption and sin loudly called for punishment.

Ver. 13. *With the earth.*—*i. e.*, With all that is on the earth.

Ver. 14. *Gopher wood.*—Doubtful what this is—perhaps cypress wood.

Ver. 16. *A window.*—Heb. a "light." It is not necessary to suppose that only one window or opening was made.

Ver. 18. *The covenant.*—The covenant which God here makes with Noah belongs to the whole human race, and not to the kingdom of God on earth; and therefore "God" (Elohim) here speaks, and not "Jehovah," as also ch. ix. It is otherwise in the command concerning clean and unclean beasts, ch. vii. 2, and in Noah's sacrifice, ch. viii. 20.

Ver. 22. *Thus did Noah.*—" I admire," says St Chrysostom, "the virtue of this just man, and the unspeakable mercy of the Lord, when I consider how he was able to live among the wild beasts—the lions, the panthers, and the bears. Consider, dear brother, what a might the first man enjoyed before the fall, and think on the goodness of God, who, after man's disobedience had spurned the dignity conferred on him, found another man who should restore the original image, and conferred on him that former dignity which the animals acknowledged, and to which they rendered obedience."

CHAPTER VII.

Ver. 3. *Face of the earth.*—To the name "Lord"—*i. e.,* Jehovah, the eternal God of the covenant of His chosen people—God joins here, in addition to the former general declaration of providential care over the whole creation, an especial promise to Noah as the appointed priest of His house and of the new race of men—the preserver and maintainer of the service of the true God on earth. On the particular occasion of the preservation from the flood, it was of great moment that the communion of man with God by means of sacrifice and thank-offering should be firmly established. This is here done by the preservation of "the clean beasts" in greater numbers than the others. As it is not stated what beasts are to be regarded as clean and unclean, we must conclude that this distinction had long ago been established by custom, and also by Divine approbation. At all events, that which was originally established by custom is here confirmed and sanctified by God. The separation of those beasts which were forbidden to be offered in sacrifice and eaten is no arbitrary invention of man's, and does not originate in an undefined loathing on the part of man towards certain beasts; but rather in the fact, that by the fall certain animals have become emblems and representatives of certain sins and appetites, so that to man reconciled to God they are objects of abhorrence (ch. iii. 15). For the same reason that the eating of blood was in very early times forbidden, is the use in sacrifice and the eating of these animals likewise interdicted—in order, that is, by means of a symbolic outward purity, to train up mankind in its state of childhood to internal holiness. Hence we perceive at the same time in what way the forbidding of certain kinds of food, has a perpetual, eternal, inward truth, which Christ has as little done away as any tittle of the law, only that, after the abrogation of the external sign, these commands are not in the letter binding on the Christian. Although therefore nothing is unclean to Christians, if it be received with thanksgiving (1 Tim. iv. 4; Acts x. 15); and although the symbols by which God expresses eternal Divine truths vary among different people and in different ages, and God never designed to appoint perpetual forms for all people alike; and although, in the general condition of the childhood of the human race, the training to holiness by means of symbolic purity was an indispensable necessity for all, which after the full revelation of Christ no longer exists,—still there remains in these commands concerning food *the* general truth for all times, that everything outward should by emblem lead us to think of what is inward—that the external symbolic purity, like every other discipline and custom, especially in the service of God, ought to prepare the way for the life of true holiness; and that therefore we can never regard with indifference the emblems of our own sins in the world of creation, nor anything, indeed, which in nature serves to remind us of death and destruction, and of the wild power of unbridled lust. Here, then, we find the continuance of that first ordinance of God by which outward discipline, good order, and morality are sanctioned.

Ver. 9. *As God had commanded.*—This of course does not contradict what was said above, but only means that the clean, as the unclean beasts, entered the ark two by two. As seven of the clean beasts went in, it is probable that they consisted of three pairs and a supernumerary, which was probably a male, and intended either for sacrifice or food. The number seven is here, as everywhere, the sacred number of the covenant between God and man. The clean beasts were intended to serve for food, since it appears that even before the flood the eating of flesh (which afterwards, in consideration of human weakness, was formally allowed) had taken place. The animals were offered in sacrifice, and so consecrated to God, before they were eaten, and in part, if not entirely, burnt in honour of Him. By this means a double purpose was served: before every meal a thank-offering was made to God, and that which was eaten itself was sanctified.

Ver. 11. *Great deep.*—The sea—the vast reservoir of the waters of the earth. This took place afterwards on a smaller scale, when, *e.g.*, the place of Sodom was occupied by the Dead Sea. Probably there the action of fire was employed, as this agent appears to have been very instrumental in the formation of our mountains.

Ver. 12. *The rain.*—It seems it had never rained before—the earth was watered with dew: ch. ii. 5, 6.

Ver. 16. *Shut him in.*—" God" takes care for His creation to preserve it; but when " *the Lord*" provides, it is only for His true servant who has found favour in His sight.

Ver. 17. *Was lift up.*—In a most beautiful descriptive manner the narrative depicts to us the gradual rising of the flood, and does not merely tell what happened. We see, as it were, the flood, swelling more and more, until it reached the greatest height.

Ver. 24. *One hundred and fifty days.*—Therefore, a time sufficient utterly to destroy everything living, and to change the character of certain parts of the earth. Some portions, however, of the globe retained, in their streams and the course of their rivers, marks of the former age of the world.

CHAPTER VIII.

Ver. 1. *Remembered.*—This does not mean, as at first sight might appear, as though God had before forgotten Noah and the animals with him in the ark, and now again remembered him; but it points particularly at the revelation of God's care for His people. God remembereth all His works at all times, and equally; but the petition, " Remember me, O Lord" (Ps. xxv. 7; St Luke xxiii. 42), proceeds from that image of God in man, through which we can find no peace until, by inward personal communion with God, we are made partakers of Him. Here the word alludes to Noah's temptations while God still hid Himself from him, and to the renewed enjoyment of His grace and good pleasure when He again revealed Himself to him. "Therefore it is no unmeaning word which the Holy Ghost spoke, 'God remembered Noah,' since it shows that, from the day when Noah entered the ark, no word, no revelation from God was granted him. He was permitted to behold no ray of the Divine grace, but was confined to the promise which he had received; and so, while the water raged around him, it was as though God had forgotten him."—Luther.

Wind.—Here was a natural means applied to bring about a supernatural effect (similarly Exod. x. 13, 19, ch. xiv. 21), as the natural wind was the sign and conductor of the outpouring of the Holy Ghost.

Ver. 2. *Restrained.*—Cf. ch. vii. 11.

Ver. 4. *Ararat* is called, 2 Kings xix. 37, Isa. xxxvii. 38, a district in Armenia, between the two lakes Wan and Urumia and the river Araxes. In Jer. li. 27 it stands for the whole of Armenia. To this day one of the highest mountains of the earth (next to the peaks of the Himalaya, the highest in the old world) is so called. Its height, according to the latest calculations, is 16,200 feet. "The Mt. Ararat has around it, at greater or less distances, the following seas and lakes, viz.:—The Red Sea, the Persian Gulf, the Lakes Wan and Urumia, the Caspian Sea, the Ural Sea, the Sea of Asoph, the Black and the Mediterranean. The mountain lies in the midst of a vast desert region, which extends almost unbroken from the embouchure of the Senegal to the east of the Gobi, north of Peking; bounded by a northern expanse of ocean which runs parallel with the desert from Gibraltar to Baikal; in the midst of the longest line of land on the globe, which stretches from the Cape of Good Hope to the Beering Straits."—K. v. Raumer's Gen. Geog. On this range rested the ark, while all the mountains were still under water; but many yet higher, to which there is an allusion in what follows, had already begun to dry.

Ver. 7. *A raven.*—The raven, which lives on carrion, is first sent out of the ark. It does not find any resting-place, but is not obliged to return. From the dove Noah seeks a surer sign.

Ver. 11. *Olive leaf.*—The olive is a low shrub which still

grows in those countries, and comes out from under water. It was a significant and merciful appointment of God's providence that the dove brought a bough from this useful tree, the oil from the fruit of which is an emblem of the grace of the Holy Spirit, and its boughs emblems of peace.

Ver. 17. *Be fruitful.*—Noah does not leave the ark except at the express command of God. God now grants him the new promise of fruitfulness, and confirms thereby all the promises made at the creation, and especially the blessing promised on marriage.

Ver. 20. *Unto the Lord.*—To Jehovah, the living, personal, true, real God of covenant. Immediately after the flood Noah brings a sacrifice, and God concludes for the first time a covenant with man, annexing to it promises and a visible sign. Hitherto had the descendants of Seth (the branch of mankind in which was preserved the service of God) remained, notwithstanding the fall, in a kind of childlike communion with Him. But now that corruption had spread so widely, and the destruction of the rest of mankind became necessary, a new era commences in the history of the kingdom of God. The period of man's first childhood was past. He stood no longer in immediate communion with God. From the distant and estranged position in which mankind now stood to his Maker must they become reconciled to Him, through some medium of atonement which He must establish. Through this typical and prophetic sacrifice of propitiation the Divine grace is renewed to them, and the first sacramental sign afforded in the rainbow. God renews the promises which had been given to Adam. He establishes man in a relation of greater authority and power over the animals, and permits the use of wine and flesh, in consideration of the diminished strength of the human race.

Burnt-offerings.—The burnt-offering (Heb. Olah, *i.e.* "the ascending," viz. to heaven), which entirely evaporated and ascended in smoke, had this peculiarity beyond all other sacrifices, that the whole of the animal was burnt, and not a part eaten by the priest or the sacrificer, as was the case with the others (in later times the priest received only the skin). It was the most ancient, the most general, and the most important among the different offerings: and its chief design, expiation, and the reconciliation of God with man, as the context in the history before us shows. The sacrificer placed his hand on the head of the animal, and thereby symbolically laid his sins upon it. To it the deserved punishment of death was transferred. There is this difference between burnt-offering and sin and trespass-offerings, that the latter were made on account of some particular sins, but in the burnt-offering a general confession of guiltiness was expressed. The burnt-offering, as the most general kind of sacrifice, comprised the others under it, and was therefore a thank-offering, though this latter was very often especially joined with the other (see, *e.g.*, Exod. xx. 24; Joshua viii. 38; Judges xx. 26; 1 Sam. x. 8; 1 Kings iii. 15). The signification of the burnt-offering in the case of Noah, was the solemn confession that he and his had been saved, not by reason of their own righteousness, but of God's grace, and that their guilt required an expiation before God; the expression of a belief that God will, of His grace, further forgive their sin; and the thanksgiving for their preservation founded on this confession and this belief.

Ver. 22. *Seed time, etc.*—This important declaration must be taken in closest connection with what has gone before and what follows. It appears at first sight astounding that God should here allege, *as the reason of His mercy*, that same deep corruption of mankind which before the flood He had declared to be the cause of that terrible judgment (ch. vi. 5). But here the expression, that "the imagination of man's heart is evil," must be understood in connection with the sacrifice. Because the Lord had smelled the sweet savour of the sacrifice, therefore— He so spake with Himself—therefore He could forgive in spite of the deepest corruption. The sweet savour (the savour of rest, *i.e.*, refreshment) of the offering is the symbol of God's acceptance of the expiation which man brought, as well as of the believing feeling and self-offering which were expressed in this emblematic act. We find in this sacrifice, and in God's covenant with man which accompanies it, an important progress in the history of God's kingdom; since here, in the symbolic act at the commencement, are expressed the necessity of an atonement, and the forbearance and mercy shown to man in spite of his deep corruption. God promises that *such* a judgment as the flood shall never return. Henceforth is the way to reconciliation more and more opened to all, until the earth shall in God's appointed time perish by fire, and from this fresh purification come forth new and glorious (2 St Pet. iii. 7).

CHAPTER IX.

Ver. 1. *Replenish* (cf. i. 28.)—A comforting assurance that, notwithstanding the flood, God had still pleasure in the increase of mankind.

Ver. 2. *Delivered.*—The words are stronger than ch. i. 26, to which they point, and clearly show that nature generally, and the animals in particular, by the progress of human corruption and by the increase of mankind, had now become estranged from man. At the first creation, man had dominion over the brutes by means of the bond by which he was more nearly united to nature, and by his own spirit, which was in closer communion with God: now he ruled through fear and dread.

Ver. 4. *Blood thereof.*—Even before the flood, through the wild, lawless, kind of life of men, the eating of flesh had come into vogue: here, on account of man's greater weakness, it is expressly permitted. The killing of the animals, which continually reminded men of " death, the wages of sin," and of him who was a murderer from the beginning, was calculated to inspire them with a certain natural horror, and required, therefore, an express Divine appointment. But in the blood is the life— the animal soul. The eating of an animal which had not first been bled, and likewise the eating of blood generally, was calculated to nourish the thirst for blood, the delight in death, and therefore is forbidden. Besides, the soul of the animal, the blood, was appointed to be offered in sacrifice as an atonement, in the stead of man's soul. After that Christ, not by the blood of goats and of calves, but by His own blood, had made an atonement, the eating of blood became a matter of indifference (cf. Lev. xvii. 11; Heb. ix. 11).—[? *Vide* Acts xv. 29.]

Ver. 6. *Image of God.*—The life of his fellow-man was to be so much the more sacred in the eyes of man from henceforth, inasmuch as God had permitted the killing of animals for his subsistence. Man was created in the image of God, that he might know and love Him, and by means of this knowledge and will freely fulfil God's will. Every individual man, therefore, stands in personal relation to God. All injury thus done to the image of God in man, will God Himself avenge on man and beast. Every man should regard another as his brother, his equal, and possessed of the same claims on life with himself. The threatening here against man and beast is to be taken generally. Yet herein we see a proof of the Divine appointment, by which every man who has killed another suffers death at the hands of the magistrate; every beast also who has slain a man receives, after a symbolic manner, the punishment of death (Exod. xxi. 28). The reason assigned, "because God made man in His own image," shows that under the Divine image is meant not merely the moral perfection of man in his communion with God (which was forfeited by the fall), but likewise his capacity for this, which could never be lost. As the nature of all punishments consists in exact retribution, the destroying of God's image in those who had themselves destroyed it, met this requirement.

Ver 17. *All flesh.*—From what is here said, it is probable that before the flood it had never rained, otherwise the sign would not have had its significance. But, if we would rightly represent to our mind's eye the full force of this sign, we must bear in view the character of the shorter, but violent storms of hot countries. Supposing, as was the case, none of these had occurred before the flood, then every fresh gathering of clouds, as long as the remembrance of that judgment lasted, would be a visible sign of God's anger. But if, after such a storm, the sun again appeared, and more than that, if it mirrored its image on the dark cloud, in the form of the bow which, with its seven glorious colours—and more particularly with the green, that colour of peace, gentleness, and benevolence—formed, as it were, a bridge from heaven to earth, then would men be convinced that even in the midst of the threatening signs of His wrath God would still let His grace descend on men, and ever be mindful of His covenant. "God looks on the bow and remembers His covenant" is a gracious mode of expressing the great truth, that God's covenanted signs, to which He has attached His promises, are real channels of His grace, and not merely before men, but *before* Himself, have power and meaning. The Unchangeable requires no continual remembrancers; yet are the signs of His covenant true and real revelations of His grace, not chance arbitrary emblems which merely in man's idea have import, but they are real, inasmuch as He remembers His covenant when He sees them.

Ver. 18. *Father of Canaan.*—Ch. x. 6. For the significant names of the three sons of Noah, see ch. v. 30. Shem (name), the forefather of the people of Western Asia, who are still called Semites; many of whom retained the knowledge of the true God. Ham (heat), the forefather of the people in the torrid zone, in Africa and Southern Asia. Japhet (spreading), the forefather of the largest portion of the human race—of the northern and western Celtic, of the Persian, Grecian, German families. It is worthy of note that the father of Prometheus, who was a giant, bears in the Greek mythology the name Japetos. The history of the first Book of Moses is not merely from the very beginning a history of the kingdom of God, but it prepares the way for the narrative of events which follow. So here is mentioned Canaan, because, among the sons of Ham, he was of the most importance in the history of the Israelites, and on him too afterwards the prophetic curse fell.

Ver. 21. *Was drunken.*—" By trying too much to excuse the patriarch, some put from them this consolation which the Holy Spirit has deemed it needful to give to the Church—viz., that even the greatest saints sometimes stumble and fall."—(Luther.) The novelty of the use of wine, and the fiery nature of the southern wines, may in some degree lessen the sin of one who in other respects walked in such close communion with God. Nevertheless the truth remains, that this sin was no slight one, in placing himself in such a situation through sensual indulgence and want of moderation.

Ver. 22. *Told his two brethren.*—" Although Noah's sin seems only a small one, it yet was the cause of a grievous offence; since not only Ham is offended thereby, but also the other brothers, and perhaps also their wives. Ham did not laugh at his father in childish levity, as boys do when they meet a drunken man in the street, and mock him: no! he sinned through the fall of his father by thinking himself a better, and holier, and more upright man than he. Thus is the thing itself a real offence, and Ham sins in judging his father, and taking pleasure in his sin."—Luther. " God had chosen eight souls as a holy and pure seed for the renewing of the earth; but Noah's sin shows how necessary it is for God to bridle men in, however excellent they may be; and Ham's godless conduct is a proof how deep-rooted was evil in man, since in God's holy asylum, among so small a number, one was a devil. Such wickedness in the prince of the new world and in the holy patriarch of the Church, as well as such wickedness in their brother, might well make the other brothers tremble as much as if they had seen the ark rend and break in pieces. But they overcame his offence with as much decision as they covered it with becoming modesty."—Calvin.

Ver. 25. *A servant of servants.*—Noah in prophetic spirit cursed that son of Ham (Canaan) who, before all the rest, was the principal propagator of his father's sins, and the most conspicuous in the history of the kingdom of God. The descendants of Ham stand, in fact, the very lowest among all the people of the earth. It is true, indeed, that from Canaan was descended one of the civilised nations of the world, the Phœnicians, as from another of Ham's sons, Mizraim, the highly cultivated Egyptian people. But the cultivation of the Phœnicians was entirely of an earthly character. They were an enterprising commercial people, with a gross, sensual religion, and infamous for utter want of good faith, without any sense of anything high or noble, and ever vibrating between tyranny and lawlessness. Even their colony Carthage was not allowed to play any great part in the world's history, but was obliged to succumb to Rome. The Egyptians, the most cultivated nation of the old world, had also an entirely earthly, sensual religion, which kept the people in spiritual and bodily bondage; and after its first period of greatness (during which the enormous power of man in his early state displayed itself), nothing great could be produced by it. All the other people of this widely spread family of the Hamites, especially the negroes in Africa, Asia, and Australia, form the aboriginal population in those lands, but are sunk in deep degradation, and almost brutalised. Where they are independent they cannot maintain themselves in freedom, but fall into abject slavery under the most cruel tyrants; but, above all, are they "servants of servants unto their brethren." It is the office of Christianity, by the power of Him who maketh "all things new," to remove this original curse when "the Morians' land shall stretch out their hand unto God:" Ps. lxviii. 31. The curse affects the whole descendants of Ham, as the sin was committed by him; but Noah mentions beyond the others that son whose descendants, by reason of accumulated guilt, were given over to destruction.

Ver. 26. *His servant*—lit. their servant, *i. e.*, of the Semites. Instead of promising the blessing to Shem, Noah praises the Lord Jehovah, the God of the covenant. He thereby signifies that on the revelation of the living God, and the continuance of His covenant, depends the blessing which should come to Shem.

Ver. 27. *Enlarge Japhet.*—The name of God is here changed, to signify that Jehovah, the revealed God of the covenant, was unknown to the descendants of Japhet; on the other hand, the Creator of the world will bless them by making Japhet broad. His descendants shall dwell in the tents of the Semites — be received kindly by them; be made also partakers of the blessing promised to them. In this prophetic glance is promised to the heathens of Western Asia and Europe the closest reception into the covenant of God, of which, at the time when Moses wrote these words of Noah — nay, even a thousand years later— there was not the slightest prospect. The Canaanites who were not rooted out or subjected by the Israelites, were, after a short season of prosperity, brought into bondage to the Japhetic nations, and never afterwards recovered power. Here, then, in a few words, is the course of the history of the human family pointed out in a prophecy which is at once the blessing and curse of a father upon his sons. At the same time, the holiness of the paternal relationship and of God's ordinances among men is solemnly maintained.

Ver. 29. *He died.*—The last who attained so great an age. But it was of consequence for the maintenance and handing down of the history, that he should die not before the year 2006, two years before the birth of Abraham.

CHAPTER X.

The genealogical table given us in this chap. is a very remarkable ancient tradition. It shows us the connection and the severance of the nations of the old world, according to their position towards the history of the kingdom of God. Those nations which had most influence on it in its course are minutely reckoned up; others, which had but a remote connection therewith, are scarcely touched on. We learn from Egyptian remains of its earliest history how extensive were both the conquests and the pacific intercourse of this land. But still there is no account of antiquity which can be compared, in accuracy and comprehensiveness, with the view of ancient nations afforded us in this genealogical table.

The names are generally, though not always, personal names. Among them may be found also the names of many nations, as, *e.g*, ver. 13, 14. The particular persons mentioned are to be understood as the forefathers or heads of the people.

The order of the sons of Noah is here reversed (ver. 2). Japhet, who was probably the youngest son, stands first, because Shem's posterity have more direct connection with the history which follows.

Ver. 1. *Shem, etc.*—By means of this repetition the genealogical table is connected with ch. ix. 18.

Ver. 2. *Gomer.*—The wide-spread people of the Cimmerians, Cymri, Cymbri, whose memory was preserved among the ancients in the name of the Cimmerian Bosphorus (the Straits of Caffa), and in modern times in that of the peninsula Crimea. Anciently they settled in the north of the Black Sea and the Sea of Asoph; from whence afterwards they extended farther to the north-west. This people is mentioned Ezek. xxxviii. 6, as one which should come with the host of Gog.

Magog.—The people whom the Greeks called "Scythians," in the north of Western Asia. In Ezek. xxxviii. and xxxix. they appear only as the emblem of the wild people, who fight against the kingdom of God; as likewise Rev. xx. 8, 9. As the Cimmerians—Gomer—were the progenitors of the original people of Gaul and Britain—the Celts, Erse, so probably were the Scythians—Magog—the forefathers of the Germans.

Madai.—The "Medes." This name occurs also Jer. li. 11, 28; Isa. xiii. 17, 18, ch. xxi. 2; and Esth. i. 19. The people which spoke the ancient Zend language, and afterwards formed the people of the Medes and Persians. According to modern researches, they are allied by origin and language with the Hindoos, Celts, Germans, and Greeks.

Javan is the same name with "Ion," which word was somewhat changed by the Greeks, and called "Iaon." The Ionians are the original inhabitants of Greece, who called themselves "Autochthones"—*i.e.*, spring from the earth, in opposition to the Dorians, who settled there afterwards. Afterwards they spread into Asia Minor, and even farther by means of colonies. Alexander is called, Dan. viii. 21, the king of Javan in a wider sense.

Mesech and Tubal generally occur together, Ezek. xxxviii. 2, ch. xxxix. 1, ch. xxxii. 26; and they are the people called by the Greeks "Moschi" and "Tibareni," on the rivers Phasis and Cyrus (Kur) in N. Armenia and Georgia.

Tiras.—An obscure name, which only occurs here;—perhaps the "Tyrseni" or "Tyrrheni," a people related to the ancient Pelasgi, or one and the same with that people, which in the most early periods wandered through Greece and Italy, and became masters of the sea. They were probably related to the Etrusci-Tuscians (in Tuscany), and even to the Dorians. Others suppose them to be the Thracians.

Ver. 3. *Askenaz.*—A people not certainly known; perhaps in Asia Minor. There is no reason for thinking of Germany, which the present Jews so name. Perhaps the Basques in N. Spain are intended.

Riphath.—The Riphaian mountains ('Ριπαῖα ὄρη, Strabo) are mentioned by the Greeks as situated in the extreme north (the fabulous Hyperborean regions), without further description.

Togarmah.—This people also is mentioned Ezek. xxxviii. 6, as marching out of the north against the kingdom of God. It brings, according to Ezek. xxvii. 14, horses and mules to the fairs of Tyrus. Ancient tradition agrees in understanding this people as the Armenians.

Ver. 4. *Dodanim.*—Four nations who sprang from the

Ionians, or are related to them. "Elis," the western territory of Peloponnesus or Hellas, the middle of Greece, is the first. "Tharsisch" (so the Heb.) is often mentioned as a distant land. We read, Jon. i. 3, of a "ship going to Tarshish;" and the ships of Tarshish in the Mediterranean receive the news of the fall of Tyre (Isa. xxiii. 1). It was a great place of trade, from whence silver, iron, tin, and lead were brought to Tyre; all which points to Spain, where Tartessus (called also Tarseiön by the Greeks) was a Phœnician colony. There are also traces to be found among the ancients of this land having been in very early times inhabited by a people who were connected in blood with the Greeks, and of their having been subdued by the Phœnicians from Tyre; and in Isa. xxiii. 10 the Hebrew has it, "Pass through like to the Nile, thy land, thou (who through the fall of Tyre art again become free) daughter of Tarschisch: no girdle holds thee any more." "Cittim" points to the island Cyprus, where was the town "Cituim," also in old times inhabited by the Greeks. There also appears in the Macedonians to have been some remains of this name, since Alexander is called (1 Macc. i. 1, and viii. 5) the king of Chittim; also the two first letters of Italy are connected with this word. "Dodanim" reminds us of the ancient oracle "Dodona," in Epirus. The other reading, "Rodanim," would make us think of the island Rhodus.

Ver. 5. *Isles of Gentiles.*—In Scripture "Islands" often mean such people as are situated on the sea-coast, or inhabit countries intersected by bays. Here are meant all the northern countries over the Mediterranean, from Asia Minor to Spain.

Ver. 6. *Cush* is synonymous with the name "Ethiopians," which was used by the ancient Greeks very indefinitely, and included the inhabitants of the middle of Africa, a part of Arabia, and perhaps even farther—the south of Asia. In later times the name was confined to Africa, and especially Abyssinia.

Mizraim.—This is the Hebrew name of Egypt—a form of the dual—either because Egypt was divided into two halves by the river Nile, or from the union of Upper and Lower Egypt. "The two Mazor" (this is the singular form, and signifies Lower Egypt), as we say "Kings of the two Sicilies."

Phut.—There is a river of this name in Mauritania, in North Africa (now Algeria and Morocco), mentioned at a later period.

Canaan.—The name signifies, probably, "the lower country—Netherlands." This is the forefather of the people who afterwards inhabited the Promised Land and the line of country at the foot of Lebanon—Palestine and Phœnicia. They were partly exterminated and driven out of a great portion of their country by the Israelites. They became, however, extremely rich and powerful by trade and inventions, and settled in Greece, Spain, and Africa; in this last country they founded Carthage. So late as the sixth century after Christ the inhabitants of the territory, now Algeria, about Hippo (the present Bona), called themselves Canaanites, as Augustine tells us.

Ver. 7. *Dedan.*—All people and places in the south of Arabia and East Africa. Scheba is supposed to be the ancient "Meroe" in Nubia, on the Nile.

Ver. 8. *Nimrod.*—The name Nimrod means, "let us exalt ourselves." By this name, which, perhaps, first was applied to him by the people because often on his lips, is the first person designated who acquired great dominion by force. He was especially "a mighty one," a hero—a word which is used in a good sense—nay, is used of God Himself. Here, however, it points to the origin of his power—by war. The "mighty hunter" denotes also his wild, unrestrained disposition—a man who delighted in bold, rash, hazardous undertakings, whether in sport or earnest. A wild hunter's life is a degenerate one as compared with the peaceful herdsman life, ch. xxv. 27. In order to understand this we must consider how different would hunting be in a peaceful, well-ordered state of society, and in a condition quite uncultivated and rude. Its consequences would be—neglect of the service of God, of the rights of property, of trade and arts. The prevalence of this occupation would contribute to bring everything down to the lowest state of barbarism. The addition, "a mighty hunter before the Lord" (Jehovah), is of importance, as it expresses, "in defiance of Him" to His face did he lead this wild, tyrannical, devastating life. This description of him, and the proverbial saying which is added by way of confirming the statement, is to be taken in close conjunction with the description of his conquests which follows.

Ver. 10. *Shinar.*—Shinar is, as the passage before us shows, a country lying south of Assyria, in which, according to ch. xi. 2, Babel was situated—the south of Mesopotamia, between

Euphrates and Tigris, called afterwards Babylonia. "Babel" is the great, ancient, mighty city on the Euphrates; in later times, under Nebuchadnezzar, the seat of the vast Chaldean Empire, the centre of the civilisation of the old world, and also of a corrupt, impure idolatry; the place from whence proceeded, first the depravation, eventually the humiliation and destruction of the kingdom of Judah—God's outward kingdom under the O. T. dispensation. It is therefore the emblem and representation of the spiritual, hostile, antichristian power in the Revelation of St John. The city "Erech" is perhaps "Arekka," on the borders of Babylonia and Susiana. "Accad" is altogether unknown; and "Calneh," which also occurs Amos vi. 2, and Ezek. xxvii. 23, as a trading city, is perhaps the "Ctesiphon" of later times, on the east shore of the Tigris, opposite Silencia.

Ver. 11. *Asshur.*—Heb.: "From this land went he forth—viz., Nimrod—towards Assyria." This, the oldest tyrant, founded therefore an important empire, which, however, reaches back to such very early times, that beyond what is said here, every other trace of it has utterly vanished; nay, of almost all the towns which were built by him we have no further certain mention, either in the Bible or elsewhere.

Ver. 12. *A great city.*—Heb.: "This is *the* great city"—i.e., the greatest among those mentioned. How far back these notices go we may learn from the fact, that of this great city, "Resen," which was greater than Nineveh, not the least trace further is given us. As the forenamed were Babylonish, so these are Assyrian towns. Nineveh is the celebrated metropolis of the Assyrian Empire, which afterwards attained such an extraordinary eminence in wealth and power, and which, for purposes of trade, enjoyed unusual advantages. According to the Greeks, it was built by the fabulous king Ninus, and is often mentioned under that name. According to Jon. iii. 3, it had a circumference of three days' journey, and accordingly was larger than Babylon. Walls of great height and breadth surrounded it. In the year 625 B.C., it was destroyed by the Medes under Cyaxares. Its ruins have been discovered in recent times on the east bank of the Tigris, opposite the great town Wosul, where the village Numa yet retains a memento of the old name. The city Rehoboth and Calah in Assyria are altogether unknown.—We have here, then, the account of the most ancient great kingdom which was founded by earthly might, and in defiance of the Lord, and which hastened the corruption of religion, whereby the call of Abraham and his leaving his country became necessary.

Ver. 14. *Caphtorim.*—Here occurs a list of people who are descended from Mizraim, *i.e.*, Egypt, of whom, however, the first four are entirely unknown, unless perhaps in *Lehabim* we may recognise the ancient name of Africa—Libya. We often meet with "Pathros" in the Old Testament for Upper Egypt, the original seat of the people. Some consider the "Casluhim" to be the Colchi in North Armenia on the Phasis, who, according to the Greek account, descended from an Egyptian colony settled there. In the following names a change of order appears to have taken place, so that properly the sentence, " out of whom came Philistim," should stand after Caphtorim, since elsewhere in the Old Testament it is distinctly said that the Philistines "came out of Caphtor" (Jer. xlvii. 4; Amos ix. 7). Caphtor is most probably Crete, now Candia, situated opposite Egypt, from whence it could be easily peopled; hence the Philistines are expressly called "Cretes," Cherethims (1 Sam. xxx. 14; Ezek. xxv. 16; Zeph. ii. 5). The name Philistine means " Emigrant," by which they were distinguished from the native Canaanites. They dwelt in the south-east of the land of Canaan, which received from them the name Peleschet—Palestina.

Ver. 18. *Canaanites.*—The Canaanitish tribes who spread themselves over the country afterwards called Palestina, over Phœnicia and a part of Syria. Zidon means "fishing;" so that this son of Canaan settled on a sea-coast, well suited for a fishing settlement, or he received his name from having done so, or the later name of the place was transferred to the founder. Zidon, called by the Greeks Sidon, now Saide, is the ancient mighty metropolis of the Phœnicians—rich by means of its inventions and trade—from whence in later times the still more powerful Tyrus, Zor or Tor, had its origin, which about the time of David began to be of importance. The Phœnicians also are especially called "Sidonians." As this place remained afterwards at peace with the adjacent settlements of the Israelites, these latter became corrupted by idolatrous Phœnician worship: Judges x. 6, 12. "Heth," properly "Cheth," the forefather of the Hethites, who dwelt about Hebron and Beersheba, in the southern interior of Palestine. The "Jebusites" dwelt on the mountainous country about Jerusalem, which was in earlier times called "Jebus," and maintained themselves in possession until subdued by David (2 Sam. v.). "Amorite," one of the greatest of the Canaanitish tribes, so that the whole people of them was so called (ch. xv. 16); but more particularly the south-western tribes bore that name, which even in the time of Moses possessed two kingdoms on the other side Jordan, under Sihon and Og. The "Girgasite" dwelt in the north; the "Hivite," properly "Chivvite," in the northern part of Palestine, at the foot of Lebanon, and over the mountainous district as far as Hamath; the "Arkite" points to the Phœnician town Arkanosh, the present Tripolis. There are traces of the "Senites" in the same region. The "Arvadites" are the inhabitants of the island "Aradus," to the north of Phœnicia; the "Zemarites" possibly those who lived in a fortified place, "Simyra," at the foot of Lebanon; the "Hamathites" about "Hamat," the later Syrian town in the neighbourhood of Damascus, on the Orontes, which still under the same name is a considerable place of trade.

Ver 19. *Lasha.*—They inhabited, therefore, in the most ancient times the whole land from the later Phœnicia to the southern and western borders of Palestina towards Arabia. Gerar lies, according to ch. xx. 1, between Cades and Sur, on the south border. Gaza is the later town of the Philistines, situated on the south-western point towards Egypt, and still bears that name. "Sodom, Gomorrah, Admah, and Zeboim," are the towns in the valley of the Jordan which were destroyed by fire, the site of which is now occupied by the Dead Sea. Lasha lay apparently on the shore of the Dead Sea, and possessed hot sulphur springs, to which it owes its name "Kallirhoe" ("beautiful spring"), given it by the Greeks. We here find the most ancient positions and relations of these regions mentioned before the Philistines dwelt in the land, such as Abraham met with in the south of Palestine before the destruction of Sodom.

Ver. 20. *Sons of Ham.*—The descendants of Ham, therefore, inhabited the southern regions of the earth, yet they penetrated as far north as Crete, Phœnicia, and Syria.

Ver. 21. *Eber.*—"Eber" occurs, ver. 24, among the descendants of Shem. He was the forefather of the Arabians and Israelites. The latter have received from him the name "Hebrews," which they bore among foreigners, as the Canaanites were called "Phœnicians" by the Greeks, and the country which was called Egypt by the Greeks was named Mizraim by the Israelites, but "Chemi" by the natives themselves.

Ver. 22. *Elam.*—Elam occurs afterwards, ch. xiv. 1, as the kingdom of Chedorlaomer; in later times, often as under the dominion of the Assyrians and Persians. We are to understand under this term the tract of country which lies immediately east of Babylon, with its warlike people the Elamites, close on the borders of Persia.—"Assur," the Assyrians. Assyria, properly speaking, is the land east of the Tigris, between Armenia, Media, and Susiana, whose capital was Nineveh, now a part of Persia; frequently, in later times, the great kingdom which sprung from this country is so called.

Arphaxad is an Assyrian tract of country, called by the Greeks Arrhapachitis.—*Lud* are the Lydians, in the west of Asia Minor, afterwards (with their capital Sardis) a busy, rich, but luxurious and corrupt people, which, under their king, Crœsus, in the time of the Persian king Cyrus, attained a rapid but transient prosperity.—*Aram,* the root of the Aramæans, who dwelt in Syria and Mesopotamia, and in language assimilated to the Israelites. This language, which divided itself into the two dialects, Syriac and Chaldaic, is still in some parts a living tongue.

Ver. 23. *Uz.*—After *Uz* was called the land in which Job lived (Job i. 1). It lay probably east of Palestine, on the borders of Edom and Arabia.—*Hul,* probably a Syriac tract of country, Chull, near the sources of the Jordan.—*Gether* is unknown.—*Mash,* possibly the region of Mount Masais, on the borders of Syria and Armenia, above "Nisibis."

Ver. 25. *Divided.*—The three names, Salah (properly Schelah), Eber, and Peleg, are very significant. The first means a missile as well as an offshoot, sprig—something discharged; the second means "on the other side;" and the third, "division"— something divided, especially by water, which is separated into channels. These names point to the wanderings and divisions of the original tribes. In this line of the Semites, in which issued the kingdom of God, the most important portion of the history of the world occurred, and so the heads of the nations bear emblematic names. With Peleg and his descendants the order of the families breaks off, since a point is now reached where, in the history of the kingdom of God, a new era commences through the confusion of tongues. Only after the narration of this event is the genealogy of Peleg's family continued.

Joktan.—The forefather of the Southern Arabians.

Ver. 29. *Jobab.*—The names are here given of Arabian tribes and districts. Among these, Ophir is known in later times as the gold country, from whence Solomon's fleet brought precious metal to increase his treasures. It was probably a haven on the south coast of Arabia.

Ver. 30. *A mount of the East.*—These indistinct boundaries seem to point, in general, to Eastern and Southern Arabia.

CHAPTER XI.

Man's "evil imagination," which remained after the flood, now took a different direction, and shows itself in an impious attempt to unite the whole of mankind in rebellion against God.

The first land peopled after the flood was Sinear (Schinar), Mesopotamia, or Babylonia. The two great rivers, Euphrates and Tigris, water this tract of country, which in ancient times was renowned for its fertility, though now a barren plain. Human skill added wonderfully to the natural fruitfulness of the district, so that it became capable of sustaining a very large population. The vast plain has a gentle declension from west to east. The Euphrates, when the snow melts on the mountains, overflows its banks, and descends into the level country of Mesopotamia. From this circumstance the inhabitants were induced, at an early period in its history, to convey the water by means of canals over the whole country; so that in time it was entirely intersected by these tributaries from the Euphrates and Tigris. Herod. speaks as an eye-witness of the astonishing fertility of Babylonia (B. 1, 193): "This country is by far the best I know for the production of wheat, for it does not attempt to grow any other plants, figs, vines, or olives; but it is so adapted for the growing of wheat, that it commonly returns two hundredfold, and when it produces the best crops, as much as three hundredfold. The blades of wheat and barley grow fully to the breadth of four fingers; as to the size that the plants of millet and sesame reach, I shall not mention, though I know it, as I am fully convinced that those who have not been there will not believe it."—In the history before us, we find the building of the Tower represented in three points of view. The builders wished to get themselves a name. Here was simple ambition. Next, they held out a defiance to God: the height should reach to heaven, His dwelling-place. Moreover, the Tower should form a centre of union for the whole family of man. Here was reliance on their own power. The punishment inflicted is very significant. Humility and love, the bonds which join us to God, could alone unite men. Self-seeking separates them. God divides them by the confusion of tongues, before they could carry their godless enterprise into execution. Hence were formed different families of nations, each confined to itself, and in hostile relation towards others. The heathen world knew nothing of the unity of the human race, until the Gospel of Christ appeared, to teach men that they were all of one blood, all had one common head, all had one God as their Father; then the tongues of men, divided through pride at Babel, were united by love and humility at Zion.

Ver. 1. *One speech.*—This original speech of mankind was, according to the Holy Scriptures, Hebrew,—since all the names which have hitherto occurred are Hebrew: a language of a simple unchanging form, of great richness in all subjects which concern man's relationship to God: a spiritual language, adapting itself readily to express the inward idea, but with few words, in which the sound imitates the thing signified,—not, therefore, pliable for the uses of practical life, nor well adapted for the expression of merely intellectual notions.

Ver. 2. *From the east,* or rather (according to margin) eastward; *i.e.,* from Armenia south-eastward.

Ver. 3. *Slime for mortar.*—In Babylonia there are no stone-quarries. The lately discovered ruins show that bricks, dried or burnt in the sun, were used for building material, which were united by asphalt. The country abounds in asphalt and bitumen. This cement is so firm, that even now the stones can only be separated from each other by hammering.

Ver. 4. *Let us build.*—In ancient Babylon there existed an enormous tower with a temple of Belus, square, a quarter of an

English mile long each side; in the middle, a square tower half as long and broad; on this another; and so on to the number of eight of them. Around all these towers there was an ascent with seats; on the last tower stood a vast temple, with a gilded seat and golden table, but without any image. Lately, the mighty ruins of this building have been discovered and described. It is now called "Birs Nimrud"—Nimrod's Hill. From the east side it appears as a longish hill, the base of which is above 2000 feet in circumference. The present height, up to the floor of the tower which stands thereon, is 200 feet; the tower 35. From the west side it has a pyramidical form. It is made of beautiful fire-burnt bricks. Only three out of the eight stories of which the tower consisted can now be discovered. This appears to be the remains of the tower which the sons of men built at the time spoken of in the text, and is perhaps the oldest ruin in the whole world.

Ver. 5. *Lord came down.*—"God cometh down when He condescends to mark what men are doing, and to punish sinners; and these confident men, who thought He was far off and did not see their deeds, found that He is very nigh to them, and can soon find means of chastising them."—Luther. Probably a visible manifestation of the Lord was made, whereby He revealed to His elect the meaning of the wonderful punishment which was to follow. At the same time, every manifestation of God on earth, spoken of in the Old Testament, is to be regarded as a pre-signification of His coming in the flesh for grace and judgment, just as His ascent is to be looked on as a forerunner of the lifting up of the Son of God in His ascension into heaven: Eph. iv. 9, 10.

Ver. 7. *Let us go down.*—The words, "Let us," point out to us the Father taking counsel with the Son: see ch. i. 26. The confusion of languages is not to be supposed to consist in the forcible, arbitrary disruption of the words and forms of speech, but in a sudden separation of the languages, all from one point. Recent philological inquiries have been so far pursued, that the original affinity of the greater part of the more known languages is acknowledged, and the common descent of all supposed. While, then, the proof of the original branching out of all tongues from one root is being sought by means of investigation, we may, according to what Holy Scripture tells us, well imagine the separation to have taken place thus: Men desired, in their presumption and defiance of God, to unite themselves against Him; but that which was intended for their union proved the means of separation. God allowed the feuds between themselves, engendered by selfishness which already existed, to express itself in their language. In the building of the great tower, which continued many years, parties had been formed among them, more and more, according to their families, dispositions, affections, and business. When these opposite interests and parties existed, it only required the impulse of a slight necessity, acting without and within, in order to alienate their language, one man's from another's. At a time when the spiritual mass out of which mankind was formed was most susceptible of every impression, God permitted this division among men to express itself, more especially in their speech; and so it came to pass that, during the building, they no longer understood each others' language,—*i. e.*, all, according to their tribes, families, and acquaintance, were severed into so many different tongues. We recognise the antitype to this history in the pouring out of the Holy Ghost, and the gift of tongues among the first Christians. "After the flood, proud men built a tower to hinder their being swept away by another flood, should it ever come, as if they could strengthen themselves against God, or as if anything were high in His sight! God saw their pride, and let them proceed in the way of error so far that they understood not each others' language,—and so was their speech confounded by pride. As pride had severed men's language, so has the humility of Christ united them: what the Tower of Babel dispersed, that the Church of the Lord has united. From one speech they became many: marvel not at it! this hath pride done. From many languages they became one: marvel not at it! for this hath love done. For, though they sound differently, still in the heart is one God prayed to, and one peace kept."—S. Augustine. We do well to remember this, that the redeemed Church on the day of Pentecost did not speak one language, but that every stranger who was there present heard *his own* language spoken. The diversity of tongues is still God's will,—is something abiding and good: but sin was the cause of the false unity and of the separation, and severed the one body into many members; so that now the members are strange and hostile to each other. This was the judgment in the confusion of tongues.

Ver. 8. *To build the city.*—It remained, of course, still a city; but the great work, which they in their arrogance had designed, was brought to nought.

Ver. 9. *Babel;* i.e., confusion. So, down to later times, the capital of a mighty empire bore in its name the memento of this event.

Ver. 11. *Sons and daughters.*—Shem lived to the time of Abram.

Ver 18. *Peleg.*—The genealogical table of the Semites was (ch. x. 24, 25) carried on in the line of Peleg, as that which kept up the true worship of God on earth, and stopped at the narrative of the confusion of tongues. After the event has been mentioned, the time is continued up to Abram. This period is remarkable for the gradual diminution of human life.

Ver. 29. *Sarai.*—She was, according to ch. xx. 12, his half-sister—from the same father.

Ver. 31. *Haran.*—The history of Terah is here brought to an end, in order to avoid the necessity of speaking of him again, and so Abram's call may be continuously narrated. What is here said in point of chronology anticipates ch. xii.—*Ur* lay, probably, in the north of Mesopotamia.—*Haran* was the town afterwards called *Chanæ*, in the neighbourhood of Edessa, where Crassus was defeated by the Parthians. From Arrhapachitis, in North-east Assyria, the ancestors of the people of Israel passed through the north of Mesopotamia and the north of Syria towards Palestine.

CHAPTER XII.

With the narrative of the call of Abram begins an entirely new era in the history of the kingdom of God. Idolatry has spread everywhere, and infected even the family of Shem. Dread of the Holy God, and alienation from His love, led men to the worship of nature: they "deemed either fire, or wind, or the circle of the stars, or the violent water, or the lights of heaven, to be the gods which govern the world:" Wisd. xiii. 3. Even Terah and his family served other gods, Joshua xxiv. 2; not that they were completely heathens, but, as was afterwards the case with Nahor's descendants, their religion was a miserable mixture of falsehood with truth. Then Jehovah, the eternal living God, chooses out of the rest of the world a son of Terah's, Eber's descendant; reveals Himself to him as the personal, only true God, Creator of heaven and earth, the Judge of the whole world: ch. xviii. 25. He enters into covenant and communion with him, bids him leave his country and home—both of them polluted by idolatry, and gives him the promise of an exceeding rich blessing. But the revelation, promise, and favour bestowed on Abram are only vouchsafed to him in order, through him and his descendants, to pour on the whole human race the same blessing of the knowledge of God, and communion with Him. While God confines His grace to a single chosen family, He declares it is intended for all men. The first revelation to the great forefather of the Israelites shows that the Old Testament knows nothing of a Jewish national God, to whom the rest of the world is alien.

The dealings of God with this patriarch and his descendants are most wonderful. Not so much by means of doctrine and exhortation which they could not understand, as by the facts of His revelation, does He purify, fit, and elevate them to be His instruments. In Abram's life especially do we see how the first dark promise is made more clear; then followed by trials of his faith, at the outset light, afterwards increasing in severity. Hardly is anything bestowed and a prospect opened, when, lo! it is apparently taken away, and the future is clouded. First is promised, indefinitely, "a land which I will show thee;" then (ver. 7) declared that Canaan shall be given to his seed. Lot is then severed by a friendly agreement from the common possession (c. xiii.). Abram, at that time childless, receives the announcement that a son of his body shall be his heir, and a covenant is made with him (ch. xv.). Ishmael, now born to him, is separated from the true seed; and, lastly, the truth of God's promise is revealed in the birth of Isaac,—soon, by the severest trial of his faith, apparently taken away (ch. xxii.), only to be restored with still richer gifts.

Abram was a wealthy independent herdsman; such as are still to be found in the deserts and pasture lands of Arabia, Syria, Palestine—the Bedouin Emirs.

Separate occupations already existed. The huntsman was the freest of all. From him were developed the warrior and the king. The men who pursued agriculture, built houses and barns, and were bound to the soil, seemed the most settled and secure. The lot of the herdsman appeared the most uncertain, as his locality was so changeable. The flocks went on increasing almost without limit, and their possessors were obliged to enlarge their pastures on all sides. The three classes appear at the beginning to have regarded each other with mutual dislike and contempt. The herdsman was an abomination in the sight of the dweller in towns (ch. xliii. 32, ch. xlvi. 34), who lived apart from the despised caste. The huntsman is soon lost from our sight in the mountain ranges, and only appears again as a conqueror and invader. The patriarchs belonged to the class of herdsmen. Their manner of life in the vast plains and deserts was favourable to freedom of mind and thought. The sight of the vast firmament under which they lived, with its myriads of stars, was calculated to give elevation to their feelings; and they experienced more than the active, expert huntsman, more than the careful, secure, busy cultivator of the land, the need of some facts on which to rely—some solid conviction that God was by them—that He visited them, cared for them, guided and preserved them. Their simple, quiet, unrestrained mode of life was adapted to render their hearts open to receive the impression of a Divine revelation; and the manner of revelation granted them was in accordance with their simple, childlike character—conveyed to them through the eye and the ear.

The "deserts" in Scripture are the uncultivated tracts of country, often fruitful pastures. Here and there towns were built on them. On these steppes the herdsmen tended, and still tend, their cattle. They drive their flocks up and down certain districts. In summer they turn to the north, to the mountainous country—in Canaan to Lebanon, whose summit is covered with perpetual snow; in the winter, to the lower lands, into the plain towards the Dead Sea. Their tents are either round, resting in the middle on poles, eight or ten feet high; or oblong, resting on seven to nine poles, of which three are higher than the others—the middle one the highest. The covering is a thick black material, made of goats' or camels' hair,—this, tightly stretched, will keep out any rain or dew. The tents have two or three divisions—for the cattle, the men, and the women: the outside compartment for the more tender of the cattle; the next for the men; and the third, inner one, Kubba—in Arabic Alkobba (alcove)—is for the women. The Emirs have separate tents for the cattle and for the women. Abram had not these, it would seem, at first (ch. xviii. 9), but afterwards he had (ch. xxiv. 6, 7). In those hot and dry countries wells are dug where the tents are pitched, which often are regarded as property, and become objects of contention (ch. xxi. 25, ch. xxvi. 15). The tents are frequently pitched under large trees for the sake of shade. Thus lived Abraham, Isaac, and Jacob, in the land of Canaan. But, though herdsmen themselves, their descendants were gradually fitted to lead an agricultural life in the Land of Promise. But they are led on step by step.

Every notice in this living wonderful description of the life of the "friend of God" is of importance. The more we realise the truth of the existence of a living personal God, Who condescends to the least wants of His children, so shall we in proportion apply to ourselves, as the apostles did, the history of the lives of the patriarchs, and, as it were, live them over again.

Their character is represented in Scripture with undisguised truthfulness. We see in them the examples of men who sinned indeed, but ever struggled against sin, conquered, and grew in holiness. We see men who now and then succumbed under temptation, but in the end overcame, and were in truth men of God.

Ver. 1. *Will show thee.*—This revelation took place in Ur, in Chaldea, according to ch. xv. 7; Neh. ix. 7 (cf. Acts vii. 3). His father, in the first instance, was willing to accompany him; but he remained in Haran, the most northern and fruitful part of Mesopotamia, where he died after sixty years: cf. ch. xi. 26, 32, ch. xii. 4. In Haran, either the call was repeated to Abram, or he determined there, as his father chose to remain behind, that he would yield full obedience to God's voice. So Abram, in the first instance, left his country, afterwards his friends and his father's house, *i.e*, his family. His first going out to Canaan was itself an act of faith; and from the outset must that land have seemed to him, in the light of promise, as a land of supernatural blessings. "Leave, He said, the visible and the present, and choose the unseen and the uncertain. See how from the beginning this just man was disciplined to prefer the unseen to the seen, the future to the present, since God saith not into what land He will cause him to dwell; but by the indefiniteness of the command He tries the patriarch's love of God."—S. Chrysost.

Ver. 2. *Name great.*—The progenitor and his descendants appear in the Bible always as a whole; therefore it is said so frequently, "To *thee* will I give this land."

Bless.—"Blessing" on the part of God always includes "benefaction," since with Him word and act are one and the same. So it is with Isaac and Jacob when they bless in the name of God.

Name great.—The name of Abraham is highly reverenced, not only by Jews and Christians, but by Mohammedans likewise. Whatever of right belief in the living God is to be found in Islamism, has been derived from the religion of Abraham, which is inherited by the Arabians.

A blessing.—Others shall be blessed through thee. This was the case even during Abram's lifetime, but the following history, which explains the promise, shows how much further it extends.

Ver. 3. *I will bless.*—The expression of most complete covenant. Not only shall his friends be God's friends, and his enemies God's enemies, but God Himself will repay every kindness done to him, and will revenge every injury by word or deed.

All families.—This expression, which is repeated four times (ch. xviii. 18, ch. xxii. 18, ch. xxvi. 4, ch. xxviii. 14), is the centre of all promises, and that round which all the others revolve. The knowledge and the love of the one, true, living God—his covenant with Him—this was the unspeakably rich blessing which Abram possessed, the source of all other benefits which he enjoyed. Neither Abram nor Moses knew in what manner this should take place. This blessing was through him to pass to all people. The beginning of the Great Promise which is annexed to his family declares this only with clearness—that the knowledge of God, and covenant with Him, shall one day be the possession of all nations through Abram; and he is therefore chosen by God to bring salvation to all. This promise has now been perfectly fulfilled in Christ, through Whom the blessing of Abraham's descendants has been extended to all people, and will continue to be extended. From the commencement was Abram by this

Word of God raised above the world which is seen, and so the earthly blessings which were granted to him gained a higher meaning. It is of moment at the same time to observe, that before any obedience on Abram's part, the free gift by grace was accorded him. The first covenant which God made on earth for the establishment of His kingdom was essentially a covenant of grace: Gal. iii. 15.

Ver. 5. *The souls.*—*i.e.*, The slaves which they had bought in Haran. Of these Abram possessed a great number: ch. xiv. 14.

Ver. 6. *Sichem.*—In the middle of the country;—a fertile territory surrounded by hills of moderate size, afterwards the capital of the Samaritans—the modern Nabulus. Even at the present day this is a pleasant and fruitful region. "The whole valley is full of vegetable and fruit gardens, with every variety of produce, watered by a number of streams which rise in different parts, and send their refreshing waters westwards. This lovely view came upon us like enchantment. We saw nothing to be compared with it in the whole of Palestine" (Robinson, iii. 315). In after times a sanctuary and memorial were erected here by Joshua: Joshua xxiv. 26.

Ver. 6. *Plain of Moreh.*—Literally, the oak of Moreh. So called probably from the Canaanitish possessor of the grove.

Canaanite.—So that Abram, without possessing so much of the land as "to set his foot on," was obliged to wander about as a stranger and herdsman. We are told (ch. x. 15) that the Canaanites still had possession of the land; and it is here repeated, to signify that Abram had not entered it in order to take possession of the same. The earlier Canaanitish people, who were chiefly occupied in agriculture and commerce, left many steppes for pasture land, which foreign nomadic tribes were allowed to pass through. In the same manner, at the present day, the Arabian shepherd tribes, with their sheik or emir at their head, wander through the uncultivated parts of Palestine and Egypt. "Moses mentions this not without a meaning; but in order that we may learn the self-control of the patriarch from this circumstance, that he was obliged to pass as a wanderer and stranger through the places possessed by the Canaanites, and as a poor man and outcast to dwell there."—S. Chrysostom.

Ver. 7. *Give this land.*—As Abram had followed God in faith, without knowing whither he went, the Lord now appears to him again, and adds to the great general promise a still more definite one. The extension of the blessing through his posterity shall take place by means of the possession of this land, which is itself the germ and type of a greater, an eternal possession.

Appeared to him.—Here begin the revelations of God in particular places. The childlike faith of the patriarchs preserved memorials of this kind, and trusted that God would often appear where He had once done. They regarded such places as a "House of God," ch. xviii. 17, and God graciously condescended to accept such faith. He willed to teach them above all things to honour none but the true living God who revealed Himself to them.

Ver. 8. *Bethel* signifies "House of God," as the place was afterwards called, ch. xxviii. 19; about 5 miles south of Sichem—three hours' journey from Jerusalem, in a rich pasture valley. The site has lately been discovered.

Hai.—An ancient town of the Canaanites: Joshua vii. 2.

Called.—As ch. iv. 26 : *i.e.*, held a solemn service to God, with his family and servants.

Ver. 10. *Egypt.*—Egypt, which is enriched by the regular overflowings of the Nile, is to this day, as formerly, the refuge of the neighbouring countries in case of famine.

Ver. 11. *Fair woman.*—As the life of men in those days was double its present length, we must consider Sarai at 70 at about half that age. The conduct of Abram on this occasion (as also with respect to Abimelech afterwards, ch. xx. 12) shows a weakness of faith, and is a warning to God's servants at all times, that they may fall just in those particulars in which they seem strongest. The want of strict truthfulness which is betrayed even by religious persons in the O. T., is a proof that, together with faith and the inner communion with God, the natural man displayed itself in gross forms, such as under the Gospel cannot be the case. Under the Gospel, either the spirit or the flesh gains the mastery, and the leaven of grace pervades the whole man in a way which it did not under the O. T. dispensation.

Ver. 12. *Save thee alive.*—Among the most cultivated descendants of Ham—the Egyptians and Canaanites or Phœnicians—we find the highest intellectual culture and skill in science combined with the lowest moral degradation.

Ver. 15. *Pharaoh's house.*—In these very ancient days was

Egypt already a highly civilised country, with customs such as afterwards prevailed in the East, where kings usually kept large harems. The context shows clearly that Sarai escaped without injury,—since there it was the custom (at least in later times it was so) that maidens brought into the harem should undergo a long course of preparation (Est ii 12).

Ver. 16. *Entreated well.*—The king made him rich presents, such as were suitable to a nomadic prince. He wished by the richness of his gifts to offer some compensation for the violence of his acts.

Ver. 17. *Plagued.*—The kind of plagues probably was of the same meaning as those narrated ch. xx. 17, 18. The king and his priests and soothsayers understood by them what God would have them learn from them.

Ver. 19. *To wife.*—We are not to conclude therefrom that Abram's suspicion was wrong; at the same time, there lies in this reproach that which Abram was unable to reply to.

CHAPTER XIII.

A further step in the fulfilment of the Divine promise. The land was to belong to Abram and his seed, and yet Lot, rich and powerful, is still in it. A contention between the herdsmen of the two relatives is the cause of separation. Abram behaves in the most unselfish way. On the separation, the promise of possession is repeated in a still more distinct manner.

Ver. 1. *South;* i.e., to the southern region of Palestine.

Ver. 2. *Very rich.*—The commencement of the fulfilment of the promise, ch. xii. 2. Outward blessing was to faithful Abraham a pledge of the spiritual, unseen blessing.

Ver. 4. *Called on the name.*—See ch. iv. 26.

Ver. 5. *Tents.*—After the manner of the present Arabian nomadic tribes.

Ver. 6. *Not dwell together.*—They could not find pasture enough on the open free steppes.

Ver. 7. *Perizzite.*—The Perizzites are not mentioned in ch. x. 15-19 among the children of Canaan. The word properly means " dwellers from Pheræsoth"—i.e., dwellers on farms in the country, in opposition to the inhabitants of towns. The land could not bear them both, because all the country was thickly covered with towns and villages.

Ver. 9. *To the left.*—Even here, it seems, is an act of faith on the part of Abram recorded. From his love of peace he allows Lot his choice, yet was he sure in his heart that God would so order it that His promise should be fulfilled. Lot therefore was quite free to choose. Nothing obliged him to depart from Canaan; but in all this was the purpose of God brought about. The humility and forbearance of Abram are herein shown, that, though Lot's father's brother, he calls him "brother," and, though the elder, leaves him the first choice.

Ver. 10. *Plain of Jordan.*—Heb.: "The whole circuit of Jordan." So was this wonderfully fruitful valley called, in the place of which afterwards arose the Dead Sea. The Jordan appears in this valley to have been divided into several arms, and the main stream to have been lost in a subterranean cavity; since, according to recent researches, it seems impossible, on account of the depth of its channel in the upper part, that it could have flowed through the valley which stretches from thence as far as the Gulf of Akaba.

Garden of the Lord; i.e., like Eden.

Egypt.—Which was then, by nature and cultivation, one of the richest countries of the old world.

Ver. 15. *For ever.*—All that God does is eternal. He never gives or accomplishes that which is perishable; since even the transitory things which we receive from Him, He bestows with reference to the eternal, and if a man receives them in faith they bear everlasting fruit. The land of Canaan is the pledge and type of the new world, which the faithful, who are the children of Abram, shall receive for an everlasting possession; and therefore did his seed after the flesh possess it, in order to make ready for the kingdom of God on the whole earth: cf. Rom. iv. 13.

Ver. 17. *Give it thee.*—He was in figure to take possession of it. In his lifetime he had not so much as where to put his foot.

Ver. 18. *Plains.*—"Under the Oak of Mamre."

Hebron signifies "covenant." It is the after-name of the place which is here given by anticipation. It was called in earlier times "Kirjath-Arba"—afterwards Anakim Arba; afterwards the royal city of David before he conquered Jerusalem.

CHAPTER XIV.

Ver. 1. *Shinar.*—Babylon: cf. ch. x. 10, ch. xi. 2.

Ellasar.—An unknown country, probably towards Assyria.

Elam.—Cf. ch. x. 22, note.

Nations, heathen (Gojim), is in the O. T. the name of all who are not Israelites. Perhaps here it is the designation of people of somewhat distant northern regions. So Joshua xii. 23, "The nations of Gilgal."

Ver. 2. *Zoar.*—Each of the more important Canaanitish towns had, as the book of Joshua shows, its king. We find something like this in the earlier Greek times. The Canaanites of the rich valley Siddim, in spite of their inferior power, trusted so much to their own strength, that they set themselves against the combined forces of the important countries of the east.

Ver. 3. *Salt Sea.*—After the destruction of Sodom and Gomorrha.

Ver. 6. *Elparan.*—Heb., "To the turpentine trees (oak, Engl. Vers.) of Paran"—to an oasis in the steppe-land, fertile in oaks, or the turpentine—terebinthus.

Ver. 7. *Hazezon-tamar.*—The march of the kings was from the north, through the land to the east of Jordan. Here we first meet in with "Rephaims," or giants, a Canaanitish people of vast size, who often are mentioned in the O. T. Their chief town, "Ashteroth Karnaim," means, Astarte with two horns, because the Canaanitish goddess Astarte, who is represented with two horns, was especially worshipped there. From thence they went southwards. The Zuzims and the Emims, in the plain of Kiriathaim (*i e.*, the double town), were the original inhabitants of the territory afterwards possessed by the Ammonites and Moabites. The Horites (dwellers in caves) were the old inhabitants of the mountainous district of Seir, whom the Edomites afterwards drove out: Deut. ii. 12. Pharan is the mountainous country, in the south of Palestine, belonging to Edom and Arabia Petræa. The stream Mispat, or "of the right," is Kadesh, on the south border of Palestine. The Amalekites are the ancient (probably Arabian) people who lived between Edom and Egypt in Arabia Petræa. Hazezon-tamar lay in the southern part of Palestine, in that part which was afterwards the Desert of Judæa. The kings, therefore, coming east from Jordan, had encompassed the Valley of Siddim, and conquered all before them. They now turn from the south-west towards the main point of their expedition.

Ver. 10. *Slime-pits.*—Asphalt, a bitumen of a dark colour, which melts easily in a moderate heat. The whole valley was full of such pits or gulleys, out of which the bitumen flowed. At the present day there arises out of the Dead Sea, to the surface, bitumen, which becomes hardened by salt and the sun, and floats in thick masses on the water. Also in Mesopotamia such streams of bitumen are found, and likewise in the neighbourhood of Baku, on the Caspian Sea, which it is not safe to approach very close to, lest the soil should give way under one's feet. On the borders of the Dead Sea are there still some such sluices in which bitumen is found.

There—viz., into the slime or bitumen pits, by which means the defeat was complete.

Ver. 12. *Sodom.*—We are not to suppose that a regular war of conquest is here described, but a kind of predatory foray, such as were the wars of the Greeks in very old times. The object of such was to capture as much booty as possible—cattle, men, etc.—to make the slaves of the latter, partly in revenge for past offences, partly as tribute for time to come.

Ver. 13. *Hebrew.*—In old times persons were distinguished by the name of their ancestor, and therefore Abram is known among the Canaanites as the descendant of Eber. Afterwards this name gave way to that of the "sons" or "children" of Israel, or Israelites; and in the O. T. the name "Hebrew" only occurs in the mouth of foreigners, or in discourse with them; and since the whole of Israel was regarded by themselves as "a holy nation," the name Israel took the significance of holy—Hebrew, that of profane. So in the N. T., and at the present day, the name "Israel," "Israelites," is the name by which they are designated among themselves—"Hebrew," the profane name, in use in their intercourse with aliens.

Aner.—These three chieftains strengthened the force of Abram.

Ver. 14. *Dan.*—This is not the town which was in earlier times Laish or Leshem, and which in the time of the Judges was taken by the tribe of Dan, and changed its name for that of their progenitor (Joshua xix. 47; Judges xviii. 29); but another place, Dan-jaan, mentioned 2 Sam. xxiv. 6.

Ver. 15. *Damascus.*—Abraham here altogether acts the part of an independent nomad chief, after the manner of the modern Arabian sheiks: these have always under them a great number of free adherents, slaves, and clansmen. All these are regularly practised in the use of arms for cases of necessity. Abram's slaves were partly bought, partly born in his house: these latter held the higher position, as the more attached and trustworthy. Abram pursued the host of the kings as they retired in disorder, flushed with their victory, and was enabled with his much inferior forces to gain an entire victory over them, by means of his superior knowledge of the mountainous country—still more by his firm, courageous faith in God.

Ver. 18. *Melchizedek.*—Heb. Malki-zedek—*i. e.*, the king of righteousness; probably a standing title, as Abimelech, Adonizedek.

Salem.—Salem is called Jerusalem, Ps. lxxvi. 3; and therefore we may suppose that afterwards famous city to be meant. Otherwise there lay a Salem north on the Jordan, which a tradition of Christian times has handed done as the city of Melchizedek.

Bread and wine.—"Not that he offered a sacrifice, but refreshed and honoured the guests with food; thereby representing Christ, who feeds the world with His Gospel."—(Luther.)

Ver. 20. *Tithes.*—Even among the idolatrous nations the worship of the one true God still survived. Melchizedek calls Him "the Most High God," or the "Exalted," *i. e.*, Who stands far above creation; as Jehovah also is often called God "who made heaven and earth"—in opposition to the gods of nature among the heathen, who were *in*, not *above*, the world. But Melchizedek does not call Him "the Lord" (Jehovah), which name Abram alone could use of Him as the God of the covenant. Yet Abraham gives to Jehovah the same name as Melchizedek to God (ver. 22), showing thereby their communion of belief. Through his priestly office, bestowed on him by God, is Melchizedek's blessing of avail (as likewise Balaam's, Num. xxiii. 24, who calls on God, not the Lord Jehovah, and speaks only in His name); and for this cause Abram gives him the tithe of the spoil.

The number ten expresses perfection—the abstract idea of totality: when the tithe of all that was acquired had been dedicated to God, then is the possession of the remainder sanctified. We here see a priest who derived his office from no earthly descent,—who, moreover, did not belong to the temporal, outward family of the old covenant, still acknowledged by Abram as *his* priest. Throughout the whole history of revelation—even to those who were brought most close to Him and were His friends—does God show that His gifts are bestowed of free grace alone, not according to any advantages one man has over another, and that even beyond His own ordinances His free will extends; and by thus overpassing their boundaries, He gives us a glimpse of the laws of a still higher dispensation. Therefore in this priest-king is typified the eternal, Divine Priesthood, without dependence, or descent, or outward appointment, which is fulfilled in Christ; and thus is explained the remarkable phenomenon that Abram, to whom were vouchsafed revelations from the Most High God, who was the first of an entirely new family of God on earth, who built altars to the God who appeared to him, and offered sacrifices and solemn service, yet bows himself here before a priest who did not belong to the covenant of grace.

Ver. 21. *Thyself*—in the belief Abram would retain the *whole*.

Ver. 22. *Most High God.*—Him upon whom the king of Salem, thy kinsman, has called.

Ver. 23. *Abram rich.*—Abram keeps himself free from all obligations to those who are not of the kingdom of God, relying entirely on God's promise;—a pattern for those who are made partakers of Christ: cf. Rom. xiii. 8; 1 Thess. iv. 12; 2 Cor. vi. 14, 15.

Ver. 24. *Portion.*—Abram acted with complete unselfishness for himself, who was rich by reason of this covenant with God, but took care of the interests of his allies, who were strangers to the motives which actuated himself.

CHAPTER XV.

Ver. 1. *Vision.*—Probably in a trance, about even-time, when the lower faculties of the soul were asleep and subdued, and the man has his powers fitted for the reception of communication from on high. In this condition of ecstasy Abram remained until he received the Divine command (ver. 9), and then he falls back (ver. 12) into the wonderful sleep.

Great reward.—God Himself. His covenanted communion is Abram's exceeding great reward. There can be no higher reward of the love of God than the love of God: cf. Ps. cxlii. 6; St Matt. v. 12.

Ver. 2. *Lord God.*—"Jehovah Lord," which is always the Hebrew expression in the O. T. when the double name of the Deity occurs.

Eliezer.—Probably the meaning is—"I go childless, and the son of the possession of my house (*i.e.*, my heir) is this Eliezer of Damascus." Abram justly thought, as he had separated first from his father's house and kindred, and afterwards from Lot, and since God has given him the promise of the possession of Canaan, it could not be the purpose of the Lord that his inheritance, and the blessing resting on it, should devolve on his distant connections, but that he should choose his principal servant in the stead of a son.

Ver. 5. *Brought him forth; i.e.*, in vision.

Ver. 6. *For righteousness.*—Without having the least grounds of human probability, he trusts, unconditionally, the Divine promise of grace. The word "believed" means properly, in the Heb., "he held himself fast to the Lord." This belief in God, which gives up itself entirely to Him, which strengthens itself in Him, God regards in Abram as righteousness—as a virtue acceptable in His sight, because such a belief in the revelation of the Divine grace unites man altogether with God, the source of all good, and so leads him on from step to step. Faith altogether renounces the natural ground of trust in oneself, in one's own sin-defiled obedience, and throws itself into the arms of revealed grace. Therefore can God count this faith, and this alone, for righteousness. This faith is therefore substantially and really one with justifying faith in Christ's atonement, which is the end of all God's revelations. Also subjectively, as the direction of man's heart, is it one and the same, since it draws away man from trust in the seen and human, and knits him altogether to the Divine promise: cf. Rom. iv. 3, 18, 23; St James ii. 23.

Ver. 8. *Whereby shall I know?*—That Abram seeks a sign here, is not displeasing to God, more than in the case of Gideon and Hezekiah (Judges vi. 36; 2 Kings xx. 8). Nay, the contrary may be displeasing to Him, as we find in the instance of Ahaz: Isa. vii. 12. It altogether depends on the mind which prompts the request or refusal, whether the request is prompted by belief, which desires confirmation, or by unbelief, which is concealed under the pretence of the uncertainty of the revelation.

Ver. 9. *He said.*—Hereon follow customs which were practised in the case of a covenant between man and man. The victims were cut in twain, and the persons who made the covenant passed between the divided pieces, and uttered the imprecation that they might in like manner be hewn asunder if they broke the covenant: Jer. xxxiv. 18, 19, cf. 1 Sam. xi. 7.

Three years old.—Animals of three years of age were considered in their prime. In the offerings there must be no blemish.

Ver. 10. *Divided not.*—As was afterwards the custom under the Levitical law, Lev. i. 15, 17: here, possibly, because they were not the proper sacrifice of the covenant, but one over and beside it.

Ver 11. *Drove them away.*—Luther's gloss: " The birds signify the Egyptians, who first persecute Abram's descendants; but Abram drives them away,—that is, God redeems them for His promise made to Abram. This is the case also with all believers, that they are forsaken and yet redeemed."

Ver. 12. *Sun.*—This statement of the time is meant to signify the supernatural character of the darkness and of the sleep, and to denote the difference between a dream and a vision.

A horror.—A prophetic sleep, full of dread before the majesty of the approach of God.

Ver. 13. *Four hundred years,* in round numbers. The time was actually four hundred and thirty years: cf. Exod. xii. 40.

Ver. 14. *With great substance.*—Together with the revelation of grace and mercy is the prospect of the many afflictions to come laid open, yet with the promise they shall terminate in triumph and joy. This prediction of certain circumstances is a sign of grace, ver. 17. The "great substance" is the spoiling of the Egyptians by the gifts which they made to the Israelites, Exod. xi. 2.

Ver. 15. *Peace.*—Thou shalt go to thy fathers or to thy people in peace, is the gracious expression for a life after death. The same occurs especially in these very early times often (ch. xxv. 8, ch. xxxv. 29, ch. xlix. 29, 33; Deut. xxxii. 50; 2 Kings xxii. 20). We here see that even in the farthest antiquity the view into the life beyond the grave was not altogether dark and gloomy.

Buried.—Burying was the most ancient, and with few exceptions the usual, mode with the Israelites in respect to their dead. It was founded on the expression, Gen. iii. 19. This custom was more calculated to remind persons of this declaration, as well as (afterwards) of the resurrection of the dead, than the heathen custom of embalming and burning the dead. Thus was Moses buried by God (Deut. xxxiv. 6); and our Lord Jesus Christ also was interred.

Ver. 16. *Full.*—Here is Abram expressly told that, personally, he shall have no part in the enjoyment of the promised blessing, and that he will partake of it only in his descendants. The Amorites, who are here mentioned as being the most distinguished of the Canaanitish nations, are still an object of the Divine mercy: their measure must be first full,—the day of grace must have passed, before God punishes.

Ver. 17. *Pieces.*—By the furnace we are to picture to ourselves a large cylindrical-shaped fire-pot, wide within in the lower part, small in the upper, with the outlet at the top, like those now to be found in the chambers and tents in the East. Such a glowing, smoking pillar, out of which a flame of fire broke, moved betwixt the pieces. In this God appeared to Abram, as afterwards to the Israelites, on their march to Canaan, in the cloudy pillar and in the fire. Here was represented the fearful and (to sinners) the intolerable majesty of God, veiled and softened to the eye by the cloud of smoke, the emblem of reconciling grace (Lev. xvi. 12, 13). The reason why *God* alone passes through, and not Abraham, is because this covenant was one of grace, and God before all gives His grace ere He requires anything on man's part. Its aim was to strengthen Abram in his sure trust that God would fulfil what He had promised.

Ver. 18. *Abram;* i.e., what is here narrated was the conclusion of the covenant in which God had promised to Abram.

Euphrates.—The river of Egypt is the Nile, whose arms, by means of canals, stretch to the eastern extremity of Egypt. In ancient days Asia reached to the valley of the Nile. In these words the bounds of the Promised Land are only given in undefined and general terms, as the length of the Egyptian captivity in round numbers, four hundred. At times the Israelites literally possessed the whole territory from the Nile to the Euphrates, as the tribe Reuben, in the south-east of Jordan, had the pasture lands in the wilderness as far as Euphrates, and carried on wars with the Arabians on the Persian Gulf (1 Chron. vi. 9, 10); and also, on the north, the kingdom of David and Solomon extended to the Euphrates, on the south to the Red Sea (2 Sam. viii. 3; 1 Kings iv. 21, 24; 2 Chron. viii. 17). In this prophecy the boundaries of the Promised Land are extended as far as they would have been, in the case that Israel had continued faithful to the Lord: the same holds good of the glowing, brilliant descriptions of the fruitfulness of Canaan.

Ver. 19. *Kenites.*—Afterwards driven to the south of Arabia. —The Kenizzites are unknown.—The Cadmonites signify the inhabitants of the east countries. The name does not occur again. The people are unknown.

Ver. 20. *The Hittites.*—In the middle of Palestine, about Hebron (ch. xxiii.) and Bethel (Judges i. 23, 26). Even to a late period they remained, dwelling among the Israelites.

Ver. 21. *The Amorites.*—The principal nation of the Canaanites in Palestine, dwelling on both sides of the Jordan.

The Canaanites.—One particular tribe bore the name of the people in general.

The Girgashites—mentioned Joshua xxiv. 11; else unknown.

The Jebusites dwelt in and about Jerusalem, in the mountainous district. Joshua overcame them (Joshua xi.). Nevertheless their chief town, Jebus, afterwards Jerusalem, was not taken before David's time.

CHAPTER XVI.

Ver. 2. *Obtain*: lit. "be builded by her." A family is called a house, and so to beget children, to build. On such a connection as this, see ch. xxii. 24. A warning against it is given Prov. xxx. 23. By the results of this and other cases of polygamy in the O. T., God warns by *deeds* against it, though by reason of their "hardness of heart" He allows the state.

Ver. 4. *Despised.*—Since barrenness was regarded as a curse, abundance of children as a rich blessing.

Ver. 5. *My wrong.*—She rashly and impatiently blames Abram, because he did not inflict punishment on Hagar.

Ver. 7. *Angels.*—Throughout the whole of O. T. there runs the distinction between the hidden God and the Revealer of God, Himself equal with God, who most frequently is called "the Messenger, the Angel of the Lord," "Malachi-Jehovah,"—one with Him, and yet distinct from Him. This Messenger of the Lord is the Guide of the patriarchs (cf. ch. xlviii. 16); the Caller of Moses (Exod. iii. 2, etc.); the Leader of the people through the wilderness (Exod. xiv. 19, ch. xxiii. 20; cf. ch. xxxiii. 14, Isa. lxiii. 9); the Champion of the Israelites in Canaan (Joshua v. 13); and also, yet further, the Guide and Ruler of the people of the covenant (Judges ii. 1, ch. vi. 11, ch. xiii. 3); or, as He is called, Isa. lxiii. 9, "the Angel of His Presence;" by Daniel "Michael" (?), and He deputes Gabriel to the prophet (Dan. x. 13, etc.); in Zechariah He measures the new building of Jerusalem, and sends the angel to the prophet, who speaks with him (see Zech. ch. i. and ii.); by Malachi, as the Messenger of the Covenant, greatly longed for by the people, whose return to His temple is promised (Mal. iii. 1). It nowhere occurs in the O. T., that an angel speaks as if he were God (since in Daniel, Gabriel, and in Zechariah, the angel who talks with the prophet, clearly distinguish themselves from Jehovah); while this Angel of the Lord, in the passage under consideration, and often elsewhere in the O. T., speaks as Jehovah, and His appearing is regarded as that of the Most High God Himself. Nay, God says expressly of this Angel, "My name—*i.e.*, My revealed Being—is in Him." His name "Messenger," or "Angel," is to be taken in a general signification, and by no means as if it denoted a class of higher created beings, of angels, which He had taken (cf. Heb. ii. 16). In the N. T. the expressions, "The Word," "Son," "Express Image," "Brightness," betoken the same, viz., the countenance turned to man, the Revealer of the Invisible God. The expressions which our Lord frequently uses, "He who hath sent Me," "I am sent from the Father," particularly refer to this name (St Matt. x. 40; St Luke x. 16; St John v. 23), as Heb. iii. 1, He is called "the Apostle" of our profession. The future appearance on earth of the God-man is gradually prepared in the O. T. in two ways: on the one hand, there is promised a mighty and glorious Human Ruler over all (in later times called "Messiah,"—the Anointed of the Lord), to whom, at the same time, in His human nature, Divine names, attributes, and works are ascribed (so ch. xlix. 10; Ps. ii. and cx.; Isa. ix. 5; Micah v. 1); on the other hand, the personal distinction in the Godhead, the Revealer of the Invisible God as a separate person, is more and more clearly made known. Therefore it was that John Baptist, our Lord's forerunner, recognised in Christ the Eternal One who was come down from heaven, and was over all: St John i. 15, ch. iii. 31.

Shur.—Probably the town called by the Greeks Pelusium, to the north-east of Egypt. She fled back to her native land.

Ver. 10. *Numbered.*—Outwardly a blessing as great as that which was promised to Abram (Gen. xv. 5); and even in the weaker reflection in Hagar's posterity may the greatness of the promise of blessing to the father of the faithful be recognised. "Arabia, the population of which for the most part consists of the descendants of Ishmael, is an abundant source of the human family, from whence have issued, for thousands of years, streams far and wide towards the east and west. Before the time of Mahomet, Ishmael's posterity existed in the whole of Asia Minor—in the middle ages, in East India; in the whole of North Africa has it been the cradle of all the wandering tribes. Through the whole of the Indian Ocean, as far as the Moluccas, had they, so early as the middle ages, settlements; likewise on the coast of Mozambique, as their navigation passed over Lower India to China. In Europe they peopled South Spain, and were masters of it for 700 years."—(Ritter.)

Ver. 12. *Wild man.*—Literally, "he shall be a wild ass

of man,"—a remarkable and peculiarly significant prophecy. The wild ass (Onager)—Hebrew, "Pere," *i.e.* a runner—is a beautiful animal, with longer legs than the tame ass, a dark flowing mane, a projecting forehead, long outstretched ears, silver-coloured hair, and a thick stripe of brown down the back, intersected by a similar one in the form of a cross. It is a swift, shy animal, which lives in the desert, and is only with great difficulty taken or tamed: see the description, Job xxxix. 5–8. The prophet describes the wilderness as "a joy of asses" (Isa. xxxii. 14). The description thoroughly depicts the intense love of freedom of the Bedouin Arabs; their unshackled roaming about in the wilderness; their contempt of every kind of regular, and especially city life; and their determined independence. Only certain parts of their country have ever yet been subdued; and the conquerors have always been obliged to solicit afresh the friendship of a people whom it was dangerous to provoke, and utterly unprofitable to conquer. "They live under the open heaven (says Diodorus, 19, 94), and call the uninhabited, waterless desert their native country. A law forbids them to sow corn, to plant fruit-trees, to drink wine, and to build houses. Any one of them who breaks the law is punished with death. The reason of this law is the notion, that all who have possessions of the kind named, may be brought into subjection by people more powerful than themselves, and made to obey their commands."

Brethren.—Even to this day the greater part of the Arabs lead a robber life. They justify themselves by referring to the hard treatment experienced by their forefather Ishmael, who was driven from his father's house, and received the wilderness as his inheritance, with the permission to take what he could find. "Against his brethren—in their presence:" he will dwell opposite to them, *i.e*, towards the east, as, in the description of a situation, one would turn the face thither. Therefore, in Arabia, the name "Jemen" stands for the south, the land to the right; and "Scham" for Syria, the land to the left. Of all the descendants of Abraham, the Ishmaelites have taken up their dwelling most to the east.

Ver. 13. *Seest me.*—"Thou (art) the God of seeing," *i.e.*, the God who revealest Thyself. Thou art not hidden, but hast made Thyself known.

Seeth me.—Heb.: "Also see I here after the seeing;" *i.e.*, "Also here even, where I have seen God, do I still behold (the light): I still live after the seeing." This saying rests on the thought, "The sight of God is so overwhelming, that he who has seen Him can see nothing more, and must die." The feeling of fear, that when God, or a God—a Divine Being—has appeared to man, that man must die, pervades the whole of heathen antiquity also. But that which among the heathen was only an indistinct feeling of the majesty and greatness of God, became in the Old Testament, at least among religious men, a deep feeling of the unworthiness of sinful man to appear before the Holy God (cf. particularly Isa. vi. 5). The belief, which is so frequently mentioned in the Old Testament, that man could not look on God without dying (Gen. xxxii. 30; Judges vi. 22, ch. xiii. 23), is confirmed by God Himself (Exod. xxxiii. 18); and yet at the same time is contravened by a number of facts (cf., besides the above-mentioned passages, Exod. xxiv. 10, 11). By reason of his sinfulness, and that utter weakness which is inseparable from sin, a creature cannot endure the sight of the Holy God, when He reveals in any visible manner His might and holiness,— even the sight of an angel coming immediately from God is terrible (St Luke i. 12, 13); yet that which is in itself impossible, from the corruption of the creature, can be made possible through God's grace and mercy, who absolves men from their sins, and makes them capable of receiving the veiled revelation of His holiness. Hence the childlike joy when man, after participation of a vision from God, has felt himself refreshed, renovated, and invigorated: until, at length, God revealed His full glory in the flesh; and now they who believe on Him may cry out with joy, "We beheld His glory; we have seen Him with our eyes; we have handled the Word of life:" St John i. 14; 1 St John i. 1.

Ver. 14. *Beer-lahai-roi.*—"Well of the seeing to life;" *i.e.*, a well, where man sees God and yet lives, and then at the same time is looked on by Him with grace, and blessed. Cf. ch. xxxii. 30: "P'ni-el," a place where one sees God's countenance and the soul is preserved.

Kadesh and Bered.—Kadesh lies on the south border of Palestine: Bered, or Barad, is unknown.

CHAPTER XVII.

Ver. 1. *Almighty God.*—It is to this place that Exod. vi. 2, etc., refers. God had revealed Himself to Abraham, Isaac, and Jacob, as "the Almighty God" (El Schaddai). His name Jehovah (which there is "the Eternal, Unchangeable, Self-existent, Faithful God) was unknown to them, *i.e.*, not in the literal sense, since from the beginning of Creation He called Himself Jehovah; but because name and meaning are never separated. [Although the *name* Jehovah occurs, yet until the meaning of the name was revealed by the fulfilment of the promises, He is said not to be known by that appellation.] To the patriarchs, God called Himself especially the Almighty, until, in the fulfilment of the promises, He proved Himself to be the Unchangeable, True, and Sure God.

He here requires unconditional trust and reliance on the Word. A view is opened into a new Future, which begins from henceforth.

Perfect.—As My might shall be thine, and altogether for thy good, if thou believest on Me; so surrender thyself up entirely to Me, that no one may have part in that which is due from thee to Me. "To walk before God," is to walk in the fruition of His grace, and in the lively consciousness of his all-present, holy love.

Ver. 5. *Father.*—Ab-ram means "high father"—a general title of honour, which other nomadic princes (Sheiks) might bear. Ab-raham = the Father of a multitude; and refers to the particular Divine promise of which he is partaker.

Ver. 8. *Everlasting.*—God makes with Abraham and his posterity an everlasting covenant; since this covenant of grace was the first germ of the new covenant in Jesus Christ. But even with Abraham's descendants after the flesh, does God ever continue in a particular covenanted relationship. Their present punishment, after the rejection of their King and Saviour, as well as their hopes for time to come, both result from God's covenant with them. Cf. Rom. xi. 29. The "eternal possession" stands, in the first instance, in contrast to the present temporary abode of Abraham in Canaan. Yet at the same time is this land, which God promised as an inheritance to Abraham and his seed, the visible pledge, the germ and prophetic type, of the new world, which belongs to the Church of the Lord: it is therefore called emphatically, "an Eternal Possession." The same holds good of all the Divine ordinances, which in the Old Testament are declared to be everlasting ordinances; and yet in the New Testament are in the letter abrogated, while in the spirit they have been really fulfilled. So it is with Circumcision, the Passover, the Priesthood, etc.

Ver. 13. *Covenant.*—Together with the solemn establishment of the covenant, is an abiding sign of covenant joined—a prophetic type of the sacraments of the New Testament. Circumcision has this in common with baptism, that the command of God does not appoint an entirely new custom, but uses and transforms to its own purpose, one which already existed. Circumcision was a custom in very early times among the Egyptians —perhaps among some other people—however, not among the Canaanites. In Egypt it was confined to the priestly caste, and perhaps a few others, who voluntarily imitated them. It was there an emblem of purity, and closely connected with the deification of the powers of nature. In the case of Abraham and his posterity there was this difference, that circumcision was not restricted to one class, but all the males were without distinction to be circumcised for a sign that all the Israelites were to be "a royal priesthood, a holy people:" Exod. xix. 6. In the next place, with them, circumcision had not the slightest connection with the Egyptian deification of nature. It was an emblem of purity, but of *moral* purity (hence the many exhortations to circumcision of the heart, Deut. x. 16, ch. xxx. 6; Jer. iv. 4, ch. ix. 26; Ezek. xvi. 30; Acts vii. 51). It reminds man of the truth, that from the first he is a sinner; and so is a continual declaration of the existence of original sin and the necessity of repentance,—at the same time a prediction of the Deliverer and Saviour from Abraham's seed. Moreover, circumcision served to keep Abraham and his descendants separate from all people round about them, and obliged them to the observance of the whole law which God had given them. For seven days did a child remain in his natural impurity; on the eighth, he entered into covenant with God.

Ver. 14. *Broken.*—The old covenant was especially a covenant of compulsion and outward discipline. The entrance therein was not voluntary: it stood open to none of Abraham's posterity to withdraw from the grace which, by means of this covenant, was bestowed on the whole people, and through them on the whole world. The punishment of "being cut off from his people," which God threatens on the neglect of circumcision, occurs very frequently afterwards, under the law, as the penalty for very grievous crimes; more particularly those against the theocracy, *i e.*, sins against God's majesty as King of His people, which involved an entire breach of the covenant (cf., *e.g.*, Exod. xxxi. 14; Lev. xvii. 4, ch. xx. 17). This punishment is a threatening, on God's part, that all the evil should overtake the transgressor, from which, through God's covenant, he was defended. It was open to every one to become his accuser, and procure his death; and even if he escaped this, he lived in continual fear that God might, in some immediate manner, bring the punishment upon him (as Exod. iv. 24). Therefore we find that on some the threatening of being cut off from the people was followed by death (Num. xv. 30, 31); while the omission of circumcision in the wilderness was visited with the general Divine chastisement, which is announced in Num. xiv 22–24.

Ver. 15. *Sarai* means "my mistress"—a title of honour on the side of inferiors. Sarah, on the contrary, simply "princess," the high lady from whom, as is afterwards promised, even kings shall issue.

Ver. 17. *Laughed.*—As God now says of the childless, aged Sarah, what He had before said of himself, Abraham is seized with the greatest amazement. This laughing was not entirely in its nature unbelief, but arises out of the feeling of wonder at the unheard-of event promised, and at the same time of deep joy; still, of course, a certain amount of doubt was mixed with it. Abraham cannot as yet believe for joy the astonishing promise. From like feelings Sarah afterwards laughs (ch. xviii. 12). But when, on the circumcision of the boy, he solemnly receives the name "Jitschak"—one laughs—this laughter was turned into pure joy (ch. xxi. 5–7).

Ver. 18. *Ishmael live*—"that he might be blessed by Thee!—that he might be inheritor of the promised blessings." In this is implied the desire that God would more clearly reveal His will.

Ver. 19. *Isaac.*—This is the Greek version of the name: in the Hebrew, "Jitschak."

After him.—The covenant with him does not relate to temporal goods only.

Ver. 20. *Twelve princes.*—See ch. xxv. 16.

Ver. 23. *Said unto him.*—Abraham evinced at all times the most exact and perfect obedience.

CHAPTER XVIII.

Ver. 1. *Mamre.*—" Under the Oaks of Mamre," as ch. xiii. 18. Mamre was an Amorite, after whom Abraham's place of residence is called the Oaks of Mamre, though occasionally only " Mamre." It was a grove of oaks in the neighbourhood of the fruitful Hebron. " The environs of this town resemble a vast, rich olive-garden. The slopes of the hills, as rich as the level of the valley, are verdant and blooming with every flower of the meadow and garden; while in different parts, especially on the side towards Jerusalem, are to be seen fruitful vineyards."— Schubert, ii. 468. God now appeared to Abraham in a form assumed for the particular object in view.

Ver. 2. *Bowed himself.*—As in the presence of very distinguished guests, particularly kings. This reverence of bowing until the face touched the ground, which in Scripture is often called "worshipping," was a posture which recognised in a superior a representative of God Himself; or, in the case of the heathen, a messenger from Him, or an incarnation of some divine person. So far as a certain degree of truth was contained in this notion, the act of reverence was not actual idolatry, though there were times when it was important to keep in view the wide distinction between God Himself and His messengers (*e g.*, Acts x. 26; Rev. xxii. 9).

Ver. 4. *Feet.*—In the East, and indeed in ancient times everywhere, the washing of the feet (which were only covered on the soles by sandals) was a mark of hospitality.

Ver. 5. *So do.*—The Lord permits the act of hospitality to be paid Himself, together with His angels, in order by this gracious proof of His love to afford the surest pledge of His promises.

Ver. 6. *Make cakes.*—Thin cakes of unleavened bread, baked on the coals, or in a kind of frying dish, are even to this day an usual offering of hospitality among the Bedouins.

Ver. 7. *Dress it.*—It is customary among the Arabs of the Desert now, as it was among the Greeks of antiquity, for the man as well as the woman of high rank to take part in household work. In Homer, we find that even kings themselves cut up and roasted the animals for food.

Ver. 8. *Butter.*—What is translated "butter" must be understood to mean a thickened milk; since in the East "butter" is only used medicinally. Oil is used in abundance in the food; but, on account of the heat of the climate, butter would never keep sweet.

Did eat.—Abraham kills a calf, bakes cakes, places a table, waits on the angels, and *they eat*: all this happened plainly as it is narrated, and not in appearance merely. Our body, so long as it is mortal, requires the renewal of its vigour, and hence the feeling of hunger is given. From our body, power is continually passing away, though unconsciously to ourselves, and must be continually renewed. As long as we bear our present bodies, we shall feel this need,—we shall hunger,—and from hunger we shall eat. But an angel does not eat from a feeling of this necessity; since it is one thing *to be able* to perform an act, quite another thing *to be obliged* to perform it. Man eats, that he may live: an angel eats to be like a man. Thus did Christ eat after His resurrection, not to supply a need of His flesh, but to convince His disciples of the reality of His body.—S. Augustine, 362 de Resurrect. v. 1422 sq. Ben.

Ver. 9. *In the tent;* i.e., in the hinder part, where was the woman's apartment.

Ver. 10. *Time of life.*—Heb.: "I will return to thee so as the year lives," *i.e.*, lives again; the present time of the year returns, therefore, from this season of the year.

Ver. 15. *Afraid.*—She had laughed "within herself," and so hoped to escape detection, since she did not as yet, at least not with certainty, know the Lord to be present.

Didst laugh.—Even the unbelief which was concealed in her breast must be brought to light, as the fulfilment of the promise depended on her trust in it. It would not be accomplished without faith.

Ver. 16. *Rose up.*—We must attentively consider the progress of the history from this point. The three men rise up and turn their steps towards Sodom. On the way they stand still; and He who already had spoken as the Lord Jehovah, announces to Abraham His purpose to inquire into the cry which had come up to Him from Sodom. The two angels then turn towards Sodom (xix. 1); while the third, the Lord, remains and listens to Abraham's entreaty for the city. The two angels arrive at Lot's house, pass the night there, and declare that the Lord had sent them to destroy the city: in the morning, they lead him out. Here the third, the Lord Himself, comes to them (ch. xix. 17). Lot, who did not yet know them, appeals to the whole three for a particular mercy (ver. 18), but only *one* out of the three answers him, and speaks now in His own name; and thereupon, as Jehovah, He rains down fire and brimstone out of heaven from the Lord (Jehovah): ver. 21–25.

Ver. 18. *Blessed.*—Even here, when God affords the greatest proof of His gracious condescension, nay, of His friendship for Abraham, the reason why He so distinguishes him is this—because through him shall all the people of the earth be blessed. In order to show him how blessed a thing it is to serve the true and living God, and to stand in the relation of childlike intercourse with Him (a blessing which is granted to all those who are blessed through Abraham), God makes known His purpose to him as to an intimate friend: cf. St John xv. 15.

Ver. 19. *Know him.*—In the Heb. the sense is different. "Since I have known him (*i.e.*, from My love have chosen him, as Amos iii. 2; St Matt. vii. 23; 1 Cor. viii. 3), in order that he may command his sons, and his house after him, and (*i.e.*, in order that) they may keep the way of the Lord," etc. Not because God knew beforehand that Abraham would teach his family the ways of God, but in order that he may do it, did God choose him; and when by the power of God's grace he has done it, then shall the rich blessing come upon him: cf. St John xv. 16.

Ver. 20. *Grievous.*—Literally, "A cry of Sodom and Gomorrah, since it is great: their sin, since it is very grievous." By placing the words "Cry" and "Sin" first, the declaration receives a very awful impressiveness: it expresses more than a mere declaration or description.

Ver. 21. *Will know.*—The perfect justice of God, the exact weighing of all which men have done, is in a most striking manner represented in this expression. God places the Sodomites on their trial. The trial was not needful for His information; but it is needful that every sin should be brought to light, to be either blotted out, or punished.

Ver. 22. *The men.*—The two angels who accompanied the Lord (ch. xix. 1). The Lord remained, and Abraham with Him.

Ver. 24. *Fifty righteous.*—The greatness and extent of the guilt of others, which admits of no forgiveness, is often incomprehensible to him who is conscious that he himself is saved by grace.

Ver. 26. *Their sakes.*—The righteous who dwell in a place together with the wicked are able to stay God's punishments, since He wills not to destroy them with His enemies. A poor obscure child of God possesses a power to turn aside the course of the world's history. So unsearchable are God's judgments.

Ver. 32. *For ten's sake.*—" Can any being be imagined more gracious than our blessed Lord? We know beforehand that we are in the wrong, and we do not doubt His justice, yet we would willingly unbosom ourselves: where can we find any one to whom we may resort? Go straight to the eternal living God, with every sorrow, doubt, care, and scruple I cannot sufficiently express my sense of the blessed privilege of communion with our Lord. I can well conceive how Abraham's long discourse over Sodom is carried on: I can picture to myself Isaac, how he comes from the fountain of the Living and Seeing One; Moses, how he speaks nothing, but cries out, Exod. xiv. 15; David, when he inquires of the Lord what shall happen at Keilah and Ziph (1 Sam. xxiii.); Hezekiah, when he expostulates on his deathbed, 2 Kings xx. 3; Daniel in vision; Nathanael under the fig-tree; our Lord, when He speaks with the Father; Peter, when he takes our Lord aside and rebukes Him; Paul, when he steers the ship against the waves and winds; and if I should think what John did on the Lord's day, when he saw the vision of the Revelations, what was it but converse with Another at table? Blessed are we who have so merciful a Lord."—*Zinzendorf's Jeremiah.*

CHAPTER XIX.

The righteous judgment of God is now declared in a fearful event, which at the same time serves to magnify still further the grace of God towards Abraham by saving his brother's son out of the overthrow. In the paradisaical region of the Valley of Siddim dwelt the most depraved of all the tribes of Canaan, on whom, more than on the rest, God's punishment was to fall. The kind and manner of the punishment were so regulated as to call into action the natural properties of the country. The springs of bitumen (cf. ch. xiv. 10, note) were ignited by lightning, an earthquake tore the ground asunder, subterranean streams of water rose to the surface, and the lately blooming valley was covered with a salt lake, deadly to everything. Its proximity to the land flowing with milk and honey would be a standing memorial of the judgment of God. So it remains to this day. Tacitus thus describes it, and his account holds good to the present time: "A lake of great extent, offering to the eye the appearance of a sea, to the smell a most offensive odour. Its evaporations are fatal to those who live by it. The water is so heavy that the wind does not stir it, and neither fish can live in it, nor bird on it. Anything thrown on its surface floats—swimmers or not swimmers, all are buoyed up. At certain times it throws out bitumen. The borders of the lake are said to have been once fruitful, and the site of large cities. They were burnt up by lightning, and the parched ground has never recovered its fertility. Everything that grows there indigenously, or is sown— weeds, or flowers, or shrubs—is black, and crumbles into ashes."— Modern investigation has discovered that the water contains 42 per cent. parts of salt, and 24 of muriate of magnesia. It gives the skin an oily surface, and then peels it off. No more jagged mountain can be seen than the salt mountain at the south end of the lake. Around are lonely shores, without vegetation, or habitation of man. Wild animals avoid the region, as they can find no food there; only vultures and eagles build their nests on the black rocks, and swallows search here and there for insects. —Throughout the whole of the O. and N. T. the overthrow of

Sodom is set before us as an emblem of all God's judgments, especially that of the last day (cf. Deut. xxix. 23, ch. xxxii. 32; Isa. i. 9, 10, ch. xiii. 19; Jer. xlix. 17, 18, ch. l. 40; Lam. iv. 6; Ezek. xvi. 46; St Matt. xi. 23; St Luke xvii. 29; 2 Pet. ii. 6; Rev. xi. 8); and so the restoration of the salt water in the Dead Sea is one of the most beautiful images of the renewing of the earth: Ezek. xlvii. 1, etc. Likewise the following history may be regarded step by step as an image of the inner giving up of the world which lieth in wickedness, and of the denial of communion with it from regard to God's threatened judgments, and in reliance on His preventing and assisting grace.

Ver. 1. *Gate.*—The covered doorways, and the piazzas adjoining (such are to be seen in modern fortified towns), were in ancient times usual places of concourse, where the inhabitants met for amusement, or to transact public business, especially the administration of justice: cf. 1 Sam. iv. 18; Job xxix. 7; Deut. xxi. 19.

Ver. 2. *Behold.*—Lot takes the angels for distinguished strangers, whose appearance inspired awe. As a good man, he is distinguished for the widely-cultivated oriental virtue of hospitality. The blessing which he gained thereby is mentioned in the N. T. as an example to ourselves: Heb. iii. 2. Perhaps he apprehended that in a place of such fearful profligacy some evil might overtake them. Only at ver. 13 do they declare themselves to be messengers of the Lord.

Nay, but we will abide.—Travellers often carried tents with them; but it was customary also to pass the night under the open heaven. They would put Lot to the proof, since it was regarded as a mark of the corruption of morals in a place to allow a stranger to remain in the streets (Judges xix. 15; Job xxxi. 32).

Ver. 5. *Know them.*—In addition to the fearful sin itself, against which God's law afterwards enacted the punishment of death (Lev. xviii. 22, ch. xx. 13), the depravity of these Sodomites is shown in their violation of the sacred law of hospitality, and the shameless manner in which they express their purpose, as if it were something allowable: cf. Isa. iii. 9.

Ver. 8. *Two daughters.*—We must regard Lot's proposal as the result of desperation, as it cannot in itself be justified any more than Abraham's lie, ch. xii. 10; yet, under the circumstances, it admits of some excuse. The sacredness of hospitality was, according to the code of the time, above everything else. Perhaps Lot hoped that, as his daughters were espoused to Sodomites, they would not proceed to extremities.

Ver. 9. *Judge.*—Lot had evidently the character of a corrector of morals among them, and was accordingly hated for it: cf. 2 St Pet. ii. 7, 8.

Ver. 10. *Blindness.*—Not literally blinded, but struck with reeling vision like drunkards. So far were they allowed to proceed, that their hopeless wickedness might be manifested.

Ver. 12. *Out of this place.*—Even Lot's sons-in-law were tainted with the prevailing depravity, which is shown clearly afterwards by the sin of his daughters. The dangerous intimacy of Lot with this corrupt people is given as a warning to ourselves.

Ver. 13. *Cry.*—The men against whom the sin has been committed, the beasts who have been abused, all cry out to God for vengeance: cf. ch. iv. 10. In this expression is contained the solemn thought, that for every violation of the Divine order a satisfaction will be required, that this sacred order must be restored in every case by the punishment of him who has violated it.

Ver. 14. *As one that mocked.*—A lively representation of those whom the messenger of the Lord warns of impending punishment: cf. St Luke xvii. 28, 29.

Ver. 16. *Merciful;* lit., " in the mercy of the Lord upon them." There is no greater love than that which, even at the hazard of being vexatious and troublesome, presses on the sinner, and says, " Escape for thy life!"

Ver. 17. *Look not.*—To look back is a sign of unbelief, and of cleaving to sin. Who, in such a case, looks behind, does not believe the threat that the danger is his own: cf. St Luke ix. 62. Here, again, we find One who speaks with Lot. *They* lead him out, but *He* speaks to him. Here has the Lord, or *the* appointed Angel of the Lord, His co-equal Revealer, again joined the other two. Lot recognises Him as the first among them; since, while he directs his words to all three, he speaks yet but with One, whom he addresses by the name of God, " Lord;" and He now declares in His own name what He will do.

Ver. 20. *Little one.*—The town is a little one, and therefore does Lot plead for its being spared, as vengeance would be satisfied with the great and flourishing towns. From ver. 21 we learn that this town was originally doomed to destruction like the rest.

Ver. 22. *Till thou.*—How forcibly is God's justice, as well as His love and forbearance, here expressed! He will not suffer one just man to perish in the judgment on the godless; but for the sake of one righteous man He spares a guilty city. He *can* not, by reason of His covenant with one man. In the decree, that for the sake of His elect God will spare a city, there is nothing arbitrary or contradictory to the Divine justice. God reserves to Himself His judgment upon individuals, and does not send His final condemnation on a community until, by the removal of the righteous, the influx of His renewing grace and mercy is barred.

Ver. 23. *Zoar,* " The little," spared on account of its smallness, lay on the southern entrance to the present Salt Valley, in the neighbourhood of which is the jagged Rock-salt Mountain.

Ver. 24. *The Lord.*—" From the Lord" clearly expresses the distinction of persons in the Godhead, as is intimated in the whole of the O. T., and clearly revealed in the N. T.

Ver. 26. *Pillar.*—From love to her former abode, and from unbelief, she would not abstain from disobedience to God's commands. She remained standing. The sulphur blast overtook her, and, like all the country round, she was enveloped in an encrustation of salt, in which state she was afterwards found: cf. St Luke xvii. 32.

Ver. 29. *Remembered.*—This short remark points out that Lot was saved for Abraham's sake, and on his account only is all this narrative given. It is worth mentioning that a resemblance of this history is to be found in the Greek fable of Philemon and Baucis. Two gods come down from heaven to know by personal experience the wickedness of the men of a certain country. They are inhospitably repulsed from every door except that of Philemon, who receives them in a friendly manner. They declare to him they are come to destroy that region. At their command, Philemon and Baucis save themselves by fleeing to a mountain, without looking behind them; and when, at last, they look on the country, it is changed into a lake.

Ver. 30. *Cave.*—The mountain district of that part abounds in caves.

Ver. 31. *Earth;* Heb., "in the land." It is altogether false to justify this guilty act of Lot's daughters by supposing they imagined all mankind, by God's judgment, were cut off from the earth. Their residence in Zoar contradicts this.

Ver. 37. *Moab;* i.e., "from my father."

Ver. 38. *Ben-ammi;* i.e., "son of my people." The descendants of these two were afterwards the bitter enemies of the Israelites, who were not allowed to meddle with them on their passage to Canaan: Deut. ii. 9, 19. Lot's descendants were excluded from the congregation of the Lord (Deut. xxiii. 3); and finally they were made "servants" and tributaries by David: 2 Sam. viii. 2.

CHAPTER XX.

Ver. 1. *Kadesh*, towards the south-east, near the Dead Sea.—Shur, towards Egypt: cf. ch. xvi.—Gerar, in the south-western part of Canaan, in the land of the Philistines.

Ver. 3. *God.*—He is not here called the "Lord," Jehovah, because one is addressed who, although a worshipper of the true God, was nevertheless not in covenant with Him, as Abraham was. At that time it would seem even these Philistines were not as yet idolatrous (just as Melchizedek was a worshipper of the true God), yet they knew not God as Jehovah, as the God who had entered into a covenant with His servants.

She is a man's wife.—We find, from ver. 7, 17, that he was sick, and by that means preserved from the sin (ver. 6). God threatened that the sickness would be unto death, if he disobeyed His warning.

Ver. 6. *Sinning.*—"Here we may observe that a sin is committed *against God* when an action is done which seems in the eyes of men of small moment, because they treat lightly mere sins of the flesh."—St Augustine.

Ver. 7. *Prophet.*—Cf. Ps. cv. 15.

Ver. 9. *Ought not.*—Abraham cannot reply to this reproach, which contains the reproof which God would convey to him.

Ver. 16. *A covering.*—To cover the sin of any one, to cover the countenance (to appease, to make him well-inclined), are very frequent expressions for atonement, justification, forgiveness. The gift was to be an atonement for the wrong done to Sarah. The king owed her a public compensation.

Reproved.—Heb.: "And she is justified." "Now have I made all restitution."

Ver. 18. *Closed.*—The subjects suffer as well as the king, since it was God's will to evidence how highly He regarded Abraham.

CHAPTER XXI.

Isaac, the son of promise, he who was begotten through the Spirit,—*i.e.*, by the power of the word of God, and of faith—is now born. Ishmael, the son born after the flesh, in a natural way, grew up with him, but as a scoffer at God's word.

In order that Abraham's natural affection might not be a hindrance to the fulfilment of His own purposes, God does not allow him "that was born after the flesh," from a bond-woman, to be "heir together with the son of the free-woman."

In all this the great truth is taught us, which runs through the whole of Scripture, and is brought forward most prominently in the N. T., that the claims of the flesh are of no worth in God's sight, but that all is of His free grace alone. This history, therefore, is a type of higher spiritual relations (Gal. iv. 22, etc.). But at the same time Ishmael is an example how God extends His guidance and blessing to those whom yet He does not receive into covenant. He vouchsafes a portion even of the spiritual blessing of Abraham to Ishmael's posterity.

Ver. 1. *Spoken.*—Ch. xvii. 19.

Ver. 6. *Laugh.*—Cf. ch. xvii. 17; Ps. xxvi. 2.

Ver. 9. *Mocking.*—Isaac derived his name from a holy laugh. Ishmael, too, was one who laughed, but with an unholy mocking. He was a stranger to the mystery of the covenant of promise, and persecuted his brother with a sinful mocking: Gal. iv. 29.

Ver. 12. *Isaac,*—*i.e.*, Isaac's children shall be thy real de-

Ver. 15. *Cast.*—She let the child lie there: hitherto she had led him by the hand. Ishmael was at that time fourteen years old: ch. xvi. 16, ch. xxi. 5, 8.

Ver. 20. *Wilderness.*—Ishmael was not banished to any distance: he dwelt in the near wilderness: cf. xxv. 9.

Ver. 22. *Phichol.*—Both these names occur again, ch. xxvi. 26. Abimelech means "father-king;" Phichol, "mouth of all"—one who commands all. They were both of them at that time general names for the kings, like Pharaoh, etc.

Doest.—The blessing of God, which rested on Abraham, moved reverence in these heathens, who still served the true God. We have here an image of the blessing which, even in Old Testament times, reached beyond the people of the covenant, and extended itself to the heathen.

Ver. 25. *Taken.*—He represented how little this conduct of his servants (of which he could not be ignorant) agreed with the assurance just given (ver. 23).

Ver. 31. *Sware.*—The sacred number seven was in ancient times the number of the covenant of God and man, as it is composed of the sacred number three and of the number four, which is a figure of the world. For this reason we find it so often used in the Divine ordinances. (Seven days form the week—after seven days children were to be circumcised, etc.) It appears, therefore, that in the solemn oath between Abraham and Abimelech it is used as an emblem, and the swearing receives its name from this number. (In the Hebrew, the word translated swear, means seven.) This solemn present of seven lambs which Abraham makes, was perhaps not customary in agreements; and, therefore, is intended here to serve for the more religious ratification of this covenant. Beersheba (properly, "the well of seven"), which became afterwards the celebrated southern boundary of Canaan, was to be a memento to the two parties of their oath. Here is the boundary of the Desert. "As we advanced (from south to north) the loose sand ceased, and the land showed grass mixed with herbs. We then crossed the bed of Wady-el-Murtubeh, a broad strip of land which bears the traces of a large quantity of water. Some miles on we reached the Wady-es-Seba, the wide water-course of a winter torrent. On the north side, close to its banks, lie two deep wells which are still called 'Ber-es-Scheba,'—both contain abundance of clear, excellent water. The ruins are here scattered over the space of a quarter of a mile, along the north side of the bed of the stream."—(Robinson, i. 337–339: he was the first traveller who, for centuries, had visited the place.)

Ver. 33. *Grove.*—Heb.: "a tamarisk tree"—a tree nearly of the size of the oak, abounding in Syria and Egypt, and useful for building purposes and for fire-wood. This tree, which Abraham planted, remained, it would seem, a distinguished tree to later times, around which were gathered the traditions concerning Abraham's residence at Beersheba.

CHAPTER XXII.

The patriarch, who has been so often proved, is now put to the severest trial of his love and faith. The child of promise granted in his old age, after so long waiting, for whose sake Ishmael had been banished, had become the chief object of his earthly love. For his sake he was a wanderer in Canaan. But God would purify this affection, by bringing Abraham to regard his son only as God's gift, entrusted to him for the purpose of advancing God's kingdom. He was bidden to render back the gift. This act, even with the hope of the resurrection, required on Abraham's part the renunciation of all present hopes. He saw before his eyes only the death of his beloved son; and nothing but firm trust in God's word could keep him from falling under his trial.

But how could God command Abraham to offer up his son, since afterwards in the law He expressly forbade such acts as "an abomination, on account of which the Lord did drive out the Canaanites from before Israel?" Deut. xviii. 10–12. To this it may be replied, that God did not intend a human sacrifice in this instance, but rather expressed His will on the subject by the course the event took. In the earliest times God taught men mostly by *acts*. By this trial Abraham's earthly love was to be mortified, while he showed that he loved God more than his son (cf. St Luke xiv. 26). Such a love to God could never be inculcated by mere words.

Human sacrifices are throughout the whole Old Testament utterly forbidden. The abomination consisted in this,—that the man sacrificed unwillingly was looked on merely as a thing, as an instrument; and such sacrifices were, therefore, only possible among the heathen, who were ignorant that man was made in the image of God. They regarded man as a mere natural *thing*. It was somewhat different in those few cases among the heathen, where a man freely died as a sacrifice and atonement for others. Here was a sort of foreshadowing and anticipation of the sacrifice of Christ, who, not in figure, but in truth and reality, bore the sins of all. In like manner, the self-denying offering up of his only son, in honour of God and obedience to Him, was a type of that act of God's love, " who spared not His only begotten Son," etc.: Rom. viii. 32. The same place where afterwards the Temple stood, and the Son of God was crucified, was the scene of the most sublime act in Abraham's life, the forerunner and figure of all after sacrifices, yea, of the sacrifice of Christ Himself.

Ver. 2. *Moriah.*—This name does again occur as indicating a country, but only is used to denote the mountain on which Solomon built the Temple, 2 Chron. iii. 1; which place was selected for that purpose, with reference to the event of this chapter. The name signifies, " shown by Jehovah," in allusion to the wonderful way in which the ram was shown by the angel, which was offered in the stead of Isaac. This circumstance was the crisis in the history of Abraham. God confirmed His promise, and crowned the faith of Abraham. From the fact, that Moriah afterwards became the mountain of the sanctuary, the name obtained in addition a particular significance, analogous to its former meaning.

Ver. 3. *Rose.*—Abraham obeyed this fearful command with the same punctual, ready promptness, with which he had followed every other Divine injunction.

Ver. 4. *Afar off.*—It was about thirty-two miles from Beersheba; the road lay through a mountainous district. The particular mountain was pointed out to him on the way by a special revelation, as before the land of Canaan had been made known: ch. xii. 1.

Ver. 5. *Again.*—This may be either regarded as an untruth into which Abraham fell, in the agitation and agony of the moment,—or rather (as is more in agreement with the tone of the whole narrative, and especially ver. 8) as an anticipation that in some unknown way God would bring about their return.

Ver. 12. *Know.*—God knows: He only learns by the trial that the man will remain faithful to Him,—without the trial his faithfulness is not made apparent. It cannot be objected against this, and similar words of God, that He knew before, since He only knew before so far as He foreknew the result of the trial. But the trial and the proof must necessarily take place, since only in its fulfilment does God recognise obedience, faith, and love as existing.

Ver. 14. *Jehovah-jireh*; i.e., "the Lord careth:" His providential care is glorified in the issue of the temptation.

Ver. 17. *Gate.*—The towns being included.

Ver. 18. *Blessed.*—This promise is in all essential points the same as that given at the beginning, ch. xii. 1-3, and afterwards repeated. What God had at the outset granted out of free grace alone, and unconditionally, He now confirms as the reward of Abraham's act of faith. This faith, which He had created, fostered, and proved, had now brought forth its fruits. God first promises, and by His revelation awakens faith in the heart; He then crowns with reward the works of this faith, which is the result of His grace.

Ver. 20. *Nahor.*—The genealogy, which was broken off at ch. xi. 29, is here resumed as preparatory to the narrative of Isaac's marriage.

Ver. 21. *Huz.*—Perhaps the land of Uz on the other side Jordan, between Palestine and Mesopotamia, was called from him: Job i. 1. Though an Uz occurs, ch. x. 23, and ch. xxxvi. 28.

Ver. 23. *Rebekah.*—Heb. Ribkah.

Ver. 24. *Concubine.*—Together with one or more wives, a man might have, according to the custom of those times, a concubine, taken out of the class of slaves. Her children did not in Abraham's case rank with the others, though in Jacob's they did. It was a kind of inferior marriage. The concubine was bound to be faithful: Judges xix. 2. Any one who committed adultery with a concubine was obliged to bring a trespass-offering: Lev. xix. 21. According to Exod. xxi. 9, 10, a father was to treat the concubine of his son "after the manner of daughters;" and if the son afterwards contracted a regular marriage, he was to regard her for the future as a concubine. We see how much there was allowable in the O. T. by reason of "hardness of heart," which, after the full revelation of the mystery of love in redemption, was no more permitted.

CHAPTER XXIII.

Ver. 2. *Hebron.*—First, Kirjath-Arba, afterwards Hebron: ch. xiii. 18, ch. xiv. 3. Abraham, therefore, was once more a dweller among the Canaanites. Cf. ch. xxi. 34.

Ver. 5. *Answered.*—In a public, solemn assembly—a general council of the tribe. So ver. 7 and 12.

Ver. 7. *Bowed.*—The customary Eastern mode of showing honour, by bowing low to the ground.

Ver. 9. *Machpelah* means "a doubling;"—a name which the cave for some cause bore.

Ver. 15. *Hearken.*—Literally, "If thou wilt only hear me." Abraham could not receive the field and cave as a gift, since the promise was present in his mind that his descendants should possess the whole land and destroy the inhabitants thereof: the sepulchre, the only spot which he possessed in the land, was a memorial of his belief in that promise. At the same time he did not choose to be indebted to the inhabitants for any gift.

Ver. 15. *What is that?*—That is, "We both are rich: as you desire it, pay this sum." The shekel (schekel) was originally, and here particularly, a *weight,* not a coin, as afterwards was the case. The Jewish historian, Josephus, reckons its value at four Attic drachmæ—about two shillings of our money. Probably it was not quite so much. But no inference can be drawn from later times as to its value in earlier. As a rule, the value of money decreases with time.

Ver. 16. *Current.*—Lit., "which would pass with the merchant," *i.e.,* with those who are judges of its fineness. The Phœnicians (Canaanites) were the first who, in consequence of their extended commerce, made use of silver as a medium of interchange.

Ver 18. *All.*—Thus the whole transaction, which was an act of faith on the part of Abraham, and carried out with stedfast regard to the covenant of promise, became, by this solemn agreement between himself and the Hethites, well known among all the inhabitants of the land.

CHAPTER XXIV.

Ver 2. *Eldest.*—This is generally supposed to be Eliezer of Damascus (xv. 2), which yet is scarcely probable, since he is not mentioned by name. If indeed it were *he*, then the disinterestedness of Abraham's pious and faithful servant appears the more conspicuous, since the birth of Isaac had deprived him of the hope of the inheritance: see ch. xv. 2.

Thigh.—A custom in making oath, which we meet with only in those ancient days.

Ver. 4. *Wife.*—This purpose on the part of Abraham was the result of his living faith in the promise. He had received no Divine revelation on this matter, and therefore could not be altogether certain, though he might feel the strongest conviction, that God would bless his way of proceeding. He feared lest Isaac should take a wife from among the inhabitants of the idolatrous land of Canaan, which was doomed to destruction. He therefore made his choice from the family in which the worship of the true God was in some measure kept alive, though not altogether in perfect purity.

Ver. 10. *Mesopotamia.*—Heb.: "Aram Neharajim," *i.e.*, Syria of the two rivers, the land between Euphrates and Tigris, particularly the north part of it, now called "Aldscheschirah."

Nahor.—Haran, ch. xi. 31, 27, 32.

Ver. 12. *Day.*—Heb.: "Make to-day come before my face," —viz., her whom I seek. In a journey which was undertaken in accordance with God's will, and at the command of His prophet, such a sign might lawfully be asked. But while he actually anticipates the fulfilment of his desire, he does not blindly follow the first impulse (ver. 21), but puts to the proof all the circumstances. The sign which he prays for is an act of humane, considerate attention on the part of the damsel, by which her good pious disposition may be in a degree tested. None other than one so disposed, he trusted, would God destine to be the wife of his master's son.

Ver. 15. *Shoulder.*—To this day in the same countries the daughters of the Arab sheiks fetch water from the wells, which are meeting-places for the damsels. Niebuhr says (ii. 410), " We found on this way between Orfa and Bu different wells, at which the maidens from the neighbouring villages, or from the tribes of the Curds and Turcmans, watered their cattle. They did not wear veils as they do in the towns. As soon as we had saluted them, and dismounted from our horses, they brought us water, and also watered our horses. I could not but be struck with this circumstance, since it was in these very regions that Rebecca performed the same kind office. Perhaps at that moment we were drinking from the very same well out of which she drew water."

Ver. 22. *Ear-ring.*—Heb., a nose ring, such as the women in the East still wear. They are often of a great weight and size, and hang down below the mouth: cf. Ezek. xvi. 12.

Ver. 30. *Well.*—This is the cause why Laban ran out (ver. 29), as it is repeated here.

Ver. 47. *Face.*—The ring in her nose.

Ver. 50. *Bethuel.*—In those ancient days the brothers appeared to have had even a stronger right of protection and care over their sisters than the fathers over their daughters (cf. ver. 53, ch. xxxiv. 13). There are still traces among the Arabs of this custom. Probably the reason lay in the allowance of polygamy, which gave rise to the fear that occasionally the father might be induced, by his preference for a particular wife, to act to the disadvantage of the daughters: cf. ch. xxxiv. 7, etc.

Good; i.e., We can say neither yes or no; we must obey. They speak of the Lord-Jehovah, whom they still reverenced, even though in their worship there was a mixture of idolatry: ch. xxxi. 19.

Ver. 59. *Nurse.*—Nurses in eastern countries are accustomed to accompany ladies of distinction, and are held in great esteem by them.

Ver. 64. *Alighted.*—She threw herself down to pay reverence: 2 Kings v. 21.

Ver. 65. *Covered.*—Before marriage the bridegroom never saw the bride except veiled: ch. xxix. 25.

Ver. 67. *Tent.*—Sarah had during her lifetime a particular tent assigned her, of which Rebecca now took possession.

CHAPTER XXV.

Ver. 4. *Keturah.*—All these are progenitors of the Arabian tribes, but are for the most part entirely unknown. The best known among them are the Midianites (ver. 2), on the east of the Gulf of Elan, a trading people (ch. xxxvii. 28), often in after times engaged in war with Israel (see particularly Judges viii.). In the time of the Kings they altogether disappeared from history.—*Shuah* is the native country of Bildad, the friend of Job.

Ver. 6. *East.*—See note, ch. xxii. 24.

Ver. 18. *Havilah*, probably in the neighbourhood of the Arabian Gulf.

Died.—The margin gives "fell," which seems the more correct version. The meaning is then—"His lot fell to him eastward of all his brethren:" cf. ch. xvi. 12, note: see also the version of the Septuagint, κατὰ πρόσωπον πάντων τῶν ἀδελφῶν αὐτοῦ κατῴκησε, i.e, he dwelt in the presence of all his brethren.

Ver. 19. *Generations of Isaac.*—A fresh era here commences in the history of the patriarchs. God first separated Abraham from his father's house, and made a covenant of grace with him: next, He distinguishes between the son of promise and "him born after the flesh:" now He chooses one of the twin sons of Isaac, the youngest, to be the heir of promise.

That which was determined, nay, declared, concerning these two sons before they were born, is verified as they grow up. In the one case, that of the younger, the work of grace proceeds notwithstanding his great faults; in the other case, his rejection is justified as the punishment of an irreligious, carnal mind. We cannot help remarking in all this narrative of Esau and Jacob, how fairly the good qualities of the rejected son, and the sins against his brother of the great ancestor of the Israelites, together with God's chastisements, are recorded.

Jacob and Rebecca seize by unjust means on the Blessing, which would in God's own way, and innocently, have been theirs. Esau shows himself unworthy of the Blessing by the light way in which he parted with the birthright. Jacob had faith to value it.

Ver. 20. *Syrian.*—Heb. " Aramaite."

Padan-Aram; i.e., of the plain country of Aram, the level land of Syria, in opposition to the mountainous Syria, the region of Lebanon.

Laban.—This is especially mentioned on account of the following narrative, in which Laban plays a conspicuous part.

Ver. 21. *Conceived.*—The birth of many remarkable men is preceded by a long period of barrenness: such was the case with Isaac, Samson, Samuel, John Baptist. Not only did God purpose thereby that the affection of the parents should be directed towards the child, and that his conduct should become a particular object of their observation; but, above all, that he should be regarded as a supernatural gift of God, and thereby a type of the birth of the Saviour from a virgin.

Ver. 22. *Inquire.*—She begged in prayer for an answer from God in a vision. The struggling of the children appeared to her to forebode the strife which should exist between the two.

Ver. 23. *Younger.*—The Lord tells her that the omen presages not merely the fate of the children, but likewise of the two people which should descend from them. Two struggling people are there represented, of whom the weaker shall be served by the stronger, in the same way as, of her sons, the younger was destined to obtain the privileges, the rank, the dominion, and the larger inheritance, which originally belonged to the elder. A prophetic enigma is here shown to Rebecca, in which is portrayed the whole nature of God's kingdom on earth. The words, " The elder shall serve the younger," relate likewise to the people; so that the forefathers are only regarded in reference to their descendants, with whom they are viewed as one. In the case of the two brothers the prophecy was not fulfilled: cf. xxvii. 27.

Ver. 25. *Esau* signifies " the hairy."

Ver. 26. *Jacob.*—The children quickly follow each other: the younger puts his hand above his head, and lays hold on the heel of the elder (Jacob signifies " a holder of the heel"). In this we have an emblem of his crafty character, as of a person who comes behind another to trip up his heels.

Threescore.—Fifteen years before Abraham's death, ver. 7.

Ver. 27. *Field.*—*i.e.*, Not one who cultivated the field, but roved about, in opposition to the quiet life of a herdsman.

Tents.—Those of the herdsmen. The word "plain man" means in the Heb. "perfect." Jacob's character and conduct appear scarcely to answer to this description; but we must bear in mind that the word more particularly has reference to his relation with God. In the more simple, quiet life of a herdsman, he walks before God, and lives in His service and in faith on His promises; while Esau, in his wild hunter's life, cared only for this world.

Ver. 28. *Venison.*—Literally, "And his venison was in his mouth." Isaac's temperament began to resemble Esau's through the weakness of age.

Ver. 30. *Red.*—Lit., "Of the red—of this red." He repeats the words in his eagerness. As these words were spoken on so remarkable an occasion, the term "red" clung to him, particularly as it was at the same time applicable to the colour of his hair (ver. 25). We learn in a subsequent verse that it was a pottage of lentils, a dish very much esteemed in the East to this day. The word "red" in the Hebrew often denotes a brown, yellowish colour.

Ver. 31. *Birthright.*—Jacob's good object cannot justify his conduct in taking advantage of Esau's weariness to extract this condition. Rather, he hereby confirmed his name "Supplanter," which was afterwards taken from him when his character was completely changed, ch. xxxii. 28.

Ver. 32. *Profit.*—The promise which belonged to the first-born had as its object the spiritual and the eternal. The blessing which rested thereon was emphatically a spiritual blessing, that through Abraham's posterity the knowledge and love of the true God should be spread on earth. As a coarse, earthly-minded man, Esau thinks only of himself, and the short space of his life on earth. Perhaps, too, he might have in view the dangers to which his hunter's life exposed him. Such a man would scarcely hesitate to sacrifice the holy privilege of the first-born for the sake of a momentary gratification. Thus is he a representative of all those who, for the lust of the eye and the lust of the flesh, sacrifice their sonship to God and eternal life. Heb. xii. 16.

Ver. 34. *Went his way*—as though nothing of consequence had taken place.

Birthright.—So that it was afterwards with justice taken from him.

CHAPTER XXVI.

Ver. 2. *Tell.*—A journey into Egypt in time of famine was accompanied with danger in the case of the patriarchs, as they might be tempted to remain in the rich pasture lands of that country, and to forget the Land of Promise. In this respect Isaac, a man of weaker faith than Abraham, was in greater danger than he. Only under the plain guidance of Divine Providence was a stay in Egypt permitted to the chosen people.

Ver. 5. *Laws.*—Here again is the promise, which was in the first instance given out of free grace, again ratified for the sake of Abraham and his obedience, since God is pleased to reward that which He works in a man by His prevenient grace.

Ver. 8. *Abimelech.*—Abimelech appears to have been a royal name common to the kings of the Philistines, as Phichol (ver. 26), the title of an officer. This history, therefore, speaks of another king than that mentioned, ch. xx. Isaac's weakness of faith (especially after the similar histories, cf. ch. xii. and xx.) is very remarkable; yet the same Divine preservation is accorded him. Weak as Isaac's conduct is, nevertheless God's blessing on him was so conspicuous, that he is honoured by the Philistines as his father.

Ver. 12. *Hundredfold.*—Examples of an extraordinary fruitfulness in the East are here and there recorded; but in the present instance such return was the consequence of an especial blessing.

Ver. 25. *Called.*—Cf. ch. iv. 26, note. In this place, which had already become of note in Abraham's lifetime, the Lord renewed to him the assurance of His grace, as He did afterwards to Jacob (ch. xlvi. 1). By the sanctification of particular places the Lord condescended to the wants of the patriarchs.

Ver. 35. *Grief.*—Esau declares his rude, undisciplined character, his alienation from God, and his contempt for the grace and blessings which belonged to his family, by taking two Canaanitish women for his wives. He was already a heathen, even before his actual separation from the line to which the blessing belonged. Between this marriage of Esau, and the history in the next chapter, there intervenes a space of thirty-seven years, as may be gathered by a collation of the statements of time given.

CHAPTER XXVII.

Ver. 4. *Love.*—In itself, there was nothing sinful in this conduct of Isaac. The trait is characteristic of the childlike simplicity of the patriarchs: but the sin which was connected with this request of Isaac, consisted in his partiality for Esau.

Die.—Isaac's faith was much darkened. He had a general conviction that he was divinely commissioned to bless the heir of promise; and it is said of him, that "by faith he blessed Jacob and Esau concerning things to come" (Heb. xi. 20); but his love for his eldest son hurries him into disobedience against the Divine command.

Ver. 13. *Upon me.*—Her faith is quite firm as to the issue. Her heart was directed towards God, though she made use of sinful means to effect her purpose. "Much as her deceit dishonoured God's prophecy, still, in the history, her distinguished faith shines forth. The anger of her husband, the hatred of Isaac against Jacob, the danger to the life of her beloved son, did not deter her, because the inheritance promised by God was before her eyes; and she knew that God had designed it for Jacob."—Calvin. In reading this history, we must ever bear in mind, that the after account of Jacob's life shows us how severely he was punished for it. Rebecca lost her son during twenty years; and Jacob, instead of being lord in his father's house, is forced to flee into a strange land, where in many ways a retribution is inflicted on him for his deceitful conduct towards his father and brother. Thus does Scripture pronounce judgment on his sin.

Ver. 15. *Clothes.*—Isaac was not totally blind; so that he might be able to recognise the dress, if not the countenance of his sons.

Ver. 16. *Goats.*—The hair of the goats in the East, we must remember, is much finer than with us.

Ver. 29. *Blesseth.*—Isaac appears here to promise only earthly things to his sons—rich harvests, peace, honour from others: no mention occurs of the kingdom of heaven. This was so, because God did not give to the fathers the promise of a future inheritance in a naked manner, and as their immediate object, but conducted them thitherward by byepaths. For this cause, He willed that the land of Canaan should be a mirror and pledge of the heavenly inheritance. In all His benefits He gave them proofs of His fatherly love, not that they might be satisfied with the earthly advantages and forget the heavenly, but that they might gradually rise up to heaven, supported by such stays as, according to the times in which they lived, were necessary for them. For, since Christ, the first fruits of the resurrection, the hope of an eternal, imperishable life, had not yet appeared, His kingdom remained shadowed forth in type and figure until "the fulness of time was come."—Calvin. This promise (as was the case with most of them) is at first annexed to things seen and present; hence it rises to the unseen future. The summit and the centre of the blessing is contained in the words, "Be lord over thy brethren;" since thereby was signified that he alone was bearer of the blessing,—the others only shared the advantage through him. The lordship over his whole race ("brethren," of whom, properly, Jacob had only one, mean here, as often elsewhere, all the relations by blood) consisted, externally, in the dominion which the Israelites exercised, in a great measure, over those descended from Esau, but *spiritually* in the rule of the Messiah, which should last for ever.

Ver. 36. *Jacob.*—Literally, "How that his name is called 'Supplanter?' and he has now twice supplanted me."

Blessing.—Esau, in his mind, separated the two. He supposed that, after the loss of the birthright, he could by his father's blessing supply all that was essential. He only thought of the earthly, carnal blessing; but he had lost it altogether.

Ver. 37. *What.*—These words show (as ver. 33) clearly what was Isaac's position in reference to the blessing he pronounced.

He was but an involuntary instrument in the hand of the Almighty and Omniscient. He it was who blessed, and therefore deceit was impossible. Though Jacob had imposed on his father, yet was God's will fulfilled, which had so overruled the matter. Had the transaction occurred in a question of right among men, the whole would have been invalid. This could not be the case here, where God's providence acted. At the same time, we clearly see how, with all his weakness, a living faith in God's presence and power filled Isaac in reference to the blessing: Heb. xi. 20.

Ver. 38. *Wept.*—Esau could not prevail on his father to make any change, though he sought it with tears (Heb. xii. 17). He had once despised that which now he only sought on account of its temporal advantages,—an image of the too late and hypocritical repentance of those who bewail, not so much their conduct, as the consequences of it.

Ver. 39. *Dew of heaven.*—The dwelling of the Edomites, the descendants of Esau, was Mt. Seir (pronounce *Se-ir*, with the accent on the last syllable), on the south side of the Dead Sea (Joshua xi. 17, xii. 7), a district stretching to the Ælanitic Gulf of the Red Sea—a rocky district, which is barren towards the north; but contains even now some fertile mountain country —once flourishing communities. Its chief town was Selah ("a rock," 2 Kings xiv. 7; afterwards called "Petra," a great town, which gave the name to Arabia Petræa), which has astonished modern travellers by its magnificent ruins. It was destroyed by the Roman Emperor Trajan. In its neighbourhood are, even to this day, "the ridges of the mountains covered with cornfields and fruit-gardens."—Burckhardt, ii. 702. The northern part of Seir is now called Dschebal (by the ancients, Gebalene); the southern part, Dschebel Schera. This mountainous region is intersected with innumerable rivulets, and is on the western side very steep. It extends from the Dead Sea in a westerly direction, close by the vast waste Wady El Arabah, the continuation of the broad deep valley in which are the northern lakes of Palestine, the Jordan, and the Dead Sea. Eastward it stretches gradually into the Arabian Desert. Towards the Red Sea the heights decrease. "The character of these mountains is altogether different from those in Arabah to the west. The latter, which do not appear more than two-thirds as high, are altogether waste and barren; while those to the east rejoice in an abundance of rain, and are covered with trees and shrubs. The Wadys (beds of rivers—valleys) abound also in trees and shrubs; while the eastern and higher districts are partly cultivated, and produce good crops. The general aspect of the land is not unlike that of Hebron, though the form of the country is very different."—Robinson, iii. 103. We gather, accordingly, that this country had not the same measure of fertility as Canaan; yet might it literally be described in this place, by Isaac, " Of the fatness of the earth shall be thy dwelling, and of the dew of heaven from above;" especially might it be pronounced " fruitful," when we think of the contrast of the vast neighbouring Arabian Desert. The earthly portion of the blessing approaches very nearly that of Jacob; and it is quite a mistake to suppose, that here is to be understood a play on the words, a contrast to what was promised, ver. 27, as if Isaac had said, " (Far) from the fatness of the earth shall be thy dwelling, and from the dew of heaven." According to that, a wilderness would be declared to be his dwelling, as in the case of Ishmael, ch. xxi. 20, 21; but this is contrary to the language, to history, and to geography.

Ver. 40. *Neck.*—In all times the Edomites appear to have been a warlike, if not a powerful, people. Their land possessed a strong town as its capital, Selah, which was defended by its almost impregnable position, and could be approached only by narrow passes. At first, and for a long time, the Edomites remained independent; then Saul subdued them (1 Sam. xiv. 47); David made them subject (2 Sam. viii. 14); Solomon " made a navy of ships in Ezion-Geber," the harbour of Edomites, " on the shore of the Red Sea" (1 Kings ix. 26); and in still later times were they under the dominion of the kingdom of Judah (2 Kings iii.). They revolted against Joram (2 Kings viii. 20, etc.). Amaziah smote them and took Selah (2 Kings xiv. 7). Uzziah also defeated them (2 Chron. xxvi. 2); but under Ahaz they made themselves independent (2 Chron. xxviii. 17). After they had been subjected to the Chaldeans, Persians, Greek-Syrians, they pushed as far as Hebron in Canaan, and possessed it (1 Macc. v. 65); so that the whole southern part of Palestine was named Idumæa after them. In later times (about 100 B.C.) the Maccabee prince, John Hyrcanus, entirely subdued them, and compelled them to receive circumcision: since which time they formed one people with the Jews, so much so, that even an Idumæan, Antipater, and his son, Herod the Great, reigned in Judæa. However, even then a national hatred against them continued among the Jews; and in the last Jewish war, the mixture of the Edomites served to fill up the measure of the misery of the Jews in the siege and destruction of Jerusalem. The last part of the prophecy is literally, in the Heb., "And it shall come to pass, as thou wild wanderest about (revoltest), thou shalt tear his yoke from thy neck."

Ver. 41. *Slay.*—This trait clearly represents to us the disposition of Esau; but his worst characteristic was not so much his fierce thirst for revenge, as his entire want of faith in God, and his determined want of submission to Him. Although Isaac, in his weak affection for his eldest son, had wished to favour Esau, contrary to God's will, nevertheless, when God had decided, he unhesitatingly submitted, nay, in what follows, acknowledges Jacob's pre-eminence. But Esau does not seek to learn anything of God's purpose in the matter: he only thinks of Jacob's deceit, and the consequences which will follow to himself. He seeks to avert these by the murder of his brother, by which means he would at the same time revenge himself on his mother for what she had done. He thus trode altogether in Cain's footsteps; and, without Rebecca's prudence and Isaac's obedience, would have followed them out to a like issue.

Ver. 46. *Jacob.*—Rebecca does not think it as yet possible that Jacob will proceed under the guidance of his father's blessing; but her faith and Jacob's are unexpectedly rewarded.

CHAPTER XXVIII.

Ver. 3. *Bless.*—This blessing is a further confirmation and ratification of that already imparted. It is designed to strengthen his faith on his journey, and on his marriage.

Ver. 5. *Syrian.*—"The Aramaite," as always.

Ver. 9. *Mahalath.*—In this act Esau continues true to his character. On the one side, he manifests therein a certain kindness of disposition in consulting the wishes of his parents; on the other hand, even more, a certain wilfulness which is determined to get back outwardly the inheritance which he has forfeited and despised, together with the blind infatuation of unbelief, which prompts him to marry among the daughters of Ishmael, who in character were congenial to himself. He is the image of a man who is determined to correct his false steps by his own strength; and, accordingly, attempts it in a wrong temper.

Ver. 10. *Haran.*—Altogether alone; not with tents and servants in a caravan, probably by reason of the secrecy and hurry of his flight. Very differently did he leave his home from Abraham's servant! He carried no presents for the bride.

Ver. 12. *Angels.*—Elsewhere the angels appear suddenly (ch. xviii. 2), and vanish (Judges vi. 21). Isaiah sees the angels hover with six wings (Isa. vi. 2). Here they are displayed more visibly to Jacob, on account of the emblematic character of the vision. By this it was certified to the patriarch—"Here, where thy head lies,—here is the point to which God sends His angels, in order to perform His commands concerning thee, and to hear what thou desirest:" an image of God's gracious, particular, unceasing providence over His servant.

Ver. 14. *Blessed.*—God repeats to Jacob the solemn promises which he had made to Abraham (ch. xii. 2, 3, ch. xiii. 14–16, ch. xv. 18). Such a reiteration places the forsaken fugitive in the same relation to Himself as Abraham, the highly-favoured "friend of God."

Ver. 15. *Spoken.*—The lonely deserted fugitive was designed to become the father of the vast host of the children of the covenant: and it came to pass. How important and necessary, therefore, was this word of promise!

Ver. 16. *Knew.*—Jacob well knew that heaven and earth belonged to God, and that He is "the Almighty;" but that He should appear, of His gracious condescension and mercy, anywhere except in places consecrated to Him, this was new to Jacob, as he had not as yet been favoured with any manifestation of God. It is, therefore, no narrow unworthy notion of God, but the want of a certain revelation from God to himself, which made him cling to the signs and covenanted promises which God Himself had given. Jacob, at the bottom of his heart, clave unto God, and sought His promises even by dishonest means. He was a yielding character, not formed to encounter great dangers and labours, but open to religious impressions. To strengthen him at this time against yielding to the feeling of being forsaken by God, it was necessary to comfort him with the assurance of God's help, and of the continuance of His covenant of grace. By a wonderful representation, God showed His unseen but continual communion with His servants, whom He ever accompanies on their way, and to whom He sends His ministering spirits. The full reality of this type has been vouchsafed to all believers through the redemption of Christ: St John i. 51.

Ver. 17. *Dreadful.*—The ancient Church called the Holy Eucharist "a fearful mystery," "sacramentum tremendum." Although the vision was most loving and comforting, still God mingles with such revelations a holy dread, which keeps the sinner in deep awe before Him, and makes the gifts and promises of His grace so much the sweeter.

Ver. 18. *Pillar.*—The heathens also were accustomed, in old times, to commemorate Divine appearances after a like manner. Cf. also Exod. xxiv. 4.

Oil, which in hot countries is needful for the health of the body, for food, for light among all people, is the ancient emblem of the refreshing and renewing gifts of the Holy Ghost; and so is the means by which everything was consecrated to God. In after times both men and vessels of worship were anointed with it.

Ver. 19. *Bethel,*—" House of God." House, in the wider signification of place, as sometimes every place of residence or rest is so called. Afterwards the town of Luz, which was in existence even then, received its name from this holy spot. Later on, God confirmed the promise here given, and the name of the place was renewed on this fresh occasion: ch. xxxi. 13, ch. xxxv. 15.

Ver. 20. *Vow.*—The vow which Jacob here made was founded entirely on the promise given to him, and served to strengthen his gratitude, faith, and obedience. In a similar manner, under the law, men vowed and offered sacrifices. Such vows belonged to the time when men were "under tutors and governors" (Gal. iv. 2). Inasmuch, however, as such outward expressions of thankfulness serve to keep alive the good resolutions of amendment and change, made often in sorrow, forgotten in the release from it, they are wholesome reminiscences for all times. "Some go too far, who would condemn all vows in order to close the door against superstition. But though the presumption of those who indiscriminately make vows is blameable, still we must, on the other hand, take care lest we condemn them altogether. In order to constitute a lawful vow, first, the object must be well-pleasing to God; next, we must not vow anything but what God esteems good; and, lastly, what He permitteth us to vow. Therefore, here Jacob's object was only to testify his gratitude to God. He promises to render to God the service due to Him; and, lastly, he does not presumptuously vow more than was given him, but only the tithe of his goods for a holy offering."—Calvin.

Ver. 21. *Lord.*—These words are not to be misunderstood, as though Jacob doubted through unbelief the performance of the Divine promise; or, as if he wished only on such conditions to determine whether he should serve God or not: rather, he impresses on himself the certainty of God's promise, and the duty of entire subjection to Him, as he vowed to be His on the condition of a fulfilment which he knew could not fail.

Ver. 22. *Tithe.*—The stone was to be a place of sacrifice, as were all the places where the Lord, by His gracious promises, had revealed Himself to his fathers. So afterwards, ch. xxxv. 6, 7; cf. above, ch. xii. 7, ch. xxvi. 25. The ancient orientals were accustomed to insert such pillars into their buildings, altars, etc. To this custom refer Ps. cxviii. 22, 23; Isa. viii. 13–15. The number ten, as being the last of the cardinal numbers, expresses the idea of perfection, of a whole. Among almost all ancient people the tenth of their goods was set apart, and very frequently as a holy offering. This was an acknowledgment that the whole was God's property; and by this acknowledgment the possession and enjoyment of the rest are sanctified: cf. ch. xiv. 20. As Jacob had not priests or officers of the sanctuary to whom he could give the tithe of his goods, we must suppose some such application of it, as that which took place among the Israelites at the end of three years: Deut. xiv. 28, 29. They invited "the Levite, the stranger, the widow, and the fatherless," to partake of the tithe of the increase of the year.

CHAPTER XXIX.

Ver. 1. *East.*—The Desert Arabia, where Laban, coming out of Haran, led a wandering life with his herds.

Ver. 3. *Stone.*—In Arabia, and other desert regions, it is the custom to close and cover up the wells, to prevent the shifting sand choking them up. The flocks must be collected together, so that the water may not become vapid by long exposure, and that a part of the flocks may not exhaust the supply intended for the whole. The narrative appears to imply that the well was not near Haran, as Jacob does not see any city: it may, therefore, probably be the one mentioned, ch. xxiv.

Ver. 5. *Son*, properly grandson—Bethuel's son: but "son" is here used, as frequently, for any descendant of every kind.

Ver. 7. *Gathered.*—Driven together: they were kept in the open air, in inclosures of hurdles.

Ver. 8. *Cannot;* not on account of the stone, but for the reason given above, ver. 2.

Ver. 9. *Rachel* signifies a sheep.

Ver. 10. *Jacob.*—This right was permitted him as a stranger, and likewise as the kinsman of a rich keeper of flocks.

Ver. 11. *Wept.*—From an emotion of joy, at having been unexpectedly guided by God's providence to meet with her: as we read afterwards of Joseph, ch. xliii. 30.

Ver. 15. *Wages.*—At first natural love prevails in Laban: he rejoices to have found his kinsman. This affection, on nearer acquaintance, is mixed with a selfish feeling, which leads him on from one act of deceit to another.

Ver. 18. *Daughter.*—As the daughters served their father in his house, he incurred the loss of a part of his possessions by her marriage. This loss the bridegroom was obliged to make compensation for. In this manner Jacob purchased his wife, as is even now the case with Arabs, Curds, etc., and other wild people. His service for seven years, perhaps, is a reference to the later law of the Israelites, according to which, a slave in the seventh year became free: Exod. xxi. 2. Accordingly, Jacob, in compensation for the daughter's services, undertook to serve the full term of seven years. That he had not brought with him from home the purchase-price, is explained by his desire not to provoke his brother; and therefore he scrupulously avoided touching anything there. He preferred entirely to trust himself into God's hands, who, by Isaac and at Bethel, had promised His blessing, rather than receive help from man.

Ver. 25. *Leah.*—Even to this day, in many eastern countries, the bridegroom sees the bride only veiled until the morning after the marriage; and so even now deceptions like this of Laban often take place. As Jacob had deceived the blind Isaac, so was he deceived. With reference to this history was the marrying of two sisters forbidden, Lev. xviii. 18; also the favouring of one wife above another, Deut. xxi. 17.

Ver. 27. *Serve.*—This was the true reason; the other only a pretext.

Ver. 28. *To wife;* i.e., immediately, not after the expiration of the seven years' service. The marriage festivities lasted seven days: see Judges xiv. 12, 17; and these Laban did not wish disturbed. Then he gave Jacob his second daughter, but, as would seem, without any pomp.

Ver. 32. *Love me.*—In ancient times we find that the mothers gave the names to the children; so we read in Homer. Reuben is properly "Re-uh-Ben;" *i.e.*, See a son. The name is given to the child in the first excitement of joy at his birth. Leah changed this cry of joy, by a slight alteration of the letters, into a thankful allusion to the consolation afforded her in her dejection. She explained the name as if Raah-beonji, *i.e.*, He has seen my affliction.

Ver. 33. *Simeon.*—Hearing. The Lord hath heard it; which significantly implies, He hath had regard to it.

Ver. 35. *Judah;* *i.e.*, "praised." In a remarkable manner did the Divine providence afterwards change the sense of some of these names.

CHAPTER XXX.

Ver. 4. *Wife.*—After the custom of the time, according to which the children of the maid, if given by the wife herself, were esteemed the wife's children.

Ver. 8. *Rachel.*—In both the names which Rachel gives to these her adopted children, there is not a feeling of reliance on God and of thankfulness expressed, as was done by Leah in the names she chose; but, to say the least, a mixture of self-exaltation and pride with her other feelings.

Ver. 11. *A troop.*—"With good fortune;" happily.

Ver. 16. *Mandrakes.*—The ancient interpreters explain the word "Dudaim" by Mandragora; English, "Mandrakes,"—a plant, with a strong whitish root, with oval spiral leaves a foot long and about four or five inches broad, and stalks which shoot immediately out of the root, and bear a light-green, five-petalled blossom. In the time of wheat harvest, in May, it bears a round, smooth apple of a dirty-yellow colour, filled with seed, which emits an intoxicating, but not unpleasant odour. These apples were used in the East from very early times, even to the present day, for love-potions; and it was, without doubt, Rachel's purpose so to use them. We have here also a mark of her self-willed disposition, which could attempt to wrest the blessing which God had denied her. And she experienced her punishment in the circumstance that Leah bears a son before her.

Ver. 18. *Issachar,* properly "Jissasachar," *i.e.,* either, "this is the reward," or, "he brings the reward."

Ver. 20. *Zebulon* means "dwelling." Sabal is "to dwell;" sabad, "to present:" so that the name is derived from "dwelling," but at the same time plays on the word "gift:" "From this gift, I see that my husband will dwell with me."

Ver. 21. *Dinah,* "the judged," in the sense, as before, ver. 6. "She who, through the highest Judge, is freed from all blame and disgrace."

Ver. 24. *Joseph.*—Also in this name, there is a double play on the word. From "Asaph," to take, he is called, "he takes:" from "Jasaph," to repeat, he is named, "he adds to." The long-expected, late-born Joseph, is, among Jacob's sons (as we are repeatedly told in the sacred history), the one of most importance in his relation to God's kingdom. In the name which Rachel gave him, there is some sign of the proud spirit noticed above. Her words were fulfilled indeed, but in the fulfilment she died: ch. xxxv. 16.

Ver. 25. *Joseph.*—Jacob had obtained the object of his wishes—a child from his beloved wife. His request contains a friendly regard for Laban.

Ver. 28. *Give.*—The selfish Laban wished to receive a worldly blessing from the service of the man of God; but he found that God is not mocked. To Laban's punishment, Jacob became with him richer than he was himself. In considering the artifices and stratagems used by Jacob, we must remember that these were not counselled him by God, but permitted and blessed, as they were not absolutely sinful. A man of a higher degree of self-denial would have learnt the lessons of patience and submission from Laban's injustice; still he might allege in his justification the necessity of defending himself, as in a state of war, that it was of consequence for the heir of promise to be in a condition of outward prosperity. In effecting his purpose at least, he did not use any unlawful means. We are to judge this history as many others in the O. T., in which, though God does not counsel or sanction the acts, He still allows them to be successful, for the sake of carrying out His designs in relation to His kingdom; as, for example, in the case of the Israelites demanding a king.

Ver. 32. *Hire.*—Laban was glad to close with this demand, since among sheep and goats which feed under the open sky far the fewest are wont to be spotted and speckled.

Ver. 36. *Fed.*—To make more sure, he separated the ring-straked cattle, and took them out of the flocks which Jacob, as Laban's servant, tended. These were committed to the keeping of his sons; and to prevent any mixture he put the greatest possible space between the speckled flocks which his sons, and the white flocks which Jacob, fed. From henceforth, only what out of the white flocks were born ring-straked, should be Jacob's property. Laban had acted here with the greatest severity and exactness, and he had no right to complain if he were dealt with according to the strict letter of the law.

Ver. 39. *Ring-straked.*—With no animal does the act of seeing during breeding-time have so much influence as with the sheep. The contrary to what Jacob here did is often practised among us, in order to procure sheep altogether white.

Ver. 40. *Flock.*—As now there were speckled sheep in Laban's flock which Jacob tended, he made use of a fresh stratagem. He put the speckled sheep before the white, and this had the same effect as the pilled rods.

Cattle.—He made his servants feed the flocks, which were now separated from Laban's.

Ver. 42. *Stronger.*—The sheep of those lands yean twice a year. In the autumn, when they have particularly rich pasture: "then the stronger cattle did conceive;" accordingly, lambs which fall in February are the most esteemed. In the spring, when the pasturage is not so rich, and the sheep themselves are weakened by the damp and moisture, they do not conceive lambs of so good a quality. Jacob, therefore, took care to lay his rods in the gutters in the autumn, but did not so in the spring.

CHAPTER XXXI.

Ver. 3. *With thee.*—We must carefully distinguish, in accordance with the narrative, between what God promises to do to him, and what Jacob himself afterwards carries into effect. God had not bidden him flee away secretly, which is the act with which Laban afterwards (v. 27) reproaches him.

Ver. 8. *Speckled.*—It appears from this account of Jacob's, that (ver. 32, 33 of preceding chap.) in the representation of the agreement about the variegated cattle, much was comprised—especially the difference with respect to the sheep and goats, between ver. 32 and 35, points to the deceitful changes of the wages practised by Laban. The words were taken in a wider or narrower sense, according as Laban found to be to his advantage.

Ver. 12. *Laban.*—Jacob had, therefore, before the concluding of the hard agreement with Laban, received from God the same promise as he had in his solitary resting by the stone at Bethel, ch. xxviii. 12. It is not, however, said that the artifice which he practised was counselled to him in this dream. It is merely promised to him that, in spite of his niggardly wages, matters shall so turn out contrary to expectation in the herds, as if there were merely ring-straked, speckled, and grizzled cattle. That Jacob, in order to possess the promise made, had recourse to a stratagem, belongs to the same weakness of faith which we before perceive in him. God permitted its success, as he acted under the pressure of self-defence, and there was no actual injustice in the act itself.

Ver. 13. *Arise.*—The two visions are clearly here joined together, since the last words were spoken only in the revelation mentioned, ver. 3.

Ver. 19. *Shear.*—The time of shearing was a great rural season of rejoicing, to which guests were invited and at which feasts were made (ch. xxxviii. 12; 1 Sam. xxv. 4; 2 Sam. xiii. 23). Laban's absence lasted, therefore, several days.

Images.—"The theraphim of her father." These images, which are mentioned through the whole history up to the Babylonish captivity, were a kind of household god, images in the likeness of men (so Michal put such an image in the bed, and pretended it was David, 1 Sam. xix. 13). From several passages we gather that they were consulted and gave oracles in some way, though we do not now know how. With the priests, therefore, they occupied the place of Urim and Thummim (light and righteousness). So Judges xviii. 5. Cf. Ezek. xxi. 21, Zech. x. 2. They seem to have been regarded as a less grievous kind of superstition (and so were found even in David's house); yet were they reckoned among the abominations which Josiah rooted out from among his people (2 Kings xxiii. 24). We gather from vers. 30, 49, ch. xxxv. 2, that idolatry prevailed in Laban's house, perhaps combined with the worship of the one true God, and that even Jacob's family was not exempt from it. Rachel took with her an image of the kind mentioned, since, in her impatience to become fruitful in bearing children, she snatched at every means; or, perhaps, she wished to hinder Laban from inquiring of his deities which way the fugitives had taken. The first supposition appears to agree best with Rachel's self-willed, impatient disposition.

Ver. 20. *Unawares;* lit., "The heart of Laban." To steal away the heart, as the seat of the understanding, means, to outwit any one. It is here said in contradistinction to the stealing away the images, in which Jacob had no part.

Ver. 21. *River.*—Euphrates.

Gilead.—Gilead was originally a mountainous district to the N. of the river Jabbok, over which Jacob did not pass until ch. xxxii. 23: then from N. to S. In after times a district of this region, and even sometimes the whole of East Jordan, was called Gilead. To this day a mountain to the south of Jabbok, abounding in oaks and other forest trees, is called Dschelaad.

Ver. 24. *Speak.*—God here also protects His servant in a wonderful manner, under the most imminent danger. Laban honoured still the true God, yet speaks of Him as if He did not belong to himself: "The God of your father" (ver. 29); because he did not stand in covenant with Him.

Ver. 28. *Kiss.*—As all this was mere pretext, Jacob knew the right answer to give in what he afterwards says.

Foolishly.—The words "folly," "foolish," have in the O. T. always the moral sense, "sinful;" as, on the other hand, "the fear of the Lord is the beginning of wisdom."

Ver. 32. *Knew not.*—Jacob acted with perfect honesty towards Laban. Henceforth we perceive no further trace of his former craftiness. The dealings of God's providence had removed his old characteristics; and the genuine trust in God, which had from the first lain dormant in his heart, is now called forth.

Ver. 34. *Furniture.*—That which is now customary among the Arabs consists of a large closed basketwork, with a place for sitting and reclining, and a window at the side. One of this kind hangs on each side of the camel.

Ver. 35. *Custom.*—She was accordingly unclean, and must keep apart. Laban would therefore avoid touching that on which she sat.

Ver. 40. *Frost.*—The alternation of heat and cold is very great in summer,—so much so, that often cold nights succeed the intolerable heat of day. In the East, therefore, clothes lined with skins are often worn at night.

Ver. 43. *What can I do?*—I should injure myself if I did any harm to aught of thine.

Ver. 46. *Brethren.*—Laban's sons, who had come with their father.

Gather.—To make seats of. People avoid evening and morning sitting on the damp ground. This is still customary in the East.

Ver. 47. *Galeed.*—Sahadatha in Aramaic, and Galeed in Hebrew, signify "heap of witness." Gilead is a slightly changed form which the word acquired in the language of the people.

Ver. 49. *Mizpah.*—The heap bore likewise the name Mizpah = watch-tower. A town situated in this region, belonging to the tribe of Gad, was thus called; it was the residence of Jephthah (Joshua xiii. 26; Judges xi. 34, ch. x. 17).

Ver. 53. *Judge;* or, "The gods of their fathers be judge." In the Hebrew the word *be* is in the plural, as a sign that not one god was meant. Laban appealed to the gods of his fathers. The worship of them did not, to his somewhat heathenised mind, exclude Jehovah, whom Abraham honoured.

Ver. 54. *Called.*—To partake of the sacrificial feast which followed many kinds of sacrifices. As Laban's family had not altogether renounced the service of the true God, Jacob could invite them to take part in the service paid to God and in the sacrificial feast.

CHAPTER XXXII.

Ver. 2. *Mahanaim.*—The two hosts appear to have encamped, the one in front, the other behind his company: the one in front as a defence against Esau; the one behind, against Laban and the other dangers from Mesopotamia.

Ver. 4. *Servant.*—The words "lord" and "servant" may belong to the extreme courtesy of the East (cf. ch. xix. 2, ch. xxiii. 6, etc.). But Jacob might also have used them with the express purpose of giving Esau to understand that he laid no claim to the lordship over his family, which belonged to the birthright of the eldest. The expression by no means implied that, from unbelieving fear, he renounced the blessing accorded him; but merely, that his eye was fixed especially on the Divine promises with respect to his posterity in the land of Canaan, without on that account making any personal claim on Esau. Nay, the trial of his faith consisted in his personally experiencing the very opposite of that which was promised to his descendants, as was the case with Abraham.

Ver. 7. *Divided.*—In the present day, the caravans are frequently thus divided to avoid the danger of being entirely plundered, so that, in case of an attack, one part may escape.

Ver. 12. *Thou saidst.*—A prayer of wonderful beauty, in which Jacob, with the boldness inspired by faith, reminds God of His promises; at the same time, in deep humility acknowledges his unworthiness of His mercies. This "weeping and supplication" (Hosea xii. 4) was the means whereby he overcame; of which he receives a comfortable assurance in the significant vision of the following night.

Ver. 15. *Milch.*—Of particular value on that account, as camel's milk is a great article of food in the East.

Ver. 20. *Present.*—By this division of the droves he wished to spread out the gift before Esau, and at the same time to give him more time for consideration and for laying aside his anger.

Ver. 22. *Jabbok.*—The Jabbok is the present Wady Serka—a bed which does not at all times of the year contain water. It rises out of the mountains of the East Hauran, and falls into the Jordan at an equal distance between the Sea Gennesaret and the Dead Sea. In ancient times it was the boundary between the Ammonites (who dwelt between Jabbok and Arnon) and the Amorites, who in the time of Moses had possession of Sihon. In later times it was the south boundary of the tribe of Gad against the Ammonites.

Ver. 24. *Alone.*—On the northern bank of the Jabbok, after all had passed over. Here a marvellous event happens to Jacob, in which his name is changed, and the crisis of the first part of his life is over. Full of fear, Jacob had sent messengers to his brother, and a threatening action is the only reply. He now does all in his power to conciliate his brother, and, that ended, he remains alone with God. Now a wonderful vision takes place. An unknown man comes against him as an adversary, and wrestles with the purpose of throwing him to the ground; but Jacob contends against him, upon which the Unknown smites his thigh, so that he limps upon it. Now the contest is at an end. Jacob, convinced of the might of his antagonist, earnestly prays for his blessing. And the Unknown blesses him, and gives him a new name significant of what has now taken place; but refuses to answer Jacob's question, What is thy name? We are to consider this event not as a vision,—something presented to Jacob's imagination and mind's eye,—not yet, again, as mere ordinary history. It was an event which took place while he was raised to a state of unusual sublimity (like that in the Temptation and Transfiguration). The meaning would reveal itself when he thought on his past history, his present condition, his anxiety, his prayer, and perceived that he halted: since the last circumstance was an abiding sign, that it was no vision, but God had spoken to him by an act, as He had done heretofore. While Jacob is full of fear on account of Esau's anger, feeling what just cause his brother had against him, He who had hitherto been his Friend and Protector—God Himself—appears as an adversary, and says, "I am thy foe: overcome Me, and thy brother shall not be able to do thee hurt!" And he does overcome, not by his own strength (that is evident from his lameness), but by prayer and trust in God's promises. He gains a blessing. His old life falls from him: purified and sanctified by God's gracious dealings with him, he is no longer to bear the old name Jacob, polluted as it was by his deceit; but he is to be called by a new name, which shall be a witness of his victory in the severest trial—a victory which he gained by his distrust of himself and firm trust in God's promise. God's manifestation to him is not destructive of life—His soul is preserved; and though he halts on his thigh, the sun rises full of blessing upon him. This history is not only full of signification to Jacob, but it represents the combat and the triumph of the soldiers of God in their severest trials. It often happens in different times of their life that God seems to be an adversary, to withdraw His grace and protection—that they find themselves in great peril outwardly or inwardly; and they have nothing on which to rely but God's promise, in naked faith, without the comforts and refreshment of His presence in their souls. These are the times when God is pleased to crown His true combatants, and for their greater confirmation to give them a new name (to place them in an entirely new relation to Himself), to free them from their perplexities and troubles.

Ver. 28. *Prevailed.*—In the expression "with men," God reminds him of the consolatory side of the events of his life—on the opposition to the fulfilment of the Divine promises which Esau and Isaac, and finally Laban, had offered—and on the entire victory over it on the part of Jacob through his trust in God's words. To this is added now the contest—the hardest of all he had encountered—the contest in which God was his adversary; but in this also Jacob's faith prevailed. He is now become a true "combatant of God"—a combatant for God in His affairs on earth, as the word may signify. To this was the people of Israel afterwards called,—to this is the spiritual Israel of all times called, after it has sustained the contest of probation and come off conqueror.

Ver. 29. *Wherefore?* as Judges xiii. 18. As if it had been said, "What need of further declaration? Dost thou not understand what has taken place?"

Ver. 31. *Penuel.*—This is only another form of the same word.

Thigh.—This is a sign of his own helplessness—that he could not have prevailed by his own power. He was to carry for a while this mark with him, as a memento of the significancy of the history. There remains with the Christian, even when he has overcome in the severest contest of faith, some mark of his former weakness, like the occasional smarting and scar of a deep wound.

Ver. 32. *Shrank.*—An ancient custom of the people (there was no law on the subject), to perpetuate the remembrance of the event in which their great progenitor and the people received the sacred name. The reason why Jacob, even after this change of his name, is still called by the old one, and indeed the whole people is often in solemn addresses to them addressed as Jacob, while Abraham, after God had so named him, is never afterwards called Abram,—the reason (I say) is this: that Abram's changed name is merely a title of honour, unconnected with any great prophetic event of his life; but in Jacob's case, God's Divine providence and preservation of him was shown even in the craft of the Supplanter, mingled as his conduct was with much that was sinful.

CHAPTER XXXIII.

Ver. 3. *Bowed.*—He throws himself seven times to the ground in such a manner as to touch it with his face, which we elsewhere meet with as a mark of respect and reverence (David does the same thrice before his preserver Jonathan,

1 Sam. xx. 41); but here the reverence paid to Esau as his superior is meant as a renunciation of all claim on the personal earthly privileges of the birthright.

Ver. 4. *Wept.*—The Holy Scripture both mentions openly the infirmities of the saints, and the admirable traits of those who are out of the covenant with God. Later Jews have taken offence at Esau kissing his brother, and the words, "he kissed him" (one word in Hebrew), are wanting in very old MSS. The narrow-hearted Pharisees who transcribed this passage could not enter into the depth of God's mercy, which allows marks of His image to remain even in those who will not be His children. In this reception granted by Esau, there lay an abashing reproof of Jacob's earlier sin against him.

Ver. 10. *Pleased.*—Heb.: "And thou hast received me graciously." The whole does not mean, "Receive it as a thank-offering for the great goodness which thou hast showed me;" but, "Therefore must thou show me such great goodness, to receive me not as one man another, but as the gracious and merciful God receives a man when he entreats Him: accordingly, thou shalt receive this from me as an offering." God has put this feeling towards me in your heart, that thou mayest receive this my gift.

Ver. 11. *Blessing;* i.e., not "the blessing which God has given me," but that wherewith I bless thee. "Blessing" is here a gift of reconciliation: 1 Sam. xxv. 27.

Ver. 13. *Tender.*—As Joseph was born when Jacob was ninety-one years old, he was at this time about six; Dinah not much older.

Ver. 14. *Seir.*—He promises him a visit in Seir, of which, however, we find no further mention. Jacob did this in order to show clearly that, in any case, it was his own fixed purpose to abide in Canaan. Notwithstanding his submission to his brother, he still holds fast to the promise made him by God.

Ver. 15. *Lord.*—Esau desires to leave Jacob some of his people to protect him. Jacob, however, declines the offer, as he knew the wild capricious character of his brother, and feared on that account some future hindrance to his settlement in Canaan.

Ver. 17. *Succoth.*—Jacob went over the Jordan, and then, in a north-western direction, up the valley through which this river runs. Here is the valley Succoth, in which was situated the town Beth-Schean, which the Greeks, by a corruption of the word Succoth, called Scythopolis. It is the present Bysan. In the neighbourhood, towards the south, are to this day the ruins of a place Succoth. Jacob purposed to dwell for some time longer in this region, and therefore he built himself a house. Succoth means, properly, booths made of branches of trees. In these hot countries, however, the sheep do not require pens of this kind. We must rather understand here hurdles fenced in with boughs and thorns. Where such are fixed, a longer sojourn than ordinary is always intended.

Ver. 18. *Shalem.*—The word "Schalem" is here most probably not the name of a place at all, but signifies "in peace and safety." Jacob reached happily the end of his journey in Shechem.

Ver. 20. *El-elohe-Israel*—According to the new name which he had received, ch. xxxii. 28. The words in Heb. mean, "God, the God of Israel."

CHAPTER XXXIV.

An event like the one in this chapter is a proof of the danger and mistakes resulting from a mere carnal belief in the privileges of Israel. The chief feeling which the sons of Jacob nourished respecting themselves as the chosen family, was the proud one, that any injury against them was to be more signally avenged than if committed against any others. Even circumcision could not atone for the wrong done. Their wild fierceness and the weakness of Jacob are strongly contrasted. His disapproval of their crime, however, did not arise only from fear. He held it in utter abhorrence on its own account, ch. xlix. 6, 7.

The narrative before us shows what the people of Israel would have become, but for the Spirit of God, which, by priests and sacrifices, and by prophets, continually kept guiding them in the right way.

The impartiality of the sacred history is evinced in the way in which Moses, the descendant of Levi, records this circumstance, and the curse which Jacob afterwards pronounced on its authors.

Ver. 2. *Shechem.*—The town received, perhaps somewhat later, its name from him, and is so called here by anticipation.

Defiled.—" Humbled" her. The word shows that he used violence. A " prince" does not denote one who was of royal extraction, but a person of power, influence, and wealth in the place.

Ver. 3. *Kindly.*—He took her, as the sequel shows, into his house, and kept her there, with the intention of making her formally his wife. The words in the Heb., "he spoke to the heart of the damsel," are the proper expression for "comforted." So Isa. xlii. 2.

Ver. 5. *Until.*—Among other reasons, for the cause given, ch. xxiv. 50. So we find afterwards that Dinah's own brothers, the children of Jacob and Leah, undertake to avenge her cause.

Ver. 7. *Folly.*—Folly, a fool, are frequently used in the O. T. to express acts of great wickedness. It is derived from a word which in the original signifies being weak, being nothing, and so weak in spirit; and the connection of thought implies this great truth, that irreligion and vice is the greatest folly, the fear and love of God the highest wisdom. So " the *fool* hath said in his heart, There is no God:" Ps. xiv. 1. "The fear of the Lord is wisdom, and to avoid evil is understanding:" Job xxviii. 28. It is still a principle among the modern Arabs, that a man is not so much dishonoured by the seduction of his wife, as a father or brother through that of a daughter or sister; since a man can separate from his wife, but cannot dissolve relationship with daughter or sister,—a view of marriage quite opposed to the Divine institution, but consonant to the notion of the natural man.

Done.—Lit. "And so is it not done;" it is against all custom thus to violate the rights of hospitality.

Ver. 10. *Possessions.*—They shall become one people, trade, and obtain firm footing therein. This would have been most dangerous to Jacob's family; thus, contrary to Divine appointment, to mingle with the heathen. The crime of the sons of Jacob was used by Divine Providence to sever this knot.

Ver. 12. *Dowry and gift.*—"Dowry," the price which the bridegroom pays the father for the daughter. "Gift," the present which the bride receives.

Ver. 15. *Circumcised.*—Although they meant this proposal

treacherously, yet it shows what stress they laid on the mark of the covenant.

Ver. 19. *Honourable.*—It belongs to the impartial representation of Holy Scripture that Shechem and Hamor should appear in an admirable and even noble light, and that the circumstances in their favour should be purposely brought forward. The act of the sons of Jacob appears so much the baser, and likewise the dispensation of Providence so much the more awful, which in its judgments on men, and in the carrying out of its designs, does not regard such excellences.

Ver. 23. *Dwell.*—They represented openly to the people the rite of circumcision, not as a new service, or as an entrance into covenant with the God of Israel, but only as an outward ceremony. So, in ancient times, one people borrowed this custom from another, without attaching any religious meaning to the observance. We may here observe how adroitly Hamor and Shechem represented to the people an act in which their own personal interest was involved as a public advantage.

Ver. 25. *Sore.*—In all sicknesses the third day is commonly the most critical, as that in which fever comes. When adults are circumcised, it is generally three weeks before they can move well.

Boldly.—We must suppose that the sons of Jacob took with them armed servants in the attack; at all events, that the town was small.

Ver. 29. *House.*—We here see the wild Eastern spirit of revenge in its full force, like what takes place in those countries even now. So likewise the heathen notion, that a whole people was involved in the crime and punishment of the prince.

Ver. 30. *House.*—Jacob here puts before his sons the motive which their carnal mind would understand;—that he afterwards spoke in different terms to them, his curse, ch. xlix. 6, 7, shows us. At the same time, these words are adduced by the sacred writer, to point out to us in what a wonderful manner God preserved the poor despised family from mixture with the heathen on the one hand, and from utter extermination on the other. The whole chapter will be full of edification to those who have a spiritual mind and eye for the understanding of the O. T.

CHAPTER XXXV.

Ver. 1. *Appeared.*—The incident narrated in the former chapter, had the effect of completely severing the family of Jacob from all connection with the Canaanites. Henceforth all traces of idolatry disappear. Jacob goes to Bethel (where in his need he had first found support in God's protection), that he might perform the vow there made (ch. xxviii 20). In this critical period of his life he pays an especial act of reverence to God. As in the N. T. we read of the "God of peace, of consolation, of hope," while one and the same God is meant, who brings peace, consolation, and hope; so with the patriarchs their faith is given to God, who has revealed Himself to them at different times. It is *the* God who appeared at Bethel, and yet no other than the God who made Himself known to Abraham at Mamre; and God here expressly confirms this kind of definite, living faith in Him. Thus we honour *the* God who has revealed Himself in Christ, in whom dwelleth the fulness of the Godhead bodily.

Ver. 2. *Strange gods.*—The household deities—the theraphim, such as Rachel took with her. At all times among the Israelites there was united together with the worship of the one true God very much idolatry, in which the unbelief, or half-hearted belief of the people sought support: just as among Christians now may be seen the refined idolatry of the worldling, or the saint-worship of the Romanist.

Be clean; i.e., wash or bathe yourselves. This is the earliest mention of a religious washing, which was in after times enforced with many particular ceremonies. In this way were the family of Jacob, inwardly and outwardly, to cleanse themselves from all defilements of idolatry.

Garments.—Even the garments were esteemed defiled through idolatry, since various religious tokens were attached to many of the clothes.

Ver. 4. *Ear-rings.*—These were used for several purposes of superstition. They were often inscribed with words and marks, which were supposed to ward off the hurtful influence of sounds.

Oak, which was in later times of much note, and held in honour, in memory of the event here narrated.

Ver. 5. *Terror.*—A fear, inspired by God, of injuring the family of Jacob. This religious obedience shown by him was repaid with the reward, that the fear of him fell on all the neighbouring people.

Ver. 7. *El-bethel.*—He did not call the place so, as he had already named it Bethel; but he named the altar after the God who appeared to him.

God.—In the Hebrew, the plural stands here: "Because the Gods had appeared to him"—the Godhead in plurality: the heavenly vision, in which he had seen God and so many angels. God (Elohim) is the ideal, impersonal expression; and therefore here, God, together with His angels, the higher Divine existence, is designated in an indefinite manner by this expression. The angels are never simply called "Elohim," but the sons of Elohim. But the heavenly beings in whom God reveals Himself, in a more perfect manner than in men, as they are without sin, are often included in the idea of the heavenly, the Divine; so that "the Deity" comprehends all the heavenly beings, God and His angels (cf. Ps. viii. 6), though neither conjointly nor singly are they in any sense called God.

Ver. 8. *Allon-bachuth.*—This event was commemorated in the name given to an oak beneath Bethel, which was itself situated on a height. We read, ch. xxiv. 59, that this nurse accompanied Rebecca to Canaan. After Rebecca's death, which is not mentioned, she appears to have taken charge of her grandchildren.

Ver. 10. *Israel.*—The occasion of the name being given (as told, ch. xxxii. 29) is supposed to be known. But God here confirms the name, because it was affixed as the covenant-name in connection with the covenant now to be made. Jacob is established as successor to the promises made to Abraham, and as the inheritor of his blessings.

Ver. 11. *Nations.*—By "nations" are also to be understood the smaller tribes of those days, which often consisted only of a few thousands. Here are meant the tribes of the Israelites.

Ver. 14. *Drink-offering.*—At most of the sacrifices there were made offerings of wine. By these were represented the sanctification of drink to God (as by the meat and corn-offerings the hallowing of food), and at the same time the dedication of the

Ver. 15. *Bethel;* i.e., he solemnly confirmed the old name.

Ver 16 *A little way.*—About four English miles.

Ver. 18. *Benjamin.*—Rachel, on her deathbed, named him "the Son of Sorrow;" but Jacob, who did not wish to have a perpetual memento of the loss of his beloved wife, and was unwilling that a name of sorrow should cling to his son, called him "the Son of my Right Hand"—the right side being the fortunate one. Perhaps, too, there is contained in the word the play on another signification :—" Jamin" (Heb. Jamim) means in the Chaldee "Days;" and Jacob would thereby signify that Benjamin was the son of his old age.

Ver. 19. *Bethlehem.*—"The House of Bread." Bethlehem lay about four English miles to the south of Jerusalem, in a very fertile district. On the way thither the grave of Rachel is to this day shown, over which a Turkish mosque is built.

Ver. 21. *Edar* means "The Tower of Flocks." It was originally a watch-tower, for the guarding and watching of the herds of cattle. Afterwards it became a town, as mentioned, Micah iv. 8.

Ver. 22. *Concubine.*—A grievous sin, which Jacob afterwards punished : ch. xlix. 3. Absalom committed the same crime, with the purpose of dishonouring his father : 2 Sam. xvi. 22.

Heard it.—There is a mark here, dating from very old times, that something is left out in the text. The ancient Greek version adds, " and it appeared evil to him." Perhaps these words really stood in this place, though it is very possible the translator might be induced to add them, from the mistaken notion, that something *must* be left out, since Israel is not said to have pronounced any judgment on the crime. But rather, from the significant circumstance that he hears of it and yet is silent, one is led to expect a punishment to come. The sons of Jacob are of a wild, ungovernable character, which their father feels himself too weak to keep under: cf. ch. xlix.

Twelve.—Here ends Jacob's earlier history. In what follows, Joseph is the main subject of the narrative. Hence, as at a conclusion, a complete list of the sons of Jacob is given.

Ver. 27. *Sojourned.*—It is not intended to be said that Jacob, the whole time he was in Canaan, had not visited his father, who was only a few days' journey distant from him; but that in the latter days of his life he went altogether into his neighbourhood, taking with him his flocks and herds.

CHAPTER XXXVI.

Ver. 3. *Nebajoth.*—Esau's wives bear different names here from those given in ch. xxvi. 34, and ch. xxviii. 9. The names are often changed in the East on eventful occasions, especially the occasion of marriage.

Ver. 7. *Cattle.*—Like Lot and Abram, ch. xiii., they lived a long time as herdsmen with the inhabitants of the land. We find indeed, ch. xxxii., that Jacob sends messengers to his brother to the land of Seir, at a time when they had not as yet dwelt together in Canaan. But it is easily explained by supposing that, at that time, Esau had given way to Jacob, for the reason assigned; since he learnt from his father Isaac, that the promised inheritance of Canaan was destined for Jacob.

Ver. 8. *Edom.*—This is often repeated, because Edom was the name of the southern neighbours of the Israelites, who exercised an important influence on that people.

Ver. 14. *Daughter; i.e.,* granddaughter.

Ver. 15. *Dukes.*—The Hebrew word is "Alluph," which means, properly, the chieftain of a thousand men. It seems to have been a peculiar Edomitish title.

Ver. 20. *Horite.*—The Horites—dwellers in caves (Trogledytes)—were the original inhabitants of Seir, and were driven out by the Edomites, Deut. ii. 12; but they appear still to have remained among them in a part of the land. Esau had a Horite, Aholibamah, as his wife (ver. 2, 25); his son Eliphaz, a Horite, Timna, as a concubine (ver. 12, 22), which would mark a declension on the part of the Horites. The families of this tribe are mentioned, because the descent of Aholibamah and Timna is given.—The Horites derive their names from the caves, many of them hewn out of the rock, and from their underground dwellings. These are still to be seen in great numbers, especially about Petra. We need not, however, regard them as an utterly barbarous people.

Ver. 24. *Mules.*—According to the old Hebrew interpreters, which our version follows, Anah was the first discoverer of the breed of mules. But the obscure word which is translated "mules" seems more properly to mean "hot springs;" since, without doubt, are here intended the streams of the place, which lies to the south-east of the Dead Sea, and was afterwards called "Callirhöe." A narrow path hewn out of the rock, on the edge of a precipice, leads down to a thicket of reeds, briars, and palms, in which a number of hot springs bubble forth; the water of which, when cooled, is fit for drinking. According to ch. xxvi. 34, the father of one of Esau's wives was called Beeri—*i.e.*, man of a spring, which agrees with this account.

Ver. 31. *Reigned.*—As there was no king in Israel in Moses' time, and for long after, this expression is remarkable. Some have had recourse to a prophetic view on the part of the writer to explain it. Yet this is by no means necessary if we understand properly the expression. The constitution of the Israelites under their patriarchal chieftains, over whom Jehovah was the invisible King, presupposed a living adherence to the law of God. But in times of falling away from this, the republican government placed them at a disadvantage among their neighbours, and both without and within paralysed the strength of the people as a nation (cf. Judges xxi. 25; 1 Sam. viii. 5). Even to Abraham, and afterwards to Jacob, the glory of a kingly power among their descendants was promised, to which the prophecies of a personal Saviour of the world were annexed (ch. xvii. 6, 16, ch. xxxv. 11). But, before this prospect of a kingdom to be established in Israel was realised, Esau's posterity, to whom no such promise was accorded, had a long succession of kings reigning over them, one of whom is mentioned in Num. xx. 14. Calvin's observation on this is a very excellent one. "We are led here to consider how those shut out from God's covenant quickly blossom, only the more quickly to wither away, like grass on the house-tops, which soon springs up, but soon likewise fades away for want of depth of root. To the two sons of Isaac was this glory promised, that kings should be born from them; and they first arise among the Edomites, while Israel appears to lag behind. But the sequel of the history shows how far better it is to strike the roots deep into the ground, than to acquire an early but evanescent glory. And so believers, who seem to move forwards but slowly, need not envy the quick, joyous steps of others, who are not as they, since the abiding happiness which their Lord promises to *them* is of far more value than what these obtain." We gather from the following record of successions, that the Edomite kings were not hereditary, but elective; and their successful leaders in war were probably chosen to be kings, ver. 35. One of these was a native of "Rehoboth by the river" (*i.e.*, the Euphrates), and consequently was a foreigner: ver. 37. The same would have been the case among the Israelites, but for the establishment of the house of David in the royal dignity. There was hereditary monarchy in the kingdom of Israel, but of a very irregular kind.

Ver. 43. *Edomites;* or, of Edom: which name Esau himself bore: ch. xxv. 30.

CHAPTER XXXVII.

Ver. 3. *A coat.*—Such as was worn by young persons of distinction: 2 Sam. xiii. 18, 19. Jacob appears by this to have wished to assign to Joseph the chief rank among his brethren, and the rights of the eldest son, of which Reuben had rendered himself unworthy.

Ver. 10. *Ourselves.*—His father supposed the dream to have arisen out of his presumption and arrogance; indications of which dispositions, Jacob, not without reason perhaps, thought he perceived in his son.

Ver. 11. *Observed.*—Cf. St Luke ii. 19, 51. In spite of Jacob's perception and rebuke of the sin manifested in this conduct of Joseph, he might still suppose that some Divine revelation was contained in these dreams. This notion was altogether dissipated after his belief of Joseph's death; still it was not altogether fruitless.

Ver. 17. *Dothan* lay twelve (English) miles north of the town (afterwards) Samaria (Schomron), which was in the neighbourhood of Sichem, at the entrance to the plain of Jezreel.

Ver. 20. *Pit.*—A cistern, wide at the bottom, with a narrow mouth to receive the rain waters. Such cisterns are often, after a long cessation of rain, without water, but filled with mud; so that any one thrown in would be in a very helpless condition. They were sometimes used as dungeons: Jer. xxxviii. 6, ch. xl. 15.

Ver. 23. *Wilderness.*—In a pit on the pasture land, in the border of the plain of Jezreel. Reuben, as the first-born, had a kind of responsible oversight of his brethren. After they had agreed to his suggestion, he withdrew to some other place, and was not present at the proposal of Judah to sell Joseph. So he could appeal to his innocence, ch. xlii. 22.

Ver. 25. *Eat bread.*—Full of satisfaction, as if nothing had happened.

Egypt.—They travelled in a large merchant's caravan from Gilead, lying to the east of Jordan, crossing over the river below the Lake of Gennesaret, through the valley of Jezreel, then towards the sea, leaving Hebron, where Jacob dwelt, to the left, and so along the sea-shore to Egypt. The products which they took with them are, in later times, mentioned as belonging to the land of Gilead. We know that from the very earliest times merchant-caravans were in the habit of travelling into the rich country of Egypt, and the kings made especial arrangements to further this traffic.

Ver. 27. *Content.*—Judah had just enough feeling of remorse to keep him from extremities, but not to restrain him from the commission of the sin.

Ver. 28. *Silver.*—The Ishmaelites—Ishmael's descendants—dwelt in Midian, a part of Arabia, near Mount Sinai; therefore the same people are also called Midianites. The price was very small, according to the later value of money. Perhaps his brethren purposely would not take a large sum, in order to avoid the reproach of having acted from love of gain.

Ver. 34. *Sackcloth* (a word found in very many languages) means in the Hebrew a thick haircloth, such as was used for sieves and corn-sacks. This was put on in mourning, when people wished by the disfiguring of their outward persons to represent the distress of the inward man.

Ver. 35. *Daughters.*—Of whom, besides Dinah, he perhaps had several. Daughters, when not the subjects of any remarkable history, are not enumerated in the genealogical register.

Grave; Heb., "to Scheol," the kingdom of the departed, upon the nature of which very little light was vouchsafed in the O. T. Only after Christ's appearance, when life and immortality were brought to light, did death become a gain to the believer.

Ver. 36. *Captain.*—"Officer" means properly, in Heb., "eunuch," but is also a general name for officers of the court. Our margin gives the literal Hebrew for "captain," chief of the executioners—of the body-guard—which will account for the circumstance that the prison was in his house.

CHAPTER XXXVIII.

The sacred narrative here mentions an event in the life of Judah, the head of a tribe destined to such great things (ch. xlix. 8-12), which was much to his discredit. This history prepares the way for the genealogical table, ch. xlvi. 12; and, as Joseph was sold at the time of the death of Judah's sons, must be inserted here. We see in this story how *one* interest—that for their families, and the preservation of them—overpowered every other feeling, even the sense of shame in a woman. The sanctity of an ancient descent, as it had been brought out of Mesopotamia by Abraham's posterity, and the establishment of the duties of the brother-in-law (the Levirate, from a Latin word, levir, a husband's brother), are forcibly put forth by this narrative. The law was, that when a widow was left childless, it was the brother's duty to marry the widow, and the first-born son of this marriage was to be regarded as the child of the deceased brother. The purport of the laws of the Israelites on the subject (no doubt derived from the patriarchs), was to preserve as much as possible the heirs in a direct line. The father lived in the son—the whole family descended from him was in a certain sense himself. And in early times religion and morality depended on the preservation of the tradition in families, through which they were handed down. They were not so much the affair of individuals, as of families and the people. As afterwards out of Jacob's house a nation arose, this duty of the brother-in-law entailed much mischief; and yet, though he was not compelled to fulfil the claim, the neglect was followed by the infliction of a public disgrace: Deut. xxv. 5; Ruth iv. 7; cf. St Matt. xxii. 23.

Although the way in which Tamar avenged herself was a shameful one, yet still, from the prevailing view of this ancient family right, the scandal rested more with Judah—who neglected, from an unfounded suspicion, to fulfil the duty of keeping up his family—than with herself. This, on God's part, is confirmed by the birth of two sons, as this unwonted blessing showed that Er and Onan had died as a punishment for their disobedience; at the same time, the difficulty of the birth, and the remarkable circumstances which attended it, indicate the sin of the mode in which Tamar gained her end. And Judah's avoidance of further intercourse with her proves that, even in those days, the act was regarded as incestuous.

Ver. 2. *Shuah.*—This marriage is not here reprehended, since it was impossible that all Jacob's sons could take wives from among their kinsfolk in Mesopotamia. But the right of the brother's widow was scarcely a Canaanitish one, but peculiar to the patriarchs.

Ver. 5. *Chezib.*—He was absent in the place Chezib, which is mentioned, Joshua xv. 44, as belonging to the possessions of the tribe of Judah in Canaan. Perhaps the circumstance of his absence is here spoken of because this son was on that account the dearer to him.

Ver. 9. *Onan.*—The sinfulness of the act consisted not merely in the shameful abuse of his members, but, above all, in the frustration of the Divine purpose of continuing his family.

Ver. 11. *Brethren.*—The early premature death of the two might well have suggested the thought of a Divine act of judgment on the family of the patriarch. But Judah, a carnally-minded man, thinks rather of some fault on the part of Tamar, probably from some kind or other of superstitious notion.

Ver. 12. *Comforted.*—The death of Judah's wife is mentioned, because with it his duty commenced to give Tamar in marriage, if he did not wish to bestow her on his son. Tamar compelled him by her artifice to the fulfilment of this duty.

Sheep-shearers.—To keep the sheep-shearing feast.

Ver. 14. *Wife.*—A wrong on the part of Judah, as she could not marry another.

Ver. 24. *Burnt.*—As head of his family and judge in his house, Judah will cause death, the punishment of adultery, to be executed on her. As the betrothed of Shelah, Tamar is looked on in the light of a wife. According to the Mosaic law, such an one was stoned: Deut. xxii. 21.

Ver. 26. *More righteous;* i.e., she is right, and I am wrong; or, at least, the wrong she had committed he could not bring against her, since he had in the first place neglected his duty, and then himself committed a sin as regards herself.

No more.—By which he showed that the connection with the daughter-in-law was in those times regarded as sinful.

Ver. 29. *Pharez:* " breach."—Cases of similar twin-births have already occurred. The first child has a wrong position, because the hand comes first instead of the head; and this child being drawn in, the second is born first, and so, in fact, the last-born is the eldest. In reading this account, and what is said in it, we must bear in mind the great privileges attached to the first-born.

Ver. 30. *Zarah.*—" Rising;" which is especially used of the sun. The name is here given to signify the first coming forth of the elder.

CHAPTER XXXIX.

An important move in the development of God's plan of salvation is now about to take place. The house of Jacob, as had been many years before foretold to Abraham (ch. xv. 13), is about to sojourn in a strange land, far away from the Land of Promise. Jacob's numerous family could not any longer dwell among the Canaanites without either dispersing, and so losing their unity and independence, or else coming into collision with the inhabitants. The sons of Jacob could not as a whole have maintained possession of the land. To prepare them for their future destiny, it was necessary for the Israelites to grow up and become a nation in the midst of the most cultivated people of the world at that time—to be closely united with this people, and partakers of all its advantages; and yet never mixed with the Egyptians, but widely severed from them.

Although God vouchsafed to the patriarchs the widest views

into the distant future, He scarcely allowed them to see a few steps before them in their immediate way. They knew that the salvation of the whole world should proceed from them, and that God's purposes with them were the greatest imaginable; yet could they not guess at the meaning of the great and momentous events which occurred in their daily lives. So must it be, in order that their faith might be roused, their mental vision exercised and proved by looking forward to the greatest and noblest object, at the same time that their human sinfulness and shortsightedness were not allowed to interfere with the wise means for attaining that end chosen by God's grace.—Joseph was called in Egypt "the Hebrew," one of Heber's descendants, who, coming from the Euphrates, had settled as nomads among the Canaanitish nations. In Egypt, Joseph served the Lord (Jehovah) his God, ver. 3. Potiphar, though he perceived that he did not take part in the Egyptian idolatrous worship, found that he was blessed by his God, and Joseph adorned his confession of the true God by genuine fidelity and wisdom.

The better to understand the following narrative, we must bear in mind the ages of Jacob and Joseph at the time. Jacob was, when presented to Pharaoh, 130 years old (ch. xlix. 9); Joseph, when introduced to the king, 30 years (ch. xli. 46): between these two periods had intervened the seven plentiful and two of the famine years. Joseph was therefore 39 when Jacob was 130. He was born when Jacob was 91. At that time Jacob had served the 14 years' service for Rachel and Leah (ch. xxx. 25): he was therefore 77 when he came to Laban—allowing for the difference in length of life, about middle age of our time. Joseph came into Egypt soon after he was 17 (ch. xxxvii. 2); he was thirteen years in Potiphar's service and in prison—of these, more than two in prison (ch. xli. 1): he was therefore something past his twenty-fifth year during the events of this chapter.

Ver. 5. *Overseer.*—It was a custom among the ancient Egyptians to place a steward over every large family, who had the control of all the servants.

Ver. 7. *Lie with me.*—We know from the testimony of the ancients that Egypt, at least in later times, was a land fearfully corrupt, in which prevailed every kind of sensuality, and especially adultery. Herodotus tells a story of Pheron, son of Sesostris, who was to gain the use of his sight again by the touch of a woman who had never been unfaithful to her husband, and could only find one, whom he immediately made his wife (Herod., B. ii. 111). The Egyptian women lived for the most part separated from the men, as is usual with the sex in the rest of the East, but they came together in the intercourse and different relations of life.

Ver. 9. *Against God.*—Joseph abhors and shuns the sin from obedience to God's laws. The trust of his master comes in as an additional motive to restrain him from the sin.

Ver. 20. *Prison.*—In Egypt the influence of the woman was greater in the house than that of the man; so Potiphar is, in a certain sense, compelled to comply with his wife's demand. Joseph's master, as captain of the eunuchs, who are the ministers of all executions, is also overseer of the king's prison; and therefore places there his slave, over whom he has the power of life and death. He does not, however, concern himself any further about him, but delivers him over to the "keeper of the prison," who, under himself, had the oversight of the particular prisoners.

Ver. 23. *Prosper.*—The Lord rewards immediately Joseph's faith with the richest blessing, so that in his need he still feels himself to be in God's grace and favour. Nevertheless His trials of him still continue; and not the least of these certainly was this, that a man so distinguished as Joseph, who felt himself called to great things, was nevertheless obliged to pass years, as overseer of the prison, in the greatest obscurity. But thus do we perceive that God often deals with His greatest instruments: so did He with Moses, with David, with Paul, with Luther— nay, the Son of God Himself lived to his thirtieth year at Nazareth. Nothing is more displeasing to God than that impatient distrust of His power which interferes wilfully with the plans of His providence.

CHAPTER XL.

Ver. 4. *Served them;* i.e., he appointed that Joseph should always attend on them, to render them what services they required, not that he should be placed over them. The chief butler and chief baker were high court officers, and therefore were treated with more respect than the rest. The choice of Joseph to serve them was a favour shown to him. This insignificant circumstance had great influence on his destiny.

Ver. 8. *Interpreter.*—They had narrated to each other their dreams; and from many concurring circumstances, and by the relation of the dreams to their office, they concluded that they were full of significance, but whether boding good or ill they knew not.

Ver. 11. *Pharaoh's hand.*—The imagery of the dream is altogether Egyptian. The Egyptians, even to very late times, drank no wine, as they esteemed it the blood of Demons; but the kings and priests drank a moderate quantity of the juice of the grape without having been fermented.

Ver. 15. *Stolen.*—He specifies only in general terms the secret violent mode of his abduction, but does not narrate the particulars for his brethren's sake.

Ver. 16. *Head.*—The Egyptian men carried the burdens on their heads, the women on their shoulders, as Herodotus tells us. Shallow baskets borne on the head are to be seen often depicted in Egyptian monuments.

CHAPTER XLI.

The important occurrence which was to exercise so great an influence on the fate of Joseph and his family, and was of such moment in the history of the kingdom of God, is brought about by a dream. We must bear in mind the great significance which, among the ancients, was attached to the dreams of kings.

Nestor says in Homer, Iliad 2, 80, "Had any other of the Achæans told us the dream, we might have looked on it as a delusion; but *he* has seen the vision who is the greatest of all, etc." The dream itself is clothed in striking Egyptian emblematic figures. Egypt is the offspring of the Nile. The fertility of the land is yearly renewed by its overflowings. The cow is a very ancient emblem of the land, and of the earth generally, and was worshipped among the Egyptians as the goddess Isis. The Nile, Osiris, is honoured under the form of a bull. The fruitfulness or unfruitfulness of a year is represented, therefore, under the image of a cow rising out of the river, the source of blessing to all around. The seven ears from one stalk point to the great fertility of Egypt, where such a phenomenon occasionally, though rarely, occurs. If Pharaoh's residence was at Zoan or Tanis, in North-East Egypt, then the scorching east wind, coming from the Arabian Desert, would be an emblem of famine beyond the power of the river to overcome, as in the first dream were the lean kine. The agreement of the two dreams in the number seven, and their internal resemblance, filled Pharaoh with the feeling that they were of pressing moment, and thus they became the occasion of the greatest events.

Ver. 1. *River.*—Lit., "on the Jeor," which is the Hebrew name for the Nile.

Ver. 14. *Dungeon.*—Lit., "the pit." It was apparently a subterranean dungeon: so the word also stands, ch. xl. 15; Jer. xxxvii. 16, ch. xxxviii. 6.

Ver. 25. *God.*—Lit., "God will answer the peace of Pharaoh." The expression "the Lord" (Jehovah) is never used in speaking to heathens. The belief in one God, which lies at the bottom of all idolatrous religions—more evidently is this the case with the religions of the most ancient times—is always presupposed by the servants of the true God to exist among heathens.

Ver. 37. *Good.*—This power of diving into the meaning of images and figures which were familiar and frequent among themselves, made a great impression on the Egyptians. It was remarkable in a foreigner.

Ver. 42. *Ring.*—All persons of distinction in the East wear a seal-ring on the finger, or round the neck.

Linen.—Heb.: "Schesch;" *i.e.*, Byssas, the finest white linen. It would appear from this that Pharaoh enrolled him into the priestly caste, or the rank next after it. Herodotus tells us (B. 2, 37), "The priests shave themselves every third day, that no vermin or other insect may be on them when they minister before the gods. The priests wear only linen clothing and shoes of byblus (the inner bark of the papyrus). They are not allowed to put on any other kind of clothing or of shoes." All Egyptians of note wore golden chains on their necks.

Ver. 43. *Bow the knee.*—Lit., " shall call out Abrek." This is probably an Egyptian (Coptic) word, properly Aperek—*i.e.*, " bow the head." Out of it is a Hebrew word made, which signifies "bow the knee." The person who called out would thereby remind the people that the outward reverence, next to that paid the king, was to be shown to Joseph.

Ver. 45. *Zaphnath-paaneah.*—This word, converted into a Hebrew term to express "a revealer of secrets," is certainly Egyptian, as it was Joseph's Egyptian name, which was given him when he was received into the rank or caste of the Egyptian priests. The ancient Greek translation of the Septuagint, which was made in Egypt, and usually renders the Egyptian words and things very accurately, has here the word "Psonthomphanech," which almost exactly answers to the Coptic "Psotomphaneh," signifying "the preserver of the world," or " of the land—kingdom." Joseph thus received a name which, by a little alteration, was made by Moses to form the Hebrew word which expressed what now occurred.

On means "the sun." It was the town called Heliopolis by the Greeks. The marriage of Joseph was a part of his exaltation in rank. In a country under a despotic form of government, where the king's power is only circumscribed by the laws and customs of religion and of the priestly class, the sudden elevation of a slave to the highest honour—especially if he is believed to be endowed with some supernatural gifts—is nothing extraordinary. Such events happen even at this day in eastern despotisms—nay, even in Russia. Herodotus tells us of a similar exaltation of a Moor by king Rhampsinatus to be his son-in-law, because, as the Egyptians excel the rest of the world in cunning, so he excelled the Egyptians: *vide* Herod. ii. 120. The greater marvel is, that we see Joseph in his exaltation maintain the fear of God, the conscientiousness, and mild, gentle disposition which he had learnt in his adversity.

Ver. 52. *Ephraim.*—Lit., "Bring forth a double blossom"—in allusion, perhaps, to his being the second son.

Affliction.—Egypt remains, even in his elevation, still "the land of his affliction," as it became to his family the land of refuge only in their necessity. We see in this expression of Joseph's a mark of his still longing after the Land of Promise.

CHAPTER XLII.

The famine now extends beyond Egypt and its immediate vicinity, and thereby becomes the means, in God's hand, of bringing down the family of the patriarchs to Egypt, in a way little contemplated.

The overflowing of the Nile, the source of Egypt's fertility, is caused by the tropical rains which fall in the Abyssinian mountain district and the interior of Ethiopia, with which we are unacquainted. These rains put the valleys of those extensive highlands under water, which flows thence into the basin of the Nile; and the single channel of this river, charged with this vast stream—the produce of a large district of 220 geographical miles in length—passes through Egypt to the sea. The reason of the greater and less swelling of the river is common to Egypt and the neighbouring countries. The great heat of Egypt, Nubia, and Ethiopia, during the later spring months, when the sun is right over those regions, and the expansion of the heated atmosphere, cause the colder streams of air and the clouds to pour in from the north (the Mediterranean Sea) in order to restore the equilibrium. This is the physical cause, which is again itself altogether dependent on the course of the sun and the stars (Ritter Geog. i. 835). When the mass of clouds from the north is less, there is a smaller fall of rain; and this affects equally Egypt and the adjacent countries.

When we consider Joseph's conduct to his brethren as a whole, we see that this God-fearing, conscientious, and affectionate man was actuated by no spirit of revenge towards them. His object was to prove them, whether they were still the same cruel, treacherous men as before. The assertion, that they were ten brethren, was in itself startling, and might well lead to the inquiry which brought about the mention of Benjamin. Joseph might, not unreasonably, suspect that from envy they had dealt with this youngest brother as they had done with himself. By causing their money to be returned in their sacks, he wished both to make a present to his father, and to prick their conscience on account of their former crime. They feel that God's hand is in this. So may we explain Joseph's conduct, without supposing he had forgotten the fear of God or love to his brethren, even though we cannot altogether excuse the mixture of cunning and artifice which is displayed in it.

Ver. 3. *Buy corn.*—In a like case, Abraham went down to Egypt with all that he had. Jacob's family do not the same—either because the journey was too long for such a family, or rather because the famine prevailed in Egypt, and corn could only be procured by purchase from the stores laid in by Pharaoh.

Ver. 4. *Mischief.*—A kind of presentiment that Joseph's brethren were not altogether guiltless in respect to his disappearance, runs through Jacob's words in this account. He knew their envy of Joseph, and had had some experience of the violent character of Simeon and Levi.

Ver. 6. *Sold.*—Certainly not himself, but by the hands of inferior officers. But this case, in which ten men from a foreign land desired to purchase (apparently) a large quantity, required to be laid before him for his personal decision.

Ver. 8. *Knew.*—About 20 years had elapsed since they had sold him. It was very natural that he should recognise them, but that they know not him. His whole appearance was changed: he was shorn, as was usual with the priestly class, wore magnificent clothing, and spake to them by an interpreter.

Ver. 9. *Remembered.*—The literal fulfilment of his dreams came forcibly before his mind. He was vividly impressed with a feeling of wonder at the wisdom, might, and love which had so marvellously brought about the Divine promises.

Ver. 12. *Nakedness.*—Nothing is more common than for this charge to be made against travellers in the East in the present day, especially if they take any note or plan of the countries.

Ver. 14. *Spies.*—The improbability of their assertion, that they are ten brethren—the strangeness of their appearance, resembling each other indeed, but utterly unlike the rest of the

Canaanites,—all this gives Joseph a plea for repeating his accusation more positively. At the same time, when they mentioned Benjamin, about whose fate he was anxious, he seizes the opportunity of proving them, and of gratifying his yearning to see his brother.

Ver. 16. *Life of Pharaoh.*—An usual adjuration among the Egyptians.

Ver. 17. *Three days.*—To give them a sort of trial of what they had deserved, and to awaken the feeling of repentance in their minds. This severity on Joseph's part was certainly more wholesome to his brethren, and more conducive to the object he had in view, than if he had pardoned them at once without any taste of punishment.

Ver. 18. *Fear God; i.e*, Ye may rely on my fear of God, that if ye will deal honestly with me, ye shall find me neither false nor arbitrary. He mitigates the threat which he had at first made, by requiring that only one should remain as prisoner.

Ver. 21. *Guilty.*—The dealings of Providence were so evident to the brethren, that they were impressed with the conviction of God's retributive justice in what happened to them.

Ver. 24. *Wept.*—Moved by the thought of God's wonderful preservation, as well as by the distress of his brethren.

Simeon, the instigator of the cruel deed against Shechem, may well be supposed to have had the greatest share of guilt in the selling of Joseph.

Ver. 28.—From all that has now happened to them, they are so impressed with a sense of Divine retribution, that they can think of no natural causes, but only of a direct punishment from God. Under this harassing feeling, they omit to look into the other sacks.

Ver. 36. *Joseph.*—He seems, with a feeling of presentiment, to accuse them of this likewise.

CHAPTER XLIII.

Ver. 2. *Eaten up.*—Probably only the members of Jacob's family partook of the corn brought out of Egypt. The slaves would be obliged to support themselves from roots, vegetables, and milk.

Ver. 9. *Blame,* and the punishment.

Ver. 11. *Fruits.*—Literally: "from the song of the land;" *i.e.,* those things by reason of which our land is celebrated in song.

Almonds.—We see here for what productions Palestine was distinguished in most ancient times, and what things it exported into the neighbouring lands. Three of the kinds of produce here named occur among those which the caravan of the Ishmeelites carried into Egypt: see ch. xxxvii. 25. The first is "Zori," balsam—a product in ancient times considered peculiarly to belong to Palestine (from the Zacchum plant). "The balsam is a moderately high shrub: as soon as the bough begins to swell, if iron is forcibly applied, the veins shrink; but they can be opened by a broken stone or potsherd, and the juice is used by physicians." So says Tacitus, Hist. B. v. 6. And Pliny, Nat. Hist. 12, 25: "The Emperor Vespasian first showed this shrub in the city of Rome (it is worth remark, that since the time of Pompey we have used boughs of trees in triumphs). It serves us, and pays tribute like its people. It resembles the vine more than the myrtle. It spreads over the hills by its shoots, like the vine, and does not require any props. The leaf is oval, and always green. The Jews have raged against it, as they have against their own life; the Romans have defended it, and a single tree has cost a combat. It is now planted at the expense of the treasury; and never was it more abundant or larger. The juice, which flows from the incision made by glass, stone, or bone, is called opobalsam, and yields a delicious perfume; but the drops trickle only scantily, and are collected on wool in small horn vessels."—Further, "D'basch," honey. This is probably not bee honey, which is neither a costly present nor rare in Egypt, but a thickened kind of grape-juice, which, even in modern times, is carried to the amount of hundreds of camel loads from the district of Hebron to the Egyptians, who are poorer in vine produce. It is called to this day Dibs. Next, "N'koth"—a kind of gum from the Tragakanth or goat's thorn shrub (a low kind of shrub growing on Lebanon), and used for smoking, or in medicine. "Lot," ladanum—a sweet, green, soft, and rich resin on the branches of the cistus rose, which in early morning attaches itself to the goats' beards, and is useful in medicine, outwardly or inwardly applied. "Botnim"— long angular nuts from a tree like the terebinth, about the size of a hazel-nut, whose oily sweet-smelling kernel was much prized by the ancients, and reckoned an antidote to the bite of serpents. "Sch'kedim" are almonds, in which Palestine was very rich.

Ver. 29. *My son.*—According to ch. xlvi. 21, Benjamin had ten sons (no doubt, from several wives) at the time the family went down to Egypt, and was indeed only seven years younger than Joseph—therefore thirty-two years old. This term is, rather, the kind expression of a superior, than any allusion to Benjamin's youth. The words contain not so much a particular blessing, but are rather an usual form of friendly salutation in the East.

Ver. 32. *Abomination.*—We have here a representation of the manner of the Egyptian castes. Joseph, as belonging to the priestly class, eats separate from the other Egyptians, apart from both the brethren. The reason of this separation (as at present among the Hindoos) lay in the fact, that foreigners and the inferior castes killed and ate beasts which were sacred among the Egyptians; so says Herodotus, B. ii. 41: "Isis is represented with the horns of a cow; and therefore all the Egyptians honour the cow more than the sheep. For this reason, an Egyptian man or woman would hardly kiss a Greek on the mouth, or use his knife, or spit, or basin; nor will he taste of the flesh of a clean cow which has been cut with a Greek knife." Whereupon he tells us how they bury with the greatest care bulls and other cattle, and, after the flesh has rotted, lay the bones in a particular place. In all this is shown the blind worship of Nature among the Egyptians, who, forsaking the living personal God, honoured certain beasts, as representatives and incarnations of the highest powers of Nature. Joseph could partake in much of their customs as indifferent and external;

but their after history will show us the great danger the Israelites incurred from their sojourn among the Egyptians.

Ver. 34. *Five times.*—The ancients ate not all out of one dish; but each received his own, which was distributed to him according to the will of the host. From the dishes which stood on his own table, Joseph commanded five times as much to be given to Benjamin as to the others.

Merry.—This is not to be taken in a bad sense, as his brethren would not give themselves up to unrestrained mirth in the presence of Joseph.

CHAPTER XLIV.

Ver. 5. *Divineth.*—The divining out of cups (chilicomantia) is a kind of soothsaying, mentioned by the ancients as practised by the Egyptians. The soothsayer drew his auguries either from the rays of light which played upon the water in the cup, or threw in pieces of gold and silver with jewels, and then pretended to see signs of future events from the figures which appeared on the surface, after an incantation had been pronounced. As the expression here, and that in ver. 15, bears upon it a certain appearance of jesting, we are not to conclude that Joseph had really practised the superstition: still the circumstance here mentioned, points out the dangerous position in which Joseph and the Israelites were placed in Egypt, the very fountain-head of superstition.

Ver. 14. *Judah.*—As he had especially been guarantee for Benjamin, so he is afterwards the chief spokesman. Perhaps we may see in this an allusion to the leadership and kingly dignity of that tribe, on which account Jacob (ch. xlix. 9) assigned to him a portion of the birthright of the eldest.

Ver. 15. *Such a man.*—Higher divine powers were attributed to kings and their chief servants by the ancient Orientals.

Ver. 16. *Servants.*—He does not venture to clear himself against the charge of theft; but it would appear, by submitting himself and his brethren to slavery, he hoped to find some means of liberating Benjamin.

Ver. 34. *Father.*—In these moving and beautiful words of Judah we perceive what a change of character had taken place in Joseph's brethren, since the most faithful conscientiousness and filial love towards their father are expressed therein. This it was which Joseph desired to see; and so with these words, when the anguish and perplexity of his brethren have reached their height, there comes in the turning-point of the history.

CHAPTER XLV.

Ver. 3. *Father.*—He repeats this question in order to give them to understand what thought above all was nearest to his heart, now that again he was their brother.

Ver. 5. *Preserve life.*—Joseph declares to them (as he does afterwards, ch. l. 20) that he saw in his fate so completely the hand of Divine Providence, as to forget the part *they* had in it. It was, therefore, easy for him to forego all retaliation. The brethren, indeed, even after this, could not but feel that their sin was not altogether cancelled; but Joseph out of love would not impute it to them.

Ver. 8. *But God.*—As ye did not gain your purpose, but only subserved the providence of God, I cannot say that ye sent me here.

Father.—In the East, to this day, the Grand Vizier is called the king's "Foster-father" or guardian. So is Haman also named "the father of the king."

Ver 10. *Goshen.*—The situation of the land of Goshen can be no longer a matter of doubt, after what the Books of Moses contain on the subject, and the researches of modern travellers tell us. According to ch. xlvi. 5, 6, it lay on the eastern boundary, and was a land of pastures (ch. xlvi. 34); at the same time the best part of the land, the most fruitful region of Egypt (ch. xlvii. 6), "where they sowed their seed, and watered it with their foot," Deut. xi. 10; where the Israelites planted and ate "cucumbers, melons, onions, and garlic, and fish," Num. xi. 5; where in the midst of the Egyptians they dwelt in large and rich towns, and took with them out of every house golden and silver vessels, and great riches, when they left Egypt. All this together will only agree with the north-east part of Egypt, the region situated on the Pelusian or perhaps Tanitic arm of the Nile—the province now called Esch-Scharkijeh. The whole of modern Egypt is like the gigantic monument of a Great Past, which, notwithstanding all its trials during the continuance of many centuries—from the Persians, afterwards the Romans, the Saracens, the Turks—is not yet destroyed, nor converted into a barren waste. Now, indeed, is the canal in ruins (though capable of restoration) which once connected the Nile with the Gulf of Suez, the Pelusian arm of the Nile filled with sand, and the artificial means of irrigation destroyed; yet still, with all this, is the province of Esch-Scharkijeh one of the most productive of the whole land. "The great fertility of this district arises from the fact, that the surface of the land lies at a less elevation above the level of the Nile than that of the other regions of Egypt; and therefore it is more capable of irrigation by sluices which are cut through it. Here is a greater quantity of cattle, large and small, than anywhere else in Egypt, and also more fishermen. The population is partly migratory, and consists of Fellahs (country people) and of Arabs from the adjoining wilderness, and even of Syrians, who retain their nomadic kind of life, and often wander from village to village. Many villages are thereby altogether deserted, where some 50,000 men could once find a habitation. A million more could be maintained in that district, and the adjoining wilderness (as far at least as the water could be conveyed) might be made fruitful." (The eye-witness, Lord Prudhoe, in Robinson, i. 87.) Accordingly, the outskirts of the wilderness was the residence allotted to the Israelites, where Jacob and his sons pursued their former pastoral life; and yet, by cultivation of the soil, participated in the wealth of the best part of Egypt. Here they lived much as the Copts now do, partly in separate villages, and partly residing with the people to whom the land belonged.

Ver. 16. *Pharaoh's house.*—The land of Goshen lay near the ancient capital of Egypt. This would be the case if we suppose it to be the Memphis situated about twenty miles south of the present Cairo; but much more so, if (as most likely) the capital of the Pharaohs was the ancient Zoan, called by the Greeks Tanis. Cf. Num. xiii. 22; Ps. lxxviii. 19, 43.

CHAPTER XLVI.

We stand now at the threshold of a fresh era in the history of the kingdom of God, for which everything since ch. xxxvii. had been preparing—the going down of Jacob and his family into Egypt. Since the ancient promise seemed extinct, and the people of Israel mixed with a heathen nation, a new and clear revelation from God was needed in order to bring the Head of the chosen people out of Canaan into Egypt. Had the Israelites remained any longer in Canaan, they must, as has been observed, have merged themselves in the Canaanites, or, at all events, have lost their united family character. They could only preserve their unity any further under the peculiar circumstances in which they went into Egypt. Here, at first being treated with great favour, they obtained room enough to spread: here they were objects of religious avoidance on account of their occupation as herdsmen, at the same time that they were enabled to participate in the riches and the high cultivation of the people among whom they sojourned. This was a country in which they came into close contact with a people, the most renowned of all heathens for the profoundness and symbolism of their religion, and for the extensive influence which it exercised. No place was, therefore, better fitted than Egypt for the revealing of a religion, so opposed in its character to heathenism as was the religion of the Israelites: no place where religious Israelites could so perfectly learn the distinction between the people of God and the worshippers of Nature and her powers. For this reason was the journey out of Canaan solemnised by a sacrifice on the part of Jacob, and by a gracious revelation on the part of God. The promise, not merely of protection on the journey, but of a return into Canaan, is expressly given. This is the last immediate Divine communication mentioned in the history of the patriarchs.

Ver. 1. *Beersheba.*—The boundary of Canaan on the south, where Abraham, and more especially Israel, had lived so long: cf. ch. xxi. 31.

Ver. 3. *God of thy fathers.*—Lit., " I am the El, the Elohim of thy fathers." Here God calls Himself by the more general name, as a new period of promise is beginning. Exod. iii. 13 and following verses afford the suitable conclusion to this history. There God, as the fulfiller of this promise, who thereby is revealed afresh as the God of the covenant, calls Himself Jehovah ("Ehjeh," I am): cf. ch. i. 1, note.

Ver. 4. *Up again.*—Here we find again how entirely Jacob is regarded as one with his posterity. God promises to bring *him* up again, although He immediately afterwards declares his death in Egypt. How completely does this suppose a life of faith on the word of God, when all that happened to the individual sank into nothing compared with the blessing promised to his seed, and through it to all the people of the earth!

Ver. 10. *Canaanitish woman.*—It would seem from this, as a Canaanitish wife of Simeon's is particularly mentioned, that she and Judah's wife alone were from this people. The other sons of Jacob had taken wives from among their kinsfolk in Mesopotamia.

Ver. 13. *Job.*—He is called, Num. xxvi. 24 and 1 Chron. vii. 1, "Jaschub." Job means the same in Arabic, "one who turns back," or is converted. He was called Job, perhaps, by an Arabian mother, and the name translated in the Hebrew tradition of it.

Ver. 23. *Hushim.*—He is the only son mentioned. The beginning, "sons," is used for the sake of uniformity in the genealogical table, as ch. xxxvi. 25.

Ver. 34. *Abomination.*—The Egyptians indeed had among themselves a caste of cow-herds and another of swine-herds, and Pharaoh even wished to put some of the sons of Jacob over his own cattle: ch. xlvii. 6. But herdsmen were generally hated by the Egyptians, partly because they could not easily be subdued and kept in subjection, and partly (in the case of foreign herdsmen) for the reason mentioned, ch. xliii. 32, note.

CHAPTER XLVII.

Ver. 9. *Few and evil.*—Jacob alludes to the many and severe trials of his life which he had suffered, especially those of his servitude to Laban, and that he had only late attained to a state of greater freedom and independence. He compares his short life—the end of which he felt approaching—not merely with the length of days enjoyed by the patriarchs before the flood, but with the life of Abraham and of Isaac, both of whom reached a much greater age than himself. He calls his life a pilgrimage—a roaming to and fro in a strange country—not so much on account of its nomadic character, as because the whole existence on earth, in relation to eternity, appeared to him to be such. The promise which had brought them down to Canaan, directed the mind of the patriarch ever towards the future.

Ver. 11. *Rameses.*—Rameses is, according to the old Greek translation, the town of Heroonpolis (hero-city), probably so called by the Greeks because the greatest Egyptian heroes had the name of Rameses. In the east, near the Pelusian arm of the Nile, commences the valley now called "Wady Tamilat." At first its direction is from west to east, then it inclines towards the south-east and south, towards the northern point of the Gulf of Suez. It is the old bed of the channel which connected the Nile with the Red Sea (cf. ch. xlv. 10, note). At the entrance of the valley, the site of the modern Abassieh was situated, the ancient Pithom (Exod. i. 11). Some 16 or 20 miles distant, to the east, lay Rameses, on the site of the modern Abu Keischeid. Both were border fortresses against Arabia, which afterwards the Israelites assisted in building. This was the southern part of the land of Goshen, which, from its capital, bore the name of Rameses. From this place, at a later period, the Israelites reached the Red Sea in two days: Exod. xii. 36; Num. xxxiii. 6.

Ver. 20. *All the land.*—At the time of the going down of Jacob and his family into Egypt, a great change in the state of the country was brought about by Joseph's instrumentality. In order to form a correct notion of this transaction, we must be on our guard against the mistake of transferring modern notions to ancient times. In Egypt, the king had always been esteemed as a sacred person. He was the visible representative of Osiris, his incarnation, and himself a priest. As king, he possessed from the first large tracts of land; and the lower classes or races of the people stood in a political and religious dependence on him. These classes had been brought into entire subjection to the priestly caste—it would seem in a peaceable manner. The priests also were great landowners; but received, besides, from the king an allowance for their support. The result of what Joseph did was this—that he procured for the king the possession of the land of the whole country, so that, with the exception of the lands which belonged to the priests, every kind of landowner was swept away; and instead of landowners, they became merely tenants or farmers of the king. Their rent was fixed at a fifth. The other change was this—that he did away with the free optional living on the land. He removed the tenants into towns, and made, it would seem, a regular and accurate division of the land. We find, from later tradition, that such a division was ascribed to Sesostris. There is nothing in the narrative to lead us to think of a personal slavery, which was out of the question. The expression, "our bodies and our fields," gives us to understand that their estates, together with their personal labour, belonged to the king, and that both were more dependent on him than before. As Herod. (B. ii. 109) says, "Sesostris is reported to have distributed all the land among the Egyptians, giving to each person an equal square portion; and from their allotments a yearly rent was paid, according to a rate appointed to each. Whenever the river washed away a part of any one's portion, he might present himself before the king and state what had taken place; and the king sent persons to measure how much the land was diminished, that the occupier might for the future pay a proportionate tribute." Even in the much later time when Herodotus lived, there were no land-freeholders besides the king, the priests, and a part of the military caste, who appear to have obtained the privilege, probably, in consequence of some war. By the Egyptians themselves, the open and straightforward conduct of Joseph was felt and acknowledged as a benefit; and in a country where the return is often thirtyfold, the tribute of a fifth was not oppressive. It is probable that from this time Egypt may date its good order and management, which excited the admiration of much later times.

This whole transaction, which did not affect the Israelites themselves, is, however, here mentioned so circumstantially, because afterwards among them a similar right was introduced in reference to their Highest King—God Himself. He had given and divided the land of Canaan to them. They were all His servants (Lev. xxv. 42, 55). Accordingly, they must pay to Him a double tithe. Of this God gave one part to the priests and Levites for their maintenance (as Pharaoh to the Egyptian priests), the other was consumed in high feasts at sacrificial meals, which were given to the Levites, the widows, orphans, and the poor. For the first, see Lev. xxvii. 30, Num. xviii. 21; for the second, Deut. xii. 17-19, ch. xiv. 22-29, ch. xxvi. 12-15. Those relations of dependence of person and property on the king, and of acknowledgment of his supreme right over all by the payment of the fifths, was Israel to transfer to its invisible King. The main principle of the whole outer life of the Israelites was always to be in subjection to Him.

Ver. 22. *Sold not their lands.*—The priests received from Pharaoh for their services a certain allowance of meat and wine. They did not therefore suffer from the famine, nor were obliged to sell their lands. And we find also, in later times, that they "received daily their sacred baked bread, and a quantity of beef and goose-flesh and wine." When the military caste also obtained possession of freehold land, those among them who had served with the king for a year had, in addition, daily rations of bread, meat, and wine (Herod. 2, 37, 168). By such regulations, without doubt, care was taken that the priestly class might not at any time suffer from want, or fall into dependence on the king, or on any other person.

Ver 25. *Pharaoh's servants.*—Servants, but not bondmen. That a sort of feudal service is here intended—the service of free labourers, not of bondmen—we may learn from the relationship of the Israelites to God, which was formed after the plan of this Egyptian model. In a political sense of the word, the Israelites were not bondmen (Lev. xxv. 42, 55): "They are My servants, which I brought out of the land of Egypt."

Ver. 29. *Found grace.*—Not as though he doubted his son's feeling towards him, but, as we would say, "If now thou wilt show me a proof of love."

Ver. 30. *Their burying-place.*—It was of consequence that

Israel, before his end, should solemnly show that he looked forward to the Land of Promise, even in the country where he and his had received such kindness. As in the cases of Abraham and Isaac, so also with Jacob, the promise of the blessing on all people, which was to be fulfilled in Canaan, was the soul of his life. This hope drew him away from this world, and was the anchor which bound him to the unseen world.

Ver. 31. *Bed's head.*—He prayed towards the bed's head, thankful that his last wish was now fulfilled: cf. Heb. xi. 21.

CHAPTER XLVIII.

Ver. 4. *For an everlasting possession.*—The chequered life of Jacob was now drawing to an end. Before his departure the Spirit of prophecy came upon him, with respect to the promises of God made to him. He announces to his beloved son, Joseph, that his portion of the inheritance was transferred to his two sons, Ephraim and Manasseh. Jacob in this verse does not mean, by this land, that in which they were then living—Goshen; but he speaks of the division of the land of Canaan. Out of Jacob's twelve sons there arose thirteen tribes; but Ephraim and Manasseh always constituted one.

Ver. 5. *Simeon.*—The first-born received a double inheritance (Deut. xxi. 17). But as Jacob had determined to deprive Reuben of this birthright (ch. xlix. 4), but might not do so exclusively in favour of the son of his beloved Rachel (in accordance with the law afterwards given, as just quoted), therefore he divided the birthright, and gave the double inheritance to Joseph, but the first rank and authority to Judah (ch. xlix. 8; cf. 1 Chron. v. 12).

Ver. 7. *Bethlehem.*—A reason added to the foregoing. I do this in honour of my beloved Rachel, who died there so early in life. The words, "the same is Bethlehem," are, like many others of the same kind (*e.g.*, Kirjath-arba, this is Hebron, ch. xxiii. 2), an addition made by Moses, explaining the name by the position of places in his own time.

Ver. 12. *His knees.*—He held them standing between his

knees. Manasseh, at that time, was at least 20 years old: cf. ch. xli. 51, ch. xlvii. 28.

Ver. 14. *Wittingly.*—Perhaps this would be more correctly translated, "he intertwined his hands"—laid them crosswise. In blessing Ephraim and Manasseh, before Jacob uttered the great prophetic blessings on his sons, the Divine Spirit of prophecy is shown in a remarkable way. By the secret guidance of God, he gives the younger the preference over the elder. This event was of great moment in the after history of the two tribes.

Ver. 15. *Fed me.*—Heb.: "Pastured me"—which is even more than nourished or fed, cf. Ps. xxiii. 1-4. Like David, the shepherd Jacob sees in the Lord his Shepherd.

Ver. 16. *Angel.*—He speaks of God and the Angel who had redeemed him as the same, and therefore clearly ascribes to this Angel Divine nature. In the Samaritan Version, this word was changed, by the alteration of a letter, from the "Angel" into the "King"—which would be an appellation of God. The Angel is He who wrestled with Jacob at P'ni-el, and blessed him there and gave him a new name. Cf. ch. xxxii. 24, and ch. xvi. 7, note.

Name.—Heb.: "And my name, and the name of my fathers Abraham and Isaac, shall be named in them;" *i.e*, May they preserve this name and spread it abroad on earth—may the fathers and I live in them.

Ver. 19. *Multitude of nations.*—A fulness. In the time of Moses this was not yet accomplished. In the first numbering of the people in the wilderness (Num. i. 32-35), Ephraim had 40,500, and Manasseh 32,200; in the second (Num. xxvi. 34, 37), Ephraim 32,500, and Manasseh 52,700, belonging to them respectively. But afterwards this proportion was much altered: Ephraim became, in the time of the Judges, the most numerous and powerful tribe next to Judah (Judges iv. 5, ch. v. 14, ch. viii., ch. xii.); and eventually, in the reign of Jeroboam, drew off ten tribes, and formed the kingdom of Israel.

Ver. 22. *One portion.*—In the Hebrew there is a play on the words. "Schechem" (Sichem) means, properly, the shoulder, the shoulder-piece, then generally a large choice portion at a feast, and thence a good piece of land. Here is the "Schechem" (Sichem) meant, which Jacob's sons had taken from the Amorites on account of the seduction of Dinah, laid waste, and possessed.

This Sichem was the chief place in the tribe of Ephraim, in a rich, fruitful region, at the foot of Mounts Gerizim and Ebal. Jacob here speaks of the act of his sons as his own, though he had by no means approved of it (ch. xlix. 6). By this gift Jacob wished to reward Joseph for the love and the benefits which he had shown himself and his sons.

CHAPTER XLIX.

As Isaac had, by Divine authority, imparted his blessing to Jacob, so do we here see the dying Israel direct his looks out of Egypt to Canaan, in order, by the Spirit of prophecy, to commit, in anticipation, the land to his twelve sons, and to appoint to each tribe his proper place among the future people of God. The twelve sons assemble round his bed. What the father had observed during the 70 years of his quiet shepherd life, will be now vividly present before their view. The germ of the prophecy —the idea in the soul of Jacob—is the prospect of the Promised Land. Thither will he turn the eyes of his mind. In Egypt he has no home. In Canaan each one of his sons shall find his place according to his peculiar character and disposition, which shall be more perfectly developed in their posterity. The Spirit of God gives light and life to the germ of prophecy in Jacob's mind. His insight into the future receives clearness; and where his natural senses might lead him astray, that Spirit affords distinctness and certainty. First, he sees Reuben stand before him, full of strength and gentleness; but by one act of sin and shame he has forfeited his birthright. It is taken from him. His tribe receives but a small inheritance, and that outside Canaan proper, in the south-eastern pastures, between Jordan and Euphrates. This tribe plays but an unimportant part in all the after history.—The fierce, undisciplined, fiery natures of Levi and Simeon come next into review. From them the first-born in privilege cannot be. They receive now the punishment of their cruelty and treachery on Hamor and Sichem. As a tribe they could not dwell together. Their inheritance is divided and dispersed among the rest.—Next comes the kingly, haughty, and powerful Judah. He receives the birthright of sovereignty taken from Reuben. His tribe possessed calm and invincible heroism, the certainty of the future royal dignity, riches and abundance in their fruitful borders.—Zebulon seems to have had a disposition for business and commerce. It was to settle on the sea-shore, and stretch to Sidon.—Issachar is a powerful, but lazy, beast of burden. His dwelling suits his character. He hazards nothing. So that he can have peace, he is content with subjection.—Dan, on the other hand, has an independent adventurous spirit, which spurs him on to bold and crafty deeds.—Gad allows himself to be attacked, but boldly turns and defeats the enemy. In his district, on the east of Jordan, this tribe was more exposed than most to continual assaults.—Asher is delicate, and prepares kingly dainties.—Naphtali is a slim hind, with eloquent beautiful language.—But all there is of outward blessing and riches is heaped on Joseph's house. Fruitful and powerful, he spreads himself on all sides. No assault can fall on him. In the fulness of his possessions he surpasses his brethren; while in Benjamin is only to be seen a spirit of lawlessness and violence, which made this tribe dangerous, and brought upon it well-deserved humiliations. This "prophetic land-chart" of Canaan is very remarkable; for, although Jacob is guided by the character of his sons in the description which he gives of their future lot, by their past conduct, by what he had observed of their disposition, and according to the kindness he had received from them, yet the Spirit of prophecy gives a width of meaning to his words, and the result turned out very differently from what might have been expected. The punishment threatened to Levi is indeed fulfilled; but it proves a blessing and an advantage both for him and the people. Judah had done nothing for his father or his brethren which should exalt him so high above the rest. Those blessings which the dreams of his childhood might have led us to expect to be reserved for the "Nasir"—"separate one" among the brethren—do not turn out so. God's purposes go their hidden way. To Joseph is only outward blessing promised. And Benjamin, the youngest son of the beloved wife, at whose birth she died, appears only as a wild, powerful beast of prey. As God drove out the eldest son of the handmaiden, and did not suffer him, born after the flesh, to be heir with him who was born after the Spirit—as God, ere the children had done either good or evil, gave the preference to Jacob above his elder brother —as God placed Ephraim before Manasseh,—so, among Jacob's sons, is that one the inheritor of the promise of whose good deeds and qualities Holy Scripture is silent, and concerning whom it narrates almost only that which is to his disadvantage.

Ver. 3. *Excellency of power.*—Jacob lays great stress on the whole dignity which belonged to the first-born, in order to make Reuben feel more deeply the greatness of the sin which had occasioned the loss.

Ver. 4. *Unstable as water.*—Jacob's address, like all Hebrew prophecy, is bold and forcible, uttered in abrupt, highly picturesque words. Literally, the sentence is, " Bubbling over as water, thou canst not be the first." As water boils over, in like manner had Reuben's self-confidence and pride led him into crime.

He went up.—The father's loathing of the sin is forcibly represented in the mode of the expression. The speaker turns away from the guilty son, and, as it were, addresses a third person. Here, where the patriarch speaks more than ever in the stead of God, the enormity of a sin is marked, which, previously, Jacob or the narrative had but slightly touched on.—This, and the curse pronounced on Simeon which follows, are of very great importance as respects the right understanding, in general, of the whole mode of speaking of transactions in these books. We might often be inclined to ascribe to the writer indifference with regard to sins which are mentioned just casually, and without any expression of disapprobation. But it is here shown that all sin sooner or later meets with its punishment, though God may long and patiently bear with it; and the reader of these true descriptions of Holy Scripture is not to look for any judgment to be pronounced at the time on each crime which is mentioned.

Ver. 6. *Mine honour.*—So in solemn and poetical language the soul, as the nobler part of man, is often called: cf. Ps. xvi. 9, lvii. 8, cviii. 1.

Digged down a wall, lit., as in the margin, "houghed oxen," whereby the animals were rendered useless. This was customary in war. The conquerors often did this to captured horses which they could not convey away. By this image the cruel deed of these brothers (ch. xxxiv.) is forcibly represented.

Ver. 7. *Scatter them.*—A most remarkable prophecy, which

shows plainly that these words were really spoken by Jacob. In the time of Moses the tribe of Levi possessed the priesthood, and so had attained great privileges. No one living then would have placed this tribe in the same rank with Simeon, or have seen, in the circumstances of it, only a punishment. The blessing of Moses shows how another act of the tribe of Levi (expressing, indeed, something of the character of their progenitor, but sanctified by its pious zeal) changed the curse into a blessing (Deut. xxxiii. 9, 10; cf. Exod. xxxii. 20-29). Still the dispersion of the tribe of Levi among the others remained for its discipline, and served to remind it of this prophecy of Israel's. In many places Moses exhorts the people to remember their duties towards the Levites, who possessed no inheritance among them (Num. xviii. 20; Deut. xii. 19, ch. xiv. 27, ch. xviii. 6-8). There were times also when, through the spread of irreligion, the people would give nothing to the servants of the Lord; and, for the sake of hire, the Levites connected themselves with idol worship: Judges xviii. Simeon, like Levi, small in numbers (Num. xxvi. 14), had not a separate and distinct inheritance in Canaan. Its towns lay among the other tribes (Joshua xix. 1). In the blessing of Moses this tribe is not named with the others.

Ver. 8. *Judah.*—Judah signifies "the commended," "the praised."

Bow down.—Judah was already in the wilderness the leading tribe, and remained so a long time, even before the establishment of the kingdom (Num. ii. 3, ch. x. 14; Judges i. 2, ch. xx. 18).

Ver. 9. *Rouse him up.*—A continuance of the image of the lion. Literally, the passage is thus: "A young lion is Judah; from the prey, my son, art thou gone up: he kneels, he couches as a lion, and as a lioness, who shall rouse him up? Judah is a lion's whelp: he goes forth to the prey, he mounts up with his prey triumphantly to the mountain-den; there he couches as a lion, nay, like the still fiercer lioness, who shall venture to rouse him?" In the description the imagery increases in force, perhaps in reference to the continually increasing power of this tribe, which received its consummation in the greatest of all Victors, in the Lion of the tribe of Judah: Rev. v. 5.

Ver. 10. *Gathering of the people be.*—Lit.: "The staff shall not pass from Judah, nor the sceptre between his feet, until the

Peace come, and to Him shall be the obedience of the people." The words "staff" and "sceptre" mean the same. The first expresses a staff which was used for walking, striking, but afterwards more particularly as a mark of authority; the second word, "sceptre," is properly "lawgiver:" so the sign of the lawgiver or king was thus named. The long staff of office was "between the feet" when the prince on solemn occasions stands or sits. So long shall a ruler of the people come out of Judah until (Heb. "Scheloh") "the peace," or "the rest," come. This is the proper name, in poetical language, of a great descendant of Judah, who is named from the blessing which shall proceed from Him, as is evident from what follows: "And to Him shall be the obedience of the people."

In this remarkable prophecy of Jacob's, the blessing which was promised to descend from Abraham upon all nations (Gen. xii. 3) is more distinctly defined. Among Israel's descendants, it is the tribe of Judah from which the promise should receive its fulfilment. This victorious tribe, full of lionlike strength, shall maintain its pre-eminence above the rest until the Prince of Peace shall come, to whom, not only the other tribes, but all people, shall yield obedience. The triumph which all nations shall enjoy in Abraham and his seed is to consist in peace, which the mighty, victorious Leader shall give to them. The "Prince of Peace," as says Isaiah (ch. ix. 5), carrying out this image, shall erect a kingdom in which peace shall have no end—peace with God by means of reconciliation, peace on earth by the spirit of love which He shall pour out.—A literal and outward fulfilment of this prophecy in all its parts is not to be looked for—as the Christ must be born at the time when Herod the Idumæan obtained the kingdom—which would not agree with facts. Rather, Judah had the first rank after the time of the Judges in the House of David—then in the kingdom, since the temple was in the midst of it. Further, after the captivity, Judah was the first tribe to return home, and it gave the name to the whole people. So it maintained the first rank until the time of Christ, when in a yet higher measure it enjoyed the privileges hitherto possessed by it.

Ver. 12. *White with milk.*—Heb., "red (lit. dark) from wine—white from milk." The great abundance of wine and milk is depicted by the fact that Judah binds his ass to the vine, and washes even his clothes in the wine,—the eyes and teeth bear witness to the fulness and richness of both. The outward blessing points to the inexhaustible source of inward blessing which should proceed from him.

Ver. 13. *Haven of ships;* i.e., he shall dwell on a shore abounding in havens.

His border.—Lit.: "And his side leans to Sidon." He not merely borders on, but has close intercourse with, the Phœnician trading towns. Deut. xxxiii. 19 also alludes to the busy character of this tribe, which "sucks the abundance of the sea, and treasures hid in the sand,"—no doubt, by commercial dealings with the skilful and industrious people of antiquity, the Phœnicians, by whom at that time Sidon, but not yet Tyre, was built. Cf. ch. x. 15, note.

Ver. 15. *Unto tribute.*—Also Deut. xxx. 19, peace is predicted to this tribe. We here see that it will lead to mean and cowardly conduct.

Ver. 16. *Dan.*—Dan means "judge." A wild determined spirit of independence appears to have been the characteristic of this tribe. Hence that lawless act, the invasion of the Danites, Judges xviii.

Ver. 17. *Adder.*—The word translated "adder" means a horned snake, still frequently found in Egypt ("Cerost;" marg. Eng. Bib., "arrow-snake"). This snake is of the colour of sand, in which it lies on the road, and perceives by means of the horn-feelers the approach of the horseman. A sharp sting in the horse's hoof causes the animal to throw the rider. From this tribe was Samson.

Ver. 18. *Salvation.*—Jacob, as it were, takes breath. Full of the predictions of salvation which God had given him, and through him to his children, he longs earnestly after their fulfilment.

Ver. 19. *At the last.*—Lit.: "Gad, a troop presses him, and he presses the heels;" i.e., he suffers himself to be attacked, but afterwards collects his force and falls on the victor from behind. The name "Gad" resembles "Gedub," which means "a troop.' The tribe dwelt on the other side Jordan, between Reuben and Manasseh; and was disturbed by incursions of the Ammonites and Arabian bands: Judges x. 8, ch. xi. 4; 1 Chron. v. 18–23. Therefore Moses calls him, in his blessing, "the room-maker," enlarger, "who dwelleth as a lion, and teareth the arm with the crown of the head."

Ver. 20. *Shall be fat.*—The fat bread which he enjoys shall come also to others. This tribe inhabited a rich, fertile country at the foot of Mt. Carmel, and on the sea-coast.

Ver. 21. *Hind.*—Lit.: "A stretched-out hind;" *i.e*, at full gallop. The gazelle, the most beautiful animal of the East. Refinement and eloquence, or poetical gifts, appear to have belonged peculiarly to this tribe, though the narrative is silent on the subject.

Ver. 22. *By a well.*—"A son of a fruit-bough (Heb., 'Phorath' —a play on Ephraim) is Joseph, a son of a fruit-bough on a stream:" of a fruitful nature; and water shall never be wanting to it.

Ver. 23. *Shot at.*—Lit.: "The lords of arrows—*i.e.*, skilful archers—vex, and shoot at, and hate." An allusion to the early lot of Joseph, which was afterwards repeated in the history of the tribe of Ephraim: Judges xii.

Ver. 24. *Stone of Israel.*—Heb.: "From the hands of the mighty Jacob; from there where the Shepherd, the Stone (the Rock) of Israel, is,"—*i.e.*, from God. The name shepherd was often applied to God: cf. ch. xlviii. 15; cf. Ps. xxiii. 1, Ps. lxxx. 2. "Rock or stone of Israel" is also very frequent: Ps. xviii. 32; 1 Sam. ii. 2. God feeds Israel; He holds and bears him. Therefore Joseph's strength is ever refreshed and renewed from God's strength.

Ver 25. *Heaven above.*—Literally: "From the God of thy father, and He will help thee; from the Almighty, and He will bless thee." Thus these words are closely connected with what precedes and follows.

Blessings of the deep; i.e., abundance of water which springs from the earth.

Ver. 26. *Everlasting hills.*—By a correct punctuation (supported by Deut. xxxiii. 15), the passage is thus to be translated: "The blessings of thy father are mightier than the blessings of the mountains of eternity, than the loveliness of the hills of former times;" *i.e.*, the most ancient fruitful mountains on earth, with their loveliness ("everlasting," for very old; rich, those which are not now for the first time carefully cultivated), do not surpass the blessing which thy father bestows on thee.

Separate.—"Nasir;" *i.e.*, consecrated, separated, the prince among his brethren; which applies here, not to the tribe, but to the person of Joseph. The tribes of Ephraim and Manasseh were the richest in vines, fruit, and pastures.

Ver. 27. *Divide the spoil.*—The comparison of Benjamin to a ravening wolf, alludes to the warlike and wild character of this small tribe. In the time of the Judges it was brought very near utter extermination (Judges iii. 15, ch. xx. 14).

Ver. 29. *Charged them.*—On another occasion—soon afterwards.

Ver. 32. *Children of Heth.*—In the cave, which has been rightfully obtained, wherein already so many of our family are buried. The purchase of the cave and the conduct of Abraham was an act of faith in the future possession of the land of Canaan by his descendants: cf. ch. xxiii., introd. Hence the strong desire of Jacob on the subject.

Ver. 33. *Gathered up his feet.*—He saw death approaching, laid himself out to meet it, and gently expired.

CHAPTER L.

Ver. 3. *Threescore and ten days.*—The funeral of Jacob, as the father of the first man in the kingdom next to the king, is performed in a very magnificent manner, after the Egyptian fashion. A part of this was the embalming of the corpse. In much later times, when the mode of doing it was probably much more elaborate, Herodotus describes it in the following manner:—
"There are certain persons appointed for the purpose, who profess this art. They ask in which of the three ways (differing in price) the relations wish to have the dead person buried. The most costly manner of embalming is this. They first extract the brain through the nostrils by means of a crooked piece of iron, and pour in spices. They then make an incision in the loins with a sharp Ethiopian stone, and take out the contents of the belly; and, after cleansing the cavity, and rinsing it with palm wine, fill it with pounded aromatics. After they have filled the belly with pure myrrh, cinnamon, and other spices, with the

exception of frankincense, they sew it up again. They then lay the body in alkali, keeping it covered for seventy days; for it is not lawful to keep the body embalming for a longer time. After this they wash the corpse, and then wrap up the whole body in bandages cut out of byssus (fine cotton), and smear it with gum. The relations then receive it back again; make a wooden chest in the shape of a man, close it, and put it upright against the wall, in the vault of the dead."—Herod. B. ii. 86. The reason of this custom was the ancient belief of the Egyptians, that the soul of man was something immortal and independent, which dwelt in the body as its house, and remained about it as long as it was preserved, but then passed in a cycle through a certain number of animals. Besides this, there was a great respect paid by the Egyptians to their ancestors; and it was a custom to bring forth these mummies on the occasion of family festivals. They thus lived, as it were, among their deceased relations— became acquainted with their features and stature. Without partaking in the superstition, Joseph might yet use for his father's body this form of sepulture, which was the most perfect kind in the eyes of the ancients. Joseph caused his servants, his physicians, to undertake this business. In Egypt, as Herod tells us, there was a particular physician for every disease. This, again, was connected with their religious views of the importance of every part of the body. The mourning for a king at a later period continued for seventy-two days.

Ver. 4. *House of Pharaoh.*—Because, in the time of mourning, when his beard was untrimmed and his person disfigured, he could not speak to the king.

Ver. 10. *Seven days.*—In no country did such long and extravagant customs of mourning prevail as in Egypt. "When a member of a family held in consideration dies, all the women cover their heads and faces with mud. Then leaving the corpse at home, they go about the town with their clothes girt up, and beat themselves, laying bare their breasts: on the other side, the men strike themselves, girding up their garments like the women."—Herod. ii. 85. In the mourning for a king, still more extraordinary customs took place—public mourning songs by hundreds of people, general fasting, etc.

Ver. 11. *Abel-mizraim*—the "plain of the Egyptians." In Hebrew, "mourning" is "Ebel," and a "plain" "Abel." From this circumstance a plain lying there received the name of "the Egyptian;" while the resemblance of sound contained an allusion to the mourning held there. This sort of play of words is not unusual in this book in the case of names. This place lay on the other side Jordan, as the Egyptians did not take the direct road (perhaps on account of the difficulty of passing through the intervening land of the Philistines), but passed round Mt. Seir, and halted in the land of Moab. From thence the sons of Israel went alone into the land of the Hittites—probably for a similar reason, not to be detained by the Canaanites.

Ver. 17. *Of thy father.*—The father, as the highest judge in the family, in weighing the doings of his sons before his death, makes this request for forgiveness. Jacob, however, could only ask, as Joseph had the power in his own hands. The last words of the brothers may well be supposed to mean: "As our father has spoken in the name of God, and we in common honour this one God, so do you regard this expression of his wish as the will of God."

Ver. 19. *In the place of God.*—God had shown His forgiveness by turning their evil deeds to the good of all. This is a sign to Joseph, and he could not therefore dare to take revenge for them.

Ver. 20. *Much people alive.*—The revelation of the most wonderful and gracious mystery of the Divine love and might, which no man could frustrate, nay, the changing of evil into good and blessing, was a thought which seems to have filled the mind of Joseph with admiration all his life through. His brothers do not appear capable of understanding his character, which was far above all thoughts of vengeance.

Ver. 21. *Kindly to them.*—Lit.: "He spake to their hearts;" so that his words dropped like balsam on their wounds. A beautiful descriptive expression often occurring.

Ver. 27. *In a coffin in Egypt.*—As the bodies of Egyptian kings are still to be found in wooden chests.—This first book of Moses concludes with an act of faith on the part of the dying Joseph, which connects it with the second, and points to the fulfilment of the promises which now follows.

THE SECOND BOOK OF MOSES,

CALLED EXODUS (MARCHING OUT).

CHAPTER I.

I. The number of the children of Israel. II. The oppression of them. III. The command of the king to slay all the male children.

In the rich and fruitful land of Egypt, and especially in that lovely part of it, the country of Goshen, had the descendants of Israel become a great, powerful people, amounting to more than two million souls. We here behold the first instance of that remarkable phenomenon, which afterwards is often presented to our view,—that God's covenanted people are placed beside and in the midst of the most cultivated and powerful nations of antiquity in order to enjoy the advantages of their worldly civilisation; at the same time, by their marked severance from the idolatry of these nations, and by their permanence (while one people after another beside them decayed and passed away), to bear witness to their own Divine origin. Egypt is that ancient kingdom which has erected monuments of its grandeur surpassing those of any early state, which still remain, and astonish us by the magnificence of their design and by the degree of cultivation displayed in them. The very nature of the country itself is most peculiar. From two great streams, one of which rises in Abyssinia, the other in the S.W. of Ethiopia, is formed the very remarkable, broad river of the Nile, from which the land derives its very existence. It receives only one great accession of water in Nubia, and thence pursues its solitary course of above 800 miles through vast arid deserts, where it scarcely ever rains. And yet, though itself alone passes through this ocean of sand, is it able by its overflowings to make the valley and the region of its passage the most productive land in the world. Here had settled, long before Abraham's time (perhaps among the original dwellers—herdsmen or fishermen), a distinguished Canaanitish people. A priestly caste (with a military caste under it) brought into subjection, by means of intellectual superiority, the rude aborigines. By means of its observance of the regular recurrence of heavenly and natural phenomena, and a more suitable arrangement of times and seasons, in respect to matters of common life, which resulted from this; by the use of rude figures of beasts and plants, which the fishermen of the Nile worshipped; and likewise by an artful employment of the sensual propensities of a gross people,—were they enabled to establish a religious and political constitution which endured and flourished for many centuries. On the vast monuments of the "hundred-gated" Thebes, and other places, have the whole mode of life and history of this people been represented in the language of hieroglyphics. And in our days, after the key had been discovered more than forty years, have these ancient inscriptions been gradually and painfully deciphered, to the great gain of our interpretation of Scripture. And now, as if out of the darkness of the grave of those early times, an ancient history rises afresh to the light of day. From these sources are we now able to perceive how cultivated, how industrious, how acquainted with the arts and sciences, was that people among whom the Israelites sojourned for more than 400 years. We are no longer astonished at the ingenuity displayed in the building of the Tabernacle, at the wealth in gold and silver and precious stones, at the frequent use of the art of writing, which the four last books of Moses mention. But as we become better acquainted with the worship of Nature, which was so deeply rooted, so highly perfected, and so interwoven in all the relations of life among the Egyptians, our astonishment is heightened at the near approach to, nay, the imitation of the model; yet, at the same time, the clearly marked line of separation which distinguished all the religious and political institutions of the Israelites from those of the Egyptians.

We may conclude from the words of Joseph (Gen. xlvi. 31, 32) that the Israelites pursued in Egypt—in the pasture lands of Goshen, on the borders of the wilderness—that patriarchal, pastoral mode of life which their fathers had done in Canaan. But we are expressly told that they likewise followed field tillage and gardening (cf. xlv. 10, note). They sowed and watered after the manner of the Egyptians (Deut. xi. 10, 11). They cultivated cucumbers, melons, leeks, onions (Num. xi. 5). There were "cunning" artificers among them, who could work in cutting precious stones, in gold and in silver (Exod. xxxv. 32, 33). They learned the arts of weaving, spinning, the preparation of leather, from the people, the most celebrated in the ancient world as the inventors of such arts. They made the bricks for the fortresses, Pithom and Rameses. They dwelt in the greatest cities of a rich nation, in the royal metropolis (ch. ii.), and even a great many of them in the same houses with the Egyptians (Exod. xi. 2). Even when living among the dominant people, they were governed by the heads of their own tribes, who had gradually sprung up from out of the original family government of the patriarchs. Moreover, we find scribes (Schoterim) mentioned (translated "officers"). These had the superintendence of the people at these works, and in the wilderness performed duties which, in after times, more especially devolved on the Levites.—Divided into separate families, the Israelites had no public place or mode of worship. It is true, indeed, that the traditions of the promises made to their fathers, and the hope of the future possession of Canaan, still survived among them; and this was doubtless the reason why the king who "knew not Joseph" was under apprehension lest they should leave the country and join themselves to the enemies of Egypt; but the Egyptian mode of thinking and living had, nevertheless, exercised a very powerful influence over them. Ezekiel describes, in general terms, their propensity to Egyptian idolatry in this time (ch xxiii., ch. xx. 7, 8), the last remains of which Joshua afterwards was obliged to eradicate (Joshua xxiv. 14). But especially do we find that in the wilderness they desired to worship the God who had saved them, after the Egyptian fashion in the form of a calf. And even after the extinction of open idolatry they secretly practised the worship of the sun and the stars, and the still more abominable Egyptian goat-worship

(Amos v. 25, 26; Lev. xvii. 7). The mind of the people was debased during the time of their degrading bondage,—so much so, that they esteemed the freedom and independence under God's guidance in the wilderness, too dearly purchased by the sacrifice of the comforts which the life in Egypt afforded them. They had become a servile, effeminate people, impatient of control, and fickle. They held in the greatest contempt that which ought to have been their peculiar privilege above all other people. Of all men they seemed the most unfit to carry out the Divine purposes of mercy concerning them (Deut. ix. 4, etc.). Such was the condition of the people which the Lord—for His promise's sake made to their fathers, and for the sake of the blessing which through them should descend on all the nations of the earth—redeemed out of Egypt with a mighty hand. Since holy Scripture only narrates the Divine acts for the preservation and blessing of His people, we are told merely those circumstances which happened to the Israelites so far as they were the immediate occasion of their freedom. There is, therefore, no gap in the history, but just a brief review of what took place from the time of Joseph to that of Moses.

Ver. 4. *Asher.*—In this enumeration the sons of Jacob's two wives are first named, and then those of the two maid-servants, in the order in which they were born.

Ver. 5. *Seventy.*—A round number, since, in order to make up literally the full sum named, we must reckon Joseph and his two sons among them.

Ver. 8. *New king.*—It has been supposed, not without reason, that the new king belonged to another dynasty, as many such ruled over the Egyptians and oppressed the people. Perhaps the Egyptian monuments will, on further inquiry, afford some additional light on the subject. (It is supposed that the dynasty of Hyksos, or shepherd kings, were rulers of Egypt when Joseph and his brethren settled there. This dynasty was expelled, and held in particular detestation by the Egyptians.)

Ver. 10. *Get them up.*—Literally, "mount up from the land," out of the lower Egypt to the higher country of Canaan. The hope of the Israelites, that they should some day possess the Promised Land, was so rife among them, that even the Egyptians were aware of it. The king feared the too great increase of the Israelites, but nevertheless was unwilling to lose them as subjects. And so afterwards, in his bloody command to kill the male children, he was still desirous of keeping the females as slaves in his land. Had any perceptible decrease of their numbers taken place, he would have put a stop to the murder of the male children. A considerable number of foreign labourers was most needful for the completion of the vast temples, palaces, and canals in which almost all the Egyptian kings were engaged. On one of the temples which the great conqueror, King Sesostris or Rameses, caused to be built, the inscription was placed, " No native hath laboured on this."

Ver. 11. *Burdens.*—A measure adopted by tyrants of ancient and modern times, especially in the East, and even now in practice in Egypt, in order to keep down all attempt at insurrection among the people.

Treasure-cities.—In the west of the most western, the Pelusian branch of the Nile, where anciently the city Bubastes stood, a valley (viz., the Wady Tumleat) intersects the Arabian chain of mountains which runs along the right bank of the Nile from south to north. Here was the canal which, in ancient times, connected the Nile with the Gulf of Suez. In this valley (probably the most southern part of the land of Goshen) were situated the two cities, Pithom, Pathumos, and to the west, Rameses, near the Greek city Heröonpolis. Now the places Abassich and Abu-Keischeid stand on their ruins: the first on those of Pithom, the latter on those of Rameses. This was the most accessible point from which Egypt could be attacked on the side of Arabia, and therefore these frontier fortresses were built there. They were intended at the same time to serve for "treasure-houses," *i.e.*, magazines and war store-houses. The principal places of the military caste were in this region, as we learn from other accounts.

Ver. 12. *Multiplied.*—Even under oppression did the Church of God in the old covenant increase and thrive.

Ver. 14. *Brick.*—A great many of the still existing Egyptian edifices are built of brick, or so-called " air-stones," *i. e.*, baked in the open air. They were made of a white chalky kind of earth, mixed with straw, and hardened in the sun, but not burnt.— Lately there has been found in the environs of the ancient capital city Thebes, in the tomb of a royal architect, a very early and remarkable painting. On it are represented workmen carrying clay in vessels, while others are shaping it with hatchets—others drawing the bricks out of the moulds—others laying them out in rows, while a great many are employed in carrying them away after they have been dried. The workmen are not Egyptians; but in complexion and dress are represented like all the foreigners from Upper Asia. In feature they resemble the Jews of the present time. It would seem as though in this painting we possessed a representation of the subject of the history before us.

Field.—Egypt was a most productive country; but, at the same time, one which required laborious care in cultivation, since its rich harvest was bestowed only in return for vast irrigation by means of canals, ducts, and other appliances for supplying water. Therefore, even up to the present time, when the magnificent works of antiquity are for the most part fallen into decay, troops of men are from time to time pressed into this kind of service. Since in Egypt the fields are not worked as with us, but the seed sown as soon as the ground is inundated, in this irrigation consists the hardest labour. In many places vast watering machines are drawn by horses and oxen; in smaller places, wound by men, or the buckets carried by them.

Ver. 15. *Puah.*—The two chief among them, through whom his command was to be communicated to the others. In a country so regulated according to caste, even in the most trifling particulars, this office had its heads, who were responsible for the others.

Ver. 16. *Stools;* or "stone vessel," in which the new-born child was received at the birth. (This by some is supposed to be the meaning of the Hebrew word, which only again occurs, Jer. xviii. 4; the Sept. merely has "when they are in labour.")

Ver. 19. *Lively.*—Or, perhaps, in the Heb., "they are beasts;" *i.e.*, as the animals, which bring forth without the help of midwives. Possibly this was not entirely a pretence. At this day there is the greatest difference in this respect between the Arabians of the desert and those who live in towns. Thus the greater part of the Israelites was employed in pastoral, garden, or field labours, and only a very small portion in sedentary occupations, which the Egyptians especially pursued.

Delivered.—The whole transaction was a secret one. Pharaoh did not dare at first to make known this command, unexampled as it was in cruelty, either because he feared an insurrection, or out of shame. For this reason he did not inflict any punishment on the midwives, as they feared God more than the king, though their faith was too weak openly to declare what they had done without any falsehood.

Ver. 21. *Houses;* *i.e.*, He gave them a numerous and blessed posterity. As they preserved the people and promoted their increase, therefore God blessed them in the preservation and increase of their families.

Ver. 22. *Save alive.*—The savage cruelty of the king increases. What at the first he had commanded and thought to execute in secrecy, he now publishes abroad. A sore trial of the faith of the Israelites, to find that the fear of God which actuated the midwives, and the blessing which accompanied this fresh increase of the people, only served to bring upon them additional persecution. But they were yet to wait a long while for deliverance, and to experience a degree of oppressive servitude more severe than any heretofore, before they were released.—But in the whole of this history, as in so many in the O. T., sin and its punishment are shown to us in a close relation to each other. As the children of the Israelites were thrown into the water, so do we find that the Egyptians themselves perish in the water. "All these plans of Pharaoh are destined to come to nought. Persecution and death cannot damage the Church of God. The Christian is not weakened thereby; but the Church ever increases under the Cross, under the tyranny of the world and of the Devil: as an old doctor of the Church, Tertullian, hath said, 'The Church is watered by the blood of Christians.'"—Luther.

CHAPTER II.

Ver. 1. *Daughter of Levi.*—Their names, see ch. vi. 20.

Ver. 3. *Ark.*—A small boat of the papyrus plant. Larger vessels made from this wood were also common on the Nile at that time.

Pitch.—Bitumen, asphalt, as Gen. xiv. 10, note.

Ver. 6. *Hebrews.*—She knew this from the fact of his exposure.

Ver. 7. *Hebrew women.*—Because an Egyptian nurse would have neglected or betrayed it.

Ver. 8. *Mother.*—So, by a merciful arrangement of God's providence, the mother received her child back again, and kept it with her until its third year, when children were wont to be weaned.

Ver. 10. *Moses.*—The name "Moscheh" is originally Egyptian, as Pharaoh's daughter could only give it a name in that language. Probably it was pronounced Mo-udsche—one saved out of the water; and so the old Greek translators, who lived in Egypt, always write it Moyses. The Israelites afterwards formed out of this Egyptian word "Moscheh," which signifies in Hebrew "a leader out." Probably the early translation of this name into the Hebrew meaning, might contribute to inspire Moses with the thought of liberating his people.

Ver. 11. *Burdens.*—Moses did this "through faith," Heb. xi. 24. He despised that which was visible, and held fast to the grace promised to his people. But right as was this beginning, yet must his faith be purified. God dwelleth with those alone who are of a broken heart. This energetic, highly-endowed man must be bowed down; his heart must become accustomed to quiet, to patience, to implicit obedience to the will of the Lord. It is the strength of the grey-headed old man, now broken, and no longer resisting God's purpose—no longer occupied with the thought of his first attempt—which can become the instrument in the hand of the Lord for the salvation of His people. According to Acts vii. 22, Moses was learned in all the wisdom of the Egyptians; which could not be otherwise with one brought up in the court of the king (the Egyptian kings belonged to the priest caste), and which, indeed, the law given by God through him attests. All the other circumstances which are narrated concerning his early life elsewhere than in Scripture,—such as, by Josephus, that he was a successful general in a war against the Ethiopians,—rest on uncertain tradition, which sought to exalt the man of God after human notions of greatness.

Smiting.—In the Hebrew the same word stands as in the following verse with respect to the Egyptian. He smote the Hebrew with purpose to kill him. The Egyptians, after the last command of Pharaoh, thought themselves at liberty to do anything they pleased against the Israelites.

Ver. 12. *In the sand.*—" He hid him in the sand," for he was in the land of Goshen on the borders of the desert.—In passing judgment on this act, we must consider that it was no murder, but a manslaughter, which by the law was leniently regarded, and permission given in such a case for the slayer to flee to the cities of refuge (Lev. xxxv. 9, etc.). The conduct of Moses may well receive some justification from the circumstances of the case, and it belongs to those actions which the world's history praises as noble; but, in the judgment of God's Word, it is a self-willed intrusion on the rights of Him to whom " vengeance belongeth" (Deut. xxxii. 35), and who on earth hath appointed His delegates, the magistrates, to execute it. St Matt. xxvi. 52. It therefore receives chastisement, and that at once. Augustine's words on this act are admirable (contra Faustum 22, 70): " If I weigh the eternal law of God, I find that he who did not possess judicial authority ought not to have slain this man, though a wrongdoer and a sinner. But noble souls, who are capable of great virtues, often commit first great mistakes, showing thereby to what a degree of virtue they are designed, after the soil has been cultivated through God's laws. So does the husbandman, when he sees a field produce an immense crop of weeds, conclude that, though this must be rooted up, still the land is well fitted for the growth of corn. Thus did the Lord call Saul from heaven while persecuting His Church: cast him down—raise him up—fill him with His Spirit—tear him up—prune—transplant—make fruitful. Thus did the Lord rebuke Peter when he drew his sword and cut off the ear of His persecutor, because he shed blood without lawful authority. And yet He makes him the chief pastor of His Church." The Jewish tradition viewed this history in a similar way, which Mohammed followed, who, in the Koran, narrates it with the following addition:—" But thereupon, after he had come to himself, he made the confession, This which I have done is a work of the devil, who plainly tempts to sin; and he prayed, O Lord, I have done a wrong against my own soul, yet do Thou forgive me. So God forgave him—the God who is so willing to forgive sin."

Ver. 15. *Midian.*—On the peninsula of Mount Sinai, between the two gulfs of the Red Sea—probably on the western coast of the Gulf of Akaba. The Midianites were descendants of Abraham (Gen. xxv. 2), and therefore, probably, servants of the true God.

Ver. 16. *Priest.*—A priest of the true God; see verse above. In verse 18 the father is called Reuel; ch. iii. 1, Moses' father-in-law and the priest of Midian is called Jethro; Num. x. 29, Hobab. It is clear from the last-mentioned place that Reuel was Hobab's father. The names Jethro and Hobab are synonymous (the precious, the beloved), and represent the same person. Accordingly, Reuel, here called "father," was the grandfather, and probably the hereditary office of the priesthood was exercised by Jethro in conjunction with his father; or, perhaps, before the events mentioned, ch. iii., Reuel was dead, and Jethro, his son, had succeeded to his office.

Ver. 22. *Strange land.*—Sign. "expulsion." Moses' explanation is to be regarded as a kind of play on the sound of the word, "a stranger" (Ger) there (scham). Moses had fled in the direction of Canaan, and had taken refuge with a people descended from Abraham. He there gave witness by this name that he still held fast to the promises made to the fathers.—In the old Latin Version the words from ch. xviii. 4 are added, "And she bare yet a son, whom he called Eliezer, and said, The God of my father is my Helper, and hath saved me from the hand of Pharaoh." "Eliezer" sign. "God is help." This name, even more than the former one, has a reference to his hope and belief. It is remarkable how, with the utter destruction of all prospects, still his calm trust on God as the God of his father, *i.e.* Abraham, increases.

Ver. 23. *Died.*—Viz., the same from whom Moses had fled. Whether this was the father of Moses' foster-mother (in which case he must have reigned more than 60 years) cannot be known with certainty. The Pharaoh who succeeds acts just in the same way as the one first mentioned in this book. Indeed the position of the king (as of the whole people) had become, quite independently of the person who occupied the throne, one of decided hostility towards the Israelites.

Ver. 23. *Cry.*—Their cry of anguish, the dire necessity of His chosen people, reached Him and moved His compassion.

Ver. 24. *Jacob.*—Cf. Gen. viii. 1, note.

CHAPTER III.

Ver. 1. *Kept.*—Heb.: "Was a shepherd of the sheep;" *i.e.*, this was his regular calling. He served for Zipporah as Jacob had done with Laban. Here, in this calm shepherd's life, did Moses become disciplined, and freed from that sinful impatience and ungodly impetuosity which had been displayed in his former life.

Horeb.—Midian lay on the western coast of the Gulf Akaba, so Horeb was two days' journey distant from thence. A wide tract of country for a shepherd.

Ver. 2. *Angel.*—The "Angel of the Lord" appears to him; but afterwards it is God who speaks to him. Cf. Gen. xvi. 7, note.

Bush; *i.e.*, he saw no form, but afterwards heard a voice, which came to his ears out of the bush.

Consumed.—The fire which lights up but does not consume points, on the one hand, to the tribulations which then visited the people of Israel; on the other hand, light and fire are constant emblems of the Divine glory. The figures combined represent, that the affliction is sent from God; that by means of it God will reveal Himself to His people, but not consume them. The emblem of the Scottish Church is a burning bush, with the words, "nec tamen consumebatur," "and yet was not consumed."

Ver. 5. *Holy ground.*—Moses, who had not as yet been visited with any Divine vision, is taught by the voice the needful religious reverence from which alone can result that calmness, that obedient spirit of willingness to hear God's words, which are required in order to become a receiver of a Divine revelation. The place is marked by God as "holy ground," as the mountain is called above (ver. 1) a mount of God, because it is destined soon to become the place of His greatest revelations: ver. 12. Horeb and Sinai form one range of mountains. In the presence of kings the dust-soiled shoes must be laid aside, and also, probably, among the Egyptians during sacrifice. With such marks of reverence is Moses to approach the great sight.

Ver. 6. *Father.*—Abraham is here to be understood as Moses' father; and thus the following words explain the foregoing, since the "God of Abraham" is the God of his covenant. It is said, not "of thy fathers," because not only are Isaac and Jacob, as his descendants, included in him, but also God's covenant with them in the covenant with Abraham. Isaac and Jacob are named in order to show that the covenanted relationship which began with Abraham, was a continuous and eternal one. In what manner, from the words, "the God of Abraham, Isaac, and Jacob," Christ deduces their personal immortality, see St Matt. xxii. 32, note.

Afraid.—Cf. Gen. xvi. 13, note.

Ver. 8. *Milk and honey.*—The land which God promises to them is here called a "good"—*i.e.*, rich, fertile—and a "large" land, in contrast to the narrow, over-peopled valley of the Nile. The fruitfulness is more closely designated by the abundance of milk and honey, which products betoken a land *naturally* productive, in contrast with the *artificial* fertility of Egypt: so ch. xiii. 5 (cf. the glorious description with which Joel draws out these words, ch. ii. 23). Still more completely is the fertility of Canaan described, Deut. viii. 7–9; and its advantages over Egypt—Deut. xi. 10, 11—are represented as consisting in this, that the cultivation is not nearly so laborious, by reason of the abundance of rain. With this description agrees that (among others) given by the Roman historian Tacitus, who says, Hist. v. 6: "The land is fruitful; there is an abundance of the same produce which grows with us, and, in addition, the balsam and date trees" (cf. Gen. xliii. 11, note). The present barrenness of the land is in a great measure the fault of its inhabitants—the Turks and Arabs—whose lot it has been, wherever they settled, to turn the most fruitful countries into deserts (cf. Gen. xi. 1, ch. xlv. 10, note). On the high grounds, in many districts, are still visible the marks of the former rich cultivation. If we add to what is here said the description in Deut. viii. 7, where it is expressly declared to be "a land of brooks and fountains, and depths that spring out of valleys and hills," and listen to the concurrent testimony of modern travellers, who describe the present country of Palestine as especially deficient in brooks and streams, we must perceive in this change, surely, the fulfilment of the oft-threatened prophetic curse; *e. g.*, Deut. xxviii. 23, 24. The instruments of the fulfilment of this have been—great natural changes, the destruction of many forests on the hills, and the barbarian settlers in the country.

Jebusites.—The most distinguished people who are mentioned, Gen. x. 15–17, as descendants of Canaan. For the Perizzites, who do not there appear, see Gen. xiii. 7, note.

Ver. 12. *Mountain.*—The commission which Moses received was this: to lead the children of Israel out of Egypt to Canaan. But as the delivery of the law on Sinai lay in the midst of it, this event was to be the greatest confirmation of his Divine mission. In leading the people to Sinai, Moses fulfilled a part, but very far from the greatest or most difficult part, of his mission. The 40 years in the wilderness were far more trying—put his faith, his endurance, his patience far more to the test—than the delivering the people out of Egypt. In this the natural disposition of Moses, his spirit of enterprise, and love of freedom, were able to find greater scope. Therefore "the sign" which God promised to him was designed to impress the seal on this portion of his life, in order to prepare and fortify him for the times of severer trial.

Ver. 13. *What shall I say?*—The heathen nations were accustomed to names for their gods. On the invention of these, and the communication of them to other people, as we learn from the Greeks, the Egyptians particularly prided themselves. The desire for a name for God contained, however, this truth, that in the name the personal, self-cognisant God reveals Himself in a distinct, actual, covenanted relationship to men. At least God gave the direction in very early times to this wish. And here, especially, where God did not indeed reveal anything afresh, but rather commenced a new order of revelations, it was very natural to inquire in what name He might reveal Himself; *i.e.*, in what relationship to man His Divine nature would now make itself known.

Ver. 14. *I am.*—This is the wonderful expression in which the name "Jehovah," or properly "Jahveh," is declared. "I shall be" means also "I am," since the future tense with names in Hebrew signifies the perpetual continuance of that which the name betokens. Thus "Jacob" properly means, "he will seize the heel;" *i.e.*, he continually lies in wait. Craft is his characteristic. "Israel," properly, "he will overcome God;" *i.e.*, he overcomes Him continually: in this lies the essence of his new man.

And here, where God explains the name, He says, "I am that I am," which He afterwards more briefly expresses by "I am." This word in Hebrew is "Ehjeh;" in the old language, "Ehveh." Thus God speaks of Himself in the first person. But when God is spoken of by others, or when He speaks of Himself, as of the already known and revealed, He says, "I am Jehovah," I am Jahveh; *i.e.*, "I am He is,"—I am He who is known unto you under the name "He is." "This name signifies 'He is existent' —that He claims exclusively the glory of the Godhead, because He is self-existent, and therefore eternal, and He alone affords its being to the creature. The single existence and being of God includes in itself all that we can imagine of things that exist; and He possesses, at the same time, the supreme power through which He rules all. In order that we may rightly understand the true God, it is necessary before all things to know that everything in heaven and on earth has its being derived from Him who alone exists. From His being proceed the power and the might. He who upholds all by His might, governs all according to His will. What would it have benefited Moses to speculate on the hidden mysterious being of God, as contained in heaven, unless he had, out of His almighty power, made Himself to be the shield of his faith? God therefore declares that to Him belongs the all-holy Name, which was profaned by being given to others; and He magnifies His boundless might, that Moses may not doubt his ability to overcome under His guidance."—Calvin. "With these words God exalts Himself above all creatures who are not God, and cannot give eternal life, since there is none who 'worketh evermore' but God alone. He says, 'I am He.' That can none else say, since all else perishes. All our life is a passing uncertain possession. I can rightly say, I pass away, but not, I am existent—I fade or change not. With this claim does God draw off our hearts and eyes from all creatures, and fix them on Himself. I only possess existence; he who leans on others passes away."—Luther. We may add the remark, that the sense of this name is not exactly that of the word with which the heathen wise men designated the Godhead: "that which is"— *i.e.*, the existent. In Holy Scripture the Godhead is the *personal* Self-existent, the only living Being, the Almighty Will; therefore the unchangeable, true, and real God of Covenant, Who is called by this exalted name. So the gods of the heathen are called, by way of contrast with Him, "Nothings," as the creations of man when he has fallen away from his Creator: cf. 1 Cor. x. 19, 20.

Ver. 15. *Jacob.*—These latter words are the further explanation and definition of the name of God. The God of their fathers is proved by this new revelation to be the Eternal, Unchangeable One, who was, and is, and is to come.

Ver. 15. *Generations.*—In the N. T. He is called "God the Father of our Lord Jesus Christ," in which name is comprehended, likewise, that of the God of covenant of the O T., since in Him, *i.e.*, in Christ, are all the promises fulfilled which were made to Abraham, Isaac, and Jacob.

Ver. 16. *Visited; i.e.,* I have exercised a special oversight with regard to them: I have interested Myself peculiarly in their state. The same word is used for visiting, for blessing, and for punishing. This visiting is the open interference of the Divine acts in the fate of men.

Ver. 17. *Flowing.*—God, as the Possessor of the whole earth, bestows on the Israelites in Egypt the land which was promised to their forefathers. This, as is afterwards repeatedly declared, rendered necessary an open invasion—a war of extermination on the part of the Israelites against the Canaanitish nations. This war, by means of which they took the land in possession, did not rest on their claim to the pasture lands once possessed by their forefathers, which the Canaanites might have refused them, nor on the offer of submission which might have preceded extermination; but rather, the ground for the destruction of these Canaanites is in many places alleged to be their utter moral depravity, which brought down God's wrath and punishment on them, as once it had done on Sodom; and of this punishment the Israelites were the instruments (cf. Gen. xv. 16; Lev. xviii. 24–28; Deut. ix. 4). Therefore that which Israel did to them is called a destruction—a hallowing of God in them through their overthrow. The consideration of the extinction of this people was calculated to fill the Israelites with a holy dread of God's righteous judgments,—and still more ourselves, when we reflect that He did not spare His own people or Temple, when "the abomination of desolation" stood in the Holy Place.

Ver. 18. *Hearken; i.e.,* As soon as they hear thy voice, this matter shall not be left in doubt.

Met.—Heb.: "Is called over us;" *i.e.*, we are called after His name—are His people. We owe Him service therefore, lest He punish us; so ch. v. 3.

Sacrifice.—It is perhaps surprising to us, that, as God purposed from the beginning to bring the people of Israel out of Egypt, He should have commissioned Moses to ask that which was not His real object. But this request was the smallest and the most reasonable that could be demanded from Pharaoh. The Israelites could not serve their God in the midst of the heathen Egyptians; and so, in order to remain God's people, they needed the permission to make a feast to Him free from the influence of idolatrous practices. No doubt the king had reason for dread, lest the people would thereby be roused to a feeling of independence and freedom, and might thus become dangerous to him. On the other hand, the Israelites were not lawfully his bondmen, and owed him no service which was incompatible with this demand. By refusing this trifling petition, and thereby intimating that he designed to perpetuate their servitude among a heathen people, he justly fell under the Divine judgment. Thus we see God fulfil His counsel, that all who fall under His correction shall be without excuse. He designed from the first to lead out the people of Israel, but He would not put any force on Pharaoh's will. His unrighteous tyranny in refusing a just demand must first be brought to light, ere God would show in him His might.

Ver. 19. *Hand;* *i.e.*, not even after the manifestation of the wonders of My power. Pharaoh did, indeed, after the last and most terrible of the ten plagues, let the people go; but he immediately retracted his permission. This does not therefore contradict what follows, because Pharaoh's resolution and declaration are counter one to the other.

Ver. 22. *Spoil.*—This command is not to be explained by supposing, either that God, as the Lord of all things, can take away, and give, as He chooses to every one; or, that He can suspend when He will His own command, "Thou shalt not steal;" or, that the Israelites looked on themselves as in a state of war, and so might lawfully take booty; or, that the Israelites, at first, only borrowed, and then, when the Egyptians followed and attacked them in a hostile manner, retained as their own that which they had borrowed. All these explanations are not worthy of the character of the Holy and Unchangeable God, as revealed to us in Scripture. In the first place, it is well to observe, that neither here, nor ch. xi. 2, ch. xii. 35, is it said that the Israelites had "*borrowed*" the vessels; nor ch. xii. 36, that the Egyptians had "*lent*" them; but the former had *demanded*, the latter had *yielded* to the demand: when the transaction took place, the journey out was determined on, and even desired by the Egyptians, and there was no thought on either side of "giving back." Moreover, this "spoiling" has not the signification of "stealing"—secretly taking away,—but that of openly and forcibly taking possession of anything. The significance of the Divine command, and of the conduct of the Israelites, is rather this: Egypt and Pharaoh had sinned, in manifold ways, by robbery and tyranny against Israel—they deny the people independence, and liberty to worship their God: their God takes the part of His first-born son, and smites, after many other signs, the first-born in the whole of Egypt. The heathen king and people are humbled, and lose courage; they entreat Israel to be gone, and drive them forth; and the Egyptians give them all they can in order to appease them. Thus it comes to pass, that without violation of right, the powerless, oppressed, poor people spoil their tyrants, and depart laden with their treasures.—In this history is typically represented to us the condition of the Church of the Lord among the people of the earth at all times. The people of God are really free, and called to serve their Lord. For a while the Lord allows them to suffer oppression, under which they sigh; but at last He leads them forth from their captivity, inflicting heavy punishment on their oppressors, and with the spoil taken from their enemies may they now glorify their Lord. Hence the intellectual culture which the Christian Church learnt from heathen antiquity was rightly called by the fathers of the Church, "The spoils of Egypt."

CHAPTER IV.

Ver. 4. *A rod.*—We find on the ancient Egyptian remains the representation of a rod, crooked at the top, being carried in the hand; and still the Arabs use such for various purposes. In the monastery of Mt Sinai is the wood of a shrub which grows in the wilderness (Colutea Haleppica) sold, adapted for such rods, and (not improbably) regarded as the kind from which Moses' wonder-working rod was made.—In ancient Egypt there existed an art of serpent-charming, which has continued even to the present day. The person who practises it restrains the serpents from biting; nay, exercises such power over them, that they will stretch themselves out, stiff and immoveable like a stick. When this power of working miracles is bestowed on Moses, he is given to understand that henceforth, through God's might, he shall be superior to all enchanters. At the same time, this miracle, like that of the burning bush, had a deep significance. "What can be more simple than a shepherd's staff? Yet My power can create from thence that which is an object of fear to all its enemies." Moses understood this from the miracle, since he himself fled in terror from the face of the serpent. But as the serpent in his hand became again a rod, so was he assured that even the most terrific power, which made Pharaoh tremble, should be to him a means of help, not of injury.

Ver. 7. *Flesh.*—The leprosy, as an incurable malady which excludes the unhappy sufferer from the society of men. That same Moses, who had been driven out of Egypt, and rejected by his own people, is destined to be restored through God's power, and to be reinstated in that office to which so early he had felt himself called.

Ver. 9. *Dry land.*—By this sign would Moses show himself, and the God who sent him, to be lord over Egypt; since the Nile is the source of all life and fruitfulness to the land, and was regarded by the inhabitants as a deity.

Ver. 10. *Heretofore.*—Literally: "Been eloquent, neither yesterday, nor the day before, nor since," etc.; *i.e.*, my deficiency has been since that time no way changed. God chooses a weak and inefficient instrument, in order thereby to glorify His own power through its weakness: 1 Cor. i. 27; 2 Cor. xii. 10.

Ver. 11. *I the Lord.*—This expresses two things:—1. Have I not created thee, and know I not what gifts thou hast? and 2. Can I not endow thee with all eloquence needful for thy mission? The latter is the primary meaning of this expression, as is seen from what follows.

Ver. 13. *Wilt send.*—" Every other whom Thou pleasest."

Ver. 14. *Levite.*—The designation, " Levite," here used, prepares the way for the future privileges of that tribe.

Glad.—He also received a vision which made him acquainted with the call of Moses, and God's purpose in respect to Israel. The coincidence of these visions, and the joyful readiness of Aaron to enter into Moses' plans, were calculated to strengthen the desponding old man, who felt so keenly his weakness and deficiencies.—We clearly gather from this history, that at first it was not God's purpose to give Moses the assistance of Aaron as his spokesman. This was done only in consequence of his repeated refusal. At the same time, Holy Scripture prominently sets forth the high priesthood of Aaron as a divinely appointed office. In this respect the whole circumstance resembles the appointment of a king in Israel, 1 Sam. viii. 7. Such a division of the office of ruler (Moses bore more the character of king, Aaron that of priest and prophet) was not in God's original design, but resulted from the weakness of faith and the disobedience of Moses. This imperfect economy typified the perfect. Moses pointed to Him who should be the Mediator of a better covenant, Heb. viii. 6: the king of Israel, who was distinct from the high priest, to the Priest after the order of Melchisedek.

Ver. 16. *Instead of God.*—As God puts the words into the prophet's mouth, who is nothing but God's instrument, such shall be the relationship of Aaron to Moses.

Ver. 18. *Yet alive.*—As Moses found with so much difficulty faith in the people of Israel, he has less reason to expect it from his father-in-law. The pretext he makes is, nevertheless, not false.

Ver. 19. *Thy life.*—After the manner of the scriptural narrative, an earlier event, with which the present is connected, is repeated (just as Gen. ii. 4, etc.). No doubt the Lord had already communicated this fact to Moses, that he might not be tried beyond his power. In the long period of his sojourn in Midian, a new king has ascended the throne of Egypt, and the relation of Moses to the house of Pharaoh had been long since forgotten. We do not find in the later history the least mention of it; how much less of so unimportant an event as the killing of the Egyptian!

Ver. 21. *Harden.*—In several places it is declared, and the declaration is repeated, that God Himself was the author of the hardening of Pharaoh; and yet in many others is the hardening ascribed to Pharaoh himself. In order to avoid making God the author of sin, it has been attempted to explain the expression, by supposing that this hardening was the result of the miracles performed on Pharaoh; so that it is only said God did these great works, which, instead of softening Pharaoh's heart, by his own fault hardened it. Others have attributed the inward sinfulness entirely, and in its fullest sense, to Pharaoh, but have ascribed the mode of its external exhibition to God; since, of course, so soon as sin passes out of the will into act and assumes any form, God must afford this form in which it appears and govern it. Thus, when David is puffed up with pride, this pride in his heart is his own sin and fault; but the *act*—that of numbering the people—in which it breaks forth, is a consequence of a temptation presented to him from God. But these explanations do not reach the meaning of the word.—When God's power and grace work on a man in vain, his heart becomes necessarily harder and harder than before; and this hardening is not so much itself a sin, as a consequence and punishment of former sin, and therefore an act of God's. The Gospel is "the savour of life unto life, and of death unto death," as one and the same savour is to some creatures refreshing, to others poisonous. But that the Gospel is unto death, is not a part of its original intention, but a consequence of perverse unbelief; but when this takes place, that it is unto death comes as a punishment from God. Thus the expression "hardening" presupposes an earlier condition when the heart was susceptible, but which ceased in consequence of the misuse of Divine revelations and gifts. As Pharaoh hardens himself, so God hardens him at the same time; and the prediction of this hardening would afford Moses and the Israelites a great consolation in their intercourse with the tyrant. They would have the assurance that the outbursts of his rage were all under the Divine control, and that the very punishment which befell him was ordained of God.

Ver. 22. *First-born.*—Of all people, has God chosen this people first and especially. The expression conveys the notion of peculiar love towards the people.

Ver. 23. *Thy first-born.*—This retributive putting to death the first-born, because he had withheld from God His first-born, would be an emblematic sign of the full real meaning of the word.

Ver. 24. *Kill him.*—This was in consequence of the omission of circumcision, as the context shows. Among the Arabs, circumcision takes place in the thirteenth year, as it does with many people who follow the practice. The circumcision of children was peculiar to the Israelites. It is very possible that the Midianites, who were descended from Abraham, had not entirely abandoned the custom, but deferred it to a later age. Moses, by living so long among the Midianites, had become estranged from the customs and ways of the Israelites, and had adopted those of the people among whom he sojourned. Then God interfered, and would have revenged the contempt of His holy ordinance, on the omission of which He had enjoined the punishment to be, " that they should be destroyed from among His people."

Ver. 25. *Bloody husband.*—So she names Moses, expressing, " I must buy thee with the blood of my child." A sign how the entrance into God's covenanted people could not be without pain for one who was an alien.

Ver. 27. *Mount of God.*—Horeb: ch. iii. 1. It appears, then, that Moses, for some unknown reason, had taken the way over Horeb into Egypt.

Ver. 31. *Worshipped.*—They fell down upon their faces: they paid reverence to Moses as to a prophet of God. Even men often received the honour of such marks of reverence, since they were regarded as God's representatives; therefore especially persons of high rank—kings in the O. T., as also Divine messengers in the N. But after that God had become man in Christ, and so the Divine and human natures were united as never before, and at the same time a more distinct line between the two drawn, the messengers of the Lord decline this honour of kneeling before them: Acts x 25, 26; Rev. xix. 10, ch. xxii. 8, 9. This first belief on the part of the people, which was elicited by the signs and wonders performed, and supported by the yearning after freedom and the joyful sense of God's mercy, would turn into a witness against the people, when afterwards they shrunk back from the will of the Lord, and resisted His commands.

CHAPTER V.

Ver. 1. *Afterward.*—After Moses and Aaron had performed their great miracles in the sight of the people, and thus attested their mission. From ch. iii. 18, it is probable that the elders of the people went in with them to Pharaoh. They served, by the outward dignity of their office, to support the claims of the Divine mission of Moses, which could not be apparent to Pharaoh. The capital of Pharaoh was either Memphis, near the modern Cairo, in which place the Jewish and Arabian traditions place the scene of our history; or, according to Ps. lxxviii. 12, probably Zoan, named by the Greeks Tanis, situated at the mouth of one of the eastern branches of the Nile on the Delta: so it would be in the neighbourhood of Goshen.

Wilderness.—Cf. ch. iii. 18, note. The demand appears to contain nothing extraordinary in it. A place has lately been discovered at Sarabet-el-Khadin, full of Egyptian buildings and pillars, with kings' names inscribed thereon. This was probably a place of pilgrimage, where the Egyptians held feasts in the wilderness. With some such custom would Moses' request be connected (Lord Prudhoe, in Robinson i. 128).

Ver. 2. *Who is the Lord?*—Lit.: "Who is Jehovah?"

Israel go.—It is by no means to be inferred from this, that Pharaoh did not know Jehovah, nor understand what their wish implied. He knew well that the Hebrews honoured Him as God. He could as a heathen have nothing to object against this; nay, he might esteem Him as really a Superior Being. But since the national deities were regarded as the defenders of a people, they appeared to him only as objects of contempt, when that people was overcome and enslaved (cf. Isa. xxxvi. 18; 2

Chron. xxxii. 13, 14, 19). These words, therefore, contain a strong expression of heathen self-reliance, as well as of proud, overbearing scorn towards a people who were utterly subjected.— Instead of completing at one blow what He had promised His people and threatened Pharaoh, the Lord commences with this refusal of the king a series of trials for Israel and chastisements for Pharaoh, by means of which the latter is humbled, and the former exalted. This mode of proceeding is very significant. It purposes neither to subdue the king by the mere exercise of Divine power, nor to assist the people without the trial of their faith in the Lord. The immediate consequence of the first attempt to redeem them from bondage is, that their condition becomes worse, and their belief in the word of promise is contradicted by the present appearance of affairs. But, especially, it was God's design not to humble Pharaoh merely as regards his outward condition, without imparting an inward sense of his sin. None of the heathens and unbelievers, who in the course of the history of God's people come in any contact with them, could do so without some personal impression being made on them by what they saw and felt. So it was with Nebuchadnezzar, Cyrus, Herod, Pilate. Especially in Pharaoh's case ought the Divine chastisements to have humbled him, and brought him to a sense of the sins for which they were inflicted.

Ver. 3. *Met with us.*—As ch. iii. 18; *i.e.*, we belong to Him: we owe Him sacred duties, from which no man can set us free. While their words expressed their sense of *religious* dependence, they declare their *national* independence.

Sword.—In this address is observable great respect towards the king—perhaps a certain degree of dread of him. They do not say that Pharaoh is responsible to God, or that punishment will fall on *him* for disobedience.

Ver. 4. *Burdens.*—In Moses, Aaron, and the elders, he addresses the whole people.

Ver. 5. *People of the land.*—By this term Pharaoh denotes expressly that they belong to the land, and wishes to imply how great injury they (Moses and Aaron) inflict on the country. Pharaoh could not mean to say that the people were *too many*. It is an observation made from very early times, that the people of Egypt would patiently endure any kind of oppression, but on the least relaxation of severity were ready to break out into revolt. These words of Pharaoh, therefore, express a well-known rule of statecraft.

Ver. 6. *Taskmasters.*—The (lit.) "drivers" were Egyptian officers whom Pharaoh had placed over Israel: the "officers" were the superior persons taken from among themselves. The word "officers" means, properly, "Scribes" (Heb. Schoterim). The duty of these latter was, we find, to take care that each one delivered in the proper number of bricks. In later times, their office was to select the men fit for the service of war, and to leave those at home who had built a house, planted a vineyard, married a wife, or who were faint-hearted (Deut. xx. 5–9). It is, therefore, not improbable that they assisted the elders of the tribes when they had to keep the genealogical registers of the families.—"I have been present at the cutting of a canal, in which everything resembled this description. The workmen came chiefly out of Upper Egypt, with their wives and children, and were distributed in bands along the canal which was forming. The whole body was under the direction of Turks and Albanians, who had put overseers over the peasants, taken from among themselves; and these were responsible for the work to be done. These latter abused their power even more than the former. Pay and maintenance were indeed promised the labourers; but the first was altogether withheld, and the latter afforded so sparingly and uncertainly, that a fifth part died under the lashes of these drivers."—Laborde.

Ver. 7. *Make brick.*—The Egyptians had no burnt bricks, but baked the clay, mixed with chopped straw, in the sun. The chopped straw was used to give it adhesiveness. For this purpose were they obliged to collect straw.

Ver. 11. *Get.*—This is the reason especially why this new command is made known to you.

Ver. 12. *Stubble.*—"Small cut straw."

Ver. 14. *Officers.*—The commands of the taskmasters were communicated to the people through the Hebrew officers, who were responsible for the correct delivery of the work.

Ver. 16. *Fault.*—They represent to Pharaoh how the whole Egyptian people are hereby guilty of a sin, and liable to Divine punishment; without, however, openly expressing this latter feeling.

Ver. 19. *Evil case.*—This "evil case" would express their hopeless despair.

Ver. 21. *Eyes of Pharaoh;* i.e., have stirred up his indignation against us, and given him a reason for inflicting punishment on us.

Ver. 22. *Sent me.*—Moses, without light, propounds his doubts in the strongest manner. He had been warned of the result—that in consequence of his mission it would go worse with the people, and that they would rebel against him. In such a position he is left without guidance and instruction from the Lord, and must therefore refresh his faith. With every fresh movement of God's grace in the inner life, fresh difficulties and questions are raised. If we will bring these before the Lord, though it should be with the expression of trembling and grief, yet are they not to be regarded as signs of unbelief, but rather of the struggles and contests of faith; and the Lord is patient towards the doubtings of human shortsightedness.

Ver. 23. *Delivered.*—Every extraordinary act of God's providence among His people begins with what, for the moment, appears its contrary. The kingdom of God is built on the ruins of earthly happiness and comfort.

CHAPTER VI.

An important crisis of the history has now arrived, for which all the preceding was preparatory. The oppression of the people, Moses' call and going down into Egypt, his first announcement of the Divine will to Pharaoh, the refusal of the king, the still harder servitude of Israel,—all this combined had extorted from Moses the almost despairing cry of complaint, ch. v. 22, 23. Now commences properly the history of the deliverance. In a solemn appearance and address, God renews the former declarations and promises. He explains more fully the name by which it was His wish to be known to Israel. Even this fresh and solemn declaration of His gracious purposes makes no impression on the people under their hard burdens, and Moses repeats his complaints. Henceforth begin the deeds of the Lord—His wonders in Egypt.

Ver. 1. *Drive.*—The answer of the Lord shows from what

spirit the complaint of Moses had proceeded. He renews His former promise yet more distinctly to His sorely-tried servant, by telling him that the king, who now refused to let them go, would be so humbled by God's almighty power as himself to drive them out.

Ver. 3. *Jehovah.*—This is thus expressed in the Hebrew: "I have appeared to Abraham, Isaac, and Jacob as El-Shaddai, 'Almighty God;' but according to my name Jehovah have I not been known to them." He does not say His name Jehovah was not known to them, which would contradict the earlier history; but He according to His name Jehovah. God calls Himself El-Shaddai (Almighty God) in the solemn revelation in which Abraham's name was changed, and the covenant established with him by the institution of circumcision—that covenant which altogether pointed towards the future. This circumstance, known from the history of the patriarchs, now serves as a foundation-stone for further revelations. The patriarchs were led to trust in Him as the Almighty God, and to believe that He will become to them Jehovah (see ch. iii. 14, note). The O. T. (and particularly the time of the patriarchs) was the economy under which God revealed Himself more by *acts* than by the unfolding of doctrines, as the instruction conveyed by an act left the most abiding impression on the feelings. So long, then, as the promise of the covenant in reference to the possession of Canaan remained unfulfilled, "God was not yet known to them by His name Jehovah." The meaning of this name was not yet revealed to them in deeds. This it is which now is about to be changed.

Ver. 4. *Strangers.*—At the same time that I revealed Myself to them as the Almighty, I have thought on the time when I would make Myself known as Jehovah.

Ver. 5. *Remembered.*—This period is now arrived: the trouble of the people is the particular and immediate occasion of this revelation as Jehovah.

Ver. 9. *Cruel bondage.*—At the first coming of Moses they received him with joy, and believed him; but as the consequences of his mission had only been increased severity, while he was commissioned to communicate nothing actually new, they cooled towards him, though they offered him no opposition.

Ver. 12. *Uncircumcised lips.*—An image taken from those

whose tongue must be cut before they can speak plainly. Such a difficulty and impediment had Moses in his lips.

Ver. 15. *Simeon*.—These two are only first named, in order to make out Levi as the third tribe.

Ver. 16. *Generations*.—The names of the sons of Reuben and Simeon are recapitulated from Gen. xlvi. 9, 10. The present genealogical register of the family of Levi is a continuation of that given, ver. 11 of the same chap.

Levi.—By this statement it is signified that in the present genealogical table the family of Levi is especially meant to be kept in view, as, by a similar announcement of the age of Kohath in ver. 18, and of Amram in ver. 20, that their lines are those to be marked.

Ver. 24. *Korhites*.—The family of Korah is here again mentioned, and his line carried further on in this place than in the others, in order to prepare for the history of his rebellion, by means of which the Divine establishment of the priesthood was solemnly confirmed (Num. xvi. xvii.).

Ver. 25. *Phinehas*.—Eleasar and Phinehas are mentioned more particularly among the sons of Aaron, since the dignity of the high priesthood was to descend in this line: Num. xx. 22–29, ch. xxv. 11–13.

Ver. 30. *Pharaoh hearken*.—All this is added only in order, at this critical period of the history, to keep before the reader's mind the importance of the two principal actors in the events.

CHAPTER VII.

Ver. 1. *A god to Pharaoh*.—" I have made thee a god to Pharaoh" is not to be understood merely figuratively. Moses in very deed stood in God's place before him: God had put His own word into his mouth—had intrusted to him His creative power for the work of his mission. "Through my word, says God, shalt thou be lord over him: let him struggle and resist as he may, thou shalt do with him as thou wilt. So it happens to him who has God's word and is God's son, Who has power over all; since a Christian is a man of such power that all creatures must obey him. Although this does not appear, yet, in truth, it is so. What on earth is more powerful than death? what more fearful than sin? what more bitter than a bad conscience? Yet a Christian can say that he is lord over all these."—Luther. Cf. 1 Cor. iii. 21. For Aaron as a prophet, see ch. iv. 16, note.

Ver. 2. *Shall speak.*—A continual source of humiliation for Moses, and memento of his weakness of faith, which was the cause of this division of offices.

Ver. 5. *Am the Lord.*—" This conviction, which is forced on them against their will, is different from the knowledge and experience of the chosen people. 'Ye shall know that I am the Lord when I have brought you out of the land of Egypt.' This is nothing but a confirmation of the faith which, before the *deeds*, had relied on the simple *word*; or God chastises its weakness when He sees that it does not sufficiently rely on the word. The ungodly, therefore, know God in such a manner, that, confounded by shame and fear, they see not that which they see."—Calvin.

Ver. 6. *Commanded them.*—All unwillingness to obey, arising from unbelief or fear on their parts, had now ceased for ever.

Ver. 7. *Old.*—In this great turning-point of the history their age is mentioned (as before, their descent), in order to throw light on the narrative. In a similar way is the age of Joseph mentioned (Gen. xli. 46). The longevity of the human race still continued down to this time, though it becomes less and less. We are to regard Moses as a grey-headed man, in the full possession of vigour and energy.

Ver. 9. *Thy rod.*—Moses' rod (ch. iv.) is here called Aaron's, because he carried it, so that he might every time accompany the act and sign with words.

Ver. 10. *Became a serpent.*—What the Egyptian wise men did by means of their enchantments, Moses effected by the power of his word.

Ver. 11. *Sorcerers.*—This word properly means those who rehearse forms of incantation. It would be plainly contrary to the word of Scripture to suppose that these sorcerers were merely deceivers, and their work a juggle. We find among many heathen people a science of incantation in the service of the false religion, in which much, indeed, depended on the concealed use of natural agents, much on deceit, but likewise much on the assistance of evil spirits. From the Grecian oracles to the arts of the Greenland Angekok, no sound judgment can conclude that these concurrent phenomena are mere tricks or the results of natural skill. Of the Greenland Angekoks, some who have been converted to Christianity have declared, " Much was mere deceit; but in much there was present a spiritual influence which they now abhorred, but could not describe."—Cranz. Hist. of Greenland, i. 273. Mention has been made already (ch. iv. 4, note) of the art of taming serpents; and even to this day one caste, which is regarded by the people as sacred, cultivate this art, which is hereditary among them. In the practice of it, they lash themselves up into a state of phrensy; and removed as is the present Mohammedan creed from such heathen arts, still they like these things to make their appearance in their great religious processions. In all this we see the remains of an art and of a class which formerly flourished on the fruitful ground of a religion which was at once a service paid to Nature and her powers, and a homage rendered to evil spirits.

Ver. 12. *Swallowed.*—Although they imitated what Aaron did, their weakness and inferiority are plainly visible. In this and the following miracles we see that the sorcerers could imitate some, but not all. They show their weakness herein, that they only aggravate, and do not keep off the ruin—more especially, that this their power at length fails them.

Ver. 13. *Hardened.*—Even the most evident miracle does not overcome his hardness and obstinacy: it only served to increase his guilt. All miracles are given for the help and support of weak faith. On the other hand, the natural and usual course of events is of more weight in the eyes of the determined and proud mind than the greatest miracles, which break in on this order.

Ver. 15. *To the water.*—The Nile received divine honours We may suppose, with a great appearance of probability, that the true God made known His power on the Nile at that very time when Pharaoh was about to offer homage to his false god. —We have now the first of a long list of plagues, after the first exhibition of God's might had triumphed over the magical power of the Egyptian idolatry, though it was without effect on the king. This first miracle left the king and land uninjured. Now begins a succession of plagues. All these are natural phenomena peculiar to Egypt. The water there sometimes assumes a blood-red hue,—frogs, lice, locusts, etc., all have in Egypt, even at this day, something peculiarly fearful. The significance of these plagues consists in this—not that things are brought forth which are utterly strange to the nature and circumstances of the country, but that well-known visitations occurred with unusual violence and in rapid succession—that they were called forth and ceased at Moses' word—that the Egyptian sorcerers at the outset can only *increase*, not *remove*, the visitation; and, finally, are obliged to declare themselves powerless and vanquished. This it is which proves to the Egyptians, under these circumstances, the mighty saying of Jehovah, "All the earth is Mine:" ch. xix. 5. At length a plague is inflicted which exceeds all the former in its awfulness, since it leaves the ground of nature on which the others were exhibited—this is the slaughter of the first-born. The number of the plagues is *ten*—the number of completeness—to signify the entire subjection of the land under its rightful Owner. In contrast to these ten plagues, Israel receives ten commandments. They are a type of the tithe which men give to the king, Israel to God. The first of the plagues assailed the Egyptians in a necessary of life. In a country otherwise so deficient in water, the Nile is the source of all well-being. Its water is drunk, not only as a necessary, but also on account of its delightful taste. It sometimes happens, at the rising of the Nile, that the water becomes red or green, by means of some mixture of (perhaps) an earthy ingredient with it. At such times it is unpleasant to drink. This plague was now inflicted on Egypt in an unusual degree, and at a time determined by the word of the Lord by the mouth of Moses. There is something very awful in this punishment (the first miracle of Jesus was to turn water into wine). Nevertheless, no immediate damage is done to the land or its inhabitants. The Lord gives time for repentance.

Ver. 17. *Blood.*—It is evident that we are here not literally to understand blood, but that the water had the appearance and thickness of blood. We are to understand in the same manner the saying of the prophet, that, on the day of the Lord, the moon shall be turned into blood, Joel iii. 4; Acts ii. 19. The blood-colour of the water would remind the Egyptians of God's vengeance for the innocent blood shed by them in such abundance.

Ver. 18. *Fish.*—That which lives in the water and derives nourishment from it shall die. Here is given a forewarning of the judgment of death which shall follow.

Ver. 19. *Streams.*—This plague reaches all the streams, etc.; *i.e.*, the arms of the Nile, the water-ducts in the canals, the water collected in reservoirs, and every single pool which remained from the inundation. These are all the different waters which, in Egypt, are derived from the Nile.

Vessels.—By which the Nile water was filtered.

All the land.—It is not added here, as in some of the following plagues, that Israel was spared participation in it. It appears rather to have reached the people of God. It was more revolting and painful in its character than actually dangerous—a sort of emblematic warning; and therefore the people of God, by fellowship in this plague, are reminded of the danger of fellowship with the heathens. At the same time, Israel had the comforting assurance that the plague was sent by the God of covenant, and was a forerunner of deliverance.

Ver. 22. *Magicians.*—The fact that the magicians, after the general change of the water, still found some which they could turn into blood, is a proof that "*all* the water" is not to be understood literally. It is possible that, in the land of Goshen particularly, there was water unaffected by the plague. How the magicians performed this, is difficult to explain. Evidently it was no mere illusion, but a secret art, which is here spoken of. But withal they possessed only the power of heightening the plague.

Ver. 24. *Digged.*—The Egyptians only drink well-water from sheer necessity, as the pleasant taste of the Nile water makes it preferable.

Ver. 25. *Smitten.*—These words must be connected with what follows,—" Seven days were fulfilled after that the Lord had smitten the river, and the Lord spake unto Moses," etc.: *i.e.*, seven days after the commencement of the first plague the Lord commanded the second to be brought. It is not said whether the first had by this time ceased.

CHAPTER VIII.

Ver. 3. *Kneading-troughs.*—In this and the following plagues, the great characteristic is the loathsome nature of the animals which bring them about. The pride of the Egyptians, who looked down on the Israelites as unclean animals, is thus significantly rebuked. This second plague is more severe than the first, though as yet it is rather annoying and troublesome than dangerous or destructive. Pharaoh finds it so, and must humble himself to entreat for its removal. A distinction would appear to be made between the Egyptians and Israelites in respect to this plague; though such is only expressly mentioned in those which follow.

Ver. 4. *Servants.*—Here, without doubt, we are to supply to the narrative that Pharaoh (perhaps silently) treats the warning again with contempt.

Ver. 8. *Sacrifice.*—The first sign of Pharaoh's pride being broken; not, indeed, of his repentance or humiliation, but yet of a certain feeling of his own helplessness, in opposition to the might of God. There might be shown, too, a recognition, though a weak one, of the Divine Majesty. Slight as is such homage, the Lord vouchsafes to receive it.

Ver. 9. *Glory over me;* i.e., "It does not indeed belong to you to determine the time; but since thou humblest thyself before God, thou canst again command me, therefore fix the time." How is God's might glorified in the willing humility of His messenger, who, by allowing Pharaoh to fix the time, puts at the same time before him a proof of the greatness of God!

Ver. 15. *Hearkened.*—A heathen, who could form no right idea of an Almighty God, might not unnaturally suppose that this last plague was the extreme exhibition of the power of the hostile Being who opposed and attacked him. As soon, therefore, as the plague had been removed, he again bid Him defiance, and the Lord, in punishment, made his heart yet harder.

Ver. 16. *Lice.*—In this plague the punishment proceeds a step farther. Instead of lice (Heb. Kinnim), it has been supposed that the insect here spoken of was a kind of very small, almost invisible gnat, which at times, when they swarmed, became extremely troublesome, nay, even most painful, by creeping into the smallest orifice—the very nostrils and eyes, and not allowing a moment's rest even in sleep. Herodotus says, B. ii. 95: "The following means are used to keep off the gnats, which are very numerous. Such as dwell in the upper parts of the fens are protected by the towers, to the top of which they ascend to sleep, as the gnats cannot fly so high on account of the winds. Those who live about the morasses have each man a net, in which he catches fish by day, and which at night he casts about his bed, and then creeps in and sleeps under it. If any one were to attempt to sleep wrapped in his clothes, or in linen, the gnats would bite through them, but they do not attempt this at all with the net." Like means are now used. The sting of the gnat leaves a feverish irritation after it. This plague, which at all times was a very troublesome one, became now so monstrous that all the dust of the land seemed changed into gnats.

Ver. 18. *Could not.*—The power of the Egyptian magicians here ceases. As with the snake-charmers a secret knowledge of the powers of nature might be combined with devilish arts, so a similar conjunction possibly acted in the production of the frogs. But neither human skill nor any power in the service of the kingdom of darkness availed to call forth the gnats.

Ver. 19. *Finger of God.*—In proportion as they recognised the bounds of their own science, did they perceive more clearly that this plague was a work of the supreme power of God.

Ver. 21. *Swarms of flies.*—This plague, that of the flies (lit., of the mixture), closely resembles the last. But here, to make this miracle more impressive, the separation between Egypt and Israel is distinctly and expressly mentioned. In a small degree this kind of plague is very general in Egypt, and is described by travellers as intolerably painful and troublesome, as the dog-fly settles in great swarms on every exposed part of the body, with invincible pertinacity.

Ver. 22. *Midst of the earth.*—The rightful Lord of Egypt, who dwells therein, and rules every province according to My good pleasure.—A direct contradiction of the heathen notions of the Godhead.

Ver. 27. *Command us.*—To one unacquainted with the fanatical, superstitious nature-worship of the Egyptians, this might appear like an evasion on the part of Moses. But all the victims of sacrifice must be most carefully chosen, and the least mistake therein might be a crime deserving death. Therefore a carefully selected sacrifice must have a seal fixed on the horns by the priests, before it could be offered. But Israel had now for centuries not offered any public sacrificial worship. To arrange such after the directions of the Egyptian priests, would be a concession to their nature-worship. Nothing, therefore, is left for Israel but to establish its own peculiar worship, if it is to enter into covenant with God as His people. This mode of worship, though outwardly resembling often the Egyptian, was nevertheless in its nature and character entirely in contrast with it: hence the necessity of this journey into the wilderness.

Ver. 28. *Very far away.*—Moses does not reject this demand. The obligation under which the Israelites were in respect to it could only be removed by God, through means of a series of events which His judgments brought about.

Ver. 32. *People go.*—From the same reason as ver. 15.

CHAPTER IX.

Ver. 6. *All the cattle.*—That this is not to be taken literally (the same is the case ch. vii. 20), is proved by the plague of hail which follows (ver. 19–21). It has the meaning of "a general mortality among the cattle," or, "the cattle of all kinds die."— The severity and awful character of the plagues now increase. Hitherto they had been painful and troublesome—this fifth plague causes death; yet still forbearance is shown, as the death is inflicted on the cattle only. The severance betwixt the Egyptians and Israelites is now more brought before our view.

Ver. 8. *Ashes of the furnace.*—Perhaps there is a significance in the instrument of the miracle (as before, in respect to the water of the Nile and the dust of the land). The pride of the Egyptians were their great and magnificent works of art: these were produced out of the furnaces of their workshops. Thus the subject of their exultation was made the means of humbling them. The "boil breaking forth with blains," which is here mentioned, is threatened (Deut. xxviii. 27), under the name of the "botch of Egypt," as a punishment on the Israelites for disobedience. It was a disease prevalent in the country; but we cannot determine of what kind, owing to the change of inhabitants, and the different mode of living in modern times. It was in any case a great miracle, that at Moses' word such a disease should everywhere break forth. And in this plague his victory over the magicians was complete, since they likewise were infected with these boils.

Ver. 12. *Lord hardened.*—Here, for the first time in the narrative after the general declaration ch. iv. 21, is it said, "The Lord hardened him." And even in this mention of the hardening, is it intimated that Pharaoh's act *went first*—God's act *followed;* since the condition of being hardened was preceded by one of feeling, and of conscious resistance to this feeling.

Ver. 15. *Pestilence.*—As continuation of the plague of the boils, and before the destruction of the cattle.—We may observe a remarkable progress in the gradation of judicial punishments, in respect to this next plague;—at the same time, we gain an insight into the position of the Lord towards Pharaoh. After six plagues have been inflicted without effect, Moses begins with an awful threatening of a general destruction, and the declaration that from henceforth God will be glorified by the sparing and by the hardening of Pharaoh. We now anticipate the infliction of that last visitation threatened at the outset; but, though all is surely pointing to that termination, the Lord still withholds the fulfilment of the last impending woe. There happens a fearful hail; but with this the Lord reveals mercy in the midst of His anger. He provides a means of preservation for the Egyptians themselves; and offers to Pharaoh yet a further inducement than hitherto had been done by the exemption of the Israelites to escape the extreme penalty, by humbling himself, in the fear of God, under His almighty hand. So did Jesus bear with Judas, and warn him until the very last, even after He knew he was a devil, and after He had predicted his end.

Ver. 16. *Throughout all the earth.*—This place St Paul quotes in the remarkable passage Rom. ix. 17. In the Hebrew there is an antithesis to the preceding: "Since now I stretch out My hand, and smite thee and thy people with the pestilence, and thou shalt be destroyed from the earth; but for this cause do I place thee up, that I may show My might," etc.;—*i.e.*, not only "thou hast deserved it, and I can so do," but even more—"I have raised up My hand to do it; and that I still spare thee, has another object—the glorifying of My might." The raised up hand of the Lord points to the death of the first-born and the destruction of Pharaoh, since this declaration is not to be taken literally, as though the pestilence would destroy all. God therefore places Pharaoh up (keeps him upright, under the blows which fall on him and his people), in order that He may cause His might to be seen. It means, therefore, taken with the context, "Thou resistest My might: henceforth canst thou see in thyself, and show to others in thee, My justice in punishing." This is not an accidental consequence of the conduct of Pharaoh, but it is contained in the Divine purpose—it is a fulfilment of a Divine judgment.

Ver. 20. *Feared.*—We perceive here the beginning of that disposition on the part of the Egyptians, which afterwards was more clearly shown in the giving of the vessels on the departure of the Israelites.

Ver. 24. *Fire mingled;* i.e., great masses of fire fell down amidst the hail.

Ver. 30. *Know.*—It perhaps surprises us that a petition for removal, and the granting of it, should follow on a merely hypocritical confession, which Moses knew to be but such. But it was not Pharaoh's personal intention or change of heart on which the matter turned; but, as king, he stood on one side— God on the other: and his public position before the world was the point to be regarded. As he now gave God the honour, and humbled himself under His hand, immediately the removal of the plague follows. So now is a national blessing the certain fruit of an open confession of the service due to the true God, on the part of the rulers.

Ver. 32. *Not grown up.*—Spelt (a kind of wheat—not "rye," as in our Version, since this was a species of corn not known in the ancient world) was the usual bread-corn in Egypt. Wheat and spelt were the principal articles of food: other kinds of corn are not met with in ancient times. The remark inserted in this verse agrees with what takes place in Egypt in modern times. The flax and the barley are ripe in the sixth month after sowing (*i.e.* in March), the wheat and the spelt in the seventh (April). Accordingly, February would be the time when the event spoken of took place. How long each plague continued we are not told. Only once is it mentioned how long a period elapsed before the beginning of the next (ch. vii. 25). It is not improbable that a time was allowed after each for coming to a better mind. A period of some weeks, therefore, might pass before the infliction of the last plague.

Ver. 35. *By Moses.*—"The boldness of Pharaoh again increases through the removal of punishment, as confidence always provides the reprobate with weapons against God. But at the conclusion Moses represents his guilt as yet greater, by adding, this had been foretold by himself. We have several times seen that the ungodly king hardened himself, 'as the Lord had said to Moses;' but here it is further mentioned that Moses himself had declared this unmoveable hardness of heart on the part of Pharaoh."—Calvin.

CHAPTER X.

Ver. 4. *Locusts.*—In order to understand what an advance in the degree of judgments is revealed in this plague, we must consider the nature of the fearful visitation which is here threatened. In the East the locusts are not found, as with us, singly, but in vast countless swarms. There have been known flights of them which have extended ten leagues in length, one and a half in breadth, and several feet in thickness. A yellow reflection in the air, cast by their bright wings, is their harbinger, often a day before their actual arrival. The air is then misty, the light of the sun obscured, so that a person can scarcely see ten yards before him, as sometimes happens in a very thick snow-storm. The locusts march straight onwards—dam up the canals—fly over the walls—enter at the windows and every crevice, in on one side, out at the other. They rush through the open stores in hosts,—nay, they can only be kept from creeping into a person's mouth by shutting it quite closely. They settle on everything eatable, and fly off with the food in their mouths. In a few hours they have devoured every leaf, every ear—have stripped bare the tender boughs and the very twigs—often gnawed the dry wood and reeds. Pitfalls, smoke, noise, clothes hung on poles, are the means used for defence, but are found quite insufficient. They invade Egypt with the east wind from the Arabian Desert; and it is mostly the south or west wind which sweeps them into the sea, or the barren steppes. This is the only certain means for their destruction. Such was the plague which, known indeed to the Egyptians at all times, now assailed the land in a degree hitherto unprecedented.

Ver. 8. *Shall go.*—In all these communications with Pharaoh, the question is—Whether the people of Israel shall be regarded as completely in vassalage, or with freedom to serve God in the way He shall choose. Pharaoh might have ruled over them as a free people, serving their own God, and with an equality of worship and of laws; and there is no sign in the history that the Israelites would have refused this submission. But these limits the people dare not transgress, or accept any conditions prejudicial to the relations in which they stood to God.

Ver. 10. *Little ones.*—Bitter scorn.

Ver. 11. *Desire; i.e.,* did not require more than this at first.

Ver. 21. *Darkness which may be felt.*—Heb., "And it (the people) may grope in the darkness;" lit., "may seize the darkness," *i.e.*, may make use of the hands to touch the surrounding darkness —a very frequent figure of speech; as Job xii. 25, "They grope in the dark without light." It shall be so dark, that persons in the day-time must find their way by groping. As was the case with the other plagues, so in this fearful judgment (fearful, not only on account of its painful or injurious effects, but by reason of the awful sense of the Divine anger it would inspire) there was some resemblance to the natural phenomena which from time to time happen in Egypt. There is the hot wind, called Chamsin, which, in its usual mode of appearing, has something terrific to Europeans unacquainted with the visitation. An oppressive heat precedes its arrival; the sun loses its natural appearance, and assumes a dull, pale-yellowish hue like the moon. The air is obscured with clouds of dust, and at mid-day it is as dark as at night. A violent storm, accompanied with lightning, damages houses and tears up trees. There are examples in history where this visitation has reached such a degree of intensity that people believed the last day was come, and now and then it has continued three days. This it is which Moses, in the name of God, brings on the land of Egypt in its most terrific form.

Ver. 23. *Light.*—We can scarcely suppose this to have been the case in respect to the dwellings of those Israelites who lived among the Egyptians, as from the history, ch. xi. 2, we must conclude many of them did, but only in the land of Goshen and the districts exclusively inhabited by the Israelites. This remark holds good of the other plagues, ch. ix. 26. Those who lived among the Egyptians needed, for their own purification, to participate in much of the judgments inflicted, since they were, without doubt, the most luxurious and corrupt among their people.

Ver. 26. *Come thither.*—An allusion to the great feast of self-dedication which the people were to celebrate in the wilderness, whereby they became His people, as God had already said, ch. viii. 12. What and how they were to sacrifice there, must then be revealed to the people.

Ver. 28. *Shalt die.*—This is the critical point of the hardening of Pharaoh, and resembles the receiving of the sop in the case of Judas, St John xiii. 27. Hitherto Moses had been at hand to entreat the Lord for help to remove the plagues; now is that resource cut off.

Ver. 29. *Spoken well.*—"We see how the ungodly king, carried away by his rage, prophesies against his will. God repays on Pharaoh's own head what he had threatened Moses. But we must carefully remember that Moses did not speak on his own impulse, but at God's command. Had he not been informed for certain that this was the last communication, he would still have been ready to do his part."—Calvin.

Ver. 29. *No more.*—It is not said that Moses went out. His departure took place ch. xi. 8; therefore that which follows, though it happened somewhat earlier, is placed after this to explain the speech of Moses.

CHAPTER XI.

Ver. 1. *Said unto Moses.*—The thread of the narrative is here broken by the insertion of these verses; as we find, ver. 4, that Moses is still in the presence of Pharaoh, from which he does not depart until ver. 8, and we hear his last threat. A similar transposition we find Gen. ii. 4, etc.

Thrust.—Heb.: " Will, when he lets you go, entirely drive you hence." He will himself not wish to keep you longer.

Ver. 2. *Borrow.*—Not " borrow," as has been wrongly translated and explained. Israel required these things for their religious worship; and they could no more depart without them than without their cattle, as these "jewels of silver and jewels of gold" were to serve in forming a sanctuary for the people's worship, and were under their circumstances quite needful. For the rest, cf. ch. iii. 22, note.

Ver. 3. *Sight of the people.*—It was not merely fear, nor yet simply the wish to be rid of the Israelites, but a feeling of reverence for so highly favoured a man, which moved the Egyptians to bestow these presents. We read before this how some among Pharaoh's servants feared the Lord (ch. ix. 20), and how they acknowledged the might of God (ch. x. 7), and would have prevailed on the king to let the people go. But the Israelites had been still more severed from the Egyptians; and the feeling which had once been roused in Pharaoh—" the Lord is righteous, and I and my people are wicked "—though stifled, was not altogether hypocritical, and must have gained more and more influence over the mass of the nation. Thus it was not merely fear which prevailed on the Egyptians, but the feeling that the Israelites were God's chosen people. They made a kind of offering to a priestly race, which was to act as an atonement, and to turn God's anger from them.

Ver. 4. *Said;* i.e., to Pharaoh.

Ver. 5. *First-born.*—Now is threatened the greatest and most awful of the plagues. The first came out of the river, the benefactor of the land; the third and fourth from the earth; the rest from the air. All stood in close connection to the idolatrous land, whose Lord the God of Israel would show

Himself to be. But now He smites them with another plague, not only far exceeding all the rest, but also coming so directly from God's hand, that none of the natural phenomena peculiar to Egypt could offer any resemblance to it. Now the Lord goes out about midnight in the midst of Egypt, and death ensues in the houses—death, not of an usual kind, as in the case of a pestilence, but the death of the first-born, because the king had withheld from God His first-born son. This plague and deliverance—comprehending all the others—is a perpetual memorial to Israel of his election, sealed for him in the institution of the Passover, and dedication of the first-born to the Lord.

Upon his throne.—As the next to him, as it were his co-regent. Cf. Rev. iii. 21.

Mill.—The service at the hand-mills was esteemed the hardest, and performed by the very lowest class of female slaves.

Beasts.—This ought to have been a corroborating testimony to the miracle, that the plague came from God. The first-born, as "the beginning of strength" (Gen. xlix. 3), has from earliest times been reckoned the most excellent. Among the patriarchs, and even now among the Israelites, and probably among the Egyptians, the first-born had particular privileges; hence in every family the grief was more bitter for the loss of one so highly prized.

Ver. 8. *Follow thee;* lit., "that is at thy feet." Moses, on account of his miracles wrought, was esteemed the king of Israel.

Go out.—To complete the humiliation of Pharaoh, Moses threatens that he will by no means, as heretofore, beg for permission to go out; but the king himself will, by his servants, entreat him to do so as a great favour.

Great anger.—"We see from this, that the servants of God, even when they execute their office faithfully and truly, are so impressed with the greatness of the sins, that they are by no means free from the feeling of anger. It is the Holy Spirit which here inflames the heart of Moses with holy zeal, and preserves it from all mixture of unholy passion. Much reason have we, when moved by righteous indignation, to pray for the spirit of forbearance and singleness of mind, to preserve us from excess. Yet we see from Moses' anger, that God does not desire that we should be cold and indifferent in the execution of His commands."—Calvin.

Ver. 10. *Land.*—This is the conclusion of the entire history from ch. vii.—a summing up of the whole; as in like manner, ch. vi. 26.

CHAPTER XII.

Ver. 1. *In the land of Egypt.*—The course of the history is here interrupted, as it was at the beginning of ch. xi. Moses, when he wrote in the wilderness the account of what happened on that memorable night, inserted into the narrative the revelation on the subject of the feast of the Passover, which he had previously received, though he had only partially made it known to the elders. He did so, in order to show that this feast was no accidental institution or after-thought, but that all rested on the Divine appointment, and had a deep significance. A fearful judgment is announced against the Egyptians: according to strict justice, the same must be accomplished on Israel; but the mercy of the Lord will spare His people, and through this very mercy and grace are they to become His people.—A new era now commences. Henceforth they shall begin their year with the month on which they were delivered · at its full moon, on the day in which they went out of Egypt, shall they repeat in commemoration the events in Egypt. All which is here appointed has reference, for the most part, to the circumstances of that Exodus. The lamb was to be roasted, not boiled: they were to eat it with loins girded, shoes on their feet, and staff in hand, as travellers in haste. The bitter herbs were to remind them of the time of misery in Egypt—the unleavened bread, of the impossibility of leavening their dough in their hurry to be gone. But this significance was not all. All the customs of this feast, resting as they did on Divine institution, had a higher meaning,—especially the lamb itself which was sacrificed. The paschal sacrifice had, in every point of view, a particular signification. It was an especial sacrifice of atonement which was here ordained, since it was the blood of the lamb alone which on the door-posts averted the destruction from the people. "The Lord saw the blood and passed by." The blood of the lamb was in the stead of the blood of the Israelites, which would otherwise have been shed. But to this meaning of the Passover as a sacrifice of atonement, there was another in addition. The lamb slain in sacrifice was afterwards eaten in common: so this repast has the character of a sacrificial meal; *i.e.*, the whole blessing which the sacrifice accorded to the people, was thereby individually appropriated by those who partook of it, which otherwise was the case only with the thank or peace-offerings, never with the atonement or sin-offerings. This was therefore at once an atonement and a thank-offering. As food of a significant and peculiar kind, it was not to be mixed with other sorts; therefore, to be eaten roasted, not boiled, and whole. No bone was to be broken, that each person might have the emblem perfect before him. Nothing was to remain, lest it should be used for unhallowed (*i.e.*, non-religious) purposes, or be the cause of any superstition. It was to be eaten by a family as a whole, that the people might everywhere be reminded that they formed one body, and that every one, as member of that one body, became participator in the benefits which were obtained and commemorated by this offering. Leaven, as the cause of fermentation, solution, corruption, was regarded as an emblem of impurity; and therefore unleavened bread, as a type of what God's redeemed people ought to be, was to be eaten seven days. To be cut off from the people was the penalty of eating leavened bread. The whole feast had thus the name of the feast of unleavened bread; and all leaven was with the most scrupulous care removed from their houses during the days of the feast. But the most peculiar mark altogether in this great act of sacrifice was this,—that the very least and most obscure Israelite was therein called to the priestly office. The whole people was to be thereby represented as a " priestly kingdom, a holy people:" cf. Lev. ix. 1. A later tradition maintained, that the marking the door-posts with blood only took place the first time in Egypt, but never afterwards; but this is plainly contrary to the words of institution (vers. 24, 25). As a feast of redemption, and of thanksgiving for freedom at the same time, the sacrifice of the paschal lamb was to be continually offered: and since so many circumstances connected with it were a perpetual memento of the trouble of the people in Egypt, and their release therefrom by the plague, this feast was intended to be a perpetual exhortation to them at all times, to teach them that they owed their preservation and continuance to the all-powerful mercy of God, which alone had saved them; and that their thanksgiving could only worthily be offered to God by means of that honest sincerity which became His people. How in all this we are to see a type of the one eternal, all-sufficient sacrifice of Jesus Christ, and how all the particulars have a deep spiritual meaning (though we must be careful not to regard them merely as types, and so explain away their historical sense), the thoughtful reader of the N. T., from comparison of the institution of the Lord's Supper, and from 1 Cor. v. 6, etc., and 1 Cor. x. 16-21, can easily perceive.

Ver. 2. *Month.*—Before this a different mode of reckoning time was practised among them. We are to understand here, and afterwards where mention is made of months, the lunar months, which begin with the new moon, and on the 14th or 15th day of which the full moon takes place: therefore the Passover was celebrated at the full moon. By means of intercalation, the Israelites made the lunar to assimilate with the solar year; so that the harvest could always begin with the paschal festival.

Ver. 3. *Tenth day.*—This command only held good in Egypt, where, in consequence of the impending judgment, and the haste of their departure, no time would have remained afterwards for the selection.

A lamb for a house; lit., "a lamb for the house of your fathers."

Ver. 5. *Without blemish.*—Whereby it was marked out as a sacrifice, in which such care was always observed.

First year.—The Jewish tradition understands this of a lamb which had not exceeded the first year; but this is against the usage of the words.

Goats.—*i.e.*, As a rule, from the lambs, but even from the goats.

Ver. 6. *Evening.*—Between the two evenings. In Hebrew it is said, "the two lights" for mid-day—"the two dawns," the two evenings; because the particular points of mid-day, of sunrising and setting, which are by us indiscriminately called morning, mid-day, evening, are divided into two halves [*i.e.*, the time when the sun sinks below the earth, leaving twilight, and its final setting out of sight]. Here sunsetting is appointed as the particular time for killing the lamb; but, as in after times this must be done for all Israel before the sanctuary, custom kept to three o'clock of the afternoon as the time for the killing the lamb.

Ver. 7. *Upper post.*—The destroying angel came from above; therefore the upper posts must be marked with blood.

Ver. 8. *Roast.*—Because roast meat can be most quickly prepared; likewise, because it can for the most part be eaten without any accessories.

Unleavened bread.—Such bread was called "Matza;" *i.e.*, pure. They were thin, smooth, round cakes.

Bitter herbs.—Heb.: "with bitter;" it being left undetermined what this bitter is: without doubt is meant bitter herbs—it is supposed, wild lettuce. The unleavened bread and bitter lettuce reminded them of the suffering in Egypt, the trouble and pain of their departure; whilst other thoughts out of the deeper meaning of the feast would be added to these.

Ver. 9. *Sodden.*—The two extremes were to be avoided: neither too much time given to the preparation, nor too great haste shown so as to render the meal unsavoury and without due order.

Legs.—It should represent completeness. Every family or neighbourhood which partook of it, represented in miniature the whole people; and before this union of families the lamb was to be placed entire, in order that thus the meaning of the whole feast might be realised.

Ver. 11. *Girded.*—The long flowing Eastern garments, which in the house were loose, being girded up, as when a journey was about to be undertaken.

Feet.—In the house, the Orientals go barefoot: before a meal they wash the feet; when they go out or travel, they bind on sandals.

Passover.—The word in the Hebrew is "Pesach," from whence afterwards in the Aramaic (the Syro-Chaldaic) was formed "Pascha." "Pasach" signifies, properly, "springing over,"—a most significant word for the act of passing over and sparing His people, which the Lord did for Israel. The same word occurs, Isa. xxxi. 5, for the gracious passing over of the people of Israel in the judgments which are inflicted on other people. The name is explained in what follows.

Ver. 12. *Gods of Egypt.*—This is, of course, not to be taken literally, as though the gods of Egypt, or generally the heathen gods, were real beings, powers of the spiritual world, which Jehovah then judged. The scriptural names of the heathen deities—" Elilim," nothings, Lev. xix. 4 ; Ps. xcvi. 5 ; " Jetzer," something made, and other terms, in contrast with the " living God"—show most clearly that they are treated in Holy Scripture as human inventions without any reality. The Word of God does not afford any support to the notion of the fathers of the Church, that certain evil spirits had the power to reveal themselves as false deities to certain nations, and to establish for themselves a worship among them. This expression is here to be understood figuratively, just as when elsewhere, Isa. xix. 1, it is said, " The idols—the nothings—of Egypt shall be moved ;" or Jer. xlviii. 7, " Chemosh shall go forth into captivity with his priests and princes together ;" or as the emblematic miracle on the idol of Dagon, 1 Sam. v. 3, 4. The " gods of Egypt" are the power of error—which is, of course, something more than human—without, however, the different gods being evil spirits : cf. 1 Cor. x. 19, 20. This explanation seems preferable to the other, which supposes that here the judgments are said to be upon the Egyptian gods, because that people worshipped animals, and the firstborn of many of these sacred animals died. Still this circumstance is of importance for the understanding of the impression made by the plague, and particularly the mention of " beast," in ver. 12.

Ver. 13. *See the blood.*—A similar mode of expression with that concerning the rainbow, Gen. ix. 16. Although the Lord " knoweth His own," and so far requires no sign, yet still by this strong human mode of expression is the great truth represented that the sign was essential, and had a power and meaning in it, and that the atonement which the sacrifice effected was a needful one. The blood, therefore, is by no means merely for a confirmation of the faith of the Israelites.

Ver. 14. *Ordinance for ever.*—This expression is afterwards repeated in many of the commandments of the ritual law; *e.g.*, ch. xxvii. 21, ch. xxviii. 43, ch. xxx. 31; as also it is used, Gen. xiii. 15, of Canaan, and Gen. xvii. 13, of circumcision. " Eternal" is often said in Scripture of an indefinite time—not for a certain period. Thus the servant who will not be free remains a servant " for ever:" Deut. xv. 17. Yet with respect to the law, we must consider that it has never been abrogated: St Matt. v. 17.

Ver. 15. *Cut off.*—For explanation of this punishment, see Gen. xvii. 14, note.

Ver. 16. *Convocation.*—The people was called on these days with the sound of trumpets into the fore-court of the tabernacle: Num. x. 2–10. There solemn prayers and hymns and different sacrifices took place, and afterwards the sacrificial feasts. On the intermediate days there were likewise sacrifices and repasts, but they served also for work and business.

Ver. 19. *Born in the land.*—The "born in the land" are the descendants of Abraham; the "strangers," those proselytes from other people who were formally received into the people of Israel by circumcision, since one uncircumcised might not (according to ver. 43, etc.) eat with them. The same punishment, therefore, is to be inflicted on all.

Ver. 21. *Called.*—Moses tells the elders only what was immediately necessary: nothing of the observances which belong to the particular circumstances of the Exodus.

Ver. 22. *Dip.*—Hyssop (Heb., Esob; Greek, Hyssopus) is an aromatic plant, of a straight, strong stalk about a foot high, with woolly leaves; grows frequently in stony ground, on ruins or old walls. It was often used in religious sprinklings or purifications; e.g., in sprinkling of the blood of the red heifer, Num. xix. 6—of the water for the purifying of the lepers, Lev. xiv. 4. The small woolly leaves of the plant, gathered into a bundle, made it particularly adapted for the purpose of sprinkling.

Ver. 23. *Smite.*—In the Heb. the word stands which particularly denotes the infliction of a Divine judgment.

Ver. 27. *Shall say.*—On this is founded the beautiful custom, which has always prevailed among the Israelites in later times, at least since the dispersion, that the son of the house, at an appointed time in the Paschal Supper, shall ask the father of the family, " What meaneth all this?" and the father answers: " We eat this Passover, because the Lord passed over the houses of our fathers in Egypt. We eat these bitter herbs, because the Egyptians made the lives of our fathers bitter in Egypt. We eat this unleavened bread, because our fathers had not time enough to leaven their dough before the Lord appeared and redeemed them. Therefore shall we confess, laud, praise, and magnify Him who hath shown unto us and our fathers so great wonders, and hath brought us from bondage into freedom, from sorrow into joy, from darkness into great light." This is called the "Haggada," the declaration—explanation.

Ver. 32. *Have said.*—Cf. ch. x. 24, 25.

Ver. 35. *Did.*—On this night.

Ver. 36. *Lent.*—Heb., "gave," made presents. How incorrect is the translation "lent" is shown from this, that this word occurs only once again, in the vow of Hannah; and there the words properly mean, "And him I *give* to the Lord all his life long, since he has been begged from the Lord," 1 Sam. i. 28, where a "lending" is out of the question.—*Spoiled.* Cf. ch. iii. 21, note.

Ver. 37. *Succoth.*—Rameses was the principal town of the land of Goshen, which was also called the land of Rameses, Gen. xlvii. 11. It was afterwards called by the Greeks Heroonpolis. Succoth means "tabernacles," a name which belonged to many places, because in former times tents had been pitched there. Its locality is not now clearly to be ascertained.

Ver. 37. *Besides children.*—According to usual computation, this would make up the whole number of the people to be about two millions.

Ver. 38. *Mixed multitude.*—There is nothing contemptuous intended in this word "mixture." We may reckon among these such of the Egyptians as had been impressed by the succession of miracles of the Lord. This multitude of strangers was to be incorporated among the people.

Ver. 40. *Years.*—Gen. xv. 13.

Ver. 42. *Night.*—Literally, "A night of observances is this to the Lord, that He has brought them out of Egypt: this is the night of the Lord, observances for all the children of Israel for their posterity." By the express repetition of the words is the great importance of the festival of this night prominently set forth.

Ver. 44. *Eat thereof.*—No one might eat of the feast of covenant of the congregation, who had not entered into covenant with God by circumcision. Yet even here is the idea very observable, which is an essential part of the later laws, viz., that the servants, the slaves, are in covenant with God; and therefore, notwithstanding all difference of position and relation, were in full enjoyment of the blessings of the covenant, and spiritually equal with the rest.

Ver. 45. *Foreigner.*—A settler, a stranger who has settled down for a long time in one place, without obtaining the rights of citizenship.

Ver. 46. *Bone thereof.*—The house shall represent one congregation, the congregation of the people. For this the Passover shall be entire, and not distributed piece by piece to this and that company. This idea of unity is also the reason why no bone in the lamb was to be broken: cf. St John xix. 36. The Christian sacrament of the Lord's Supper, founded on the typical Paschal Supper, is to correspond to the Passover in all these particulars set forth in this passage. If we consider that in the N. T. the circumcision of the heart, and not outward baptism, corresponds to the rite of circumcision, so the discipline of the Christian Church, and its application to the sacrificial meal of the new covenant, is rightly founded on these precepts. Although from this place we cannot conclude that every private communion is irregular (since the ancient Church, by its practice of distributing the Lord's Supper to the sick, maintained the notion that the bread, first consecrated and partaken of in the church, was carried out of the church to the sick, and they became partakers of one bread), yet certainly it is to be recommended that at every private communion, either by the drawing together other persons who were absent, or by the connecting the private communion with that in church, the Divine intention of the union of His people at this holy sacrificial feast should be fulfilled as far as possible.

CHAPTER XIII.

Ver. 2. *Sanctify;* i.e., declare by thy word Israel to be holy: just as, according to Lev. xiii. 3, the priest, in respect to the leper, was "to make him unclean" (so the Hebrew). Here is at the same time an allusion to the creative power of the Divine word.

First-born.—In the First Book of Moses, we see throughout a prominence given to the right of the first-born, who received a double inheritance and authority over the family. The reason for this was chiefly founded on the great importance attached in ancient times to the keeping together of families—the transmission of their traditions—the maintenance of discipline and morality, of stedfastness and community. This family relationship had clearly continued in Egypt, and preserved Israel from disruption. It was in after times one of the foundation-stones of the Israelitish political constitution. But God could take away the right of the first-born, and choose the last to be first, and He had chosen Israel as His first-born son before all people (ch. iv. 22). As a retribution upon Pharaoh and Egypt for withholding this from Him, He had slain the first-born of Egypt. Among the people of God the right of the first-born was a holy one. Of Isaac's sons the first-born was the channel of transmission of the Divine promises of grace, and to this birthright appear to have been attached early privileges, which, if not priestly, had a resemblance to the Levitical. At all events, the first-born was the head, the centre of unity in the family, and so God's representative. After the judgment on the Egyptian first-born, Israel was now in a double way God's peculiar possession. He had spared them of His mercy, as He had punished the Egyptians. As a thank-offering, were all the first-born to be given up to Him. This sacrifice consisted in the perfect surrender to the service of the Lord; in which respect the tribe of Levi in later times stood in the place of the first-born, Num. iii. 13, and the first-born were hence under an obligation to tax themselves for its support; at the same time, the first-born was yet further released by an express offering. In all this we perceive a type of Him who is "the first-born of every creature," Col. i. 15; who gave Himself to God by the sacrifice of His own will once for all, for the sanctification of all, and not merely as a typical service. His death became at the same time the effectual sin-offering for men: cf. Heb. x. 5–10. This is the deep significance of the law before us, by means of which Moses was led to a clearer understanding of what took place before his eyes.

Ver. 3. *Said.*—He had, according to ch. xii. 21–27, only spoken to the people of the slaying the lamb, and striking the posts with blood. When in the haste of the journey they were compelled to eat the unleavened dough, he made known to them this commandment, which gave a deep meaning to an apparently accidental circumstance. When Moses in this place, and afterwards very often, speaks with "the people," with "the whole congregation," we are to understand thereby that he called the elders to him in presence of the people (ch. xii. 28), and these communicated to the people what he had told them.

Eaten.—Because the Lord hath preserved, made you His own, and sanctified you, ye shall observe this sign of purity.

Ver. 4. *Abib* means "month of ears of corn." On this month the harvest began, the first-fruits of which were brought on the feast of the Passover. The mention of it here is not to be regarded as a mere date; rather, the name signifies that the people in the month of harvest was earned as the first-fruit by the Lord.

Ver. 5. *Honey.*—Cf. iii. 17, note.

Ver. 7. *Seven days.*—Repeated for the sake of emphasis, as Gen. i. 27.

Ver. 9. *Memorial.*—From this passage, as from the similar places, ver. 16, Deut. vi. 8, ch. xi. 18, the custom of the Rabbinical Jews has its origin (of those among them, at least, who assign to tradition an equal weight with Holy Scripture), according to which the Jews write on strips of parchment certain passages out of the law—Exod. xiii. 2-10, 11-16; Deut. vi. 4-9, ch. xi. 13-21; according to Jerome, the ten commandments—and hang them between their eyes, and bind them on their hands (Thephillin, called phylacteries St Matt. xxiii. 5): while the Caraite Jews, who follow Scripture only, explain the passages figuratively. In the place before us, it is plain, at the first glance into the context, that the precept was never meant to be understood literally, since at ver. 16 the feast itself is called "a token upon the hand," etc. In the same way it is said, Prov. iii. 3, "Bind them about thy neck, and write them on the table of thine heart." The figure is derived from the amulets which the heathen were accustomed to hang about them to avert evil, or attract the influences of divine mercy. What this kind of superstitious service was supposed to afford the heathen, that should Israel by the solemnisation of the holy feast really obtain, as in this it gave itself anew to God as His covenanted people. The other passages mean the same. The Jewish custom originated at a time (probably after the return from Babylon) when

Israel, by means of its traditions, had perverted the holy spiritual commandments of God into doctrines of men: cf. St Matt. xv. 6.

Ver. 13. *Ass.*—Afterwards, when the laws concerning the unclean beasts were given, it is added, "of every unclean beast."

Ver. 18. *Led the people about.*—In the leading of the children of Israel, there is a manifest difference between what was God's original purpose in respect to it, and what afterwards took place as a punishment of their rebellion. This first journey into the wilderness to Mount Sinai was a compassion to the people, and at the same time to prove them, and was very different from the forty years' wandering, to which they were condemned (Num. xiv.) when about to invade the Promised Land. By the straight line of march through the land of the Philistines, the Israelites would have had not much more than three days' journey to the frontier. But the Philistines, of all the people who had migrated from Crete, were the most powerful (cf. Gen. x. 14), and were never entirely subdued by the Israelites. It is only after the Babylonish Captivity, and amid the revolutions of the great Asiatic empires, that the Philistines entirely disappear from history. The judgment of God was not destined especially to fall on them, as they were not Canaanites.

Red Sea.—"The reedy sea" (Heb., Suph), on account of the quantity of sea-weed which grows therein. It is often called the Red Sea in the O. T., and also in Egyptian.

Harnessed as for war; prepared for a hostile attack.

Ver. 19. *My bones.*—Gen. l. 25. So long as Joseph's services were kept in thankful remembrance among the Egyptians they would scarcely allow his body, like that of Jacob (Gen. l. 5), to be interred in Canaan. Foreseeing this, Joseph had made the elders swear that oath mentioned in Gen. l., and thereby kept alive among them a continual remembrancer of the fulfilment of God's promises made to their fathers. We perceive from the narrative before us how vividly these promises were preserved in an unbroken tradition by the Israelites in Egypt.

Ver. 22. *Took not away.*—At Etham, at the entrance into the wilderness, when their march began to be through a trackless land where God alone could direct them, does the mention occur for the first time of the miraculous guidance of Israel by means of the pillars of cloud and of fire. Among many ancient nations, smoke by day and fire by night were signals in time of war. Among the ancient Persians, "the holy eternal fire," which was to them the visible appearance of the godhead on earth, was carried on silver altars before the army in time of war. The appearance, in which the Lord afforded to His people not merely a memorial sign of His continual presence and guidance, but in which He truly dwelt among His people, might well bear a certain resemblance to this and other customs of heathen nations. It was one and the same cloud which cast a shadow by day and gave light by night (cf. ch. xiv. 19, 20). This outward sign had an inward emblematic meaning. In the desert, under the hot burning sun, the sight of a shady cloud is most pleasant and refreshing—it acts as a screen in front, and so a defence against the enemy; while the pillar of fire in the dreary pathless desert at night, during which the march for the most part is made, affords a comforting sense of security. Moreover, the cloud veiled the Divine Majesty, and was a continual remembrancer to Israel that they were not to make any image or likeness of their God. There is frequent mention made of this cloud and pillar of fire in the O. T.: Ps. lxxviii. 14, xcix. 7, cv. 39; Neh. ix. 19. And the prophet perceives in the defence of the shadow of the pillar and cloud a type of the eternal, all-protecting, and glorifying presence of the Lord, Isa. iv. 5. The people, by passing through the sea under the cloud, "were baptized unto Moses," 1 Cor. x. 2.

CHAPTER XIV.

Ver. 2. *Turn.*—The dwelling-place of the people of Israel in Egypt had been Goshen, called from its principal town "the land of Rameses." It is probable that the people had collected for the most part here, and they marched out from that town, for which they had for more than eighty years been obliged to make bricks. Their route lay through the valley which afterwards formed the bed of the great canal between the Nile and the Red Sea, even at that time affected commonly by the overflowings of the Nile. From thence the Israelites could easily march to the head of the Gulf of Suez in three days, the distance being about thirty-six or forty miles. Moses began to lead the people this way, which was the accustomed one from Arabia to Egypt, and which was sufficiently familiar to him from his own journeyings. Etham, the exact site of which cannot be determined, lay, therefore, probably in the neighbourhood of the only harbour of this part, Suez. But suddenly he receives a command from the Lord not to pursue this road any farther. The whole army turns towards the south, where a range of hills—on the west now called Mokattam, on the east Attaka—runs from the Nile to the Red Sea. In this waste region of coast-country they had on their right the sea, on their left the range of mountains, behind and before them the wilderness. When Pharaoh perceives this change in their line of march, he believes that they have lost their way, and are given into his hands. He follows after them, and, humanly speaking, all hope was at an end. Then the miracle of the dividing of the Red Sea takes place. Opposite Ras Attaka, the last peak of the range of hills, the sea is from W. to E. about twelve miles broad. If the east wind made a road in this part, the water standing up like walls on either side, in that case the alarmed people might by haste effect a passage in one night; so that, when Pharaoh in the morning pursued after them, they had reached the other side. The supposition of modern travellers, who place the spot of the crossing in the neighbourhood of Suez, north of this place—where the gulf runs out into a narrow strip, about 1500 paces wide, which at ebb-tide could be easily waded—is altogether in contradiction to the history, and rests on unsuccessful attempts to explain the miracle by natural causes. We find here the same miraculous guidance of the Lord which at all times attends God's kingdom on earth. He might have permitted His people to gain the wilderness by the accustomed route, and there by simple means have defended them from the power of Pharaoh; but He willed to make known His glory on this self-willed heathen, and at the same time, by a mighty miracle of deliverance, to sever His people, and for ever, from fellowship with the heathen. When the need has reached its highest point, the Lord shows Himself a deliverer in the mightiest way. He brings about the conversion of the people, and thereby sets forth this passage of the Red Sea as an image of Christian baptism

(1 Cor. x. 1, etc.), which separates us from the world and the prince of the world, and hands us over to the guidance of the Lord through the wilderness of earth to the heavenly Canaan.

Pi-hahiroth means " mouth of the caves ;" but is probably only turned into Hebrew from the Coptic, where it has the signification " place of the green turf."

Migdol.—This word, which often occurs as the name of places in Palestine, means " Tower ;" in the Coptic, " multitude of mountains." This place is often spoken of in the prophets, but is otherwise unknown.

Baal-zephon.—This word means in Heb., " Lord of the North." However, we may recognise therein the Egyptian god Typhon, " Place of Typhon." This was the evil spirit which came in the hot wind out of the desert to destroy the creations of Osiris in the valley of the Nile. The place lay on the naked range of coast on the Red Sea.

Ver. 3. *Entangled.*—The Divine guidance had so ordained, that by thus thinking he should run to his own destruction.

Ver. 4. *Honoured.*—God is glorified in His enemies by their destruction. God's governance of the world, which they would put away, brings them to nought, and thereby proves its own Divine, eternal origin.

Ver. 5. *Turned against.*—Ch. xi. 3, ch. xii. 36. So this change of mind might constitute the apparently unwise alteration of plan of marching to Pi-hahiroth, with the Red Sea on their left. They might imagine, therefore, that Moses was no true prophet, and that the guidance of God had forsaken His people.

Ver. 7. *Captains.*—Heb. : " And all the chariots of Egypt, and three combatants on each." We do not, among the ancient Egyptians nor the most ancient Greeks (in Homer, *e.g.*), hear of cavalry, properly so called ; but what was afterwards a horse-soldier (as Hippotes in Homer), was a combatant in a war-chariot. In every one of these there were three men, of whom one guided the horse—the two others fought : here the name translated " captains " is three combatants.—We know, from authentic information of the ancients, that the main position of the military caste lay on the eastern frontier, where Egypt was most exposed, so that Pharaoh could on the spot summon a large force. We know, likewise, that the kings of Egypt kept up a considerable body-guard. And although the force here named appears inconsiderable against the vast mass of the Israelites, yet we must take into consideration the great superiority every disciplined army has over even so vast a number of undisciplined men; and likewise, more especially, the circumstance, that in Egypt no one but the military class was allowed to carry arms. Thus Israel was at that time without weapons. For this reason, they were obliged to prepare arms in the wilderness for the conquest of Canaan, as they did not possess them before.

Ver. 8. *High hand;* i.e., boldly, joyfully, openly: though it must be confessed that this boldness was soon succeeded by as great fearfulness, which, indeed, was often the case in the after history of this wayward people.

Ver. 12. *Better.*—They had been bold, and had rejoiced in the continued enjoyment of God's miraculous protection; but their faith has so little root, that it cannot stand against the first assault. However, here there is no mention of any rebuke to His people from the Lord. He trains with patience His self-willed children, and passes over their first outbreak without reproof.

Ver. 15. *Criest unto Me?*—It is here implied that Moses had at that time prayed unto the Lord. He tells him the help for which he asks is at hand: let him stand up and act.

Ver 19. *Angel of God.*—According to ch. xiii. 21, it was the Lord Himself. It was the Angel in whom His name, His whole revealed nature, dwelt: cf. Gen. xvi. 7, note.

Ver. 21. *Stretched.*—Every one must see that here a miracle of the most wonderful kind is narrated. The ebb of the tide, though very prolonged, could never have produced the effect here narrated, viz., the passage on dry ground of two millions of men, with their herds, during a space of twelve hours. The result is quite inconceivable, that "the people should hear and fear," had nothing else happened than the march of the Israelites at ebb-tide under the guidance of a skilful and prudent leader; and Pharaoh would not have ventured into the sea at the flow of the tide. Whoever receives the account as true, will feel even now, on reading it, an awe in thought of the Divine Majesty which then revealed itself. The eyes of his faith will be opened to behold the same wonders in the history of God's people, and of His own children, happening even now about him.

Ver. 24. *Pillar.*—He revealed Himself to them in a fearful

manner from thence. The Egyptians had pursued the Israelites in the thick darkness, which was so much the easier, as the water at first remained divided for them. But when the morning came, the pillar of the cloud, which was floating before them, would fill them with an anxious foreboding of their fate, and with the feeling of the presence of some awful mystery.

Ver. 26. *Egyptians.*—By morning (in twelve hours) the Israelites had reached the opposite shore, distant about three miles. The Egyptians, closely following on them, filled the whole sea-way which had been dried up.

Ver. 27. *Fled.*—On the western shore the east wind first began to cease. The water therefore returned back there first to its bed. The Egyptians, flying from the Israelites, met the returning waves.

Ver. 30. *Hand of the Egyptians.*—An expressive summing up of the great miraculous event, similarly with ch. vi. 26, 27, ch. xi. 9, 10, ch. xii. 51.

Ver. 31. *Servant Moses.*—It was not only a feeling of awe at God's Majesty, but likewise one of confiding trust in His merciful protection, which now filled the whole congregation of Israelites; though, indeed, with the majority the feeling had no permanence. The Lord and His servant are here most closely associated, because all revelations of God to His people came through Moses; and one main object of the guidance by his hands was, to convince them of the Divine office of this servant of the Lord.

CHAPTER XV.

Ver. 1. *Sang.*—Israel was now in safety; and at once its awakened and confirmed faith pours itself forth in a song of thanksgiving and triumph. Moses was the inspired leader of the song: the people followed after him. The entire hymn consists of two parts. The first looks back on the past, on the mighty deed of Jehovah just experienced; the other looks forward with confidence to the future—the rest and peace in Canaan, and so becomes at the same time a prayer. Thankfulness for the mercy received, is the ground of hope that the Lord will not leave the work He has begun. The thoughts and the imagery of the song are simple and forcible. They dwell on the great event which has happened. They are derived from what they have seen with their eyes, without much movement or variety, as belongs to songs of very ancient times, and as under these circumstances was likely to be the case.—We find, in this hymn, the first traces of that arrangement of Hebrew poetry which divides each verse into two, and often more, lines. Apparently these hymns were sung from the first responsorially or antiphonally. As soon as the chorus of men had finished, the chorus of women repeats the whole; Miriam, as prophetess, reiterating the same in a more general way. The song, by the peculiar force and beauty with which it sets the whole history before us, had also the purpose of being a living, continual witness of the people to the great event. It was intended to declare to posterity through all ages, that so many hundred thousands beheld the great works of the Lord which gave existence to His people, and which would leave behind them such a monument for their children. Therefore we find in many poetical parts of the prophets, echoes, as it were, of this song of Moses.

Triumphed.—Heb.: "He is high exalted," or, "He has exalted Himself;" *i.e.*, revealed Himself in His great Majesty.

Ver. 2. *Salvation.*—At the very commencement is all honour in the redemption of the people ascribed to the Lord. In the Heb., the position of the words gives even more expression: "My strength and praise is Jah, and He is salvation to me" (Jah is the contracted form of Jehovah or Jahveh). The meaning is: "All my feeling and thoughts are now directed to the One Being."

Exalt Him.—With the praise of the sole majesty of Jehovah is connected the elevating and animating feeling, that it is the God of covenant who has fulfilled for His people the promise made to their fathers.

Ver. 3. *Name.*—Lit.: "He it is" is His name: cf. ch. iii 14. He is the true "Man of war," because He alone exists: everything which is, has being and existence only from Him; therefore all His enemies are but chaff before Him.

Ver. 5. *Sank.*—They could not save themselves by swimming. The greatness of the miracle is hereby graphically described, as ver. 10.

Ver. 7. *Consumed.*—God's anger is likened to a consuming fire: as the stubble is to flame, so is the opposition of His enemies to the almighty power of God.

Ver. 8. *Congealed*, lit., "curdled" like milk.

Ver. 11.—Lit.: " Who is as Thou among the gods, Jehovah? who is as Thou, glorious in holiness, fearful in praises, doer of wonders?" Seized with wonder, he inquires, who is like the Lord? His matchless greatness forces itself on the observance of those who consider His deeds. "Among the gods," does not at all mean among the heavenly, the angelic natures; but he compares the Lord with all heathen deities. The writer does not attribute to these deities real existence, as though they were to be regarded as higher beings, as powers of the spiritual world, who have fallen away from God. The expression is rather a bold poetic figure of speech, by which the nothingness of the gods is designated. God is glorious in holiness: all the glorious attributes of His Divine nature are pervaded and animated by His holiness. "Fearful in praises;" *i.e.*, celebrated with the deepest reverences by hymns of praise.

Ver. 13. *Hast guided.*—Since in the miraculous commencement of the guidance of the Lord lay the certain pledge of its fulfilment.

Ver. 14. *Palestina.*—" Sorrow took hold of Pelescheth:" the Pelischtim, the Philistines, the inhabitants of the southwestern low country on the sea in Canaan (cf. Gen. x. 14, note). The nearest were the first named. It seems as though it were concealed from Moses at the time that these, in particular, were not to be attacked.

Ver. 17. *Have established.*—A prophetic view cast forwards to a (then) distant future; since a long time elapsed before the sanctuary obtained an established dwelling-place in Mt. Zion. The mention of this in the oldest and most known song of Israel, must afterwards have proved a great confirmation to the belief that the sanctuary stood on no place arbitrarily chosen, but on that spot which the Lord had appointed. The words, then, "which Thy hands have established," refer to the eternal continuance of Zion. The people shall be planted "on the Holy Mountain"—while, elsewhere, the whole of Canaan is called its dwelling-place, and actually afterwards so was—because from the sanctuary the Lord governed and blessed the people. The mountain of the sanctuary is the place where this tree takes root, which spreads itself over the whole land and overshadows it.

Ver. 18. *The Lord shall reign.*—These words, which sum up the contents of the song in reference to the past and future, seem to form the conclusion of it. The following words are a prose addition, not so much for the purpose of explanation, which was not required, as for concluding corroboration, as ch. vi. 26, ch. xi. 10, ch. xiv. 30. God is here for the first time called a King (shall reign), (the patriarchs knew Him as the Lord, the Shepherd), because He now had formed for Himself a people and kingdom on earth. This name forms the leading thought in the whole constitution of the people.

Ver. 20. *Miriam.*—Her name is written Mariam by the Greek translators, and appears afterwards to have been so pronounced. It is the N. T. name Maria. She is called a prophetess, by which we are to understand not an office of any kind, but the peculiar endowment of the Holy Ghost: and this was not so much the power of predicting future events, as an inward suggestion and guidance of the Spirit, for the purpose of arousing, exhorting, comforting, rebuking, in inspired and poetic language. Several prophetesses of this description are mentioned in the O. T., as Deborah the judge, Huldah, etc. The raising up of such prophetesses was at all times an exception to the rule, and was altogether to cease in the N. T. dispensation; but the whole prophetic office was itself also an exception, in which, so soon as a rule was established, fresh exceptions started forth (cf. Amos vii. 14). Over and beside the regular guidance of His people through the priestly and kingly offices, God willed to interfere in an extraordinary manner with the government of them, when these offices by man's sin lost their vitality, and were deprived of their sanctity. Miriam is called here Aaron's sister, as he himself performed the office of Moses' prophet, and probably had taken the lead in the chorus of men as Miriam in that of the women: cf. iv. 14.

Ver. 20. *Timbrels.*—The song was accompanied by the hand-drum (tambourine)—a ring with skin stretched over it, and with little bells attached. The same kind is at this day carried by Oriental women in processions. Miriam went first, the others followed " in rows"—made a solemn procession in a tricircular dance. The manner of expressing enthusiastic religious emotions by regular graceful movements and postures of body, is often mentioned in the O. T.: Judges xxi. 21; 2 Sam. vi. 14; 1 Sam. xviii. 6; Jer. xxxi. 4, etc. Dances not of a religious character, appear to have been unknown to the Israelites. Similar religious processions of women, with song and dance, still take place in the East; as, *e.g.*, in Egypt when the Nile begins to rise. The degradation of the dance into an instrument of vanity, has estranged it from the service of God, as has been the case with so many of the fine arts. But we may expect, from the strengthening of the Christian Church, that it will again, in time to come, consecrate to the Lord whatever has been withdrawn from Him: as some particular sects (in North America) have introduced, though certainly after a most objectionable manner, the dance into their worship.

Ver. 21. *Answered*—viz., the men; *i.e.*, she sang an antistrophe to the preceding song of the men. The same thing occurs 1 Sam. xviii. 7, and is alluded to Cant. vi. 13. The whole was a repetition in prophetic fervour of the main thoughts of the song, the two lines being sung antiphonally.

Ver. 22. *Moses brought.*—Israel now entered on the long march in the wilderness, through which he was to reach the Promised Land. The Red Sea is divided on the north side into two long bays, that of Heroonpolis and Ælan—or, as they are now called, of Suez and Akaba. Between these two is situated the peninsula which, together with the slip of desert to the north, on the Mediterranean and south border of Palestine, is called Arabia Petræa. To the south, between the two arms of the sea, runs a range of limestone and sandstone hills, the chief of which is a granite mountain, now called Tur—in Holy Scripture, Horeb. The wilderness begins at the point where the effects of the overflowings of the Nile cease, about three days' journey from the sea-coast. It is not sandy in every part; but a wide extent of surface is often to be met with, covered with a silicious earth. In some few spots there occur scanty, and frequently salt springs: by the side of the sweeter waters are pasture-grounds, with their palm-trees—garden spots—little oases: elsewhere, scarcely anything beside acacias and tamarisk trees are to be found. At the present time from about 4000 to 6000 Arabs inhabit this peninsula. Northwards from Sinai, where the granite pass into the sandstone mountains, the heights are less considerable, the peaks more rounded, and the valleys more genial. Still farther north there runs a barren, sandy plain, bounded from W. to E. by a long ridge of hills of nearly equal altitude, from Suez to Akaba. On the other side this ridge, called El-Tieh, runs the just named dreary wilderness up to the Mediterranean. Here the streams are extremely few, and far and wide not a tree or a shrub, and not a single village from Sinai to Gaza. This march of the Israelites in the wilderness was certainly of great importance for the training of the people. The Lord "allured her, and brought her into the wilderness to speak comfortably to her:" Hosea ii. 14. Then was Israel a beloved young bride. Jer. ii. 2. No other discipline could have freed them so entirely from the former bands of heathenism and irreligion. But that which, in the original design of the Lord, would have been a short time of trial and purification, became extended to a long period of punishment, as they had tempted the Lord ten times, and He sware in His wrath that none of those who came out from Egypt should see the Promised Land. So their wanderings became forty, instead of the two years originally designed: Num. xiv. 23. And yet the blessing of this guidance of their fathers was not lost on the following generation. We behold, under Joshua, an era appear, the like of which seldom is to be found in the history of the people of God. At the very beginning of their journeyings we meet with a rule of God's dealing with the people, which is constantly carried out. For while He by miracle and immediate revelation guided and supported His people, yet natural means are not excluded, but rather Israel is continually referred to them. Thus the advice of Jethro, ch. xviii.—the pointing out of resting-places in the wilderness by the same (Hobab), Num. x. 31.—the means of nourishment from the natural products of the wilderness, besides the manna. Thus was it likewise with respect to water. Modern travellers have very justly mentioned the fact, that so great a host of men could not at present live on the peninsula, merely on account of want of water. Now we find that they often meet with springs—that water gushes out of the rock at the command of Moses; still all this would, under the ordinary course of things, have been insufficient. We must necessarily conclude from what is told us, according to analogy, that God made use of the natural products of the wilderness by supernaturally multiplying them for the support of the Israelites. But as the pillar of cloud and of fire did not exclude the guidance of Hobab, nor the continuous revelations the counsel of Jethro, in like manner, the water, the pasture, in short all that the wilderness afforded, were miraculously blessed to suffice for the support of His people and their herds. But amid all the rich supply of blessings, interruptions often occur for the trial of the people: the water did not suffice—it was denied altogether—it was bitter. The Lord treats the first natural outbreak of discontent in our history with forbearance; and at the same time, by the miracle on the water, He points to the inexhaustible source of all life, of all health, which the people have in Him.

Shur.—A town on the borders of Egypt, in the direction of Palestine, from which the adjacent wilderness was named. It is improbable that it should have been Pelusium, situate on the right mouth of the Nile: most likely, a town in the neighbourhood of the present Suez. The wilderness called after it lay on the east shore of the Gulf of Suez, whence the Israelites now marched in a south-easterly direction to Sinai.

Ver. 23. *March.*—If we suppose that, after the passage through the Red Sea, the first days' journeys of the Israelites were short, and that they landed in a part now called Ajun Musa, then they would have reached in fifteen or sixteen hours a place now called Howara. "We travelled over rough, hilly, gravelly, flinty ground, and came to the springs Howara, round which some date-trees grew. The water is so bitter that men cannot drink of it; and the camels, unless very thirsty, refuse it."—Burckhardt, 770. The scriptural name is now there unknown.

Ver. 25. *Sweet.*—No Arab could tell modern travellers of a tree which had the power to make the bitter water sweet. The knowledge of such would be very welcome, as all the springs of the peninsula have more or less a brackish and sulphureous taste. However, the history says expressly, the Lord showed Moses a tree: not by His word, or any other display of His almighty power, did the water become sweet. Even if such a tree is unknown, we may not conclude that it did not then exist in the place. Burckhardt supposes the change might have been effected by means of the berries of the Gharkad (wild rue, Peganum retusum), which grows in some valleys of the wilderness; but this will not quite agree with the narrative. But anyhow, the rare occurrence of the last-named shrub, or the slight effect of the berries, will be no argument against it; since the blessing on means, naturally inadequate to produce great effects, is altogether in accordance with the laws of the history before us.

Proved them; i.e, in this first trial He gave them a representation of all future ones, both in the weakness they displayed and in the mercy He showed, so long as they openly expressed their discontent, and did not proceed to defiance and disobedience of Him.

Ver. 26. *Healeth thee.*—As I have now made the bitter waters sweet (the same expression is used of the Dead Sea, which instead of salt water obtains sweet, Ezek. xlvii. 8).

Ver. 27. *Elim.*—This place has, with probability, been supposed to lie in the Wady Gharendel, 42 miles S.E. of Suez. "In the rainy season there is a strong stream here, which flows into the gulf. It was dry now (September); but we obtained tolerably good water at 2 or 3 feet in the sand, as it had not rained for a long while. As here there is no lack of water, we find also abundance of trees—a pleasant sight for one coming from Cairo."—Niebuhr. The 12 wells of water and the 70 palm-trees correspond with the 12 tribes and the 70 elders—a gracious mark of God's loving-kindness.

CHAPTER XVI.

The provision which the Israelites had taken with them, on entering the dreary wilderness that extends to Mt. Sinai, was sufficient only for a few days. When the people vehemently express their discontent, the Lord begins in a miraculous way to provide food for them in the wilderness. He gives them flesh and bread; but both in a form which peculiarly belonged to their place of abode. In all the East, especially in Arabia Petræa, the bird translated "quail" (Tetrao Alchata, Linn.) abounds. It is about the size of a partridge, and the natives are very fond of its flesh. "In the mountains of Belka, Kerek,

Dschebal (in the land of the Moabites and Edomites, close to the scene of the narrative before us), the bird called Katta is met with in great numbers, particularly in May and June. They fly in such dense flocks that the Arabian boys often kill one or two at a blow, by merely throwing a stick at them" (Burkh. 681). From the time of this history the name of manna has been given generally to a thick, glutinous, sweet juice, which oozes out of many kinds of shrubs. But more particularly is there at this day, in the Sinaitic peninsula, a shrub of the tamarisk genius (Tamarix mannifera), from the leaves of which a gummy substance exudes, when pierced by the sting of the cochineal (coccus). This juice curdles, and falls to the ground in a granulated form. It must be collected in the morning before the sun is up, else it will melt. This is eaten as honey on bread. These are the two natural products which formed the ground-work of the Divine miracle. And here, as in the case of the miracles in Egypt, God shows Himself to be the Lord of the whole earth, and of this land in particular, not by creating something new and altogether unknown, but by affording to existing nature a richness, a fulness, and also qualities which it could not else have possessed. Manna furnished the ground-work of this miracle; yet was it at the same time bread from heaven—a food wonderfully provided by God Himself. For, in the first place, it is quite clear that all the quails and all the manna of the Sinaitic peninsula, taken together, would scarcely have supported the enormous host of men more than a few days, since the natural manna can only be collected sparingly under a few tamarisk shrubs, scattered here and there. Next, it is, generally, only found in rainy years (often not for five years), and then only in the months of June and July. In the wide sandy valley of Ghor, where afterwards the Israelites wandered for so long a time, there is none at all. Besides, it is nowhere mentioned that Israel had nothing but manna in the wilderness. They had brought their flocks and herds out of Egypt. The land poor as it is, possesses still some means of nourishment. Later' we find that they wished to buy food from the Edomites (cf. ch.' xii. 38, ch. xvii. 3, ch. xxxiv. 3; Num. xx. 19, ch. xxxii. 16; Deut. ii. 6, 7). Still all this would not have sufficed to support a twentieth part of the multitude in the most fruitful years. And therefore we must regard the miracle from a similar point of view as the corresponding one in the N. T.—the feeding of the 5000 with five loaves and two fishes—and explain it as the supply of water, ch. xv.—But beyond this external view of the miracle there lies a higher meaning. It was "spiritual food," the Apostle says, as the water out of the rock was "spiritual drink:" 1 Cor. x. 3, 4. The object of the miracle is told us by Moses himself, Deut. viii. 3. Israel should know that man does not live by bread alone, but by every word that proceedeth out of the mouth of God. The people of God are nourished and cared for day by day by the Lord and God of covenant. This great truth, concealed from the natural man—since God's providential care acts through the creature, and is thus veiled—was to be made known to Israel, and the people thus placed in personal communion with the Almighty God of nature, the Lord who had redeemed them from heathen nature-worship. And so far, manna afforded something more than mere bodily nourishment. The fathers indeed did eat manna in the wilderness and died—it was not bread which by itself could be the food of immortality. But for those who partook of it in faith, it was a veritable channel of Divine grace—a sacrament. Ever afresh was the people confirmed by this daily, perpetual miracle of love and grace, in their faith in the Creator of all things, who needeth not bread in order to support His people,—on the God of covenant, who giveth to His people all that they can need.

Ver. 1. *Sinai.*—According to Num. xxxiii. 10, they halted first at the Red Sea. They had passed through a very mountainous region, to the entrance of what is now Wady Taibe. Soon afterwards a broad plain begins, which stretches almost without interruption to the south point of the entire peninsula, at present called El-Kaa: this is the wilderness of Sin. From this plain they marched into the mountains, through the Wady Feiran to the Wady es-Scheikh. This is the district where the manna is especially found.

Ver. 3. *Would:* lit., "Who gives us that we," etc.

Ver. 5. *Daily.*—While the Lord miraculously provides for His people, He will at the same time have them exercise their own diligence. Every one must be up in the morning as soon as the dew has fallen, and collect diligently. But He will at the feasts, and at the assembling of the Sabbath, try their faith in His providence. The greedy man, who, by keeping the manna to the following day, would save himself an act of faith, is put to shame. In all these miracles is mirrored forth the mystery—hidden from the natural man—of God's daily dealings in providing food for His creatures.

Ver. 10. *Appeared.*—It seems as though this appearance of the Lord "in the wilderness" is not without significance. The "pillar of the cloud" never departed from them by day (ch. xiii. 22). It guided the march of the host—belonged thereto. Here the Lord appears in especial glory without the camp, to signify that through their murmurings His presence had departed from them—was adverse to them: as afterwards the tabernacle is pitched "without the camp" (ch. xxxiii. 7).

Ver. 15. *Bread.*—Manna is called, in Heb. and Arabic, Man, and means, gift, present. When the Israelites, in compliance with the preceding command, went forth from their tents, they called out one to another, as they had no name for it (the words may also be taken interrogatively), Is this the gift? And Moses assures them of it, with the explanation, that it is the bread of God. "The Israelites give a proof of thankfulness by calling the food which was given them from heaven, Man; and thereby silently condemn their perverse, thankless murmuring, since it was so much better for them to collect food offered to their hands than to procure it for themselves by a laborious husbandry. But Moses shows they had not inquired concerning something altogether unknown to them, but represents their notion as a mixture of ignorance and knowledge. Before their eyes was manifested the power of God; yet the veil of unbelief hung over it, that they did not behold clearly the grace promised to them."—Calvin.

Eat.—In order to form a just notion of the miracle here narrated, we must keep in view the especial object of the bestowal of the manna; viz., to impress, by means of an extraordinary dispensation of Providence, a lively sense of God's ordinary dealings on a people who had been brought up in a nature-worship, and were addicted to it. In the collecting of the manna, the Israelites were made to depend partly on their own industry and care. But many cases might occur in which these did not suffice to provide what was needful. Want of skill without any fault of their own, or delay, or distance, might allow many to collect only a small quantity. In these cases the Divine care was at hand to make all equal: the most favoured did not collect any over,—his utmost industry was necessary for the providing a needful supply; and the least favoured was not a whit behind, —he, too, obtained all that he and his required. This is a law of the Divine governance generally, but he alone comes to understand it who looks beyond the outward appearance of things. The truth, therefore, is revealed to this people in a simple emblematic manner. As love is the soul of this Divine law, so ought the love of God in the souls of Christians to make this the law of their dealing one with another.

Ver. 20. *Wroth with them.*—Step by step God puts them to the test; yet He bears patiently with them, and suffers His deeds to speak to them. "To care for the morrow brings no blessing to the people of God." This great truth God causes to be preached to the sight and feeling of His people.

Ver. 30. *Rested on the seventh day.*—From the whole account it is clear that the Sabbath had not hitherto been kept by the Israelites. In all of the first book of Moses, we do not find any trace of its observance. It is only when Israel became a people that this important ordinance of God—so beneficial for the inner and outward life of the congregation of His people, and of such deep consequence in the development of the kingdom of God— came into operation. Still Moses speaks of the holy rest of the Lord as of something well known to the people. The tradition of the very ancient revelation (Gen. ii. 23) still continued among them; and, dividing their moons into four parts, like the other nations of antiquity, they might, on the seventh day of the week, well remember that original revelation. But of a distinct command, of any regulation forbidding work on that day, is there no mention. Here was the Lord the immediate guide of His people. His direct ordinances regulate their whole outer life; and so was the law respecting the Sabbath most naturally ordained in connection with the gift of manna. As work and diligence were needful even in the obtaining of this gift, so was work forbidden on the Sabbath day; still in a way the most considerate for this perverse people,—viz., that they should receive a double supply on the sixth day. It is the discovery of the greatness of this gift which leads the rulers to make the inquiry, and occasions the declaration of the law. All these circumstances are of eternal import, and show forth a rule of God's dealings; for in them the people of God have the sure pledge, that the blessing of the Lord will richly compensate all loss of labour incurred for the sake of His holy day. After the people have thus learned by their own experience the blessing with which the Lord rewards obedience to His ordinances, the rest of the Sabbath is solemnly ordained in the ten commandments, and the reasons for its Divine appointment given.

Ver. 31. *Honey.*—The same is the nature of the natural manna.

Ver. 36. *Ephah.*—The last words (ver. 32–35) were evidently not written on this occasion, since the "Testimony" (ver. 34) were the tables of the law in the Ark of the Covenant, which did not at that time exist. It appears that the idea of a book, containing all the great events of the Exodus, very early presented itself to the mind of Moses, under the direction of God (ch. xvii. 14, note). But though each circumstance was at once recorded, the arrangement of the whole might well be reserved for times of quiet. When this happened, is doubtful: but that it did not take place until after the entrance into Canaan, is from ver. 35 by no means necessary to be supposed; since, after two years, the doom of forty years' dwelling in the wilderness is declared (Num. xiv. 34). That now the manna was to be laid up before the Lord, shows that this miracle is of eternal import to the people of God. Not merely are they reminded thereby of a remarkable dispensation—a great benefaction from the Lord, but rather a deep principle of the loving care of Providence is therein made known for all times. It was a kind of sacramental covenant, withdrawing man from the service of Nature, and placing him in living and blessed communion with the personal Lord and Creator of the world. The ephah is as much as a "measure," metretes, St John ii. 6, which contains 1985·77 Parisian cubic inches (according to Böckh and Berthean): the weight of an omer, the tenth part thereof, might at least amount to a pound. The ephah is the standard measure from which the reckoning was made. The statement therefore in this place, of what an omer is, would serve to give to all times a notion of what Israel had received at God's hands in the wilderness.

CHAPTER XVII.

Ver. 1. *Rephidim.*—The people are now drawing near to the first great goal of their wanderings—Mount Sinai; since the stations Dophkah and Alush (Num. xxxiii. 12, 13) lie between the commencement of the wilderness of Sin (ch. xvi. 1) and Rephidim; and Rephidim, as the history shows, was also close to Sinai, perhaps in the long and wide valley, Wady es-Scheikh. As here the people experience the want of water, they tempt the Lord; *i.e.*, dissatisfied with the proofs of Divine guidance they have hitherto received, they put Him to the test, whether He be really among them or not. All belief that rests on evidences afforded to the senses is ever insatiable in its demands. God grants them water out of the rock, but at the same time gives them to understand that it is not the natural rock which produces the supply, but He Himself, the Lord who went with them. The rock out of which the water gushed, is called "a rock in Horeb" (ver. 6): it is therefore evident that Rephidim, though a day's journey from Sinai, must lie in the commencement of the range of hills, as in these books the name Horeb is given to the whole mountain country, of which Sinai forms a particular hill. Burckhardt describes this region (ii. 798): "We gradually ascended in a south-easterly direction. The valley became narrower. In a couple of hours we came to a thick wood of tamarisks, or tarfa shrubs, and found several camels browsing on the prickly pods. From this ever-green tamarisk, which grows so luxuriantly nowhere in the peninsula as in this valley, is the manna collected. We approached now the heights of Sinai, which stand as the central point of the whole, and which we had kept in view for several days. These granite cliffs, 6000 to 8000 feet high, the surface of which is blackened by the sun, inclose the passes which lead to the elevated platform, called in a narrower sense Sinai. The cliffs shut in the holy mountain on three sides, and leave open to sight only the north and north-eastern sides towards the Gulf of Akaba. On either side of the tamarisk forest there runs a range of lower hills, formed of a material which looks like white clay. After the lapse of three hours, we reached the above-mentioned cliffs through a narrow defile of granite rock, about 40 feet wide. In a broad part of the pass is shown an isolated rock, some five feet high, forming a sort of natural seat. This is named "Moses' Seat." Farther up the valley widens, the mountains recede from the path on both sides, and the Wady es-Scheikh penetrates yet more into the height, in a southerly direction. In the neighbourhood lies the well Abu-Szuehr, and not far from this a wide open plain surrounded by low hils."

To drink—They had just left the fruitful and well-watered Wady Feiran. Some water, indeed, is now found there; but without the extraordinary blessing of the Lord, all the water of the wilderness had been totally insufficient for the great multitude. As Jesus, after He had been miraculously sustained without food for forty days in the wilderness, "afterwards hungered," so did the Lord permit in this case a time of trial to succeed a time of plenty.

Ver. 2. *Give us water.*—Moses and Aaron were both addressed, because the latter in Moses' name was spokesman to the people.

Ver. 5. *Before.*—In the face of the danger which threatened.

Ver. 6. *Stand.*—Probably, as at all times, in a cloud. This took place, for a visible proof that it was the Lord's power which caused the water to gush out.

Ver. 8. *Amalek.*—The nations around, especially the Edomites and the Philistines, had heard with terror and astonishment of the mighty acts of the Lord in Egypt (ch. xv. 14, 15), and none had ventured to assail Israel. But the Amalekites (an Edomitish nomadic tribe, Gen. xxxvi. 12-16), who had wandered from Mount Seir (1 Chron. v. 42, 43), in South Palestine (Gen. xiv. 7) and the Petrean peninsula, at that time in the flower of their vigour—"the first of the nations" (Num. xxiv. 20), undertook, in reliance on their own strength, to attack the people of the Lord. They were animated with the same jealousy and hostility against a people nearly connected with them by descent, as afterwards we shall perceive, though in a less degree, was the case with the Edomites, and were certainly under apprehension that they would at some time be brought into subjection to Israel: Gen. xxvii. 29. Here begins with the people of God a new and important series of events. Hitherto the Lord had fought for them, and they had remained still (ch. xiv. 14); but now were they, though in reliance on the might and presence of God, and in constant dependence on Him, to learn themselves to fight and to conquer. This was a hotly contested fight; and, as in all such cases, the result was for a time uncertain. It was only the banner raised by Moses, and the faith in this, which at length overcame all opposition. The memory of this wonderful and significant event was perpetuated by an altar set up on account of it, and by the first command of writing a memorial in the book of this history. At the same time, also, the judgment is recorded against the sin of this people, which henceforth is destined to be "utterly put out of remembrance;" which doom was by degrees accomplished on them: Deut. xxv. 17–19; 1 Sam. xv. 2, 3, etc.; 1 Chron. iv. 43.

Ver. 9. *Joshua.*—A foreshadowing of his future election to be the leader of the people of God: as yet we have not heard that he was the servant of Moses. His human talent for command, as well as his faith and reliance on God, are here to be exercised.

Mine hand.—It is not related that Moses held up his hands in the posture of one praying; rather, he held up one arm, and raised on high the wonder-working rod as a banner for the people in battle. In ordinary human battles, the banner is the rallying point of the army, and the sight of it a continual stimulus to hope (as Isa. v. 26, ch. xi. 12, and other places, show): in like manner was this sign to be a pledge to the Israelites of the wonder-working presence of God.

Ver. 11. *Let down.*—The natural weakness of the servant of the Lord must become apparent, that the might of God may in him and through him be more glorified.

Ver. 12. *One side:* exchanging hands—now one hand, now the other, being held up.

Going down.—Although this sounds like a mere appeal to the outward senses, and as if the banner raised on high had gained the victory as by a charm, yet we must always bear in mind that the people at that time required outward signs, in order for them to realise the presence of the Lord. We nowhere afterwards read of such a banner; and yet the people fought and gained victories through the Lord, just as they received food and drink in Canaan without the manna and the water from the rock. The Lord bestowed His blessing, in the first instance, without requiring unconditional faith from the people, or, at least, without making His miraculous help to depend on this faith. It is otherwise in the N. T.: St Matt. viii. 10, note.

Ver. 14. *In a book.*—Heb., in *the* book. From this it is evident that already the recording of the great events of the people of God had begun (perhaps first with the hymn of triumph, ch. xv.); although it is not said that Moses at that time composed the book we now possess, paragraph after paragraph.

Joshua.—As the future leader.

Ver. 15. *Jehovah-Nissi.*—Moses continues the custom of the patriarchs (Gen. xii. 7) until the mode of worship is instituted for the people. The name of the altar expresses accurately the purport of the whole history.

Ver. 16. *Generation.*—Heb.: "Because he hath laid his hand on the throne of the Lord, therefore," etc. The throne of the Lord is among His people, or, rather, is His people itself. Amalek wished to put it to the proof, whether the living God really was King of this people. Therefore, because he has attacked the kingdom of the Lord, the Lord fights against him even to his extermination.

CHAPTER XVIII.

Ver. 1. *Jethro.*—We find in Jethro a servant of the true God not belonging to Israel: of such, since the time of the patriarchs, there were still some, though they were fewer and fewer. Still he can scarcely be supposed to have kept the worship of God quite unmixed with heathen errors. For such men as these, were the mighty deeds shown by God to His people a strengthening of their faith. So we find here a communion with a stranger in the worship of God, such as does not again occur.

Ver. 2. *Sent back.*—He had sent her back home, as we here find, before the breaking out of the Egyptian plagues; perhaps because, as an alien, he did not fully confide in her firm adherence to the communion of the people of God, which was so needful to make her fit to be a companion in the Exodus.

Ver. 3. *Strange land.*—Cf. ch. ii. 22.

Ver. 4. *Sword of Pharaoh.*—The name of the second son is here mentioned for the first time; perhaps because only now the full meaning of the name had received a fulfilment.

Ver. 7. *Tent; i.e.,* of Moses: cf. Gen. xii.

Ver. 11. *Lord.*—Jehovah.

Proudly.—The Lord has proved His might in overruling the tyranny and oppression of the Egyptians upon the Israelites. We perceive in this, that Jethro was under the influence of a heathen mode of viewing the matter, which regarded the subjection of a whole people by another as a mark of the weakness of its God. Now, on the contrary, had he seen that never had any God done such wonderful things for the preservation of his people as had been done for Israel. Jethro scarcely worshipped God under the name Jehovah, which is not found among the descendants of Abraham, the Arabs; but he might so speak to Moses of the true God, whom he honoured after the manner in which He had been revealed. Nay, more: he was also deeply impressed with the feeling of His glory, and clave to His service, not without blessed consequences for the future.

Ver. 12. *Burnt-offering.*—The "burnt-offerings" (of which we shall speak more fully afterwards) were entirely burnt: in them the meaning of atonement was the prevailing one. The "sacrifices" were, without doubt, thank-offerings, part of which was consumed by fire, part was eaten,—in later times, by the priests and the persons sacrificing.

Before God.—A great, solemn sacrificial meal was prepared, as a common public thanksgiving for their preservation.

Ver. 14. *He said.*—The counsel of a man who did not himself belong to the people of the covenant leads to an institution which, in the after-development of the Israelitish constitution, was of considerable importance. Since the Lord Himself was King of His people, and Moses His sole immediate vicegerent, the whole governing power must, under God, be in his hands. Greatly as Moses, in all that he did, enjoyed the blessing of the Divine guidance, still by degrees a distinction must come in between what he did at God's immediate command, and what he made known according to the general measure of light afforded him. By this means the office of lawgiver would distinguish itself from that of judge. This was now effected by the advice of a prudent, sensible man, who, perhaps, thereby first brought home to Moses' mind the fact of this distinction.

Ver. 19. *Godward.*—In all the things in which there is no Divine decision made known, and in which no man can decide, there stand thou before God for the people.

Ver. 21. *Able men,* of unimpeachable character.

Rulers of tens.—By this appointment there was formed among the people an office independent of the patriarchal mode of government. These judges were, as we see from Deut. i. 13, chosen out of the people, placed before Moses, and by him inducted into their office; but at the same time they are there called "heads of the tribes"—*i.e.,* generally, fathers of families. Moreover, in this election regard was especially had to the chiefs of the families; yet, as the choice was regulated according to personal qualifications, the order of rank by birth was no more decisive. The electors in the tribes and in the particular divisions were, without doubt, the heads of families. That the officers are appointed in relation to numbers merely, and not to property, was owing to the fact that Israel in the wilderness was a military constitution. It is evident in Canaan these circumstances were changed. But even in this division according to numbers, the family constitution was not without its influence, which is here not mentioned, as being a sufficiently well-known fact.

Ver. 23. *In peace.*—Every one will go to his house satisfied.

CHAPTER XIX.

From Rephidim, on the fore-mountains of Horeb, the people proceed a day's march into the wilderness of the Sinaitic range, which forms the centre of the whole peninsula. The wonderful granite formation of hills, with its variety of strange shapes, wild, abrupt peaks, blackened by the sun—with its lovely, well-watered, and fertile valleys abounding in fruit,—has three summits in particular which have obtained great note. The two front ones are the northern and southern extreme points of a ridge of hills between two valleys, Wady-Shueib and Wady el-Ledscha: the northern point, situated on the table-land, now called Horeb, rises steep and rocky to a height of 12,000 to 15,000 feet; by the side of this runs the valley Wady-Shueib, in which is the celebrated monastery of Mount Sinai, lying in a lovely oasis. Almost due south of this lies the now called Dschebbel Musa (Hill of Moses), generally regarded as the ancient Sinai, the southern extremity of the lofty ridge: on the flattened top there is a small mountain valley. South-west from thence lies the St Catherine hill, the highest point of the peninsula, more than 8000 feet high. From recent researches there seems to be no doubt that, of the three celebrated points, the more prominent northern one, now called Horeb, and particularly the heights of it, at present named Ras Sufsafeh, may be regarded as the mount of the giving of the law. In front of this mountain is extended a valley of about two miles in length, and in some places one in breadth, adjacent to which are other wide, broad valleys. Arriving from the north-west, the approach is through a wild desolate pass. The interior higher peaks of the great circle of Sinai—black, wild, desolate ridges—are seen in front: at every step the dark threatening cliffs of Sinai. The valley widens and gradually ascends, environed by wild, jagged, granite rocks and peaks: then is extended before the eyes of the traveller, on the elevation where the streams separate, a lovely wide valley, shut in by rough, solemn-looking, dark granite hills, naked cliffs, and ridges of indescribable sublimity: some distance behind, the boldly precipitous wall of Horeb. "The scene around," says Robinson, "was a glorious and sublime one, altogether unexpected, and such as we had never witnessed. He proceeds to say: "The great difficulty, and even danger, in the ascent to the Ras-Sufsafeh (the rocky summit of Horeb), was amply repaid by the view which opened upon us. The whole plain land, er-Rahah, with its adjacent wadys and mountains, lay stretched before our feet; while to the right Wady es-Scheikh, and to the left the bend towards the Ledscha valley, both joined with the table-land, and running out from it to a considerable distance, almost doubled the whole tract. Here, or on one of the adjacent cliffs, was the place where the Lord descended with fire, and proclaimed His law. Here lay the plain where the whole people could be assembled; here stood the mountain which could be approached, which could be touched, if it were not forbidden; here was the mountain-top where the lightning and the thick cloud were visible, and the thunder and the sound of the trumpet could be heard, when the Lord came down in the sight of all the people on Mount Sinai." Consequently, the whole mountain-range is called in Holy Scripture Horeb; as even a day's journey from Sinai, at Rephidim, mention is made of the "rock in Horeb," ch. xvii. 6. But Sinai must be the mountain which rises immediately above the table-land, now called Horeb; since, from the Mount of Moses, which is commonly called Sinai, it is impossible to see any part of the valley, as it is concealed by the intervening heights of Horeb.—Before the Lord proclaims His law, He makes a solemn covenant with His people. He offers to be their King and Lord; and if they will be His people, they shall become a kingdom of priests and a holy people. Moses is commissioned to declare this to the people, and to bring back their assent. Then follow the sublime preparations for the giving of the law.

Ver. 1. *Same day.*—The word "month" is in the Heb., properly, "renewing,"—namely, of the moon: new moon, because with every new moon the month began. On the first day, therefore, of the third month they arrived, about six weeks after the Passover. According to Jewish tradition, the giving of the law commenced on the sixth day of this month.

Wilderness of Sinai.—The wider and more extended valleys in the vicinity of the mountain.

Ver. 3. *Mountain.*—As the mountain now called Horeb has several peaks, Moses probably ascended the mountain-ridge, and heard the Lord speak to him from one of the heights. Doubtless the pillar of the cloud stood on the mountain, and afforded there the sign of the presence of the Lord.

Children of Israel.—The repetition of the synonymous terms, "House of Jacob," "Children of Israel," prefaces a solemn address.

Ver. 4. *Eagles' wings.*—When danger threatens the young ones, or when they cannot as yet fly, the eagle will take them on her strong wings and support them: Deut. xxxii. 11.

Ver. 5. *All the earth.*—These words point out how God's choice of the people of Israel is founded on His right of possession over the whole earth. And hereby the heathen notion of a God whose power is confined to His own land and people, is entirely removed from the minds of the Israelites. As the

Almighty power is declared to the whole earth, so has it been to the Egyptians. At the same time, an intimation is afforded that the peculiar privileges of Israel stand in relation to the salvation of the whole world. If God be Lord of the whole earth, and yet chooses for Himself a peculiar possession before all other nations, He can only have His object, in doing so, to care for the welfare of all through this chosen people.

Ver. 6. *Kingdom of priests.*—God first calls Himself the King of His people, and establishes Israel to be His peculiar dominion. He calls the whole people "priests," as selected from the whole of mankind for His especial service, and to bring salvation to all men; at the same time, He reminds Israel of the particular end of its existence as a people, which consists in the service of the true God. Other people had received other gifts, and were destined for other purposes; but Israel had no other destiny than first to preserve alive on earth, and next to spread, the knowledge and worship of the true God.

Holy nation.—Cf. Deut. vii. 6, ch. xxvi. 18. " Holy," in Holy Scripture, always includes the idea of separation from what is common and unclean, "and the surrender to God and His service." In the O. T. the more external signification appears to prevail, of being dedicated to the outward service of God. But as this outward service of God bore a continual reference to the inward, the express relation of the holiness of the people to the holiness of God, Lev. xi. 44, ch. xix. 2, which is represented as the direct opposition to all that is evil (Ps. v. 5), alone explains the perfect, entire meaning of the expression.

Ver. 8. *Returned.*—He went back to the mountain, as the people's ambassador for the solemn making of the covenant. The uttering of the words is afterwards mentioned. There was no need that God should learn through Moses what the people had spoken; but this was a great and solemn act of covenant, at which each party must distinctly express the conditions under which the covenant was concluded.

Ver. 10. *Sanctify.*—Let them, by putting away all that is unclean, and by bodily purification, place themselves unto that position of holy reverence which they owe to the Divine Majesty.

Clothes.—Even the clothes—much more themselves.

Ver. 13. *Shot through.*—As an offender, he has become liable to the Divine anger; so that even by touching every one has sinned or committed defilement.—In all this the awfulness of the Divine law is revealed to man. "The mountain of Sinai shows, and God through the mountain, what the heart feels when the law is laid open to it, and it is touched by the judgment of God. Since, like as the Israelites saw lightning, thunder, smoke, earthquake, so that their heart stood still as if they should now die—they had no other image than death before their eyes,—so also does a heart left to itself regard God as an executioner and jailor. None other than Christ can raise it up, whom I must know as a friend and brother, and be able to say to God, 'Lord, I know no one, neither in heaven nor on earth, in whom I may have consolation and confidence than Thyself through Christ.' "—Luther.

Trumpet.—Heb.: "By the blowing of the trumpet;" lit., "by the sounding of the jobel" (cornet), which last word signified a horn, by which a loud protracted sound could be produced. A note, therefore, such as a war-trumpet sends forth, and which in the valleys of the lofty mountains would cause a fearful reverberation, accompanied the appearance of the lightning, making its sound to be distinguished from that of the thunder.

To the mount.—There is an emphasis on "*they.*" These words cannot relate to the people, who were forbidden to touch the mount: they appear, therefore, to refer to the "elders," mentioned ver. 7, who do ascend (ch. xxiv. 1) the height of the mountain-ridge where Moses receives the tables.

Ver. 15. *Wives.*—In like manner as Moses was commanded to take off his shoes on Horeb, must that act be omitted, which at other times is permitted, nay, commanded by the Lord, in order that the soul, free from the influence of the senses, may occupy itself entirely with the holy manifestation now granted: 1 Sam. xxi. 4.

Ver. 18. *Furnace;* i.e., as if the whole mountain had been a burning furnace.

Ver. 19. *Voice;* i.e., in thunder. We are either to suppose that they were words sounding like thunder, yet distinctly uttered, or that it was an answering sign from God. The latter is the more probable, as it is not told to us what Moses and what God spake. Perhaps they were the words of the covenant menoned before, ver. 9, joined with the prayers of Moses.

Ver. 21. *Perish.*—The meaning of this fresh prohibition is, no doubt, to exalt the holiness and majesty of the law in the eyes of the people; but at the same time to show God's mercy towards a stiffnecked and rebellious nation, Whose love willed not that on the solemn day of the giving of the law any judgment should fall upon them.

Ver. 22. *Priests.*—The mention of "priests" before the institution of the Aaronic priesthood is very remarkable. Some have thought that here was meant the priestly dignity of the firstborn; but of this nothing elsewhere is said. Below, at ch. xxiv. 5, young men are mentioned who offered sacrifices; above, it is said of the elders that they should go up to the mount with Moses (ver. 13). It seems, that in connection with the dignity of the elders, something resembling the priesthood at that time existed among the people of Israel, though, in what it consisted, we cannot more particularly determine. Those elders who, as priests at that time, drew near to the Lord, were not to suppose that they were at all pure in God's sight, and needed no sanctification. They themselves also must undergo the same emblematic purification as the people.

Ver. 24. *Break forth.*—If the priests are the same as the elders, ver. 13, this may be reconciled by supposing that they came nearer than the people, and yet were not permitted to ascend to the highest point.

CHAPTER XX.

Before any particular law is given to the people of the covenant, the Lord puts before them in the ten commandments, afterwards written on two tables of stone, a summary of His will. In the form in which most of them are conveyed—"Thou shalt not," and also in the word, "Remember," with which the Sabbath commandment begins—we may perceive how God, through the law, speaks to a sinful people, which could render submission to His will only by an inward struggle against its own. We see how the main object of the law was to lead to the knowledge of sin. But, at the same time, the task is imposed on the people of gathering from everything which is forbidden, that which is commanded, and which is really the groundwork of the prohibition, as afterwards in the law they are led to understand.

The commandments are divided into two main heads. The first contains the duties towards God; the second, those towards our neighbour: the first comprised in the precept, "Thou shalt love the Lord thy God with all thy heart;" the second, in that, "Thou shalt love thy neighbour as thyself." To the first part, as to the second, there belong five commandments. For so did the Jews in the time of Christ consider them to be divided, as Josephus tells us (3, 5, 8): "He showed to them the two tables on which were written the ten commandments, on each five." And therefore the commandment, "Thou shalt not make to thyself any graven image," has been unreasonably regarded by a part of the Christian Church as a portion of the first commandment. And likewise the commandment, "Thou shalt honour," etc., which is looked on as belonging to the second table, containing the duties to our neighbour, really belongs to the first, since it speaks of our parents, not of our neighbour; it speaks of those who have authority over their children as God's representatives, and who demand honour by reason of this sacred relationship, but do not seek respect as part of the duty man owes to his neighbour.

According to this general division, we now perceive how the first two commandments of the first table have regard to the honour due to God in general; the third inculcates obedience to Him in word; the fourth and fifth, obedience in deed. The fifth forms a point of transition to the second table, by speaking of the honour paid to God in the person of His representatives among men. The second table then speaks of the duties towards God's image—our neighbour. The expression "neighbour" is derived from that childlike relationship in which the people of the covenant stood to God: therefore is every one "the neighbour," i.e., literally, fellow, companion, friend of the other, because all stand in the same relationship to God. The first commandment of the second table speaks of wrong done to our neighbour by injury inflicted on himself, on his person; the second and third, on injury by deed on his wife, on his property; the fourth, of injury done to our neighbour by word; the fifth, by sinful desire. In all these commandments (this is particularly observable if we compare heathen laws with them) every duty is regarded directly as in reference to God, and proceeds from the relationship towards Him. There is no trace of the threatening of punishment from the magistrate, nor of the advantage of obedience to God for temporal purposes. On the contrary, while this law formed the groundwork of the whole political constitution of the people, it will become perfectly clear to us, that the object of all the other commandments was to bring these ten commandments to bear on every particular of daily life. As the Lawgiver Himself is a Spirit, and holy, so are all these commandments holy, and to be understood, not according to the letter only, but after a spiritual, moral, and inward sense. No doubt the prohibition proceeds by gradation from "Thou shalt not kill," to "Thou shalt not covet," and in the first three commandments of the second table, *acts* are especially spoken of; but at the same time that the prohibition goes on from deed to word, and from word to desire, it is quite clear that murder is not to be understood merely as the outward act, but is regarded in its inmost root—in hatred, and anger, and envy—as an offence against God. In like manner, every unchaste act is forbidden as the beginning of adultery, as the first expression of the sinful propensity. So covetousness, before it proceed to theft, as its inward cause, is forbidden. The flagrant, open transgression of the commandment is expressly forbidden; and thence it became gradually clear that every other smaller or more secret transgression was therein included, while the prohibition of the more secret sins, as the root of the open ones, would have made a far less living and sensible impression. The amplification of the ten commandments, in the laws which follow, shows also clearly to the rude understanding, in how deep a sense they are to be received. Thus the Lord gave in these "ten words," to an uncivilised people, nearly sunk in the darkness of heathenism, the first outlines of a holy law, which the eternal Son of God Himself did not annul, but fulfil—which He has not even exceeded, since He quotes the two great commandments on which hang all the law and the prophets, and which form the foundation of the two tables, in the very words of the Mosaic law itself: St Matt. xxii. 37–39. And in the Sermon on the Mount even, He only removes the barrier which circumscribed laws given during the time of nonage.—The law is usually distinguished as the moral, the ritual or ceremonial, and the civil law; and it is assumed that the two latter parts of the

Mosaic law were abrogated by the introduction of Christianity, but the first not so, and that this first part is contained in the ten commandments, which are therefore permanent and binding on Christians, even to the most minute detail. But such a distinction is nowhere mentioned in the law itself. Even in the ten commandments something of a ritual character is contained, as in the law respecting the Sabbath; and likewise the great principle of civil legislation for the Israelites, which consists in the covenanted relationship of the people to Jehovah, is declared therein. On the other hand, the ritual law is not full of arbitrary chance ordinances; but all its injunctions embody those relations of the people to God, which have their foundation in the ten commandments. And even in the remarkable civil constitution of Israel, in those limits which it imposes on the law, we still see the deepest expressions of the moral law confirmed. Thence is deduced a very important principle for the right understanding of the whole of the Old Testament. In the same sense that the law has not been destroyed but fulfilled by Christ, has the ritual and civil law of the Israelites *not* been destroyed; but in the same sense that these have been annulled, has the law of the ten commandments also been annulled. The purpose of the ritual law, as also of the ritual precepts in the ten commandments, was, in the first place, to teach by signs and actual observances, at a time when teaching by language was not understood; in the next place, by means of these emblems and usages, all of which referred to Jehovah as King, to instil into the minds of the whole people the feeling that every relation of life, every movement of nature, every detail of human intercourse, placed them in constant dependence on God, and by means of this feeling to separate them widely from their heathen neighbours and from everything heathen; and lastly, the object was, by the unsatisfactoriness of all mere outward service, by the burdensomeness of all these typical and preparatory observances, to point to "the fulness of time." What the law said in word, this the observances and external rites expressed in figure: the tabernacle, the priests, the sacrifices, the laws about outward purity and purification, declared in a more diffuse manner, and in the language of that time and people, the eternal truths which the ten commandments briefly utter, and which other laws more minutely enunciate. But as little as a Christian is commanded to address God only in the words of the Psalms, is he bidden to speak always in this language of sign and emblem. They are the shadows of things to come—the substance is in Christ. But how marked was the outward distinction between the Israelites and the heathen nations occasioned by this ritual law, the ancient heathens themselves attest; as, for example, the Roman historian Tacitus (Hist. 5, 4): "Moses, in order that he might secure the people to himself for the time to come, gave to them novel customs, and such as are opposed to all other mortal practices. With them all is profane which is considered holy among ourselves; and, on the other hand, that is permitted among them which is forbidden with us. Thus they have introduced circumcision in order to make themselves easily recognisable by means of the distinction." The same testimony is borne by the counsellors of King Antiochus Sidetes (Diodorus, 34, 2): "They alone of all men wished to live without communion with any other people; they regarded all others as enemies; they desired to have laws quite opposed to those of other people; they would not eat with them, nor show them any act of kindness." Those of the ten commandments which have a most intimate connection with the civil law are extremely remarkable. In them the eternal, Divine law of the covenant is the groundwork; but, at the same time, the law circumscribes this principle during the time of nonage, and thereby declares its own merely preparatory character. The grand principle of the civil law of the Israelites is this: the Lord Jehovah is supreme King and Lord of the people and of their land; He, to whom the whole world belongs, has chosen this people for His service and possession. This principle had the greatest influence on all their civil relations. So, in matter of personal right, did an equality prevail of all the children of covenant before God. While of the slaves the ancient Roman laws say, "We find among all people, without distinction, that the master has power of life and death over his slave, and that all which the slave earns belongs to the master," both these marks of slavery were unknown in Israel. "They are My servants, which I brought out of the land of Egypt: they shall not be sold as bondmen:" Lev. xxv. 42. "If thy brother be sold unto thee, thou shalt not compel him to serve as a bondservant:" Lev. xxv. 39. Cf. Exod. xxi. 20, 26, 27; Lev. xxvii. 1–8, ch. xxv. 49; 2 Sam.

ix. And, therefore, the same distinction of rank did not exist among them as with other ancient nations. At the same time we see certain restrictions in the law itself, by which it clearly declared that slavery should continue, and the slave had only the possibility of being freed on the sabbatical year—yet could he, by a certain legal form and expression, become a slave for ever. Although the whole people were a kingdom of priests to the Lord, yet there existed a priestly class exclusively regulated by birth. But the most surprising of all is, that the law had foreseen the establishment of the kingly dignity in Israel: Deut. xvii. 14.—The original institution (Gen. ii. 18, etc.) so defined the nature of a proper marriage as to exclude polygamy and divorce; and marriage was hallowed by being an image of the communion betwixt God and His people. Moses, while in his first book he records the institution of marriage, permits, but restricts, the power of divorce, and places difficulties in the way of polygamy.—Jehovah is the supreme possessor of the whole land: this is the great principle of the law of property. Strictly speaking, there is no actual possession of property: the land is the Lord's—all Israelites are in the relation of strangers and guests, Lev. xxv. 23; hence it followed that, properly, they could never sell the land, but only the produce for a certain time. In the fiftieth year all property of land reverted to its original owners, to whom the Lord had apportioned it. Herein is therefore declared the principle of eternal Divine Right, that in the kingdom of God every man is only God's steward, to administer His goods for Him and His. But as sin has made men selfish, so must there exist by the side of the Divine right a temporal, formal right, the needful limit of the Divine law among sinful men; and this right the law sanctions in the command, "Thou shalt not steal;" while the sabbatical year and the year of jubilee, by their peculiar regulations, reminded men of God's supreme right of possession. Even in respect to the law of debts, the same ruling principle is expressed in the prohibition of usury: "If thou lend money to any of *My people*, thou shalt not be to him an usurer:" Exod. xxii. 25. To the same purpose was the release of all debts in the fiftieth year. In respect to the penal law, the principle of retribution and retaliation is that on which every punishment rests. Yet the retaliation must come from God at the hands of His representative, the magistrate: Deut.

xxxii. 35. But even here the right of revenging blood remained, as belonging to a rude and infant state of society, though the right was circumscribed by many limitations.—Among crimes, those against God stand at the head. Idolatry, therefore, is treason. It assails the state of God at its foundation; and was therefore punished by stoning, Deut. xvii. 2: and for the same reason were blasphemy, false prophesying, Sabbath-breaking, and witchcraft punished. In a similar way were crimes against God's vicegerents treated: so, to blaspheme God, and to curse an elder, stand together (ch. xxii. 28). The judges are called "gods," or deity. David dreads to lay his hand on the Lord's anointed: 1 Sam. xxiv. 5, etc. To strike parents, to curse them, nay, to withstand them, are crimes punishable with death. The punishment for murder is inflicted, because it is a violation of the image of God: Gen. ix. 6. For the same reason, the dishonouring God's image in others by sins of uncleanness, is visited with the heaviest punishment. Death was also the punishment for incest, by which the sanctity of the family bond, and so the respect due to parents, was destroyed.—In all this, it is shown how the whole civil law was nothing else than a carrying into practical effect of the moral law. The distinction of sins and of crimes, which of course has a certain propriety, was nowhere made, because every Israelite, from his birth, and in virtue of an outward compulsion, was a child of God's covenant. But everywhere are shown in the law itself the restrictions and limitations placed upon it in this particular, chiefly, that Israel was severed as a peculiar people from all others, and to this people alone was confined that which, by the rules of justice, was intended for other men. Divested of these restrictions and of the mere outward motives, the law is still valid every whit of it; and the main principles, in every particular of the law, are those which hold good for ever among all Christian people.

Ver. 2. *I am;* or, more correctly, "I, Jehovah, am thy God." In the introductory words, God distinguishes Himself with the great name, "I am,"—begins with the promise and assurance that He is the God of covenant, the God of Israel.

Brought thee.—Every covenant of God with man commences with some benefit, which He, out of pure grace, has conferred on him. God bestows before He requires. He never reaps where He has not first abundantly sown. He here reminds them, not of the benefit which was most recent and most vividly in their memory, but of that connected with the covenant made with their fathers, whereby Israel became a people—the people of God. This blessing of redemption was not merely a type of the greatest of all, the redemption through Christ from the bondage of sin, but the latter is contained in the former, as the flower in the blossom; therefore the Christian does not attach any strange meaning to the commandment when he paraphrases the words: "Who have redeemed thee, through My only Son, from the power of sin, death, and the devil."

Ver. 3. *No other gods.*—Heb.: "Thou shalt have no other God before My countenance." Every word is here of weight. "Before the countenance of the Lord," reminds us not only of His all-seeing eye, but speaks of the defiance, the deliberate insult offered to the gracious and merciful Saviour by the sin of idolatry. In this first commandment is the unity of the true God most absolutely maintained. The heathen worship of Nature never led to the notion of such unity. It distracted the trust, the reverence, of men into different directions, according as the thirsting heart of man in proportion to its hopes and longings sought for peace and satisfaction, but in vain. A kind of unity of the many gods—Fate, or the all-producing, all-absorbing Nature—could awaken no love, no confidence. It was itself without consciousness. But the one, the living God, could do this; and therefore this prohibition is one and the same with the first and chief commandment, Deut. vi. 4, 5; or, as Luther well expresses it, the purport of the first commandment is, "We must fear, love, and trust God above all things." And in his Great Catechism, "What is the meaning of, 'To have one God?' To have one God, is to rely on Him for every good thing, to have recourse to Him in every need; so that to have one God, is nothing else than to trust and believe in Him with all the heart. For that on which thy heart hangeth, and to which it trusteth, is thy God."

Ver. 4. *Under the earth.*—This command does not merely repeat what was said before, but adds to it something besides. Israel was not allowed to make any image of God, either of the true or of the false. In after times there occurred two gradations in the people's apostasy: first, the worship of the true God under an image, as especially the worship of the calf in the wilderness, and afterwards by Jeroboam in the kingdom of Israel; next, the worship of false gods—of Baal, of Astoreth. Before all is the "Image"—*i.e.*, a graven or molten idol—mentioned, as the usual mode of idolatry: however, in order to prevent every evasion, it is added, "nor the likeness of anything." This command had the purpose of preventing the religion of Israel from becoming a worship of Nature, which first honours God under the form of some creature, and then loses in Nature the idea of Him, and itself altogether.—"In heaven" alludes to the worship of the sun and stars; "on earth," to that of men and beasts; "in the water," to that of the inhabitants of the water, the objects of worship in Egypt; "under the earth" means the water, because it lies deeper than the land, as in French one says, "A town lies on the sea, on a river." We find, indeed, that afterwards God caused the cherubim in the sanctuary to be made; but these images were an actual defence against idolatry, as the meaning of them was to show how the very highest powers in Nature were entirely subject to God, and that He Himself is enthroned above them in invisible, incomparable Majesty.—Every representation of God, in Christianity even, which would visibly exhibit God, "who dwelleth in light that no man can approach unto," 1 Tim. vi. 16; but, above all, everything which would degrade the Creator of all, who is exalted above all Nature, to a level with Nature, and which, in anything whatever, honours, not God's work, but God Himself, is absolutely forbidden in this commandment. So long, therefore, as there is danger of God's holy, invisible essence being dishonoured by any image or likeness, and of the creature being honoured instead of the Creator, so long may we appeal to this commandment against any such error. Of a different character are the representations of the God-man Jesus Christ, in whom God Himself has taken human nature, and who has become for us the Visible Image of the Invisible God. Luther says: "I know for certain that God wills that man should hear and read His works, especially the sufferings of Christ. But if I must hear and consider them, it is impossible but that I should form in my heart images thereof; since, whether I will or no, when I hear Christ, there is traced in my heart a human figure which hangs on the cross: if it be not sinful, but right, for me to have an image of Christ in my heart, why should it be a sin when I have His image before my eyes?" Here only begins the sin: when in any sense there is ascribed to the image a Divine power—a power of communicating salvation, and so it is itself honoured as Divine. But when there is no danger of this kind, then are images, even in sacred places, a proper expression of Christian devotion.

Ver. 6. *Keep My commandments.*—The threat and the promise are directly connected with that command which the Israelites were most tempted, and which it was most dangerous for them, to break. In general, it is said, God's grace extends much further than the chastisements of His justice. But the declaration, that the fathers' transgressions should be visited on the children, has its reason in that unity which existed in families in old times much more than at present. It is not said that the innocent children shall suffer for their parents' sins; for the contrary is most expressly declared, Ezek. xviii. 20. But the awfulness of the sin, as of the punishment which descends from father to son, is pointed out. At the same time, such outward chastisements are here meant, which continue, even where the conversion of the children has changed them into a blessing: as, for example, it has been observed that the leprosy, one of the most fearful visitations in the East, usually is transmitted to the third and fourth generation.

Ver. 7. *The name.*—Literally: "Not bring to a lie," not utter for that purpose. This is, therefore, in the first place, directed against all false swearing. But Christ shows, by His explanation, that therein is contained a prohibition of *all* swearing, so far as it proceeds from ourselves; since, from man's natural proneness to falsehood, it may easily happen that in every self-imposed oath, taken in a light-minded manner, a lie may be sworn to. And next, since without naming God's name, every "yea" is spoken in His presence, and ought to have equal weight with an oath. The explanation of Christ is contained in this commandment; but, for the time, hidden from view by the outward mode of its delivery.

Ver. 11. *Hallowed it.*—Cf. Gen. ii. 3, note. Hitherto there had been given to the people no express command concerning the Sabbath; and there appears, so far, no trace of this day being hallowed. Only in respect to the manna was the people reminded of the institution of that day by a Divine act (ch. xvi.

5, etc.). But, as the history of the creation lived in the minds of the generations who feared the Lord, so there would surely be some honour paid to this day. The present embodying of this command about the Sabbath in the laws of the covenant, was of the utmost significance. It was expressly declared, and by a continued ordinance kept in mind, that the God who had brought Israel out of Egypt was the Creator of the whole world. The sanctification of the Sabbath preserved Israel from all heathen worship, and from all superstitious notions that they reverenced a mere national God like the other people. Hence the great weight which is again and again laid on this Divine command; hence the name "sign" and "covenant," which is given to the Sabbath (ch. xxxi. 13–15; Ezek. xx. 12; cf. Neh. ix. 14). Hence the dishonouring of the Sabbath appears as a sin of apostasy from God (Ezek. xxii. 8, ch. xxiii. 38). Of what is of temporary and what of perpetual obligation in this command, we have already spoken on the institution of the day.

Ver. 12. *Giveth thee.*—Parents, as God's representatives, are here invested with an honour above all other men; for while we are to "love" our neighbour, we are commanded to "honour" our parents. They are to be regarded not as persons who, for certain definite temporal objects, are invested for a time with a power over their children, to nourish and foster them, but as persons who administer an office from God, carry out His will, command in His name,—as persons, therefore, from whom children are to receive the first impression of the governance of the Lord of the world and the Father of men. As the constitution of the Israelitish people and its different membership entirely rested on the patriarchal form, this commandment enforces the duty of reverence to those in authority, as well as to parents. Hence all that is said elsewhere of "elders," of "the rulers of the people," belongs to this commandment: ch. xxii. 28. The promise of long life in the land which God should give, is now, that the whole earth has become the land of God's kingdom, to be understood of every kind of earthly blessing. "Even for the Israelites, long life in that land was not in itself a blessing, but only so far as it was a pledge of Divine grace. Therefore, if God early removes from this life an obedient son, He is no less mindful of His promise than if He had given an hundred acres of land to every one to whom He had promised one. All depends on our understanding that a long life is promised us, so far as it is a blessing of God: but it is a blessing so far as it is a pledge of grace; and this God can often accord more richly and more certainly to His servants in their death, which leads to eternal life."—Calvin.

Ver. 13. *Kill.*—Every kind of killing is not here meant, as the magistrate puts to death, and in war an enemy is justly killed, and in a later place express mention is made of unintentional killing. The Hebrew expression is the appropriate one for intentional killing of another with malicious purpose. The true reason for this prohibition is expressed, Gen. ix. 6, viz.: because our neighbour is the image of God; with which must be joined what is said, ch. ix. 5: because our neighbour is our brother. And it follows naturally, from the reason on which this prohibition is built, that it is equally commanded, that "the preservation of our brother should be to us as our own." Whatever assails his life, assails ours: his well-doing is ours.

Ver. 14. *Commit adultery.*—Literally taken, this command enjoins:—"The marriage of thy neighbour shall be esteemed holy by thee: thou shalt not have any unchaste communication with his wife." It belongs to the narrowness of the law in the time of nonage, to understand under adultery in the O. T. only an offence with a wife—not that of a husband with an unmarried woman. In the rude sensual view taken of marriage, the crime of the wife appeared of so much more heinous character, as the consequences for the family were more important. Thus also, in Homer, is the chastity of Penelope lauded, while the repeated adulteries of Ulysses are mentioned with unconcern, as something quite indifferent. This is suitable to a state of things in which divorce lay at the option of the husband, and was not regarded as adultery. But Christ shows, in this latter example, what is to be understood by adultery, by referring to the original institution of marriage; and explaining that every breach of the marriage-contract, as well as every unchaste act, was either itself adultery, or prepared the way to adultery. From this point of view, we may perceive why the law of Moses was more opposed than any other law of ancient times to every kind of harlotry, and put obstacles in the way of divorce and polygamy. In this prohibition also is contained the command to hold marriage as sacred. And the reason of the prohibition is this,—that marriage is not an union for a short time, for the gratification of carnal lust, or the procreation of children; but, as the creation of the woman out of the man shows, is an union of the whole life, for the training up of the images of God, the heirs of His kingdom, and shadows forth the union of love betwixt God and His creatures. Hence, clearly, all that follows whereby this union is a continual exercise of love, humility, patience, and hope. All this the command of marriage tells us.

Ver. 15. *Steal.*—As the earth is the Lord's, no one besides Him can be in a full sense the owner of his possession. Yet is this possession lent by God: it is His holy appointment, and no mere human invention, which can be done away with at man's pleasure. Accordingly, that which He has so lent on earth ought to be holy and inviolable in our eyes, as He has granted each a portion of His goods in stewardship: cf. Lev. vi. 2. This view would be most promoted and kept alive if each man did not say of *his* goods, "It is mine," but, because it is God's, would resign part of it cheerfully for the sake of others. Both duties are contained in this commandment: to have respect for that which belongs to another—to hold light by our own.

Ver. 16. *False witness.*—This command is far too much limited, if we suppose (which the words by no means authorise) that in it is simply contained a defence of our neighbour's good name. Every injury inflicted on our neighbour is forbidden, by the utterance of any falsehood concerning him, whether it be to the damage of his honour, or of his substance, or intentional deceit. The deeper view of the command teaches us, that every intentional deceiving of our neighbour, though with a kind purpose, in order to help him—every so-called lie of necessity out of love to him—still does really do him an injury, since it destroys the reverence for truth, the confidence of fellowship between man and man, and the open interchange of Divine gifts and benefits. Only a false code of morals, which sees man's highest good in momentary, temporal welfare, can maintain the lawfulness of lying for the benefit of others, or out of so-called necessity, since the law of truthfulness and of charity are essentially one and the same. Therefore, this commandment enjoins full, entire, unequivocal truthfulness towards our neighbour in every relation, although the practical understanding of its meaning was very imperfectly attained to in the O. T., where we find that so many servants of God allow themselves, in their perplexities, to have recourse to lying, which the Word of God narrates, but never excuses.

Ver. 17. *Thy neighbour's.*—Neither in the word " covet," nor in anything else, is there the slightest hint which should lead us to suppose that by "coveting" is meant anything else than a purely inward desire. Even the other commandments cannot be fulfilled by an external obedience only. " Thou shalt not kill," includes likewise, Thou shalt not be angry, shalt not hate, as the seed of the evil; and so on with the rest. But it is a matter of great moment to observe, that here the evil desire is itself expressly declared to be a sin, not only inasmuch as it leads or can lead to an act, but also simply in itself. Envy, which grudges another man his life, the impure desire, the greediness of gain, the inward insincerity—even though they should not be strong enough to break out into acts, or should be hindered by circumstances from doing so—are sins. There is no such thing as a purely involuntary bad thought. All such spring from the ground of a corrupt heart. They proceed from the inward desire to be free from God's laws, and to follow their own desire or vainglory. Even the evil thoughts and desires which are roused in us by outward circumstances, or inspired by the devil, are sparks which fall continually on prepared tinder. This last commandment is really the keystone of the whole law of the ten commandments, and so St Paul quotes it (Rom. vii 7) as the main idea of all that is prohibited. Those Israelites, therefore, whose eyes God had enlightened, must, through this commandment, have felt their hearts filled with a longing desire and prayer for " a clean heart :" Ps. li. 12.

Ver. 19. *Lest we die.*—The awful character of the outward signs was calculated to impress on the minds of the people the unapproachable holiness of the Lawgiver, and the greatness of the punishment which would befall all those who broke His commandments. So the people now feel the need of a mediator between themselves and God; and in this confession is expressed the most entire submission to all which Moses, in the name of God, might reveal to the people. Thus the purpose of the Lord, mentioned ch. xix. 9, was attained.

Ver. 21. *Where God was.*—The feeling of awful dread, which had seized even Moses on the first apparition of God to him (ch. iii. 6), appears here entirely to have left him, as we find afterwards (ch. xxxiii. 18) that he made the bold request that God would show him His glory. Something was revealed in the manner of the Lord's appearing, which bridged over the mighty gulf that lies between the sinful creature and the holy Creator—some especially great and encouraging assurance of His favour.

Ver. 23. *Gods of silver.*—The setting up of the golden calf afterwards, shows how the people, on having been constituted into an independent community, was seized with an inclination to act like the other nations, and so to have a visible national god at their head as leader. The establishment of the first king proceeded from a similar wish: 1 Sam. viii. 20. The Lord reminds the capricious people of the deep impression which His appearing had made on them, distinguishes Himself from all gods worshipped by idols, and forbids every mode of service which was calculated to degrade His nature to a likeness to the creature.

Ver. 24. *Bless thee.*—The word "altar" is in the Hebrew "place of sacrifice." A temporary large heap of earth was to serve for the first requirements of sacrifice. But with respect to the more precise regulations which should afterwards be given, it is expressly determined that it does not depend on the material, whether the altar is of wood or of stone, but on the word of the Lord, which commands the people to make mention of Him in such a place, and on the obedience of faith which follows the bidding of the Lord.

Ver. 25. *Polluted.*—The altar in the fore-court of the tabernacle was made of wood, with wooden staves overlaid with brass, the interior of the framework being filled with earth. The altar in Solomon's Temple was entirely of brass: 2 Chron. iv. 1. After the captivity, and in the time of the Maccabees, as we learn, 1 Maccabees iv. 45, 47, the altar in the Temple was of unhewn stones, probably because, without express Divine command, they did not wish to depart from the command here given. The same was the case with the altar in Herod's Temple. Properly, then, every altar ought to have been made of earth, and the wood or brass plates were only the framework into which the earth was heaped. If it was made of stones, these must be unhewn, that they might resemble earth as much as possible.

Probably the reason why the sacrifice was to be offered on an altar of earth, or of stone resembling earth, was this—because such altars were erected for the offering of burnt sacrifices to do away sin; and sin, which was committed on earth, was on earth likewise to be atoned for. With the rising up of the smoke of sacrifice from the earth, was represented the surrender of the earthly man to the heavenly King, in order that God's will might be done in earth as in heaven. It was somewhat different in respect to the golden altar of incense in the sanctuary. The lifting up of the knife on the stones, therefore, pollutes them, inasmuch as a main idea and chief emblem in the sacrificial service is thereby lost, and a mere arbitrary employment of human art takes its place.

Ver. 26. *Discovered.*—A law of extreme bodily purity and modesty, as an emblem of inward purity; therefore, also, the command, ch. xxviii. 42.

CHAPTER XXI.

From ch. xxiv. 4, 7, we see that all the laws from this chap. as far as ch. xxiii. 19, and the promise which follows, were an explanatory supplement to the ten commandments, and therefore the groundwork of the whole legislation of the covenant. In the laws which now follow there is no exact order observed; only they fall into certain divisions, in which ten appear generally to go together, after the pattern of the ten commandments. It is very possible that the questions which came before Moses, when he sat in judgment, or when appeals were made to him, and the particular necessities of the people at the time, might have occasioned the promulgation of these several laws. But yet, together with such laws as might be peculiarly wanted in the wilderness, are ever connected others which have a more general application, and which meet every conceivable case; so that everywhere the marks of the Spirit are to be found, which embraced in one view both the present and future destinies of the people.—The first division treats of laws which concern the slaves and Israelites. Slavery was in all ancient nations a common and acknowledged right, as we find the case with Abraham, Gen. xii. 5 (Heb.). The ancient Romans regarded it as a national right; *i.e.*, as an institution common to all people. The Mosaic law found this relation of master and slave existing among the Israelites, and a fourfold manner in which persons became slaves: by war, by purchase, voluntary surrender, and birth. All the change which the law effected in respect to slavery tended to its mitigation; and this proceeded from this great principle, that *all* Israelites were God's servants, and brothers one with another. The mitigations of the condition of slavery, as compared with the practices of other nations, are the following:—1. Every Israelite who was a slave could either become free in the seventh year, or might bind himself, of his own free will, before a magistrate, to perpetual slavery. 2. That every slave enjoyed protection not only of his life, but of his person. 3. That he might earn property, and thereby purchase his freedom. 4. That every week he had one day of rest from labour. Besides these, there were many other regulations which enjoined mercy and kindness towards slaves from a higher point of view; *e.g.*, their being invited to the sacrificial feasts: Deut. xii. 17, ch. xvi. 11.

Ver. 2. *Buy.*—An Israelite might sell himself out of poverty, Lev. xxv. 39; Deut. xv. 12; a creditor might take him for a slave for his debt, 2 Kings iv. 1; the thief who could not make restitution was sold, ch. xxii. 3. In other cases, the prohibition held good, that the Israelites were not to buy slaves from among their brethren, but from the nations who lay round about them: Lev. xxv. 44.

Seventh.—In the two services of Jacob for seven years each, there appears to be a sign that perhaps this period was an ancient one for voluntary servitude. Here, by this law, *all* slavery, without distinction, is limited to that period. It has been long a question, whether the freedom was gained in the seventh year of service, or in the actual seventh year, that is, the sabbatical year. As in the express command concerning the sabbatical year, Lev. xxv. 1–7, nothing is said of the emancipation of the slaves, the first view seems the truer one, especially as else the term of servitude would have been to many a very short one. The law is given more fully Deut. xv. 12–15.

Ver. 4. *By himself.*—These regulations bear indeed on them, in a high degree, the marks of the severity of the ancient relations of slave and master. It must, however, be kept in mind, that this wife and her children belonged to the master, and otherwise the slave would have taken away a considerable portion of his property without possible compensation. And the severity is mitigated by the condition which follows—the slave might prefer his wife and child to freedom.

Ver. 6. *For ever.*—A solemn legal ceremony, therefore, was part of this surrender into perpetual servitude, in order that it might not be the result either of intimidation on the part of the master, nor of inconsiderate haste on the part of the slave,—a ceremony which, at the same time, left an abiding mark on the body of the slave. " Before the gods," lit. in Heb.; or rather, before God. The judges are not called gods; but the place of judgment is the place of God's presence, whose office the judges represent, as we particularly see this from the fact that, Deut. xix. 17, it is said, "The people who have a controversy" shall stand before the Lord (Jehovah), before the priests and judges (cf. Deut. i. 17). Therefore is the word to be understood as " God " (not gods); so also ch. xxii. 8, 27. The boring of the ear, an emblematic custom which still prevails among Eastern nations, was meant to signify its being open continually to hear and to obey. So its application to our Lord, Ps. xl. 6. This took place at the door-post, to represent the slave's abiding relation to that house.

Ver. 7. *As the men-servants do;* i.e., she shall not be again free in the seventh year. It appears that afterwards, before the entrance into Canaan, the severity of this rule was mitigated: Deut. xv. 17; cf. Jer. xxxiv. 9, 10. We may, perhaps, herein perceive a gradual diminution of the hardship of the slave-condition, to which the Mosaic law was in general unfavourable.

Ver. 8. *Be redeemed.*—This was, even then, an exception from the rule just established. If the master will not himself take her in marriage (as a concubine), nor give her to his son, to another, he has not the power to compel her to remain unmarried as his slave: in this case he must, at her desire, " let her be redeemed;" i.e., especially, he may not refuse should any one wish to buy her free. But, perhaps, this expression also includes his letting her go free.

Strange nation.—" Strange nation " does not mean here a

foreign heathen people. Unto such no Israelite could be sold, as in this case the right of being free again would be altogether lost—he would have become out and out a heathen. When Herod promulgated a law that robbers should be sold as slaves to foreigners, this transgression of the Divine law caused a violent outbreak among the people. "People" often signifies, in Hebrew, also "a family"—("gathered to his people," synonymous with "to his relations, his fathers.") He might not sell them to a strange house, but must afford them the same rights as the men-servants had.

Ver. 11. *Without money.*—A relationship which Moses found in existence (as it everywhere prevailed in the East), was, besides polygamy, the lower kind of marriage, concubinage, as we find with respect to Abraham. Especially was it usual for the father, before the complete regular marriage, to give his son a slave for his concubine. In this case, she was to be treated in the house as a daughter; but if the son contracts a regular marriage, he shall still after it, as before, treat her as his concubine, and grant her, together with the other, nourishment, clothing, and conjugal rights; or, if not, she had a claim to be let go free without money. This was, therefore, a case in which a kind of divorce complaint was allowed the woman.

Ver. 12. *Put to death.*—In these laws which here follow respecting injuries inflicted, the great principle enforced is that of retaliation, which lies at the foundation of all judicial punishment. The criminal has violated the order of God in the life and property of His people, and that order must be restored again *in him* by recompense made. Such recompense extends, according to this original law of right, to the smallest particular—"An eye for an eye," etc.—in which, however, according to the analogy of all other legislations, it is supposed that the injured party may remit the retributory punishment, or receive restitution in some other way; and thus it holds good of these, as of all similar Divine and human laws, that the general principle is laid down in certain definite plain examples, which principle, legal usage and custom extended to all similar cases, and more clearly explained.—In the killing here spoken of, intentional murder is not meant (the homicidium dolosum), but that kind of death-blow which is inflicted by any one with the hostile purpose of doing an injury; and which, according to the usual course of things, *may* cause death, as it is explained in reference to several particular cases, Num. xxxv. 16-21.

Ver. 13. *Shall flee.*—This, therefore, is a case of killing by an accidental blow without intention of injuring. The law points to the appointment of the cities of refuge at a later period, and supposes the relation of the avenger of blood, which existed from the earliest times: cf. Gen. iv. 14. Even to this day, in certain parts of Arabia, the relations of the slain man have the choice, whether they will arrange the matter with the connections of the slayer before the magistrate, or have the murderer delivered into their hands that they may themselves put him to death. Mohammed expressly confirms this in the Koran: " Kill no man whom ye ought not to kill according to the law of God; but if any one is killed contrary to the law, then his nearest in kin is appointed as avenger of blood against the murderer; but he may not, in his manner of putting to death, under the defence of the law, transgress the law."—Koran, Sur. 17, Wahl. In the law of Moses this ancient right is recognised and allowed to stand: Num. xxxv. 21. It was one out of the many remains of the patriarchal time, when the whole state was included in the family. Only gradually could the idea of a governance of God over His whole people, and of the exercise of His judicial right by means of His representatives, overpower every idea of self-redress. It was a step in that direction to give the general law for putting the murderer to death, and also to appoint the cities of refuge for the protection of the unintentional slayer.

Ver. 14. *May die.*—The intentional murderer shall nowhere find protection. The altar of the Lord is not profaned, but honoured, when the law of the Lord is fulfilled (cf. 1 Kings ii. 29-31).

Ver 15. *Put to death.*—Among the commands which determine the punishment on murderers, men-stealers, and violent injurers of men's persons, there are two which appoint the punishment of death for much smaller offences committed against parents—this one, and at ver. 17. Afterwards, obstinate incorrigible disobedience to parents also came under the list of crimes worthy of death · Deut. xxi. 18-21. The reason is to be found in that divinely hallowed reverence towards parents which is implanted in us by God's will, whereby any injury by deed, or a cursing of parents, is a violation in their persons of God's majesty.

Ver. 16. *Stealeth.*—A land so completely a thoroughfare for merchants as Canaan and Arabia Petræa was, must have offered particular facilities to this crime. He who in this manner not only deprived an Israelite of his liberty, but also sold him to a heathen people, was certainly a criminal worthy of death. According to present national law, this crime committed by slave-dealers on negro slaves is also punished with death.

Ver. 17. *Curseth.*—The curse was regarded not merely as an injurious affront by words, but as an especial wrong, since he who curses invokes the aid of a higher power against the other. As God has sanctioned reverence towards parents, no curse from Him at the summons of the child could touch them. It was an evil power, therefore, with which the children allied themselves against the parents, and therefore against Him. Hence the punishment of death.

Ver. 20. *Punished.*—It is not said what should be the nature of the punishment. As the master possessed the right to strike his servant, and in this case, therefore, merely the excess of the chastisement had caused death, without any intention on the part of the master, the punishment of death, of which ver. 12 speaks, would have been here an injustice. Nevertheless, as the master ought to be made aware that he had killed not simply his own, but God's, servant, the choice of punishment might be left to the discretion of the magistrate.

Ver. 21. *His money;* i.e., he pays already a fine by the loss of his services.

Ver. 22. *Judges,* who here act as arbitrators.

Ver. 25. *Stripe for stripe.*—This law is afterward extended to every kind of bodily injury: Lev. xxiv. 19, 20. It was the ancient law also among the Greeks and Romans, with the last of whom a law of the Twelve Tables ran thus: "If any one breaks another's limb, and they do not come to terms on the matter, a reprisal must take place." The same exception must naturally be presupposed. Retaliation is the groundwork of all judicial punishment; but as civilisation advances, its literal carrying into effect will more and more disappear. Thus, for example, according to Solon's laws, any one who had destroyed the eye of a one-eyed person, for punishment was to lose both his own. In this great principle of retribution, the law particularly expresses its own inward nature; for without this principle there could be no justice, nor belief in a Divine judgment of the world. In the stead of the arbitrary pleasure or will of the individual stands the Divine rule, the violation of which is made good by the violator receiving the same as he has inflicted. It is, therefore, only an interpretation and elucidation of the principle on which the law of retaliation rests, when Christ (St Matt. v. 39, etc.) forbids the individual the power of avenging himself. The same Lawgiver who avenges every wilful transgression of His ordinance, closes up also the source of such violations by forbidding every withstanding of the injurer.

Ver. 27. *Tooth's sake.*—A gentleness so entirely unknown to heathen antiquity, that it was only in the second century B.C. that any punishment was decreed against masters for the violent misusage of their slaves.

Ver. 28. *An ox.*—The following laws treat of wrongs and injuries done by or to the property of another, and have in them a certain unity. The law places a wall of defence about the possessions of every one, and visits the violation of it by enforcing compensation of one or more of the same kind. In like manner, every one must be responsible for the damage done by means of his property.

Ver. 30. *Laid upon him.*—As an exact retribution for the injury, the ox must die. Of course, this is only figuratively a punishment as far as the ox is concerned, since an exact one could not be inflicted on it: cf. Gen. iii. 14, ch. ix. 5; Lev. xx. 15; but, in order to maintain in every instance before the people the great principle of Divine retribution in punishment, this is therefore to be extended to the beast even. The case here mentioned is the only one which occurs in which a money compensation for a death-blow inflicted might be taken. This was else forbidden: Num. xxxv. 31.

Ver. 31. *Son.*—Children in the father's power, not yet independent.

Ver. 32. *Shekels of silver.*—As compensation for the loss of his property. Shekel was originally a weight, and not a coin. It has been differently reckoned, as valued according to what is said in the O. T., or according to the coin of the time of the Maccabees, still in existence. According to the lowest computation its value was about fivepence—at its highest, one shilling and tenpence.

CHAPTER XXII.

Ver. 4. *Double.*—It appears that the punishment of a double restitution was the usual and regular one: that of four or five times the value formed the exception; at least so it was in later Jewish law, and ver. 4 points to it. This punishment of double restitution, which probably Moses found already in existence, rested on this—viz., that by a theft, not simply the thing stolen was lost, but also that which might have been gained or produced by it. Among a people which then depended for subsistence on its herds, and was destined to live by tillage, the stealing of cattle must be punished with peculiar severity, not merely to inspire fear, but from the circumstance that, in reliance on people's honesty, the same care was not bestowed on cattle as to other things. The ox, therefore, which was essential for ploughing, enjoyed a greater legal protection than the smaller cattle. If the ox or sheep remain still alive in possession of the thief, then restitution and repentance are possible on his side; hence, then, only the usual punishment of restoring double.

Ver. 6. *Thorns*, which are burnt for the purpose of cleaning a field. At the approach of the rainy season, towards the end of July, it is customary in the East to burn on the field the dry grass, weeds, and brambles: from carelessness or malicious intention, great damage could often be occasioned thereby.

Ver. 9. *Pay double.*—Cf. ch. xxi. 6.—Before "God," in the holy place consecrated to God, must the accused appear, and the matter be inquired into. In what manner this was to be done, we are not told. The sentence pronounced is, then, God's own judgment.

Ver. 15. *Hire.*—The hire is in this case sufficient compensation. The hirer of the cattle is possessor in the place of the real owner—exercises his right of possession; but if the owner be himself present, it is presumed that he can protect his own.

Ver. 17. *Dowry.*—This law concerning virgins is here placed with the foregoing ones about property, because the daughter was so regarded by the father, and was bought in marriage from him (so the German word for marrying, "heirathen," comes from "heiren,"—Eng. hire). The bridegroom made to the father a certain payment, either in money or goods, or in service, as Jacob did for Laban, or other gifts and performances, as Shechem for Dinah, Gen. xxxiv., and David for Michal, 1 Sam. xviii. Afterwards the highest demand which in the above case could be made, was specified: Deut. xxii. 29.

Ver. 18. *Witch.*—This law briefly forbids (as under the present circumstances was proper) that which afterwards (Deut. xviii. 10, 11) is condemned more particularly. The Lord God would reveal Himself to His prophets by word or by vision, and by the "light and justice" of the high priest, to all of His people who came to inquire. He therefore who, by other means learnt from the heathen, sought to know the future, or to work miracles, was guilty of rebellion against the true God.

Ver. 19. *Put to death.*—The revolting crime mentioned in this verse was practised in Egypt, as an honour paid to their false deities. Probably it is mentioned in this place on account of its connection with the abominations of idolatry. It appears, likewise, to have prevailed among the Canaanites: Lev. xviii. 3, 4, 22–28.

Ver. 20. *Utterly destroyed.*—Lit., "dedicated to the Lord;" *i.e.*, to destruction. A similar form of expression existed among the Greeks and Romans. Such a dedication was fulfilled in war, or even on Israelitish towns which had lapsed into idolatry, as a Divine judicial punishment; and in this case it was not lawful to take any prey, which would be to commit a sacrilege (Joshua vi. 17–19). The same was done to particular persons and fields, which could not in that case be redeemed (Lev. xxvii. 28, 29). The meaning of the punishment is therefore this,—that a man who has carried his idolatry to the extreme of offering sacrifice, may not under any circumstances escape the severest punishment.

Ver. 21. *Ye were strangers.*—The purpose of this humane law (which is repeated, ch. xxiii. 9; Lev. xix. 33, 34; Deut. x. 18, 19) was, as these words show, to keep Israel in mind, that it was only of God's grace that he had been chosen above all other people; and that they, who were now defenceless strangers, might also some day become God's people. All other ancient nations, especially the Egyptians, were notoriously unkind to strangers. The contrary sentiment only occurs in a Greek verse as a rule of worldly prudence: "Be hospitable to strangers: you also may be a stranger."

Ver. 24. *Fatherless.*—Here also shall full retribution be the punishment: cf. Isa. i. 17. In the people of God, the Lord is the Husband of the widow, and the Father of the fatherless. Hence their share in the second tithe: Deut. xiv. 28, 29, ch. xxvi. 12. In this, and similar institutions, are to be seen the germs of the Christian care for the poor, which was unknown to heathen antiquity, and which, when Christianity spread, it sought in vain to imitate.

Ver. 25. *As an usurer.*—Heb.: "Thou shalt not become to him as a creditor."

Usury.—The prohibition of all usury is likewise extended (Lev. xxv. 36) to produce of the land. In both these places the reason of the prohibition appears to be the oppression of the poor by taking usury: Deut. xxiii. 19. Usury is generally forbidden, but the taking of it from strangers is at the same time permitted. The relation of all Israelites to God as their common Lord, was plainly the ground of this prohibition. From "His people" should no usury be taken; and so far the prohibition is a result of the general brotherly love, by means of which the use of all earthly goods ought to be common to all men. The limitation of this right to Israelites, and the permission to take usury from strangers, was a necessary act of defence, in respect to those people who themselves had no prohibition about usury. The practicability of the prohibition of usury was rendered more easy among the Israelites by the circumstance, that among them possessions in land could not be alienated, but only a succession of harvests might be sold; while a number of other laws and regulations made the carrying on of trade very difficult. And so it was, that even in times of its greatest prosperity, the trade of the country, for which Canaan was so conveniently situated, was almost entirely in the hands of the neighbouring Phœnicians—a people of Canaanitish origin. The law does not determine any particular punishment for the usurer. It appears to have been this, that he had no legal redress in claiming his interest. Although this law, taken literally, relates to circumstances very different from our own, and which were of a peculiar character—the condition of the people of God on earth, in the time of its nonage, "under tutors and governors"—yet has it still a perpetual meaning for all times and countries. That the lender should receive compensation for the risk he runs, and the advantage he confers on the borrower, is not only fair, but likewise mutually advantageous. A literal prohibition of usury would make loans very rare, and thus act injuriously on the borrower, to whom the possibility of a loan on interest is of the greatest service. But in its spirit the Christian will still faithfully observe this law. He ought to regard himself simply as the steward of goods which do not belong to him, but are only entrusted to his keeping. Therefore, *so far as lies in him*, he may not deny any one a participation in the enjoyment of his substance, unless the denial be to the benefit of him who would borrow from him.

Ver. 27. *Sleep.*—The upper coat, the only clothing the poor had—consisting of a large piece of cloth, six ells long and three wide, fastened about the body with a girdle—still, to this day, serves for bed likewise among the Bedouins and wandering Arab tribes. This property, so absolutely necessary to him, is not to be taken in pledge from any poor man.

Ver. 28. *Gods.*—Heb., God. The judges are not here meant, who are nowhere merely called "God," or gods (cf. ch. xxi. 6, note), but God the Lord Himself. "The ruler of the people" is mentioned together with Him, to show that he is God's vicegerent.

Ver. 29. *Liquors.*—Lit., "tear." Here is meant the harvest of every kind of fruit, and the juice of the olive and grapes,—the first of the garner and the wine-press, which are here mentioned together with the first-born son. The first of every sort of possession is to be given to God, in order, by this figurative surrender, to sanctify the whole. The son likewise is the father's property, and is therefore to be given up to God: but he is at the same time more than any other property: he stands, as an image of God, in an independent relation to God, and is therefore not in person to be offered up as a sacrifice, but figuratively to be consecrated to God by means of another gift offered in ransom: cf. ch. xiii. introd.—This command is no longer binding on Christians in its literal sense, but it is in its spiritual. They are not only bound to serve God, and not themselves, with all that they possess; but they shall also manifest this service by the express surrender of their best and their dearest, for the sake of God and His kingdom.

Ver. 31. *Dogs.*—The meaning of this, and of other prohibitions with respect to food, is explained, Gen. vii. 3, note.

CHAPTER XXIII.

Ver. 1. *Raise.*—" Thou shalt not receive a lying report." This command, like many others of the following, refers particularly to judges; but there were not always at that time (as ch. xviii. shows) established persons in authority. Every one also was judge in his own house; and, therefore, these commands were given with a general application. The prohibition to receive false accusation is directed against the hypocritical justification of a judge or arbitrator, who would excuse himself by saying he had received this or that report, of which he nevertheless knew that it was false.

Ver. 3. *Countenance.*—Simple truth and justice do not permit any deviation from the right path, either through a false report, nor from friendship to the unrighteous, nor from regard to the multitude, nor yet from false sympathy with a poor man who is in the wrong.

Ver. 5. *Help.*—In these commands a true practical love of their enemies is taught. They show how false it is to ascribe without consideration the declaration, St Matt. v. 43, to the O. T. A similar command is given, Deut. xxii. 4.

Ver. 7. *Justify.*—Think not that thou as judge can with impunity slay the innocent: thy judgment will not make the wrong to be right.

Ver. 9. *Oppress.*—This command is similar to that in ch. xxii. 21; but the earlier one is a general commandment, while this especially refers to the dealings of persons in power and authority in their official capacity.

Ver. 11. *Oliveyard.*—This is only a short preliminary direction: afterwards, Lev. xxv., the same thing is spoken of more fully, and in connection with the year of jubilee.

Ver. 13. *Other gods.*—This general exhortation would impress upon them, that these directions here given are the signs of the covenant of the chosen people; that their obedience to them excludes every kind of worship of strange gods.

Ver. 14. *Three times.*—This threefold order of feasts points to the establishment of Israel to be the chosen people—his continued preservation and maintenance, and his glorious destiny; and it declares God to be the Creator, the Preserver, the Perfecter of His people. The first feast is one of atonement and purification; the second, a feast of thankfulness; the last, of rejoicing. In all three are united the remembrancers of natural and spiritual blessings. The feast of the beginning of harvest, of its completion, and the feast of the vintage, are connected with the feast of thanksgiving for their preservation out of Egypt, of the giving of the law, and of their support during the dangers of the journey through the wilderness.

Ver. 15. *Empty.*—With offerings of sacrifice, as marks of homage to their King. The particulars of the offerings at the feasts are given later.

Ver. 16. *Hast sown.*—It does not mean that at this "feast of harvest" the harvest had only begun, and the first reaped sheaves been offered; since, from Lev. xxiii. 17, it is clear that two wave-loaves of the new corn were offered. Rather, the bread is called, Lev. xxiii. 20, "first-fruits," because it was baked of the first of the fruits of the field.

Ver. 18. *Unleavened bread.*—In no sacrifice might unleavened bread be offered: cf. introd. ch. xii.

Ver. 19. *Mother's milk.*—There is something obscure in this command, which again occurs in ch. xxxiv. 26, and also Deut. xiv. 21. The Jewish tradition of the Thalmud understands the words to mean, that by the "kid," animals of every kind are intended; and by the mother's milk, it is not meant that of the particular animal itself, but a general prohibition is given of dressing an animal in the milk,—*i.e.*, the butter—of another animal. The moderns have found a somewhat farfetched reason in the prohibition: they suppose that Moses would wean the Israelites from the use of butter, which they had learnt in Egypt, and would accustom them to the use of oil in Canaan, thereby to make the land pleasant to them, and the return to Egypt unwelcome. But the command is here, and in the place where it next occurs, ch. xxxiv. 26, given in connection with the festive offerings: in the latter, it is mentioned together with the beasts which were forbidden. It is, therefore, not improbable that this law had a double object in view: in the first place, to promote a certain gentleness and tenderness towards the animals themselves, as there appears a degree of brutality in dressing the kid in the mother's milk, which has been its nourishment. In this respect, it is similar to the command that the beast should rest on the Sabbath day, and to the law with regard to bird nests: Deut. xxii. 6, 7. But, moreover, the brutality against which it was directed, seems to have been practised not without a meaning, but to have had its origin in a heathen superstitious custom, of which marks elsewhere are found, ascribing a magical power to the use of such milk.

Ver. 20. *Behold.*—The first great division of the laws of the covenant concludes with the last commandments. After such laws had been delivered to them as were necessary for the guidance of their present way of life in the wilderness, and for time to come, promises of grace follow in respect to the defence and help to be afforded the people on their entrance into the Promised Land.

Ver. 21. *My name.*—These words, compared with others of similar import, are of great consequence in bringing us to a knowledge of the nature of this Angel. God will send an Angel before the people whom Israel is to obey: He will be angry with them if they transgress: He has the power of forgiveness. All this is declared in the expression, "My name is in Him." In the person of this Angel, God goes before, and with, His people. God declares, ch. xxxiii. 2, 3, He will *not* go up with the people, "lest He consume them in the way;" *but* He will send an angel before them. Between these two angels, therefore, a great difference must exist. In the one is God's name, *i.e.*, His whole revealed Being: whoever displeases Him, displeases God Himself: so likewise He forgives in God's name, without the mediation of any other. The other, on the contrary, is a subordinate servant of God: an offence committed by Israel against him is not directly against God Himself, but against a creature. In the place before us, Scripture speaks therefore of a messenger of the Lord equal to the uncreated God, whose acts are the acts of God Himself. By means of Him, Israel stood in a different relation to God from all other people. As they enjoyed a higher degree of grace and blessing, so did they run far greater risk if they transgressed against God. On the other hand, if God had carried into execution the threat at ch. xxxiii. 2, 3, the people would then have been placed on a like footing with the heathen, in a lower relation with God, and at the same time with less responsibility like them. This, therefore, is the Angel who led the people out of Egypt (Num xx. 16), who appeared to Joshua as "Captain of the host of the Lord" (Joshua v. 14), as the "Presence of the Lord" (ch. xxxiii. 1, 4), the "Angel of His Presence" (Isa. lxiii. 9), the "Angel of the Covenant" (Mal. iii. 1),—in whom even then was the Duality in God's nature revealed. The full revelation of this truth was made known in the sending of the only begotten Son into the world, followed by the revelation of the Spirit, proceeding from the Father and the Son, and uniting the Two, made known by its pouring out on all flesh. That Scripture does not here speak of an impersonal, visible appearance (like the pillar of the cloud, or the burning bush), which God calls His angel, and by which He speaks, is evident from the words, which denote most forcibly a Person. "Provoke Him not:" He will "not forgive:" which can only by great violence be regarded as a form of expression for what God Himself will do.

Ver. 24 *Break down.*—This prohibition is particularly directed against *the* heathen superstition, which regarded the gods as closely bound to the land, and the land as belonging to them; and so in cases of any public calamity, or of invasion, the protection of the gods of the country was propitiated. Thus, in later times, the invading heathens, the progenitors of the Samaritans, honoured Jehovah, together with their own deities: 2 Kings xvii. 24.

Ver. 26. *Thy days.*—Shall not die an unnatural, premature death

Ver. 28. *Hornets.*—Two instances occur in Eastern history of an immense swarm of insects contributing to the decision of a battle. We might therefore suppose that this promise was to be understood in this manner,—that God would direct and increase in a miraculous manner a natural occurrence, to assist in conquering their enemies. But it is remarkable, that Joshua, xxiv. 12, after the conquest of the land was accomplished, speaks of the driving out of the Canaanites by hornets, without the slightest mention occurring of such an incident in the history of the invasion. We may therefore conclude, that under this name were intended all the various visitations and alarms whereby God brought about the destruction of those nations.

Ver. 30. *Inherit the land.*—Only after the people of Israel had spread abroad and multiplied, and begun to cultivate the conquered territory, were the heathen to be extirpated. The *gradual* driving out of them was of God's express purpose, and would have taken place under all circumstances. It must not, therefore, be confounded with the people's sparing many tribes out of unbelief, weakness, or an inclination towards heathenism, of which mention is made, Judges i. 21, etc.

Ver. 31. *River; i.e.*, the Euphrates. So, from the Red Sea and the Mediterranean through the wilderness, even to that great river. These were, in fact, the boundaries of the land of Israel in the time of their greatest prosperity under David and Solomon; and if it were otherwise in after times, the fault was that of the people themselves. It is evident that the deserts in the east and south were not allotted as dwelling-places, but notwithstanding the claim of Israel remained as neutral spots. Hence the possession of the oases, and other places of pasture in the deserts, were continually subjects of strife.

Ver. 32. *Snare;* a cause of falling into sin—of falling away from God.

CHAPTER XXIV.

Hitherto Moses had been in the darkness on the mountain wherein God was (ch. xx. 21), after the people had heard God Himself deliver to them the ten commandments: he now receives the further interpretation of them in his mysterious intercourse with the Lord, where he probably laid before Him all which at that time seemed to him of moment, and obtained His decision thereupon. At the close of the delivery of these great fundamental laws of the covenant, he is commanded, after solemn offering of sacrifice, to come up together with the elders of Israel into the immediate presence of the Lord, in order to receive there the documents of the covenant, the two tables of the law written by the finger of God. There, on the mountain, he passed forty days, that he might thence, living exclusively in mysterious communion with God, contemplate his whole future mission; might prepare himself for it by fasting and prayer; and might, in anticipation, pass through his struggles and difficulties which were to come. But as the old covenant represented especially, in significant types and shadows, future heavenly blessings, we perceive from what immediately follows, that the ark of the covenant with its furniture, and the service of the priesthood, were the things more particularly which were shown to him on the mount.

Ver. 1. *Come up.*—After the sacrifice (of which mention is made afterwards) had been offered. The people had already promised to do all that the Lord should say to them (ch. xix. 8): therefore no further mention here of the renewal of the vow, but only of the solemn act which followed thereupon, and which is immediately connected with the delivery of the tables of the covenant.

Afar off.—From the body of the elders were seventy (or rather seventy-two, since seventy is a round number), six out of each tribe, to be chosen, who should come up with Moses into the mount. These elders afterwards (Num. xi. 16) received an office under Moses. Here are they chosen only as a number of representatives—perhaps with a reference to those seventy who came with Jacob down into Egypt (ch. i. 5). In all this narrative is manifest the wide distinction betwixt the old and new covenant. In the New Testament, all believers are called on to enter with their Forerunner into the holiest through the veil (Heb. x. 19); while in the Old, merely the chosen representatives of the people, and they only to a very limited extent, may come into the presence of God. Still, however, the general priestly dignity of the whole people is declared in the fact, that not consecrated priests, but elders out of every tribe, enjoy this high privilege (ch. xix. 6).

Ver. 3. *Judgments.*—Those contained in ch. xxi. 23.

Ver. 4. *Wrote.*—Moses must (ch. xvii. 14) have first written at God's command an important and remarkable history in the book, which was to serve for the people as a perpetual memorial of these great events of its early origin. Now, he is commanded to write anew (on a papyrus roll) the whole laws of the covenant, which begin with the ten commandments, and continue to the end of the last chapter. This was the more ample book of the covenant; the purport of which the tables of stone represented. The books of Moses were afterwards composed in the wilderness, from the subject-matter contained in these two portions.

Ver. 4. *Israel.*—The tabernacle, with the great altar in the fore-court, was not yet erected. This is, therefore, a temporary altar, according to the direction in the laws of the covenant, ch. xx. 24. Twelve pillars—*i.e.,* stones heaped one upon another—surround it, in order to mark it as the altar of covenant for the whole people in its twelve tribes.

Ver. 5. *Sacrificed.*—Thanksgiving was the main object; but we also afterwards find that burnt-offerings are always joined with solemn thank-offerings, in order to keep ever in view the notion of self-surrender and propitiation which prevails in the burnt-offerings.

Ver. 6. *Sprinkled.*—This was the great sacrifice of covenant, such as took place in ancient days in every making of agreements. We see, Gen. xv., that the Lord Himself condescended to this custom of confirming a covenant. The different customs of different people, in their sacrifices at covenants, all had the meaning which is expressed in the prayer of the two armies in Homer: "O Jove, most glorious, most great, and all ye immortal gods, whoever, of the two, first breaks these sacred oaths, let his brain be poured on the ground like this wine!"—Iliad, iii. 298. The sprinkling of the blood which followed on the sacrifice, was the act of appropriating and applying it. One half only was sprinkled on the altar, the material representation of God's presence at this sacrifice; the other half is sprinkled on the people, which by this means ratifies the covenant.

Ver. 7. *Book.*—Even in the O. T., where God spake so much to His people, yet but children in understanding, by means of figure, this solemn act was not complete without the word of explanation and instruction. Before the promise was renewed on the side of the people, and so the covenant concluded by both parties, the whole laws of the covenant were read in the ears of the people. "This act shows us clearly the true nature of the sacraments, and their right use. If the word goes not first as the bond of mutual union betwixt God and man, then are they empty acts, whatever name of honour people may assign to them."—Calvin.

Ver. 8. *All these words.*—The solemn establishment of the old covenant. With these words are naturally connected those of the institution of the holy Eucharist (St Matt. xxvi. 28; St Mark xiv. 24), in which we receive the sprinkling of the blood of Jesus Christ (Heb. x. 22; 1 St Peter i. 2), and the participation in all the blessings of the sacrifice of His death.

Ver. 9. *Went up.*—The elders now ascend to the middle height of the mountain, in order, in the name of the whole people, to behold Him who had made the covenant with them. We might here suppose that, like Isa. vi. 1, and Ezek. i. 27, they saw a glorified human form before them; and the mention of His feet (ver. 10) seems to favour the supposition. But it is expressly said (Deut. iv. 12), "The people heard His voice, but saw no similitude,"—which is applicable to the elders also; and though it need not have surprised us if the Lord, who appeared in human form in Paradise, and afterwards to the patriarchs, and in later times revealed Himself in like fashion to the prophets, thereby to prepare for His perfect manifestation in human nature, had likewise here shown Himself in a glorious human form; still the reason is quite obvious why such a revelation of Himself at this time would have been very unsuitable. It was of the greatest importance that a people so imbued with a heathenish Nature-worship should be impressed with the feeling that God's nature is raised far above anything which can be seen and known—that He dwelleth in inaccessible light. If God were thus recognised in His perfect sublimity, as far above all things created, then, and then only, in its due time, might be comprehended His condescension out of love to man, whom he had made after His own image—then would be seen in the assumed human form only a type of His glory, which nothing created could adequately represent; and thus did the human nature which was in after ages truly and really assumed by God, appear as inseparable from, yet unmixed with, the Divine nature. For this cause they saw no similitude. Hence was the throne of God on the ark of the covenant empty: hence Moses drew near to God in the darkness, wherein he saw nothing, but could only in unspeakable, spiritual communion hear and perceive what God revealed to him.

Ver. 10. *Sapphire stone.*—A blue transparent precious stone.

The heaven itself, the most sublime thing in creation, lies at the feet of the Most High, whom no creature can represent. If the elders had seen any form, they would have enjoyed a privilege greater than Moses did, ch. xxxiii. 28. Therefore the Sept. gives the translation, "They saw the place where God stood:" above it, no doubt, a glorious lustre of light.

Ver. 11. *Laid not His hand.*—The same expression as Gen. xxii. 12. Although they had seen God in a degree such as was not granted to the rest of the people, by an immediate revelation of Himself, and as sinners must fear to be brought so near His presence (Isa. vi. 5; Gen. xvi. 13, note), yet He harmed them not. He who had called them to Him, justified them, and cleansed them from their sins in this His word of calling.

Did eat and drink.—They solemnised a sacrificial festival of the sacrifices which were offered beneath on the mountain. On this solemn occasion is shown the unity which existed betwixt every kind of sacrifice. The sin-offering is made in the burnt-offering, and the thank-offering also has the nature of a sin-offering by means of the sprinkling which followed thereon; but at the same time a sacrificial feast is made of the victims, as was else only the case in thank-offerings, thus representing the enjoyment and the assurance of the blessing. In these words we perceive an intimation of a difference between Moses and the elders. *He* fasted forty days on the mountain, miraculously sustained by God's power, and thereby was distinguished above the elders, who "did eat and drink."

Ver. 12. *Teach them.*—"*The* tables of stone," saith God; although there has not been mention made of them, because henceforth they were about to become the well-known records of the covenant. The law of the ten commandments is engraven on stone to show their imperishable character; and since God Himself first spake these words, and not Moses, He gave the law written by His own hand, without the intervention of a man. In the N. T. the law is said to have been "ordained by angels" (Acts vii. 53; Gal. iii. 19); since God, in all His dealings in the creation, and especially in reference to His kingdom, makes use of the service of angels. And therefore, highly exalted as is this law-giving of the Mosaic covenant, it is infinitely beneath the greatness of the revelation of the new covenant; since in this last God does not make use of the service of angels to declare and to confirm His covenant, and there is no mediator between the two parties; but the Son Himself becomes man, and makes known what He has heard in His Father's bosom; and He who enters into communion with God is One with God, and Himself God.

Ver. 13. *Mount of God.*—They went up from the part of the mountain whence the elders on its highest point had beheld the glory of the Lord. Moses' servant Joshua had from the first accompanied him; but because he had personally no independent rank, but had only to minister to Moses, mention is not made of him before. But at the same time Joshua also was by this service distinguished beyond the others, as he was permitted to penetrate farther than they; and herewith likewise he received the beginning of consecration to his future office of successor to Moses.

Ver. 14. *Come unto them.*—As Moses' deputies, they were to arrange every doubt and every dispute among the seventy.

Ver. 17. *Devouring fire.*—A cloud, from which on every side shot forth lightnings. God, therefore, here dwelt in darkness; and yet a darkness which no man could with impunity approach unto, except he whom His word had sanctified.

CHAPTER XXV.

The minute and detailed description of the sanctuary, now to be erected, requires us to look on this event as one of the most important in the giving of the law. If Israel is to form one united people, it must also have one national sanctuary: only by these means could it be freed from the slavery of that Nature-worship to which the heathens were subjected, and in consequence of which they regarded every particular revelation of the Divine in nature differently, according to peculiarity of place and people, and received it among the subjects of their worship.— The names of this tabernacle are full of significance: it is called the "house" or "dwelling-place of God," the "tent of assembly," as the place where God Himself dwells among His people, and through which He enters into communion with them (ver. 22, ch. xxix. 42, note)—"the tent of testimony," Num. ix. 15, as the place where the law was kept—"the sanctuary," as the place which belonged exclusively to God, the Holy One, being severed from all that is earthly, human, sinful. The place where the Holy One of Israel revealed Himself, and entered into communication with His people, consisted of two parts :—(1.) The holiest of all, God's especial dwelling-place, which, both in this tabernacle and in the temple afterwards, was completely dark. Into this the high priest only, on the day of expiation, might enter, veiled in a cloud of incense.—(2.) The holy place, where the people, through their consecrated mediators and intercessors the priests, might draw near to their King. Therefore the whole people is represented, if righteous, as dwelling on the holy hill in the tabernacle of the Lord (Ps. xv. 1, xxiii. 6, xxvii. 4). But because the whole people dwelling in the sanctuary is still sinful, the tabernacle, with all that belonged to it, was to be purified on the day of expiation: Lev. xvi. 15, 16. And therefore, when the Lord breaks off all communion with His people, He Himself destroys the temple (Amos ix. 1); and when this communion shall again be restored after a glorious manner, then the Messiah builds up the temple again (Zech. ix. 12), then He anoints the Most Holy: Dan. ix. 24.—All the vessels which are therein refer to this meaning of the sanctuary. In the holy of holies was the ark of the covenant, with its records, the tables of the law, or the "Testimony,"—this declared the will of the Lord, and bore witness against the sins of the people. Above this was the covering of reconciliation, or the mercy-seat, which covered the testimony that condemned: upon this was God enthroned above the cherubim as the gracious and merciful One. This is the mode of God's dwelling among His people. But His people appear before Him with the light kindled by Him in the holy candlestick—with the incense of prayer upon the altar of incense—with the nourishment well-pleasing to God, the virtues which are acceptable in His sight, typified in the shew-bread. All these things remind the Israelites what manner of people they ought to be when they desire to come before God, and what they really *will* be if they serve Him in the right way. But as yet the way into the Holy of holies is closed by a curtain, and only once a year does the high priest enter therein with the blood of atonement. This is the point on which the typical meaning of the sanctuary turns, as the Epistle to the Hebrews fully explains. Cf. Heb. ix.

Ver. 2. *An offering;* or heave-offering.—A free gift oblation.

Ver. 4. *Blue.*—The colour which is taken from the purple mussel in the Mediterranean, hyacinth-coloured.

Scarlet.—Heb., "shining worm." This is the cochineal, an insect which lives on the holly, also called kermes, and used in dyeing.

Fine linen.—Heb., "Schesch," the whitest and finest kind of cotton, called Byssus, the material of clothing for the very rich: St Luke xvi. 19.—The four materials, therefore, which are mentioned here and elsewhere frequently, are—worsted dyed in blue, reddish-purple, and kermes, together with the finest white cotton. Blue, a dark and a bright red, and white, are the four sacred colours which have been imagined to represent the four elements—air, earth, fire, and water. At all events, the number four—the number of the divisions of the world, and of God's revelations in the world—is significant.

Goats' hair.—Goats in the East have black hair, which is spun or woven for the coverings of tents.

Ver. 5. *Rams' skins;* i e., Morocco leather.

Badgers' skins.—It seems uncertain whether this is the skin of badgers, which is seldom used in the East, or that of the seal.

Shittim-wood; i.e., the wood of the Egyptian acacia, which grows to such a size in the deserts of Egypt and Arabia that boards are cut out of it. It is indeed the only tree in those places. It grows to the height of our willows, and has broad-spreading boughs. The wood is very durable, neither liable to be worm-eaten or to decay, and thus very suitable to be used in the building and furniture of the sanctuary. No particular significance is to be attached to the use of this wood. Where afterwards the "fir-wood" is mentioned, we are to understand this wood of the acacia.

Ver. 7. *Breastplate.*—These things will be spoken about more particularly in the following chapters.

Ver. 9. *Make it.*—Moses saw on the mountain a pattern of all the things which he afterwards caused to be made. But here an important question suggests itself: Did Moses imitate a mere external pattern—did he copy a heavenly original design—or did he, from understanding that which these things represented, and by spiritual comprehension of the wonderful relation between God and His people, build the sanctuary? The right answer here, certainly, is to say, Both are comprised. In his intercourse with God, he attained to a deep view into the spiritual, eternal relations which existed between God and His people; but these relations were revealed to him under the veil of type and emblem, which veil neither he nor any Israelite could altogether take away. Many thousands were kept by such outward service, with its minute details, in a certain external discipline and reverence towards sacred things, without entering into their meaning (the Jews, Philo and Josephus, in the time of the apostles, had altogether lost the key to it); while the really spiritually-minded found a continually elevating employment for heart and spirit in the beautiful and appropriate symbols, which so harmonised with the doctrinal teaching of the Word. And even for him who understood perfectly the meaning of all the figures and emblems, to behold such things,—to hear and speak by means of symbols was an absolute necessity, as is now the case, even after the substance has come in the place of the shadow of heavenly "good things."

Ver. 10. *Ark.*—The ark of the covenant was the principal thing in the Holy of holies. As an ark or chest, it had no particular significance, but derived its importance from the tables of the law which it contained. It was a chest of ordinary wood, surrounded by a crown of gold for ornament. The tables are the groundwork of the whole relation betwixt God and His people—His witness to them, the declaration of His will, and His testimony against them in their transgressions.

Height.—The length of a cubit we may most naturally suppose to be the length of the arm, as far as the elbow—whence the measure originally was derived.

Ver. 11. *Overlay.*—To be understood of thin gold plates placed on it, not of gilding, after our manner.

Crown.—A rim of gold on the upper edge for ornament; perhaps, also, to strengthen the lid.

Ver. 12. *Corners.*—Heb., "its four feet." The ark had therefore feet on which it rested, as appears fitting, in order that it might stand more firmly and might not touch the ground. By this means also it was more conspicuous when carried by the rings fastened in the four feet.

Ver. 15. *Taken.*—In order to prevent the ark being touched by human hands.

Ver. 17. *Pure gold.*—This cover of reconciliation (Kapporeth) over the ark of the covenant was the most important and sacred of all that was in the sanctuary—the centre of the whole kingdom of God in the O. T. The more prominent we observe this to be, the more significant appears the circumstance, that in His chief revelation of Himself in the O. T., God appears as requiring atonement and as reconciled. Of this atonement especial mention is made Lev. xvi. The mercy-seat is not to be regarded as a supplement to the ark, but has its independent meaning, even if it stands in close connection with the other. Therefore the Lord begins afresh, "Thou shalt make," etc. Over this mercy-seat stand two cherubim: between and above them is the Lord enthroned: Ps. lxxx. 1. The covering is called propitiating cover or mercy-seat, because its principal meaning was seen on the day of atonement. The cherubim (cf. Gen. iii. 24) are the representation of what is most glorious in the creation. There must be *two* of them, as one might easily have been taken for an image of God, and at the same time to signify that the plurality of the creature has its unity in the Creator. Above that, therefore, which the whole heathen world at that time worshipped under various forms—above the most glorious beings of the whole creation—is God enthroned: the most glorious creatures are but the supporters of His throne: they turn their faces one to the other, that they may alway behold the Lord and do Him honour. The Holy of holies is called, after this throne of God, "the house or place of the mercy-seat," 1 Chron. xxviii. 11. From this place, between and above the cherubim, did God reveal Himself to Moses, ver. 22.

Ver. 20. *Cherubims be.*—The cherubim have already been mentioned, Gen. iii. 24, as the guardians of the garden of Eden after the fall. Their form is nowhere distinctly described—most fully, Ezek. i. 10. It seems, from the passage before us (ver. 20), that the cherubim on the mercy-seat had only one face and wing, while in the temple of Ezekiel they have two faces, turned towards the two sides, the one of a man, the other of a lion; but in Ezekiel's vision, ch. i., they have four faces—of a man, of a lion, of an ox, of an eagle. In the Revelation of St John they appear as four distinct living beings. Among many Eastern nations we find the forms of beasts joined together. The most known were the Egyptian sphinxes, with the head of a man and body of a lion. These bore, no doubt, the nearest resemblance to the cherubim. If they resembled these, we may suppose the cherubs to have had one face—to have been forms with the countenance of a man, the neck and mane of a lion, the body and feet of an ox, and the wings of an eagle.—Among all Eastern nations there is a fulness of thought in their religious creations, which does not succeed in making a perfect and beautiful figure,—nay, often only affords a representation of form which, if actually copied (as in the instance of many of the prophetic visions), would be revolting to our ideas; while the Greeks, who attain to their notion of heavenly things from earthly, never sacrifice the beauty of the human form to the religious thought. For this reason, as is clear from what has been said above, the cherubim—as represented in the tabernacle, afterwards in the temple, and further in the visions of Ezekiel and the Revelation of St John—have made different impressions on the minds of the readers as to what was their real shape, while the main idea appears to be the same in them all. The significant *four*fold form also has never been wanting, even where it is not expressly mentioned.

As regards their signification, the meaning of all such emblematic figures is, that they denote an union of the powers and qualities of the creatures out of which they are formed. The sphinxes in Egypt represent the qualities of the deities before whose temples they lie, or of the kings, who are regarded as incarnate gods. But here a distinction is to be made between the signification of the Israelitish figures and the heathen. The former unite the highest things in creation—the thinking man; the soaring, far-seeing eagle; the powerful lion; the useful, beneficent ox. But in this union they still only represent what is highest in *creation*, the highest *created beings*, typifying by their fourfold form the divisions of the world, the four winds, or the four portions of the globe. And the fact is very significant, that at the beginning man was appointed to dress the garden of Eden and to keep it (Gen. ii. 15); but when man had fallen, then the Lord placed at the east of the garden of Eden cherubims, to keep the way of the tree of life: Gen. iii. 24. The highest beings in creation came in the stead of man. The blessed home of the first man, and the office originally committed to him, is now transferred to higher beings, and Paradise itself removed from earth to the invisible world. These cherubim on the mercy-seat showed the immeasurable distance between the highest created being, nay, the whole creation, and the Creator Himself, whose throne they bear, and to whom they pay honour. The figures wrought in the tabernacle and the temple remind men that the Church of God on earth is to be regarded as one with the Church in heaven, and that in the sanctuary the Church invisible is joined with the visible in celebrating the worship of God.—That there are really higher beings, just such as the cherubim are represented—that these are angels—can nowhere be shown from Holy Scripture. The emblematic figures of animals are only the outward expression of the Divine idea, which no single form of earth can as yet adequately represent. The name "angel," messenger, is not at all suitable to the cherubim, as they are not spoken of in Holy Scripture as despatched to do God's commands, but as the bearers of His throne or His chariot, inseparable from His appearing. And quite as little can it be shown that they are not real existences, only creatures of the imagination, since, though their outward shape may have some resemblance to the Egyptian and Persian figures, yet is the main idea of their being quite dissimilar. We are justified in regarding them as the very highest of created beings, who, in God's immediate presence, receive His most perfect revelations, and combine in themselves the glory of the whole creation, as those to whom God has intrusted the blessed home of the human race, until man, restored to his original purity, can again take possession of it.

Ver. 22. *Meet.*—The word denotes "I will place Myself there, as I have agreed and promised."

Ver. 23. *Table.*—The distinguishing mark of the table was the shew-bread which was to be laid on it. The people of Israel were not to appear empty before the Lord, but to do Him homage after the manner of the Eastern nations (ch. xxiii. 15): it was therefore enjoined that they should, figuratively, bring a gift for the table of the Lord in the tabernacle (as was done to earthly kings: Gen. xlix. 20; 1 Kings iv. 7). For this cause they were bidden to place continually before the Lord twelve loaves, after the number of the tribes. Together with these loaves, there were on the table bowls of wine (ver. 29). Thus the people offered perpetually before the Lord bread and wine, the main representatives of the gifts of His creation. "Side by side with the prayer, 'Give us this day our daily bread,' and the promise on which it rests, runs the command, Give Me daily My daily bread, as God never asks without giving, and never gives without asking. This command is complied with when the Church of God offers that to which He has given strength, blessing, and continuance."—(Hengstenberg.) By the shew-bread was the people reminded to hallow—by a daily offering the bread and wine, the fruits of the earth procured by the sweat of the brow—their whole earthly life to God; *i.e.*, by a holy life to do that which is well-pleasing to God.

Ver. 25. *Border.*—This might be the border under the surface of the table which joined the four feet.

Ver. 29. *Make them.*—The first word, "dishes," signifies the vessel in which the food was carried. The loaves were laid on them. The second word, "spoons," is literally "hollow hands;" an utensil therefore of this form, probably for the incense: Lev. xxiv. 7. The two last vessels, "covers" and "bowls," appear intended for wine—the covers, or larger deep bowls; and the bowls, smaller drinking-cups. To both these the words, "to pour out withal," belong (as in margin of Engl. Bible)—"bring a drink-offering." We see, therefore, from the vessels, that besides the shew-bread, there was also wine on the table; and that a drink-offering was made therefrom, perhaps when the priests changed the bread on the Sabbath day, and ate the old loaves: Lev. xxiv. 8, 9. There is no further mention of this elsewhere: cf. 1 Kings vii. 50.

Ver. 34. *Candlestick.*—Therefore the candlestick itself, the stem from which the four branches separated, was to have four bowls, each with knop and flower.

Ver. 35. *Candlestick.*—So under every two branches, which separated on the two sides from one point of the stem, was a knop which bound the two together.

Ver. 37. *Against it.*—The burning lamps were all to be turned to the front, that they might lighten that which was opposite to the candlestick. On every branch, and on the fourfold ornamented stem, was there a lamp casting its light in front.

Ver. 38. *Snuffers.*—Into which to throw the refuse.

Ver. 40. *Showed.*—Cf. ver. 9, note.

CHAPTER XXVI.

The sanctuary is called here and in the following chap. a dwelling—tabernacle. It was the dwelling-place or tent of God among His people, who themselves lived, like other nomadic tribes, in tents. It was needful, therefore, that they should have such a portable sanctuary. Like most nomadic tents, it had two divisions, separated by a curtain, and the whole was covered with the usual roofing for tents. This kind of tabernacle was most suitable to the manner of life and the wants of the Israelites at that time. The magnificence of its furniture and utensils served for the glorification of Him to whom every Israelite was prepared to offer his best. The sources of their great wealth in precious stones, and the artistic skill presupposed in the erection of such a building, have been pointed out in the beginning of this book.

Ver. 1. *Curtains.*—Four kinds of coverings of the tabernacle are mentioned here, ver. 7 and ver. 14. The first forms the "dwelling-place;" the second, of goats' hair, is afterwards called "the tent above the dwelling-place." The costly and highly wrought covering of finest linen (byssus, schesch, cf. ch. xxv. 4, note), and of three coloured materials—blue, red, purple and kermes, *i e.*, scarlet—with cherubim woven in, formed the inner hangings, and was to be seen on the side-walls and ceiling; the second one of goats' hair hung above it, on the outside of this first covering; the third and the fourth served the purpose of protection from wind and rain. In like manner, afterwards, the cherubim were depicted on the side-walls of the temple.

Ver. 6. *One tabernacle.*—This covering, therefore, consisted of two great equal parts, which were united by loops or rings and hooks, each part being composed of five curtains. The breadth and the height were ten cubits each; but the length of the curtain twenty-eight cubits, two cubits short of the thirty, probably because it did not quite reach to the bottom. The curtains were joined lengthways, each four cubits broad; so that the whole five were twenty cubits in breadth, which was the length of the holy place. The two great parts—the five and five curtains—reached to the veil which separated the holy place from the Holy of holies. The Holy of holies was about ten cubits shorter than the holy place; and as the five curtains, twenty cubits in breadth, would be likewise affixed to this part, it would seem that the last ten cubits hung down the hind-wall of the Holy of holies in folds.

Ver. 7. *Goats' hair.*—Goats' hair was formerly, and is at present, a material often used in the East for tent-coverings. It seems that here the shining white hair of the goat of Angora is to be understood, since this covering was part of the adornment of the sanctuary, and did not serve for a defence against weather.

Ver. 9. *Fore-front.*—The difference between this and the other covering spoken of before was, that instead of ten curtains divided into two main parts of five each, there were eleven; five belonged to the hinder, six to the fore-part: of these latter, this sixth curtain was doubled and wrapped over, and might possibly be for the purpose of ornament over the entrance. Moreover the length of this curtain was thirty, instead of twenty-eight cubits, which still were not sufficient on account of the thickness of the boards (of which more hereafter); so that it likewise on both ends fell a cubit short of the ground.

Ver. 11. *May be one.*—This was, therefore, likewise above the veil which separated the two divisions of the tabernacle; and of the forty cubits of the hindmost curtain, nearly the half hung down the outer hind-wall in folds.

Ver. 13. *Cover it.*—The covering of goats' hair was to hang down behind, so that the overhanging curtain hid the corners.

Ver. 14. *Badgers' skins*, or seal skin, as ch. xxv. 5.

Ver. 15. *Standing up.*—The boards were planks, or beams, a cubit thick. The Greek translation calls them "pillars," στύλοι.

Ver. 19. *Two tenons.*—Under every board or beam were placed two silver pedestals, with holes into which the tenons or hands of the beam were fixed. These appear to have been level with the floor, into which, indeed, they were fastened. Perhaps they were sharpened on the ends; otherwise the building would not have stood firm, or been raised enough. All this was a part of that reverent propriety which took care that the beams themselves should not touch the earth, or be exposed to any defilement from beneath, but with these silver sockets should rest on their own framework.

Ver. 24. *Coupled together.*—Heb.: " And they shall be coupled (properly twins) from beneath, and together shall they be coupled each one up to his head, to a ring; thus shall it be to them both, to the two corners shall they be." As the entire length of the tabernacle (from within) was thirty, the breadth ten cubits; but behind were six boards, each a cubit and half broad, together nine cubits—in addition, the two boards at the corners, both together three cubits—so that the breadth of the tabernacle outside was twelve cubits: of this, two cubits are to be taken off for the inner room, as every board was a cubit thick. The expression, that they should be twins, must mean that their connection was a double one. They belonged more particularly to the hinder wall; but from their thickness, to the side-wall also, and below and above where they met, were they joined together by means of a ring with the boards of the side-wall.

Ver. 28. *End to end; i.e*, one bar was to go right through; the other four probably only halfway each, so that three bars kept the boards together.

Ver. 31. *Cherubims.*—Wherever the eye rested in the sanctuary, it beheld the figures of the cherubim. On every side the worshipper found himself in the presence of the highest of God's creatures who worship before the throne, who are the guardians of Eden. From the outside nothing of these cherubim was visible: hence their significance is most clear.

Ver. 32. *Hooks.*—For fastening the veil. As no mention is made of rods on which to roll the veil, we may suppose that the high priest, when he entered within, removed it. This would not be difficult, as it was made of such fine material.

Ver. 33. *Under the taches;* namely, those which are described, ver. 6—the golden hooks whereby the two greater divisions of the curtains were fastened together.

Ver. 35. *North side.*—The candlestick and the table, therefore, stood on the two sides, the altar of incense in the middle of the holy place. If the candlestick with its shaft and branches stood parallel with the veil, and of equal height and breadth with the table (whose height is not given)—the altar, which was of far greater height, in the middle, the lamps casting their light in front,—then the impression on the person entering must have been a beautiful and elevating one. The whole aspect of the interior seemed to call upon him, in the midst of God's highest creatures who surround His throne, to come before the Lord anointed with the unction of the Holy Ghost, and enlightened by His grace to come with the offering of a holy life—above all, with the incense of heartfelt prayer.

Ver. 36. *Hanging.*—The material was the same as that of the veil of the Holy of holies; but the cherubs were wanting, for the reason mentioned ver. 31.

Ver. 37. *Brass,* instead of silver, as in the pillars of the veil of the Holy of holies, ver. 32. The pillars, without doubt, stood within, as also the beams of the tabernacle were not visible from the outside.

CHAPTER XXVII.

Before the sanctuary, in the fore-court, stood the great altar of burnt-offering, so called in distinction from the altar of incense within the tabernacle. Even in very early times we find mention of the erection of an altar on the occasion of a solemn sacrifice, or a covenant being made: Gen. viii. 20. These were made, as appears from ch. xx. 24, 25, of earth, or unwrought stone: see note there. They were erected most usually on a mountain,—on which, for example, Abraham was commanded to sacrifice, Gen. xxii. 2, where Balaam sacrificed, where the temple was built. So likewise, in after times, Israel offered sacrifices on the "high places;" and the heathen nations for the most part made sacrifice on mountains in general, or on some specified sacred mountain, and almost everywhere the name "altar" signifies a height, or raising up (Bomos [$B\omega\mu\delta\varsigma$], from bao, is equivalent to a base, a height; altar itself from altus). On such a place the sacrificer, while on earth, was raised nearer to heaven. And thus likewise on the altar, the place raised from the earth and on the earth, was put the victim for sacrifice to God. Hence ascended the flame and the smoke of the sacrifice, a sweet savour unto God, typical of a spiritual offering. But all this happens only in the case where God, by the revelation of His grace and mercy, has been man's guide. The erection of altars on high places without express direction was in later times forbidden, as in these man thought, in his notions of self-righteousness, of doing God service without the intervention of any covenant of grace.—From what is gone before, we can explain the four-cornered shape of the altar as of the sanctuary: it is typical of the world—a part separated by God, and representing the whole. On this, sin, which has been committed on earth, is on earth to be expiated. Hence the material of the altar to be earth or unhewn stone. The altar stood *before* the tabernacle, to signify that entrance into communion with God was only to be obtained by the sacrifice of the covenant. Here must every sin (typically) be removed, every vow paid, before the Church on earth could unite in a holy service with the Church in heaven.

x

Ver. 1. *Shittim-wood.*—See ch. xxv., note.

Ver. 2. *Of the same.*—These words signify that the four horns were not made separately and then put on, but made out of one piece with the brass covering. It is evident that these horns were not merely for ornament, but had an important typical meaning, from the circumstance that at the sacrifice of atonement the priest was to put the blood on the horns of the altar (ch. xxix. 12), and also that persons who fled to the altar for refuge laid hold on the horns thereof (1 Kings i. 10). The horn, as the offensive and defensive weapon of animals, was an emblem of strength (hence " horn of my salvation," Ps xviii. 3). Horns were used to express rays of light: hence a horn was an emblem of glory. The horns, formed out of one piece with the altar itself, the emblem of strength and glory, the refuge of fugitives, represented in the highest degree the very character of the altar itself; and so, according to Jewish tradition, without the horns the whole value at once was lost: the altar ceased to exist.

Ver. 5. *Compass.*—The altar had in the middle a compass, a board covered with brass. From the extremities of this was a grate of network of brass. This compass served for the functions performed on the altar.

Ver. 8. *Hollow.*—The altar, therefore, was a mass of earth, which was placed in a hollow framework of boards covered over with brass as often as the framework was laid down. The main part of the altar was the earth, which, as ch. xx. 24 shows, was put into it, while the framework only served the purpose of giving it a distinct and becoming shape. The frame of boards was three cubits high; at the height of a cubit and half there ran a compass a way round (how broad it was is not known), and from this the network descended, and covered the lower half. The ascent was made not by steps (according to ch. xx. 26), but probably by a mound of earth.

Ver. 9. *Court.*—Around the sanctuary was a court in which the people offered up their service to God. The way into the holy, and still more into the holy of holies, was closed to the people. They could only enter the holy place through the priests, their consecrated mediators; and these, again, could enter the holy of holies only through the high priest. The people sacrificed in the fore-court by means of the priests, and prayed with them if they offered incense. In this fore-court, besides the altar of burnt-offering spoken of above, was the "laver of brass," described ch. xxx. 17-21.

Hangings.—This word is translated in the kindred dialects, and in the Greek version, "sails."

Ver. 11. *Hooks.*—The hangings were fastened to the pillars with silver nails; but, besides this, they were bound together by fillets, *i e.*, poles of silver. The pillars were, no doubt, made of acacia-wood, as those ch. xxvi. 37.

Ver. 16. *Gate.*—The entrance to the tabernacle and to the court was on the east side. Here was the wall, with the pillars and hangings, only fifteen cubits broad on each side. There remained therefore twenty cubits in the middle for the doorway, which was closed with a curtain (the colours as ch. xxv. 4).

Ver. 19. *Brass.*—That is, every kind of instrument used in its erection which has not been particularly described—especially the tent-pegs to which the ropes were fastened, which in a storm served to keep its balance,—whatever was used in the sanctuary, or in the pillars of the court, should all be of brass.

Ver. 20. *Oil.*—Oil, which gives light and refreshes and invigorates the body, is an oft-recurring emblem in the O. T. for the Holy Spirit, the source of life and light, with whom God anoints especially His servants in the O. T.—*all* His children in the N. T. With this emblematic oil were the seven lamps on the holy candlestick to be continually supplied. Olive oil was reckoned the purest. It was to be beaten in a mortar, not ground in a mill, that it might be as fine as possible.

Ver. 21. *Congregation.*—This is the first place in the text where this expression occurs. It means "tent of the (appointed) meeting." The sense of this word is explained, ch. xxv. 22; but more particularly, ch. xxix. 42, "At the door of the tabernacle, where I will meet you, to speak there with you." It is the place of God's revelation of Himself on the one hand, and of the people's communion with God in worship on the other (not of assembling of the people). This communion is derived from an appointment, an ordinance, a promise on God's part. The old Greek version incorrectly gives it, "tent of the witness, or testimony." "It means," says Luther, "a place like a church, where the people might assemble to hear God's word, not run hither and thither on mountains, etc., to sacrifice to God."

Order it.—In the holy place it was dark, with the exception of this light: in the holy of holies there was no light at all. It is not here said that the lamps on the candlestick were always lighted, as ch. xxx. 7 and 1 Sam. iii. 3 (cf. 2 Chron. xiii. 11) seem to prove that they were extinguished in the morning. According to Josephus, the middle lamp and two on the side burnt by day also. But this might be a custom more lately introduced.

CHAPTER XXVIII.

The command is now given to make Aaron and his sons priests, and to prepare vestments of office, which accordingly are minutely described. Every religion, however disfigured by error and sin, awakens in men's hearts a consciousness of alienation from God, and a feeling of the necessity of reconciliation to Him. But everywhere the efforts of man to draw near to God, depend on an act of drawing nigh on God's part—on a revelation of the creating, sustaining, blessing influence on man. This power in the heathen religions was shown in the regular recurrence of natural events which were interwoven with their history. With the people of Israel, on the other hand, it was declared in the covenant which God makes with His chosen ones, in order that He may sanctify them to Himself, by the knowledge and love of Him. Among all nations of antiquity, we find that a certain order, sometimes an hereditary caste, is the channel by which this relationship betwixt God and His people is carried on; and that it is regarded by God as chosen and consecrated to that office. But, as all intellectual energy, all laws and institutions, had their source in religion, in the surrender of man to God, and the consciousness of dependence on Him, and were engendered by religion, we naturally find in the early state of society and of political life—as, for example, when a people emerge out of the patriarchal, pastoral life, the age of unconscious childhood,—that a priestly class stands at the head of social order, exercises more or less influence over it, and, from being in possession of all the wisdom and learning of the day, acts as the soul in the political body. Everything which contributes to overcome natural hindrances, to unravel social difficulties, to promote an orderly and happy life in a country which, though fertile, requires laborious cultivation,—all this proceeds from the priestly class, which, by a Divine law committed to it (a portion of the general law of the universe), points out to every one, from the king to the lowest slave, his place among the people. At the very time when the Israelites were passing from the patriarchal and pastoral to the national life, they were sojourning among the most cultivated people of the ancient world, the whole of whose existence in the productive valley of the Nile (which still required skilful husbandry) was governed by a priestly class, which fixed laws and regulations for the most minute particulars of daily life. If the Israelites are to become a nation like the rest of the world, their requirement of some means of mediation with God, through an order of priests, must be satisfied. But here is a great difference apparent between God's covenanted people and the heathen worshippers of Nature. With all heathens, the relations of Nature to the world are those in which the priests adjust: observations of the sun, of the changes of the seasons, of the ordinary or unusual natural events,—these are the matters in which they are engaged. For this reason the priests invented fables of a race of gods, who represent the creation and development of the world; they observed the course of the planets as the governors of the world; they regulated the ranks and order of life according to their laws, and, in case of violation of them, sought to reduce again such disorder into harmony with the whole. All this was effected by a secret traditional wisdom which was preserved in their order. But in Israel it was clearly announced at the beginning, that only sin had separated between God and man, and that man's communion with God depends on his holiness. The priestly class, therefore, is the class which is chosen and sanctified by God, in order to bring about the sanctification of the whole people. In a certain degree, this sanctification of the people had already begun by God's choice of them. So the whole people are called, ch. xix. 6, a kingdom of priests. This wide outward severance between priests and people is not therefore an eternal division, or by an unalterable law of Nature; but only according to degree, and for the time of preparation until the people shall be perfectly sanctified. This sanctification, although embodied in an outward worship, and in minute regulations suited to the age of childhood and of sense, carries with it still, as a soul, holy love, which not only requires the reconciliation of the sinful people, but likewise graciously brings it about. And this holy love is revealed, not in some secret science and art, but in the written law, which, while committed to the priesthood for accurate understanding, interpretation, and administration, is still accessible to the meanest among the people. The tribe of Levi, although separated from the rest, is still a tribe *with* the others, not above them; and its outward privileges were calculated quite as much to humble as to exalt it. And even Moses himself, who was put over the whole house of the Lord, was no priest, but king and prophet; and he likewise foretells that a Prophet should come like himself, to whom the people will listen (Deut. xviii. 18). Moreover, he appoints, by the side of the priesthood, and in a certain sense above it, the office of extraordinary messengers, whose duty it was to rebuke the degenerate priesthood and people, and to remind them of their duties, nay, sometimes themselves to exercise the priestly office And as the time arrived for the prophetic office to be set up side by side with the priestly, so did the season come for the kingly office; thereby severing between the spiritual and secular. And at the same time preparation was made for the period when the ever-changing priesthood of sinful men should not altogether cease, but become merged into the everlasting priesthood after the order of Melchisedek—the order of the Eternal Mediator and Intercessor, the Prophet and King, Jesus Christ.

The priests who are chosen out of the people are Aaron and his descendants. But, together with them, the rest of the tribe of Levi discharged the less significant, inferior duties. Among these descendants of Aaron, there was one particularly distinguished, who at first is merely called "the priest," or the "anointed priest;" but is afterwards named "the high (more properly "the great") priest." This person alone performs the great atonement of the people at the feast of atonement, described in detail Lev. xvi. 14; likewise unites in himself the whole priestly office, both as regards its higher privileges and dignity, and also its outward sanctity. He therefore stands in the place of the whole people: if "the priest who is anointed do sin, the whole people is guilty," Lev. iv. 3 (Hebrew). The prophet (Zech. iii. 1) sees the high priest in the temple accused by Satan for the sins of the whole people. This is the high priest, whose vestments and official insignia are here so especially described. His clothing was to be an honour and ornament. Their unusual splendour was intended, like that of the tabernacle, to exalt the priestly dignity in the eyes of a sensuous people. But at the same time this splendour was likewise full of significance, and by the most exalted symbols reminded both priests and people continually of the relation of the Lord to the people of His covenant.

Ver. 1. *Sons.*—The first two were afterwards slain: Lev. x. 2. The last two were the progenitors of the priestly family. Out of the whole tribe of priests, the especial priestly family is here chosen, which was empowered by a peculiar consecration to be the mediators before God of the whole people.

Ver. 3. *Wisdom.*—Just as was the case with the gifts of the Spirit in the Church of the N. T., do we find in the O. T. all natural gifts employed in the service of the kingdom of God ascribed to the Spirit of God. If they are truly to be of service in the kingdom of God, their sanctification thereto and their renewal are needed, by which they may become essentially different from what they were before.

Ver. 6. *Ephod.*—First in the description of the priestly garments stands the ephod—a clothing over the shoulders, with which was closely connected the breastplate (Choschen). These were the signs of administrative and judicial dignity; and yet not mere signs, but likewise Divine promises and pledges.

Ver. 7. *Joined together.*—Therefore a short garment without sleeves, in which, besides the four materials so often named (blue, red purple, kermes, and white byssus), gold threads were likewise worked in.

Ver. 10. *Birth*; *i.e.*, according to the ages of the sons of Jacob.

Ver. 12. *Memorial.*—The ephod was the sign of the office of leadership over the children of Israel; and therefore the breastplate (Choschen) was attached to it as a mark of the judicial office. The high priest bears the children of Israel on his shoulders; *i.e.*, he rules them. "The government shall be on His shoulders:" Isa. ix. 6.

Ver. 13. *Ouches.*—Rings: borders for the two onyx-stones.

Ver. 14. *Wreathen chains.*—The use of these appears ver. 25.

Ver. 15. *Breastplate.*—Literally, "the ornament of justice;"

Heb., Choschen—a four-sided worked pocket or bag, as will be seen in what follows, covered in front with the most precious stones, the signs of the highest judicial dignity.

Ver. 16. *Doubled.*—The stuff being doubled as a pocket, in order to put the "light and judgment" in front, ver. 30.

Ver. 17. *Row.*—The particular names are difficult to understand, and are differently explained. They were the most precious stones then known. The Israelites had learned in Egypt the art of setting and engraving stones, where it had been known from very early times.

Ver. 26. *Inward.*—The first rings were fastened above in the breastplate, and from thence they bound the chains with the precious stones to the shoulders. These were below and towards the inner part.

Ver. 27. *Girdle.*—Therefore there, where underneath the shoulders close above the girdle the two pieces met, these rings were to be inserted.

Ver. 29. *Heart.*—As the shoulder carrying burdens denotes governance, so is the thinking wise heart (according to Biblical, more particularly Old Testament mode of speaking) the source of all judgment which is pleasing to God: 1 Kings iii. 9–11.

Ver. 30. *Continually.*—In the breastplate—probably, therefore, in the fold or pocket formed by the rings—was the "light and judgment" (Urim and Thummim) to be placed. From the entire silence of Holy Scripture concerning the form of that which was placed in it, we can only now venture to conjecture concerning its fashion. We learn from a number of places that, by means of this "light and judgment," the high priest gave sentence in all difficult and important matters in the name of God; but *how* this took place we have no information. Among heathen nations we find something similar, both as regards its outward and inward character. In Egypt, the high priest, when he acted as supreme judge, hung round his neck a figure of truth, cut out of sapphire-stone, with closed eyes. And among almost all ancient nations we find certain priests or priestesses who regularly, in important national circumstances, gave oracular answers. We may therefore fairly conclude, that God drew near to His people in the same way. But that the Urim and Thummim were (as Philo Judæas, who lived in the time of Christ, says) two woven figures enthroned on the breastplate as a base, contradicts the words, "*put in* the breastplate," which words altogether correspond to those which speak of putting the tables into the ark (ch. xxv. 16). Perhaps they were two worked figures, or more properly, after the manner of the cherubim, one worked double figure, which represented light—the knowledge of truth and judgment—moral purity. The Egyptian figure was called only "truth"—the Israelitish, "truth and judgment;" which seems to intimate that holiness is the characteristic of the religion of the covenant in opposition to the heathen Nature-worship. We are not to suppose the manner in which illumination was communicated to the high priest by the light and judgment to have been a questioning of the figure or the precious stones, which returned answer by a certain mode of glittering; but rather, that the high priest had in this figure or image a Divine pledge and assurance that, in all matters appertaining to the right and welfare of the tribes of Israel (and only in those things which did concern the twelve tribes was he allowed to ask of the Lord and to judge in His name), the Lord would never leave him, on his faithful asking for it, without a certain knowledge of what was His will. Thus did Joshua, after the death of Moses, go before the high priest Eleasar, and inquire of him from the Lord by means of "the light." According to the same judgment were the whole congregation of Israel to go in and out, Num. xxvii. 21. Thus God answered Saul no more after his rejection by the "light," 1 Sam. xxviii. 6. After the Babylonish captivity there was no longer a high priest with "light and judgment;" and the people waited in difficult questions for the time till a high priest stood up with Urim and Thummim (Ezra iii. 63), or till a prophet arose (1 Macc. iv 46).

Ver. 32. *Rent.*—This garment also was not sewed together, but woven out of one piece—a symbol of entireness and perfection.

Ver. 33. *Pomegranates.*—The pomegranate is one of the most beautiful kinds of fruit. Both the blossom and fruit of the pomegranate is an emblem of beauty and abundance; and, therefore, is used as an ornament and significant image even by the heathen. Life, blossom, fruitfulness, are therefore symbols of communion with God, who is the Source of all true life. These pomegranates were made of thread of bright colours, and hung between the golden bells, which were probably open below.

Ver. 35. *Die not.*—These words, "that he die not," do not refer only to the bells, but to the whole dress. Aaron might not appear before the Lord except robed in these holy garments, which He Himself had consecrated. The sounding of the bells was a sign to the people in the fore-court of his entrance and employment in his priestly functions. They were in this manner enabled to accompany these ministrations with their thoughts and their prayers, although the veil concealed them from their view. Cf. Ecclus. xlv. 10, 11.

Ver. 36. *Plate.*—The Hebrew word signifies "flowers." It appears, therefore, that the form was perhaps that of a wreath of flowers. This often occurs in sacred objects (the rod of Aaron which blossomed—the calix shape of the head-dress), and it was to remind men of the true Divine life which is in holiness. Everything which is sanctified to God—which comes into His more immediate presence, is full of life, flourishes and blossoms. Whoso walketh in the law of the Lord "shall be like a tree planted by the rivers of waters, that bringeth forth his fruit in his season:" Ps. i. 3.

Holiness, or sanctified to the Lord. The word holiness relates not to the plate, but to him who bears it. It denotes him as sanctified to the Lord. As the whole people out of the mass of the world—the tribe of Levi out of the people—the priests out of the tribe—so is the high priest entirely separated out of the body of priests, and consecrated to the Lord to be a mediator between Him and His people.

Ver. 38. *Hallow.*—The high priest alone is able to bear the iniquity, because the holiness of the Lord takes it away. Sin clings to all sacrifices, either because they, as sin-offerings, take on themselves the sin of the people, or, as thank-offerings, are ever only imperfectly that thing which they represent. But all sinfulness which belongs to the sacrifices, to the gifts of atonement and sanctification of the people, is removed by the holiness of the Lord, which triumphs over every obstacle and takes away all imperfection. But as the high priest can only do this by outward sign, and not really, since he himself is a sinner, and in mind not always sanctified, we perceive here how he and all that he does is only a type of the Holy One whose whole life even to death was sanctified to the Lord.

Ver. 39. *Coat.*—The name of this coat is in the Hebrew

"K'thoneth." It was, according to Jewish tradition, a long garment reaching to the feet, with long sleeves. According to ch. xxxix. 27, it was woven; *i.e.*, not sewn together from different pieces, but altogether the work of the weaver. A garment which was woven was regarded as more perfect in distinction from one sewn. The material was the finest white cotton—byssus; the colour, that of holiness, purity.

Mitre.—A turban of byssus, different from the coifs or bonnets mentioned afterwards.

Girdle.—The girdle holds the long clothes together, and girds them up; so that it alone makes the wearer fit for the discharge of his duties. At the same time, different instruments and signs of office were put in the girdle before the commencement of the discharge of his functions. For this reason the girdle itself is a mark of office, and was, according to tradition, only worn by the priests in the discharge of their office.

Ver. 40. *Aaron's sons; i.e.*, the ordinary priests, in distinction from the high priest.

Coats.—The same word as ver. 39 for the narrow coat of the high priest.

Bonnets.—The priestly head-dress (Migbaah, *i.e.*, elevation, hill) had the form of an inverted calix. It appears to have differed from that of the high priest (Mitznepheth) only by being less high.

Ver. 41. *Consecrate.*—"Fill their hand." This is the frequent expression for the solemn institution to the priestly office. It stands in direct reference to the first sacrifice of consecration, at which the pieces of the sacrifice were given into the hands of the priests. "To fill the hands of the Lord" signifies to offer Him gifts. With respect to the priests, therefore, this filling of the hands signifies "laying gifts in them to be presented to the Lord;" therefore, consecrating them to be sacrificers.

Ver. 42. *Breeches.*—As the coat, the K'thoneth, reached to the feet, these breeches had rather a symbolical meaning, and served to remind men of the origin of the feeling of shame, Gen. iii. 7.

Ver. 43. *Iniquity.*—For which they have no atonement, as, according to ver. 38, they have for the iniquity of the people. The same expression, to "bear the iniquity," may therefore, in respect to the sin of another, signify, to remove it, to wipe it away; in respect to their own, to "bear the punishment of it."

CHAPTER XXIX.

The mode of consecrating the priests to the office follows the description of their garments. This consisted of ablution, of a solemn robing, of anointing, and the sacrifice which followed thereon. Here, also, is observable the use of the number four, as is the case with respect to the colours, the pieces of their garments, the component parts of the oil of consecration, and of the censor. Each particular act has its own special signification. The ablution signified their preliminary purification from daily sins; their garments, their investiture with their office; the oil, the gifts of the Spirit granted them; and the sacrifice, the forgiveness of their sins, and their entire sanctification to the Lord. The sacrificial meal which follows is the enjoyment of the blessing received in their priestly office, and more especially in the sacrifice of reconciliation, and an emblem of their close, intimate communion with the Lord, whose guests they are.

Ver. 1. *Blemish.*—All the particulars of the sacrifices will be fully explained in connection with the laws concerning sacrifices, which follow in the next book.

Ver. 5. *Robe of the ephod.*—These belonged to each other, but so that the ephod or shoulder-garment was the main part.

Ver. 7. *Anoint him.*—Oil not only beautifies man's person, but it likewise improves all the bodily powers. The skin is made soft, and defends the body from the effects of heat; the limbs are rendered supple, the head lighter. Oil not only is the cause of light, but likewise of life; and is, therefore, in the O. T., the emblem of the Holy Spirit, especially of His gifts to men for the purpose of serving the kingdom of God. The oil was poured on the head of the high priest: of the other priests it is only said that they were anointed—*i.e.*, probably with the finger dipped in oil.

Ver. 9. *Consecrate.*—Cf. ch. xxviii. 41, note.

Ver. 10. *Head.*—Whereby the sacrifice was solemnly dedicated. All the details in the next book.

Ver. 12. *Finger.*—Cf. ch. xxvii. 2, note.

Ver. 20. *Ear.*—The ear, the hand, and the foot, are the three great instruments of obedience in the human body. They are purified and consecrated by the blood of the sacrifice.

Ver. 24. *Wave.*—This word, which often afterwards occurs, and which will be more fully explained as to its significance, means, "to move hither and thither on all four sides;" "to heave" (ver. 27), on the other hand, signifies, "to move up and down" in a perpendicular direction, cf. Lev. vii. 34, note.

Ver. 29. *Sons.*—Namely, the sons who succeed him in the office of the high priesthood; not the ordinary priests, who likewise are descended from him.

Ver. 39. *Even.*—At sun-setting: ch. xii. 6, note.

Ver. 42. *Meet you.*—Here is the name of the tabernacle, as a place of the Lord's meeting with His people, again confirmed.

Ver. 45. *Their God.*—It is only possible that the Lord shall dwell continually among the unholy people when He has hallowed to Himself a sanctuary and priests by an especial act of consecration. This is the main condition of the everlasting covenant.

CHAPTER XXX.

After the description of all the furniture of the tabernacle, of the priests' garments and their consecration, next follows that of the altar of incense—apparently somewhat late and detached—not as though this part of the sacred things was of less importance and significance than the others, but because all the preceding sacred furniture contains everything needful to prayer and the service of God. The people reconciled to God are they who send forth daily to Him the incense of prayer. In the East, in king's houses, at feasts, the whole air is redolent with incense, as, where so much flesh was daily sacrificed and in great measure burnt, incense was a real necessity to the senses. A symbolical meaning is attached to this.—All reconciliation with God by means of sacrifice, all light of knowledge, all surrender of the earthly active life to the Lord, would still leave a sensible void in the life and service of the people of God, without the incense of prayer rising out of the sanctuary—out of the hearts of the congregation of God. While the priest offered the sacrifice of incense in the sanctuary, the smoke ascended towards heaven through the curtain (as there was no opening) before the eyes of the people, who were praying in the fore-court (St Luke i. 10). Its ascent was both an exhortation to them to pray, and an assurance their prayers would be heard.

Ver. 2. *Of the same.*—The regular altar was of earth, with a wooden framework. This was such a frame overlaid with gold, without the filling up.

Ver. 3. *Top.*—This top or roof was flat and smooth (as eastern roofs usually are), with a low border, which latter, by the side of the table, was intended to prevent the falling of the incense.

Crown.—Apparently in the middle of the raised part.

Ver. 6. *Mercy-seat.*—It is significant that it is not said of the table and the candlestick that they stood before the mercy-seat (ch. xxvi. 35). Immediately before the mercy-seat, yet separated from it by the veil (because the way into the Holy of holies was not yet opened), the incense of prayer daily ascended to God. And thus, under the New Covenant, ought the daily, unceasing prayer of Christians to rise up to God before the cross of Christ, "whom God hath set forth to be a mercy-seat in His blood," Rom. iii. 25.

Ver. 8. *Lighteth.*—This conjunction of offices is significant. In the morning were the lamps of the candlestick set up (snuffed, trimmed). In the clear day the people of the Lord are to trim His lamps, that the light from the Lord in the dark places may shine thereon. But every step in the light of holy knowledge ought to be connected with prayer.

Ver. 9. *Strange incense.*—The preparation of the sacred incense is afterwards very particularly described. This might not be applied to any common use (ver. 32); and in like manner no unhallowed incense might be offered on the altar, since everything was significant. In the New Testament, God will only hear prayers offered in the name of Jesus. There is no ground of assurance except in His word, His promise, and His mediation. St John x. 23.

Drink-offering.—Prayer is to be an especial service in the worship of God, not mingled with the sacrifices. The sacrifices without prayer are wanting in an essential part; but prayer, together with all that the sacrifices express, goes forth as something independent. In the N. T. the sacrifice of the children of

God is their heart, their will, their body. This sacrifice without prayer cannot be well-pleasing in God's sight; but, at the same time, prayer can by no means make up for the want of the offering of the heart and life to God.

Ver. 10. *In a year*, on the great day of atonement, which is spoken of fully, Lev. xvi. Even the altar of incense must on this day be purified, because it also was defiled with the sin of the people. Even the prayer of the children of God is not in itself pure and acceptable in His sight; but this their service needed to rest on the atonement of the Mediator of the New Testament. The more any one lives an inner life, the more does he perceive how sin defiles and corrupts the most religious acts. He would, therefore, have no confidence in the acceptableness of his prayers without an ever fresh appropriation to himself of the merits of the atonement.

Most holy.—This oft-recurring expression does not, of course, mean every time, exclusively, the "most holy, but the " very holy." They are, therefore, the most exalted and sacred places, persons, things, and acts, which form the centre of the whole Divine plan of revelation and sanctification, which refer immediately to the renewal and maintenance of the relation to God. That which relates to God, and is rather a holy ordinance established by Him among men, is called simply " holy."

Ver. 12. *Numberest them.*—The numbering of the people had a religious meaning. While the whole body of the people was interceded and atoned for by means of the priests and the sacrifices, at the numbering every individual stood personally and for himself before the Lord, the Holy One. The Lord stood before him, and asked, Whether he also belonged to His people? A ransom, therefore, must be paid for the life of each Israelite, at this time of immediate appearance before God, lest he be smitten with punishment. It is clear that this was also a symbolical act (cf. Ps. xlix. 8)—a recognition of each person's continual need of redemption—a continual awakening of the consciousness of sin, in order to keep alive the thought that no one could dare to stand before God without some mediation ordained by Himself.—We may gather from these words, that numberings of the people often took place, as at God's command is the case Num. i. But whether such census was taken at regular periods is not known, but not probable: still in the time of

Christ the payment here appointed had become a regular one, as appears from St Matt. xvii. 24, and is known from other sources; and it is scarcely possible that the maintenance of the magnificent tabernacle and the service of God could be provided for except by a regular tribute. But the numbering of the people (for the reason given above) was ever regarded as something very hazardous; and for this cause David committed a sin when he presumed to do this of his own accord, and so the punishment here threatened befell the people: 2 Sam. xxiv.; 1 Chron. xxii.

Ver. 13. *Shekel.*—The calculation of weights, and of the value of money which depends on weight, is very difficult in such very ancient times. A shekel has been reckoned to be the forty-sixth part of a fine Cologne mark, or something above seven good groschen. Accordingly, each Israelite paid not quite four good groschen as tribute. The common shekels, which were different from the shekel of the sanctuary, were considerably lighter. (Calmet thinks the value of the silver shekel to have been 2s. 3¼d.—Trans.)

Ver. 15. *Atonement.*—The soul of the one needed atonement just as much as that of the other. That which in this appointment lay heavily on the poor, it was the part of love to lighten; as Christ pays the money procured by His miracle for Himself and *Peter.*

Ver. 19. *Feet.*—In the dress of the priests no shoes are mentioned. But it appears from ch. iii. 3, that no one might come into the presence of the Lord with shoes on his feet, but all Divine service was to be performed barefoot. Hence arose the necessity of the priests' washing their feet before they entered the sanctuary.

Ver. 21. *Wash.*—This purification had also here a symbolical religious meaning. Although they were washed, and therefore were altogether clean (St John xiii. 10), yet did they need to wash the feet—to put away the impurities which touched them again and again in the daily walk and work of life.

Ver. 23. *Pure myrrh.*—Heb, "Mor flowing from itself," or myrrh, smyrna. This is the juice which exudes from the stem of a small shrub that grows in Arabia and also in Canaan (Amyres), very like to the acacia-tree. When the bark is slit a gummy liquor flows out, and the fragrance from it was very highly valued among the ancients. The myrrh which flowed from the tree, and not the extracted juice, was esteemed the best. "Cinnamon of sweet scent;" *i.e*, not the common kind, but an aromatic sort. "Calamus," a reed with a sweet odour, frequently met with in Arabia.

Ver. 24. *Cassia.*—Heb., Kiddah, a kind of cinnamon much prized by the ancients as a precious sweet spice.

Oil-olive.—The oil for sacred anointing was, therefore, pure olive oil, compounded with the most precious perfumes. The oil was the emblem of the Holy Ghost—the perfumes of the favour of God. The number four of the perfumes signifies the revelation of the Divine Spirit in the world, in which this number continually occurs.

Ver. 25. *Apothecary.*—A perfumer. The art of preparing precious spices, perfumes, was a particular trade in ancient times.

Ver. 32. *Man's flesh;* i.e., not to be used for the purpose of ordinary anointing, to make the body supple. Even in those cases where the holy customs most nearly approached the acts and usages of common life, there was still a wide external line of demarcation, that the typical meaning of the sacred customs might always be conspicuous as the proper sense.

Like it.—This does not mean that the oil of anointment was prepared then for all times, and no new was to be made; nor that only Aaron and his sons, and no one of his posterity, was ever to be anointed—as both these opinions are a misunderstanding of the Jewish interpreters,—but that nothing like it should be made for ordinary uses.

Ver. 33. *Cut off.*—Because this would be an act of open rebellion against the Lord, a breaking of the covenant with Him: Gen. xvii. 14, note.

Ver. 34. *Frankincense.*—The incense also which was offered on the golden altar in the holy place was compounded of four substances (ver. 24, note). The first (Hebrew, Natap, *i.e.*, "drops") is probably the gum from the tree which in Heb. is called Libneh, in Greek, Storax,—a plant about twelve feet high, like the quince. By means of slitting the stem a sweet gum is obtained, called in Greek, "Stacte." The second material (Heb., Sch'cheleth) is the name of the covering of a shell-fish (Anguis odoratus), which is met with in the Red Sea. This fish had not itself a pleasant scent, but afforded to other perfumes strength and continuance. The third, " Chelb'nah "—galbanum, is a resin from a shrub which grows on the Syrian mountains, and which, when lighted, has so strong and disagreeable an odour as to drive away snakes, but, mixed with others, increases the sweetness of the perfume. The fourth, " L'bonah," frankincense, is the very highly prized resin of a small shrub, about ten feet high, which grows in Arabia, but more particularly in India. It was used by the ancients, for the most part, in the service of the temple. L'bonah means " whitish," because the whitest kind was the most prized and most used in the service of God.

Ver. 35. *Tempered.*—Heb., " salted, pure, holy." Salt was used in every sacrifice. Of its significance there will be occasion to speak Lev. ii. 13, note.

Ver. 36. *Before the testimony.*—Therefore a dry incense-powder, which stood on the golden altar of incense before the testimony—*i. e.*, in the holy place, before the curtain which concealed the ark with the tables of the law, and from thence was put in a pan when the incense was burnt.

CHAPTER XXXI.

Ver. 2. *Bezaleel,* sign.: " In the shadow of God." The choice of the artificers forms the conclusion to the list of commandments about the tabernacle and its furniture. They were sanctified to this work. Their natural gifts were exalted by the Spirit of God which was bestowed on them, whereby they were enabled to do the work not merely in a more beautiful and comely manner, but also to work in the continual consciousness that they were engaged on holy works, destined for the kingdom and service of God.

Ver. 3. *Wisdom.*—Wisdom is the highest faculty, the faculty of perception (of contemplating the beautiful); understanding is the gift of discrimination, the power to discern which is the most beautiful of two or more things presented to the perceptive faculty; knowledge, outward, practical knowledge; and workmanship, skill, the power of executing that which the mind has conceived.

Ver. 4. *To devise.*—Lit., "to conceive thoughts" (*i.e.*, to conceive what is ingenious), "to work in gold," etc.

Ver. 5. *Set them.*—Lit., "to cut in stone for the fittings," settings.

Ver. 6. *Aholiab* means "tent of the father."

Wise-hearted.—This is very forcible, literally rendered—"And unto the heart of every one, in the heart of the wise have I given wisdom;" *i.e.*, have sanctified his natural gifts by My Spirit for this holy work.

Ver. 10. *Clothes of service.*—Heb., "the clothes of the weaving;" *i.e.*, the woven carpets and hangings of the tabernacle and the court.

Ver. 11 s. *They do.*—There were certainly separate persons for each part of the work, who had learnt the craft in Egypt; in which country all kinds of work were divided among different persons, and one man undertook only one particular branch of a trade. But two artificers stood at the head of the whole as the "devisers of thoughts," in order to do all in an exact manner after Moses' description, and to give the pattern to the workmen.

Ver. 13. *Sign.*—As the sanctuary just described was to be God's dwelling-place among the people, so should the Sabbath be on the part of the people a perpetual confession of the covenant with God, the Creator of all things

Sanctify.—Separate you from all other sinful people, who are strangers to the true God. To that purpose the Sabbath served, which had so peculiar a position in the regulation of their mode of life, by its direct reference to God as the Creator.

Ver. 14. *Cut off.*—Herein was not yet clearly expressed what should be done to him; afterwards the punishment of stoning was decreed: Num. xv. 32.

Ver. 15. *Put to death.*—The reason of this punishment becomes most clear from the reason assigned and the context. It was not because the sin in itself was so great; but because, in the case of a people like the Israelites, who were governed by outward ordinances, and necessarily bound to them, and more kept in union with God and separate from Nature-worship by the discipline of fear than of knowledge, the violation of the Sabbath was a violation of the inner sanctuary, an actual breach of the covenant with their God.

Ver. 17. *Refreshed.*—Heb., "He drew breath," refreshed Himself. See explanation of this expression, Gen. ii. 2, note.

Ver. 18. *Finger of God.*—Here also, as ver. 3, it stands, "with God's finger;" not "His," or "the finger of the Lord.' A superhuman work, one of Divine, almighty power is generally signified. The ten commandments, as the peculiar records of the covenant, the root of all other laws, were hewn in stone, the others were written in a book. These laws written in stone, bearing witness before man of God's will, and so condemning him, were intended to stand before him until the time came when they were written in the heart: Jer. xxxi. 31, etc.; 2 Cor. iii. 7.

CHAPTER XXXII.

Scarcely had the giving of the law concluded, together with the call of the lawgiver, and the ratification of the sabbatical rest as sign of the covenant—hardly were the records of the covenant delivered to them—when the first great apostasy of the people took place. The occasion of this was the long delay of Moses on the mount. Remembering the dread which had overwhelmed themselves at the former Divine manifestation, they believed Moses to be dead. We may remark, with respect to the idolatry of the people of Israel, two gradations of it. One was the worship of the true God under the form of some image: this was the calf or ox-worship, of which the Egyptian Apis-worship formed the prototype (cf. Deut. xxix. 17). This was the idolatry which Jeroboam in after times established in the kingdom of Israel (1 Kings xii. 28, 29). The other kind of idolatry was the worship of the gods of other nations—Baal, Moloch, Astoreth, etc. The first kind led directly to the second, since the worship of Jehovah through an image never showed itself adverse to the worship of strange gods. The common ground of both forms of idolatry is Nature-worship—the reverence of God as the power of Nature; for the calf is the early emblem of the productive power of Nature, and is represented both as male and female. But since a beast can only be the emblem of Nature or the powers of Nature, never of the Creator Himself, the Holy and the Just One who hath created man to know and love Him, and made him lord over nature,—so, in the most noble kind of symbolical animal-worship, man pays honour not merely to a fellow-created being, but worships that very creation which is destined to serve himself. It thus becomes a worship of the world in the fullest sense of the word; which, as a necessary consequence, gives man over to serve all manner of worldly and fleshly lusts. In this way is the apostasy of the people easily to be explained. The impression made on their senses by the miracles on Sinai had soon vanished: the object of these miracles, in bringing the people to obedience to the commandments of the Lord, had not been attained. The people now felt especially the need of a visible leader to go before them—a god who should dwell among them, not merely shrouded in the pillar of the cloud, as was the Holy, Unapproachable One, whom no image might represent, but a god clothed in bodily form, to be recognised and understood by all. They desired a god by the sight of whom their strength might be roused, and to revel in the exercise of that strength, without their conscience being awed by the feeling of his holiness. We here see Israel on the brink of the precipice—on the point of losing all which constituted their peculiar privilege beyond every other people. Hence the terrible punishment and the after effects of this great event. There is a truth in the Rabbinical saying, "No punishment happens to Israel in which there is not an ounce of the transgression of the calf."

Ver. 1. *Go before us.*—In the marches or wanderings of the nomadic people, it was customary to carry the images or altars of their deities before them; so that they figuratively led the people. Thus was Israel guided by the pillar of the cloud. But this pledge of the Divine presence, because it reminded them of God's unapproachable holiness, was distasteful to this undisciplined, heathenly-disposed people.

Become of him.—Of course the long, inexplicable delay of Moses on the mount was intended as a trial for the people, by which they should show whether or not the spirit and meaning of the holy commandments of God had made an impression on them.

Ver. 2. *Unto me.*—Aaron felt in great perplexity, and did not know how to escape from it except by a concession. Probably he soothed his conscience with the thought, that it was after all the true God whom they wished to worship, through an image—that without this concession Moses and himself would be deprived of all power—that Moses could afterwards remove and forbid the worship. The fact, too, is perhaps significant, that he bids them bring their most costly ear-rings, with the supposition this demand would be sufficient to restrain them from their idolatry.

Ver. 4. *Graving tool.*—"He formed it with a chisel," after he had first melted it up in mass; and the words which follow mean, "And so (after he had first melted, then chiselled it) it became a molten calf."

Land of Egypt.—Cf. Neh. ix. 18; Acts vii. 40, 41. "Gods" is here in the Hebrew the same word as elsewhere, God, also in the plural; but generally the number is in the singular. Here, on the contrary, it is in the plural: "who have led thee." In every kind of Nature-worship the feeling of the unity of the Godhead is easily lost. Both the images and the powers represented are separated and multiplied. The unity is only dimly imagined by some of the more enlightened, but never becomes a clear belief. Nature has its unity only in the Creator. The people, now overjoyed at having a visible leader like the rest of the nations, loudly exult and ascribe to it the happiness which filled all hearts.

Ver. 5. *Feast.*—Aaron seizes the opportunity to call God by His covenant-name (Jehovah), with the intention, as far as in him lay, by means of this feast, to keep the people in allegiance to the true God.

Ver. 6. *To play.*—They celebrated a sacrifice with feasting and heathen games, since both went together in every heathen Nature-worship. The games were usually of a free, lascivious kind—a necessary consequence of the worship of Nature: cf. 1 Cor. x. 7.

Ver. 7. *Said unto Moses.*—Before the Lord chastens and cleanses the people from their sin, he puts Moses to a severe trial of his faith. In the position of God to the people as now described, the representation of it on the human side comes forth very prominently. God *sees* from this history how disobedient the people are. He tells Moses *to let Him*—not to hinder Him from destroying the people; afterwards, at Moses' supplication, He *repents* of the punishment He had threatened. All this is not merely a figure, which, from condescension to the rude ideas of the Israelites, is applied to God, but it contains essential truth. God learns from trial the mind of man, not as though He had not known it before, but really, because He pays respect to man's freedom of will conferred by Himself, even up to the open outbreak of sin, and so far regards this source of evil (*i. e.*, sin) as not in existence. The wrath of God is His holy horror of sinners, which then has its full truth and reality when it is overcome by His grace and mercy. Therefore the repentance of God represents the true and actual side of God's relation to this sin of His people. For this latter, cf. Gen. vi. 6, note.

Thy people.—So completely is the bond betwixt the Lord and the people broken, that He says, "Thy people," etc. The covenant was in its origin a covenant of grace: when the Israelites, on the strength of this covenant, were formed into a nation, it became a covenant of law, which was annulled as soon as the people broke their part of the conditions of the covenant. And so all that God had done on the strength of the covenant is treated as though it had never taken place. Israel's Exodus from Egypt becomes a mere ordinary migration of the people under a human leader: cf. the remarkable passage, Amos ix. 7. Through this fearful threat, Moses saw himself altogether bereft of Divine aid. He had, it would seem, done all in vain, which he had undertaken at God's command. At the same time, God puts him to the proof, whether he has most regard for the salvation of the people or for his own greatness.

Ver. 9. *And the Lord.*—Moses is silent from consternation, and the Lord begins altogether afresh.

Stiffnecked.—A very frequent image, taken from a beast of burden which will not bend its neck to the yoke: so, a self-willed, rebellious people.

Ver. 10. *Great nation.*—A promise which is afterwards repeated in the case of the great punishment in the wilderness: Num. xiv. 12.

Ver. 13. *For ever.*—"The saints, when they pour out their cares before God, often stammer in their prayers; as when they ask, 'How long sleepest Thou—forgettest Thou us?'"—Calvin. But in fact that judgment of God was a true and right one, which must be overcome by His grace. When God first threatens to punish, and then rescinds the threatening, because His covenant of grace takes on itself strict justice, and so at the same time removes it, He allows the inward purposes of His mind, which in Himself are eternally one, for man's sake, to be separated, that thus man may be able to understand them. In like manner, Christ allows Himself to be overcome and changed by the prayer of the Syrophœnician woman: St Matt xv. 24–26. That which in the Eternal Mind is ever one, is separated according to the order of time; and thus it seems as though God allowed His purpose to be changed at the petition of Moses. In this last circumstance is, however, contained a great truth, inasmuch as without this intercession, to which God's forgiveness is annexed, the people would assuredly have perished. First, Moses reminds God of the triumph of His enemies, who would believe their gods had taken revenge on the people of Israel: but next, he appeals to the main point, to the covenant of grace with their fathers, which had promised a free gift on the part of God without any conditions.

Ver. 16. *Upon the tables.*—This is circumstantially and emphatically repeated, in order to show the great significance of the act which immediately follows.

Ver. 17. *Joshua.*—Joshua was with Moses on the mount (ch. xxiv. 13). Yet we find from this, that he has not received the revelations with him, nor heard God speak: cf. ch. xxxii. 11.

Ver. 19. *Brake them.*—Moses' anger was a righteous, godly anger—a reflection of that which God had just now declared to him: cf. Deut. ix. 8, etc. The people might perceive the enormity of their offence depicted by this action.

Ver. 20. *Drink of it.*—Chemical means were necessary for burning the gold and reducing it to powder; and these Moses might easily have learnt in Egypt. Nothing was to remain of the golden calf, that its destruction might be as complete as possible. But the main point was the sprinkling the dust upon the water, and making the people drink thereof: for while so many foreign nations were held in abomination by the Egyptians, because they ate the animals which were sacred among themselves, how much more did the Israelites declare their abhorrence of idolatry by consuming, every one of them, the image in which the deity was supposed to be incarnate!

Ver. 24. *Came out.*—Aaron represents himself as carried away by the violence of the people, so that he scarcely knew what he did.

Ver. 25. *Naked.*—"That the people was unbridled, since Aaron had unbridled them unto their shame among their enemies." He had himself freed them from their restraint, that the people which ought to have promoted God's honour on earth might be exposed to the scorn of all heathen nations. Josephus, the Jewish historian, passes over in silence the whole of the event of this worship of the calf, from a deep feeling of the shame brought on the people by it.

Ver. 26. *Sons of Levi.*—Who, by reason of their relationship with Moses at that time, especially placed themselves at the service of the sanctuary. But, as the sequel shows, there were many among them who had been tainted with the idolatry.

Ver. 27. *Neighbour.*—Who has been guilty of the sin; *i.e.*, let no one hesitate even to slay his nearest neighbour. Every Levite was made a judge in this state of affairs, in which no one was to be trusted, as all had defiled themselves. The necessity of the circumstances called for proceedings which did away with all inquiry and examination, as is the case in a war of extermination.

Ver. 29. *This day.*—Moses spoke these words at the outset, when he summoned the Levites to carry the punishment into execution. But they are put at the close of the narrative, thus more emphatically to show the importance of the circumstance. "To fill the hands to the Lord" (to consecrate), means to offer a sacrifice acceptable to Him. He requires them to enter, as it were, on the duties of the priestly office appointed by the Lord (cf. ch. xxviii. 41, note); *i.e.*, to render themselves worthy of that office by this act of impartial self-denying obedience. The words in Moses' blessing, Deut. xxxiii. 9, refer to this circumstance.

Ver. 32. *Out of Thy book.*—This remarkable petition of Moses shows, more than anything else in the event before us, what a crisis this was in the history of the kingdom of God. "It is very surprising that Moses appears to prescribe a law to God, to call on Him to annul His eternal decree, and to wish to deprive Him of His justice. Would not all condemn the expression as a very arrogant one: If Thou wilt not spare the wicked, then count me no longer among Thy servants? Does it not appear as the extreme of daring, to wish to annul God's eternal decrees? And is it not to confound all distinctions between good and bad that he should wish to be included in the same punishment? I do not deny that Moses is here carried away by so strong feelings as to speak like one beside himself. But it is well to observe, that when believers pour out their cares into the bosom of God, they do not always speak with clear distinctions and accurately-chosen words; but sometimes they are incoherent, sometimes they utter irrepressible sighs, sometimes they are anxious about and press one request beyond all others. Nothing certainly was less in Moses' thoughts than to prescribe a law to God; and quite as little would he have hesitated to confess that God's decrees, made concerning His elect before the foundation of the world, cannot be reversed; and quite as sure was he that the Judge of the world cannot condemn the righteous with the sinners. But since his whole mind was full of care for the people intrusted to him by God, he can think of nothing but the desire to save it, and he can let nothing stand in the way of the fulfilment of this his great hope. And thus it is that he takes all on himself: he offers himself as surety for the people, he forgets God's decree of grace concerning himself, and does not consider that which alone may become Almighty God Himself. St Paul goes still further, when he wished himself accursed for his brethren's sake (Rom. ix. 3). Their hearts being fixed solely on the salvation of the chosen people, neither of the two are chiefly solicitous about what may concern themselves, and are willing to sacrifice themselves for the whole of the Church; because this general truth is impressed on their souls, viz., if the whole body be preserved, then each member will be in health. We need not wonder that they were in such perplexity, since in the destruction of the chosen people was involved the loss of God's truth and righteousness. God would then have denied Himself, if the eternal election vouchsafed to Abraham's children had come to nought."—Calvin.

Ver. 34. *Upon them.*—Hereby God distinguishes the sins of the individual from those of the whole people. He will still have mercy with His people for His promise's sake made to the fathers; but on those who have sinned He will take vengeance in His appointed time.

Ver. 35. *Plague.*—The death of the 3000 already mentioned (ver. 28) is here meant.

CHAPTER XXXIII.

The terrible chastisement had humbled the people. It was, however, to be feared, that if the Lord still further chastened them, they would throw off all bonds. Therefore the Lord repeated the old promises of the covenant, though one important privilege was taken from it: they should possess the promised Canaan indeed; but He Himself would be no longer in the midst of them, as His presence could only be terrible to them. All these threatenings are to be understood with the silent condition of their removal, if the people should repent.

Ver. 2. *Will send.*—This promise or threat (since it is both at once) is essentially different from that, ch. xxiii. 20. The angel of whom mention is now made is one distinct from the Lord Himself, whereas that spoken of above is represented as equal to Him. Cf. note there.

Ver. 3. *Consume thee.*—The people, on ceasing to be a peculiar possession of the Lord's, and on passing into the more general and remote relationship towards Him, such as the other nations had, was no longer liable to the same amount of responsibility as before, or exposed to the same great dangers, on transgression of His laws.

Ver. 4. *Ornaments.*—The chastisement and this threat had, in truth, awakened in the people whatever genuine fear and love of God remained. They felt deeply the loss they had incurred, in being made like the other nations, and put in possession of the temporal benefits only which God had promised them. As a sign that they felt their true ornament, their distinguishing honour, was taken away, they remove also from off them all their external ornaments.

Ver. 7. *Tabernacle.*—The people had probably a moveable sanctuary from the commencement of their journey through the wilderness,—perhaps the tent before which Moses was accustomed to sit for the administration of justice, and to offer the sacrifices for the people. This tent had also the name of tabernacle, though we read nothing about any service being performed in it. This tent, then, on which the pillar of the cloud regularly appeared during the sojourn of the people at Sinai, Moses now removed outside the camp, in order to give the people to understand that the presence of the Lord had departed from among them, and he who wished to inquire of the Lord must go out in order to do so. At the same time, the Lord distinguished Moses by fresh and greater marks of His grace and favour. For explanation of the name, "tabernacle of the congregation," see ch. xxvii. 21, note.

Sought.—It appears, therefore, that the chief judgments were at that time regularly pronounced by Moses before this tent, and that he inquired of the Lord in the tabernacle.

Ver. 11. *Face to face.*—This is spoken of in a later place more fully, and a distinction made between this manner of intercourse and that to the prophets: Num. xii. 8.

Ver. 12. *Moses.*—Here we have the most sublime incident in the life of Moses. Moses seeks afresh the countenance of the Lord in the tabernacle outside the camp, which now lies under the Divine displeasure; and begs of Him once more to turn His whole favour towards His people. As he himself has found grace, and stands in the relation of a highly-favoured servant, he could not rest satisfied with the commandment laid on him, and with the general promise, if God will not once more go with His people. When God has promised this, Moses becomes bolder, and begs to behold the glory of God. But God refuses him this. He will let all His goodness pass before him, then shall he see behind Him. Upon this, He renews the tables of the covenant. And now, while Moses stands in the rock, the Lord Himself proclaims the Divine names in which is declared the depth of His holy love for man. No doubt, Moses expected to obtain by this petition a vision of God with the bodily eyes. Every visible supernatural apparition by which God's glory, might, and grace are revealed, is rightly named, "beholding God's countenance," "God's glory." Many before Moses had already seen somewhat of this glory (cf. Gen. xvi. 13, note); so likewise (ver. 11) it is said of Moses himself, The Lord spake to him face to face; and (ch. xxiv. 10) it is said of the elders, "They saw the God of Israel." But every higher, clearer revelation through the senses (which cannot be supposed without an exaltation of the spiritual vision), fills the beholder with a longing still more to know God as He is. (For either we shall see God with the eyes of the glorified body, so that they have something resembling spirit, by which the incorporeal existence can be seen, which it is difficult or impossible to show by any examples from Scripture; or, what is more probable, God will be so known and visible to us, that He will be seen by every one of us in ourselves—be seen in others, be seen in Himself, be seen in the new heaven and new earth, and in all creatures who then shall exist—be seen also through the bodies in every body to which the eyes of the spiritual body shall with piercing keenness direct themselves.—St August. de Civit. Dei xxii. 29, 6.) In this full and perfect sense can no one, so long as he is on earth, see God. As the eyes must be protected from a dazzling light, so must God keep His favoured servants from such a vision, for which sinful man is not yet meet. They can only hear of the existence of His holy love, what he has announced concerning it, as He passes by; they can only look behind Him, and so behold the traces of His presence. This is granted to Moses; and at the same time is vouchsafed a fulness of knowledge of the Divine salvation, and a renewed certainty of the Lord's covenant of grace with His people.

Ver. 12. *In My sight.*—God had spoken in general terms, ver. 1, of an angel whom He would send with him. But as now the Lord had said, "He knew him by name"—*i.e.*, stood in a conscious, personal covenanted relation to him—therefore now it is Moses' prayer that He would not remain at a distance from him and from the people as He did from the heathen, whom He led only by the dark incomprehensible way of His providence, without any personal covenant mediator.

Ver. 13. *Show me.*—All this clearly means that Moses prays for a certain knowledge and direct guidance, such as belongs to a child of the covenant.

Thy people.—What he prays for himself, he will also now apply to the people.

Ver 14. *Presence.*—The "presence of the Lord" is not a general term for His being present with them, but it is His presence by means of a Mediator of the covenant, co-equal and of one nature with Himself—by means of the "Angel of the Lord," who is called, Isa. lxiii. 9, "The Angel of His presence," and Mal. iii. 1, "The Angel of the covenant:" in the N. T. He is called "the likeness of the invisible God," Col. i. 15; "the brightness of His glory, and the express image of His person," Heb. i. 3; "the Word, who was with God, and who was God," St John i. 1; in whom is God's name, ch. xxiii. 21. And so Moses afterwards speaks in like terms of Him, "*Thou* goest with us." We see, therefore, how clearly and distinctly is expressed, in the oldest books of Holy Scripture, the thought that the redeemed people of the covenant of the Lord is guided by a Mediator who is equal with God, and that the mediation which this people requires is an immediate Divine revelation of this co-equal Mediator. The difference between *this* mediatory covenant and that of the New Testament consists only in this, that in the former, notwithstanding the condescension of the Lord and His Angel of the Covenant to the ways and form of man, still, by reason of the continuing discipline of the law, He remains apart from man in the distance of an angelic nature.

Ver. 16. *Separated.*—The peculiarity of the relationship of the covenant consists in the gracious presence of God among His people. Moses here does not pray for anything new, but only reiterates and enforces his petition for the reinstatement of the people in the covenant of grace.

Ver. 17. *Will do.*—Not a fresh promise, but a confirmation of what was said, ver. 14.

Ver. 18. *Show me Thy glory.*—This petition suitably follows the former ones. God had promised to him and the people His immediate guidance by means of "His presence;" but Moses knew that still God would not reveal Himself unveiled, but in the Cloudy Pillar, or invisibly in the tabernacle. In the visible tokens of His nearness, indeed, he had certain pledges of its reality; but still he must by faith spring over the chasm which yet separated him from perfect communion with God. As mediator of the covenant with the people, he hoped that God would grant to him what He had as yet denied the rest, but which would be imparted to him only for the sake of the rest.

Ver. 19. *Goodness.*—God first shows that which He grants to him before He limits the favour, and, in part, denies the request. The "goodness" is not at all here, as some have believed, the glory, the bright appearance which passed before Moses, but the revelation of the grace of God, ch. xxxiv. 6; which, however, from the nature of the case, is made known more in word than to sight—rather to the attentive belief than to the inquisitive vision. The appearance, therefore, which he shall see as it passes by, is to be a revelation of His grace. But the main part is this, that he will hear God "proclaim" His peculiar name—that particular portion of His being by which He will be known as the true God of men. He adds most impressively to this promise, the truth, that it is a no less great than free act of grace. Cf. Rom. ix. 15.

Ver. 23. *Shall not be seen.*—We must accordingly suppose that Moses, when he had to hew out two tables of stone and give them to God, must have been placed on the mount, in a cave of the rock, or behind a hewn cliff of rock. Here he beheld the glory of the Lord, as it passed by, through a cleft of the rock; but even then, during the time of its passing by, his eyes were holden by God, so that he only heard, but did not see anything. Only when the glory had passed by did he behold the appearance from behind, when a cloud probably covered it. While in the places where mention is made of a "seeing God face to face," this can only be understood comparatively with reference to the ordinary knowledge of Him, in the present case it is meant in the full peculiar sense. All knowledge of God is, in this life, only a mediate knowledge ("an enigma," 1 Cor. xiii. 12). We see God from behind—we know Him from His works, His dealings, by His word, by comparisons, by inferences, etc.; but face to face we cannot behold Him, since then we must be holy even as He is holy. In order to know Him in His governance of the world in all its steps—in order perfectly to be able to distinguish that which He *does* from that which He merely overrules, ordains, and permits, His holy will must hence become the perfect law of our whole life.

CHAPTER XXXIV.

Ver. 1. *Hew thee.*—It is remarkable that Moses himself is obliged to hew out these tables, while the former were given to him written by God, ch. xxxii. 16. It appears, that though nothing essential was withdrawn from the people, yet in this difference between the two tables they are reminded of their sin.

Ver. 3. *Before that mount.*—The circumstances are like those of the first solemn covenant-making.

Ver. 5. *Proclaimed.*—This did not take place in order that he might know this was the glory of the Lord, but in order to proclaim at this solemn moment the names by which God would reveal Himself to His people.

Ver. 6. *The Lord.*—The Lord Jehovah Himself: the word repeated (the Lord) is in both cases, in the Hebrew, "Jehovah," though the first may be referred to what precedes, viz., "the Lord proclaimed." In this case the word would be repeated in order to express distinctly that Jehovah, and not Moses, uttered what follows.

Truth.—All which follows after "the Lord" is a description of the nature of God literally, "a merciful and gracious God, longkeeping from anger, and rich in grace and truth." In the most solemn moment of the highest revelation, the mediator of the Old Testament beholds God as Love, who, without having first received anything, is full of the desire to communicate His holy and blessed nature to sinners, in order to make them partakers of His perfections: He is not only ready to forgive, but He also waits for their repentance, and remits the punishment. On the word "truth," cf. St John i. 14, note. At this moment He wishes especially to show how, and why, He will again turn His grace to the stiffnecked people.

Ver. 7. *For thousands*—namely, of generations; *i.e.*, even for ever: as similarly, St Matt. xviii. 22. This is closely united with the "grace and truth," and is an explanation of them. The covenanted truth of God never ceases, even when He punishes His children of the covenant. And, therefore, even now the relation of God to the apostate people Israel is that of their covenant God, who punishes and tries them differently from all other people.

Clear the guilty.—Lit.: "And speaking clean, He speaks not clean." He does not declare them free from sin, which is repeated for the sake of emphasis. This appears to contradict what has gone before. The word means, "to declare pure, guiltless," and is intended to add the attribute of holiness to that of the love of God. Because God is merciful, and the truth of

His covenant endures for ever, let no one suppose that he shall be without punishment. Even within the covenant of grace He can and will punish individual sinners terribly. Scripture does not here speak of a less punishment which will even still overtake those whom God has forgiven; but it is a warning not to turn the grace of God into lasciviousness, as God will not leave impenitent sinners without punishment. The words of Jer. xxv. 29 and xlix. 12 seem an allusion to this declaration.

Fourth generation.—Upon this visiting to the third and fourth generation, see ch. xx. 5, note.

Ver. 8. *Worshipped.*—As soon as the Appearance was manifest.

Ver. 9. *Go among us.*—Heb., "in our middle," in reference to the revelation made of God's never-ending forgiveness, grace, and covenanted truth. "If Thou art such an one among us, then have we nothing to fear; then will Thy people find in Thee not only defence, but in Thy forgiving love, notwithstanding all chastisements, ever afresh access to Thee."

Thine inheritance.—Literally, "and possessest us." As among the Israelites all land-property was inherited and actually inalienable, in a similar manner is the people to be an inheritance and possession.—"The '*and* take us,' etc., is as much as to say, 'And lettest us, *therefore*, in this way be Thine inheritance:' by which he says, God can keep this possession on no other terms than those of forgiveness of sins; since so great is the people's sinfulness, that they must immediately fall out of the grace of God if they are not ever anew reconciled to Him. And, therefore, not only is the beginning of our salvation of God's free reception of us to the rank of children, but we cannot continue to the end in this relationship of children, unless God of His grace reconcile us to Himself."—Calvin.

Ver. 10. *I make a covenant.*—The Lord has renewed the promise of the covenant; but in order to remove every doubt concerning the establishment of His former engagement with the people, He renews also briefly the lawgiving of the covenant. The "ten words," or commandments, God writes yet again on the tables of stone (ver. 1, 28); but, besides this, He gives in ten other commandments (the first, ver. 11–16; the second, ver. 17; the third, ver. 18; the fourth, ver. 19, 20; the fifth, ver. 21; the sixth, ver. 22; the seventh, ver. 23, 24; the eighth, ver.

25; the ninth and the tenth, ver. 26), the contents of the laws of the covenant which had been written in the Book of the Covenant (ch. xxiv. 4), and commands this to be recorded as a second and explanatory memorial of the covenant. It is very significant that nothing new is contained therein. The repetition and the rewriting of them is meant as a confirmation of their authority, just as is the repetition of so many laws in the Book of Deuteronomy.

Do with thee.—This promise also has a reference to the breach of the covenant by the people, and to its present renewal. The great wonders by which the Lord had preserved His people out of Egypt were in a manner undone. For the perfect restoration of the former relation between them, it is requisite that the Lord should promise as great and wonderful miracles to His people as before had taken place. It is to be observed that the Lord does not yet say He will make a covenant *with* His people; but, *before* the people, as below it is said, "That I will do *with thee.*" Moses therefore is to be regarded as he with whom the Lord makes the covenant, who in this manner acts as mediator for the people. This manner of expression is intended to remind the people of their unworthiness, and to increase their affection for the great servant of the Lord, who was the only pledge among them of the covenant of grace made by God.

Ver. 12. *In the midst of thee.*—The main part of all this was said at the conclusion of the first giving of the laws of the covenant.

Ver. 13. *Their groves.*—Luther translates (as our version) "destroy their groves;" but in the Heb. it is, "thou shalt cut down their Ascherim." Aschera was the name of a Canaanitish idol, which probably was formed of a large perpendicular stem of a tree made fast in the ground. This, as the image of productive Nature, was set up partly by itself alone on high places and in woods, partly by the side of other images and altars, and was a very impure emblem, as was indeed mostly the case in Nature-worship. In the O. T., "Aschera" is usually put only for the statue, a trunk of the tree, not for the deity; therefore it it is said, "to hew down, to break down the Ascherim." As by the preceding word "images" we are to understand pillars of stone, so by "the groves" are meant these wooden trunks. At all times, when Israel fell from the true God, it was accustomed to erect such emblematic pillars, and thereby to open the doors to all the abominations of Nature-worship. Gideon hewed down a great trunk of this kind (Judges vi. 25). In the kingdom of Israel there were prophets of the same (1 Kings xviii. 19); nay, sometimes in the very house of the Lord, women worked tent "hangings" (called "houses" in the margin) for this goddess (2 Kings xxiii. 7).

Ver. 14. *Jealous.*—Jealous signifies one who will not endure any rival; and is one of the many expressions which represent the marriage-relation of the Lord to His people. By the covenant with the people is the Lord become the Husband of His people: He suffers no one else beside Himself: He will possess the undivided love of His people, as He has already bestowed on it the full love of a bridegroom.

Ver. 16. *A whoring after their gods.*—This word belongs to the same circle of thought. A marriage can only take place with the true God, because He is one. All polytheism is to be compared to the union of a woman with many husbands, and therefore this expression of the heathen. The word does not refer to the sin of unchastity, which was so often closely connected with idol-worship.

Eat of their sacrifice.—A slight degree of communication is here put, and not at present absolute idolatry, but only participation in their sacrificial feasts; but from this to perfect apostasy the step was not a wide one. How great was the danger of such communication even in times of far higher cultivation, we see from the warnings of St Paul to the Corinthians, 1 Cor. x. 19, etc.

Ver. 16. *Thy sons.*—By reason of the communion of the whole life which is entered on in matrimony, it was, and still is, at all times a sacred duty not to enter on such a connection with any one who is the follower of a false worship.

Ver. 17. *Molten gods.*—Ch. xx. 23, ch. xxxi. 4.

Ver. 18. *From Egypt.*—Ch. xxiii. 15.

Ver. 20. *Empty.*—Ch. xiii. 12.

Ver. 21. *Thou shalt rest.*—The command of the Sabbath was of such eminent importance, that each time it is mentioned it forms a distinct subject. Even the most necessary field labours are to cease on the Sabbath: cf. ch. xxxv. 3.

Ver. 22. *Ingathering.*—In Lev. xxiii. more particular mention is made of these feasts.

Ver. 23. *God of Israel.*—Ch. xxiii. 17.

Ver. 24. *Thrice in the year.*—The theocratic constitution of the Israelites exercised unceasingly on so many sides their faith. We read in the after history of no instance where the enemies of the Israelites made use of these feasts as a time for assailing them. It was only when the people was destined by the Lord to destruction, when the Romans had got possession of a large portion of their country, that the occurrence of the feast of the Passover served to heighten the famine of the besieged in Jerusalem.—See review of Jewish History in Appendix, in the last volume.

Ver. 25. *Morning.*—Ch. xxiii. 18.

Ver. 26. *Mother's milk.*—Ch. xxiii. 19.

Ver. 27. *Write thou.*—We may therefore well suppose that the new ten commandments of the covenant, whose substance was certainly in a great measure contained in the earlier Book of the Covenant, must be recorded afresh as a document of the covenant now restored again; while the history written at a later period, which was inserted between the two, explained the whole matter.

Ver. 28. *Eat bread.*—As in the case of the shining of his face (ver. 35), so was this miraculous abstinence of Moses intended to be a pledge both to himself and the people of his divine mission. During his communion with God, in his intercourse with Him, he was removed above the wants of the earthly life, and received a foretaste of the vision of God in the eternal world: cf. St Matt. iv. 1, introd.

He wrote.—That is, as has been expressly said, ver. 1, not Moses, but the Lord. "The words of the covenant, the ten words," also, are evidently not the ten laws just mentioned, but the well-known ten commandments. With this, as has been already explained, it is quite consistent that it is said of the first, the Lord "has made a covenant with Israel according to them."

Ver. 29. *Shone.*—Lit., "radiated:" rays shot from it. Because the horns of animals resemble rays, the word "to shine" comes from "horn;" and so Moses is often represented with horns: more properly, and in accordance with the word, with two horn-like rays proceeding from his head. In order to fill the people with deeper reverence for Moses, God ordained that his countenance should shine as often as he came to the people from His presence. A double signification was conveyed by this: In the first place, it was signified that the law proceeded from a higher world of light (of knowledge and of holiness), since its very gleams were to be seen outwardly on the minister of the law: in the next place, since the people could not bear the shining of light, it represented how fearful, condemnatory, and fatal the law was for a sinful people. For this cause Moses was obliged to put a veil over the lustre of light (a type of the veil which, in the O. T., lies over the full revelation of the Divine truths of salvation), until the light again gradually vanished: cf. 2 Cor. iii.

Ver. 31. *Returned.*—The lustre had something so blinding and terrifying, that, notwithstanding the veil (ver. 33), Moses was obliged to reassure them by an especial calling of them to him.

Ver. 34. *Came out.*—He himself was, during his intercourse with the Lord, so entirely absorbed by means of the revelation accorded to him into the condition of the glorification, that the light did not blind him, and his eyes and countenance were able to bear its lustre.

CHAPTER XXXV.

Ver. 2. *Put to death*, entirely, as ch. xxxi. 14, 15.

Ver. 3. *Kindle no fire.*—The commandment is here repeated on account of this addition. Fire for purposes of cooking is here spoken of. As the eastern people took their chief meal soon after sunsetting, and the Sabbath lasted from one sunsetting to another, this commandment could easily be kept by a somewhat later preparation of the meal, after the close of the Sabbath, without much disturbance of their usual mode of life.

Ver. 9. *Breastplate.*—A carrying out of the command of ch. xxv. 1.

Ver. 10. *Hath commanded.*—As helpers to the two principal artificers of the work: ch. xxxi. 1, etc. All the particulars have been explained already at chs. xxv.–xxx.

Ver. 22. *Tablets;* i.e., nose-rings, golden rings which were placed in a hole bored through the middle of the nose: cf. Gen.

xiv. 22, note. [The Sept. uses a word (emplokion) which rather means some ornament entwined in the hair.—Trans.]

Ver. 24. *Offering of silver.*—In respect to the great riches which we here find in the hands of the Israelites, we must always bear in mind that they had sojourned in the richest part of Egypt, the wealthiest country of the ancient world; and that, on their exodus, they had received from the rich Egyptians gold and silver. Moreover, no doubt they traded in the wilderness, which was so continually traversed by caravans.

Ver. 35. *Cunning work.*—Cf. ch. xxxi. 1, etc.

CHAPTER XXXVI.

Ver. 7. *Too much.*—It was altogether in the character of a sensuous, easily excited, but inwardly obstinate people, to contribute their offerings with the same willingness as they had a short time before shown, in bringing costly gifts for the making of the calf. At that time was their faith tried: after so violent an agitation of their senses, they saw and heard nothing more. Here was it intended that they should possess a visible and splendid sanctuary, which they might regard as a national possession. We perceive herein the reason why God established so gorgeous a service in Israel.

Ver. 38. *Of brass.*—Cf. ch. xxvi. In the command of God, the ark, the table, the candlestick are first described, because they are of the most importance; and the tabernacle is built for their sake; but naturally, in the description of the preparation and construction, the building must precede the furniture thereof.

CHAPTER XXXVII.

Ver. 5. *Bear the ark.*—Ch. xxv. 10–16.
Ver. 9. *Mercy-seat.*—Ch. xxv. 17–22.
Ver. 16. *Cover withal.*—Ch. xxv. 23–30.
Ver. 24. *Vessels thereof.*—Ch. xxv. 31–39.

Ver. 28. *Overlaid.*—Ch. xxx 1–5.
Ver. 29. *Apothecary.*—Ch. xxx. 23–25, ch. xxx. 34–38.

CHAPTER XXXVIII.

Ver. 7. *Hollow.*—Ch. xxvii. 1–8.

Ver. 8. *Women assembling.*—We learn from this passage, in the first place, that a number of ministering women lived by the tabernacle, who were altogether employed in the service of Divine worship. From 1 Sam. ii. 22 we learn that this was a regular constant calling; and the history of Jephthah's daughter (Judges xi. 39), as well as the account of Anna in the N. T. (St Luke ii. 37), show that there were vows for women similar to those of the Nazarites, by which virgins and widows bound themselves (like nuns) to a constant service in the sanctuary. It is uncertain whether such as the latter were meant in so ancient times as the passage speaks of. Perhaps this custom was of Egyptian origin, and left remaining by Moses in order to bring them round to better things. The looking-glasses of the ancients were all of metal, and hollow. They were, as the context shows, made of brass. This kind of mirror the women in the East carried in their hands. On certain festivals, the women who were dedicated to the service of the Egyptian goddess Isis were accustomed to assemble themselves before the temple, clothed in white linen, and with mirrors in their hands. The Israelite women may have imitated that custom, without any intention to continue an idolatrous service; but now that the tabernacle of the true God was built, may have given it up of their own accord as unsuitable to be used before it, and have offered their mirrors for the making of the great laver for the priests.

Ver. 24. *Talents.*—A talent has 3000 shekels; therefore the whole sum amounted to 87,730 shekels of gold, which, according to the highest reckoning of the shekel, would amount to about 300,000 ducats.

Ver. 25. *Silver.*—According to the highest mode of reckoning, 300,000 thalers (in Engl. money, L.45,000).

Ver. 28. *Filleted;* i.e., they were overlaid with silver, as otherwise the sum would not have been sufficient. So the altar of burnt-offering is said to have been of brass, and the altar of incense of gold, though the one was only overlaid with brass and the other with gold.

CHAPTER XXXIX.

Ver. 2. *Twined linen.*—Therefore blue-purple, red-purple, and kermes-coloured thread and byssus. Upon the whole, comp. ch. xxviii. In the description it is sometimes said "he," sometimes "they made," according as one of the two chief artificers, or both together, were employed.

CHAPTER XL.

Ver. 15. *Everlasting priesthood.* — Jewish tradition has grounded on this passage its mistake, that only Aaron and his sons, but no other priest after them, were anointed. But the words can very well also signify that this first anointing guaranteed their future consecration to the priestly office for all generations to come.

Ver. 17. *Of the month.*—After the Exodus from Egypt.

Ver. 34. *Filled the tabernacle.*—The cloudy pillar which went before the host of the Israelites removed and covered the tabernacle. At every fresh breaking up of the camp, it again went before the van of the host.

Ver. 38. *By night.*—The cloud, which was dark by day, became light by night, as ch. xiii. 21.

LEVITICUS.

CHAPTER I.

AFTER the giving of the laws of the covenant, and the subsequent erection of the tabernacle with its furniture and vessels, and the robes and consecration of the priests had been revealed, and all had been executed in accordance with the command, now followed a more minute direction of the sacrifices. Sacrifice was the peculiar main point and essence of all worship both in the Old Covenant religion and in all heathen services. We find that sacrifice was brought out of paradise in the family of Adam, Gen. iv. 4, note. We saw Noah offering burnt-sacrifice aft e the flood, Gen. viii. 20, note. But as Israel became a people only under Moses, the whole service of sacrifice did not receive before his time its full and complete form. For although there were in the times before him thank-offerings, yet certainly there did not exist sin-offerings and sacrifices of atonement, as a particular distinct kind of these holy customs. The general meaning of all sacrifices, even among the heathen, is a representation under a material form of the act of devotion to God. Man, justly enough, was not satisfied with a mere inward feeling, a purely spiritual disposition of the heart—he felt that he needed in his relation to God *an act* of self-surrender, and for this act he made use of symbolical means. As one who prays is not satisfied with merely inwardly thinking and feeling, as he pours out his thoughts and feelings in words, and by posture and gesture bears witness to what he is doing, even when he is alone with God; so is an actual union with God by means of an outward act a real necessity of human nature. But this act takes a twofold form, according as man is conscious especially of an obstruction, a severance dividing God and himself; or as he more particularly desires to express thanksgiving for a benefit received, or petition for one he hopes yet to receive. *Both* are united in the burnt-offering, the earliest and most comprehensive kind of sacrifice. The animal to be sacrificed is placed before the sacred place: he who is to sacrifice it lays his hand on its head, in order thereby expressly to appropriate it to himself as his sacrifice, and also symbolically to transfer to it that which he ought to offer in its stead. The soul of the animal which has not sinned, and cannot sin, is, as it were, an empty vessel, in which he places his own guilt. Under the feeling of this his guilt, and with the longing after an entire surrender to God, he thereupon himself slays the sacrifice; expressing by this act that he for his own sins has deserved death, the punishment of sin, which God now will remove from him. The soul of the animal streams forth to death in the blood, the seat of animal life, in his own stead, and its blood now covers, atones for, the sin of the sacrificer. As a sign that God has received this vicarious offering, the priest sprinkles the blood of the animal about the altar. And now is the animal's flesh, freed from its sin-burdened life, laid whole on the altar, and consumed by the sacred divine flame; and the smoke of the sacrifice ascends to the Lord as a well-pleasing savour, as a symbol and a bearer of the offerer's perfect devotion to the Lord.—With this was then a meat-offering connected. As the table with the shew-bread (cf. Exod. xxv. 23) was the food which the people offered to God in a holy life; so every meat-offering added to the other sacrifices was a similar symbolical offering of good works. The burnt-offering had almost all this in common with the other sacrifices. The peculiarity of it, however, was, that *all the flesh* of the animal was burnt: wherefore it was called in Greek "a whole offering;" in Hebrew, "mounting upwards," *i.e.*, a sacrifice altogether ascending in smoke (the skin which was given to the priests made no exception. This was only a tribute of what was in itself insignificant, as an acknowledgment that of every sacrifice a portion belongs to the priest.) As the entire burning of the victim was the main thing, it clearly follows that the utter surrender to the Lord which belonged to every sacrifice was in an especial manner represented in this; and on this account this sacrifice was made daily: it was the general sacrifice on all solemn occasions, and presupposed that the sacrificer had not by any particular sin broken his union with his covenant God.—Even with the heathen, the sacrifice was the chief point of the Divine worship. But as this itself was a worship of Nature, so was the atonement not that of the sinner with the Holy One, but of the individual man or of the people with the general life of Nature which the heathens honoured in their sacrifices, in which the expiation of a sin appears only here and there as a subordinate object. But especially the great " whole offerings," or burnt-sacrifices, in most of the heathen religions, had the meaning that a beast which represented the whole of Nature, or a distinct part of it, was sacrificed, in order thereby to bring all individual life into harmony with the general life. At the time when Nature awoke out of her winter sleep, in the majority of the heathen religions a beast was offered which represented this productive power of the creation. Every natural object and gift was thereby sanctified, and man blessed in them and by them. In every sacrifice of the people of God, a self-offering to God by a figurative act took place, which embodied as it were the inward act between God and man. But as an animal could not really take on itself sin and expiate it, as the sprinkling of its blood did not really wash away sin, therefore these typical sacrifices pointed to the true perfect sacrifice of the Son of God, the holy and spotless Lamb, who truly bore the punishment of the sinner in his stead, and took it away. The sacrifice of the N. T. is not merely one which took place once for all, but it is a sacrifice so living, so eternally efficacious, so continually present, that every Christian ought to have it before him in spirit and in faith, as if it had even now been offered for himself. Then he experiences the blood-sprinkling—*i.e.*, God-acceptance of this sacrifice—in his justification before God. To this every sacrifice of the O. T. more or less pointed. But of all the sacrifices, the burnt-offering especially places us in *the* position and *the* act of faith of the Christian, when he is conscious of standing in communion with God, and yet, oppressed by the common guilt, needs to seek full forgiveness; when he desires, indeed, to give up his heart entirely to God, but requires the flame of Divine love to consume the sacrifice; and when he vows to God continually in all his works to do that which is well-pleasing in His sight. This burnt sacrifice of the Christian is the general offering of his whole life which is made every day, which includes and sanctifies all other offerings. The fire of this can never be extinguished. The Church of the Lord must without ceasing offer up this sacrifice.

Ver. 3. *Without blemish.*—The latter was a requirement in every sacrifice; the former, of the burnt-offering especially. The male animal, as the more powerful and perfect representation of its kind, was not to be wanting in this chief sacrifice particularly: that it should be " without blemish"—fault—was to signify the holiness which ought to belong to this gift, which stood in the place of the sinner.

Ver. 4. *Atonement for him.*—The laying on of hands occurs in the O. T. on the occasion of pronouncing a blessing, and of instituting to an office. In both cases is this custom meant to express that he who lays on his hands communicates, transfers, something to the other. This imparting can here be nothing else than all that which the man wished to lay on the sacrifice. He transfers to the sacrifice his sin, his guilt, the believing surrender of the thankful heart, the vow, the petition which he would lay before God, in order that he may in the sacrifice utterly give up himself to God, that his sin may be wiped away, his debt of gratitude paid to God. The Jewish doctors say on this,—" He who lays on his hand, must do so with all his might; he must put both hands on the *head* of the animal, not the neck or shoulders, etc., and may not let anything interpose between his hand and the animal. He lays his hands betwixt the two horns; and in the sin-offering he confesses the iniquity of his sins; in the sacrifice of propitiation, the misdeeds of his guiltiness; in the burnt-offering he confesses his fault, that he has done what he ought not to have done, and not done what he ought to do." " To atone" is, in the Hebrew, " to cover." Sin is covered, that God from that time forth does not as it were see it; *i.e.*, that He treats man as though he had no sin in His sight. Of course, properly speaking, this word cannot be applied to God, from whom nothing can be hidden,—nay, it is even God Himself who has appointed the sin-offering, the means for covering the sin. But if in the nature of God no change can take place by means of the atonement (as is self-evident), yet a change may happen in His relation to the sinner. He, the same holy

God, cannot hold the same relation to the sinner when his sin still remains upon him, and when it is atoned for. When, therefore, the sin is covered, the wrath of God towards the sinner ceases, and His good pleasure, as was just said (ver. 3 and 4, Heb., " to his well-pleasing before the Lord," *i.e.*, that he thereby is made acceptable to the Lord), is turned towards the reconciled one. This is the point to which the German word to expiate, " versöhnen," corresponds, which answers more to the " making acceptable" than to the " covering."

Ver. 9. *Wash in water.*—Shall over and above, especially, purify, as being the unclean parts of the animal.

By fire; lit., " a firing,"—a sweet smell caused by the burning. On this, see Gen. viii. 22, note.

Ver. 13. *Unto the Lord.*—The burnt-offering was preferably to consist of cattle; but it might also be taken from the sheep and goats, and, in case of necessity, even from less costly animals, turtle-doves, or other doves. Of clean animals, those were especially to be sacrificed with which man had become as it were most united in his domestic life. These are the best fitted to stand in his stead, as being those which are nearest to him in the whole animal kingdom. In the custom practised in the burnt-offering of sheep and goats, there is no difference from that in the case of cattle.

Ver. 15.—*Wring off;* Heb., " break with the nail;" since we see, from ch. v. 8, that the head was not torn off.

At the side of the altar.—In the offering of the dove, no laying on of hands took place, but the sprinkling of blood; likewise not the offerer, but the priest, killed the birds. The reason, without doubt, was, because in the tearing away of the head too much blood would have been shed to admit of the after solemn sprinkling of it. The whole business was curtailed, and the most important part retained, which was the atoning acceptance of the sacrifice with the promise of grace by means of the sprinkling of blood.

Ver. 16. *With his feathers;* or, more correctly, " the crop with the filth,"—whatever of food was therein.

Ver. 17. *Not divide it.*—For the same reason that the head was not wrung off, but broken, were the wings only split, not cut off. The sacrifice was not to be divided, but offered as a whole. It was otherwise in the case of the cattle, the sheep, and the goats; and therefore this custom is not significant, but had its reason only in a sense of beauty and propriety, which would have been wanting in the dividing of the smaller animals.

CHAPTER II.

Immediately after the burnt-sacrifice follows the law of the unbloody or meat-offerings (called in Heb. "Mincha," *i.e.*, gift), since these were the usual supplemental gifts to the burnt-sacrifice, as also to the other sacrifices, but (with the exception of the first-fruits) never stood by themselves alone. The most distinguished of all meat-offerings was the shew-bread, which continually lay before the Lord in the holy place. The main signification of all was the same. The meat-offering consisted of the most necessary articles of nourishment—meat, either baked or roasted, or of the first-fruits—and was anointed with oil and salted. A drink-offering was joined to it. They contained, therefore, on the whole, the elements of a repast. Like the shew-bread—that "meat-offering" which was always in the holy place, the unbloody offering, which was always made together with the other sacrifices, reminded men that the people of God were always bound to offer to their Lord and King with every sacrifice their food; to consecrate to Him continually their whole daily life, and by this consecration to hallow to Him every enjoyment of it. It is well to observe that they were not completed good works which were offered to the Lord, but the holy resolution of the will to perform them, since the meat-offering followed immediately on the burnt sacrifice, which expressed atonement and self-surrender. The meat-offering, therefore, had the purport (as has been observed of the shew-bread, the candlestick, and the offering of incense) of reminding the sacrificer of what he ought to be, and to what his sacrificial service bound him. In the life of the Christian, the meat-offering receives its spiritual interpretation thus—that no renewed self-offering to the Lord can be acceptable without the resolution, and likewise the commencement, of a new obedience; *i.e.*, "fruits meat for repentance."

Ver. 1. *Frankincense.*—The oil here, as Exod. xxx. 22, is the emblem of the Holy Spirit—the frankincense, of prayer. The meaning is, that no offering of new obedience, no work, can be well-pleasing to God without the unction of the Holy Spirit penetrating and hallowing them. In like manner, no sacrifice can rise up to God without the accompaniment of prayer.

Ver. 2. *Memorial,* "remembrance," means generally the part of every sacrifice which was burnt; because (to speak after the manner of men) God, smelling the sweet savour, was moved to think graciously of the sacrificer: so, *e.g.,* the incense is thus called, ch. xxiv. 7, cf. Acts x. 4. The meaning, therefore, is: the offering of man to God in a new obedience, sanctified by the Holy Ghost, supported by prayer, makes him partaker of all the promises of grace of the covenant of God. It is well to consider that these gifts were an addition to other sacrifices, and never stood by themselves. This, therefore, excludes the notion of men's own righteousness.

Ver. 3. *Of the offerings.*—The priests were in the sacrifices the mediators between the Lord and the people. As they offer also on their own behalf, and then are reminded of their place among the people; so did they, in many sacrifices (as in this especially), represent the place of the Lord Himself. They who served at the altar were to live by the altar; and the priests receiving a part of the sacrifices, the people presented them to the Lord. In the New Testament there is no more a human mediator between God and man. But in the place of the priests, stands that which is the channel of the sinner's relation to God —the Christian Church itself—as an institution for the sanctification and training of sinful men in their search after holiness. In every repeated surrender of the heart by fresh obedience in good works, is the Church of the Lord, the priestly people of God, to have its share in our sacrifices, and in the church, its servants, offices, institutions for spreading the Word, etc.—Of the sacrifices, which are called "most holy," the priests alone received their portion; of the thank-offerings, which are called merely "holy," the sacrificers themselves partook together with the priests. The "most holy" is all which exclusively refers to the restoration and establishment of man's relation to the Lord; the "holy" is that wherein man appears in union with God.

Ver. 11. *With leaven.*—Leaven was regarded as unclean, because it was the cause of fermentation, and so of decomposition, corruption: cf. Exod. xii. 1; and the general prohibition, Exod. xxiii. 18, ch. xxxiv. 25. The same appears to have been the reason for the prohibition of honey. This is also a means of fermentation—was, at least, used for this purpose by the later Jews, as an excess of it produces acidity in the stomach. Every kind of corruptness ought to be far from the new obedience which we offer to God, whether it be originally sour or sweet to the carnal appetite.

Ver. 12. *Be burnt;* because both were in and for themselves not impure; because good and useful under circumstances, an emblem of corruption only when mingled with something else.

Ver. 13. *Offer salt.*—Salt is the exact opposite of leaven and honey, fermenting materials. Salt imparts life, preserves from corruption, and makes every kind of food wholesome and savoury. Plants cannot thrive in a ground or from moisture whence all saline property is extracted. Salt at sacrifices is called "covenant salt;" since from the earliest times to the present the tasting of salt is customary in all agreements in the East, and signifies the truth and permanence which belongs to a covenant: cf. in N. T. St Matt. v. 13, note; St Mark ix. 49, note.

Ver. 14. *Beaten out;* lit. Heb., "beaten out of the garden;" *i.e.*, a kind of meal or grits of the finest field-fruits, and therefore such as are planted in the garden.

Ver. 16. *Frankincense.*—The priests received a portion of the corn and oil, but, as is evident, not of the frankincense, since this, as an emblem of prayer, could only be pleasing to the Lord Himself; while in the sacrifice which the other gifts represented the ministers of the Lord could and ought to have their portion. —The firstlings, therefore, of all fruits, as of the cattle also, were sacrificed, and thereby a solemn confession made, that the Lord is the supreme Possessor of the land, to whom they must give all did He require it. To Him they offered the first and the best in acknowledgment of this truth. These gifts of the first-fruits were also the chief maintenance of the priests, which were at the same time marks of respect to them, as they only formed a part of the offerings made to the supreme Lord of the land, the Creator of the world. The priests were by every such gift attested afresh as intercessors with God for the people, and every property received thereby its consecration. The only rightful claim to it was now established by the declaration that it was possessed from the Lord and for the Lord. Cf. upon this in the book of the laws of the covenant, Exod. xxii. 29, note.

CHAPTER III.

Another and a much smaller class of sacrifices are the thank-offerings. Their name ("Schelem;" in the plural, "sch'lamim") has the sense of "payment," "recompense," "compensation," "removing of a debt," out of which issued the condition of peace (Schalom); and so these sacrifices were called also "peace-offerings." Indeed, they cannot with propriety be called merely "thank-offerings," since we find distinct traces that they were also offered as prayer-offerings, though only together with burnt-sacrifices (cf. Exod. xxiv. 5; 1 Sam. xi. 15; 2 Sam. vi. 18; 1 Kings viii. 63; and the notes on Judges xx. 26 and ch. xxi. 4). By means of the burnt-sacrifice man made an entire surrender of himself to God; by the trespass-offering was his particular sin cleansed; by the compensation or payment-offering he laid before God his own peculiar thanksgiving, or his peculiar petition. Although the burnt-sacrifice was the most comprehensive, because the original, sacrifice, yet was the thank-offering generally distinguished from it. Hence burnt-offerings and peace-offerings are often mentioned together for all kinds of sacrifices (Joshua viii. 31; Judges xx. 26; 1 Chron. xvi. 1, 2). In this offering man desired (emblematically) to remove the distance which existed between God and himself through benefits shown or to be shown him by God. And so in this offering the vicarious representation and the atonement is not wanting, and the self-surrender takes place. But there follows on this, as the peculiarity of this kind of sacrifice, a sacrificial meal: an emblem of the communion of peace now completely restored between the Lord and man, God now making man to sit down at His table (Deut. xii. 12, 17, 18, ch. xiv. 23, ch. xxvii. 7). From this main signification of the thank-offerings are explained all its particular customs, and its different kinds,—the thanksgiving-offering (ch. vii. 12), the vow-offering (ch. vii. 16), and the free-will offerings (ch. xxii. 23).—The first and most important of all acts, in its relation to God, is the entire surrender of their own person by propitiation and consecration represented in the burnt-sacrifice. But, together with this, man feels his need expressly to give utterance to his thanks, partly for general, partly for especial benefits of the Lord towards him, and to make known before Him all his sentiments, and then to rejoice in the consciousness of renewed communion with God. While the "most holy" sacrifices (the burnt-offerings and trespass-offerings) had especially in view God's honour in the doing away of sin, and in the surrender of man to Him, this "holy" offering aimed likewise at the sanctification of man in relation to Him, which follows from reconciliation and self-surrender.

Ver. 1. *Male or female.*—For the thank-offerings, in distinction from the burnt-offerings (ch. i. 3), female animals might also be taken, because they were not so holy.

Without blemish.—This rule was not without exception, namely, in one kind of thank-offering—the free-will offering (Nedaboth, ch. xxii. 23).

Ver. 3. *Inwards.*—The fat about the peritoneum and the fat about the entrails.

Ver. 4. *Caul.*—All the fat, which on the opening was immediately severed, was to be sacrificed as the choicest part of the animal, not the fat with which the flesh has mixed.

Ver. 5. *Upon the burnt-sacrifice;* i.e., in addition to the burnt-sacrifice—properly, "on the burnt-sacrifice."

Sweet savour.—The customs used in the thank-offering are not here circumstantially described. In a later Jewish writing on the sacrifices, they are thus detailed:—"After the priest has sprinkled the blood and taken out the entrails, he cut the flesh into pieces, and divided the breast and right shoulder from the rest (ch. vii. 30, 32), and laid the entrails with the breast and the shoulder in the owner's hand, and the priest laid his hands under those of the owner and waved all before the Lord on the east side of the altar. Then he took the bread which was brought with the sacrifice, and laid all, with the breast, the shoulder, and the entrails, on the owner's hands, and waved all on his hands. First he laid the fat on the owner's hands, then the shoulder, and then the breast on it; thereupon he salted the entrails, and burned them all on the altar: but the breast and the shoulder the priests ate, and the rest the owner—but they did not get them until the entrails were burned. In like manner, the bread which was waved with the sacrifice was eaten by the priests, and the rest by the owners. If two or more persons together brought a thank-offering, one waved it for all. If a woman was the sacrificer, she did not wave it, but the priest. A woman never waved except in the jealousy-offering, Num. v., and a Nazarite vow, Num. vi."

Ver. 9. *Backbone.*—The fat tail of the sheep of the East, which was esteemed the best piece: cf. Exod. xxix. 22, note.

Ver. 17. *Neither fat nor blood.*—The context shows that this prohibition was no rule for the sake of health, nor a prescript which was intended to separate Israel from the heathen; but the fat was to belong to the Lord as the best part of the victim. The reason of the prohibition of blood is given, ch. xvii. 10–12; viz., because the blood was intended as an atonement for the life of the sacrificer. It is self-evident, therefore, from this, that after the cessation of sacrifices, the prohibition of the apostolic council at Jerusalem (Acts xv. 20, 29) must cease.

CHAPTER IV.

There now follows a class of sacrifices which belong to "the most holy" (ch. vi. 25, ch. x. 17), because they were the channel of the whole relation of the people to the Lord (cf. Exod. xxx. 10, note). The yearly great sin-offering on the day of atonement (ch. xvi.) was the chief act of sacrifice of the whole year. But as in this sacrifice the Divine completion of the atonement was performed by the act, by the sprinkling of blood, in the most solemn manner possible, so was it also in the ordinary sin-offerings. The idea of atonement was marked by a particular solemnity. The high priest was, at his own sin-offering, to sprinkle the blood seven times in the holy place, towards the veil of the sanctuary (ver. 6). The same was done for the congregation (ver. 17). The horns of the altar were besmeared with the blood of the atonement for the princes and the congregation (ver. 25, 34). Moreover, it was peculiar to the sin-offering, that all of the animals whose blood came into the holy place, or the most holy, with the exception of the fat, the skin, the flesh, and the dung, was burnt on the heap of ashes before the camp. But of the other animals, only the fat was burnt; the flesh, on the contrary, was eaten by the priests in the holy place. All which the blood had touched must be cleansed (ch. vi. 26-28). Lastly, it is nowhere said that a meat-offering was an adjunct to the sin-offering.—All this was significant. The sprinkling of blood, the Divine completion of the atonement, is here more prominently set forth. Seven times (the sacred number) is the blood sprinkled in the holy place. It is put on the horns of the altar, which denoted the altar's strength and meaning. The blood which had served for the most holy means of atonement might nowhere remain visible, not because it was reckoned unclean (since it was already shed, the sin-laden soul was given to death as the punishment of sin), but because, as the most holy means of atonement, it would have been defiled in any other place. The flesh of the sin-offering of the high priest and of the whole congregation was burnt without the camp, in a clean place, on the heap of ashes. It could not be eaten by the priests if the most holy among the people, or if all the people, were to be atoned for; but it must in some way, though after a clean fashion, be removed. It might not be burnt on the altar, because it was intended to represent, not a gift to God, as in the case of the burnt-sacrifice, but an atonement above all else. And although, in the other sin-offerings, the priests in the name of the Lord consumed the victim, still this act was a part of the atonement to be completed. Those who were consecrated to the Lord (not their families, ch. vi. 29) ate it, in order thereby to wipe away the sin of the people, ch. x. 17; since, through their holiness granted them from the Lord, their sin was as much expiated as, through the forehead-plate of the high priest, the sinfulness which clave to all sacrifices (Exod. xxviii. 38, note).—In this way were all the sins atoned for which did not imply a purposed rebellion against the Lord. He who sinned "presumptuously" (Heb., "with a high hand," Num. xv. 30), that soul shall be destroyed. As such presumptuous sins, were regarded all intentional violation of the ritual laws, because in this there lay an open rebellion against the supreme authority. For murder and adultery there could in like manner no sin-offering be brought.

For these the punishment of death was appointed, and sacrifice was the giving of an innocent life for a guilty one. Other civil offences—as theft, cheating, even in certain cases perjury, adultery with a female slave (ch. xix., xx., xxi., xxii.)—were atoned for by the trespass-offering, and were therefore also cases for sin-offering. Accordingly, we may suppose that such transgressions of the social laws for which there was no punishment at all, or none specified in the law—as usury (Exod. xxii. 25), or mistake in the observance of the ritual law (as when any one continued his work after the Sabbath had begun without his knowing it)—these were the most frequent cases for the sin-offerings. Sins were therefore atoned for through it, in which a man was by no means guiltless—not merely had taken part in others' guilt—but sins of *culpable* weakness and ignorance. Further, the sin-offerings relate to certain definite sins. They were not the channel of the entire communion with the Lord, but the restoration of it after its violation by some definite act. In this point of view, they teach the Christian the necessity of seeking in every single sin (as soon as he is aware of it) the renewal of pardon through the all-sufficient atonement of Jesus Christ. They show how this act of daily renewal and forgiveness belongs to the most holy part of our spiritual worship, and how all which relates thereto is most sacred. Also the men consecrated to the Lord have their parts and duties in this sin-offering. The Lord has ordained even in the N. T. that the assurance of forgiveness should be conveyed through men; and although no priest has the exclusive right to impart this, yet is it a consolatory, faith-strengthening institution, to receive this assurance through the appointed servants of the Lord in His congregation.

Ver. 2. *Through ignorance.*—A sin is therefore meant, of which, at the time of its commission, a person was not perfectly conscious that it was a sin. Here it is the part of the law especially to inculcate the truth, that not merely the conscious participation in any act is a sin, but the act in and for itself, as an offence against God, as a violation of His order, as the first example shows.

Ought not to be done.—Lit., "sins (and does one) of all the commandments of the Lord, which ought not to be done;" *i.e.*, one of all the prohibitions.

Ver. 3. *Anointed; i.e.*, the high priest. The high priest, by his sin, can no longer be the person capable of sanctifying the people to the Lord. He has accordingly, by his sin, brought guilt on the whole people; he has committed an (objective) violation of, the Divine order which he must make good again. For more on this subject see ch. v., introd. on trespass-offerings.

Ver. 7. *Tabernacle.*—This is not the sprinkling of blood, which has already been done, but merely the pouring away of what remains over and above in a holy place. The atonement takes place here in an especially solemn manner. As the priests in the people's stead perform their service to God in the holy place, so the sprinkling of blood is made here, and not at the altar of burnt sacrifice. The blood is sprinkled towards the veil, behind which are the ark of the covenant and the mercy-seat, in order to represent, as it were before God, the life which is given to death for sin. The blood is put on the horns of the altar of incense, which is the holier one, instead of the altar of burnt-sacrifice. From the former at other times only prayer arises.— What could be a stronger exhortation to spotless holiness in the high priest than this act of sacrifice, which clearly bore witness that sin was not less flagrant in him, but far more so, than in any one else?

Ver. 12. *Ashes* of the other sacrifices.

Be burnt.—From the circumstance that the flesh of the sacrifice was burnt without the camp, we are by no means to infer its uncleanness, any more than from the customs at the feast of atonement (ch. xvi. 27, 28). A "clean place" is expressly prescribed, on which it might be burnt with fire. Every other place within the camp would rather have exposed the holy flesh to pollution, as for this cause also the blood was carefully taken away.

Ver. 15. *The elders,* as representatives of the whole congregation.

Ver. 21. *For the congregation.*—Up to the laying on of hands by the elders, all is here done as in the former sin-offering. In the former case the priest, here the elders, lay their hands on the bullock. It was intended to represent by this how the high priest stands in the place of the whole congregation, and again, how the whole people is a kingdom of priests (Exod. xix. 6).

Ver. 22. *A ruler.*—A head of a tribe.

Ver. 25. *Pour out.*—Cf. ver. 7, note.

Ver. 28. *A kid of the goats.*—This is the difference (cf. ver. 32), while the ruler is only to bring a male animal.

CHAPTER V.

The trespass-offering is yet distinguished from the sin-offering. Only a ram—no female sheep (ch. iv. 32) as it seems, and no other animal—could be taken for the trespass-offering. In the sprinkling of blood it was like the burnt-offering (ch. vii. 2). In respect to the burning of the fat and the portion of the priest, it resembled the sin-offering (ch. vii. 7). The first shows that the offering was of more weight and significance than the sin-offering; the second, that in reference to the atonement, which was the main point in the sin-offering, it was not equal to this latter, but its chief importance lay elsewhere. Besides the occasions here brought forward, mention is made of a trespass-offering in the case of unchastity with a slave (ch. xix. 20–22); of unintentional defilement during a Nazaritish vow (ch. vi. 9–12); and on the occasion of pronouncing the cleanness of a leper (ch. xiv. 12, 21); also, in later times, in the case of those who had taken to themselves strange wives (Ezra x. 19). The word "sin" means in Heb. a wandering from the right way; the word "trespass" signifies a violation of a right—a robbing, which requires restitution—a debt. By every sin man transgresses against God, and is bound to make restitution. But a trespass may be imagined which is without sin. The whole law, with all its institutions and regulations—an emanation from the will of God, *His* perpetual ordinance—might even without man's knowing it be transgressed by him. The ritual law was given to the people of God for the very purpose of reminding them of the statutes and guidance of God, which encompassed them at all times. If now this holy, irrefragable ordinance was broken by man even without sin, yet thereby man had committed a trespass against God, for which he was bound to compensate. And therefore the cases in which a trespass-offering was to be made were of two kinds: those where, in the sin, the idea of guilt was peculiarly prominent, where God had been robbed of something, and where, therefore, besides the customary atonement and repentance, a restitution ought to be made to God; and those, where a man had contracted guilt quite unconsciously without sin, but had thereby violated what belonged to God. In the first named cases of our chap. (ver. 1-13), the compensation for the offence consists not of a trespass, but of a sin and burnt-offering. As every sin was a trespass, so was every sin-offering likewise a trespass-offering. On the other hand, in the rest of the cases narrated, and in the others mentioned in the O. T., a particular trespass-offering is prescribed as restitution of a robbery directly or indirectly committed against God.

Ver. 1. *Voice of swearing.*—An oath, adjuration. The manner of the swearing of a witness was this: the judge administered a form of oath to the witness, who thereupon brought forth his depositions, which were then regarded as an oath.

His iniquity; *i. e.*, the guilt of a trespass lies upon him. The case is this: If any one has been a witness to any act, either an eye-witness or in any other way, and is summoned before the judge to give his evidence on oath, but has, for some reason or other, either been silent on some point or denied his cognisance of it.

Ver. 2. *Hidden.*—And therefore has omitted the legal purification, treated himself as one clean.

Ver. 4. *Knoweth of it.*—The case is this: A man, from inconsiderateness, swears that he will do some person harm, and he perceives afterwards that he may not do it; or to do good, and he perceives afterwards that he cannot keep his promise. In both cases the person is not guilty of anything; but the oath contains at the same time a vow to God,—towards Him is he bound to make payment as for a trespass, in punishment of his inconsiderate oath. In the four cases here mentioned, there stand together two trespasses committed unknowingly and without guilt (ver. 2 and 3), and two out of inconsiderate haste—of which the first approaches very nearly the sin of a wilful breach of an oath. That which the four cases have in common is this: that both in the oath and in the legal defilement, God's (objective) ordinance has been broken—has been violated. Independently of the particular sin, the son of the covenant of God is bound to keep inviolate the property and rights of his Lord and King, and to do by way of restitution all which God prescribes; otherwise, an act which at first was an unwitting commission, or which has before men been made good, becomes a positive sin. Every other which has not been kept,—even that which we ought not only not to keep, but which we are bound to break (as, e g., the oath of Herod, St Mark vi. 23),—this brings upon us guilt in the sight of God. We are also, as Christians, bound in such a sad case, by an open, solemn act, to preserve God's honour inviolate before men—to sanctify the Lord.

Ver. 12. *Sin-offering.*—The sin-offering which is to be made in this case, is called his "trespass" (his "Ascham," the name also for the trespass-offering); he brings it thereby to the Lord, as afterwards (ver. 7) by the burnt-offering to be added to the offering of birds, or the unbloody offering (ver. 11). As the sin-offering is always at the same time a trespass-offering, the trespass may also be wiped away in every one of that kind, i.e., sin-offering. It is, however, remarkable, that in the regulations concerning the sin-offering in general (ch. iv. 27, etc.), nothing is said of an offering of birds or meal; consequently, only in this case, where the sin-offering is especially designated as a trespass-bearing, is that exchange allowed. This would represent the trespass-offering not as less than the other, but as even more needful, since the poorest person, who could only bring meal, was bound to make it.

Ver. 14. *Spake unto Moses.*—From this place follow the cases in which a trespass-offering with its particular customs was to be brought, not by way of compensation as a sin or burnt-offering.

Ver. 15. *Trespass-offering.*—Lit.: "When a soul commits a trespass thereby, that it sins in error against the holy things of the Lord, it shall bring its trespass to the Lord: a ram without blemish out of the flocks according to thy estimation, silver in shekels according to the shekel of the sanctuary, as its trespass" (or "its trespass-offering"). This refers particularly to the holy payments of all kinds, the holy head-money (Exod. xxx. 12), the tithes, the first-fruits, etc. The case is that, not of innocent, but of blameable ignorance, and would, accordingly, properly belong to a sin-offering. But not the (subjective) forgiveness, but the (objective) wrong done to God's possession, here comes under consideration. This requires express compensation, which is afforded, not through a sin-offering, but by a ram as trespass-offering. The priest estimates the trespass in the sacred money, and the ram must be of this value. If one ram did not suffice for removing the trespass, then it seems more must be offered.—Whether in this and the following cases a sin-offering went before or with the trespass-offering, is not said; but it may fairly be inferred that not every trespass was a sin, and not every trespass-offering to be regarded as a sin-offering; and where, for other reasons, it was a case for a sin-offering, that then the guilty person was not exempt from it for the sake of the trespass-offering.

Ver. 16. *Forgiven him.*—The trespass-offering was the symbolical payment, the compensation in a higher sense to God. To this must yet be added the outward payment, that the two might not be confounded. A fifth was added thereto, as something more is always offered in every compensation. The priest received it as God's deputy, to whom the purloined or withholden gift ought to have been made.

Ver. 17. *Wist it not.*—This must be carefully distinguished from the "ignorance" in ver. 15, and ch. iv. 13, 22, 27. Here is meant a not knowing which is entirely without blame, as with the people in the case, ch. iv. 3.

CHAPTER VI.

Ver. 2. *Fellowship.*—Lit., " or inlaying of the hand;" *i. e.*, in a solemn promise, namely, such an one as concerns the property.

Ver. 6. *Priest.*—Lit.: " And his trespass shall he bring to the Lord, a ram from the herd according to thy estimation, a trespass-offering to the priest." Together with full restitution to the possessor, which in particular thefts amounted to double, nay, to four or five times as much (Exod. xxii. 1), restitution was also to be made to the Lord God, since, according to ver. 2, the transgressor had laid hands on the Lord's possession. Nothing could more completely than this regulation keep alive and strengthen the belief that God is the supreme and only Possessor, and nothing could more completely impress on the mind the holiness of social order.

Ver. 9. *Burning in it; i.e.,* it shall be the nourishment for every fire that comes on the altar. It is evident that the fire burning continually, which was kept up by the daily burnt-offering (Exod. xxix. 38), had a symbolical meaning. As the daily burnt-sacrifice betokened the daily renewed gift to God, in like manner did this continually burning fire denote the unceasing, uninterrupted character of the same. Similar customs with the heathen had a different signification. Among the Persians (and among the Parsees in India at this day), fire was the visible representative of the godhead; the continual burning of it, the emblem of eternity. The perpetual fire of Vesta (the "oldest goddess") among the Greeks and Romans, was the emblem of the inmost, purest warmth of life, which unites family and people—the hearth, as it were, the heart of the house or of a state. In both is shown the essential difference which existed between these and the Divine covenant-religion.

Ver. 10. *Upon his flesh.*—Exod. xxviii. 39, 42. The garments of the finest, brightest linen or cotton, showed immediately every speck, whether caused by the things used in sacrifice, or by impurity of any other kind. The under-garments typified the subjugation of all fleshly desire during the sacred service.

Ver. 11. *Other garments.*—Therefore, at every fresh burnt-sacrifice, consequently twice a day, the priests changed their clothes.

Ver. 18. *Shall be holy.*—The participation in the sacrifices was certainly a gift of the people for the maintenance of the priests; but this was only a secondary object in it, since the eating of them itself had a symbolical meaning. The unleavened food (not in a state of fermentation or corruption), eaten in a holy place and only by the consecrated priests (with the exception of their families), typified the participation acceptable to God, which the people's gifts prepared for Him. The priests partook thereof, properly, in God's stead. There were, therefore, different relations of man to God and of God to man represented in the burnt-offering which was entirely consumed, the smoke of which ascended to heaven as a well-pleasing savour, and in the meat-offerings which were only partly burnt, but chiefly eaten by the priests. Upon the surrender, the reconciliation, the acceptance of the whole man, followed the particular virtues and works well-pleasing to God, which were the Lord's daily, perpetual joy in His people.

Ver. 20. *Anointed.*—When he or one of his descendants is anointed as high priest.

Ver. 21. *Made with oil.*—Heb., "often turned in oil," that it may be completely saturated with it. The emblem of the oil is everywhere conspicuous in this ceremony.

Ver. 22. *Wholly burnt.*—Quite naturally, since no one could stand in stead of him who consumed the sacrifice in the name of the Lord.

Ver. 28. *Broken.*—Because in earthen vessels which were not glazed the blood would unavoidably penetrate. The blood did not defile the vessel; but could itself, as the holy means of atonement, be defiled in and on the vessels.

Rinse.—As in the sin-offering the atonement was the main point, this was done here more than in the other sacrifices, in order to point to the blood as the means of atonement.

Ver. 30. *Burnt.*—For the same reason as ver. 23.

CHAPTER VII.

Ver. 4. *The liver.*—That which hangs over the lobe, as ch. iii. 4.

Ver. 7. *One law*—In this respect, that all the flesh falls to the priest, they are both alike.

Ver. 8. *Hath offered.*—The burnt-offering is peculiarly a whole sacrifice, and therefore the skin is to be regarded as the least significant part in it. It was to fall to the share of the priest, in order that not the least portion of the sacrifice might be withdrawn from the Lord, but only that to which no sacred meaning was attached.

Ver. 10. *As another.*—This offering is to be equally divided among all. That which is mentioned in ver. 9 is immediately to be partaken of, and might spoil by being kept longer; the dry part, or the meat, which is merely rolled in oil, not so. But nothing which has in any way undergone fermentation or corruption may be eaten as a sacrificial meal.

Ver. 12. *Thanksgiving.*—Here the different kinds of thank-offering are enumerated—praise-offering, vow-offering, free-will offering. The name of the first shows how unsuitable the term "thank-offering" is for the whole kind, as these praise-offerings were peculiarly, exclusively thank-offerings, gifts in thankfulness for a Divine favour.

Ver. 13. *Peace-offerings;* i.e., in addition to the slain praise- (peace-) offerings. A particularly rich meat-offering was to be brought as an additional gift to the thank, and especially to the praise-offering (a rich vow and offering of acceptable works), because in this kind of sacrifice the meal was a prominent part. It is remarkable that here leavened bread is offered, while the prohibition of all leaven in the sacrifices (Exod. xxiii. 18, ch. xxxiv. 25) appears to be general. But herein exactly is shown the significant peculiarity of this kind of offering. Even here, indeed, the leavened bread might not be burnt on the altar, and so that early general prohibition (ch. ii. 11) is expressly explained; but as first-fruits (ch. ii. 12), leavened bread might be offered. But in this sacrifice the repast was to be the most prominent feature, as the most significant sacred custom; and for this purpose the leavened bread was more suitable than the unleavened. It was in every respect to be partaken of like an ordinary meal.

Ver. 18. *His iniquity.*—It is to be inferred from this, that of the three kinds of thank-offering the praise-offerings were the most holy. These were the offerings literally "of confession" —the acknowledgment of the reception of an undeserved benefit from God. A vow-offering, to which also the vow of the Nazarites belonged (Num. vi. 14), was brought at the expiration of the time to which it referred. A free-will offering appears to have had more the character of a prayer-offering. The reason why the flesh might not be kept longer was plainly the putrefaction, which in hot countries sets in sooner than with us, and which makes the flesh unfit for holy uses. In the most holy kind of the three even the least taint was to be avoided; in the others the greater degree. The greater holiness of the praise-offering evidently consists in this, that it was more independent of the will of the individual—that it referred to an act on God's part which man merely acknowledged.

Ver. 19. *Eat thereof.*—The last part of the sentence is literally, "And (concerning) the flesh every clean person can eat (sacrificed) flesh." After it has been determined that such flesh of the sacrifice as has touched anything unclean shall be burnt, it is added, that besides this there is no bar to the eating of the flesh of the thank-offerings. Every one who has not made himself unclean may eat of it.

Ver. 23. *Cut off.*—The reason is likewise added. All fat belongs to the Lord, the fat, therefore, of the beasts which are not sacrificed, or which may not be sacrificed, must not be eaten, lest the people should desire that which it is unlawful to touch, and lest an opportunity should be given to transgress this holy commandment.

Ver. 27. *Eateth.*—The reason is the same as in the former prohibition, and is further explained, ch. xvii. 10, etc.

Ver. 30. *His own hands.*—There is a particular emphasis laid on the fact, that the same person who laid his hands on the victim must bring the gift to the priest, because in this sacrifice the act of bringing it was particularly significant.

Ver. 34. *Wave-breast.*—The breast and the shoulder were the best part of the victim, which therefore the priest received. They are called "wave-breast" and "heave-shoulder" on account of the ceremony of waving and heaving which took place with them. "Waving" means to move the pieces of the victim in an horizontal, "heaving," in a perpendicular direction. The first was, according to some, only in front and back again; but according to others (and this is the more probable opinion), also to the right and left. The priest laid the pieces of the sacrifice on the hands of the sacrificer, and his own under them, and so made these movements. The "waving" took place with the breast, and the "heaving" with the shoulder-piece. Similar to this movement with the pieces of the sacrifice was the ceremony which, according to Num. viii. 11, etc., was performed in the consecration of the Levites with respect to themselves, as they were moved or waved to and fro. To this a custom refers which occurs among the Jews during the end of prayer on their departure from the synagogue; namely, that they take a couple of steps forwards, and to the right and left. The "waving" betokened the world which is the Lord's—the "heaving," Himself who dwelleth on high. The pieces were thus consecrated to the High and Lofty One to whom belong the ends of the world. In like manner, the Jews believe that, by this movement in prayer, the benefit of it is bestowed on the whole world. The first-fruits of His people, the first of the fruits of the earth, and the best pieces of the thank-offering, were therefore dedicated to the Lord of the world, in order thereby to hallow the whole to Him: in these sacrifices to consecrate more especially the whole sacrificial meal which followed thereupon.

Ver. 35. *Anointing.*—Heb., "the appropriated portion;" because "to anoint" is to stroke with the hand over something, the same word means "to apportion."

Ver. 38. *Wilderness of Sinai.*—With these words is therefore both concluded the part of the commandments which relate to the priests' share in the sacrifices, and that which relates to the sacrifices themselves.

CHAPTER VIII.

Ver. 4. *Of the congregation.*—The whole congregation in the literal sense could not possibly be assembled before the door of the tabernacle in the fore-court. But we find also expressly mentioned, Num. i. 16, ch. xvi. 2, "the renowned of the congregation," who at the same time are called " princes (heads) of the congregation." From the first place we see that they were heads of families. These appeared, therefore, in the name of the different families of the congregation, and conveyed to them what was told themselves in personal conference with Moses. There is no trace whatever of freely chosen deputies.

Ver. 9. *Commanded Moses.*—Upon all this see Exod. xxviii.

Ver. 15. *Reconciliation upon it.*—At the sin-offering of the high priest, which is described ch. iv. 1, etc., other customs are commanded. The high priest carries the blood into the holy place, sprinkles it towards the veil, and besmears with it the horns of the altar of incense; while here all takes place at the altar of burnt-sacrifice before the tabernacle. The reason is the following—that this, the consecration-sacrifice, is generally for the sins of the high priest to be consecrated: here he still stands without, together with the people, before the tabernacle, and only later (ver. 33) is it entrusted to him. All the sins of the high priest before his entrance on his office are not so great as those which follow after it, and therefore for these latter there is need of a greater atonement. The reconciliation of the altar, as if all the sacred vessels had the significance that the sins wherewith the people from whose hands they have come have defiled them, were taken away from them.

Ver. 34. *Atonement for you.*—They daily offered the full—*i.e.*, the consecration-sacrifice. Hence it is evident that by the door of the tabernacle can here be meant not the door of the holy place, but the gate of the fore-court, as the sacrifices were made in the fore-court. In the tabernacle itself they might not even sit, far less could they sleep there. The seven days are either the number of the covenant generally, or perhaps they are intended yet more distinctly to bring to remembrance the seven days of creation, so that the priests therein were consecrated to the service of the Creator of the world.

Ver. 36. *Hand of Moses.*—Cf. Exod. xxx.

CHAPTER IX.

The custom of sacrifice had arisen in the earliest times out of the immediate childlike intercourse of man with God, so that there needed no express establishment of it on God's part; but at the beginning the essential point was, that the Lord should express by a significant act His acceptance of the sacrifice, as was the case in respect to Abel, Gen. iv. 4. But now, when a new period in the service of sacrifice began, when for the first time sacrifice was regulated even in its minutest particular by a Divine messenger, this centre of all worship of God required a solemn attestation. The fire, which henceforth was never to go out on the great altar of burnt-sacrifice, was kindled by a stroke of lightning, and burnt as a holy Divine fire on it for ever, in order to do away with the emblems of the individual, God-estranged life, and to consecrate His people as well-pleasing to the Lord.—Of the genuine coin, the Divine impress of which is certified by this history to every one who enters deeply into it, many false imitations have existed among the heathen. The frequent occurrence of narratives of fire fallen from heaven shows the necessity existing in human nature which this event was intended to satisfy; *e.g.*, the fable that on some altars the sacrifice was never set fire to, but that it was consumed by means of fire called down from heaven.

Ver. 4. *Appear unto you.*—All kinds of sacrifices were, on this solemn occasion, made together. First comes the sin-offering, which removes all hindrances to access to the Lord (the trespass-offering is comprised in this, see ch. v., introd.); then follows the burnt-offering, the expression of entire surrender of all to the Lord; upon this the thank-offering, which does not here refer so much to benefits received, but rather, as elsewhere is the case at the ceremonies of consecration (Exod. xxiv. 5; 2 Sam. vi. 18; 1 Kings viii. 63; 1 Macc. iv. 56), to those which are yet to be sought and expected from God; and as additional offerings to the two last, comes in the meat-offering, the offering of a life well-pleasing to God. All these offerings are to be made "because the Lord will appear'"—they are to be offered, as it were, for dedication and confirmation.

Ver. 7. *Commanded.*—It is to be observed that in the first sin-offering the high priest is to reconcile both himself and the people; afterwards, in the second, to offer for the people more particularly. This results from the relation alluded to before, ch. iv. 3, that by the sin of the high priest guilt passed on the whole people, and thereby its relation to God was interrupted. The high priest, therefore, first atones for his own sin, and for the guilt which, by means of it, has overtaken the people; then, yet over and above this, he makes atonement for the particular sin of the people.

Ver. 9. *Bottom of the altar.*—The atonement takes place here at the altar of burnt-sacrifice (as ch. viii. 15), not at the altar of incense, and for the same reason as there.

Ver. 22. *Blessed them.*—In blessing, the hands were properly laid on the head, Gen. xlviii. 14, as a sign of the transferring of something. Where this was impossible, as here, then the lifting up of the hands expressed the same thing, just as the leading about of the Levites stood in the place of the waving, ch. vii. 34, note.

Came down from the altar.

Ver. 23. *Tabernacle.*—As all kinds of sacrifices were offered before the tabernacle, it seems they made here the first burnt sacrifice, which, under these circumstances, was to carry up especially prayer to the Lord for the appearing of His glory.

Appeared.—It is uncertain whether this glory is to be imagined as a particular appearance—a descent of the cloudy pillar on the tabernacle—a bright effulgence from the same or something like it, or whether it consisted merely in the simultaneous descent of the fire.

Ver. 24. *And the fat.*—It is literally, "The fire went forth from before the countenance of the Lord." The same took place at the consecration of the altar of Solomon's temple, 2 Chron. vii. 1. According to Jewish tradition, this fire continued up to the reign of Solomon, and that which was then kindled, to the days of King Manasseh, 2 Chron. xxxiii.; from which time to this it has disappeared from among the people, as have all similar visible pledges of the Divine presence: the glory of the Lord which appeared in the cloud, the ark of the covenant, the tables of the law, the spirit of prophecy.

On their faces.—It was not so much the confirmation of the priesthood of Aaron, as of the sacrifices, which took place in the descent of the fire. The people rejoiced in the certainty that they, by means of the sacrifices, had now a continual access to God.

CHAPTER X.

The whole service of sacrifices had just been hallowed by means of an act on God's part. From the fickle and changeable character of the people, it still could not but be that the impression made by the mighty miracle would soon be effaced from their minds. For this reason did the Lord desire to show His presence in His sacred things, to be both the cause of great blessing and also of terrible punishment. It was of great importance that the fire which consumed the sacrifice was not of man's creating, but of God's sending—not merely as a solemn recognition on the Lord's part, but also on account of the whole significance of the sacrifice. The act of surrender to God which was figured by the sacrifice, and fulfilled in the believers, was intended to be the work of God through man, not of man alone. This pledge of Divine favour in the sacrifice was as much destroyed by the strange fire as in the case of the similar interference with the emblem, Exod. xx. 25, note. So far is the symbolical meaning of this history very deep and comprehensive. Every gift to God, every sacrifice for Him, every act of zeal in His service, however it might otherwise outwardly be right, is displeasing to the Lord so soon as the fire of self-denial ceases to originate from the Holy Spirit: 1 Cor. xiii. 3, note; St John xiii. 38.

Ver. 1. *Commanded them not.*—A prohibition to use "strange fire" (*i.e.*, that which was not taken from the altar) has not yet been mentioned; it has therefore been regarded as included in the command, ch. vi. 12. It will be expressly prescribed in a later place (ch. xvi. 12), concerning the act of burning incense on the great day of atonement —The Angel in the vision of St John, therefore, takes fire from the altar for burning incense (Rev. viii. 5). We may conclude from the context and the meaning of the history, that they purposed in the offering of strange fire a particular service before God, wishing to add something of their own over and above what was present there. This self-chosen service to God must on this occasion, when the fire fallen from heaven was of so great significance, be most severely punished as an act of rebellion against the Lord.

Ver. 2. *Died before the Lord.*—It is not without significance that the very fire at whose appearing the people had before rejoiced, was fatal to them, as they had despised it. The same Gospel is to one a savour of life, to others a savour of death: 2 Cor. ii. 16. It "devoured," *i.e.*, it killed them; since, according to ver. 5, their clothes were not singed. They died "before the Lord"—before the tent of His dwelling, in which He had shown Himself as present by means of the fire: as in the case of Uzzah (1 Chron. xiii. 10, cf. 2 Sam. vi. 7). The history reminds us of Ananias and Sapphira, Acts v.

Ver. 3. *Glorified.*—The Lord "is sanctified" by showing mercy on those who are His, Ezek. xx. 41; and likewise by punishing those who despise Him, Ezek. xxxviii. 16. In both cases He shows and reveals Himself as the Holy One: cf. St Matt. vi. 9, note.—The Lord has "said" this actually, Exod. xix. 22, ch. xxix. 34; and it is also implied in the words so often appended to the commandments relating to the priests, "that they die not:" Exod. xxviii. 35, ch. xxx. 21; Lev. viii. 35.

Held his peace.—As fear came on all the people: Acts v. 11. Here reference is particularly made to the circumstance, that it was the custom to lament the dead with loud cries.

Ver. 4. *Camp.*—They are called "brethren," as being near relations, as Gen. xiii. 8. Their nearest relatives, their father and brothers, might not touch them, lest by being defiled they should interrupt the service of the priesthood; as afterwards this is expressly commanded, ch. xxi. 1.—To the commandment for the especial occasion is now a general prohibition appended. Communion with God, the Holy One, is simply life. Death has come into the world by sin: therefore, God's representatives, who are to bear the sin of the people, have no communion with death. The life from God effaces from their minds the thought of the death even of their nearest kinsmen. Hence is explained Christ's word, St Matt. viii. 22.

Ver. 6. *Uncover not.*—To uncover the head was a mark of grief, as ch. xiii. 45. Nothing therefore can here be meant about shaving the hair, or, as others translate, "letting it grow," because the priests wore turbans which covered the hair. These, it was commanded them, they should not remove on account of their sorrow.

Rend your clothes.—Another mark of grief—ch. xiii. 45 and ch. xxi. 10—which often occurs; *e g.,* Gen. xxxvii. 34; 2 Sam. xiii. 31; St Matt. xxvi. 65.

Ver. 7. *Anointing oil.*—The Spirit of life, which overcomes all death, is given you. The Spirit, whose emblem is the anointing oil, is also called particularly a Spirit of joy; the anointing oil, therefore, the oil of gladness, Ps. xlv. 8. Afterwards this general commandment is made more stringent— that the high priest was allowed to mourn no one: the other priests, their nearest kinsfolks: ch. xxi. 1-4, 11.

Ver. 9. *Strong drink.*—Heb., "Schekar." So was every intoxicating drink called, made from barley, honey, and dates. It is remarkable that this prohibition of drinking wine follows directly on the prohibition to mourn. By this connection is taught, that as no external event was to depress with grief the priest, so ought he to apply no artificial means to his senses to promote exhilaration: his whole thoughts and attention are to be directed to the sacred offices which are commanded him. We are reminded of the antithesis, Eph. v. 18.

Ver. 11. *Moses.*—There was in the O. T. no distinct office of teaching. At this time, when God instructed by deeds and symbolical acts, the teaching of the priests consisted in the occasional description and explanation of the necessary holy offices. In order that they might have ability to do this, they should themselves above all, in the performance of the sacred rites, be possessed of the most sound understanding of what they were doing.

Ver. 15. *Hath commanded.*—All this had Moses already said, ch. ii. 3, 10, ch. vii. 34, and he need hardly now have repeated it; but he does so in order to prepare for the history which follows.

Ver. 18. *Holy place.*—In the fore-court of the tabernacle, ch. vi. 26.

I commanded.—It is not told us more distinctly what kind of sin-offering this was. The sacrifice of consecration was, according to ch. ix. 8, a calf—the flesh and skin of it had been already burnt. According to ch. iv. 23, a goat was brought for a prince as sin-offering. It is therefore to be supposed that, for a cause not further given, some such was offered on the same day on which Aaron's sons had been killed on account of their transgression.

Ver. 19. *Sight of the Lord.*—Moses made, perhaps, out of consideration towards Aaron, his sons responsible for the mistake. By eating of the sacrifice, they expiated, on the one hand, the sin of the sacrificer; on the other hand, they appeared therein as the guests of the Lord. This participation also (as yet more in the thank-offering, the more general sacrificial meal) was an expression of joy after the completion of the atonement. In the midst of such terrible grief, Aaron could not resolve to perform this act. Although, therefore, Aaron was here guilty of some irregularity, yet he hopes that the spirit of the law will relieve him from a fulfilment of the letter.

Ver. 20. *Content.*—Moses affords him the indulgence for which he begs. It satisfies him that Aaron has recognised the rule, and the more so, inasmuch as he himself characterises what he has done as an exception.

CHAPTER XI.

There now follows a long list of regulations with respect to pollution. One kind of this pollution was the result of man's wilfulness, viz., the eating of unclean food. The other kinds were natural and bodily conditions. These concern the relations of the sexes, child-bearing, certain inevitable fatal sicknesses, and death. The object of the law, in all these cases, is continually to remind the people of God of sin, and of their own call to holiness. Sin has its seat in sensuality; it has made man carnal and worldly, since itself proceeded from the spirit of self-exaltation (Gen. iii. 4-7, note). Although now generation, birth, nourishment, sickness, and death, are all God's ordinances, and therefore good, still there clings to them, partly, sinful lust, partly they stand in distinct relation to it as its punishment (thou shalt bring forth with sorrow, Gen. iii. 16; with sorrow shalt thou eat until thou return again to the earth, ver. 18, 19). For this reason, during the time of nonage, laws must be of the greatest consequence, which both taught men to regard these conditions with a holy awe, and made them see in bodily uncleanness emblems of spiritual defilement, in bodily purification the image of cleanness of heart.

The prohibitions respecting food follow immediately on the laws about sacrifice, because a part of the sacrifice was eaten, and this sacred eating was a channel of direct communion with God. From this eating of the sacrifices, the law then passes on to all kinds of eating in general. The main object of the prohibitions respecting food was by no means to separate Israel from other people; since, long before the election of any family or individual, we find a distinction of clean and unclean animals (cf. Gen. vii. 3, note). Rather, all heathen nations were acquainted with such distinctions, in which they expressed the fundamental ideas of their religion. In the heathen Nature-worship (especially among the Egyptians), the purity and sanctity of the animals had reference to the relation in which they were supposed to stand to a distinct deity, of which they were esteemed to be the revelation: their uncleanness, to the relation in which they stood to the disturbing kingdom of the evil spirit. They were either too holy to be eaten, or too unclean. The opposition of good and evil lay altogether in the province of nature. All was good which furthered and maintained the order of the world—all bad which disturbed it. In the Divine law, on the contrary, "filthiness" or "abomination" was the expression of an inward, moral loathing: and if nowhere any being has been given up to be the work of an evil spirit, still many animals have been unmistakeably the bearers of human passions, and as such are an object of dislike to man engaged in the work of sanctification. God Himself has, by His curse, given the most loathsome form to the serpent, and put enmity between his seed and that of man (Gen. iii. 15). Among all prohibited animals, the swine is the one most repulsive to the Israelites. This and others have been an abomination to them on account of their feeding on mire; others, on account of their eating blood; and others still, by reason of a certain feeling which does not belong to us, but was peculiar to the country and the views of the age. While, therefore, they abhorred the emblems of sin, and thereby endeavoured to attain outward purity, they were to learn to accustom themselves to inward holiness, to which this outward purity was designed to lead them.

Ver. 3. *Cheweth the cud.*—Lit., "bringeth up the fetching up," brings up its food again. It is difficult to find in these marks any symbolical meaning: they occur in the domestic animals which offer the emblem of purity, and are easily recognisable.

Divideth not.—Has therefore one of the marks by which the clean and unclean are distinguished.

Ver. 4. *Camel;* namely, not entirely. His hoof is divided in front, but hangs together behind by a skin.

Ver. 5. *Coney.*—Heb., "Schaphan;" probably the lemming (mountain-mouse), an animal with very long, three-toed hind-feet, which occurs also Ps. civ. 18, Prov. xxx. 26, as inhabiting the clefts of rocks.

Ver. 6. *Hare.*—It has a double, while other animals have a quadruple, stomach. Even among the physicians of antiquity, we find the notion that the flesh of the hare produced thick, heavy blood. Perhaps also its unusual philogenitiveness caused this animal to be regarded as unclean.

Ver. 7. *Swine.*—Swine's flesh produced and fomented leprosy, according to the view of heathen writers, and might even on that account become the object of abhorrence. But certainly it was more especially so, as an emblem of impurity and sensuality (it was sacred to Venus). Of all prohibited animals, this was at all times the most detested by the Israelites. Even among neighbouring heathen nations it was esteemed unclean. Still it was sacrificed to certain deities, as, indeed, was very suitable in Nature-worship. The swine-flesh eating ministers of idols are mentioned at a later period as the objects of particular detestation: Isa. lxv. 4, ch. lxvi. 17.

Ver. 9. *Fins and scales.*—Here the idea appears to be, that fish with scales and fins seem the most natural proper water creatures, while the rest live in the depths, holes, and bottoms of rivers and of the sea; and in order to distinguish between the clean and the unclean, it was necessary to lay down some simple rule.

Ver. 13. *Fowls.*—All winged animals are called "fowls;" therefore, as will be seen in what follows, also four-footed creatures and insects.

Ver. 14. *His kind; i.e.,* generally all birds of prey. The particular names are differently translated; some are difficult to decide on.

Ver. 16. *Night-hawk.*—According to others, the male and female ostrich.

Ver. 18. *Pelican.*—The Greek translation, written in Egypt, has the "Ibis."

Gier-eagle.—Here stand in the Hebrew three birds. The first is by some supposed to be the swan,—by others, a kind of falcon (in a later place, ver. 30, the same name stands for an animal resembling the locust or lizard); the second, "Kaath," is supposed to be a pelican; the third, "Racham," a kind of hawk.

Ver. 20. *Creep.*—By this expression, "which creep" (Scherez), are designated all animals which crawl upon the earth, especially insects.

Ver. 22. *Grasshopper.*—These are all different kinds of locusts, a common food of the poor in the East: cf. St Matt. iii. 4. These were the only insects allowed to be eaten, probably because they were known to feed on fruits, leaves, etc.

Ver. 24. *Until the even.*—This is the less degree of pollution which is frequently mentioned. The evening began a new day. The uncleanness therefore continued during the whole day on which it had occurred.

Ver. 27. *Paws.*—Properly "hands;" the animals which have not hoofs, but paws, as those of the feline kind, bears, etc.

Ver. 29. *Creep.*—Four-footed animals, indeed, but with very short feet. The reason of the aversion from these lies in their short feet and creeping motion close to the earth, by means of which they come in contact with everything that is in the dust and mud. Hence the curse upon the serpent, Gen. iii. 14.

Ver. 29. *Weasel.*—More correctly speaking these three animals are the mole, the mouse, and the land-crocodile (called scincus). The next five are most probably species of lizards; the last, the chameleon.

Ver. 32. *Cleansed.*—The person was unclean by contact with these clothes or this vessel, and could do nothing therein or therewith. In order to save himself this, these things were to be avoided.

Ver. 36. *Their carcase.*—"Their" carcase; *i.e*, that of the wells, cisterns, etc.,—the beast which has fallen into them. In a land where water was so scarce, and cisterns are the only means of saving it, it would have been a great grievance to have declared the whole water unclean. Here, then, is allowed a similar exception of necessity from the ritual law with that in the case of the Sabbath, and reminds us of Christ's saying, that these commandments were for men, and not men for these commandments.

Ver. 37. *To be sowed;* because this did not come into immediate contact with man.

Ver. 38. *Unclean.*—When the seed is not employed for sowing, but used for food. The reason of the command is clear from the preceding.

Ver. 39. *Any beast.*—A clean beast which had not been killed. No animal that died of itself might be eaten, because its blood had not been poured out: it defiled as a human corpse.

Ver. 40. *Until the even.*—Evidently, he who had done so unwittingly; since any one who did this knowingly would, as every other transgressor of the law, be cut off from the people: Num. xv. 50.

Ver. 42. *An abomination.*—In the Heb. there are three different kinds of animals: those which creep on their belly without feet, as the serpent: thereupon further it is said, such as go on four feet, together with all which have more feet. Among the first are those four-footed animals to be understood who have so short feet that they touch the earth with their belly, as those mentioned, ver. 29; among the last, insects and worms of different kinds. These words, therefore, are partly repetition of what has been said, partly an emphatic adding of a general law, which formed the transition to the yet more general concluding words in what follows.

Ver. 45. *Holy.*—This conclusion plainly shows what is the particular meaning and object of the prohibitions respecting food. God has, after man's fall, imparted to certain animals (which are good in themselves, and even in this their mark of punishment are good) a kind of stamp by which they become emblems of sin for man. At a time when the pure spiritual knowledge of sin could not yet possibly be communicated to the people of God, it was intended that they should through these emblems of sin be filled with a loathing of sin itself,—that the people should be awakened to the consciousness that no sinner can stand before a holy God, or hold communion with Him. As, therefore, God is holy, who by saving them from Egypt has made Israel a people, and revealed Himself to them as their God; so should there dwell in the children of His covenant a horror of sin of every kind.

CHAPTER XII.

Among the pollutions which do not arise from what is outward, as from food, but lie in man's natural condition, and indeed in his procreation and birth, that is first mentioned which had the most effect of all, and therefore needed the greatest purification. Sin, as well as its punishment, has peculiarly taken its seat in the sexual relations. Immediately after the fall, mankind discover that they are not masters of their own bodies, and clothe themselves. And the birth of children is accompanied with the sharpest punishment, of which the woman is the bearer, as she was the first to break the commandment. This is the reason why procreation of children, but more particularly the act of child-bearing, was a defilement; just as a sense of shame causes us to hide all these connections, though we know that they are not sinful in themselves. The bodily impurity is an image of the moral defilement, which belongs to them more than to any other natural act, and makes it even to the Christian an object of holy dread, lest by a too close spiritual contact he should become spiritually and not bodily defiled. As in the whole province of unclean meats (all of which God has created) man was not internally defiled, but was continually reminded of the desecration of the creation by sin, and as the prohibition about unclean meats was a call to abstain from all communion with sin and its consequences, in like manner is to be regarded the declaration of uncleanness in these natural relations which are not sinful in themselves, but are especially liable by misuse to become sinful, and which carry with them the stigma of sin. With no other people of antiquity was marriage so honoured, founded as it was on express Divine institution. Among no other people do we find, through their religious idea of death, so reverential a care for the rites of sepulture. If, then, procreation, birth, death, caused defilement, we perceive therein, in emblem and germ, the doctrine which was more clearly revealed in the N. T., which teaches us that the flesh created by God, and originally good, has nevertheless, by sin which dwelt in it, been made the means of exciting sinful desire. The different degrees of uncleanness in these relations are determined, not according to the greater or less defilement in them by sin, but according to the greater or less prominence of the carnal appearances in these relations: therefore, on this account, the female sex is that which most needed purification The natural consequences of the sexual relations continue with them the uncleanness for a longer time, and require more purifying; and in the birth of a female child the uncleanness remains longer than in that of a male. It is now evident also why a burnt and sin-offering must be made. Burnt-offerings, which betokened the renewal of the perfect surrender to God, were offered on every important event of life (cf. ch. iv.), not merely for particular sins, but for transgressions of the ritual law which were not of the nature of wilful perverse acts of disobedience, and yet were not altogether involuntary. This condition was, therefore, thus to be viewed, and by the sin-offering the remembrance of sin was kept alive.—Even among the heathen, women after child-birth were excluded from certain religious rites; but in this exclusion there was no reference to sin, but to that finite existence into which man entered by his birth, from which he passed by his death. This entrance into and passage out of life, was a disturbing of the order of nature, which for the restoration of concord needed an atonement, and so rendered persons unclean; *e.g.*, among the Greeks, in respect to the sacred rites of Hestia (Vesta, ch. vi. 9, note), which was the holy fire, the cause of life; and also of Artemis (Diana), who was Nature, the mother and nourisher of all: cf. Acts xix. 27, note. We could scarcely anywhere else meet with so great an outward similarity, and yet so decided an inward opposition, as we find in these laws about purification.

Ver. 2. *Have conceived.*—Heb., "brings forth seed," bears a child. In what follows a distinction is made between the male child and the female. The same expression occurs Gen. i. 11, for the bringing forth seed in plants.

Ver. 4. *Purifying*; *i.e.*, in the blood which purifies her; not, from which she is to be purified. The days of the flowing of blood are the days of purifying (cf. ver. 6), because the blood takes with it the uncleanness: this consists in the birth itself. The thirty-three days are naturally to be added to the seven (ver. 2), as the sixty-six to the fourteen, so that the time of separation on the birth of a male continued forty, on the birth of a female eighty days. It is self-evident that we are not to look for the reason of this in any bodily or medical cause.

Ver. 8. *Young pigeons.*—Cf. St Luke, ii. 24, note.

CHAPTER XIII.

Of all pollutions, that of leprosy is mentioned with especial detail—certainly not for the purpose of giving sanitary regulations, but by reference to this bodily evil to awaken an inward horror of sin, and its kingdom—death. From this way of viewing it arise the great care and minuteness with which this ailment was distinguished from all others of a similar kind. A deadly poison was not allowed to spread among the people of God. Everything smitten of God, and become subject to the dark, unclean dominion of death, was to be put away from the midst of them. From the carrying out of this principle, no doubt, important consequences as concerns the health would follow. It is somewhat remarkable, that of all sicknesses leprosy (elephantiasis) is distinguished as peculiarly unclean. In order to understand this, we must bear in mind that this fearful malady, which is indigenous in Egypt and Asia Minor, both in its deeply latent commencement and in its certain, nearly incurable progress and horrible effects, has nothing like itself, and so even by the Greeks was called " the first-born son of death." It is an ever-progressive dying. Its pollution, therefore, was of an equal character with that which resulted from touching the dead.— Egypt has ever been the main seat of this evil, from very early times to the present day. Moses could only from actual experience and from observation of the evil have been able to lay down the particular and accurate description in this chapter, and was the many wise regulations against it. Later observations have verified the accuracy and clearness of the account of the symptoms of the malady which distinguish it from other kindred diseases. Leprosy is a poison which often lies latent in the system for years, and shows itself in a skin disease. When inherited or produced by contagion, it causes death sometimes not until after the lapse of twenty years or more. The disease, for the most part, breaks out suddenly in the form of a small white spot or blotch, which arises often quite quickly under the influence of fear or some other emotion. Afterwards the spot extends and spreads; the skin sinks; the hair changes colour; the cellular membranes and fatter parts of the body gradually corrupt; the nerves are deadened; sensation is lost; melancholy, distressing dreams, despair, torment the sufferer; the breath stinks; digestion is destroyed; the deep-seated, fatal poison then seizes the joints; the whole limbs rot, and death comes slowly, though at last, very often, suddenly. Of the different species of this disease the white leprosy, (Heb., Zaraath) is the most noted in the O. T. The black leprosy was probably Job's malady; and the tuberous kind (elephantiasis) is that mentioned, Deut. xxviii. 27, 35, as the sickness peculiarly Egyptian. All kinds of this malady are, as a rule, hereditary, and continue to the third and often fourth generation, when it then merges into some peculiar appearances, as in the breath, of the teeth, in languor and feebleness of body. The leprosy which is really seated in the constitution and has broken out, is regarded even to this day as incurable. The leper is therefore looked on as already a child of death. He is excluded from all communion with his fellow-man. He must go about as a person in deep mourning (ver. 45), and alone; his dwelling must be without the camp (ver. 46). But as every contact with the leper did not produce the uncleanness, nor even a very close one, therefore all these regulations are to be regarded as of a religious character and not as medical precautions.—Cf., on the miraculous healing of the lepers, what is said St Matt. viii. 1, introd. As we are there reminded, this disease is to be regarded as an image of sin, which view may be followed up deeply and widely.

Ver. 2. *A rising.*—Those little spots which sometimes, though very rarely, pass away.

Bright spot.—A white spot, which is a symptom of the white leprosy.

Plague of leprosy.—The leprosy has in Hebrew the very descriptive name "scourge;" fully, "blow of the scourge." So completely was this evil regarded as the greatest of all Divine visitations.

The priests.—We see from this duty which was imposed on the priests, that their office necessarily required some knowledge of medicine, and must have made them the physicians of the people, as we find was the case with the heathen nations. But their business in the matter was essentially a religious one; and we do not find that in other maladies they had such functions to discharge.

Ver. 3. *His flesh;* i.e., when it is seen that the tumour goes deeper than the skin, presses into the flesh.

Unclean.—Lit., "defile him." As the expressions "to purify," "to sanctify," often occur for declaring "clean," "holy." Under the term is implied that the judgment of the representative of God was the judgment of God Himself.

Ver. 6. *Be clean.*—It is remarkable that modern physicians prescribe just the same mode of proceeding in the examination of this malady. "It is difficult," says one of them, "to pronounce a decided opinion upon this disease, until the spot has increased to the size of a bean. It often happens that the spot remains in the same state a long while, and does not widen, since the progress is quick or slow according to the constitution. If it remains stationary judgment must be deferred. Even in the event of its turning out to be a harmless eruption, still the least degree of legal purification must follow, since the mere suspicion has placed the person infected in contact with the kingdom of the Impure.

Ver. 8. *Leprosy.*—There is here a certain mean observed in the severity of the inquiry and exclusion. He is secluded and watched long enough for the eruption to show whether it be of a malignant character or not: if it should be so, then the pronouncing clean goes for nothing.

Ver. 10. *Raw flesh.*—Heb.: "A spot of raw flesh." In one kind of leprosy there is no moisture in the ulcer, but under it a thick skin and red tuberous flesh, which sometimes grows to the size of a mulberry.

Ver. 13. *He is clean.*—This is the case in the same kind of leprosy when the disease comes to an end. Then the whole skin from head to foot is covered with white scabs like scales, which fall off in the course of ten or twelve days, upon which the skin becomes clean and the disease is over. This is one of the very rare cases when, by the complete outbreak of the poison at once, the body gets freed from it. The same holds good of the change of the red, raw flesh into white, of which there is mention immediately after.

Ver. 23. *Pronounce him clean.*—The case, therefore, is that of an ulcer which at first is harmless, and is not seated in the flesh but only in the skin, but in which afterwards something of a leprous character is visible.

Ver. 24. *Reddish.*—Lit.: "And there arise a suppurating spot of burning, reddish or white;" *i.e.*, a pustule with white matter, which on the outside has a reddish or white hue. Such small or harmless sores very easily turn into leprosy.

Ver. 30. *Head or beard.*—The leprosy broke out very frequently in the hair, and there were some peculiar previous symptoms, for which cause it is particularly treated of.

Ver. 39. *He is clean.*—They are harmless pustules—head-disease.

Ver. 45. *Upper lip.*—Heb., "the beard veiled." This was also a sign of mourning.

Unclean, unclean.—He shall warn any one approaching him from a distance with these words.

Ver. 46. *Without the camp.*—So afterwards was Miriam excluded from the camp, Num. xii. 15; and in like manner, at a later period, was King Uzziah or Azariah obliged to dwell in a house apart (2 Kings xv. 5). In the synagogues, the lepers had particular seats appointed them: they were obliged to enter the first and to leave the last. It is remarkable how well even the Jewish teachers themselves understood the symbolical meaning of this regulation; for thus speaks one of them on this place. "If a man considers this, he will be humbled and ashamed on account of his sin; since every sin is a leprosy, a spot upon his soul. And, as it is written of the leper, his clothes shall be rent, etc.; in like manner, the defilement on his soul, which is far removed from the holiness on high, shall equally separate him from the camp of Israel. And if a man turns to repentance in order to be cleansed from his spots, behold he is clean from his leprosy, but otherwise the leprosy remains clinging to his soul; and in this world, and in the world to come, he is far removed from the whole camp there above until he has become cleansed." The law instructs how to know leprosy, pronounces the leper unclean, shuts him out from the congregation, but it has not power to heal him: this was reserved for the Son of God, to cleanse bodily in figure, and spiritually also, as the true Redeemer from sin and its consequences.

Ver. 59. *Unclean.*—In the East, similar appearances to those of the leprosy in human beings which are found in trees, houses, and garments, are called by the same name as the human disease. We are not in this to suppose anything about an infection from men, of which not a word is said. The thing itself has not yet been sufficiently inquired into in the East; and, therefore, there are only suppositions on the subject, of which the most probable is this,—that the spots here described in woollen stuff, originate in the so-called morling (dead wool), that which comes from sheep who have died of disease. Others suppose the spots to be those caused by insects. But, whatever may be the reason of this mischief in wool, linen, and leather, in any case this law is not to be regarded as a police regulation against the use of damaged articles, but as a command which would place before the eyes of the people an image of sin and of death in a fretting disorder, which raised general disgust.

CHAPTER XIV.

The purifying of the leper has an affinity to some other customs—to the purifying of those who are unclean by touching the dead (Num. xix.); to the sin-offering on the day of atonement (ch. xvi.); to the covenant offering (Exod. xxiv.); to the sacrifice of the Nazarite who is made unclean (Num. vi.); and to the consecration of the priest (Exod xxix.); which customs are to be considered in their significance, and carefully to be compared. The purifying of the lepers consisted of two degrees; the first made it possible for the person to be cleansed, again to enter the camp, and to be received into the congregation of the people (ver. 1–8); the second reconciled him to the Lord; and was made in different manners, according as he was rich enough or not, to bring the greater sacrifice (ver. 9–31). As the leper was altogether regarded as a dead person, the sin-offering was made for his first purification, like to that of the red heifer, outside the camp. The first bird killed for the purification was intended to receive the impurity to itself. Together with its life, streaming forth in the blood, was the uncleanness poured out. The blood was mingled with the purest, that is, with running water, in order, together with the peculiar atonement, to point especially to the *purifying*. With this was mixed cedar-wood, as the most vigorous of all woods; and hyssop, a frequent emblem of purification; and scarlet-coloured wool, the most brilliant among the sacred colours of the tabernacle (Exod. xxv. 4), in order to strengthen the life-renewing, purifying, sanctifying, power of the blood and water. But this was not enough. The atonement must be made equal to the greatest of all—that on the day of atonement. A second living bird was dipped into the blood, and then let go free, in order to carry away the uncleanness altogether. The leper (as in the case of the covenant sacrifice) was sprinkled with the blood, as a sign of his appropriating to himself the atonement and renewing the covenant with God (Exod. xxiv. 8). The whole solemnity is not called "sacrifice," since it did not take place in a sacred place; nor was the leper yet in a position to appear before the Lord. For that purpose he must again be received into the congregation of Israel. Still, this purification had the characteristics of a sin-offering, as is seen by a comparison with the (expressly so-called) sin-offering of the red-heifer; and also shown by the expression to "cleanse" (or "to atone for" "entsündigen") in the case of purifying the houses, ver. 49. After the former leper had undergone other cleansings, he now again entered the congregation of the Israelites, yet at first after a more external manner. Now he must bring his trespass-offering—which kind of offering was here altogether in its place; because the leprosy was not of the nature of a personal moral guilt, but rather had been a disturbance in the life of the people—a robbery, for a time, of one of God's subjects, for which restitution must be made (cf. ch. v., introd., and especially ch. v. 15, etc.). In this particular, that this offering was a trespass and not a sin-offering, the act resembles the purification of a Nazarite, and is distinguishable from the consecration of the priests. It differs from the latter in the circumstance, that no thank-offering takes place, and the trespass-offering precedes the others, the reason of which is obvious from the nature of the relation. But now was the person to be purified (just as the priests at their consecration), to be touched on the ear, the thumb, and the toe, with blood and oil. The pieces of the sacrifices also must be waved, doubtless, in order to mark the act as a new consecration—a reinstatement among the people of priests (Exod. xviii. 6). After what has been said on the subject of the purifications in general, and the leprosy in particular, in the introd. to chs. xi.–xiii., the meaning of the purification which takes place here cannot be doubtful. Like the uncleanness of women after childbirth, the leprosy was not in the individual a personal, criminal, evil; but as death is the punishment of sin, so is this malady as the main instrument of death, a continual memento of the general guilt of all men, and of the sin of the particular person; hence the necessity of a symbolical purification, and of a renewed consecration after the person had been received into the congregation of the living.

Ver. 5. *Running water;* i.e., as the sequel shows, in such a manner, that the living water (drawn from a brook or stream) was put into a vessel. Water is the often recurring emblem of the purifying and reviving power of the Holy Spirit, cf. St John vii. 39, note. We are reminded by the circumstance, that the purifying was by water and blood, of Him who came "not by water only, but by water and blood," 1 St John v. 6, note.

Ver. 7. *Seven times.*—To this, as to the offering of the red heifer, do those passages of the N. T. refer, which speak of the sprinkling with the blood of Christ, Heb. ix 14, ch. xii. 24; 1 St Pet. i. 2. Seven times is also here the number of the covenant, which also occurs in the case of the cleansing of Naaman, who dipped himself seven times in Jordan; 2 Kings v 10.

Loose.—This custom is expressly explained in the case of the goat on the day of atonement (ch. xvi. 21, 22); namely, that the sins are thereby to be borne away. This meaning of the action is clear, from the circumstance that the bird has been dipped in the blood and water which is intended entirely to take away the uncleanness. The explanation altogether misses its meaning, which supposes that the resurrection of the leper from his social death is thereby intended, since the main point in the same, the restoration to the congregation is certainly not signified by this action, for the bird flies into the open air and does not return again. Rather, the restoration follows as a matter of course, so soon as all hindrances are removed. This is just now represented by the flying away of the bird. This meaning of the letting the bird loose is, moreover, confirmed by the command to perform the same act in the case of purifying the houses, ver. 53.

Ver. 8. *His hair.*—Because the leprosy has especially its seat in the hair. But this was not a sanitary regulation, and was not done in order to show that a man was clean, but it had the symbolical significance of a sacred purification. For the same reason the Egyptian priests shave the whole body.

Seven days.—Partly because he was not yet fully clean; and this was to be denoted outwardly, but more particularly, in order that the person cleansed might not again, in this time, defile himself afresh: according to ch. xv. 18.

Ver. 18. *Make an atonement.*—Upon all this cf. Exod. xxix. 19.

Ver. 19. *Uncleanness.*—Here, therefore, is the atonement clearly distinct from the removal of, and compensation for, the trespass.

Ver. 21. *To be waved.*—This also, as in the consecration of the priest, Exod. xxix. 24; only that there the pieces of the sacrifice are laid in the hands of the priest to be consecrated, and are waved by him, which here, naturally, the priest must do for the leper.

Ver. 35. *In the house.*—The disease of the houses, or of the walls, of which mention is here made, is, probably, one still frequent in Egypt, and, therefore, at that time, sufficiently well known to the Israelites. The great abhorrence with which leprosy was regarded, had probably long ago directed their attention to this malady in houses; and so the regulations on this subject are naturally annexed to the laws respecting leprosy in the human being.—It is supposed, almost with certainty, that by this leprosy of the walls, we are to understand what is called by us the salpetre rot. It is thus described:—"It is found especially on damp walls, which stand on wet ground, or which have not been sufficiently dried. It appears on the walls in the shape of a ring, causes the mortar to break out like great boils, and eats it away so that it falls out and leaves great holes. Green and other spots, likewise are observable on such walls. If the dampness increases, the saltness passes on to the water which flows down the walls. All which stands in the neighbourhood of the wall decays. If the mortar is removed, and the house fresh plastered, it is of no avail, the wall-rot returns again. The only remedy is to pull down the wall, and to build another in its place, of dry brick."

Ver. 36. *In the house.*—At first the furniture of the house is not yet attacked by the disease, and is not unclean.

Ver. 40. *Unclean place.*—It is clear from this, and also from the uncleanness attached to the men who touch the house, that the evil should be represented as not simply shameful, but as a type of sin, and so far an object of inward abhorrence. The ashes of the sin-offering were put in a clean place, this dust in an unclean.

Ver. 41. *To be scraped.*—Also the rest of the wall, besides the place manifestly leprous, in order to see whether, under the plaster, the poison might not also show itself on the stones.

Ver. 53. *Shall be clean.*—The surprising part, which at first sight appears in this, is, that a sin-offering was to be made for the house, as also for the purification of a leprous human being; but it leads again to the conclusion, that every disorder which sin has caused among men—and leprosy was peculiarly regarded as such—should be covered by God's means of healing—withdrawn from His sight—and so His grace again turned towards man. The sin of man has, as it were, here taken a bodily form, and entered into his dwellings, just as in the unclean animals it manifests itself in the creation. This sight, offensive before God, is to be removed from before Him, the uncleanness of the house to be exterminated by the most powerful means of purification, and to be taken entirely away, and thus the house to be restored to an object well-pleasing in His sight.

CHAPTER XV.

Hitherto the greatest degrees of pollutions—by means of unclean meats, of child-birth, of leprosy—have been spoken about: now the lower degrees of pollution follow, which also require only a less kind of cleansing and atonement. The cases which immediately succeed, refer generally to the sexual relations; partly, as the first and last, to those which have the character of disease; partly, as the two middle cases, to those which are natural, but which still point to a certain condition of weakness and disorder in human nature. The reason and the significance of all these pollutions has already been explained, chap. xii., introd.

Ver. 12. *Rinsed with water.*—It would be a misunderstanding of these regulations to suppose, that in such cases the fear of infection was the reason of declaring the person unclean. Similar rules are afterwards given respecting the blood-flow in women, where it is impossible to think of infection or any bodily harm. The commands rather refer to the holy awe with which all things relating to sexual intercourse should be regarded, and to the horror of every irregular appearance in the same.

Ver. 13. *Shall be clean.*—Here also, as in the case of the leper, we see two degrees of purification: the first cleanses a person rather outwardly and bodily, and so far as men are concerned, but does not excuse him from that before the Lord, which can only be obtained by the second.

Ver. 15. *For his issue.*—By the first is the interrupted relation to God to be restored; by the second the renewed surrender to God to be completed.

Ver. 18. *Until the even.*—In both the cases here named the slightest degree of uncleanness took place, which was to be removed without atonement or purification—merely by the lapse of an interval of time. And, in respect to both (the first can happen altogether involuntarily, and, therefore, be without sin), it is well to remark, that neither on the man or the woman is the least reflection thrown, nor is it maintained that their act has, in the remotest sense of the word, anything sinful in it. Children were highly prized as a gift of God—the unmarried condition is nowhere praised, but, on the contrary, is esteemed a Divine punishment and a disgrace, and, therefore, there could be nothing sinful in the procreation of children. But, in doing the acts here mentioned, a man ought well to consider that he is entering into a province which, more than any other, has become the seat of sin, and which, in its present condition, will cease with the removal of sin. He should, therefore, consider, while he obeys the most powerful passion of his fleshly nature, in an act in itself altogether innocent, that he may not, without preparation, venture to touch holy things which belong to God; that he ought not, without seriously composing his mind, and without a consciousness of his natural distance from God, to enter into communion with Him and with His congregation. What a wholesome influence on chastity and self-restraint must this law have exercised! Now, in figure, are Christians still exhorted not to come behind the people of the Old Covenant in this respect.

Ver. 19. *Seven days.*—The number of days which exceeds the

usual time, at least in our climate, appears to signify, that in the fixing of the duration, what is natural was not so much considered as the proper regard to the covenant of God which had been broken.

Ver. 24. *Unclean.*—For this kind of pollution also, as for that of ver. 16-18, no legal purification is prescribed—only during the continuance of it was the woman to withdraw herself from the congregation. The uncleanness last mentioned, if it took place wittingly, involved "the being cut off from the people," ch. xx. 18.

Ver. 25. *Unclean.*—Two cases: when it took place at an irregular time, or when it continued beyond the usual length.

Ver. 29. *Congregation.*—Just as in the case of the man, ver. 14.

Ver. 31. *Among them.*—This is the last reason of all these laws of purification, which, at the conclusion, is strongly brought forward. In the time of their uncleanness they shall not come in contact with the sanctuary, which, without separation, had been unavoidable.

CHAPTER XVI.

We now enter on the centre point of all the atonements and purifications which the law prescribes to the people, on the ordinance of the great day of atonement. Its name is literally the "day of atonements" (ch. xxiii. 27). The plural shows that it includes every other kind of atonement. It is called the "festival of festivals," the "sabbath of sabbaths," ver. 31. By the later Jews it was called "Joma," day, as the day of all days. As there was a higher, greater atonement, which was to take place in the holy place (ch. iv. 6, 17), so must this, the most important of all, be performed in the Holy of holies. It might not be made by a common priest, but only by the high priest, whose distinguishing office it was to offer it. And, on this day, he was to wear a particular dress, which, both by its colourlessness, was a remembrancer of the great solemnity of the day; and, by its whiteness, of the highest point of holiness on which he was standing, in order to atone for the sins of the people. Highly exalted as he was, he was still, at the same time, deeply humbled, since, before the atonement made for the people, he was obliged to reconcile himself and the whole priestly order to God. But the atonement for the people, which now took place, had the peculiarity, that a very remarkable addition was made to the sacrifice of atonement. Two goats were solemnly presented before the Lord for a sin-offering, which were separated into two parts. Lots were cast on the goats, the Lord Himself, who decides how the lot shall fall (Prov. xvi. 33), determined that one should be for Himself, to be slain; the other for the "Asasel" so in (Heb. v. 8, x. 26); *i.e.*, for the banished, rejected, driven out. Thrice thereupon the high priest goes into the Holy of holies: the first time with the golden censer, in order to take fire from the altar, and to raise a cloud of incense before the mercy-seat; the second time, in order to sprinkle the blood of his own bullock; and the third time, to sprinkle the blood of the goat, the people's sin-offering, upon and before the mercy-seat. When, then, all things of a sacred character have been cleansed, the High Priest, figuratively lays the sins of the people on the live goat, and causes him to be led by a man into the wilderness—into a "separated" land, in order that there as "Asasel," it may bear the sins of the whole congregation.—While all the other circumstances of the solemnity explain themselves, this remarkable addition to the sin-offering should be more closely examined. The sins of the people are already done away by the sin-offering of the first goat; but, in order to symbolize more forcibly its entire removal, were these sins, which were already forgiven, to be laid on the goat which was to be driven into a waste, *i. e.*, a "separated" land; *i.e.*, to be driven from a region which was inhabited and set apart by God's blessing, into one which was distant from, and rejected by, Him. That this goat is now considered as a person, an evil spirit, is very probable, by the opposite position of the two goats in the casting of lots (ver. 8). The Egyptians also, and the Persians, believed in an evil spirit which inhabited the desert neighbouring countries, Lybia, Turan, and they sent to him those offerings from the blessed valley of the Nile, from the kingdom of light—Iran. But in their case, the contrast which lay in the province of Nature, we find here in the kingdom of revelation to be altogether in the province of sanctity. The wilderness is only an emblem of death as the wages of *sin*. As Adam, after the fall, was obliged to till the ground out of which he was taken; Cain, after his crime, to wander into the desert barren land of Nod, which even, when cultivated, should give him no pleasure—in like manner, the "banished one," the rejected by God, dwells in a land which is altogether severed—in a desert land into which sin has brought him who has seduced man into sin. In later times, a purple-coloured thread was bound round the head of the live goat. All conceivable kinds of invectives were poured upon him; and the man who led him into the wilderness was obliged to throw him down a precipice. This last act (though it might likewise have its origin in superstition, which converted the symbolical into the actual) arose, perhaps, from a misconception which existed among the later Jews, to which the whole circumstance ought to have been a contradiction—as if the goat which was taken away was a sacrifice made to the devil, in order to pacify him, that he might not interfere with the blessing of the other sacrifice. But this solemnity contained the exact antidote to such sacrifices as were offered by the heathen to Typhon and other evil spirits, since both animals were presented before *the Lord*, and at *His* command the goat carried away the sins to Asasel, in order to remove them from the people. Whoever considered this must be vividly impressed with the conviction, that it was the Lord who sanctified His people, Who banished the scape goat, and now had afresh taken away all sin—that His people ought not to stand in the slightest relationship to an evil spirit, which could have no power over them. This great solemnity took place once a year, in order that an entire atonement might be offered for the sins of the whole year. But it must be repeated yearly; because the atonement could take place only in figure, only symbolically, since the High Priest himself was a sinner, and the sacrifice itself but the sacrifice of an animal. Now, once for all and for ever, has the sacrifice of His own life been offered to God by the sinless High Priest, and an eternal reconciliation been thereby effected. By this ceremony of the goats is the Christian reminded, that by the great atoning sacrifice on the cross sin has both been forgiven him, and likewise far removed from him as a member of Christ, into the far distant and separated land—into the kingdom of darkness.

Ver. 1. *Died.*—As the most important laws were revealed on marked occasions, so it appears also, that the death of Aaron's sons gave rise to this law. A deep impression of the inviolability of the sacred institutions of the Lord was thereby made. This impression, it was intended, should be kept alive and strengthened by the separation of the Holy of holies from all service excepting on the day of atonement. The command therefore commences at once with this point.

Ver. 2. *Mercy-seat.*—In all temples of the ancient world, there was an inner sanctuary, which bore the name, "unapproachable" (Adyton, Abaton), and into which alone consecrated persons were allowed to enter. Only there was this difference in Israel—the prohibition referred altogether to the sin of the people; in the case of the heathen, to the apparition of the Godhead, so overpowering to finite, circumscribed mortals; cf. Gen. xvi 13, note. The cloud in which the Lord appeared was the pillar of the cloud in which He had gone before the Israelites on their journey, and which sank down on the tabernacle at its consecration. It is not distinctly said that it rested perpetually on the mercy-seat, as the later Jews supposed (who called it "Shechina," the dwelling of God among His people). Notwithstanding that God appeared in a cloud, yet was the high priest obliged to envelop the whole Holiest place in a cloud of incense, that he might not behold too near the veiled majesty of God.

Ver. 4. *Holy garments.*—The priests among the Egyptians also wore linen garments.

Ver. 6. *Make atonement.*—On which occasion, according to later Jewish tradition, he is said to have uttered the words, " O Lord I have transgressed, done amiss, and sinned in Thy sight, I and my house! O Lord cover my transgression that I have sinned against Thee, I and my house, as it stands written in the law of Moses Thy servant, since on this day is the atonement, etc." (ver. 30).

Ver. 8. *Scapegoat.*—Heb., "And a lot for Asasel." This word was rendered by the old Greek translation, "the remover away;" and the heathen idea of a God, who removes evil away, got mingled with the expression. Afterwards this translation was so misunderstood, as if it were meant, "the sent away;" and so arose the explanation of the "free goat" (as it is in Luther's version). But the word has rather the sense of an adjective, "the removed far away, the banished." In the O. T. there is rarely mention of the devil. In the older books only in a dark, indistinct manner; no doubt, for this cause, that the people, with their inclination to heathenism, might not, by the doctrine, be misled to the notion of an evil deity. And, therefore, at the fall, the devil appears under the form of a serpent, "which God made," Gen. iii. 1, and here, under the indistinct, mysterious name, "the removed," rejected. He is not put in juxtaposition with the Lord; but the goat which is sent to him is a part of the sin-offering which is placed before the Lord, and which removes all uncleanness out of the midst of His people, into the unclean, into the devil's kingdom. In like manner, in the offering at the purification of the leper, one of the two birds removed far away his uncleanness.

Ver. 10. *An atonement with him.*—Namely, the goat; as afterwards, the holy place (ver. 16), and the altar (ver. 18), must be atoned for, because those who dwelt about them were sinners, and, in the atonement made, they were to have a vivid remembrancer of their own sin. In this most complete offering of purification, whatever of the effects and consequences of sin still clung to the goat, as to everything earthly, must be wiped away. And this was done, by its being presented before the Lord.

Wilderness.—The wilderness, as the image of the dead on earth, was regarded as the dwelling-place of evil spirits, Isa. xiii. 21; St Matt. xii. 43; Rev. xviii. 2.

Ver. 11. *For his house.*—His descendants, the priestly family. In the case of the following high priests this was the collected priestly order.

Ver. 12. *Sweet incense.*—Heb., "Incense work of a sweet savour." He should spread abroad the savour of holy acceptable prayer. This it was which was to cover the mercy-seat.

Ver. 16. *Remaineth.*—Altogether he was to sprinkle eight times—once on the mercy-seat itself, then seven times before it. The completion of the atonement on this great day of all atonements, had reference to the sacred places themselves, which had been polluted by the sins of the people. The first blood sprinkling was to cleanse the mercy-seat itself; the second, seven times, the Holy of holies, from the sins of the priests; as the sprinkling eight times, which followed upon this, was intended to cleanse it from the sins of the people. The main symbolical idea of the whole tabernacle was that of a dwelling of God among His people, which drew nigh to Him in the person of the common priests as far as the holy place; in that of the high priest, as far as the Holy of holies. As all these persons were sinners, they polluted the holy places, and their defilements must be covered by the atoning blood. But the priests, appear in this case, in a double character,—they have defiled the sanctuary in the first instance as individual, sinful men, and next as mediators of the people, and both must be atoned for.—This significant type tells the Christian that there is nothing in itself so holy as not to need intercession and atonement. God's own ordinances, as the preaching of His word, the sacraments, by means of which He dwells among us, ought never to be approached without the consciousness that, only through the power of Christ's atoning blood, are they pure to us, and the channels of grace. "Since whoso eateth and drinketh unworthily, eateth and drinketh damnation to himself" (1 Cor. xi. 29). Thus, here we have the greatest and most momentous type of Jesus Christ, "whom God had set forth to be a mercy-seat in His blood." He is the mercy-seat sprinkled with blood, the sight of which affords to faith the certainty of the full forgiveness of sins.

Ver. 21. *Head of the goat.*—A similar, yet at the same time an essentially different, custom took place in Egypt. Herodotus narrates, ii. 39, "After they have brought a drink-offering and have called on the god, they kill the animal and cut off its head. They then flay the body; but on the head they lay a number of curses, and either give it away, when possible, to a stranger, or throw it into the river. The curses are of this kind—"That if any evil impend over them, the sacrifices, or the whole of Egypt, that it may be laid on this head." According to Jewish tradition, the high priest prayed thus, "O Lord, Thy people have done amiss, have transgressed and sinned in Thy sight. Be Thou propitiated for the misdeeds, the transgressions, the sins, which Thy people, the house of Israel, have committed. As it is written in the law of Thy servant Moses, when it is said, For on that day shall the priest," etc., ver. 30.

Ver. 22. *Wilderness.*—According to the tradition no one might at the last be present with the man. He led the goat up a steep hill, threw him down, and before he had reached half down the hill, he was broken in pieces. This superstition must have arisen from the return of a goat which had been sent out into the wilderness.

Ver. 24. *His garments.*—His priestly robes—the garments of his office.

An atonement.—The atonement through the burnt-offering was a peculiar one, which was not rendered superfluous by the sin-offering, since in the burnt-offering reference was not so much made to actual transgressions and their removal, as to the entire render and sacrifice to God, cf. ch. i. introd.

Ver. 28. *Into the camp.*—It is plain that these two men are on this account obliged to purify themselves, because the one had taken away, the other had burnt, the animal upon which the sins were laid, and which was therefore unclean. We find even among the heathen the same custom, that such sacrifices which were the averters of evil omens rendered the offerer unclean, and, consequently, he was obliged to wash himself. The reason that the high priest, by slaying the sin-offering and sprinkling the blood, did not render himself unclean, was this, that the very streaming forth of the sin-laden life took away the sin, while the sprinkling of blood was a sign of death, having fully ensued. The remainder of the animal, which no consecrated priest might consume (ch. vi. 26) was burnt outside the camp, and there in an unhallowed place. That the sprinkling of blood must take place in a holy place, was on account of the reverence due to the sacrifice, as generally in the case of the sin-offerings, both the sanctity of the offering and of the act of sacrifice (it is the "Most Holy" (ch. vi. 29); and the uncleanness of the remaining part are at the same time represented. Here, also, the burning of the fat must not be omitted; in order, by the offering up of the finest and best part of the victim purified from blood, to betoken the renewal of the self-sacrifice of the sinner. The sin-offering was made for the people on this great day, in other respects, altogether according to the directions given: ch. xiv. 13, *i.e.,* the flesh is not eaten by the priests, because the blood was taken into the sanctuary. Since here this higher degree of atonement was both required, and had actually taken place, there was no necessity for the sacrifice to be eaten by the priests.

Ver. 29. *Afflict your souls.*—With deep fasting and mourning were the whole people to prepare themselves for the great act by which the Lord did away all their sins. In what these exercises of humiliation consisted, the law does not further tell us. Tradition says, that fasting formed a great part of it, together with abstinence from ablution, anointing, wearing of shoes, and conjugal intercourse; all signs of mourning, which are mentioned elsewhere (ablution and anointing, 2 Sam. xii. 20, 21; going barefoot, 2 Sam. xv. 30; the last, 2 Sam. xi. 11). But fasting was regarded so much as the main thing, that, Acts xxvii. 9, the whole day is called from it. Fasting was a religious practice, which is met with among all people. On the great feast of Isis at Busiris, in Egypt, a fast preceded the most solemn sacrifice; and it was accompanied by self-torture of other kinds. But, with the heathen, these would represent symbolically man's sympathy with suffering nature, and were therefore properly a sinking down and yielding to the world; whereas, among the Israelites the fasts, in conjunction with the general confession, were the outward marks of mourning for sin; and, at the same time, through mortification of the fleshly lusts, the means of discipline to direct the spirit with less hindrance to dwell on the spiritual object of the solemnity: they therefore served the purpose of freeing the spirit from the service of the flesh and the world. This fast is the only one commanded in the law. In after times others were added, *e.g.*, that in remembrance of the destruction of Jerusalem by the Chaldees, and there were other extraordinary general and private fast-days. It is a deficiency in every religious community to be without such general days of humiliation.

Ver. 31. *Sabbath of rest.*—Lit., "the Sabbath of sabbaths:" the feast of feasts. But this word does not signify merely the greatest Sabbath, since it stands, Exod. xxxi. 15, of every weekly Sabbath, in order to express the full religious rest.

Ver. 32. *Father's stead.*—The existing high priest: cf. Exod. xxix. 7, note.

CHAPTER XVII.

It was of the greatest consequence for a people just released from heathen bondage, like the Israelites, that it should possess only one centre of public worship—only one sacred place. There was nothing so likely to promote the polytheism of Nature-worship, as that every place should be regarded as holy, according to its natural peculiarities, its situation, its historical associations, the customs of its inhabitants, nay, even according to the prevailing different notions of the Divine Being. By these means a multitude of deities would be produced. But, without unity of worship, the people, so long as it was without a king, could not be kept together as one state. And so, in after times, this "sacrificing on high places," always was the beginning of apostasy to false worship (cf. Exod. xxv., introd.). In order, therefore, now to oppose effectually the tendency to this, it was commanded that the Israelites should not only not sacrifice animals without the fore-court of the tabernacle, but should not kill animals for food elsewhere. Hence, of every animal that was killed, the fat was to be burnt, the breast and the shoulder given to the priest, and the rest to be eaten as a sacrificial meal. This law was abrogated before the entrance into Canaan (Deut. xii. 15, 22), as naturally it could not be observed there. The law is an example for all times, reminding us that all food is sanctified to us by thanksgiving and prayer: cf. 1 Tim. iv. 4, 5, note.

Ver. 4. *Imputed.*—It shall be reckoned to him as if he had committed a murder.

Peace-Offerings.—The thank-offerings only are mentioned, because these alone were connected with sacrificial feasts.

Ver. 7. *Unto devils.*—For "devils," stands in the Heb. the word "goats." Animal worship was spread throughout the whole of Egypt. As the constellations and stars were very early distinguished by the names of animals, so was the land as it were a symbolic mirror of the heaven. Thus, a particular sacred animal was worshipped in every district. In its peculiar characteristics was seen a form of natural life; and in its bodily condition were represented the different changes of nature. In a north-easterly district of Egypt, which was named from the town Mendes, which again had its name from the goat-deity Mendes, not far from the ancient capital Tanis, and the land of Goshen, a goat was worshipped, and a living animal of this kind always kept in the temple. The abominations connected with this worship are unspeakably horrible, but are fully authenticated; and the Egyptian priesthood held it in such esteem, that every one who aspired to the office of priest must first be initiated into its mysteries. The Israelites lately come out of Egypt, were at that time given to this idolatry, and practised it secretly in the wilderness. In later times they appear to have connected with it notions of goblins, in the form of goats, who haunted the wilderness, and laid in wait for women (Isa. xiii. 21, ch. xxxiv. 14); and hence the translation, "field-devils" (in our version " devils"). Of the proneness of the Israelites to Egyptian idolatry during the passage through the wilderness Amos speaks, v. 25, 26.—The words, "with whom they have gone a whoring," means literally, "after whom they go a whoring," or after whom they run with adulterous desire. In the words themselves there is no reference to the impure lusts which were practised in that worship: cf. Exod. xxxi. 15, note.

A statute for ever.—The pith of this statute was the unity of Divine worship; the appointment that sacrifice should be made nowhere else except before the tabernacle. The mere external part, on the contrary, was the command to offer in sacrifice all flesh which was killed. The latter command has very little that was burdensome in the wilderness, where the Israelites lived chiefly on manna.

Ver. 10. *Eateth blood.*—This prohibition occurred before in ch. vii. 26-29. Here the reason is more fully given.

Ver. 11. *For the soul.*—Literally, "since the blood atones *through* the soul," the soul which is therein is the ransom, the means of atonement. The meaning of these words in conjunction with what follows is this: "The soul is the seat of desire and feeling, of pleasure and pain, and as such the seat of sin in the individual man, and at the same time the especial recipient of the punishment of sin—evil and death. In the body the blood is the seat of the soul—it is that which gives life to the body, and as soon as it streams forth life ceases. The harmless animal soul which lives in the blood of the animal, God has now given in the place of the sin-laden human soul to be (symbolically) a means of atonement for the sinner; so that when its life is poured out to death in its blood, the punishment of sin is removed from man. The prohibition of eating blood was promulgated originally when permission was given to eat animal flesh, and was enforced as a preventive against ferocity, cruelty, and murder (Gen. ix. 4, note). Now, on the more perfect establishment of the service of sacrifice, a still deeper significance is attached to the prohibition. The symbol of the channel of your most sacred relation to God, the most holy part of your most holy acts of worship, that which the believing Israelite can never regard without reverence and awe, may ye not profane by any common use.

Ver. 13. *Cover it with dust.*—A hunted wild animal was to be killed on the spot, and his blood poured out; but even then there should remain a religious reverence towards its blood. It was to be covered with earth, that it might not be licked up by any other animal. No blood should be profaned where man could prevent it.

Ver. 15. *Eateth.*—Obviously, unwittingly, since a wilful sin of the kind was punished with death.

Ver. 16. *His iniquity.*—To bear his iniquity, to expect the punishment thereupon. Here, as in so many places where the cutting off from the people is threatened, we are not thereby to understand any distinct judicial punishment, but a threat of a Divine chastisement, either that of death, or of some lighter kind.

CHAPTER XVIII.

This chapter forms by itself a complete whole. On the laws concerning sacrifice and symbolical purifications, which conclude with the ordinance for the full atonement on the great day of atonement, there follows a series of commandments which again appertain to the moral life. First, and especially, the prohibition of incest, under which is included both the act without marriage as well as with marriage; since, although the conclusion of the marriage is not expressly mentioned (this is done in the similar passage, ch. xx. 14), and the words used about the crime rather imply unchastity, yet verses 17 and 19 clearly prove that only marriage can be intended, and those words are purposely used in order to point out wherein lay the particular abomination of such a connection. As reason for the prohibition of these marriages in a too near relationship, we find nothing assigned beyond this very degree of relationship itself—" She is thy flesh—thy mother, thy sister"—at first in general terms, ver. 6, and then in the particular instances. The meaning of the reason is this—that by marriage the nearest relations of kinsmanship would be disturbed. The daughter, the sister, cannot at the same time be daughter or sister and wife; and without the strict prohibition of such marriage, the domestic life would altogether forfeit its sanctity, and be continually exposed to the greatest danger of disorder through lust. The family relationship is itself ordained by God. It is the birth-place of the children of God—the first school, and generally the source, of all chastity and good manners. Any injury inflicted on it would undermine the temporal and eternal welfare both of individuals and of the people. In this lies the abomination of incest. This is the reason of that natural horror of it which God has implanted in us. This is the reason that, among all nations, marriage within certain degrees was forbidden, though the laws of the most moral nations wavered in respect to the exact boundaries. This is the reason that such marriages in degrees of near relationship as cannot be called exactly forbidden, still excite in us a feeling of aversion. Because this was the reason of the forbidden degrees, we see also why, in the family of the first men, when there was as yet no difference between family and people, brothers and sisters might marry without sin; while, at the same time, the history of Abraham seems to show that his marriage with his half-sister must have had something very strange in the eyes of the Canaanites and Egyptians, who were yet at that time very corrupt, and, according to the testimony of the portion of Scripture before us, in later times practised these very abominations. And even Isaac, by giving out that Rebecca was his sister, wished to make it incredible that she could be his wife (Gen. xxvi. 7).—In these commandments, also, we must distinguish between the essential and non-essential. It cannot be proved that their literal acceptance is binding on Christians. But since the forbidden degrees can by no means be far extended, and in the settlement of them a tender regard should always be paid to the sanctity of relationship, and since there is no especial reference to the people and the time when they were given,—for these causes every Christian legislature acts wisely in keeping closely to these commands, and in not permitting a departure from them.

Ver. 4. *The Lord your God.*—The permission of marriage in near relationship, which occurs among the heathen nations, usually stands in close connection with the teaching of their religion, which mentioned (though, for the most part, under the veil of figurative language) deeds of this kind of their gods. Philo Judæus, who lived in Egypt in the time of our Saviour, says, concerning the prohibition of marriage with a sister: "Solon of Athens permitted marriage between halfbrothers and sisters of the same father only, but not among those of the same mother: the Lacedæmonian lawgiver just the reverse. The Egyptians, on the other hand, overstepping the scrupulousness of the two, went further in licentiousness, and permitted all brothers and sisters to marry, both the half and those who were related on both sides—and not merely the younger ones, but those of the same age, and older; nay, often even twins, whom nature from their birth had severed, were by licentious lust brought into an ill-sorted union, a jarring harmony" (de leg. spec. p. 780). Diodorus expressly maintains (i. 27), "The Egyptians gave this law against the general custom of nations, because Isis had been so fortunate in this." The Lord, therefore, particularly reminds His people that they had nothing to do with the idolatrous worship of Egypt, and therewith takes from them the ground on which these immoral customs were built.

Ver. 5. *Live in them.*—Shall be blessed in this world, and in the world to come. The keeping of the commandments is nothing else than the truly divine, and therefore blessed life. But it is not here said that a man is able to become blessed by observance of the commandments.

Ver. 6. *Near of kin.*—Literally, "no one shall approach to any flesh of his flesh." The repeated word "flesh," are in the Hebrew two separate but synonymous expressions (scheër basar), which are intended to betoken the fleshy union, as Gen. ii. 23. Men stand in relation to "their flesh" in the divinely appointed connection of father, brother, etc., which they may not tread under foot. The general prohibition is first given, and then is more particularly mentioned what is to be esteemed as "his flesh."

To uncover.—The connection of the nearest relations with one another is derived from birth; and therefore the whole province of the sexual relations among them is to be esteemed sacred. They are to keep far away from it, otherwise they trench on the family sanctuary, the common ground of union.

Ver. 7. *She is thy mother.*—" And she would cease to be so by this thy abomination: thou wouldest thereby destroy the sacred relationship." For this reason, the unwitting crime of Ædipus appeared such a monstrous thing even to the Greeks, that the mother thought she must atone for it by death, the son, by the loss of his eyes. He thus declared himself unworthy any longer to behold the temples of the gods. In these prohibitions the man is continually addressed with "Thou:" the marriage of the daughter with the father is not therefore here forbidden; but this is regarded as something so utterly horrible that it is not mentioned, as it did not occur even among the Canaanites and Egyptians. "The father's nakedness" is that of the mother, who belongs to the father.

Ver. 8. *Father's wife.*—Therefore, after the death of the father, the step-mother was not to be married, because she was one with the father; and even after death the parental relationship is not destroyed.

Ver. 9. *Daughter of thy father.*—Half-sister by father or mother. It is remarkable, that here the very kind of marriage is forbidden in which Abraham lived with Sarah (according to Gen. xx. 12). Here is one more proof how, from the mere silence of Holy Scripture in respect to an action, we are by no means to infer its approbation of it: cf. Gen. xlix. 4, note.

Born at home; i.e., born of a wife with whom thy father lives at home, or of one with whom he cohabits away from home. Relationship from a wife or concubine shall equally hinder the union.

Ver. 11. *Her nakedness.*—It would be surprising if the prohibition to marry the half-sister from one father, which is already expressed in ver. 9, were repeated here. We must then suppose that this marriage—the marriage of Abraham and Sarah—required a double and altogether unmistakeable prohibition. But even then it would be strange that ver. 10, containing another command, should intervene. It is, therefore, more correctly supposed that the words are thus to be connected: "Thou shalt not uncover the shame of the daughter of the wife of thy father (she is the child of thy father, and is thy sister)." Then, the properly so-called step-sister (comprivegna) would be meant, and the marriage between children brought up together be forbidden. This may be well imagined, in consideration of the strong prominence given in the Mosaic law to the paternal dignity and authority, so that the child of his wife was fully regarded as his own child; and therefore the marriage of his child with this child would be forbidden.—Although, on account of the less degree of reverence paid to paternal authority among us, the law may not in the letter be binding on us, still this prohibition represents such marriages as very objectionable.

Ver. 14. *Thine aunt.*—From these three prohibitions the question has arisen, whether they were to be extended to cases of relationship on another side, which in point of nearness are equal; and so, not only whether marriage with paternal and maternal aunt was forbidden, and with the widow of the mother's brother, but likewise with the brother and sister's daughter, and the widow of the nephew, as well as of the mother's brother. Doubtless the prohibition is not to be extended to these cases. The reverence felt towards the father's sister was the cause that she was regarded as more nearly related to the nephew than, on the other side, the niece with the father's or mother's brother; and traces of the same view of relationship are found among the Arabs. The same holds good of the nephew's widow. But the brother of the mother did not belong any more to the family: his widow stood much farther than that of the father's brother. The question, whether such marriages are allowable among us, must be settled much less from the letter than from the spirit of this law. The decision will be directed according to the opinion, whether among us the relationship between uncle and niece is equally near with that between aunt and nephew. In this, as in other cases, the prohibition may properly be extended beyond the letter of the Mosaic law, as the Christian Church has everywhere done in this respect.

Ver. 16. *Brother's wife.*—The law declares this marriage as not permitted, but does not pronounce it to be incest. The punishment therefore of barrenness was only threatened against it (ch. xx. 21). It is evident that it was regarded not as in itself sinful, but as inexpedient, from the fact, that the so-called Levirat marriage (cf. Gen. xxxviii., introd.), which was in existence from very old times, is expressly confirmed in the law:

Deut. xxi. 10–14. As, however, the reasons for the Levirat marriage no longer exist with us, it may be more in accordance with the spirit of the Divine law to forbid marriage with a sister-in-law, as is done, for example, in England.

Ver. 18. *Vex her.*—Heb., "in addition to her," besides her. The meaning is by no means that the sister can permit it. Here also a marriage is forbidden in which the patriarch Jacob lived; but his history shows clearly the soundness of the law while polygamy still existed. If there are more wives than one, which is always the cause of jealousy and contention among them, it is better that the two or more should be taken from different families than that they should be nearly related. This, however, is only a sound by-reason, not the main reason of the law. This consisted in the fact, that as man and wife are to be regarded as one, the sister of the wife is to be esteemed the sister of the husband. This brotherly relationship ought to be regarded as holy and inviolable, like the case with the brother's widow.

Ver. 19. *Uncleanness.*—Ch. xx. 18. The punishment of being cut off from the people is threatened. The reason was no sanitary police one; but consisted in the position of the law to this condition, of which mention has been made, ch. xii., introd.

Ver. 20. *Defile.*—The punishment of adultery, see ch. xx. 10.

Ver. 21. *Molech.*—Molech (king) was an idol of the Ammonites and the Phœnicians likewise, which was also worshipped under the name Malkam or Milkom. Children were offered to it in fire as sacrifices. The Rabbins pretend it was a brazen figure, hollow within, with the head of a bull and outstretched arms, in which image a fire was kindled. The O. T. knows nothing of this. That the children were really burnt to Molech is quite clear from many passages (Jer. vii. 31, ch. xix. 5; Ps. cvi. 37). Molech appears to have been the same with the planet Saturn, which, according to Amos v. 20, the Israelites worshipped in the wilderness. The object of burning their children was not the purification of their souls, but in order to make the greatest atonement, and, by the offering of what was dearest, to avert harm. The surrender of the first-born to the Lord has some similarity to this notion (Exod. xiii. 1), only that in the offering of the first-born the abomination of human sacrifice is abolished. The worship of Molech is here not so much forbidden as human sacrifice, which was in defiance of the doctrine of man being made in the Divine image (cf. Gen. xxii. 1). This is evident from Deut. xviii. 5, where no mention is made of Molech, and from the above-quoted words of Jeremiah. For the punishment of this crime, see ch. xx. 2–5.

Ver. 22. *Abomination.*—The crime of the Sodomites (Gen. xix.) was very frequent among the Canaanites, and even practised in their idolatrous worship, as in the temples of Astoreth there were men appointed for the purpose. Deut. xxiii. 17; 1 Kings xiv. 24. The crime also mentioned in the next verse was practised in Egypt in their idol-worship.

Ver. 30. *I am the Lord your God.*—This general warning and threatening applies to the incest, adultery, unnatural sins, and the human sacrifices which are mentioned in the foregoing. The mention of human sacrifice occurs in the midst of completely sexual sins, on account of its unnatural and detestable character, since here the sacrifice of children by their parents (*thy* seed) is spoken of. Such a crime was a violation of God's holy ordinance in respect to families, just as much as were the other abominations mentioned in this chapter.

CHAPTER XIX.

The beginning and the end of this chapter shows that it forms a consistent whole. Scarcely any division can be found in it. It gives particular laws more in full, others already given are merely repeated, and much that is new is added. It contains particular statutes, as they were required for the settlement of difficult cases, or when the inroad of some evil custom was observed.

Ver. 5. *At your own will;* i.e., that ye may thereby be well-pleasing to God.

Ver. 8. *Cut off.*—Ch. vii. 16.

Ver. 14. *The Lord.*—These are commands, suggested by particular cases, which afford a sort of reflex of the general character. Every kind of advantage taken over innocent helplessness, in order to injure another, or for one's own benefit, is hereby forbidden. The addition, "shalt fear thy God," points out that He it is who has made the deaf and the blind, and who can punish every sinner in a like manner. In the latter point of view, this prohibition brings to our minds what is said St Luke xiii. 1.

Ver. 17. *Sin upon him.*—Upon this also is founded a saying of Christ, St Matt. xviii. 15–17. No one is to bear a secret grudge against his neighbour, but to tell him of his sin; otherwise he has part in it;—a prohibition which is particularly applicable to communities which stand in close relationship to each other.

Ver. 19. *A garment mingled.*—This latter is, literally, "a garment of twofold (Schaatnes) may not come on thee," which is explained, Deut. xxii. 11, by "woollen and linen together." What kind of stuff is meant is uncertain.—These three prohibitions, which are here placed together, all clearly rest on the same ground, and are not enjoined for the mere sake of utility. Nature, as God has created it, was to be held in reverence by the Israelite, and he was not to deal artificially with it, or introduce confusion into its different species. But as all natural things were to be to him a type of spiritual relations, there was contained in this prohibition a forbidding likewise of everything contrary to nature in man himself,—all misuse of the limbs bestowed on him by God, or of His creation, to any other purpose than that ordained by God Himself. The Jewish doctors remark thereon: "Whoever causes cattle of different kinds to gender, he acts as if God had not created all that is necessary, but as if he must bring forth new creatures, and so help Him in the creation of the world. He who mingles different kinds, falsifies the impress on the king's money." Philo Judæus says, "He exhorts men from a distance, as from a watch-tower, to be chaste, that men and women, learning this beforehand, may restrain themselves from forbidden intercourse." The addition of the law respecting garments to that about beasts and plants, reminds us of the house and clothes leprosy, which, as an image of sin, is to be treated in the same manner as the human disease. In clothing, everything needlessly artificial is to be avoided; and by the simplicity of the material is reverence to God's creation to be evinced. The same holds good of this prohibition as of other similar symbolical commands—of the unclean animals, of the uncleanness contracted through natural and bodily conditions,—the outward command is to lead to the feeling of heart-purification. When this exists, the commandment in the letter becomes superfluous. The Apostle Paul sees in this prohibition a type of a spiritual evil, namely, that of believers having fellowship with unbelievers (2 Cor. vi. 14). Yet his earnest remark upon it is only a typical application, and not an interpretation, of this prohibition.

Ver. 20. *Because she was not free.*—The meaning is: In the case of slaves, with whom a regular marriage cannot take place, a punishment still shall be inflicted on the woman's sin, and on his who has committed it with her, when she has lived in a condition similar to marriage. In this respect also the Mosaic law is distinguished from the most moral law of the ancient world, the Roman, which had no punishment for such an offence. The reason of the slighter degree of punishment for the adultery consists in the looser character of the union which the relation of slave entailed, while in the punishment itself it is indicated that the union is a true marriage.—" Not at all redeemed, nor freedom given her," refers to the twofold mode of gaining freedom—by purchase, or by manumission without payment. The first was made from the property of the slave, or by another person. The punishment is not expressed. According to tradition, it was to be scourging inflicted on both parties. (She shall be scourged, is not in Luther's version, but "she shall be punished." —Translator.)

Ver. 22. *Forgiven him.*—Cf. the introd., ch. v., on trespass-offering. As the proper punishment appointed for adultery was death, which in this case was not inflicted on account of the adulteress being a slave, there was the more need of a solemn confession that the holy law of God had been broken, and must be restored by doing away the offence; hence the "ram of the trespass-offering."

Ver. 25. *The Lord your God.*—The design of this law is altogether similar to ver. 19. The people of Israel was to have in nature everywhere a mirror of God's moral governance, and a guide to Him. As every child from his birth was unclean, until by the covenant of circumcision he was given to God and sanctified, so are all the fruits of the earth to be regarded as unclean until they have been sanctified. Moreover, as nothing small, unripe, imperfect, might be sacrificed to the Lord, the full perfection of the fruit in the fourth year was to be waited for before the consecration followed. If the fruit was not eaten for three years, the blossoms might be broken off, and thereby in the following year greater fruitfulness produced. This, however, was certainly not the reason of the law, but a gracious consequence of it.—"By this religious use was that pointed out which St Paul, 1 Tim. iv. 5, says,—'Everything is sanctified by God's word and by prayer.' Not as though anything were in itself unclean, but because through man's sin the earth had as it were become defiled, and thus, in respect to us, its innocent fruits are regarded as contaminated with the uncleanness of uncircumcision. And therefore it is said, that for the same reason they themselves are sanctified to God, must the fruits also of the tree become clean."—Calvin.

Ver. 26. *With the blood.*—The prohibition, already often given, is perhaps here repeated because, likewise, nothing was to be eaten "with blood" in it—added to it: ch. xvii. 10-12.

Use enchantments.—Heb.: "Ye shall not predict from serpents and clouds." Serpents were esteemed in Syria and Egypt sacred animals, and were kept and observed for the purpose of soothsaying. As this, however, was not very frequent, the two words had perhaps a cognate, more general signification: "Ye shall not whisper enchantments, or practise secret arts of divination."

Ver. 27. *Round.*—Lit.: "Ye shall not go round the extreme part of your head in a circle;" *i.e.,* ye shall not shave the extremity of your head in a circle. As this appears to have been a prevalent custom among the ancient Arabians in honour of the god whom the Greeks called Dionysius.

Beard.—Lit.: "Nor cut off the extremity of your beard"— the whiskers.—This prohibition had the same reason—to forbid a superstitious custom.

Ver. 28. *For the dead.*—Lit.: "Ye shall not make a cutting in your flesh for a dead person, nor a writing (or engraving) of burning on you,"—not burn in your flesh any marks or letters. Incisions, as marks of grief, signify that in the blood which flows a kind of sacrifice for the dead is made. This prohibition, then, is of the same kind as that respecting human sacrifices. It is well known how prevalent to this day is the custom of tatooing among heathen nations in connection with superstition of every kind. The prohibition appears similar to that, ver. 19; and the meaning and object to have been, besides the prevention of superstition, to inspire likewise a reverence for God's creation. It is remarkable that the South Sea Islanders, among whom the art of tatooing had arrived at great perfection, after their conversion to Christianity, would have nothing more to do with this custom.

Ver. 29. *Wickedness.*—Lit.: "Thou shalt not profane thy daughter to whoredom," in order that the land may not follow the example. Perhaps here an allusion might be made to prostitution in honour of some deity. Then would the word "profane" be purposely used, because the expression for such a woman of the temple was "the consecrated." But we may suppose that acts of this kind took place, without open idolatry, to excuse the sin and greed of gain. Cf. Num. xxv. introd.

Ver. 31. *Familiar spirits.*—The necromancers. Such was the witch of Endor, 1 Sam. xxviii.

Your God.—All these could know future events only through God, who had revealed nothing thereof to them; consequently their soothsaying was a Nature-worship, an act of apostasy from the true God.

Ver. 32. *Rise up.*—Although there were no differences of rank among the Israelites, except the distinction of priests and people, still the heads of the tribe enjoyed an hereditary dignity. It was the more necessary, as a counterbalance to this, to put the general reverence to be paid to age, which the Lord Himself had invested with its honour. The same custom existed in Egypt.

Ver. 34. *As thyself.*—Here is the love to their neighbour expressly extended to strangers. Even in the first lawgiving of covenant was there a similar commandment, Exod. xxii. 21; cf. Deut. x. 18, 19, and below, ch. xxiv. 18, note.

Ver. 35. *In measure.*—Unjust judgment is put on an equality with unjust measure, as a similar comparison, in a saying of Christ's, shows: "With what measure ye mete it shall be measured to you again:" St Matt. vii. 2.

CHAPTER XX.

The commandments of this chapter are, likewise, not arranged in order. However, here especially grievous offences against God and heinous carnal sins are put together as an especial abomination in His sight, and the particular punishment assigned, which in the earlier mention of many of them was not added.

Ver. 5. *Cut him off.*—This place clearly shows what is signified by the expression, which so often occurs, of "cutting off from the people." First, the ordinary punishment of stoning is fixed; but, as the crime was hardly conceivable without a widely-spread apostasy, the threat of being cut off by God is added. The person to be cut off had fallen under the judgment of Divine punishment, which, sooner or later, by an especial guidance of the people of God, must overtake him. Meanwhile, he was declared outlawed. Every one could execute the judicial punishment threatened against him, if the magistracy neglected their duty; cf. Gen. xvii. 14, note. Upon the crime itself, see ch. xviii. 21, note.

Ver. 6. *Familiar spirits.*—The connection with them was in every case joined with idolatry: ch. xix. 26, 28, note.

Ver. 9. *Upon him;* i.e., May the guilt of his death fall upon him, as ver. 11.

Ver. 10. *Committeth adultery.*—Lit.: "And the man who committeth adultery with the wife of a man, who committeth adultery with the wife of his neighbour, they shall both die the death, the adulterer and the adulteress." The repetition is not intended to suppose a fresh case (for then must the word "and" interpose), but to enforce still further the heinousness of the act. He commits against his neighbour an act which, committed against himself, he would never endure.

Ver. 13. *Shall be upon them.*—Ch. xviii. 22. According to Roman law, any one who had compelled another to the crime, was (if this person were a freeman) punished with death. He who was a party to the crime lost the half of his property and the right of making a will. In the Mosaic law, the chief view was directed to purity and sanctity: in the heathen law, the prevailing consideration was social honour.

Ver. 14. *Wickedness among you.*—Ch. xviii. 17. A sin not uncommon, even among us, for a man to undergo a sham marriage with the mother, but really to cohabit with the daughter.

Ver. 16. *Upon them.*—Cf. ch. xviii. 23. Punishment was also figuratively to be inflicted on the beast which had been contaminated by the man's sin: cf. Exod. xxi. 28. That this was the meaning, and not merely to produce a greater abhorrence of the crime, is clear from the expression, "their blood shall be upon them."

Ver. 17. *His iniquity.*—Ch. xviii. 9, note.

Ver. 18. *Among their people.*—Ch. xviii. 19.

Ver. 19. *Their iniquity.*—The expression is here more indefinite than in the form, "shall be cut off from among his people." God threatens to them punishment in general, which they had cause to dread even when the magistrate neglected his duty. He might punish him as he chose, only not with death.

Ver 20. *Childless.*—"What does this mean, since children have been born from such unions in earlier times, and are still born? Is it at all determined by God's law, that they who come of such a marriage shall not be esteemed as children,—*i.e.*, shall not inherit the rights of their parents?"—St Aug. So a king is called childless who yet had children, but none who succeeded him on the throne: Jer. xxii. 30. However, it seems more probable, that here a Divine curse was to be pronounced, which justified the judge in inflicting such a punishment: so also ver. 20.

Ver. 21. *Unclean thing.*—The Hebrew expression is, "it is an uncleanness." The punishment also is less, as this marriage was even commanded in the case of a childless brother's widow.

Ver. 27. *Upon them.*—Ch. xix. 26, 31.

CHAPTER XXI.

As the whole people—in bodily purity, in the avoiding of all pollution, in the sexual relations, or through touching the dead—were continually reminded of sin and exhorted to inward holiness; so was the priestly order, and among them the high priest, to be distinguished from all the people by higher requirements, to a more perfect separation from all that was defiling, either actually or figuratively, and also by outward faultlessness. Even his kinsmen were not to stand nearer to him than his sacred office. The requirement of bodily cleanness from the priest was not simply out of a sense of propriety, but contained likewise, as in the case of the sacrifices, a deeper symbolical meaning. There was to be nothing of a bodily kind in the servants of the Lord, which, by its unseemliness, could remind them of the kingdom of sin, from which all evil, as well as death, had its origin.

Ver. 4. *Profane himself.*—Heb.: "He shall not pollute himself as housemaster (head of a family) in his people." "His people" are his relations, as in the well-known form of speech, "to be gathered to his people." Among the heathen also, the priests were not permitted to pollute themselves, either by touching the dead, or by taking part in their interment, or by mourning.

Ver. 5. *Cuttings in their flesh.*—A strong growth of hair is a sign of physical power. The case of Samson (Judges xvi. 22), as well as of the Nazarite vow, may occur to our thoughts (Num. vi.). In mourning, it was usual to shave the head and the beard (Isa. xv. 2; Jer. vii. 29). Herodotus mentions (B. 2, 36), as a peculiarity among the Egyptians, that "in other parts the priests of the gods wear their hair long, but in Egypt they shave. Among all other people it is customary in mourning for the near relations to shave their heads: on the contrary, in Egypt, in cases of death, they suffer the hair to grow both on their heads and chins, although at other times they go shaven."

Ver. 6. *The bread.*—By this are to be understood not merely the shew-bread (Exod. xxv.), but all offerings. They are called bread, food, ch. iii. 11. In order to place before the Holy One that which rejoices His heart, they themselves (the priests) must not be defiled with any heathen superstition.

Holy.—Lit., "let them be holy,"—as it were a sanctuary, wholly belonging to the Lord.

Ver. 7. *Holy unto his God.*—With respect to their marriage, the priests, and among them the high priest, were to observe the highest degree of purity. To a harlot (a public person), and to a profane (a fallen woman), there always clings a moral stain; and, although she may really have amended her life, still it is, at least, not so certain but that suspicion often again might arise. The divorced woman may be unjustly left by her husband (cf. Deut. xxiv. 1, note); still, as cases of that kind were not inquired into, the man had the supposition of a right separation on his side; and the priest ought not to contract such a marriage, which, to say the least, was open to suspicion.

Ver. 9. *Profane herself.*—Heb., "profane herself to play the whore." The daughter of the priest partook likewise in the holiness of her father. Every kind of harlotry is to be understood under this, and not merely that which was open, for money.

Burnt with fire.—According to Jewish tradition, the body was first strangled, and then burnt; and the participator in the crime was also strangled.

Ver. 10. *Among his brethren.*—Lit.: "The priest who is great (*i.e.*, greatest) among his brethren." This is not a particular title, "high" or "great" priest. This title was derived in later times from this place.

Rend his clothes.—The context teaches, that this was merely forbidden him as a sign of mourning. Caiaphas therefore (St Matt. xxvi. 65), did not break this commandment.

Ver. 12. *Go out.*—In order to attend on mourning. Cf. on the whole, ch. x. 6, 7, note.

Crown.—The golden crown, Exod. xxviii. 36. There it was said how this band, with the inscription, "holiness of the Lord," was designed to remove all unholiness from the sacred acts of the Israelites. As God's representative among the people, must the priest stand apart from all earthly engagements.

Ver. 14. *A widow.*—The high priest was distinguished from the others in this respect, that he might not marry a widow, because there was at least the possibility of greater sexual uncleanness in such a marriage.

Ver. 18. *Flat nose.*—With a short nose.

Ver. 20. *Hath a blemish.*—The reason of these commands is the same as in respect to the offering up of perfectly sound animals. This perfectness was an emblem of inward sanctity, and so a type of the "undefiled" High Priest, Heb. vii. 26.

Ver. 23. *Unto the veil*—namely, if he is high priest. At eating of the sacrifices, it was not necessary to appear in the

Divine presence at the altar, or in the sanctuary. As a man afflicted with the above-mentioned defects is not suitable to the service of a king, to appear in his presence, but yet elsewhere may be useful; so, in like manner, this personal defectiveness, as symbol of inward deficiency, excluded from all service which was to offer atonement for men to God, and to apply His favour to them.

CHAPTER XXII.

In this chapter, former commandments are in part repeated, but more definitely and fully. The first part is a general warning against touching any of the holy things while in a state of uncleanness; and then proceeds further to declare which among the household of the priest may eat of that which is holy,—not of the most holy. This was reserved for the priests themselves: cf. ch. vi. 18.

Ver. 7. *Shall be clean.*—From this it is evident that the explanation of St John xviii. 28 is incorrect, which supposes that it means that the Pharisees feared they should be excluded, as unclean, from eating of the paschal lamb, which was to be eaten after sunset, if they entered the judgment-hall.

His food.—This food is intended for his maintenance. Here also the rule holds good: "The Sabbath was made for man, and not man for the Sabbath."

Ver. 13. *No stranger.*—The whole house of the priest was sanctified through him; but in this sanctification was also to remain separate from all strangers.—To the rules respecting freedom from blemish on the part of the priests, is annexed the instruction respecting the perfection of the sacrifices. As, figuratively, the animal who had done no sin atoned for the sinner, and the costly gift of the burnt and thank-offering was meant to represent the offering of the noblest and best which man has—his soul, created after God's image,—in like manner must the sacrifices represent by their external perfectness the same thought. They were so far types of Him " who, through the Eternal Spirit, offered Himself without spot to God:" Heb. ix. 14. This perfectness was to be on two sides: partly, they were not to be too young or too old, but in their full natural vigour; and, next, there must be no blemish in them. So likewise were they a type of the sacrifice of Christ, who entered on the path of self-sacrifice in the vigour of His manhood, and without blemish of body or of mind.

Ver. 19. *Of the goats.*—The sacrifices were therefore to be made of the animals on which depended the whole outward existence of the people—of the most valuable, clean, domestic animals. Of these, male animals were to be offered, as the stronger and the more perfect, with the exception of the thank-offering, ch. iii. 1. The reason of this exception not being mentioned here is, because the thank-offering did not belong to the most holy, to the peculiar and most important sacrifices.

Ver. 22. *Broken.*—If it has any broken limb.

Ver. 23. *Superfluous.*—Heb.: "Too long or too short limbs."

Accepted.—The "free-will offerings" were less than the "vow-offerings," because these latter rested on a covenant existing between the Lord and man. No other defect than this only was allowed in the least kind of offerings. Moreover, all these blemishes are mentioned by way of example, as is clear from this, that, Deut. xv. 21, lameness is added.

Ver. 24. *Cut.*—These are expressions for the different kinds of mutilation known to the ancients.

In your land.—These words might be understood of the sacrificing these animals, but then it would be a mere repetition of the foregoing. The Jewish tradition, therefore, more correctly understands it as a general prohibition to mutilate animals. The reason of this prohibition is not the more sure prevention of like acts towards men, but (as the comparison of this passage with such as ch. xix. 9 shows) in order more vividly to impress on men's minds a reverence for the creation of God, which man is indeed to be lord over, but which he may not wilfully alter or disarrange. This prohibition, then, has especially a symbolic significance, like that about behaving in this way towards men: cf. Deut. xxiii. 1.

Ver. 27. *Accepted.*—The reason, no doubt, is, because then it begins to be eatable; but the command is given, not for the sake of its really being eaten, but figuratively.

Ver. 28. *One day.*—The old Chaldee Paraphrase makes here the following addition:—"My people, as your Father in heaven is merciful, so be ye also merciful on earth." A cow and a sheep shall ye not kill on one day with its young." It is parallel to the prohibition Deut. xxii. 6. There is an indication in this, that as God preserves the different species in creation, man may not exterminate them, but use them for the service of God, and for his own advantage. One step to such extermination would be this way of killing the mother and her young, if the practice became general.

Ver. 30. *On the same day.*—As the most holy of the thank-offerings: cf. ch. vii. 15.

CHAPTER XXIII.

The law now once more places the feast-days of the whole year together, and, indeed, after a short repetition of the institution of the weekly Sabbath, in the order of time. The holy seasons of the Israelites consisted of a fifty year Sabbath cycle, and in a yearly cycle of feasts. The number seven, as the number of the covenant, ran through the whole Sabbath cycle; it was closely connected with the week, the origin of which (as all divisions of time followed the changes of the moon) rested on the quarters of the moon. This natural division, which was common to the Israelites with most ancient people, was, however, sanctified to them by a higher thought, to which it served as the ground-work. The seventh day of the week, the first of the seventh month, the seventh and the seven times seventh year, were sacred seasons, because the Lord rested on the Sabbath day after He had finished the work of creation. The remembrance of the Eternal One, who is raised above all change, and who, after the completion of the work of creation, rejoiced therein that all was very good, this was to lead man up to his own origin from God by the cessation from all work. As the bodily refreshment restored his physical energies, so should the consciousness of union with the Almighty and the Eternal restore the true life to his soul. In the order of months, this holy rest of refreshment to body and soul was not celebrated to the full. Israel was not to rest the whole month, but on the first of the seventh month trumpets were blown; it was the Sabbath of the blowing of trumpets, which, as it appears, was intended to proclaim this month solemnly as that of reconciliation and reunion with God—of return to Him. In this month fell the day of deepest humiliation, the day of atonement, and the feast of greatest joy, the feast of tabernacles. The Sabbath of the seventh year, and of the seven times seventh year, was closely connected, in ever-widening circles, with the weekly and monthly Sabbath. These are mentioned, ch. xxv.—The three feasts referred especially to the beginning and the end of wheat harvest—to the vintage, the oil and fruit harvests. Their groundwork was a natural one; only that the Israelites did not, as the heathen, hold feasts in honour of the course of Nature, as their deity; they did not enslave themselves to its changes, and become intoxicated with joy or overcome with grief on account of the variation of the seasons, but, regarding them as the gifts of creation on which their temporal being depended, they reverenced God with thank-offerings. But, besides this sign, by which they solemnly declared that they owed their senses and their being to God, there was a still higher meaning of the festivals as memorials of the historical revelations of God, for the redemption, preservation, and blessing of His people. The first was a memento of Israel's election to be a people, by means of their preservation from the destroying angel, and escape from Egypt; the second feast was closely connected as harvest feast with the first, and was a memorial (at least according to later tradition) of the Divine blessing, whereby the preservation from Egypt received its accomplishment—the lawgiving on Sinai; the third was, according to its natural position, the main harvest feast. It celebrated the conclusion of the gathering in of all fruits, as well of the barn as of the wine-press (Deut. xvi. 13). At the same time it represented, as an historical national feast, what Israel as the people of the Lord had become, under His guidance—on the one side, the journey through the wilderness, with God's wonderful leading of the people—on the other hand, the joy of receiving the promise in the fulness of the "land flowing with milk and honey." But for this feast the day was preparatory, which itself rested on no historical event—the day celebrated a little before, the great day of resting, and fasting, and repentance, and atonement. Only when the people were fully released from their sins were they allowed to rejoice in their continued guidance by the Lord—the type of guidance from earthly necessities to heavenly rest. Thus, in all these feasts is the Lord praised as the Giver of all earthly gifts, the Creator, Preserver, and Ruler of His children of the covenant. While the cycle of Sabbaths raised the mind from the constant change of time above all earthly affairs to the Eternal, Unchangeable Creator, and was intended as a foretaste of eternal rest, in like manner the cycle of feasts brought the mind into the midst of the revelations of the Creator of the world, both in nature and in the history of His covenant people.

Ver. 3. *Sabbath of rest.*—Lit., "the Sabbath of Sabbaths;" which in this position merely serves to add to the force of the meaning, "the entire full Sabbath."

Ver. 4. *Holy convocations.*—Heb.: "These are the appointed times of the Lord" ("appointed time"—Moëd, the same word as is used of the "appointed assembly," the tabernacle [cf. Exod. xxvii. 21, note]), "holy convocations, which ye shall call at their appointed times." The first word, "appointed time," has the particular meaning "feast-time;" the second the original.

Ver. 8. *No servile work.*—The paschal festival has already been spoken of more in full, Exod. xii. Here mention is again made of it only on account of its connection with the subject in hand. The offerings which are to be made during the eight days' feast are described Num. xxviii. 16, etc.

Ver. 11. *After the Sabbath.*—For the meaning of the waving, see ch. vii. 34, note. By the Sabbath we are here to understand the feast Sabbath, the first feast-day: Exod. xii. 16.

Ver. 14. *Parched corn.*—Cf. ch. ii. 14, note.

Your dwellings.—The natural relation of the paschal festival is subordinate to that which results from the history of the kingdom of God. For the meaning of the offering of the first-fruits, see ch. ii. 10, note.

Ver. 21. *Your generations.*—This feast is elsewhere called "the feast of weeks," Exod. xxxiv. 22. The Hebrew word for week is "Septenary," a time reckoned after the number seven. Since the whole festival has its name from "week," the whole time from Easter to Whitsunday, as a time determined by the number seven, is denoted as a week of weeks. By this division the harvest-time was to be represented as a week, and the harvest festival as the great harvest Sabbath. The whole festival consisted, therefore, only of one feast-day as the concluding Sabbath of this great week. As on the paschal feast the beginning, so on the feast of weeks was the end, of the harvest sanctified: the former with the offering of a sheaf, as a sign that the harvest was begun; the latter with the offering of two loaves, as a sign that it was completed.

Ver. 22. *The Lord your God.*—Cf. ch. xix. 9. This is here repeated, in order to show whereby the festival may be well-pleasing in God's sight.

Ver. 24. *Blowing of trumpets.*—The blowing of trumpets served to announce the great festivals, and to call together the people. So had the giving of the law on Mount Sinai been announced, Exod. xix. 19, etc. The same took place on the anointing of the kings, 1 Kings i. 34; and on the assembling of the army, Isa. xviii. 3. The feasts of these months were the conclusion and crown of the yearly feasts. As the Sabbath was the conclusion of the week, so were these feasts of the yearly cycle. Therefore the blowing of trumpets was a "memorial," to call the attention of the people to this great season, as "memorial" often signifies a reminding sign. So, *e.g.*, the stones of memorial on the shoulders of the ephod, Exod. xxviii. 12, cf. Exod. xiii. 9.

Ver. 32. *Your Sabbath.*—This festival has been spoken of more fully, ch. xvi.

Ver. 38. *Give unto the Lord.*—Which is here added, in order to remind the people that no one can sufficiently honour God by private acts of worship.

Ver. 40. *Seven days.*—The customs of this festival were especially joyous, and in later times there were constant additions to them: cf. St John vii. 37, note; ch. viii. 12, note. The tabernacles were in after times erected on the flat roofs, in courts, streets, and squares. Boughs of beautiful trees—probably fruit-trees, with fine fruits on them—palm-trees, and especially branches of the leafy willow, were taken for the purpose; but not, as the later Jews misunderstood this place, carried in the hands of the feasters. By leaving their ordinary dwellings and pitching tents, they transported themselves as it were into the wandering life of the wilderness, while the fulness of the beautiful foliage and of the fruits symbolised the blessings of the promised land. Although it was a general harvest feast, yet more particularly the conclusion of the vintage and of the oil harvest was celebrated, as these productions more especially typified the richness of the country. In later times the customs of drawing water and of lighting lamps were naturally and significantly added to the rest—all emblems of the grace and goodness which the people enjoyed under the guidance of the Lord, and at the same time, as festive rites, pledges of the continuance of His guidance and blessing of the people on the way to the promised rest, of which Canaan was only the type: cf. Heb. iv. 1–9. In no other festival were the natural and historical relations so closely allied to one another.

CHAPTER XXIV.

Ver. 4. *Pure candlestick.*—That which was made of pure gold. The same word used of the table, ver. 6.

Ver. 9. *Perpetual statute.*—The shew-bread was laid before the Lord during the week, and eaten on the Sabbath day by the priests, because the loaves were meant to represent, as food well-pleasing to God, the whole life of the people, the day-work of the same, which corresponded to the day-work of the creation of God. The eating by the priests near the altar of incense denoted its acceptableness in God's sight, answering to the joy of the Sabbath after the completion of the creation.

Ver. 11. *Cursed.*—In the Heb. " the name" merely stands, in order, in the case of this crime, to evince a greater reverence of God's name by silence. It lies in the very essence of a Nature-religion, which is at the same time idolatry, that it should enter in the war of oppositions which is being carried on in nature, and therefore at times can blaspheme the same gods whom at other times it honours, since all the while the attribute of holiness is wanting to these deities. We know, indeed, that a blaspheming of the gods took place at certain sacred customs in Egypt. So Menelaus, in Homer, when his sword broke in the critical moment, says, " Father Jove, none of the gods is more hurtful than thou."—Iliad, B. iii. 365. The occasion of this blasphemy very likely was such as the Jewish interpreters give —that this man had been refused permission to pitch his tent among the tribe of Dan, and his complaint had been rejected by Moses' decision.

Ver. 14. *Upon his head.*—By this act they declared solemnly that the crime and the uncleanness should fall only on the offender. The idea here prevails, which has been more fully discussed chap. v., introd., that by such a heinous offence the ordinance of God has itself been violated; and so, in a certain degree, guilt is incurred by the people as a whole, from which they designed to free themselves by this laying on of hands. The custom of laying on of hands in the case of sacrifices is thus more clearly explained.

Ver. 16. *Put to death.*—The word which here occurs, and is translated "blaspheme," signifies also "to pronounce clearly;" and thus the later Jews have found in this passage the command, that no one might utter the name Jehovah (or Jahve). It is, however, altogether improbable, that at any time the punishment of death would have been inflicted for the merely pronouncing the name of the Lord; which, moreover, is contradicted by the whole of this history, but especially by such songs as that, ch. xv. (Exod.). The stranger among the Israelites partook in many privileges of the people of God; he enjoyed, in general, not only a mild treatment, but celebrated the Sabbath and the feasts with the people. On this account no difference ought to take place in relation to crimes betwixt him and a born Israelite.

Ver. 22. *Lord your God.*—This last sentence is the reason why those laws which are mentioned before (Exod. xxi. 12, 23, etc.) are here repeated. In respect to murder, as to every other injury, the stranger is to stand on an equal footing with the born Israelite.

CHAPTER XXV.

To the weekly Sabbath and the Sabbath of months (cf. ch. xxiii., introd.) was added the Sabbath of years. This had also, as all the feasts, a natural groundwork. As man is to rest one day each week, in order to raise himself above the changes of earth to the Eternal, Unchangeable Creator; but as this higher meaning of the Sabbath was supplemental to the natural requirement of rest after work, in like manner was one year of cessation after six years of cultivation a necessity to the land. With this, however, was the higher thought connected, that the land also, by means of this rest, should do homage to its Lord and Creator; and the people acknowledge that, in its natural relation, it belonged to the Creator of all things. But, as the weekly Sabbath was especially destined for the refreshment of men-servants and maid-servants, in like manner the produce of the uncultivated fields during the year of jubilee served for the refreshment of the poor: it represented in figure the all-embracing love of God, which levels all differences, and which belongs to all His children,—which love men were required to imitate.

Ver. 5. *Undressed.*—Lit., " of thy Nazarites." The unpruned vines were so called, because the Nazarites did not shave their hair during the time of their vow (Num. vi).

Ver. 7. *Be meat.*—The apparent impracticability of this command, which at least after the return from Babylon was exactly observed, appears lessened by the fact, that where this rule was introduced, scarcity was provided against by the previous accumulation of provisions, and the rest from field labour could be employed in other necessary work. Still, however, such possible advantages are by no means the reason for this command. The year of jubilee—the year of the restoration of the order of things appointed by God—formed the close of the cycle of Sabbaths. This year also was to be a sabbatical year, and was connected with the ordinance just now described; but, at the same time, it had this one thing peculiar to itself, that the original division of property was restored, and thereby especially the servant who through poverty was unable to regain his liberty, returned into his possession. As the weekly Sabbath and the Sabbath of years was intended to raise men from the changeableness of earthly affairs and events to the life in eternity, by restoring through rest strength to man and to the land, in like manner the year of jubilee was designed to raise the whole people, in respect to their rights and possessions, from the changeableness of outward circumstances to the unchangeableness of the Divine appointment,—to produce an equality in the distinctions of life,—to make men conscious of their common dependence on the Lord, and of the freedom of all men. As in the case of the other Sabbaths, this, however, took place rather figuratively than actually. Much remained still probably unaccomplished of this law. But by its very deficiency it predicted (as did the other types of the O. T.) the future perfect remission of debts, and restoration of all Divine appointments, in the eternal rest of the people of God.

Ver. 8. *Forty and nine years.*—The question arises, Whether by this is meant the seventh sabbatical year, or the year following it; or, in other words, whether the forty-ninth or the fiftieth is intended? Some have tried to solve this question by saying that the forty-ninth was also the fiftieth year, since the Israelites reckoned both by the lunar and the solar year, and in this period of the fiftieth year the difference between the two was settled. However, no traces of such double reckoning are found; but rather the rule of the division of time seems to have been this: the year consisted of twelve lunar months, which began with the new moon; but they were so far bound to the course of the sun by the regulation that the year should begin with the harvest month (according to Exod. xii. 2), and on the full moon of the same, the 15th, the Passover should be celebrated with offering of the first-fruits of barley. The Israelites were thereby under the necessity of intercalating; the new moon being chosen as the beginning of the harvest month, on the full moon of which the barley harvest was to commence. It is unknown how soon this rule of intercalation was formed. Accordingly, the lunar year was the groundwork of these years, which was only here and there made to square with the solar year. Thus, then, forty-nine years are the time of the great sabbatical period; and the name, "the fiftieth year," occurs for this cause, that the last jubilee year from which the reckoning began was counted in, just as it is said, Christ rose again on the third day; and thus the number seven is not violated, and the unnatural supposition is needless, that by this regulation two years of rest followed each other. How ver. 21 is to be made agree with this, see below.

Ver. 10. *Inhabitants thereof.*—Heb.: "And ye shall call out (proclaim) freedom to all who dwell in the land."

Jubilee.—Lit., "shall be Jobel to you." This name of the year came from the jubilee-trumpets, so called from a sound they made like the word Jobel. The trumpets on this day (figuratively) summoned the whole people solemnly together, that they might be restored by the Lord Himself.

Ver. 12. *Out of the field.*—The command from ver. 4 is here repeated, and nothing new appointed. This repetition takes place, in order more expressly to place the year of jubilee on a level with the others.

Ver. 13. *Unto his possession.*—Therefore all property of land returned to its original possessor, without paying back the purchase-money. In all states of antiquity which had in view the close fellowship of all the citizens, we find laws which were designed either to preserve the equality, or from time to time to restore it. Among a people which was to be regarded as God's peculiar possession—all its members as His servants—it was so much the more necessary, from time to time, to bring about such a reinstatement of condition. The prospect of it would from the first help to preserve equality.

Ver. 15. *Sell unto thee.*—No sale generally of the property itself took place, but only of the harvests, and a renting of the land for a number of years reckoned beforehand.

Ver. 22. *Of the old store.*—As in the seventh year they were prohibited not merely reaping, but sowing, the sixth year (which began with the month Abib, the end of March or beginning of April) was obliged to provide first for itself, next for the sabbatical year, and lastly for the year after the sabbatical year. In case of general faithfulness to the covenant on the part of the people, this would have been the regular course; but, besides this, the Israelites were frugal and industrious, and by economy provided against the danger of famine.

Ver. 24. *Redemption.*—The possibility of purchase before the jubilee year. To provide against all mixture of the tribes, permission was to be given to every one to purchase back his land within the period between the jubilees.

Ver. 27. *Possession.*—The fruits which the buyer has already received are deducted; the rest, which the buyer would have obtained up to the year of jubilee, is paid him.

Ver. 30. *In the jubilee.*—The whole Israelitish commonwealth was founded on agriculture; and in the case of landed property, which was of the most consequence, no changes were allowed. But it was different in respect to property in towns, in which at that time no distinct usufruct could be purchased. To insist on their return into the original hands in the year of jubilee, would have needlessly obstructed intercourse. Here, then, simple re-purchase took place.

Ver. 36. *Usury.*—On the prohibition of usury, see Exod. xxii. 25, note.

Ver. 43. *With rigour.*—In respect to persons the same principle held good as in reference to land. It was not so much slavery, as an agreement of service of every kind for a number of years. That the slave might not be obliged to serve beyond this time through poverty, he received then back his property in land.

Ver. 53.—It is surprising that in all these regulations respecting the manumission of the Israelite bondmen in the year of jubilee, no mention is made of their being free in the seventh year, of which it is spoken in the giving of the laws of the covenant (Exod. xxi. 2, etc.). But the one does not exclude the other. It was the right of every bondman, after six years of service, to be free on the seventh; but as he did not then receive back his inheritance, he might very likely prefer the state of servitude, and wait for the fiftieth year. In every case, the promise of being free in the fiftieth year was only of consequence to those who were near this term, since the prospect of fifty years' servitude would take away all value from the hope of freedom. This whole chapter has therefore in view those slaves who, in the fiftieth year, had not yet served their six years, or who, on account of poverty, had prolonged their time of servitude after the lapse of the six years.

CHAPTER XXVI.

We have here arrived at the conclusion of the lawgiving on Sinai, since that which follows in the next chapter is the redemption of particular things. This book, like the book of the lawgiving of the covenant, concludes with solemn promises, threatenings, and warnings, which afterwards, on the occasion of Moses' decease, are still more fully repeated. Those refer, however, only to the taking possession of Canaan: but here the people appears, with the progress of the lawgiving, as already in possession of the promised land. There are blessings *in* that land which are here promised to Israel. The last portion of the chapter (from ver. 40) is particularly remarkable, and is peculiarly prophetic. It shows how the relation of the Lord to His people is an eternal one, which does not cease even through that people's apostasy. Even in His punishment, which never entirely destroys the hope of the people being received back again, the Lord shows Himself as the covenant God of Israel.

Ver. 1. *Image of stone.*—Heb.: "No stone of aspect;" by which is to be understood a stone carved, or with hieroglyphics of religious signification, such as were in great numbers in Egypt.

Ver. 2. *I am the Lord.*—These two precepts by no means belong to the preceding, but form the introduction to the promises and threatenings which follow. Out of the whole range of the commandments, two are brought forward as the sum of the whole, which relate to the honour to be paid the one true God and to His service, by observing His Sabbaths and other customs of His sanctuary. That this is the meaning of "reverence My sanctuary" is evident from this, that all public service and religious ceremonies were given in order to make it possible for the Lord to dwell among His people. These were, therefore, to be observed with reverence for His sanctuary, in which He dwelt.

Ver. 5. *Until the sowing-time*; *i.e.,* Ye shall reap such a full harvest that ye shall have work from the threshing-time, which begins in April, to the grape-gathering in September, and in like manner from the vintage with the wine-press to the time of sowing.

Ver. 10. *Old store.*—Ye shall have so rich harvests, that the first shall not be consumed when the new arrives.

Ver. 12. *My people.*—This is the essential point of the blessing. All outward blessing is only the earnest of God's continual dwelling among His people. The gracious, merciful, holy, and just God can never confer mere outward blessing. All such outward blessing is only the inducement for children who are led by the senses to walk in communion with Him.

Ver. 18. *Seven times.*—This is repeated four times besides, so that there are five degrees in the ever seven times more severe punishment. God punishes so, that He always in His wrath remembereth mercy, and gives time for repentance. But no punishment is so great that a greater cannot follow it. These Divine fundamental laws of all punishment are made known here also, since the last of all, the perishing from out of the promised land, leaves room still to a return (ver. 40), until the final hardening brings on the irreparable destruction.

Ver. 29. *Eat the flesh.*—Repeated Jer. xix. 9, cf. Lam. ii. 20. This was literally fulfilled, 2 Kings vi. 28, 29, and at the last destruction of Jerusalem.

Ver. 30. *High places.*—" High places" are called properly places on mountains or hills where Divine worship was paid, and then the small sanctuaries, chapels, there erected. The history of the Kings, both of Judah and Israel, shows how prone the people were to this kind of worship on high places, which appeared to have a more exciting effect through the senses on the religious life. It allowed greater liberty to their caprice; but, above all, paved the way to the idolatry which attached particular sanctity to certain places.

Your images.—Lit., " your Chammanim," Canaanitish sun idols.

Carcases.—There seems here an allusion to an idolatry such as the Egyptian was, in which mummies of animals were kept and worshipped. The worshippers of such deities should be slain, and their carcases cast on these objects of impious worship.

Ver. 32. *Astonished at it.*—2 Kings xvii. 24, etc.

Ver. 34. *Her Sabbaths.*—Heb.: " The land will pay her Sabbaths." It shall now be as long uncultivated as it before had been tilled by the disobedient people in the sabbatical years.

Ver. 39. *Pine away.*—They shall receive at the same time the punishment for their own sins and for their fathers' sins.

Ver. 44. *And yet for all that.*—This " yet for all that" (Heb., " aff") is regarded by the Jews in their dispersion as of the very greatest importance, since on it rest all their hopes of the covenanted grace of God towards them. Accordingly they call it " the golden affen;" and it is sung forth in their synagogues with a loud voice, and great expressions of joy. And, indeed, this prophetic word declares that Israel, even in its banishment, still remains God's people, and that His particular intentions in relation to them have not come to an end with their apostasy from Him.

The Lord their God.—God's gift and calling are not capable of retractation, Rom. xi. 29.

Ver. 46. *By the hand of Moses.*—Herewith is concluded the whole of the lawgiving on Mount Sinai. That which immediately follows is perhaps not received into it, because it treats of something of a peculiar character, which does not lie within the design of the law.

CHAPTER XXVII.

As the whole people of Israel, their land, and all that they had, was the Lord's possession, and yet a priestly class was set apart from among them to stand nearer to the Lord than the rest, in like manner it was in the power of each individual to make a free-will offering of himself to the Lord. The same held good of every kind of property, which was thereby dedicated to the sanctuary or the service of God's worship. The motive for such a vow is to be sought in the unsatisfactory feeling attending the religious service of the O. T. in the hearts of those who wished by means of it to draw nearer to God. The consciousness that the sacrifices could effect only an outward cleansing and pardon, could only figuratively reconcile and unite to God, urged some among the Israelites expressly and entirely to give up themselves, and what belonged to them, to the Lord. In such a case any one could only now become a servant of the sanctuary, who, like the Levites, was employed in it, but in still lower offices than theirs. Samuel (1 Sam. i.) was such a person dedicated to the Lord, only that he as a Levite (1 Chron. vi. 28) was there employed in higher duties. In like manner the Gibeonites were servants of the sanctuary. It appears as though something similar to this vow existed even in earlier times, and that in the following chapter the liberty to absolve themselves from them only was intended to be preserved to the Israelites.

Ver. 2. *A singular vow.*—Lit.: "When a man sets apart a

vow"—when he will do something over and above the usual service of sacrifice.

For thy estimation.—From vers. 9, 10, it is evident that a beast vowed to the Lord must be sacrificed and was altogether holy. The "estimation" of the men who were vowed to the Lord had, therefore, altogether the same meaning as the redeeming of the first-born (Exod. xiii. 13). The man, in truth, was dedicated to the Lord; but because human sacrifices were an abomination in God's sight, his life must be redeemed. By the words "by thy estimation," we are not to understand the person dedicating himself (cf. ver. 15), still less the whole congregation, because in the case of each particular vow the congregation could not be called to estimate it. But rather Moses is addressed, and in him the priest (cf. ch. v. 15, ch. vi. 6), who in a particular case (vers. 8, 12) is expressly mentioned, because the estimation was more difficult, and he must see the animal itself; but, in the case of men, he made the estimation according to years. That in ver. 2 all the children of Israel are addressed, does not prove that by "thy" they must be intended, since the address at the commencement delivers an already prepared commandment to the people. There is also no example that such a mode of address as "thy" can refer to the people.

Ver. 6. *A month.*—Females were estimated at a little more than a half, or at half as much as the men. The woman is the weaker vessel (1 Pet. iii. 7), created after the man, out and for him (1 Tim. ii. 13; 1 Cor. i. 8, 9), and she was the first in the transgression (1 Tim. ii. 14). But in Christ Jesus there is neither male nor female, but all are one in Him, Gal. iii. 28.

Ver. 8. *Poorer;* i.e., if he does not possess enough to pay such a ransom for himself or for what belongs to him, his child or slave.

Ver. 9. *Shall be holy.*—According to Jewish tradition this is to be understood thus: If any one had vowed a clean animal that may be sacrificed, then must it, if it be a male, be sold for a burnt-sacrifice and offered as a burnt-sacrifice; if it be a female, must be sold and offered as a thank-offering, and the price falls to the sanctuary for its support.

Ver. 13. *Fifth part.*—If the vow is so far void to any one that he may keep the animal for his own use, in this case he must pay the price of it, and by way of punishment or compensation add the fifth part (cf. ch. v. 16, ch. vi. 4, 5, ch. xxii. 14).

Ver. 14. *Stand.*—Even in the case of a vow with respect to a house or other thing, the main point is not its value or the sum to be paid for it, but the renunciation of right in it—the inward redemption of it, which is declared openly by the offering of it.

Ver. 17. *Thy estimation.*—Simply, without reckoning the harvests.

Ver. 20. *To another man;* i.e., if the priest to whom the field has been made over has already sold it to another. The owner cannot here be meant, as he had renounced his right to it until the year of jubilee.

Ver. 21. *Devoted.*—All is " devoted " which was taken by the Lord against the owner's will or confiscated to Him—an involuntary consecration. So afterwards in war: cf vers. 28, 29.

Ver. 23. *Thy estimation.*—Here Moses is distinguished from the priest, since at that time the affair must be brought before Moses. It is not inconsistent with this, that at a later period the priest alone made the estimation.

And he; viz., who had made the vow.

Ver. 24. *Did belong.*—Under the pretext of a vow could no one be deprived of his inheritance. That was only possible in the case, ver. 21.

Ver. 25. *Of the sanctuary.*—In order that the estimation might be the same in case of alterations in the value of money.

Ver. 26. *It is the Lord's.*—Cf. Exod. xiii.

Ver. 29. *Put to death.*—At first sight it seems as though it would have been free for every one to devote anything of his possessions, or of the persons who were in his power; and the vow of Jephtha has very mistakenly been referred to this command. What was devoted could never be offered in sacrifice; but in all places where mention is elsewhere made of the ban laid on anything (Num. xxi. 23, ch. xxxi.; Deut. ii. 34, ch. xiii. 13, etc., ch. xxv 29; Joshua vi. 17; Mal. iv. 6), this appears as a dedication to destruction, as a fulfilling of the Divine vengeance, as an honouring of God *on* those *in* whom He cannot show Himself holy and glorious. Jephtha's vow cannot be of this kind, as he has vowed his daughter for a " burnt-offering," since here it is not said that the thing devoted should be offered in sacrifice, but that it should be put to death. In like manner the devoted town was to be made " an heap for ever," Deut. xiii.

16. The same took place, therefore, in every case in the holy war against the Canaanites; e.g., Num. xxi. 1-3. In the case supposed in the place before us, we are therefore to understand that the punishment of God was to be executed on a town in which were persons or things which belonged to individuals dwelling outside it—to innocent Israelites. In this case none should have the right to treat "the devoting" as "vowing," and by redemption to withdraw what was devoted from punishment. The ban of devotion is the counterpart of the burnt and sin-offering. As these "most holy" sacrifices might not be eaten by the sacrificers, but must be altogether burnt or consumed, so must that which was "devoted" be destroyed. The sacrifices could not be eaten, because the Lord was to be propitiated by the entire surrender of them before any communion with Him was possible: the devoted thing could not be redeemed, because only its entire destruction could satisfy the retributive justice of God.

Ver. 30. *Holy unto the Lord.*—From these, no more than from the first-born, could anything be vowed to the Lord, ver. 26.

Ver. 31. *Fifth part thereof.*—The tithes of natural products might, therefore, be exchanged with money, only on this condition, that a fifth part of the tithe must be added. The subject of tithe has been generally spoken about, Gen. xxviii. 22, note.

THE FOURTH BOOK OF MOSES,

CALLED NUMBERS

CHAPTER I.

THE lawgiving on Sinai was now completed, since what occurs, Lev. xxvii. and Num. v. vi., and in the other chapters, consists either of some particular supplemental directions, or of commands which relate to their march into Canaan. Israel, the people of the Lord, is now also to become His army, to carry on His wars, and to execute His judgments. The people, therefore, is reckoned in martial order; and hence is plain what is the right relation of the numbering which here takes place in reference to that which was given in the case of the payment made to the sanctuary. A comparison of the numbers in Exod. xxxviii. 26 and in this place, shows them to be exactly equal, viz., 603,550. But as it is not likely (without a miracle, which is not mentioned, and is not probable) that, after the lapse of about a year, the number would be exactly the same, we may suppose that probably the old numbering, taken at the erection of the sanctuary, and there recorded, is the groundwork of this fresh one; and that this latter related only to the division into tribes and families, according to which the army was arranged. And the case so stands in the numbering of the host, that all the sums of the particular tribes can be divided by ten, as probably the army was arranged in divisions of ten, and those which were over and above were omitted. In this manner the few changes which in the course of a year had taken place among the men of age to bear arms, could be supplied by the supernumeraries.

Ver. 2. *House of their fathers.*—"House of their fathers" was the name of the greater, more comprehensive families; "families," of the particular lines.

Ver. 3. *By their armies.*—According to the particular divisions of the army.

Ver. 5. *Stand with you.*—Heb.: "Those called into the congregation:" cf. Lev. viii. 4, note.

Ver. 16. *Renowned.*—Heb.: "The heads of the thousands of Israel." The tribes were divided into thousands, as in Germany (and in England and North America the division was customary into hundreds); a round number, to express the approximate size of a tribe. This division appears from the beginning to have referred to the host, or afterwards to have been applied to it. In later times every such thousand had a centre in a larger town; therefore was Bethlehem too small to be among the thousands of Judah: Micah v. 1.

Ver. 18. *Number of their names.*—Lit.: "According to their families in the house of their fathers, in the number of their names"—*i.e.*, of individual persons.

Ver. 20. *Number of their names*, proceeding from the individual to the more general, as always afterwards.

Ver. 47. *Levites.*—Because they did not belong to the host.

Ver. 51. *Set it up.*—Heb.: "Let it down;" *i.e.*, the scaffolding and curtains. "Stranger;" *i.e.*, one who is not a Levite.

Ver. 52. *Wrath.*—If the sanctuary is profaned.

CHAPTER II.

In order to give Israel still more the form of an army, a distinct order of encampment is prescribed it. In the middle is the tabernacle. Around this is arranged the camp in the form of a square, so that three tribes are arranged on every side. Among these the middle, as the most distinguished, carries the standard. The eastern side is the foremost. The main direction of the march of the host was towards the east. There was the entrance of the sanctuary. On this side Judah, as the prince among his brethren (Gen. xlix. 8), carries the standard; on the south side stands the standard of Reuben; in the middle, next to him, his own brother Simeon, and Gad, the son of his mother's maidservant. Dan receives the chief post on the north side, as the judicial tribe in Israel (Gen. xlviii. 16); on the west are Rachel's descendants—Ephraim the standard-bearer, as the selected firstborn, Gen. xlviii. 19.

Ver. 3. *Standard.*—The standard belonged to all the three tribes; but besides this each tribe had its own ensign.

Ver. 33. *Levites.*—As they did not give any service in war.

CHAPTER III.

Around the tabernacle, in the middle of the whole, is encamped the tribe of Levi. And in order to show that this tribe is, as it were, the heart of the whole people, it was to be arranged in four divisions, each of which corresponds to one of the four divisions of the tribes. The Gershonites, behind the tabernacle, had the charge of the coverings and hangings; the Kohathites, on the south side, the sacred vessels and furniture; the Merarites, the boards, bars, sockets, and pillars. Before the tabernacle, towards the east, were encamped Moses, Aaron, and his sons, as the immediate guardians of the sanctuary.

Ver. 1. *Generations.*—With these words commence many narratives of these books, which contain far more than a register of genealogy; *e.g.*, Gen. xxxvii. 2. The reason is, because in these very ancient books the table of the generations forms the thread of the history: cf. Gen. v. In the case of Moses, who in so many respects stands by himself in the history of the kingdom of God, we find this peculiarity, that his children are merged among the rest of the Levites, and have no part in the priesthood, so that, as the passage before us shows, he is continued in Aaron's posterity. The reason perhaps might be, either that the mother of his children was a Midianitish woman, or because at the first Moses had refused to be sent, so that

Aaron, contrary to God's purpose, was appointed his colleague. Exod. iv., note on ver. 14.

Ver. 3. *Priest's office.*—Cf. Exod. xxviii. 41, note.

Ver. 7. *Charge of the whole congregation.*—This word signifies not merely "to watch," but "to do the service." The whole people were called to this sacred service; the Levites performed it in their stead.

Ver. 9. *Children of Israel.*—It is here intended expressly to be signified that they were only servants of the priests.

Ver. 10. *Stranger.*—Therefore even a Levite himself.

Ver. 12. *Shall be mine.*—Cf. Exod. xiii. 1; Lev. xxvii. 26. According to the intimation in Exod. xxxii. 29, the particular time of conferring this blessing was on the occasion of the vengeance executed by the tribe of Levi on the idolaters.

Ver. 25. *The tabernacle.*—"The tabernacle" are the curtains on the sanctuary inside; "the tent," the outward coverings: cf. Exod. xxvi. 1, 7, note 2.

Ver. 27. *Kohath.*—The Kohathites, to which Aaron and his family belonged, had the most sacred offices.

Ver. 39. *22,000.*—When we reckon the particular sums given, vers. 22, 28, 34, we find a total sum of 22,300; therefore 300 more than here. We must either suppose an error in transcribing the numbers, or a round sum to be mentioned, or that the 300 above the number were themselves first-born, and therefore could not come in the place of other first-born.

Ver. 43. The very small number of the first-born is surprising, as it is only one in every 27. Various ways of accounting for this by way of deduction have been resorted to; as, for example, that in all the families where the first-born was a daughter, no first-born was reckoned. But, perhaps, the most correct way is to suppose that only the first-born after the law, Exod. xiii., had been given were reckoned. In that case the number, of course, would be very great; but this, perhaps, may be accounted for by supposing that, in the latter period of the great oppression in Egypt, the people had not much multiplied, but afterwards in the wilderness the increase had been proportionably great.

Ver. 51. *Commanded Moses.*—Subsequently all the money for the redemption of the first-born fell to Aaron, ch. xviii. 15.

CHAPTER IV.

After the general view of their position given in the former chapter, there follows now the particular business of each division of the tribe of Levi. The priests held the most holy offices, which the other sons of Levi might not touch, "lest they should be destroyed;" the next holy, the Kohathites, from which family Aaron was. Their business is most fully described, and Aaron's eldest son set over them: the younger over the two others.

Ver. 3. *Thirty years and upward.*—According to ch. viii. 24 they are fit for war and for the service of the tabernacle from their twenty-fifth year. But for the carrying of the holy things, as the most distinguished office, whereby they were most highly honoured and placed most near the Lord, they were only considered mature from their thirtieth year. The reason was, not on account of their bodily strength being insufficient for the purpose before that age, but this maturity had a figurative signification. The service of the Lord claimed a person in the perfection of manhood and the bloom of his years The Jewish tradition believed that in the five years they had enjoyed a training for the full duties of the office—which perhaps was the case in later times.

Ver. 4. *Most holy things.*—Cf. Exod. xxx. 10, note.

Ver. 5. *Cover.*—Cf. Exod. xxv. 5.

Ver. 6. *Wholly of blue.*—Heb., "A blue purple (hyacinth-coloured) covering:" as Exod xxv. 4. In order that the greatest sanctuary of the covenant might, in the march of the host, be prominent and distinguished, it had a peculiar beautiful covering over it.

Ver. 7. *Continual bread.*—Cf. Exod. xxv. 29, 30.

Ver. 10. *Upon a bar.*—An instrument for carrying it which might be laid on the shoulders.

Ver 14. *Staves of it.*—In the oldest versions this addition is found,—"And they shall take a blue purple covering, and place therein the stave, and shall place it in a covering of badger skins, and place it on a bar:" which words in the Hebrew were perhaps afterwards left out by oversight, and originally stood in it.

Ver. 16. *Daily meat-offering.*—According to Exod. xxix. 38, a meat-offering was joined to the daily sacrifice. If, during the march of the host, this latter must be omitted, yet at least the former should be continued without interruption.

Ver. 48. That of the 22,000 Levites there were 8580 of the age between 30 and 50, is somewhat unusual; and, perhaps, may be explained by supposing that this tribe had been spared in the great chastisement, Exod. xxxii., in which men in the prime of life especially perished.

CHAPTER V.

Ver. 3. *Without the camp.*—That was now carried into execution which had been commanded, Lev. xiii. 46.

Ver. 8. *To the priest.*—This completes what had been said on the thing itself, Lev. vi. 4. Here it is only added in what way, in the case of the impossibility of restitution to the injured person, satisfaction shall follow. Since, in such a case, every one had committed a sin especially against the Lord (ver. 6), it was natural that to Him, *i.e.*, to the priest, satisfaction should be made.

The following remarkable regulation gives us a deep insight into the teaching of the law of marriage. The state of marriage appears as a Divine institution immediately after the creation. The human connection of the sexes is most clearly distinguished from that of the animals as a holy and indissoluble union; and in the course of the history we see how the great comprehensive covenant-relation of God to His people is represented to us as that of marriage—the type of which, in a small degree, is human marriage. We find, among the covenant people, adultery forbidden in the ten commandments, and, in the more full explanation of the law, threatened with death. The prohibitions of marriage in cases of near kinship are intended to protect the holy family bond, which is founded on marriage. The whole constitution of the people of Israel, with their tables of genealogies, resting, as this constitution did, on the patriarchal family unity, necessarily inculcated the great importance of a pure and unmixed descent. Hence, now, the appointment of the jealousy-offering, which was intended to bring to light the truth of the suspicion of adultery. Later tradition thus describes the proceeding:—" The husband comes to the judge of his place, and says to him, This, my wife, has had intercourse with another man, and these are the witnesses; and she says she is innocent, and is willing to drink in proof thereof. Then the judge examines the witnesses, and appoints two persons to watch the man that he does not have any intercourse with his wife until she has drunk. Then she is sent to Jerusalem, since the suspected woman is not allowed to drink, except in the high council of the seventy elders in the sanctuary." It is remarkable that now the woman must appear with an offering before the Lord. This was an offering of barley with wheat-meal—no oil, no frankincense, might be on it. She lay under grave suspicion. In this, at least, she was not blameless. In the meat-offering she presented her walk of life—her works to God (cf. Lev. iii., introd.). This she could only do in the feeling of her unworthiness, without the emblem of joy in the Holy Ghost, and of prayer well-pleasing to God. Yet she might bring the offering, since she was only *suspected*, not judged. By making the offering, she confessed herself pure before God; she appealed to Him, in case her small offering was pleasing to Him, to defend her innocency; in case of guilt, she challenged His judgment to fall upon her more heavily. Holding the offering in her hand, she must take the oath that she is clean, which is the main point of the whole transaction. All besides is intended to make the perjury in this case the more fearful. Therefore she must now drink the water wherein is placed dust taken from the floor of the sanctuary, and figuratively charged with a curse. The meaning is not that the water has thereby received any actual power to do her any injury: it was rather an earnest and token of the Divine judgment which now passed over her. From the moment of drinking it she might be sure that, as certainly as the curse had figuratively passed into the water, and the water into her, so surely would God know how to find her out with His punishments, and that in the very parts of the body with which she had sinned.

Ver. 14. *Spirit of jealousy.*—The "spirit of jealousy" is the spirit which in this relation will endure no rival. It appears here as by no means a sinful feeling. On the contrary, it is only by the conduct here prescribed that the man is "guiltless from iniquity" in respect to his wife (ver. 31). He would become a participator in her guilt if he let it pass unnoticed. Nay, there is in the words, "come upon him," an indication that a holy indignation was well-pleasing to God, and therefore indifferent acquiescence displeasing to Him. Moreover, the man only had the right of this appeal to the oath, the woman not so. She was in the husband's power as his property, and must endure the presence of a concubine. A relation like this, having its origin in the fall, could not abide in the Christian Church.

Ver. 15. *Her offering.*—The husband brings the offering; *i.e.*, he does not present it to the Lord as his offering, since the woman must do that, but he must give it her out of his property —place her in a condition to make it.

To remembrance.—Namely, before the Lord. Since the offering, in case of guilt, calls down the punishment of the Lord on the sin. With this may well be consistent that in the mind of the woman it was a meat-offering in the usual sense.

Ver. 17. *Holy water.*—Water from a brazen vessel in the fore-court: Exod. xxx. 18.

Earthen vessel.—Of a common, despised material.

Into the water.—There must, as an emblem of the Divine presence, be put into the water something holy, consecrated to God. But on account of the heavy suspicion against the woman this might be nothing but the meanest of things, the dust from the floor. The serpent was sentenced to eat dust, Gen. iii. 14; and mourners disfigured themselves with it, Job ii. 12.

Ver. 18. *Uncover.*—The uncovering took place by way of disfigurement; but, at the same time, it was to signify that the woman, so long as she lay under suspicion, was not united with, or in the power of, the man: 1 Cor. xi. 5, etc.

Bitter water.—The bitterness does not relate to the taste, but to its power to bring destruction in case of a false oath.

Ver. 21. *A curse and an oath;* *i.e.*, an example of the fulfilment of the threatened curse.

Ver. 22. *Amen, Amen.*—The priest administered the oath— put it in her mouth—and she ratified and made it her own by her Amen. This word, which occurs in the O. T. both at the beginning and end of a speech by way of confirmation and affirmation, means properly, "firm," "certain," and was rendered by the old translators, "so be it;" but in the N. T. we find the Hebrew word itself in the Greek, whence it has passed into our Church language. In respect to the oath, see Deut. xxvii. 15; Neh. v. 13, ch. viii. 6.

Ver. 31. *Bear her iniquity.*—The punishment of death decreed against adultery.

CHAPTER VI.

As God ordinarily revealed Himself to His people through His priests, and especially His high priest—but, beside them, occasionally raised up prophets as Moses, Deut. xviii. 18, who interfered with a corrupt and irregular state of things—so, on the other hand, was it permitted to some out of the people, as being a kingdom of priests, at their own option to partake, by means of a vow for a time or for their life, in certain privileges of the consecrated order. This was the relation in which a Nazir—*i.e.*, one set apart—stood. Like the priests when they were about to enter the sanctuary (Lev. x. 9, 10), a Nazarite abstains for a time from wine and strong drink, as if he desired ever in spirit to live before God in His service. He lets his hair grow in token of fulness of life, which flowed to him from God. Like the priest, he might not mourn for the death of his nearest kinsman. Samson and John Baptist were exceptional cases of such persons set apart to the Lord for the whole of their life. In them, as in the best of the Christian monks, and in their influence on corrupt times, the meaning and the working of such an institution may be perceived, which, if it belongs, as it does, more to the time of the law and of childhood, yet may in certain limits be revived in all times. Therefore God speaks of it as one of His benefits conferred on the people, that He had "raised up of their sons for prophets, and of their young men for Nazarites" (Amos ii. 11); and He represents them as the flower and ornament of the people, Lam. iv. 7.—Two particular customs in sacrifices are appointed the Nazarite. If he has accidentally made himself unclean by touching a dead body, he must, on account of the sanctity and conspicuousness of his peculiar relation to God, bring a trespass-offering, besides the burnt and sin-offering (cf. Lev. v., introd.). When the time of his vow was past, the Nazarite was, besides this burnt and sin-offering, above all to bring the thank-offering, which is made in the case of every vow (cf. Lev. iii., introd.). But into the fire of the thank-offering the especial token of the votee must be thrown, namely, his long hair, which is now cut off. The other customs in sacrifices are like to the consecration offering of the priests (Exod. xxix.), but naturally have not the meaning of consecration, but of the thank-offering of one consecrated after a priestly manner, who partly will acknowledge the blessing he has received, partly will show his joy and thankfulness for the same.

Ver. 2. *When either.*—Lit., " When a man or woman does something extraordinary to vow the vow of the Nazir (the separated), to set himself apart to the Lord," etc.

Ver. 3. *Strong drink.*—Under the "strong drink" is all kind of fruit-wines to be understood, which were in those times made from dates or from the juice of palms; also a kind of beer from barley.

Ver. 4. *Husk.*—As, under things forbidden, much not properly speaking intoxicating is mentioned, we perceive herein the emblematic meaning of the abstinence.

Ver. 5. *Grow.*—From the history of Samson especially, we perceive the meaning of this custom. It is not for a moment to be regarded as a token of mourning. A strong growth of hair is an emblem of the vigour of strength and life, and hence often in pictures is represented as " blossoming, sprouting." This is again an emblem of communion with God, the source of all life.

Ver. 7. *Consecration.* Cf. Lev. xxi. 11.—" Vow." " Neser" signifies, properly, " separation ;" but then also, what in this circumstance appears as its peculiar token, " the strong growth of hair."

Ver. 12. *Days of his separation.*—From the day of the sacrifice, the eighth day.

Ver. 14. *Peace-offerings.*—The most precious animal for the most important of the three sacrifices.

Ver. 15. *Drink-offering.*—Each of the sacrifices had its own.

Ver. 17. *Unleavened bread.*—Cf. Lev. viii. 26.

Ver. 20. *Heave-shoulder.*—The waving, which denoted the

surrender to the Lord, the consecration of the sacrificer (cf. Lev. vii. 34, note), must here be prominent, where a consecration similar to the priestly took place, and where it was intended to be especially marked by the sacrifice. When the sacrifices were prepared which the fire from heaven consumed, Aaron felt himself impelled, as it seems without express command of God, to bless the people (Lev. ix. 22). The Lord confirms what was then done, by giving *His name* as the particular purport of the blessing which was to descend on the people. Here also the name of the Lord appears as something real, creative. It is His revealed nature—God Himself in His attributes made known to His covenant people, who, when the blessing is pronounced, communicates Himself to the faith of His own, and unites Himself with them. In the form of blessing here appears for the first time the Divine number Three, which so often occurs in the N. T., and following each other in the same way as in similar passages in the N. T. First, God generally, as the source of all good, and the defence against all evil: next, the same God as revealing Himself from without, and, indeed, in His grace; and lastly, the same as inwardly uniting Himself with His own, and sending them His peace ("the love of God, the grace of Jesus Christ, the fellowship of the Holy Ghost," 2 Cor. xiii. 13).

Ver. 24. *The Lord bless thee.*—A notification that these words continued in use is to be found 2 Sam. vi. 18; cf. Ecclus. xxxvi. 17.—That the *Lord* blesses, the *Lord* defends—this is the main point in this first division. He it is from whom all good proceeds, and He will grant all good to His people.

Ver. 25. *His face.*—A further repetition of this, see Ps. lxvii. 1. The countenance of the Lord lightens upon every one when He reveals to them His grace, as this last is expressly added. In the fullest sense of the word, He has personally revealed His grace in the Angel of the covenant, the Mediator also of the N. T. · cf Exod. xxxiii. 14, note.

Ver. 26. *Lift up.*—The "lifting up of the countenance on any one" expresses an actual powerful working of the personal God on this man. In "making His countenance shine on any one," He remains standing before him, although as the Gracious One; in "lifting up His countenance on him," He works on him or in him. The same expression occurs, as spoken of God's anger, Jer. xxi. 10, ch. xliv. 11. But what is added shows, that as in this blessing the gracious countenance of God shines on man, so is it lifted up upon him in order to give to him peace, the essence of all blessing to sinful, fighting, struggling man.

CHAPTER VII.

Ver. 9. *Bear.*—Cf. ch. iv. 15. All their burden might not be drawn, but must be carried.

Ver. 11. *Dedicating.*—Cf. Exod. xxv. 21, 22. This is repeated here, in order to show that notwithstanding these gifts, with which the people in the person of their princes drew near to God, yet Moses still remained the mediator between God and the people in the old way.

CHAPTER VIII.

Ver. 2. *Lightest.*—The office of lighting the lamps is hereby expressly conferred on Aaron, while, Exod. xxvii. 21, the general care of the tabernacle is only spoken about.

Ver. 5.—The tribe of Levi, which had already been set apart in the ordering of the camp, and placed in the middle, now receives here its consecration. It is severed from the rest of the people; the office conferred on it, which it has to perform, but which it dare not undertake without express consecration; and it is appointed to assist Aaron and his sons as their ministers. A ceremony similar to the consecration of priests (Exod. xxix.) is performed. It consists of an ablution, a double act of sacrifice, and a waving of the sacrifice.

Ver. 7. *Water of purifying.*—Atoning water as "sin-offering;" a sacrifice betokening the taking away of sin.

Shave.—So the Egyptian priests, for the sake of purification, shaved off every hair from their body.—*Wash their clothes.* The washing was a kind of external, preliminary purification, before the deeper and more entire one through the sin-offering: Exod. xxix. 1. The washing of the clothes in the case of the Levites corresponds with the putting on of their robes by the priests: Exod. xxix. 5.

Ver. 10. *Upon the Levites.*—As upon the sacrificial gift: cf. Lev. i. 4, note.

Ver. 11. *Offer.*—Wave: cf. Lev. vii. 34.

Ver. 12. *Atonement.*—For the cleansing from their sins and offering of them to the Lord.

Ver. 19. *Unto the sanctuary.*—The atonement takes place by means of a covering of sin. The unsanctified people would in the service of the sanctuary have had to suffer the punishment for their sins; but the Lord allows to be presented to Him by them the tribe of Levi, which covers their sins. Thus, on a later occasion, Phinehas atoned for the people: ch. xxv. 13. The offering of the Levites in place of the first-born is distinguished from the sacrifice (Exod. xiii.) for the same by this, that the sacrifice did not offer to the Lord any especial compensation for the service of the first-born. The Levites afforded this once for all, while in addition the sacrifice continued, that it might never be forgotten that the first-born must be offered to the Lord for the whole people.

Ver. 24. *Tabernacle.*—Cf. ch. iv. 3, note.

Ver. 25. *Serve no more,* *i e.,* shall be free to serve no more. According to Jewish tradition, this command related merely to the service in the wilderness. In Canaan, on the contrary, they were not free therefrom.

CHAPTER IX.

It appears that for the celebrating of the Passover in the wilderness an especial revelation was on this account necessary, because on its establishment the festival was expressly intended for the land of Canaan (Exod. xii. 25), as afterwards no Passover was celebrated in the wilderness. Now, because on the Passover the continuance of the covenant with God depended, a question connected with it was this—What were they to do who were hindered by reason of uncleanness? and for them a formal particular after-festival was commanded.

Ver. 13. *Appointed time.*—It is clear from this and from ver. 13, that the Passover was a proper sacrifice, and therefore the paschal meats, the meats of the sacrifice.

Ver. 15. *Testimony.*—So is the Most Holy called in a narrower sense, because the testimony was kept therein. On this rested the cloud, as also from thence Moses received the Divine commands: ch. vii. 89.

Of fire.—Cf. Exod. xiii. 22, note.

Ver. 19. *Kept the charge.*—Heb., "they observed the observance of the Lord;" *i.e.*, they performed the service of sacrifice as prescribed by Moses, which had necessarily been interrupted during the march. When the cloud rested only a short time, the tabernacle was not pitched.

Ver. 20. *A few days.*—Heb., "days of number"—days which could be counted; *i.e.*, a few days.

Ver. 22. *Or a year.*—Heb., "days;" *i.e.*, not easily counted, an indefinite long time.

CHAPTER X.

The Lord Himself appoints the preparation of the trumpets by which the different signals for the people were to be given, that in all which they did as a people, they might have the certainty they stood under God's immediate guidance. Every assembling of the people or of the council, every expedition in war, was thereby marked as holy.

Ver. 2. *Of a whole piece.*—Heb.: "Thou shalt make them turned (rounded) of silver."

Ver. 5. *Blow an alarm.*—Lit., "a broken (extended) sound."

Ver. 7. *Ye shall blow.*—As ver. 3, a short sound.

Ver 8. *Generations.*—Not the princes. The Lord Himself was the Ruler. At His command His immediate servants did it.

Ver. 9. *From your enemies.*—As when God saw the rainbow He will remember His covenant with men (cf. Gen. ix. 17, note), in like manner will He at the sound of the trumpets remember His people: *i.e.*, the blowing of the trumpets was to be no mere human signal, but, as resting on a Divine appointment, a pledge and a channel of the grace of God.

Ver. 10. *Before your God.*—As it were for the confirmation of their act of worship. Just as the ascending smoke of the sacrifice was " a sweet savour," so was this an awakening sound, in order to remind God of His covenant. This mode of expression after the manner of men is explained, Gen. ix. 17.

Ver. 21. *Against they came.*—Therefore, in the march, the Gershonites and Merarites go before with the poles, etc., of the tabernacle, behind the camp of Judah; the Kohathites follow after Reuben, in order that the tabernacle might be pitched before they arrived with the sacred vessels, and that these might not remain in the open air, but as soon as possible be brought into the tabernacle.

Ver. 29. *Midianite.*—Cf. Exod. ii. 16, note.

Ver. 32. *Unto thee.*—Notwithstanding the pillar of the cloud showed them the way, yet Hobab's guidance might be of essential consequence to them. The pillar of the cloud indeed gave the signal for marching, and afforded a general direction as to the route; but in the wilderness, intersected by mountains and valleys, the tribes must certainly disperse in quest of springs of water. We find even in the case of the manna, that in collecting it the activity and diligence of the people were not dispensed with (cf. Exod. xvi. 5, note): how much more must this be the case in respect to water, for which no provision was made by any like regular supply!

Ver. 34. *Out of the camp.*—It seems that the cloudy pillar especially stood over the ark of the covenant and moved with it, but likewise during the march spread itself as a defence over the host. In like manner, it is allowable to suppose that the pillar of fire by night diffused a radiance over the host, so that they all had it, not merely as a guiding token, but as a light on their way.

Ver. 36. *Thousands of Israel.*—Moses uttered a prayer of faith both in the marching and at the standing still. It was at once a petition from the mouth of the mediator of the covenant, and contained at the same time an earnest encouragement to the people themselves, reminding them of their entire dependence on God.

CHAPTER XI.

The people of Israel now break up from Sinai. There were two roads to Canaan: the one runs along the Ælanitic Gulf, but this is unsuitable to the march of a large host, on account of its narrowness and the proximity of the mountains to the coast; the other leads through an inhospitable desert, et-Tih. "From the mountain of the same name, the land, which is composed of chalk, gypsum, and flint, falls off into uniform terraces towards the Mediterranean Sea, into which its waters in the rainy season flow—the most horrible and melancholy of all wildernesses."—(Laborde.) As in the list of the stations (ch. xxxiii. 16), there is only mention of one place, "the graves of lust" (Kibroth-hattaavah), it appears that Taberah is one and the same with it.—While the people were receiving the law in the wilderness of Sinai, peace had altogether prevailed. Fear in the presence of the wonders which were seen on the holy mount—the punishment which followed immediately on contempt being shown towards them—the comparatively more lovely and fertile region in which they then were,—these might have been motives so far to restrain the outbreaks of fleshly lust. But hardly had they set out on their march to the Promised Land, when their perverse, unsubdued, carnal mind is once again roused. This time it does not break out against the Lord Himself, and so proceed to open apostasy and idolatry; but it is expressed against His dealings with them, against the kind and degree of that food which He provided for them on the way. This is the commencement of a long series of temptings of God.

Ver. 1. *Complained.*—Lit.: "And the people were as evil-complainers in the ears of the Lord." The reason is not here given. It was a general discontent, dissatisfaction with the providences of God.

Of the camp.—By "the fire of the Lord" we are most likely to understand lightning, as often; especially Lev. x. 2. The "end of the camp" (so literally) is the extreme border of it; where, perhaps, the lightning fell among the circumjacent bushes, and consumed a number of tents before it could be extinguished.

Ver. 3. *Taberah;* i.e., a burning. The chastisement just narrated was a light warning, meant to check at the outset the evil disposition of the people. The murmuring now took a more distinct direction—it was aroused by a craving desire after change and variety of food. The manna had a pleasant taste, an agreeable appearance, it was a direct gift from God; but it wanted the flavour which imparts its piquancy to human viands, and which men long after in this restless, sinful, changing life. What a wonderful type of that of which the manna generally was intended to remind us (Exod. xvi.)—the moral and spiritual nourishment imparted in God's revelation, both by His Word and His Providence! And quite as remarkable is the issue of this history. Moses, as ever faithful in his intercession, receives, on his complaining that the burden was too heavy for him, a council of seventy elders to assist him, who were endued with the Holy Spirit; the people also receive what they desire. But after God has showed them what He is able to do, He changes, by a chastisement annexed to the gift, the blessing into a curse. Thus does the kingdom of God proceed to develop itself, as much furthered by man's sinfulness as by the prevailing intercession of the servants of God.

Ver. 4. *Mixed multitude.*—The mixed rabble which had marched with them out of Egypt (Exod. xii. 38). The murmuring proceeded first from these, but soon spread among the people.

Ver. 5. *Garlick.*—In all these productions Egypt was, and indeed in a measure still is, remarkably rich.

Ver. 9. *Fell upon it.*—This account of the manna here inserted, is intended, by describing its beauty and pleasantness, to show in stronger colours the unthankfulness of the people. It was like to the fine, elegant coriander-seed; it resembled the beautiful, fragrant bdellium (cf. Gen. ii. 12, note); it could be prepared in many ways; but, what was the main thing, it was an immediate gift from Heaven. But all this was insufficient to stay the longing desire after food more stimulating to the appetite.

Ver. 12. *Nursing father;* as a lulling mother.

Ver. 15. *Wretchedness.*—The Lord permits even the stronger language of dissatisfaction in His servant, as already before (Exod. xxxii. 11). The wish to die was certainly a despairing, and therefore a sinful wish. But God would rather that His servants should lay open before Him, in their prayers, even such unholy movements of their heart, than that they should express their sorrow in any other way. In no way can this hidden sin of murmuring, of fear, of despondency, be so completely removed as by making it known to the merciful and gracious One—by declaring to Him that we cannot understand His unsearchable ways. To complain to Him is already the beginning of a return of faith and confidence: cf. Gen. xviii. 32, note.

Ver. 17. *Thyself alone.*—We here find the first beginning of a prophetic office among the people of Israel. While the priests were instituted to their office by an outward consecration, and the council appointed at Jethro's advice was only a judicial tribunal in human affairs, these elders received at their calling the Holy Ghost, which immediately manifests itself in the gift of prophecy. It is expressly said that they received of Moses' spirit, in order to betoken their necessary union with him. That these elders formed a permanent corporation, which afterwards was continued in the high council, the sanhedrim, is neither here said nor does it appear afterwards. But we have the first trace of a connected society of prophets, such as was in later times still further carried out by Samuel.

Ver. 18. *Eat flesh.*—The flesh was a Divine gift: in order to be able to receive it aright the people must sanctify themselves, as they came by means of it in direct contact with God. See Exod. xix. 10, note.

Ver. 20. *Wept before Him.*—The gift itself shall become a punishment to you; the sinful lust shall, by its very gratification, become a pain.

Ver. 22. *To suffice them.*—We find here quite a similar occurrence with what took place in the case of the feeding of the 4000, where the disciples had altogether forgotten the former miracle (cf. St Matt. xv.), just as Moses here forgot the former sending of quails (Exod. xvi. 13). Here, however, there was this in addition, that the first miracle only had in view to feed the people once in a way; but in the present case, to supply them with provision for a long while.

Ver. 25. *They prophesied.*—The prophesying took place by their being raised to a condition of soul in which their lower mental faculties were kept bound, and the higher ones fitted to receive more fully the revelations of the Divine Spirit. In this condition the inspired person spake words of exhortation or poured forth devotions, of which he was incapable in the ordinary circumstances of life; and even the bodily gestures bore witness to what was inwardly taking place. Cf. especially 2 Sam. xix. 20-24. We are by no means compelled to suppose that this inward change befell the elders of a sudden. No doubt Moses chose out such of the elders as had not taken part in the outbreak of the people.

Did not cease.—Heb., "and did not add thereto;" *i.e.*, the prophesying was not again afterwards repeated. This gift was displayed in them only on this occasion, in order to invest them with a sacred dignity in the eyes of the people. The same was the case in the early days of Christianity, when, on the laying on of hands after baptism, the gifts of the Holy Spirit manifested themselves in every one, which afterwards were repeated only in the case of a very few.

Ver. 26. *In the camp.*—On this occasion, also, it was intended to be shown that the Spirit of the Lord is bound to no human order, but acts as He lists. So it was in the instance of the preference of Jacob before Esau, of Ephraim before Manasseh; so was it instanced in the case of the outpouring of the Spirit before baptism in the house of Cornelius (Acts x. 47).

Ver. 28. *Forbid him.*—In a similar spirit with John (St Mark ix. 38).

Ver. 29. *His Spirit upon them.*—Moses, who himself possesses the greatest fulness of the Spirit, is likewise on that account the most liberal: for, "where the Spirit of the Lord is there is liberty." He recognises in this free pouring out of the gift a prophetic sign, that the whole people of God will some time be partakers of it.

Ver. 30. *Elders of Israel.*—They all came together.

Ver. 31. *Quails.*—The same as was given to the people, Exod. xvi.

Ver. 32. *Ten homers.*—An homer contains about two cubic feet; therefore a rich measure for one month.

Ver. 33. *Very great plague.*—The outward gift was here, therefore, no pledge of the Divine favour; just as it often happens that a wish, which has long been perversely and eagerly cherished, when in the providence of God it is brought to pass, brings with it at the same time a judgment of God.

CHAPTER XII.

To these first outbreaks of the people, through their lust of flesh, are added the still more dangerous one resulting from ambition. But what must have proved the greatest trial to Moses was, that they began among his own relations, who had been deemed worthy with himself of so much higher favour, but who on that account presumed to think they could be raised above him. Miriam the prophetess, the first among the Israelitish women (Exod. xv. 20, 21), is the prime mover of the sedition; and Aaron, who on every occasion showed himself weak, followed her. The trial, however, ends in the greater glorification of Moses, and in a clear distinction of that which was peculiarly his own above all other prophets, and in the deep humiliation of Miriam.

Ver. 1. *Ethiopian woman.*—Lit., "since he had taken a Cushite." Zipporah was a Midianite, and so not of Cushite descent. She can, therefore, here hardly be intended. After her death (for, since polygamy was discountenanced by the law, it is hardly likely that Moses practised it, especially when advanced in life), he had taken a wife of a Cushite descent, no doubt designedly, in order by this example to foreshadow the future union of Israel with the most distant heathen. Miriam and Aaron, who did not understand this, treated him with most foolish scorn on that account.

Ver. 2. *Also by us.*—Regarding that marriage as a blot on him, they wished to degrade Moses as a prophet, and to elevate themselves.

Ver. 3. *Very meek.*—Moses here says of himself what Christ with still greater truth said, St Matt. xi. 29. By mentioning this in connection with the history, he would intimate that he did nothing to justify, far less to avenge himself, but committed his cause entirely to the Lord. He did this so fully that he is able calmly to relate, as a fact with which he had nothing to do, what was necessary for a full understanding of the narrative. To this utter silence and patience of Moses the sudden interference of the Lord is a striking counterpart.

Ver. 7. *In all Mine house.*—To whom I commit My whole

house, and no particular office therein; and he is a faithful steward in it: cf. Heb. iii. 2.

Ver. 8. *Shall he behold.*—Lit.: " I speak mouth to mouth with him, and not in riddles (parables); and he beholds the face of the Lord." In the revelations made to the other prophets, whose commission referred to some particular subject, the powers of their souls were fettered, and an image or a parabolic saying was presented to their spirit: Moses, on the other hand, was raised to that condition in which he could clearly understand the things revealed to him. He beheld them "apparently," without the help of any intervention. That to " behold the similitude of the Lord " is said only comparatively, is plain from Exod. xxxiii. 20; cf. the note there. This distinction is thus explained by the Rabbins :—" It is a fundamental principle in our law that God vouchsafes the gift of prophecy to the children of men; but that the gift of prophecy only rests on a man who is great in wisdom, mighty in virtue, so that in no particular do his desires domineer over him. In such a man the Holy Ghost dwells, and his soul has communion with the angels, and he becomes a different man: 1 Sam. x. 6. The prophets were different in degrees, as one wise man is greater than another. All saw their visions only in a dream or a nightly apparition, or in the daytime when a deep sleep had fallen on them; and when they prophesied their limbs trembled, and their bodily strength sank, and their thoughts became restless, and their spirit was withdrawn, as it is said of Abraham (Gen. xv. 12) and of Daniel (x. 8). The things revealed were given in parables, and, together with them, the explanation was written in their hearts. So Jacob's ladder to heaven (Gen. xxviii. 12), so the beasts of Ezekiel (ch. i.), the seething-pot and the rod of Jeremiah, etc., all prophesied in figures and dark words. No prophet prophesied at every time and when he would; but they prepared themselves for it with joyfulness of heart, and with meditation, and with psalteries and harps (1 Sam. x. 5). And when they had prepared themselves it came upon them, and at times also it did not come upon them. This holds good of all the prophets, with the exception of Moses. All prophesied through dreams and visions; but Moses waking and standing (ch. vii. 89). All prophesied through angels, therefore they saw their countenances in likenesses and dark words; but Moses without this.

He knew Divine things. All the rest were terrified; but God spake to Moses as a man speaks to his friend (Exod. xxxiii. 11). All the rest did not prophesy continually; but Moses was at every time when he wished endued with the Holy Spirit, and he had no need to prepare himself beforehand; but he stood like the ministering angels before God, as it is said, 'Stand still, and I will hear what the Lord will command'" (ch. ix. 8). Even in all this Moses was a type of the Mediator of the N. T.; since, while all the above can only be said comparatively of Moses, it is absolutely true only of Christ.

Ver. 10. *White as snow.*—The leprosy befell Miriam here as the most terrible, direct Divine scourge for an offence committed against the Lord and against His holy servant: cf. Lev. xiii., introd.

Ver. 12. *Mother's womb.*—Heb.: "That she be not as a dead person, from whom, as he comes out of his mother's womb, already the half of his flesh is eaten"—as an already corrupt stillborn child, the extreme of impurity and nullity.—The punishment is inflicted on Miriam as the instigator; in Aaron the priesthood is spared and reverenced, but he feels that, nevertheless, he is a participator in the punishment, and confesses his own sin together with hers.

Ver. 14. *If her father.*—If an earthly father had done this and must be ashamed, how much more it, etc. etc.

Ver. 15. *Seven days.*—The exclusion of the leper lasted this time, for the proving whether he were cured or not: Lev. xiii. 4, 5.

CHAPTER XIII.

Here we arrive at an important crisis in the history of the Israelites. They had often tempted God, and He has chastised them with a moderate, though, it may be, marked visitation; but now came the trial which should determine whether they who were come out of Egypt have a personal interest in the promises, or were to leave them to their successors—whether they should march at once into the Promised Land and take possession of it, or should die on their long, wearisome, and dangerous wanderings in the wilderness. And herein also is the guidance of Israel an image of similar critical periods in the life of nations and of individuals—whom God desires to lead by less rugged roads, and had begun to do so, until some necessary trial, under which they fail, clearly manifests to them that they require a more severe mode of dealing. According to Deut. i. 22, the whole people first desired Moses to send spies to Canaan, according to which the command of the Lord here mentioned is a granting of their petition. Although He might have required of them to trust unconditionally His word without using this plan, still He makes a concession to their weakness, so long as it does not display unbelieving opposition to His will. But they do not know themselves what they ask; since, when God grants their wish, they lose sight of the truth of God and His almighty guidance in the human means which they employed. They thus place themselves in conscious opposition to God, which they carry so far, that they would prefer to return back into Egyptian bondage rather than undergo the trouble and the perils of conquering the Promised Land.

Ver. 16. *Jehoshua.*—His family, see 1 Chron. viii. 27.—Hoshea signifies "help;" Jehoshua (for so is the word fully), "Jehovah helps." The first servant of Moses, the future accomplisher of so great undertakings, was by his very name to be placed in a distinct relation to the covenant people of Israel.

Ver. 20. *What the land is.*—God had already long ago, by His promises, repeatedly and expressly spoken about most of these things, so that no inquiry seemed to be necessary. Still Moses would not curtail their liberty. They should learn from their own experience the truth of God.

Ver. 21. *Hamath.*—The wilderness Zin is the part of the wilderness Paran which adjoins Canaan. The most natural supposition is, that the stations in the wilderness which are mentioned ch. xxxiii. 16–36, fall in the time before the return of the spies and the events at Cadesh-barnea. Like the nomadic Arab tribes of the present day, the people wander from one stream and pasture to another, and halt in, altogether, twenty-one different places before they arrive at the south boundary of Canaan at Cadesh, where they again receive the spies. From this point the sacred history is altogether silent respecting the journeyings in the wilderness; the stations are not again named; and we find, after thirty-eight years, the people once more at Cadesh, but now no longer for the purpose of pressing into Canaan, but in order by negotiations to obtain the way through the land of the Edomites.—" Rehob" or Rechob lies (according to Joshua xix. 28; Judges i. 31) in the part of the land which afterwards fell to the lot of the tribe of Aser, not far from Sidon, on the north-west end of the land. Hamath is the well-known Syrian town on the east of Lebanon, the northern end of Canaan.

Ver. 22. *Hebron.*—The old town in the neighbourhood of which Abraham lived, Gen. xiii. 18.

Zoan in Egypt.—Zoan—by the Greeks, Tanis—in the north-eastern part of Lower Egypt, on a branch of the Nile, the capital of the Pharaohs of that day, was about seven years younger than this oldest city of Canaan.

Ver. 24. *Brook Eshcol;* i.e., Cluster of grapes brook. Even now, when the cultivation of the land has been so much neglected, are found bunches of grapes from ten to twelve pounds weight.

Ver. 26. *Kadesh.*—Kadesh was situated on the borders of the land of Edom (ch. xx. 19), on the south extremity of Canaan, not far from the Dead Sea. The people of Israel had therefore passed through the modern Wady-el-Arabah in a northerly direction towards Canaan, on the west side of the mountain-range of Seir: cf. Gen. xxvii. 39, note.

Ver. 29. *Coast of Jordan.*—All parts of the land are strongly peopled and defended.

Ver. 30. *Before Moses.*—As at the terrible news brought by the spies dissatisfaction was immediately expressed against Moses.

Ver. 33. *Eateth up the inhabitants;* i.e., The inhabitants of the lands must be continually armed, as they are exposed to the unceasing attacks of their neighbours, and cannot even thus defend themselves from them. We know, in fact, that before the incursion of the Israelites the Philistines had come from Caphthor (Crete) and subdued the Avites (Deut. ii. 20); and in like manner the Amorites had conquered all the land of the Moabites as far as Arnon. In later times, also, the country continued to be the scene of unceasing small and great wars, which was, indeed, inseparable from its position. Such was the place which Israel was destined to maintain, and from which unbelief would fain make it draw back in terror.

Ver. 33. *In their sight.*—A particular large race of men really dwelt there, though, from the exaggerations of the spies, nothing can be drawn with certainty.

CHAPTER XIV.

Ver. 4. *Return into Egypt.*—The most determined rebellious attempt of all which had as yet taken place, that they should purpose to return into Egypt under another leader; unmindful of their former bondage there, and of the severe fate which, without doubt, awaited them if they went back.

Ver. 5. *Fell on their faces*, in prayer.

Ver. 9. *Their defence.*—"Their shadow"—the defence of God's long-suffering, which had hitherto been accorded them. They are now subjects for the justice of God. If we consider that the extermination of this people took place through the instrumentality of the Israelites when the measure of their iniquity was full (Gen. xv. 16), the signs of this might be observable to the spies even in the breaking up of their internal condition.

Ver. 14. *Of this land.*—Arabia.

Ver. 17. *Be great.*—In order to bring the people into their land, ver. 16,—not, the power of Thy mercy. The connection with what follows is this—"Suffer this people still longer for Thy mercy's sake, and now let Thy whole power be shown mightily among them."

Ver. 18. *Fourth generation.*—See Exod. xxxiv. 7, where also the particular words are explained.

Ver. 22. *According to Thy word.*—It is wonderful that the Lord can have forgiven the people even while He threatens so fearfully to punish them. But we must remember that threatening and punishment related to the people as a body far more than to individuals. The Lord had threatened (ver. 12) to destroy the whole people, and to cancel altogether His covenant with them. This it is which He withdraws. But besides this, His long-suffering is still vouchsafed to the guilty, that the Lord does not suddenly destroy them by pestilence, but lets them gradually die out in their long wandering in the wilderness.

Ver. 22. *Not hearken to My voice.*—" Ten times" might in itself, as a round number, signify the full measure, since this number, as a perfect whole, means perfection; but in actual fact the temptations mentioned in the previous history are exactly ten: (1.) The murmuring at the Red Sea, Exod. xiv. 11, 12; (2.) At Marah, ch. xv. 23; (3.) In the wilderness of Sinai, ch. xvi. 2; (4.) In the case of the manna, ch. xvi. 20; (5.) In the same case a second time, ch. xvi. 27; (6.) In Rephidim, ch. xvii. 1; (7.) At Horeb, ch. xxxii.; (8.) At Taberah, Num. xi. 1; (9.) At the graves of lust, Kibroth-hattaavah, ch. xi. 4; and (10.) Here at Kadesh. Thereby was the measure of their sin really full, and the day of grace past.

Ver. 25. *In the valley.*—On the other side of the mountain now facing the Israelites. They will dispute with you the entrance into Canaan, and ye shall now no more be able to overcome them. This actually took place in the perverse attack which the Israelites afterwards made.

Ver. 26. *Moses and Aaron.*—A second time, after the first preliminary announcement. With these words a fresh revelation every time begins.

Ver. 33. *Your whoredoms.*—The punishment of them. By this expression is elsewhere idolatry peculiarly signified. But it can signify every unfaithfulness, every apostasy from the true God, which must of necessity sooner or later lead to idolatry.

Ver. 37. *Died by the plague.*—A sudden chastisement, a miraculous act on God's part. The seducers died suddenly, the rest gradually.

Ver. 45. *Hormah.*—In their rebellion against the Lord, this people are at one time as foolhardy as they had been at another cowardly. A quick transition from one extreme to another, lightness of mind, a tendency to insurrection, sudden change— these were the characteristics of the people of Israel in the wilderness, as at all times. A steady, calm obedience, therefore, very little marked their conduct.—Hormah did not receive this name until afterwards, ch. xxi. 3.

CHAPTER XV.

The people had fallen away, yet was their sin forgiven and themselves again accepted. Those who were grown up were not, indeed, to enter the Promised Land, but their children should inherit it; and in token of this, grace expressly again assured in the foregoing chapter, the command respecting the sanctification of all fruits of the land by meat and drink-offering is here further renewed, to which is added a more precise command about the sin-offering. The law was thus a pledge of the continuance of the covenant of grace. That to this a peculiar regulation is annexed about sin-offering of the congregation (ver. 22), may perhaps have its reason in the many chances of such sinnings in the wilderness, by which it might become doubtful how far the whole congregation was to be regarded as tainted with this guilt. In reference to this, the necessity of a sin-offering of the whole congregation is enforced.

Ver. 10. *Unto the Lord.*—This fresh regulation is added to the former ones respecting the offering of the first-fruits—that not merely the fruits themselves, but likewise flour, should be offered in testimony that the right of possession of the Lord extended not only to the land, but also to that which by man's labour was produced out of the fruits of the field.

Ver. 12. *According to their number.*—In the laws concerning offering (Lev. ii.), meat-offerings have already been spoken of in a general way. Here it is now determined that they shall be added to every other sacrifice. By these offerings it was solemnly acknowledged that meat and drink, all fruits of the field, all daily nourishment, belong to the Lord. By acknowledging this in the case of every kind of gift in sacrifice, all the works of man's daily life were consecrated to the Lord.

Ver. 16 *Sojourneth with you.*—Cf. Lev. xxiv. 16.

Ver. 24. *By ignorance.*—Heb. literally, "When anything is done away from the eyes of the congregation for forgiveness;" *i. e.*, when any one, without the cognisance of the congregation, has done anything out of ignorance.

Ver. 26. *Were in ignorance.*—In this law the same case is by no means supposed as Lev. iv. 13, etc., where the sin-offering of the whole congregation is treated of; rather (cf. ver. 24, note) the case is here put, that by the transgression of the individual the whole congregation has been defiled, while there the whole congregation was itself implicated in the sin. The whole congregation might, for example, commit sin when it was led by the fault of its rulers (without being fully conscious of what it was doing) to some idolatrous act, or to participation in some forbidden connections, or the like. In this latter case the sin was of a more heinous description, and the atonement belonged to those of the greater and more solemn kind, like that of the high priest. But in the case before us, the congregation was not a participator in the crime, but was nevertheless, through the sin of the individual, contaminated by it. A sin had been committed in the midst of it which had not been atoned for, and an offence given, the weight of which did not fall entirely on the individual. Here there was required not merely an atonement for the transgressor himself (also perhaps as such was cut off from the people, and not therefore atoned for), but one for the whole people, which nevertheless in solemnity stood below that other atonement spoken of.

Ver. 28. *Forgiven him.*—This is here only briefly and allusively repeated; it is the same as was more fully declared, Lev. iv. 27, etc. A transgression is intended which in no way affects the whole body of the congregation.

Ver. 32. *They found a man.*—The great punishment on the spies has humbled the people. They wish no more to transgress the commandments of the Lord, and bring an open violator of them to be punished by Him.

Ver. 34. *Should be done to him.*—The general punishment of being cut off from the people was threatened for the offence (Exod. xxxi. 14); but it was not said whether this punishment should be executed by a judicial sentence, and in what manner.

Ver. 36. *Commanded Moses.*—In the judgment of this case we must carefully keep in view the significance of the Sabbath as the sign of God's covenant with His people. An intentional transgression of the prohibition to work, was an open breach of the covenant, an act of rebellion against the Lord.

Ver. 37. *And the Lord.*—The last apostasy from the Lord leads to a fresh inculcation of all His commandments. The Israelite is to wear on his garments a continual remembrancer of the commands of the Lord, which shall bring his senses back from worldly aberrations, and deeply impress on him his calling as a member of the kingdom of priests.

Ver. 38. *Of blue.*—Heb., "purple blue," hyacinth colour, as Exod. xxv. 1.

Ver. 39. *Fringe.*—Tassels (Heb. Zizith), the threads of which were joined at the top, but open below. These were fastened by a hyacinth-coloured fringe to the corners of their garments. The tassels must by their movement attract their sight. The colour of the fringe reminded them of the dress of the high priest, Exod. xxviii. 5.

Seek not.—Heb., "wander about," inquire, spy out, that your senses do not become lost in the world, in order to seek there something new, attractive, pleasing. What follows explains it still more fully.

CHAPTER XVI.

The following circumstance, with its immediate consequences, is the only event which the sacred history has recorded out of the nearly forty years' life of wandering in the wilderness, to which the people were condemned since their last great rebellion (ch. xiv.); and, no doubt, this event is to be placed in the early part of this long period of chastisement. A dreary blank followed it, in which nothing essentially new could be contributed towards the history of the kingdom of God in this generation, now doomed to die out. After that, in the first instance, Moses' nearest kinsmen had risen up against him, the same rebellious spirit seizes on the Levitical tribe, to which Moses and Aaron themselves belonged, and which was entrusted with the highest service in sacred things. The nearer they stood to the priesthood, so much the more did they feel their distance from it. With them distinguished men out of the tribe of Reuben ally themselves, probably in order to assert the natural right of primogeniture in opposition to God's election, both in respect to Levi and to Judah. Moses' behaviour here is the same as ever. We see him, as in the former outbreaks, firm and dauntless, full of holy anger against the godless sinners, full of intercession and love for the thankless covenant people of God. And the punishment inflicted by God justifies and attests his authority afresh, while it shows most clearly the hopeless corruption of that generation of Israelites.

Ver. 1. *Took.*—What he took is not mentioned in the Hebrew. He took *men*, has been added with probability. He assembled them together for the purpose of an insurrection.

Ver. 3. *Ye take too much.*—" Ye have too much," ye are preferred in an unjust manner. In order to understand how again and again, after so many proofs by the most public miracles, any doubt on the subject of the prophetic and priestly dignity of Moses and Aaron were possible, we must place ourselves in the mind of the ancient heathens. They, notwithstanding the greatest miracles (which they themselves believed) of their gods, still did not regard them as all-powerful and unchangeable in their decrees. In certain cases they defied their authority, and sought for help elsewhere, or endeavoured to change their will. Such a notion as this, we must suppose, existed in the minds of the more hardened part of the people, even when they did not fall into open idolatry. From such heathen notions of God, it is very intelligible, how on the one side Corah deduced the holiness of the whole people from the dwelling of God among them, and yet at the same time rebelled against the ordinances of the Lord. Imagining God to resemble weak, sinful man, he thought Moses had usurped too much authority from Him, and that by a determined assertion of his own rights the Lord might be compelled to change His statutes. In proportion as God dealt with His people more after the manner of men, were the more corrupt part in danger, in their ideas of this human side of God's dealings, to mix up ideas of sinfulness—just as under different forms the same evil has manifested itself even in Christianity.

Ver. 7. *Shall be holy.*—He transfers to them a chief office of the priesthood—the offering up the prayers of the people in the incense-offering, in order that therein the choice of the Lord might be declared.

Ver. 9. *Near to Himself.*—The same word stands, ver. 10. Nothing is here said of sacrificing. Ye are allowed, he says, to draw near to Him as no other tribe: ye are the chosen of the whole congregation, their representatives before God.

Ver. 12. *We will not come up.*—To judgment, for which the expression "come up" elsewhere frequently stands. Deut. xxviii. 7. Moses endeavoured to sever these two, as misled persons, from the authors of the rebellion.

Ver. 13. *Milk and honey.*—It is not without bitter mockery that they call Egypt by a name which Canaan bears in all the promises of God.

Kill us.—Because they were condemned to die in the wilderness.

Ver. 14. *Put out the eyes.*—Treat them as blind persons, who must let themselves be led wherever you choose—who do not see that you perform nothing of your promises.

Ver. 15. *Hurt one of them.*—Have not as a king exacted gifts from them. Moses therefore lived among the people quite like an equal.

Ver. 19. *Tabernacle of the congregation.*—At ver. 16 the band of Corah was called "his company," but here it is said simply "the congregation." Without doubt, therefore, the whole congregation of the people is to be understood. Corah wished in his audacity to have them all as witnesses.

Ver. 21. *This congregation.*—It was a great sin on the part of the people that they had assembled at Corah's invitation. Even if they had not yet taken part in his rebellion, they still were willing to be neutral, and to see how matters would turn out. It was on account of this unthankfulness and unbelief that God would have destroyed them with the insurgents.

Ver. 22. *Of the spirits of all flesh;* i.e., Thou who hast given to every one life and breath; Thou the Creator and Preserver of all. They would restrain Him by that attribute which seems to them irreconcileable with the general extermination of them all. Here also holds good what has been said, Exod. xxxii. 7 and xxxii. 13.

Ver. 25. *Rose up.*—He went out to them to the camp of the Reubenites, while Corah and his party, as Kohathites, dwelt immediately behind the tabernacle.

Ver. 27. *Little children.*—They wished in their bold self-confidence to await the issue. Their children perished; but Corah's separated themselves from their father, and were preserved, ch. xxvi. 11. From this Levitical family proceed many of the most beautiful psalms: Psalm xliv.-xlix.

Ver. 30. *A new thing.*—Lit.: "But if Jehovah will make a creation," will interfere with the usual course of things by an extraordinary wonder. Similar words stand Exod. xxxiv. 10; Isa. xlviii. 7.

Ver. 30. *Into the pit.*—That the pit swallows them up without their first dying. The death of the body, as it is a punishment of sin, is also a mild form of the punishment which follows on sin, since, in the circumstances which precede and accompany it, it has an especially great power to draw the soul away from sin, and to preserve it from the worst consequences of sin. The new thing that God now makes is this—that He passes over this interval, and at once hurries the soul out of the sinful life into the pit of destruction. The event which occurred before their eyes, that their bodies go alive under the earth, was a figure of this destruction.

Ver. 35. *Offered incense.*—While this took place in the camp, those 250 (ver. 2), the leaders of the insurrection with their censers, were before the tabernacle; and Moses had probably returned to them when the punishment overtook them.

Ver. 38. *Against their own souls.*—A remarkable expression, which explains the doctrine of punishment and atonement in the O. T., and especially the expression which so often occurs, "the Lord is sanctified in His enemies." The censers tainted with sin are, by the death of those who had defiled them, cleansed, nay, even hallowed. Through the punishment, God puts His holy law in the place where lately sin was. The censers are now made into plates, and hung on the altar. The words, however, in the Hebrew would be more correctly thus recorded: "And that he take the censers out of the burning (since they are holy), the censers of those sinners against their souls," who by their sin have perished. The sense, however, is the same, since in any case the words will signify, viz., that their souls, *i.e.*, their death, have hallowed the censers. (In the German Bible the words "against their souls," etc., are translated, "since the censers of such sinners are hallowed *through their souls;*" which will explain the meaning of this note.—Translator.)

Ver. 41. Once more the people are rebellious, and by reason of the very punishment inflicted on Corah. How this could be possible, after the manifest miraculous dealing of God, is only to be explained (as in ver. 3) by the heathenish feelings of the people. They regarded Moses as a mighty magician, like the Egyptian magicians, to whose art even the Divinity itself could not refuse its aid, and they consider him to be responsible for the consequences. It becomes more and more clear from the whole history, that the old people who had been brought out of Egypt were hopelessly hardened, and had fully deserved their chastisement to die in the wilderness. Nevertheless no revelation of the righteous judgment of God is ever in vain: it remains reserved for the instruction of the generation growing up, and the blessing which it brings to that is seen in the sequel of the history.

Ver. 45. *Get you up.*—Cf. ver. 4, note, vers. 21 and 22.

Ver. 48. *Was stayed.*—It was the intercession of Moses and Aaron which saved the people; but it was necessary that the power of this mediation should be made manifest in the eyes of the people by a visible sign, and thereby the truth declared. The same burning of incense which in the hands of him who is not a priest brings death, gives life in the priest's own hands. It was also intended that the people should receive an impression of the greatness of Aaron's loving devotion by his placing himself between the living and the dead.

Ver. 50. *The plague was stayed.*—When it was ended Aaron came again to declare the effect which his intercession had by God's grace brought about, and to return thanks to the Lord.

CHAPTER XVII.

The priesthood was to be confirmed to Aaron not only by the destruction of those who had presumed to take it, but also by a miracle, which signified in a beautiful manner the holy fulness of life which God vouchsafed to this order of men, and so an abiding memorial of it (as well as of Corah's punishment) might be preserved. God is the source of all life: whom the Lord sanctifies, to him He imparts in the sanctification the fulness of His life, which needs not proceed along the gradual way of nature. This is the thought which is figuratively expressed in the following history.

Ver. 3. *One rod.*—There were, therefore, in all thirteen rods. Aaron's was added to the other twelve.

Ver. 8. *Almonds.*—The almond-tree, as that which most quickly brings forth blossoms and beautiful fruit, is an emblem of the mighty power of the Divine word, which is ever fresh and unfailing in its fulfilment (Jer. i. 11, 12). For this reason this fruit appears most significantly on Aaron's rod, to whose house the revelation of God was confided for the good of the people.

Ver 13. *Consumed with dying.*—Not an expression of faith and thankfulness indeed, but still of wholesome fear, of dread of God. This cause of rebellion ceased from this time.

CHAPTER XVIII.

After that on the occasion of the insurrections,—first, that of Miriam and Aaron, then, more particularly, that of Corah and his company,—the divine right of the priesthood had been established, there follow more particular enactments concerning the incomes of the priests and Levites, about which detached regulations have already been given. The nature of this income is very remarkable and significant, and stands in striking contrast to all that we find among the neighbouring heathen people. For while among all the heathen, with whom a ruling priestly caste has existed (as at this day in India), this class is uncommonly richly endowed, especially in landed property (just as though, being priests of a Nature-worship, they were intended to thrive in the natural land as its more distinguished members), the Levites, on the other hand, were to hold no inheritance in the land of the Israelites (ver. 20). They dwelt dispersed in different towns among all the tribes, and even in the towns they mixed with the other inhabitants. The Lord Jehovah Himself was to be their inheritance. Their property, their outward lot, their position among the people, their power, was, in its essential character, spiritual, and referred to the unseen, to the world beyond this; but even for this very reason was it to be an ever-living, present power, which penetrated and governed everything. Jehovah, as the Lord of the whole earth, had given the land of Canaan to His people. He required therefore, as the recognition of His supremacy, the tithe of all produce of the field or of the trees, as also the first-fruits of all crops (cf. Gen. xxviii. 22, note). This tithe He gave as an abiding right to those who had Him as their "inheritance and part" (ver. 20), who entirely depended on Him in all that relates to their subsistence. Considerable as this portion appears to be, when this single tribe, which was not (at least in the wilderness) so numerous as the others, received the tithe of the whole land-produce, over and above that which accrued to those who were priests, nevertheless we find the Levites often recommended to the love and benevolence of the others as being a needy tribe (Deut. xii. 12, ch. xiv. 27); because at that time, just as little as in the Middle Ages in any Christian people, was the letter of the law of tithe fulfilled, and the produce actually given to the tribe of Levi. Only when the pure reverence for God flourished among the people, which in a great measure was dependent on the zeal and faithfulness of Levi, might they hope to receive as a body outward respect. Their spiritual power was, however, so much the more considerable, since the priests (and with them all the Levites) were appointed to "teach the people the difference between the holy and the profane," and, where a cause came before them, they were to judge and speak according to the law of the Lord, and to celebrate all festivals: Ezek. xliv. 23, 24. It was their duty, as being learned in Scripture, to keep the genealogical tables. The regulations concerning leprosy and similar appointments in Egypt, lead us to conclude that they were also the physicians of the Israelites. In later times they had also in part a military organisation; and at the same time they exercised, in the more perfect temple worship, the fine arts which flourished among the people. But the root of their power lay in the faith of the people. When they themselves became entangled in unbelief and idolatry, they sank into miserable circumstances, as we find represented in the history, Judges xvii. 7, etc.

Ver. 1. *Iniquity of your priesthood.*—This expression is explained by Exod. xxviii. 38. The bearing (the same as taking away, removing) signifies the covering, cancelling of sin, by means of the holiness attributed by the Lord to the priesthood, and is a remembrancer that the nearness of Jehovah is unbearable for all whom He has not sanctified, as the former history has proved. By the addition, that they shall bear also "the iniquity of their priesthood," they are reminded that they, just as much as the other Israelites, are sinners, and must atone for their own sins with those of the people.

Ver. 2. *Minister unto thee.*—In this expression there is a play on the word. Literally: "The Levites shalt thou bring with thee, and they shall be joined to thee (Jillavu) and serve thee." Their name shall always remind them that they belong to the priests.

Ver. 6. *A gift for the Lord.*—Lit.: "Also a gift, a gift to the Lord." Prominence is always given to the fact that they are servants to the Lord, and never to the persons of the priests.

Ver. 10. *Holy.*—The most holy of the sacrifices belonged to the priests alone, and might not be eaten by any but the male members of their families in a holy place, Lev. vii. 6.

Ver. 11. *Eat of it.*—Here is meant the thank-offerings, the holy, in distinction from the most holy. Of the former every member of the priestly house might eat: cf. Lev. vii. 28–34.

Ver. 14. *Devoted.*—Lev. xxvii. 28.

Ver. 16. *Month old.*—Because it then can be weaned; and so out of compassion to the mother.

Ver. 19. *Covenant of salt.*—An incorruptible covenant. Cf. Lev. ii. 13, note; 2 Chron. xiii. 5.

Ver. 20. *Children of Israel.*—This is repeatedly given as the reason why Levi and Aaron had received no inheritance in Israel: Deut. x. 9; Joshua xiii. 14, 33, ch. xviii. 7. In truth, the grant of the tithe so much turned their minds to the unseen world, that without a firm trust in the Lord, without faithfulness in His service, it would even become a punishment: cf. Gen. xlix. 15, note.

Ver. 26. *Tenth part.*—Since the Levites themselves are not priests, but required, like the rest, the priestly mediation, they were also to give the tenth part of their tithe to the priests. Thereby were they sanctified, and their near approach to the sacred things expiated.

Ver. 27. *Fulness of the wine-press.*—As though ye had reaped it yourselves.

CHAPTER XIX.

The destruction of Corah and his company, and the plague which followed upon it (ch. xvi.), had carried off a great number of Israelites, and the need was more urgent than ever that they should become certified, how the members of the people of God might be cleansed from so general and so often recurring a pollution as that which resulted from touching a dead body. For this purpose an especial sin-offering is ordained. A red heifer was to be chosen: it must be *red*, because that fierce, flaring, blood-like colour (in Egypt, the colour of Typhon, the prince of evil) was an especial remembrancer of sin. A *heifer*, in distinction from the other sin-offerings (Lev. iv. 13, 14), because it represented the whole congregation; while, in other cases, this representation was less taken into consideration than the perfectness of the victim. The other marks—those of freedom from all blemishes—must exist in every sin-offering, which was to stand in the stead of the sinners. The heifer must, as laden with the sins of the whole people, be brought outside before the camp, and, after the blood-sprinkling, be entirely burnt. The means of purification which have already occurred, cedarwood, hyssop, and scarlet wool, are added to the sacrifice by way of adding force to its significance. (The customs, in many respects similar, in the purifying of the leper [Lev. xiv.], and on the day of atonement [Lev. xvi.], should here be compared.) The ashes of the heifer thus burnt, were mingled with fresh (flowing) water, and then used for a water of sprinkling, in order to cleanse therewith every one who, by the touching of dead bodies, was defiled. The reason of this, the chief of all purifications, was, no doubt, to represent to the people of God death, the consequence and punishment of sin, as the greatest of all the defilements of human nature. Nothing tends so much to remind men of sin as that which sin has brought on all men—death. Nothing ought man so much to avoid as that which has brought him in contact with the dark realm of sin.

Ver. 2. *No spot.*—Literally, "perfect;"—*no blemish* does not differ from this.

Yoke.—Never been used for common purposes. The less it

has come in contact with men, sinners, so much the more was it suitable to stand in the stead of the sinful people.

Ver. 3. *Slay her.*—As this sacrifice is afterwards expressly called a sin-offering (vers. 9, 17), assuredly the significant custom of laying on of hands was not omitted, but the mention is passed over as being something well known.

Ver. 5. *Shall he burn.*—As in the case of this sacrifice the entire purification of the whole people from the greatest of all defilements was to be made the prominent matter, the victim was therefore brought forth without the camp. It must also be entirely burnt, as was not the case with the other sin-offerings: Lev. iv.

Ver. 6. *Scarlet.*—For the meaning of these three means of purification see Lev. xiv. 6.

Ver. 8. *Until the even.*—As was the case on the great day of atonement with the high priest, and with him who carried out the goat into the wilderness: Lev. xvi. 23–26.

Ver. 9. *Purification for sin.*—The two marks of the sin-offering here meet—that it must be in, and for, itself clean—but becomes unclean through the sin laid upon it. The heifer, therefore, must be clean and without blemish in itself; but all is impure which has to do with the act of sacrifice—*i.e.*, with the laying on of sin upon it, with the whole process of purification: only when all is accomplished which is to serve for the purification does the water of sprinkling defile no more. Then is sin and death overcome by the Divine power of life. In all this may we easily perceive a type of the true offering for sin: Heb. ix. 13; 2 Cor. v. 21.

Ver. 17. *Running water.*—Literally, "living water." An emblem of life triumphant over death.

CHAPTER XX.

This chapter transplants us all at once into the last period of the forty years' wandering of the Israelites in the wilderness, as they have again arrived at the borders of Canaan and prepare themselves for its conquest. It is the manner of sacred history to relate only the events of most weight and consequence in the progress of the kingdom of God, and so it passes over in silence the long time which was spent in the wilderness by the generation destined to die out there, after the narration of its last violent outbreak. A new time begins for Israel. Still, indeed, at first the old rebellious and capricious spirit meets us; nay, even Moses and Aaron waver. Repeated disobedience brings fresh punishment after it. Nevertheless, these outbreaks are not of so bad a character as the former ones. A fresh, enterprising spirit inspires the new generation, full as it is of rich hopes, and destined to take possession of the Promised Land. The people march with eagerness to battle and to victory. Songs celebrating their triumphant march are sung. These are collected in a Book of the Wars of the Lord, and the fulfilment of the great promise draws nigh.

Ver. 1. *Kadesh.*—On the south border of Canaan, where, ch. xiii. 27, the Divine punishment had been declared to them. Miriam also, on account of her rebellion, must suffer the general doom; still she was permitted to come to the borders of the land.

Ver. 3. *When our brethren.*—Lit., "in the death of our brethren before the Lord." The punishment of death which took place thirty-eight years before in the same spot, is here intended.

Ver. 8. *And their beasts.*—In the case when a bodily want has led to the murmuring, the punishment of God is never so great as where pride and perverseness have been the cause of the rebellion.

Ver. 12. *Shall not bring.*—The sin of Moses and Aaron consists in the question, ver. 10. The meaning of it was—that Moses, though it may be with a good intent, wished to show the people their sin, and on account of it to make it appear doubtful whether God would fulfil their desire. But for this he had no Divine command. God would here bear with the impatience of the people, and Moses and Aaron ought to be nothing but instruments of His almighty power among the people. They ought to sanctify Him, by showing Him as the true and faithful Fulfiller of all His promises. In Moses himself, who had been thought worthy of so high grace, the very least imperfection must be chastised in the most severe manner. And in this very punishment he appears as the greatest servant of God in the Old Testament.

Ver. 13. *Sanctified.*—He showed Himself to the people to be the Holy One in His faithfulness to His covenant; and to Moses and Aaron as the Holy One in His punishment.

The people now purpose to press into the land of Canaan. They were not to march against Gaza, the most southern town of the Philistines. The contest was not to begin with this people, who were then in the full vigour of their power, and who continued for a long time a powerful nation. The war of extermination was in the first instance directed against those who were, properly speaking, Canaanites. The Israelites might now have attempted the invasion northward—as they had before tried (ch. xiv. 39)—from Arabah, the long deep valley which intersects the wilderness from Akabah to the Dead Sea, and from thence to the north, in which also lies the wilderness of Zin. But here is a rugged precipitous chain of mountains, the wall of defence of Canaan. They prefer therefore to ask of the Edomites, a people closely connected with them, a free passage, since a forcible entrance into their land at this point was not to be thought of. "The Mountain Seir (cf. Gen. xxvii. 40, note) rises precipitately from the valleys Ghor and Arabah, and is intersected by a couple of narrow wadys from the west to the east: of these, the Wady Ghoeir alone offers a not very difficult route for a hostile force. This was probably the road by which Moses, who perceived how difficult it would be to force his way, and who hoped to attain his object by negotiations, desired a passage from the Edomites, on the condition of buying provisions from the inhabitants. When the Edomites refused this request, nothing remained for the Israelites, than to follow the valley Arabah, in a southerly direction, towards the head of the Red Sea."—Burckhardt. "Mount Seir has at the base low eminences of limestone; then succeed porphyry strata, which compose the main mass; upon this, sandstone torn into irregular ridges and grotesquely grouped crags. East from these mountains stretches the unbounded plain of the great eastern wilderness. We reckon the height of the porphyry cliffs at about 2000 feet above Arabah: the elevation of the Wady Musa above the same is about 2200 feet, while the ridges of limestone farther behind are probably not under 3000 feet high."—Robinson, iii. 102.—It is remarkable how vividly the traditions from the time of the patriarchs still remained in the recollection of the people, since Edom was regarded as Israel's brother, but still retained the spirit of hostility which existed in their ancestor.

Ver. 19. *Said unto them.*—They send a second embassage.

Ver. 21. *Turned away.*—Cf. Judges xi. 17, 18. The march of the Israelites was now to the south, to the Red Sea. Here they appear to have traversed as much of the fruitful valleys of Mount Seir as the Edomites allowed them, since the Mount Hor, at the foot of which they arrived, is, after a very ancient tradition, still shown in the neighbourhood of the later capital, Sela or Petra. On this the Arabs to this very day reverence Harun or Aaron. Here Aaron died, after the Lord had once more declared death to be the chastisement of his sin; but he died a calm, blessed death, brought to his rest by God Himself. It was of importance that on this occasion the priesthood should be solemnly transferred to Aaron's eldest son, as a proof that all the commands and promises appertaining to it did not belong to Aaron personally, but to the priestly office which was bestowed on his family.

Ver. 22. *Mount Hor.*—"To our left we saw Hor, as it stood out prominently among the front cliffs of the eastern range of mountains. Its form is that of an irregular blunt cone, with three jagged points. Of these, that on the north-east is the highest, and distinguished with the Mohammedan Wely or grave of Aaron."—Robinson, iii. 54.

Ver. 24. *Gathered unto his people.*—This beautiful expression of the patriarchal time occurs here once more, after a long interval, at the death of this, perhaps weak, but faithful and constant servant of the Lord (cf. Gen. xv. 5, ch. xxviii. 8).

CHAPTER XXI.

The new generation of the children of Israel is now full of eagerness to press forward into the land of Canaan. It appears impossible to do this from the south. The negotiations with the Edomites are broken off. The people have turned from Kadesh in a south-easterly direction, along Arabah, towards the Mountain Hor. The Canaanitish king of Arad considers this a favourable moment (when the Israelites are encompassed on the north and east by the naturally strong borders of Canaan and Edom, on the west, by the inhospitable wilderness, and threatened on the south by the Amalekites) to attack them from behind, remembering the former victory obtained, when the Israelites had perversely made an attempt to conquer the country (ch. xiv. 15). Hormah lay to the south of the proper boundary of Canaan. It is reckoned, Deut. i. 44, as belonging to Seir. Israel conquered this place therefore, which lay outside the Promised Land, and its natural defences—a presage of what was destined for this doomed people.

Ver. 1. *Way of the spies.*—Or "by the way of Atharim." This word is certainly a proper name, but the place is no further known.

Ver. 2. *Destroy.*—Consecrate to the Lord, give to destruction (cf. Lev. xxvii. 29, note), as already there a chastisement had been inflicted on the Israelites.

Ver. 3. *Hormah.*—Ch. xiv. 45. This place had already been, by anticipation, designated by this name, which was only now given to it. The Israelites, naturally, did not at the time maintain this conquest, but they completed only the judgment upon it by destroying it, in order to proceed in their march to the Ælanitic Gulf of the Red Sea.

The heights of Mount Seir, which are considerable and very precipitous in the north, flatten towards the Red Sea; so that Israel hoped by a circuit round the hills to obtain the object in which it had failed by the way of negotiation. Here, out of weariness of the sameness of the food with which they were supported, the manna, a fresh murmuring breaks out, similar to that, ch. xiv. 2, which is followed by a more severe punishment, and one corresponding to the nature of the country in which it happened: cf. Exod. xvi. 1. "Everywhere on the sand of the shore were seen trails of the serpents which had crawled there in every direction. Some of these trails appeared to be made by animals whose bodies could not have been less than two inches in diameter. I heard that snakes were very common in this region—that the fishermen were very much afraid of them, and at night, before they went to rest, extinguished the fire, because it is known that the light attracts them."—Burckhardt, ii. 814.

Ver. 5. *Light bread;* i.e., worthless, wretched stuff.

Ver. 6. *Fiery serpents.*—Lit., "burning serpents," with burning bite. The article stands before the fiery serpents ("*the* fiery serpents"), and shows that something well known is meant. They are the serpents which were called by the ancients, when in the water, "hydrus," when they came to land, "chersydrus." In the dry time of the year (as Aaron died, ch. xx. 28, at the beginning of July, it must now have been the end of August) these serpents come to land, and then their bite is more dangerous than at other times. That which is a natural event in the country, is now raised into a miraculous chastisement. And perhaps in the kind of punishment there is a sort of reference to the sin which called it forth. They who found the taste of the manna too insipid, who longed after more sharp, biting food, are themselves bitten by the burning serpents. But, above all, do the serpents remind them of the war which is being continually carried on between man and the serpent (Gen. iii. 15), and likewise of the enemy who made use of the form of a serpent to tempt the first of mankind to sin, and to bring death into the world.

Ver. 8. *Upon a pole.*—A brazen serpent is set up like that which had inflicted the injury—of brass, probably, because this metal, with the sun's rays shining on it, served as a memento of the burning serpents. The healing of the burning bite by looking at the burning serpent, expresses a similar notion of intercession with that contained in the sin-offering. In consequence of sin the serpents had been sent: God forgives His people their sin, yet not unconditionally, but upon their looking up to the brazen serpent, which, lifeless and harmless, overcomes the bite of the serpents; just as, in the case of the sacrifice, the looking on the life of the victim which is given in the stead of the sinner's life, removes the punishment of death which belongs to sin. The circumstance that the serpent at the same time serves as a memento of man's tempter, adds force to the idea of intercession: it is the likeness of sin which itself comes in the place of sin ("the likeness of sinful flesh," Rom. viii. 3), and, by Divine intervention, destroys sin. Hence the typical meaning of this history: St John iii. 14, 15, note.

Shall live.—Faith in this Divine appointment of grace was therefore the hand which took hold of the miracle, and appropriated it to the Israelites.

Ver. 9. *He lived.*—For every fresh wound there was ever a

fresh healing by looking on the brazen serpent. It is not said that the fiery serpents were destroyed, but that they were made innoxious. In this also there is a typical meaning.

The moment was now arrived when the Israelites were to march towards Canaan. They had now "compassed Mount Seir" long enough; they were now to turn from the most northern point of the Red Sea "towards the north-east," Deut. ii. 3; but there they must touch on the territory of the Edomites, and, according to the will of the Lord, keep the same terms which they (ch. xx. 14) had promised them, Deut. ii. 5, 6. Although now on the undefended side of their territory, the children of Esau "were afraid before them," and let them pass through. So they marched in a north-easterly direction to the Arnon, the river which falls into the Dead Sea, and at that time formed the boundary between the Moabites and the Amorites, who stretched beyond the borders of Canaan. Here it is where mention of the songs takes place, in which the youthful Israel, eager for combat, celebrates the acts of the Lord.

Ver. 10. *Oboth.*—The name means "the sluices;" perhaps because it was the place, after the waterless desert, where these were again filled with water.

Ver. 11. *Ije-abarim.*—Ije signifies "ruins:" perhaps the site of a ruined town. Abarim is unknown: only so far we see that the Israelites compassed eastward the whole land of Moab, which at that time reached to Arnon, and, in a north-easterly direction from it, wished to enter the territory of the Amorites.

Ver. 12. *Zared.*—This brook also is unknown. It has been supposed to be the present Wady el-Ahsa, or el-Ahsy, which, coming from the west, falls almost due south into the Dead Sea. Its rocky valley is full of extremely dangerous clefts, and was no doubt crossed by the Israelites in the upper shallower part. According to others, it is Kerek, which lies more to the north. In this region the last men capable of bearing arms died: Deut. ii. 16.

Ver. 13. *Arnon.*—The Arnon is supposed to be the present Wady Modscheb, which falls into the Dead Sea somewhat about the middle of its eastern coast. The lower part of its course is through rocky clefts, the upper part through the flat regions of the Desert. In the Heb. (as in Engl. Version) it is "on the other side," since in this and other places the word is to be understood as spoken from Canaan. Here it is equivalent to "south of Arnon." Although Moses did not write his history in Canaan, he here, and in many places, always writes as taking his position there; just as a person living in Lower India always calls the country, for the sake of general distinction, "India on the other side the Ganges." The most decisive proof that such a mode of speech really belongs to the books of Moses, may be seen, Deut. i. 1 and Num. xxxii. 19.

Ver. 14. *What he did.*—Heb.: "Vaheb in the storm and the brooks, the Arnon, the pouring out of the brooks which stretches to the head of Ar, and leans to the borders of Moab." This is a picturesque description of the march which the host of the Lord made without ceasing as far as the point named, ver. 13. "Vaheb" is an unknown place. "In the storm" is a description of the unceasing manner in which Israel marches forward and occupies all those points. "Ar" is the old capital of Moab, on Arnon: before the invasion of Sihon, ver. 26, lying in the middle of this land, now on its northern border.

Ver. 17. *Lawgiver.*—A joyous song, preserved in the "Book of the Wars of the Lord."—It literally runs, "Ascend, ye wells; sing ye unto him: ye wells, the princes dug it, the nobles of the people opened it, with the sceptre, with the staffs." Here we find nothing of the old murmuring; on the other hand, youthful gladness and poetic enthusiasm. "The princes dug it with the sceptre, with their staffs," inasmuch as they excite and urge the people to it, and overlook the work.

Ver. 20. *Jeshimon.*—All these places are situated no more in the wilderness on the other side the land of Moab, but in the territory of the Amoritish king Sihon. This list of stations anticipates the following narrative, which places us on the borders of the wilderness from whence the message is sent to the king.

The territory on the other side of Jordan, which the kings Sihon and Og possessed, did not, properly speaking, belong to the Promised Land, as this especially appears from the transactions of ch. xxxi. Other places seem to contradict this, where all the land between the Euphrates and the river of Egypt is promised to the Israelites (cf. Gen. xv. 18, note). There is, however, a distinction to be made between that which formed the exact substance of the promise, and that which is added as an after-gift for the greater glory of the kingdom of God. Canaan proper is the land this side Jordan : to this district belonged more or less of the lands between the Euphrates and the valley of the Nile—at the time of Israel's greatest glory, all this region. Since now the war of extermination as a Divine punishment threatened only the Canaanites proper on this side the Jordan, Sihon and Og became implicated in it by their refusal of a passage through their country, and at the very outset the land of the people of God was extended far towards the west. Especially did the Israelites possess the fruitful hill-country of Gilead with its many towns, and the rich pasture land of Basan.

Ver. 22. *Past thy borders.*—They offered them the same conditions as before to the Edomites : ch. xx. 17, 19.

Ver. 24. *Was strong.*—And besides, they were forbidden to take possession of their land : Deut. ii. 19.

Ver. 27. *In proverbs.*—Lit.: "Therefore say the poets" (the authors of proverbs). The following verses are out of the book quoted ver. 14. Every new victory awoke new enthusiasm, which expressed itself in songs of triumph.

Ver. 30. *Medeba.*—The meaning of these triumphant proverbial sayings is this: "Heshbon, the chief city of the Amorites, lies overthrown. Victorious Israel challenges all to build her again as its capital. In order now better to depict the greatness and glory of the city, the poet alludes to its former power, when from thence Ar, the capital of Moab, and Bamoth (the heights) on Arnon, were conquered and destroyed—when the sons and daughters of the Moabites, the people of the Moabitish and Ammonitish idol Chemosh, were led captive by Sihon. Israel has now destroyed the glory of this town—has thrown down the mighty people with their spears."—Heshbon is still found on the end of the Wady Hesban, as also are places under the names Diban and Madeba. Hesban is entirely in ruins, but these bear evidence to the considerable circumference and splendour of the ancient town. Madeba lies on a hill, and is about two miles in circumference.

Ver. 35. *Possessed the land.*—This victory is more circumstantially related, Deut. iii. 1, etc.

CHAPTER XXII.

Before the Israelites, now on the threshold of the Promised Land, can enter into it, they experience in a wonderful way the protection of their God in a situation which altogether transports us to the spirit of the farthest antiquity. After the victories obtained over Sihon and Og, the people seem in the eyes of the Moabites to be extremely dangerous. King Balak does not venture to attack them; but he has recourse to a genuine heathen means of defence. He hires, for a great sum, a celebrated soothsayer to curse Israel. The person and the history of this man are in every point of view very remarkable, and appear full of strange inconsistencies. He stands in the service of the true God, without whom he does not venture to speak anything; and yet he soothsays for hire at the bidding of a heathen prince. God forbids him to go, yet lets him go, and then threatens him with death for going. In the prophecies uttered by Balaam (which are some of the most poetic, sublime, and instructive in the O. T.), he shows the deepest insight into the destiny and future fate of Israel, as well as the most accurate acquaintance with their past history. And the end of this man, who uttered such glorious prophecies, which could proceed from God only, is death by the sword of Israel (ch. xxxi. 8). All this is explained, if we think of the matter thus: Balaam was a heathen, dwelling at Pethor on the Euphrates, and for a long time famed as a great soothsayer and sorcerer. It would be altogther a mistake here, as was remarked before, in the case of the Egyptian magicians (Exod. vii. 11), to regard this gift as mere fancy, and its effects as trickery and superstition. With a natural faculty for spiritual impressions, Balaam might well be supposed, by aid of the powers of darkness, which really had influence in the heathen world, to have worked wonderful effects. But, at the same time, either what had been preserved from earlier times of God's revelation among the family of Eber, or what Balaam had heard of God's doings for the freeing of His people from Egypt, had made so strong an impression on Balaam, that he, like Jethro (Exod. xviii. 11), acknowledged Jehovah to be mightier than all gods.

He acknowledged Him for his own God; and the knowledge of this, that Balaam served this God—that he, after the heathen notion, partook of His might, and was in a position to have influence with Him, moved Balak to hire him against the people of Jehovah. He was, therefore, to be compared with those who cast out devils in the name of Jesus, but did not follow Him (St Mark ix. 38; St Luke ix. 49); as likewise in disposition and intention with Simon Magus (Acts viii. 18). Just as we find in the case of Laban the worship of the true God mixed up with the worship of idols; and as we see that Melchisedek, who did not belong to the covenant-religion, was a priest of the Most High God; in like manner could God have a prophet even among those who were without, in whose mind and belief there was a miserable mixture of truth and falsehood. We find even in the N. T. a gift of prophecy, which made those who possessed it capable of uttering divinely-given revelations, but on whose minds, in the time of inspiration, also occasionally, strange evil spirits worked; therefore the apostles frequently exhort their converts to try the spirits (Rom. xii. 6; 1 Cor. xii. 1; 1 Thess. v. 20; 1 St John iv. 1). From such the prophets, who were God's regular instruments in His Church, are to be carefully distinguished. These spoke constantly under the influence of the Holy Spirit; and though they did not foresee all the future in the kingdom of God, but each one had his appointed measure of knowledge, "yet God did nothing in His Church which He did not reveal to His servants the prophets" (Amos iii. 7); moreover, their predictions were founded on pure doctrine, and had no other object in view than the entire glory of God's kingdom on earth. But in Balaam we see a prophet who possessed a certain gift nearly allied to a natural endowment, by means of which he said what was true in the service of God; but he used in addition his dark unholy art, through which he was unable to discern the truth with clearness. His greediness after reward, nourished as it was by his practice as soothsayer, blinded his eyes; and as king Balak, in a regular heathen manner, regards him as a power whose workings reach into the spiritual world, nay, even had influence enough to effect a change in the purposes of God, so does Balaam, although as a prophet concerning Israel he knows himself to be in God's power, still hope to unite the service of God with the service of the king, perhaps to bring about a change in God's designs, or to be able to wait for it; perhaps he intended, after the manner of many heathen oracles, to have recourse to double meanings in his answer. At first, before he had fully given up himself to the power of sin, God forbids him to go with the messengers; but the more he, though actually obedient, longs after the wages of sin, so the more does God give him over to the power of darkness,—puts him to shame by means of his ass, and compels him at last to give utterance to the very opposite of that which he, in his evil desire, wished to say.

Ver. 1. *By Jericho;* i.e., in the part of Arabah which belonged to Moab before Sihon had conquered the land as far as Arnon, which the Israelites had taken from him.

Ver. 4. *Elders of Midian.*—Scarcely here the same people, dwelling on the Sinaitic peninsula, to which Moses fled out of Egypt; but a branch of the same race, which, according to Gen. xxxvi. 35, lived a considerable time with Moab,—was made tributary by Sihon (Joshua xiii. 21), and afterwards in connection with other people oppressed the Israelites.

Ver. 5. *By the river;* i.e., the Euphrates. The name of the place does not elsewhere occur.

Ver. 6. *Is cursed.*—That the power should be given to Balaam to curse in the name of Jehovah, the true God, His own people, is of course altogether absurd. But it may perhaps be imagined that he who, like Bethuel and Laban, together with the true God honoured also other gods, had in their name by his arts often spread blessings or curses; and so that after a time, when he had become blinded by the greed of gain, he hoped the same power might be allowed him by Jehovah. From this is explained Deut. xxiii. 6.

Ver. 7. *Elders of Midian.*—Both people had a government of their tribes similar to that of the Israelites, above which, in the case of the Moabites, a king was placed.

Ver. 7. *Rewards of divination.*—The soothsayers were always accustomed to offer their art for sale for money. Even among the Israelites this was the practice (no doubt in corrupt times), to take a present to the seers, 1 Sam. ix. 7. The word "soothsaying, soothsayer," which always is used in speaking of Balaam (Joshua xiii. 22), shows that he could not be a genuine prophet of the true God; that at all events, together with the service paid to Him, he made use of arts which the law and the prophets constantly rejected: Deut. xviii. 10; Ezek. xiii. 9, 23; Jer. xiv. 14. Still it may be supposed that God, while He forbade to His people, to whom He revealed Himself by His priests and prophets, the whole dangerous province of heathen magical art, was more indulgent to the heathen because they had not His guidance: cf. Balaam's words, ch. xxiii. 23, and the whole place, Deut. ix. 9–19.

Ver. 8. *This night.*—Because he received his revelations in visions by night, as, afterwards, he falls down with his eyes closed in a kind of trance (ch. xxiv. 4). Similar appearances happened also in the case of the real prophets; only with this difference, that these latter were able to declare and explain consciously and clearly that which they had received in a vision or a trance, because it agreed with the revelation they had hitherto had, and with the word of God within them.

Ver. 9. *What men are these?*—This question is a reproof to Balaam's conscience. It was designed that by means of his answer he should become conscious of the rising feeling of greed of reward concealed in his heart. The after prophecies of Balaam show how well acquainted he was with the doings of God towards this people. By them he had been led to acknowledge the power of Jehovah. It was sinful, then, that with such knowledge he should yet inquire of the Lord.

Ver. 13. *Give me leave.*—Balaam did not report the answer of the Lord truly to the messengers. Had he told them that the people, as one blessed by the Lord, could not be cursed by His prophet, they would not have returned. The same disingenuousness is afterwards repeated in the discourses of Balaam.

Ver. 14. *Refuseth.*—Here also, perhaps, there is an untrue suppression. The words were intended to convey, which, perhaps, the messengers might have observed, that Balaam was eager after the reward.

On Balak's second invitation, God permits Balaam to go with the messengers, but at the same time is angry with him because he went; both of which agree perfectly well with what Balaam, ch. xxiii. 19, says of God. By the first decided and satisfactory refusal God willed to repress his avarice, and to give a helping hand to his better feelings. But when the greater honours and gifts excite Balaam's avarice, sin obtains the upper hand, and so God can be no more glorified by his obedience; and thus He will, as Avenger of his disobedience, be sanctified in him, and yet in such a manner that, step by step, He gives him room for repentance, while He holds him as it were by a chain, and does not suffer him to give more than He pleases. This is especially the object in view in the incident of the ass. On this depends its deep significance. Balaam is confident in his gift of soothsaying, as though it was his own property. Possessed of this, he thinks he cannot miss the reward, when suddenly, by this event, his true relation to the gift is made known. The seer who boasts that the eyes of his mind are open (ch. xxiv. 4, 16) becomes blind. In his stead the beast receives the higher vision; and thus is declared to him that it is God's free grace to which he owes the gift of second sight, and that his beast is more capable of perceiving things out of the higher world than an impure man, whom sinful desire has blinded. Nay, the punishment goes beyond this: the prophet who can no longer see anything becomes also dumb, and the ass prophesies in his stead. This is clearly the meaning of the history, whether we consider it as an event which really and outwardly happened, or as a vision represented by God before the mind of the prophet, by which the conduct of the ass was explained. An argument in favour of the opinion that it was not a mere vision but an actual event, seems to be this—that the transaction is related just like the rest of the history, but more particularly, because God designed to show Balaam how He could take away a gift from the prophet and transfer it to his beast; but this a vision, however significant, would not have told him; nay, when afterwards he understood it to be a vision, that very impression must have been destroyed. What the ass says is merely the expression of her animal feeling, only uttered in human language; but it is not the expression of any thought, since an animal is incapable of this.

What the ass therefore says, is of less moment in the history than the fact that she really has spoken. That the organs of speech are wanting to an animal, is no more an objection against the miracle than that human skill was not applied to supply bread for the 5000, or wine at the marriage-feast of Cana, and must be replaced by God's creative power.

Ver. 17. *Promote thee.*—Probably at the first message Balaam's ambition had been seen through.

Ver. 20. *Shalt thou do.*—As God ofttimes appears not to

hear the prayers of His servants, so sometimes does He appear to hear the prayers of the ungodly; but the event explains the mystery.

Ver. 22. *Two servants.*—Some event might very well outwardly happen while their eyes were holden from seeing, just as the companions of St Paul before Damascus saw a light which blinded them, and heard a voice yet saw no form and understood no words: cf. Acts ix. 7, ch. xxii. 9; and also St John xii. 29, note.

Ver. 29. *Would kill thee.*—The reason that Balaam does not show any astonishment at the speaking of the ass, was because the appearing of the angel, though without his being conscious of it, placed him in that higher state, in which he not only heard what took place, but was able to comprehend the meaning of the event, whereas mere alarm at a supernatural event would have hindered his doing so.

Ver. 32. *Perverse before me.*—The angel treats him as responsible for not having seen anything. It was Balaam's sin that he had lost the gift of higher vision. By this meeting of the angel, Balaam ought to have perceived his great guilt, and that the Lord had given him permission to go, notwithstanding his former prohibition, because He saw that he lusted after the wages of unrighteousness. Still he might understand that his way could never lead to happiness and blessing.

Ver. 33. *Saved her alive.*—The ass had thus saved him. She is therefore represented as more obedient than himself.

Ver. 34. *Back again.*—Without real confession of his sin, and without repentance on account of it, excusing himself merely on the plea of ignorance, Balaam would return: but with such a disposition as this, he is rather designed to become an example of God's chastening punishment than of repentance.

Ver. 36. *A city of Moab.*—The city of Moab, elsewhere also called Ar of Moab, was situated on Arnon: formerly the centre of the land, but, since Sihon's conquest, on its extreme northern boundary.

Ver. 38. *Shall I speak.*—Here we see the double-mindedness in Balaam's conduct, by which he hoped to serve God and Mammon. Though he knew full well that God had forbidden him the journey, he makes as though he had wished him to come, and only the fear of not being able to please Balak had withheld him. At the same time he provides for any future chances, in case this double-minded conduct should not succeed.

Ver. 39. *Kirjath-Huzoth.*—City of Streets—a good name for a large place.

CHAPTER XXIII.

In order to obtain a prediction favourable to his wishes, Balak brings at first a sacrifice for himself alone. Then he places Balaam on the height of Baal, a distant point, from which he sees the end of the people; *i.e.*, overlooks the whole. Balaam goes aside—he receives a divine revelation in a vision, and what he then receives he is obliged afterwards to utter. The bodily glance has opened to him, through the power of God's Spirit, an insight into the spiritual state of Israel. He recognises the marks which form the peculiarity of Israel, and utters them in impassioned words.

Ver. 2. *A ram.*—Balaam, as he also entertained heathen notions of the true God and of his relation to Him, caused an offering to be brought by Balak, to determine whether it were perhaps possible to make Him as favourable as he wished Him to be; or, perhaps also, by an unfavourable result, to justify himself, that nothing on his part had been neglected.

Ver. 9. *Behold him.*—He saw Israel, indeed, from the height with his bodily eyes, but here especially is the glance of the spirit meant. He beholds, as he overlooks the tents of the people, guided by the Spirit, his spiritual existence, his glorious destiny. The "for" is here very significant: I see him as one blessed by God; therefore can I not curse him.

Among the nations.—The dwelling alone is explained by this. In the midst of its intercourse with the nations, should Israel form a people by itself. Its peculiarity should consist in the fact, that it should walk a road by itself through history. This token is naturally not to be taken outwardly, as though it belonged to Israel as a people; but it belongs to that peculiar destiny which is expressed, Gen. xii. 3. This mark has now, since the earthly Israel has fulfilled its purpose, passed on to the spiritual Israel, the covenant people of the New Testament. The congregation of the Lord is a peculiar kingdom among the kingdoms of the world, and will outlast them all. But as Israel often resembled the heathen and lost its independence of them, so has the Christian Church, by outward and inward corruption, often forfeited its privileges which were promised it; and, accordingly, these words contain an exhortation as well as a prediction.

Ver. 10. *Fourth part of Israel.*—The immense increase and spread of the people is the second thing which he sees. This token, likewise, is not to be confined to the temporal ancient Israel; the whole Church of the Lord, that also of the New Testament, is included under it. The whole multitude of the people whom Balaam saw before him was the occasion of his looking forward to the fulness of time, when this host shall have multiplied more than a thousandfold.

Like his.—He calls Israel "the righteous"—*i.e.*, the upright, just—because the Lord, the Holy and Just One, who is Himself designated by these words, "just and right" (Deut. xxxii. 4), dwelt among them and sanctified them. That the fact often contradicted the name, is, in the case of this token as the two other forenamed ones, quite true; but the suitableness of the appellation is not therefore lost. It was Israel's lot to be the congregation of the Lord; and by means of this lot, determined by God, they were His congregation before all other people. This privilege also has passed over to the spiritual Israel. The life of these righteous ones appears to Balaam so blessed and happy, that their end, as the peaceful conclusion of a glorious day, is the subject of his longing—perhaps not without a foreboding of his own premature, violent death.

The ground which Balak now causes him to take, is nearer than the former. Perhaps he believed that by the nearness he would be able to work his incantations with better effect, if now the Lord shall have changed His purpose through the sacrifices of His servant. But the second prediction even exceeds the first. Here the people appears as the holy people, because the Lord dwells among them. He has led them out, He makes known to them continually His will: He gives them irresistible power and victory over all their enemies.

Ver. 14. *Pisgah.*—This height lay, according to ch. xxi. 20, near the former encampment of the Israelites before they came to "the field of Moab," ch. xxii. 1, and therefore nearer than the former point, but still distant. He overlooked, indeed, the extremity of the host from thence, but not the whole, as compared with what follows.

Ver. 18. *Rise up.*—Equivalent to "Observe!"

Ver. 19. *Not make it good.*—These magnificent words relate especially to God's unchangeable counsel, as He had revealed it in the preservation of His people out of Egypt, and in the covenant which after that He had made with them. Balak shall not be able, with all his bribes, sacrifices, etc., to alter this. This expression is a confirmation of the truth, that God has never in the history before us changed His purpose. A repetition of the same expression, 1 Sam. xv. 29, has a similar meaning.

Ver. 21. *Perverseness in Israel.*—Heb.: "No wickedness in Jacob, no grief in Israel." The former word expresses the sin, the latter the punishment of it. The same holds good of this expression which was remarked of Israel in the first prediction. Balaam sees the glorious destiny of the people, and its future fulfilment in the congregation of the saints.

Shout of a king.—The shout of a king betokens the solemn festive music at his appearing. Joy reigns at the perpetual presence of this great king among the people.

Ver. 22. *Unicorn.*—Heb.: "His vigour is that of a buffalo."

Ver. 23. *God wrought.*—Because God is among them the people did not need the uncertain, deceptive arts of divination and soothsaying. When the proper time arrives, God makes known to them His counsels.

Ver. 24. *Of the slain.*—This invincible strength tells Balak, therefore, what he has to expect from every attempt against this people.

Ver. 25. *Nor bless them at all.*—If thou wilt not curse, thou oughtest at least not to bless them. Balak thereby intimates that it was treacherous on Balaam's part to act against the very purpose for which he was called.

Ver. 28. *Jeshimon.*—Lit., "The wilderness." Peor is the mountain which rises above the wilderness which stretches northward from the Dead Sea to Jordan. Balak at first thought it good for Balaam not to overlook the whole encampment of Israel. Now, however, he is more and more impressed with the notion, that the nearer he stood the more would he be able to work with

CHAPTER XXIV.

Ver. 1. *To seek for enchantments.*—Heb.: "To the meeting of signs"—auguries, omens. We find, accordingly, that in his former predictions "he went if the Lord met with him;" therefore he used his accustomed means, in order, by the appearance of certain signs and the application of certain means, to put himself into a state of greater spiritual elevation. Now, when he was certified that he should receive no other answer from God, and that the Lord, so soon as he offered himself as an instrument, would fill him with His Spirit, he remained in his usual state, and merely allowed the sight of the Israelitish camp to work its influence on him.

Ver. 2. *Spirit of God.*—Expressly to designate what follows as a Divine revelation.

Ver. 3. *Are open.*—Heb.: "Of closed eyes;" as also ver. 15.

Ver. 4. *Falling into a trance.*—Balaam announces his prophetic gift in exalted language. His prophecies become more elevated as more glorious and extended prospects are revealed to him. The state of his own mind likewise appears to have undergone a corresponding change. He calls himself the man "of closed eye" in order to depict the condition of rapture, in which the outward senses are closed, the inward are opened. That this opening takes place when "he falls into a trance," is signified by the violent agitations under which the revelations are imparted to him. Of this we have examples even in the case of genuine prophets (cf. Rev. i. 17), though in their case this was not the rule, as it appears to have been with Balaam.

Ver. 5. *Tabernacles.*—The sight of the actual tents in the camp of the Israelites transports his view to the dwellings of Israel, crowned with all manner of blessing from the fulness of the Lord. Their whole earthly well-being has its source in the unfailing streams which flow from God to His people.

Ver. 6. *Lign-aloes.*—The tree (Ahalim) here meant is that which the Greeks called Agellochus, the moderns the Tree of Paradise—a fragrant tree which flourishes especially in the Moluccas and in India, and is there highly prized. These trees and the cedars are often mentioned in the O. T. as the most noble which the vegetable kingdom produces.

Ver. 7. *Of his buckets.*—Lit., "water shall flow from both his buckets." The people is thought of as a water-drawer, from both of whose buckets, as he carries them, the beneficent stream pours forth.

Many waters.—His whole posterity shall continually dwell in the abundance of all means of life. Every kind of fruitfulness is in the East connected with water, and hence the frequent and strong figures drawn from it.

Agag.—Agag was the name or standing title of all kings of the Amalekites (cf. 1 Sam. xv.), as Pharaoh was of the Egyptians. Balaam in spirit sees a king at the head of the people, who had hitherto lived in the patriarchal constitution of tribes; and that with the rise of this dignity the power of Israel would receive a fresh impulse. With this kingdom also was the eternal kingdom connected, which the promised Son of David founded on earth.

Ver. 9. *Stir him up.*—The words are out of Jacob's prophecy about Judah, Gen. xlix. 9. There they are spoken of the kingly leading tribe; here very suitably repeated in reference to the power which will proceed from Israel's kings.

Ver. 10. *Smote his hands.*—A sign of his displeasure and contempt—that he would dismiss Balaam from his presence.

Ver. 14. *And now behold.*—The last prediction of Balaam exceeds in every respect the earlier ones. The blessing of God and His power are not merely spoken of in general terms, but one neighbouring people after another having been compared with Israel, and their future destiny declared, the kingdom of Israel stands forth clearly as the eternal kingdom of God on earth, out of these ruins of the powers of the world.

Ver. 17. *Not nigh.*—The vision of the spirit into the far future of the kingdom of God is opened to him. He whom he sees is the Star whose rising he afterwards depicts.

Children of Sheth.—Heb.: "All the sons of tumult;" all the warlike, unquiet people around. This Star and this sceptre is, primarily, the kingdom in the visible people of Israel, which should unite and rally round it the entire power of the people, and come forth to attack other powers. In actual fact, with David, the first king of Israel after God's heart, there began a power and vigour of the people never yet known. He subdued under him Israel's restless neighbours, particularly Moab. But it is not this particular king, nor his outward victory over Moab, which is alone meant. The King of Israel is generally designated whose completion appears in Jesus Christ; and the people whom He subdues are the heathen nations generally, of whom Moab and Edom are types. This Star out of Jacob is to be regarded as the soul of the whole prophecy; the subjugation of the rest of the people, which is now narrated, is His work.

Ver. 18. *Do valiantly.*—Lit., "Israel practises might," as Ps. lx. 14, cxviii. 15, 16. Edom is the people, Seir their land: cf. Gen. xxvii. 39, note. Israel, indeed, has expressly been enjoined to maintain peaceable and friendly relations with the Edomites (Deut. ii. 5, 6). But as the Edomites repeatedly attacked Israel, they were first subdued by David (according to 1 Sam. viii. 14). In the prophets they often are regarded as the emblem of the heathen (who are to be subdued by, and incorporated into, the kingdom of God), especially in the principal place, Amos ix. 12, which St James explains of all the heathen, Acts xv. 17.

Ver. 19. *Of the city.*—Who, in the taking of the city, has escaped destruction.

Ver. 20. *Looked on Amalek.*—In spirit; since, from the situation he occupied, he could not see this people, who dwelt on the Sinaitic peninsula connected with the Edomites.

Perish for ever.—This people, who then were in the flower of their vigour, and were by far the most eminent among these petty nations, had at their first attack of Israel, indeed, been overcome, but on the attack, Num. xiv. 45, have vanquished their former conquerors, and appeared to themselves great beyond all others. But Balaam foresees their overthrow, more especially by the hands of Saul, 1 Sam. xv.

Ver. 21. *Kenites.*—A Canaanitish people, who lived probably in the southern, mountainous, hill country. They are mentioned, Gen. xv. 19, as among the nations to be subdued by Israel. They are here (as elsewhere the Amorites) named as a single Canaanite people for the whole, because they lived in the neighbourhood, and perhaps in their distant mountain land could be descried from Mount Peor.

Thy nest.—Nest is in Heb. "Ken." There is a play on the name of the people, although this name is, as the following shows, to be derived from their ancestor Cain.

Ver. 22. *Kenite.*—Heb.: "O Cain!"—wasted, destroyed.

Asshur.—The question arises, Who is here addressed in the second person? Just before, the words were of course applied to the Kenites; but here, Balaam speaks of them in the third person, and it appears, therefore, that the "thee" must be referred to another people—to the Israelites themselves. "It is a harsh and forced construction to understand these words of the Kenites, and so the most persons refer them to the Israelites. It was surely the purpose of the Holy Spirit—as if, so to speak, He corrected Himself and made a digression—to teach that the happiness predicted should still be mingled with great misery. Servitude is bitter, but banishment still more so."—Calvin.

Ver. 23. *Doeth this.*—"Alas! who will live from the placing of these things from God?" *i.e.*, from the time when God brings these things to pass. The exclamation Alas! shows that it is a fearful misery which the prophet sees in spirit, so that it seems as though no one could escape it. The Assyrian and Babylonish captivity was by far the heaviest calamity which had befallen the Israelites. It would seem as though they were now utterly undone. He connects the remarkable end of his predictions with these words.

Ver. 24. *Coast of Chittim.*—Lit., "From the side of Chittim." By this name the island Cyprus is always designated in the O. T. It is not here said that the power which was to humble Asia should come from thence, but only that it should come from that side.

Shall afflict Asshur, shall afflict Eber.—By both these names is one and the same people and kingdom designated, as before in the case of the names Israel and Jacob. Eber signifies "on the other side;" *i.e.*, the land lying on the other side Euphrates. Here, then, does a prophet in the fifteenth century before Christ see events which took place in the fourth, which were brought about through the instrumentality of Alexander the Great, and of the Romans at a later period; moreover, events which no one at that time, nor, indeed, so long as Israel flourished, could sur-misc as probable, from the appearance of the relation of the different people of the world. The main thought of this prophecy is therefore this—the people of God will be raised again out of the most severe humiliation, since the Lord, according to His promise, will show Himself " an enemy unto their enemies, and an adversary unto their adversaries" (Exod. xxiii. 22). Israel, as the people of God, alone has the promise of eternity.

Perish for ever; i.e., Asshur shall perish as all the people whose overthrow he has caused.

Ver. 25. *Returned to his place;* i.e., he set off on the way towards his home, but he remained among the Midianites, as the following history shows, and gave them, out of revenge, the advice to seduce the Israelites by means of sensual lust, and thereby secured his reward. The more glorious the prophecies which he was obliged to utter, so much the more, under this compulsory office, did his heart become alienated from God, and he now returned to the heathen position in respect to Jehovah, regarding Him as one among many powerful Beings. He had been obliged to experience that he could not cope with God Himself; but His people was, as he knew, a weak, fickle, sensual people, and if he could not reverse God's promises, yet he hoped to alienate this His people from Him, and thus to undermine His power. It is possible that in the meanwhile he went to the Israelites, and carried to them his prophecies (which had been immediately written down by his followers), in the hope of winning them in this way by flattery, but without success. But even without this supposition, we may well conceive how, by different witnesses of this wonderful transaction, which must at once excite the greatest interest among the Israelites, an accurate account of it was put together, or communicated to Moses.—Thus had the attempt to destroy by supernatural powers the ground on which Israel's salvation was built, ended in a fresh glorifying of God, and a strengthening and confirmation of His people.

CHAPTER XXV.

Balak designed to attack the Israelites openly by calling in question their election by God and His defence of them, and attempting to assail this by means of magical arts. On this side, as it was shown, the people were invulnerable. Another device was to assail them as it were covertly, by withdrawing certain numbers of the people from their allegiance to God by means of the enticements of a sensual idolatry. The people felt severely the loss of a worship such as the heathen around them had, in which, from time to time, full licence was given to their sensual appetites, and in which these received a direct sanction. This is the kind of abomination here spoken of. Certain young women, even of higher rank, hired themselves out on certain days in honour of the gods, and gave the wages of their prostitution to the treasury of the temple. It seems that a feast held in honour of Baal-Peor (the god of the sun worshipped on Mount Peor [ch. xxiii. 28]) gave the occasion to this fearful apostasy, in which the Moabites and Midianites appear again to have been allied: as ch. xxii. 3.

Ver. 1. *Shittim.*—The last station of the wilderness, called afterwards Abel-Shittim (the affliction of Shittim), after the punishment which followed there. It lay in the country of Moab, opposite Jericho. Here the people remained a long time, and received the second giving of the law.

Ver. 4. *Against the sun.*—The most ignominious punishment of death—one and the same with the crucifixion of a later time. The persons to be executed were first put to death, then hanged up, and that before the Lord; *i.e.*, as accursed persons in whose destruction He had sanctified Himself. At sunsetting the bodies were to be taken down: cf. Deut. xxi. 22, 23; 2 Sam. xxi. 6.

Ver. 5. *Unto Baal-Peor.*—It is remarkable that the command of the Lord is not carried into execution. It is probable that these judges were from among the heads of the people (cf. Exod. xviii. 25), and by their faithful fulfilment of this command they might have averted that threatened punishment. Every prince who did not therefore punish his people was made answerable for it, and received the severity of the punishment of death.

Ver. 6. *Tabernacle of the congregation.*—Already was a portion of the people before the tabernacle, calling on the Lord to avert the plague. But as yet no one had dared to fulfil Moses' severe command; and that in these circumstances, in defiance of the heads of the people, and of the people who were weeping, a prince of Israel could continue the iniquity with a distinguished Midianitish woman, proved the frightful extent of the corruption, and the danger for the whole people.

Ver. 8. *Into the tent.*—Heb., "the Kubba," the alcove, the projection in the hinder room of the tent.

Ver. 11. *For My sake.*—Lit., "he was jealous with My jealousy"—words which are taken from the relation of marriage in which the Lord stands to His people.

Ver. 13. *An atonement.*—" The covenant of peace " is a peculiarly near relation of God to him, as Ps. cvi. 31 it is expressed, "It was counted to him for righteousness." The dignity of the high priesthood should, by way of eminence, remain in his family. The reason is, because he " has made an atonement for Israel." He has covered their sin, so that God can again be gracious to His people.

Ver. 14. *Simeonites.*—A Simeonitish head of a family.

CHAPTER XXVI.

As Israel was on the point of entering the Promised Land, it was necessary for the proper dividing of the inheritance that a fresh numbering of the people should take place. The old generation had now entirely died out; no one survived of it, with the exception of Joshua and Caleb, besides Moses, who, after the completion of the important duties still incumbent on him, was about soon to take his leave and depart hence.

Ver. 3. *Near Jericho.*—Cf. ch. xxii. 1, note. He spake with them; *i.e.*, he summoned them.

Ver. 7. *Were numbered.*—The number of the Reubenites appears 2770 less than in the numbering ch. i. 21, probably because this tribe had taken especially part in the rebellion of their princes Dathan and Abiram.

Ver. 12. *Nemuel.*—This word is written elsewhere also with a variation, Jemuel.

Ver. 13. *Zerah.*—This person appears also to have borne the name Zochar, 1 Chron. iv. 26; Gen. xlvi. 10; Exod. vi. 15. Similar variations are to be found likewise in some names which follow.

Ver. 14. 22,200.—This is the most considerable diminution of all, as this tribe, according to ch. i. 23, numbered at that time 59,300. Probably the plague, occasioned by a prince of this tribe, Zimri (ch. xxv. 14), had fallen most heavily on it.

Gad.—About 5150 less than ch. i. 29.

Ver. 22. *Judah.*—About 1900 stronger than ch. i. 27.

Ver. 25. *Issachar.*—About 9900 stronger than ch. i. 29.

Ver. 26. *Zebulon.*—About 3100 stronger than ch. i. 31.

Ver. 34. *Manasseh.*—In this tribe the greatest increase had taken place—about 20,500.

Ver. 35. *Ephraim.*—About 8000 less than ch. i. 33.

Ver. 38. *After their families.*—In this statement some differences from Gen. xlvi. 21 occur, perhaps arising from the fact that some families of the tribe had died out, or were so diminished in number that they were incorporated into others.

Ver. 39. *Huphamites.*—These names are written somewhat differently, Gen. xlvi. 21. In the following, also, some variation occurs, originating probably in very ancient errors in transcription in this register.

Ver. 41. *Benjamin.*—About 10,200 more than ch. i. 37.

Ver. 43. 64,400.—About 1700 more than ch. i. 39.

Ver. 46. *Was Sarah.*—Probably here mentioned as heiress, who had married into this family, and brought its inheritance to it.

Ver. 47. 53,400.—About 11,900 more than ch. i. 41.

Ver. 50. 45,400.—About 8000 less than ch. i. 43.

Ver. 51. *The numbered.*—By comparison with ch. i. 46, the number of the whole people had decreased about 1820 men capable of bearing arms. It had, therefore, on the whole, remained nearly the same. After so many destructive visitations, the power of the Divine promise to Israel had been proved by the continual renewal of the people.

Ver. 55 *Divided by lot.*—After the size of the inheritance of the particular families had been determined according to their number, the choice of it was still to be settled by lot. Here, as ever in the guidance of the people of God, God's decree and man's judgment were to work together.

Ver. 62. *No inheritance.*—The Levites are not numbered, because this numbering was taken with reference to the division of the land. Their numbering also is not complete, as the register of the families breaks off with Aaron, as the most distinguished of all. His mother Jochebed is called Levi's daughter, but only in a wider sense, as she might perhaps be his great-granddaughter.

CHAPTER XXVII.

An important case of succession to inheritance is laid before Moses, and a more comprehensive law on the subject is the result. As a general rule, the males had the precedence over females in the inheriting of property in land. Only where there were not sons, did the daughters inherit in their stead, to the exclusion of the collateral branches.

Ver. 3. *Died in his own sin.*—He had not seduced others to sin, but died in the general condemnation, merely on account of his own part in it.

Ver. 11. *Of his family.*—Therefore only the agnates—relations on the father's side—not the cognates, had any possession.

Ver. 12. *Said to Moses.*—The time is now arrived when the great servant of the Lord shall depart this life. But, in order that his death may not be altogether unexpected either to himself or to the people, and that he might complete the whole commission laid on him by God in respect to them, God solemnly apprises him of his approaching death, and reminds him of his former sin. Care is taken for that most necessary matter, the appointment of his successor.

Abarim.—This range of mountains, as the whole position of the Israelites so far shows, is to be looked for over "against Jericho," between Hesbon and the Dead Sea. That town itself lay about twelve miles eastward of the mouth of the Jordan, on a point commanding an extensive survey of the surrounding country on all sides, to a distance of from 25 to 30 miles. Jerusalem and Bethlehem can be seen from thence. The district between this town and the Jordan has never been investigated in modern times. The discovery of the real Mount Nebo in the range of Abarim is still to be made.

Ver. 18. *Thine hand upon him.*—Cf. Lev. i. 4, note.

Ver. 20. *Thine honour upon him.*—The ruling power which proceeds from God.

Ver. 21. *Judgment of Urim.*—Joshua's office is at the same time limited: while Aaron was Moses' prophet (Exod. iv. 15), Joshua is referred to Aaron's successor, who had to obtain the oracles of God for him.

CHAPTER XXVIII.

The two next chapters give a detailed and particular order of sacrifices. The occasion of this was the approaching invasion of Canaan. It was necessary to give rules for the observance of the customs of daily service to God; and accordingly these regulations must be given in this place. At the same time the Israelites, after conquering so considerable a district and taking so much booty, would be in possession of a sufficient abundance of cattle to carry out in a becoming manner all which was commanded them.

Ver. 2. *My bread.*—All the sacrifices are called the "bread of God," especially the burnt-offering which ascended to heaven entire, as generally all flesh which was sacrificed: Lev. iii. 11.

Ver. 3. *Day by day.*—Exod. xxix. 38.

Ver. 4. *At even.*—Lit., "between the two evenings:" see Exod. xii. 6, note.

Ver. 6. *Ordained in Mount Sinai*, *i.e.*, As ye there first offered it.

Ver. 11. *Beginning of your months.*—The new moons do not occur as especial feast-days in the list of festivals (Lev. xxiii.). They were not distinguished by rest from labour, but by particular sacrifices, as we here see. Therefore there was no especial religious meaning in these days. They were only, as important periods according to which the year was divided, not to pass without express consecration. Cf. on the new moon, 1 Sam. xx. 5, 6; 2 Kings iv. 23; Col. ii. 16.

CHAPTER XXIX.

Ver. 1. *Blowing the trumpets.*—See Lev. xxiii. 24. The sacrifices of the feast following, but especially of the Feast of Tabernacles, show that this was the most solemn month of the whole year.

Ver. 7. *Holy convocation.*—The great day of atonement: Lev. xvi.

Ver. 14. *Thirteen bullocks.*—On each of the eight feast-days was one of this great sin-offering of thirteen bullocks omitted.

CHAPTER XXX.

For the purpose of arousing them from lethargy, and of keeping them in remembrance of especial duties and of their relationship towards God, the Israelites were allowed to make also especial vows, of which a distinguished one, the Nazarite vow, has been mentioned, ch. vi. The general obligation to keep every vow to the Lord is naturally limited by the yet more general principle, " that obedience is better than sacrifice (1 Sam. xv 22), as only that which is well-pleasing to the Lord can acceptably be vowed to Him. But if the thing vowed is not only permitted, but the person who vows recognises God's will in respect to himself therein, then is he bound to keep it, with the exception of the case of dependence, concerning which express rules are here given.

Ver. 13. *To afflict.*—Lit., " to humble his soul," as Lev. xvi. 29.

Ver. 15. *Bear her iniquity.*—He will be regarded as having himself broken the vow.

CHAPTER XXXI.

Of the two nations who had shown themselves hostile towards the Israelites—the Moabites and Midianites—revenge is now taken on the latter. The reason why the first were spared, seems to be because the Midianites had taken the lead in the crime of seducing Israel to the practice of the licentious idolatry, and Balaam, the instigator to the act, was found among them and killed; and, moreover, the Moabites, from fear of the enmity of the powerful people, were incited to deceit, but the Midianites had no such excuse. The sin in Israel had been stemmed by the act of Phinehas: so had judgment begun at the house of God; but now likewise must the purified people of God take vengeance on His enemies. The conduct of the people in the war, the division of the spoil, as well as their wonderful preservation, are related with particular detail, since this battle was to serve as a kind of example for the war of conquest which was now immediately before them.

Ver. 2. *Gathered unto thy people.*—This was the last act of Moses as leader of the people.

Ver. 6. *Phinehas.*—In honour of Phinehas, as the first who had stood up and stayed Israel's apostasy and the plague, and at the same time to sanctify the war by the guidance of a priest.

Holy instruments.—What these were, is not mentioned; but from ch. xiv. 14, 1 Sam. iv., it is not improbable that it was the ark of the covenant with the things belonging to it—the covering with the cherubim, and the tables of the law. It is a mistake to suppose they could be the "Light and Right," Urim and Thummim, because Eleasar the high priest, and not Phinehas, had these.

Trumpets.—"Ye shall be remembered before the Lord your God, and ye shall be saved from your enemies:" ch. x. 9, note.

Ver. 18. *Keep alive for yourselves.*—This command shows that it was a holy revenge which the Israelites took—a judgment which they as the instruments of the Lord fulfilled. The putting to death all the male children has for its object the extermination of the whole people who were not continued in the females.

Ver. 24. *Come into the camp.*—All this is here so circumstantially commanded, because these prescribed rules were ever afterwards to be observed in the wars of extermination which followed.

Ver. 30. *Tabernacle of the Lord.*—The share of the priests stands in about the same proportion to that of the Levites, as did the tithes of the one to those of the other.

Ver. 33.—It is evident from this that the Midianites were a rich Arabian nomad people.

Ver. 49. *Not one man of us.*—This is in some measure to be explained by the fact, that the Midianites were not a warlike people, and had been suddenly attacked by the Israelites: still it was certainly a wonderful preservation of the people, which never failed them when they entirely did the will of God.

Ver. 50. *For our souls before the Lord.*—As the Lord had graciously recognised the obedience of His people, and had rewarded it by the preservation of them all in the war, the consideration of this mercy awakens in the leaders of the people a feeling of holy fear and thankfulness. Under the feeling that the souls thus preserved were not worthy of this grace, they offer a sacrifice to the Lord " to cover them "—to atone for their sins.

CHAPTER XXXII.

In all the promises made to the people, the Promised Land properly is always Canaan, this side Jordan. The Euphrates and the Nile also are often given as the boundaries of the land (Gen. xv. 18); but this is not to be understood of the dwelling of the people, but of the countries tributary and subject to them. But now Israel did not find, as had originally been the case, the Moabites and the Ammonites in possession of the land beyond Jordan, but two powerful victorious kings of the Amorites, whose people were especially marked out for the judgment of the Lord: Gen. xv. 16. The war of extermination had therefore begun with this people, by which means the boundaries of the land of Canaan had of themselves been extended. It is remarkable in this transaction, how the first decision of Moses rests on a misunderstanding, and therefore is wrong, but immediately is withdrawn by him and corrected.

Ver. 3. *Beon.*—These names are partially to be recognised at the present day in small places, hills and ruins. Ataroth is to be found in Mount Attarus, north of Modscheb, the ancient Arnon. An hour's journey from that river, to the north-east, Burckhardt saw the ruins of Dibon. To the north of this the same traveller found ruins, the name of which was given to him as Szyr, in which, perhaps, Jazer is to be recognised. Nimrah (elsewhere Beth-nimrah: Joshua xiii. 27; Isa. xv. 6, "the place of clean water") lay in the valley of Jordan, north of the part in which the people now were—now called Nemrin, in ruins. For Heshbon, now Hesban, see ch. xxi. 26, note. Elealeh is now called El-Al, near to Heshbon, on the summit of a hill and commanding the plain. From thence may be seen the whole land named Belka, east of the Dead Sea. Shebam or Sibma was celebrated for its vineyards; now unknown. Nebo appears to be connected with the mountain of the same name, which most probably lay between Heshbon and the Jordan. Beon is also called Beal-Meon; and is at this day in ruins, which are called Myun.

Ver. 16. *Came near to him.*—From these words it may almost be supposed that they had not really at first the intention which they here express, but only on second thoughts came to a better mind.

Ver. 19. *Is fallen to us.*—Here they use the word "yonder side," from their present position.

Ver. 30. *Land of Canaan.*—*i.e.*, Well, they shall in that case receive no peculiar inheritance, but shall be incorporated into the poorer tribes after they have been driven out of their present possessions.

Ver. 33. *Manasseh.*—The participation of this half-tribe in the possession is established by ver. 39.

Ver. 38. *They builded.*—Rebuilt after the conquest. All the names were not changed.

Ver. 41. *Havoth-Jair.*—*i.e.*, "Villages of Jair:" cf. Deut. iii. 14;—a name which for the sake of a descendant of Jair, who had the same name, was afterwards renewed.

CHAPTER XXXIII.

As the people has now finished its wanderings through the wilderness, Moses mentions the express command of the Lord to write down the stations of its encampments. Among these many are related which occur in the history; but it is especially remarkable that the whole period of the thirty-eight years' wandering, with all the stations, is entirely omitted. In the sacred books only the steps in the stage of development and the progress of the kingdom of God are recorded; the time during which the generation assigned to the curse of God was to die out, is therefore necessarily wanting. This history is here, as it were, blotted out. This record, therefore, proceeds from the beginning to the end in a direct manner as if God's original plan had been carried into effect, teaching us that man's sin cannot in the end frustrate the purpose of God.

Ver. 1. *Journeys.*—Lit., "breakings up"—the places from which they journeyed. The march is divided, not according to the encampments, the stations, but according to the decampments.

Ver. 16. *Kibroth-Hattaavah.*—Here follows the long stay at Sinai, from whence they broke up, Num. x. 11. From thence two ways into Canaan were open to them; one on the west coast of the Ælanitic Gulf, and the other through the mountain district and the wilderness Et-Tih. But the first is a very narrow coast path, close by precipitous, jagged rocks, and therefore altogether unsuited to the passage of a vast host; the other way leads at the beginning through a mountainous district, but soon arrives at the wide inhospitable desert. The latter, without doubt, was the one chosen; and the first station of the Israelites, which is called, ch. xi. 3, Taberah (burning), and ch. xi. 34, Kibroth-Hattaavah (graves of lust), was not a town, but only an uninhabited part of the mountain-desert, which received its names from the events occurring there.

Ver. 36. *Kadesh.*—These stations as far as Kadesh are as good as unknown. It may be supposed, with some probability, that the people did not march through the wilderness by a straight route, but diverged on both sides for the purpose of procuring sustenance for their herds. The last stations have with the greatest likelihood been looked for in the neighbourhood of Mount Seir, therefore in Arabah. From thence they pass on to Ezion-geber, which lay on the Red Sea; and from thence again back northward toward Kadesh, on the south borders of Canaan. There occurred the event related ch. xiv. It has been supposed that, perhaps, while waiting for the spies, the people marched round Mount Seir, until they met with them at Kadesh. The supposition that the thirty-eight years' wandering in the wilderness is described by the stations from Bnejaekan to Ezion-geber lacks all probability, and has only arisen from the wish to unite Deut. x. 6 with the account before us. The reason why on the long road from Ezion-geber to Kadesh no station is named, may perhaps be because the people visited their former places of encampment, whose names are therefore not repeated.

Ver. 39. *Aaron.*—Ch. xx. 23.

Ver. 41. *Zalmonah.*—An Edomite town on the east side of Mount Seir, lying north-east from the present Akaba; perhaps the modern Maan on the road from Damascus to Mecca.

Ver. 42. *Punon.*—This is also an Edomite place. In the fourth century after Christ a village in the wilderness, near the Dead Sea; perhaps Kalaat Phenan.

Ver. 49. *Plains of Moab.*—All these places show that the Israelites went round Edom first in an easterly, then in a northerly direction, until they reached the level land of the valley of Jordan, opposite Jericho.—Although it is quite true that in the whole history of the people of God there is a type both of the guiding of the Christian Church and of the individual Christian, yet it is altogether arbitrary, and unwarranted entirely by Scripture, to interpret the particular stations in the wilderness, or their names, by the signification attached to them, as though they represented a list of the particular steps of the Christian life.

Ver. 54. *Tribes of your fathers.*—Cf. ch. xxvi. 52.

Ver. 56. *To do unto them.*—That I should destroy and drive you out. The more there is left in the new life of the Christian of old sins, so much the greater is the danger of the contest which is certain to ensue, and at last the risk of entire apostasy.

CHAPTER XXXIV.

Ver. 4. *Kadesh-barnea.*—The boundary, therefore, was to go from the south point of the Dead Sea southward to Ghor, along the range of Mount Seir, through the heights of Akrabbim to Kadesh. It comprises accordingly all the fastnesses which hitherto had barred the entrance of the Israelites.

Ver. 5. *At the sea.*—From Kadesh the boundary turns to the east, with a slight inclination northward; here it intersects the wilderness in which Adar and Azmon must have been situated, the localities of which cannot be determined. The river of Egypt (which must not be confounded with "the Great River," Gen. xv. 18) is most probably the Wady-el-Arish, which empties itself near the ancient Rhinocura, the present Kelat-el-Arish.

Ver. 6. *The Great Sea.*—The Mediterranean.

Ver. 7. *Mount Hor.*—An unknown mountain in the Lebanon range. "Hor" is another form for the Hebrew "Har," mountain; Greek, "Oros;" and therefore common to many mountain peaks. A particularly well-known lofty point was Hermon.

Ver. 8. *Hamath.*—The well-known Syrian town on the Orontes —afterwards Emesa, now Hems.

Ver. 11. *East side of Ain.*—All these places are unknown, except Riblah, which to this day is called Ribleh, a place on the Orontes south of Hems.

Chinnereth.—In the N.T., Gennesareth, or the Sea of Tiberias.

Ver. 15. *Near Jericho;* i.e., opposite Jericho.

CHAPTER XXXV.

The tribe of Levi, which had not received any inheritance among the others, but which was to be dispersed among them (Gen. xlix. 6), obtains here in each tribe six towns, with pasture round them for their cattle, in order in this way to penetrate and sanctify the whole people with their influence.

Ver. 2. *Suburbs.*—By this we are to understand an unoccupied space around the towns.

Ver. 8. *Which he inheriteth.*—They were not therefore divided among the tribes in an equal measure, but there were a greater number in the richer and larger ones. The total sum of them, however, pointed to the number of the tribes, which was twelve.

Ver. 11. *Cities of refuge.*—Among all ancient nations, even to the Christian era, there were cities of refuge—asylums which afforded protection to those who had reason to fear punishment or revenge for any deed they had committed. Among the heathen the asylum was, for the most part, afforded unconditionally; while by the Divine law no wilful murderer was allowed to enjoy it (cf. Exod. xxi. 14). But six cities of the Levites were appointed "cities of refuge" for those who had unintentionally inflicted a blow causing death. They were placed as sanctuaries in the midst of the people, as elsewhere the altar was such, which served for a place of refuge (1 Kings ii. 29). The appointment of these cities as about to take place had already been hinted at (Exod. xii. 13). It is there remarked, and more particularly explained, how this institution presupposes the existence of the principle of vengeance for blood. We must, in reference to this principle—which was not introduced by the law, but allowed to stand—always bear in mind, that while the modern notion of judicial punishment is, that it is better to let a murderer go unpunished than to punish an innocent person, with the ancient law, on the contrary, the escape of a murderer appeared so horrible, that nothing was esteemed too great a stretch to secure his punishment. Even the unintentional man-slayer had committed a fearful deed, though he was personally innocent. He was not, indeed, to be put to death, but he was regarded as civilly dead until the death of the high priest. This death was a kind of termination of a period. With the death of the supreme judge, was the remembrance of the deed committed during his term of office to be wiped away.

Ver. 12. *Avenger.*—Lit., "the redeemer of a pledge;" sometimes with the addition, "redeemer of the pledge of blood." The kinsman who redeemed a possession was called by the same name, Lev. xxv. 25. As the one paid money for the possession, so did the other pay death-blow for death-blow, and made atonement by retaliation for the crime.

Ver. 15. *Killeth;* i. e. (as also in the following verse), a murderer. Even an unpremeditated man-slaughter was punished altogether as murder: cf. Exod. xxi. 12, note.

Ver. 33. *That shed it.*—It is regarded by the present Arabs a disgraceful act for the avenger of blood to take money from the relations. Even with them the notion is still prevalent that the impunity of a murderer is something horrible. Much more would this feeling exist among the Israelites, with whom the reason for it was expressly derived from their view of the violation of the Divine image: Gen. ix. 6.

Ver. 34. *The Lord dwelt.*—Lastly, all is traced up to the dwelling of the Lord among His people, who could not dwell in a dishonoured and defiled land. Thus do all these laws in the end refer to their Author.

CHAPTER XXXVI.

It was a great point with the people of Israel, that their possession should always appear as one lent to them by God. But the division of the tribes was essentially connected with this view. This division would be done away with, if the inheritance was allowed to pass into other tribes by marriage; and this so much the more, as the small states which formed the tribes rested altogether on the family constitution. The geographical boundaries, therefore, could not be regulated otherwise than by the possessions of the families constituting the tribe.

Ver. 4. *Jubilee;* i. e., although the year of jubilee comes, the possessions do not, however, fall to the tribe of Manasseh, but to the heirs of the daughters of Zelophehad.

THE FIFTH BOOK OF MOSES,

CALLED DEUTERONOMY (THE REPETITION OF THE LAW)

CHAPTER I.

With the preceding book is concluded the whole of the giving of the law, together with those additions to it which were made in the country of Moab. Now had the time arrived for the people to pass over into the Promised Land, and for Moses to take leave of them. As Christ, the Mediator of the new covenant, must leave His disciples even before they had received the promised Comforter, and were endued with power from on high for their new life, in like manner must the mediator of the old covenant take leave of his people without seeing them in possession of the Promised Land, or witnessing the fulfilment of God's word, and without being himself the accomplisher of it. But as Christ, before He went to His death, once more put His disciples in mind of what He had said to them in His farewell discourses, and confirmed them by the repetition of exhortations and warnings, in like manner did Moses clearly and emphatically lay before the people once more the whole counsel of God in the election of His people,—how He had saved them by miracles out of Egypt, led them through the wilderness, made them to triumph over the Canaanites, as it was contained in the law itself. The "repetition of the law," therefore, includes the memorial of these events, as well as here and there interweaves some new rules of conduct. Two somewhat long discourses of Moses open the whole book, which are written down by himself, as his last legacy of wisdom and love. The first of these (ch. i.–iv.) is altogether of a general character; it recalls to mind the acts of the history of the covenant, adding an earnest exhortation to obedience. God's great promise of grace stands first (ver. 6–8): then he begins the history with the appointment of the heads of the tribes to the office of judges, by which means the whole people was divided into separate departments (ver. 9–18): hereupon he narrates, among all the deeds of the sinful people, that momentous one, the sending out of the spies, and the disobedience following on it, which involved as its consequences their stay at Kadesh, and the thirty-eight years' wandering in the wilderness.

Ver. 2. *Kadesh-barnea.*—These names are intended to give a general view of the country through which the Israelites had lately passed. The place from which Moses now speaks is "the field," the Arabah; for thus is called all that deep, desolate valley which stretches from Lebanon to the Red Sea, in which the Jordan flows into the Dead Sea through the lakes Merom and Kinnereth, being in its middle part deeper than the surface of the sea. This Arabah lies "over against the Reedy Sea," and runs towards the south as far as the Ælanitic Gulf of the Red Sea. "Paran" is the more highly situated wilderness, Et-Tih; Tophel, the modern Tofyle, a well-watered, fruitful place on the south of the Dead Sea, at the commencement of the range of the mountains of Seir. "Laban" and "Hazeroth" are mentioned, Num. xxxiii. 17 and 20, as stations of Israel on the way from Sinai to Kadesh. "Di-Sahab" is perhaps the present Dhahab, a harbour on the Ælanitic Gulf.—The last statement, "eleven days' journey," etc., is intended to signify the distance of Arabah from Horeb. In Kadesh (cf. Num. xiii. 14) they had arrived at the south borders of Canaan; and it was their own fault that they did not enter, and were only now on the point of effecting an invasion from another side of the same Arabah.

Ver. 5. *Declare.*—The Hebrew word means, properly, to engrave, to hew in stone; which is thus used of the deeper impressing and imprinting on the heart by means of exhortation and explanation.

Ver. 6. *This mount.*—These words refer to Num. x. 11.

Ver. 7. *Amorites.*—The Amorites, as the most warlike and powerful people, stand here for all the Canaanites, as Gen. xv. 10, etc.

Euphrates.—Cf. in respect to these boundaries, Gen. xv. 18, note.

Ver. 9. *I spake unto you.*—It seems that in the following account two histories are comprised in one: the appointment of the judges at the advice of Jethro (Exod. xviii.), and the installing of the seventy elders by the communication of the Spirit to them (Num. xi. 16). The first institution, which was of man's origin, received its consecration by the latter act. The division of the whole people into corporations, under heads also inspired by the Spirit of God as Moses, made the whole unformed mass really into one people.

Ver. 19. *Kadesh-barnea.*—Num. xiii. 27, ch. xxxiii. 36.

Ver. 23. *I took.*—According to Num. xiii. 3, the Lord Himself gave the command, which may be easily explained as the other view of the same transaction.

Ver. 28. *Whither.*—Not an inquiry, but a murmur of complaint.

Ver. 36. *Wholly followed.*—Lit., "that he hath fulfilled after the Lord;" *i.e.*, has entirely followed Him, as it is said in Hebrew, "They were speedy after Him," for "they followed Him speedily."

Ver. 37. *For your sakes.*—Here again we see, as it were, the other side of the event narrated Num. xx. 10, etc. There the unbelief of Moses and Aaron bears the blame; yet this unbelief was called forth by the invincible perverseness of the people. Moses, therefore, was punished because he had not kept himself entirely free from the infection of the sin of the people, but the people had reason to reckon this sin on the part of Moses as occasioned by their fault.

Ver. 39. *Shall possess it.*—Cf. Num. xiv. 3, 31.

Ver. 44. *Hormah.*—Num. xiv. 39.

Ver. 46. *Ye abode there; i.e.*, They marched for 38 years from that point round about, in the neighbourhood of Kadesh; and therefore, in the description of the encampments, Num. xxxiii. 36, a resting-point was made there, and the objectless wandering through the wilderness is passed over.

CHAPTER II.

Ver. 1. *Many days.*—In Arabah to the west of it, from Kadesh towards the Red Sea.

Ver. 4. *Afraid of you.*—Cf. on the whole passage, Num. xxi., introd.

Ver. 5. *For a possession.*—Gen. xxxvii. 8, 43.

Ver. 6. *May drink.*—Since Israel provided continually, both for themselves and their herds, food over and above the manna.

Ver. 8. *Ezion-geber.*—A harbour on the Ælanitic branch of the Arabian Gulf, from whence Solomon's ships sailed to Ophir, 1 Kings ix. 26, and where the merchant-vessels of Jehosaphat were wrecked, 1 Kings xxii. 48.

Ver. 9. *Ar.*—The principal town of the Moabites, which lies near to Arnon: Num. xxi. 15.

Ver. 12. *Lord gave unto them.*—The words from ver. 10 appear most probably not to belong to the speech of Moses, but are explanatory remarks of the person who, after his death, wrote the conclusion of the book, and arranged the whole narrative. There are many similar instances in this book of the insertion of remarks of the same kind.—The aboriginal people who, before the Canaanites, dwelt in Palestine on both sides of the Jordan, are described as of great bodily strength and stature. Their names also appear to intimate this; as, *e.g.*, "Emim" means "the terrible." Over these rude hordes the more civilized nations got the upper hand: in the east, the Moabites and Ammonites; in the south-west, the Philistines; in the other parts, the Canaanitish tribes; and the aborigines only survived in some places in a few remnants and families. The Horites were the inhabitants of the many caves of Mount Seir: see Gen. xxxvi. 5, note.

Ver. 20. *Giants.*—Or, "of the Rephaites"—a name of a giant-like people, as the Emims and the Anakim: cf. Gen. xiv. 5, note.

Ver. 21. *Destroyed them;* i.e., through their means. It appears that in these words is expressed a nearer relation of the Lord (Jehovah) to this people, the descendants of Lot, whom God blessed for Abraham's sake.

Ver. 23. *Caphtorims.*—Cf. Gen. x. 14, note.

In their stead.—The same is applicable to the words in brackets, from ver. 20, as of vers. 10-12.

Ver. 30. *Appeareth this day.*—There is the same condition in the above proposal as in that made to Pharaoh, Exod. iii. 18, 19.

CHAPTER III.

Ver 9. *Shenir.*—Cf. ch. ii. 12, note.

Ver. 11. *Cubit of a man.*—Upon this also, ch. ii. 12, note, may be referred to. While the old giant people were subdued, and reduced to a small, scattered remnant, a giant race had been maintained in the kingly dignity. The excessive size of the bed may be explained by the attempt to make a display of great bodily height, without being obliged to suppose that he was really so huge. Nine cubits are thirteen feet and a half. At Rabbah the bedstead might have been left to relatives as a curiosity, and preserved by them.

Ver. 14. *Unto this day.*—Cf. ii. 12, note; and for the thing itself, Num. xxxii. 41, note.

Ver. 16. *And the border.*—Heb.: "Even to the brook Arnon, the middle of the brook and the border;" *i.e.*, the middle of the brook and its end, its mouth in the Dead Sea, shall be its border.

Ver. 17. *Eastward.*—The "plain" is in the Hebrew "the Arabah;" the deep valley of the Jordan, with the two lakes Cinnereth and the Dead Sea.

Ver. 20. *I have given you.*—Their own offer, which Moses accepted in the name of the Lord and confirmed, is here comprehensively represented as the command of the Lord: cf. Num. xxxiv. "Beyond Jordan" stands here in its proper local signification, not as a name: cf. Num. xxxii. 19, note.

Ver. 27. *Top of Pisgah.*—This command was complied with: ch. xxxiv. 1.

CHAPTER IV.

Ver. 6. *Surely.*—Such an impression is made, for example, on the Arabian queen, 1 Kings x. 6.

Ver. 7. *Call upon Him for.*—All the religions of the heathen have proceeded from the necessity felt of a communion of man with God; and in all of them do we find traces that this necessity has not been satisfied. Thus, for example, there runs through the old Greek religion, as we find it represented in Homer, a tradition of a near and intimate intercourse of the gods with men; but already in the time which the poems represent, this communion is on the wane. The highest God nowhere himself visibly appears, and the other gods rarely; so that it is evident the poet in his own time knew of no such communion. But it is otherwise in the covenant-religion, in which God's revelations do not cease until, midway in the history of the world, they reach their crowning-point in Christ.

Ver. 11. *Midst.*—Lit., "unto the heart of heaven."

Ver. 13. *Midst of the fire.*—Cf. Exod. xxiv. 9.

Ver. 20. *Iron furnace;* i. e., the glowing, melting furnace as an image of their hot tribulation.

Ver. 21. *Was angry.*—Cf. ch. i. 37, note.

Ver. 24. *Jealous God;* i. e., One who will not suffer any rival. An expression taken from the marriage relation of the Lord to His people: cf. Exod. xx. 5.

Ver. 28. *Shall serve.*—The sin itself will be the greatest punishment of the sin: cf. Rom. i. 24, note.

Ver. 31. *Sware unto them.*—Cf. the similar expression, Lev. xxvi. 40.

Ver. 33. *And live.*—Cf. Gen. xvi. 13, note.

Ver. 36. *Instruct thee;* i. e., taught,—educated partly by the contents, partly by the mode and way of His revelation.

Ver. 41. *Then Moses.*—Agreeably to historical fidelity and accuracy, there follows the separation of the cities of refuge in the east of Jordan, after the introductory discourse of Moses just given, when he ceases, in order next with yet more solemnity and fulness to repeat the main purport of the law.

Ver. 42. *Might live.*—Cf. Num. xxxv. 14.

Ver. 43. *Manassites.*—These three cities are also elsewhere mentioned. We find Bezer as a Levite city in the tribe of Reuben, Joshua xxi. 36. Its situation cannot be further determined. Ramoth is mentioned also as a Levite city in the tribe of Gad, Joshua xxi. 38. There the kings of Israel often engaged in war with the Syrians: 1 Kings xxii. 1; 2 Kings viii. 28. It lay fifteen Roman miles to the north-west of the later city Philadelphia on the Jabbok. Golan was situated in Bashan, and afterwards gave the name to the north-western district Gaulanitis: Joshua xx. 8, ch. xxi. 27.

Ver. 44. *This is the law.*—After the introductory exhortation now follows the "second law," and begins with a repetition of the ten commandments. In order to distinguish it as a solemn act on the part of Moses, by which he once for all delivered to the new generation that which their fathers had received on Sinai, the place and the exact time are first minutely given. Many explanatory additions are to be found in the case of the mention of the historical circumstances, as is suitable to a continuous discourse. These additions afford a more graphic account of the whole matter, and here and there adduce even new facts. It is remarkable that such alterations and additions should occur in the repetition of the ten commandments, of which that said ch. iv. 2 must above all hold good, since they were written by God Himself on tables of stone; but they are signs that in this and other similar repetitions of the word, in the Word of God itself, the Spirit of the Lord still operates with ever fresh power.

Ver. 49. *Plain.*—The Arabah. See ch. i. 2, note.
The sea of the plain.—The Dead Sea.

CHAPTER V.

Ver. 15. *Sabbath day.*—Very remarkable alterations occur in this commandment. The difference of the mode of beginning is of less importance; of more consequence is the circumstance, that the rest of the Sabbath day is founded, not on God's rest after the creation, but on the deliverance out of Egypt. The reason of this may well be—that the people are now on the point of entering the Promised Land, after the afflictions endured in Egypt and in the wilderness; and this entrance into Canaan is an emblem of the rest of God after the creation, and a type of the heavenly rest: cf. Heb. iv. 7–9. Since God has now given this rest to His people, in like manner ought a day of rest with joy to be granted to all those who were wearied with the burden of their labour.

Ver. 31. *Possess it.*—Cf. Exod. xx. 18.

CHAPTER VI.

Ver. 2. *Mightest fear.*—Every relation of the sinner to God must begin in fear, and therefore in so many places it is described as the beginning of wisdom: Job xxviii. 28; Prov. i. 7, ch. xv. 33, ch. xxiii. 17. It is the feeling of awe in the presence of the All Holy, Almighty, ever near God.

Ver. 5. *All thy might.*—Moses proceeds from fear to love. Fear makes man stand in holy awe before God; love unites him to God in closest communion. In this centre-piece of the whole law the duty of love of God above everything else is in a sublime way made to depend on His unity. Because the only, the living God, the fulness of all life and of all holiness, has revealed Himself as the covenant God of His people Israel, and has bestowed on them His dearest love; therefore now must His people not be divided in their love to Him, but give themselves up to Him with their whole heart. Already in the ten commandments had God promised His favour to them "who love Him" (ch. v. 10), and He repeats this many times; as He also, in the highest of all His revelations, especially makes Himself known to Moses as Love: Exod. xxxiv. 6, 7.—With the whole of this compare St Matt. xxii. 34, where Christ lays no other ground of holiness and morality than this which is here already laid in the law.

Ver. 9. *On thy gates.*—Cf. Exod. xiii. 9, note. The "writing on the posts of the house" recalls to mind a superstitious custom of the kind in Egypt. A commandment literally to be observed is assuredly not given here, although, applied in a free spirit, such an inscription might arise out of it. This the pharisaical spirit in later times understood quite in an outward sense.

Ver. 12. *Forget the Lord.*—The enjoyment of the good things of this life which God gives, is accompanied with the danger of forgetting Him, and of clinging to the gods of nature, as has been the case with many heathen people. The remembrance of God's benefits and chastisements, and of His interference in their history, was to serve to the people of Israel to counterbalance this danger.

Ver. 20. *When thy son.*—Cf. the beautiful custom at the feast of the Passover, Exod. xii. 26. By these ordinances was the training of the young in the fear of the Lord recommended in the most persuasive manner.

CHAPTER VII.

Ver. 2. *Destroy them;* i.e., as devoted to the curse of the Lord. Cf. Lev. xxvii. 28.

Ver. 5. *Cut down their images.*—Cf. Exod. xxxiv. 13, note.

Ver. 7. *Fewest of all people.*—That is, when the Lord chose their fathers they stood alone, and only had become a numerous people by His mighty blessing. God's free grace, which for the sake of His people had become bound to an oath of promise, made them what they were, and of this they ought always to be mindful.

Ver. 15. *Diseases of Egypt.*—Egypt was in ancient times, and is still, noted as the seat of certain diseases, particularly skin diseases, and of a peculiar kind of blindness.

Ver. 19. *Great temptations.*—The miracles whereby the Lord tried the Egyptians, whether they would let Israel go or not.

Ver. 20. *Hornet.*—See Exod. xxiii. 28, note.

Ver. 22. *Beasts of the field.*—See Exod. xxiii. 29, 30, note.

Ver. 25. *Be snared.*—That thou dost not begin to honour these images or their adornments.

CHAPTER VIII.

Ver. 2. *Whether thou wouldest keep.*—The wandering in the wilderness had this double purpose—the punishment of the incurable who were condemned to extermination, and the trial and purifying of the generation now growing up.

Ver. 3. *Out of the mouth.*—Heb., "what the mouth of the Lord brings forth;"—"that God is not tied to the laws of His earthly governance of the world, but preserves thee by His creative power." Israel was to know that it was not nature, but God the Creator of nature, who nourishes us through her; and for this purpose the people were not to be fed by the usual productions of nature, but by an extraordinary work of God's almighty power. Cf. Exod. xvi., introd., and the application of this passage, St Matt. iv. 3.

Ver. 4. *Foot swell;* i.e., ye have had no need of shoes.

Forty years.—In connection with the foregoing there seems to have been a miraculous preservation of them, though the mode and manner cannot be determined.

Ver. 8. *Honey.*—On the fruitfulness of Canaan here commemorated, and the contrast of its present unfruitfulness, see Exod. iii. 8, note.

Ver. 9. *Dig brass.*—The latter explains the former. The stones of the hills are full of iron-ore. This holds good especially of the basalt mountains in the east of the land of Jordan, the very stone of which is ferruginous.

Ver. 16. *To do thee good.*—Lit., "that He may do good on thine end." The end among the people of God is always good and blessing.

CHAPTER IX.

Ver. 4. *For the wickedness.*—Gen. xv. 16; Lev. xviii. 24, 25. The extermination of the heathen was a Divine judgment on their sins; but it by no means followed that the Israelites were in themselves better than they.

Ver. 6. *A stiff-necked people.*—There is scarcely any place in the O. T. which is so utterly subversive of self-righteousness as this. As the ungodly are excluded from the heavenly inheritance by reason of their sins, and the righteous are made partakers of it; even so was it to be the case in reference to Canaan. The free grace of the Lord chose the fathers, and brought out all the good that was in Israel; but yet it was not this goodness for which the people were preserved, since they had a hundred times perverted all God's gifts of grace.

Ver. 8. *Horeb.*—In these discourses of Moses the Mount of the Law is usually called Horeb, which was the comprehensive name for the whole mountain district. Some additions are made in what follows to the history which is here repeated from Exod. xxxii.

Ver. 20. *The same time.*—This circumstance is not mentioned in the original narrative; but it is probably noticed in this place in order that the people might not imagine the high priest on account of his consecration could not be punished, or that he had by reason of it been the means of saving the people.

Ver. 23. *Hearkened.*—For the circumstances mentioned above, see Num. xi. 1; Exod. xvii. 7; Num. xi. 4; Num. xiv.

Ver. 25. *Would destroy you.*—Not at Kadesh-barnea, but at Horeb; to which earlier narrative Moses again reverts.

Ver. 29. *Stretched-out arm.*—Cf. the two prayers of Moses, Exod. xxxii. 11, and Num. xiv. 13; out of the latter of which something here is repeated.

CHAPTER X.

Ver. 4. *Gave them unto me.*—Exod. xxxiv. 1, etc. The connection of this narrative with the preceding is this:—that Moses would show how on account of his prayer, *i.e.,* out of free grace, the Lord has received His people into favour again, and renewed the covenant with them, by means of the new tables, the ark and the appointment of the Levites, until He gives him the commission to lead the people into the Promised Land

Ver. 7. *Rivers of waters.*—These two verses interrupt the connection of the narrative, and do not give any appropriate meaning; moreover, they do not agree with the list of the encampments, Num. xxxiii. 31. They appear, therefore, to have come into this place through some misunderstanding or oversight in very early times.

Ver. 8. *At that time.*—Taken in connection with ver. 5, at the time when the covenant was renewed. Cf. Exod. xxxii. 29, note.

Ver. 9. *Promised them.*—Num. xviii. 20, ch. xxvi. 53.

Ver. 16. *Circumcise.*—Cf. ch. xxx. 6; Gen. xvii. 13, note; Rom. ii. 29. Take away the old natural corruption: renew and sanctify yourselves to the Lord.

CHAPTER XI.

Ver. 2. *Know ye.*—He addresses the older generation,—of whom Joshua and Caleb had been eye-witnesses of the wonders in Egypt; the others, of those in the wilderness.

Ver. 10. *Garden of herbs.*—In Lower Egypt it rains very seldom; in Middle and Upper Egypt, sometimes not for a whole year. The watering of the fields, though very remunerative, is still uncommonly wearisome, and effected by means of pumping machines.

Ver 14. *First rain.*—The " first rain " is the rain of autumn, in October, which falls on the freshly sown seed, after there has been almost an entire cessation of rain in the summer. The " latter rain " falls in March, not long before harvest-time.

Ver. 20. *Doors.*—Ch. vi. 6–9.

Ver. 29. *Mount Ebal.*—The mountains Gerisin (or Garizim) and Ebal rise in steep walls of rock immediately out of the valley of Sichem, the present Nablus, about 800 feet high on each side. They are both of them somewhat barren, but Garizim has a ravine full of streams and trees. Each of the mountains has a table-land which affords room to a considerable number of men.

Ver. 30. *Goeth down.*—Behind the western road.

CHAPTER XII.

The repetition of the command to destroy utterly the false gods, and all belonging to them, serves here as a preparation for the enforcing of the unity of the worship of God. The reason for this command was very apparent. In the wilderness, where Israel formed one great camp under definite rules, it was not possible to set up, at all events, separate places of worship, however much idol-worship might be practised in secret. But after the separation of the two tribes and a half in the land east of Jordan, when the people were now about to be scattered over a wide tract of country, then it was needful to make this commandment stringent. The way for it was already paved by the statute, like to it in spirit, which forbade the killing of animals except for sacrifice during their march through the wilderness (cf. Lev. xvii., introd.). This was now revoked, and the statute concerning the one place of worship put in its stead. This command is of such essential consequence to the whole religion of the Old Testament, that its existence without it is not conceivable. After therefore, as in later times, it was transgressed—nay, although these violations of it were at times the rule, and even men of God did themselves depart from it—still every deep investigation of the connection of the covenant religion shows how the belief in the unity of God, and the purity of His revelation, could be maintained among the people only on this condition. It is remarkable, moreover, that in the command which follows, mention is especially made of the thank-offerings which were joined with the sacrificial meals (see Lev. iii., introd.), and of the second tithe, which had an affinity to these. It was clearly of importance, in the case of a statute apparently severe, and quite opposed to the wild variety of heathen life, when one uniform dark hue was imposed on the Israelitish community, that a "rejoicing before the Lord," a sanctification even of earthly joy in the holy festivals of the people, should be declared to be well-pleasing to God. This is a point of very great importance in every religious constitution, and cannot be neglected for a length of time without bringing a punishment.

Ver. 2. *Green tree.*—Mountains and groves were, as is well

known, everywhere the especial places of idolatrous worship. The "green trees" we find often mentioned in the prophets, as, e.g., Jer. ii. 20, ch. iii. 6; Ezek. vi. 13.

Ver. 3. *Out of that place.*—The idolatrous names of a place were often changed into others, as is mentioned of the Reubenites, Num. xxxii. 28. This was so much of the more consequence, since often with these names were associated historical recollections, customs, popular feasts, which might gradually favour idolatry.

Ver. 9. *Giveth you.*—It is evident from this passage, that in the wilderness a great many of the statutes given were not obeyed. This happened partly, indeed, by reason of the lawlessness of the people, but partly because compliance with them there was difficult, if not impossible. Under this neglect came not only many of the regulations about the sacrifices, but also, as we know from Joshua v. 3, etc., the observance of circumcision.

Ver. 11. *Your tithes.*—Concerning these second tithes, see ch. xiv. 22.

Ver. 15. *Of the hart.*—Which animals were clean indeed; *i.e.*, allowed for eating, but might not be sacrificed. This is the rescinding of the statute given, Lev. xvii., for the Israelites while in the wilderness.

Ver. 17. *Firstlings.*—Here it appears that as, ver. 11, there is a second tithe, so also a second gift of the first-born is commanded, since the usual one fell to the priests. Perhaps we may suppose, since a gift of both the first-born is not mentioned, and would, moreover, have been very hard, that probably the female first-born of the animals were given for these thank-offerings (while "every male that openeth womb" was holy to the Lord), as the female of animals was allowed in the case of thank-offering: Lev. xvii. 1.

Ver. 31. *Burnt in the fire.*—Whereby human sacrifice, independently of its being offered to idols, is declared to be an abomination: cf. Lev. xviii. 21, note.

CHAPTER XIII.

Even when a prophet performs a miracle for the sake of seducing the people into idolatry, they shall not believe him, but punish him. Such a false miracle is referred to the Lord, who thereby will prove His people, ver. 3. In like manner miracles are mentioned in the N. T. as about to take place in the time of Antichrist (2 Thess. ii. 9, 10). They are produced by the influence of superhuman spiritual powers on the earthly order of the world; but since they cannot happen without Divine permission, they are therefore, in this respect, like all devilish temptations, ascribed to God Himself. This precept is of great importance, because it shows that even in the O. T. a miracle was only of an introductory and preparatory character, and never was meant in and for itself to work as a sufficient proof of the truth (cf. St Matt. iv. 21, note). Every miracle points to something; and if that to which it points is shown by other yet more undoubted signs to be false and mischievous, then the miracle itself is a lying miracle. Therefore the N. T. also warns us against false prophetic spirits: 2 Cor. xii. 1, etc.; 1 St John iv. 1.

Ver. 2. *Serve them; i.e.*, which he had promised for the confirmation of this his invitation.

Ver. 5. *From the midst of thee.*—In these words, so often repeated in this book (ch. xvii. 7, ch. xix. 19, ch. xxi. 21), the expression is stronger than in the usual, and in the main equivalent, one, "that soul shall be cut off from his people" (see Gen. xvii. 14, note). As that first decision of the law made the transgressors outlaws, so in this commandment the meaning certainly is not that every transgressor of this kind shall be brought to death in a judicial manner, but the words, ver. 9, are to be taken literally. The revenge of blood was allowed in the case of murder, which was in the eyes of the law less than this. That in later times a regular process took the place of this mode of punishment, is very natural, especially as the persecution of the true prophets had shown the danger of this summary carrying out of the law. The stoning of Stephen was under pretence of this command.

Ver. 13. *Children of Belial.*—This word, which so frequently occurs, signifies literally "sons of worthlessness;" *i. e.*, base, worthless men. "Belijaal," generally, "worthless," ch. xv. 9. According to some, this was the origin of the name Belial, which St Paul applies to the devil, 2 Cor. vi. 15.

Ver. 16. *Not be built again.*—This command goes, therefore, further than in the case of customary banishment, where the spoil was divided after that the Lord had received a portion, as took place in the case of the conquest of the Midianites (Num. xxxi. 32), naturally, because the guilt was far greater.

CHAPTER XIV.

Ver. 1. *For the dead.*—Cf. Lev. xix. 28.

Ver. 3. *Abominable thing.*—Cf. for the whole of this, Lev. xi., from whence this is a brief recapitulation.

Ver. 5. *Roebuck;* i. e., the gazelle, as is always its meaning in the Bible.

Chamois.—The names of these animals are hard to explain. Probably they were different species of the hart and deer kind.

Ver. 21. *Holy people.*—Here, for the first time, does a distinction occur between "the strangers," which in after times was developed into the double classes of "proselytes of the gate and the proselytes of righteousness" (cf. St Matt. viii. 5, note). Before this it is repeatedly said (Lev. xxiv. 22; Num. ix. 14), that those born in the land and the strangers should have one ordinance: here a freedom is given them (cf. Lev. xvii. 15) which no Israelite had, and which must tend to lower them in the eyes of that people. The germ of this is found in the regulation, that strangers might partake in the paschal meal only on the condition of having first been circumcised: Exod. xii. 48. It was natural that when they had now begun to receive their future habitations, such regulations must increase; and to these other privileges and customs were joined (ch. xv. 3). Uncircumcised strangers, who merely resided among the Israelites, were compelled to observe certain general commands, but were free from the rest, purposely to make a distinction between them and the Israelites.

Ver. 29. *Which thou doest.*—Therefore, besides the tithe which was paid to the Levites, there was also a second tithe, so that every Israelite gave a fifth of his fruits (see Gen. xxvii. 13). This, whether consisting of natural product or of money, was destined for two years for sacrifices and sacrificial meals in the holy place of Divine worship. In the third year this tithe was not brought there, but laid up at home, and there works of love towards the Levites and the poor were exercised from this store. What a spirit of holy, brotherly love, and of firm union of all members and classes, must have been cherished by this law, the like of which is nowhere to be found among the heathen!

CHAPTER XV.

In the former chapter practical love and kindliness towards the poor is, by the appointment of the second tithe, put in close connection with the service of God. Here it is interwoven with the institution of the sabbatical year, commanded Lev. xxv. 1. As in this year nothing was to be reaped, so likewise could no debt be called in from an Israelite—for of this is it spoken, not of the *remission* of debt. It is somewhat surprising that at ver. 4 it is promised there shall be no poor in the land, while at ver. 11 (in agreement with Christ's word, St Matt. xxvi. 11) the direct contrary appears to be said. But this is one of the many points (like, for example, the fruitfulness of the land, the victory over enemies, the security and extension of their kingdom) in which, by reason of the disobedience of the people, the promise, which was given under conditions, never came to be fulfilled. Here, therefore, Israel had a continual remembrancer how far it fell short of its destined blessing. The sight of the poor among the people of God was designed to be a continual penitential sermon, both for individual Israelites and for the whole nation.

Ver. 12. *Free from thee.*—Here is not meant the year of release, or the sabbatical year spoken of before, but the seventh of service, which for the individual answered to the sabbatical year: cf. Exod. xxi. 2, note.

Ver. 17. *Shall do likewise.*—The earlier command is extended by two further regulations: that a present be given to the servant when leaving service; and that the ceremony performed in the case of continuance in service should be extended to the maid-servant.

Ver. 18. *A double hired servant;* because a slave was bound to more service, and, besides, stood considerably lower in his privileges, than a hired labourer.

Ver. 20. *Thou and thy household.*—Here, also, we are to bear in mind the distinction which was observed, ch. xii. 17, note. The male firstlings were sanctified to the Lord: they could be partaken of by the priests alone. The female firstlings were used for the sacrificial meals. Others put a strained interpretation upon this eating of the first-born, by supposing that it was done by the priests in the name of all, which is not possible, as clearly here it is spoken of sacrificial feasts.

CHAPTER XVI.

Ver. 2. *His name there.*—Sacrifices of sheep and cattle are here expressly named "Passover," as elsewhere only the lamb is so called. Among these are to be understood the free-will offerings which the Jews call "Chagiga" ("feast-offerings"). Cf. 2 Chron. xxxv. 7–9. These were offered partly as burnt-sacrifices, partly as thank-offerings; and of these latter were sacrificial feasts made. In order to eat these, the Pharisees would not defile themselves: St John xviii. 28.

Ver. 7. *Unto thy tents.*—This is not to be understood as a command, but as a permission. The eating of the unleavened bread might be at home, outside the Holy Place. Every one, therefore, who was hindered by pressing business from celebrating the rest of the feast, might return home after having partaken of the paschal lamb.

Ver. 8. *No work therein.*—On the seventh day also unleavened bread was eaten (vers. 3, 4); but it had, moreover, this peculiarity, that on it a solemn assembly took place.

Ver. 15. *Shall choose.*—In distinction from the Passover (see

Ver. 7, note), all were to remain on this feast seven days in the Holy Place.

Ver. 18. *Officers.*—The same name (Schoterim) as Exod. v. 6; " scribes—writers," who probably kept the genealogical tables and lists of primogeniture.

Ver. 21. *Grove.*—Lit., " no Aschera of any wood." This place particularly has given occasion to the translation " grove." Here, however, a rude image of generative Nature, made of the trunk of a tree, is spoken of: see Exod. xxxiv. 13, note.

Ver. 22. *Image.*—A stone pillar, often only a rough unhewn stone, was the object of worship.

CHAPTER XVII.

Ver. 1. *An abomination.*—A short summary of the statutes, Lev. xxii. 19.

Ver. 7. *From among you.*—Above, ver. 13, the false prophet who seduced to idolatry had been spoken of; here, those who were seduced to it.

Ver. 9. *Thou shalt come.*—From the beginning, since Aaron, as priest, had been appointed Moses' coadjutor (Exod. iv. 1), the spiritual and temporal power had been distinguished in the constitution of the people of Israel. Moses, as the servant entrusted with the management of the whole house (Num. xii. 7), stood of course above Aaron even: afterwards, however, there is no such subordination of the priests in matters pertaining to God's worship. The law was given, and could not be altered; and the interpretation of it belonged in the main to the priests. However from the first there were, besides them (Exod. xviii.), judges from the order of the laity. Among these, oftentimes, one was more prominent than the rest, who was manifested as God's vicegerent to the whole of Israel, as Moses himself placed Joshua with Eleasar. This part of the temporal constitution was not at the first settled by God. A long troubled time transferred the power of supreme judge to many hands, until more and more the want of a king was demonstrated. For each smaller matter there were tribunals in particular places; but in the place of the sanctuary the high priest sat, in conjunction with other priests, as judge; and, besides him, there might be a chief judge elsewhere, before whom the more difficult cases were brought, and to whom appeal was made from the inferior judges. As to the difference of the power of these several authorities, nothing more precise is mentioned. We find the power of the kings and of the judges often stretched very far. Many of them, if they had shown themselves to be God's extraordinary messengers, executed, as Moses and other prophets (Elijah), even the offices of divine worship; *e.g.*, Samuel, Solomon; while without such credentials intrusion into the priestly office was severely punished (2 Chron. xxvi. 16, etc.). It is left to the course of the history to develop these relations: sometimes we find the kingly authority the more prominent; sometimes the high priest executed the functions of the secular power together with his spiritual offices, and obtained a council of priests and elders to assist him. Out of the patriarchal government of heads of tribes, even before the time of Moses, had the kingly power arisen in many people allied by descent to the Israelites, though, certainly, the foundation of this power was very different among different people. The Pharaohs in Egypt, who belonged to the priestly caste and governed in accordance with its laws, could, in their state, which was ruled in so absolute a manner, have little except the name in common with the many insignificant Canaanite kings in Palestine. There we find, *e.g.*, together with the heads of the tribes (Num. xxii. 4), who possessed great power, and acted quite independently, five kings in the not very important people of the Midianites (Num. xxxi. 8). In Basan there was one king (a descendant of the ancient race of giants), who probably, as among the ancient Greeks, had the reputation of a higher, perhaps of a divine descent. Among the Edomites we find elective kings, who were even chosen from foreigners (cf. Gen. xxxvi. 37). In the great Eastern kingdoms, as in Egypt and afterwards in Persia, the kings were regarded as a kind of incarnation of the deity; which view, as the power of the people increased, had for its consequence despotic authority and unbounded extravagance. Such were the circumstances which surrounded the Israelites as they were on the point of invading Canaan. Every thought expressed in the following law about kings has reference to these.

Ver. 15. *Shall choose.*—The merely natural foundations of kingly authority, descent (to which, in ancient times, a fancied relation with the gods was joined), or the choice of the people, in which was expressed the sinful desire of the multitude to be "like the heathen,"—these reasons might not decide the matter. The Lord Himself must speak by the prophets, or the high priest. Cf. the choice of Saul, 1 Sam. ix., and David's, 1 Sam. xvi., in whose family the throne was established.

A stranger.—Thereby would the kingdom and people of Israel have lost its whole significance and purpose, as salvation was promised to the descendants of Israel after the flesh. For this reason, the house of Herod the Idumæan was not regarded as an Israelitish kingly family, although at that time his people had received circumcision, and were united with the Israelites.

Ver. 16. *No more that way.*—The reason here assigned relates to that particular period, since the danger here mentioned was at that time a very pressing one, cf. Num. xiv. 4; but in later times it no longer existed. The land of Canaan knew no horses in more ancient times. Among the riches of the patriarchs, the presents which they received, we do not find any mention of them. In the war of conquest under Joshua, we do not meet with them among the southern, but only among the northern tribes. In the time of the Judges, still no mention of them. Under David they appear again. On the other hand, we meet with them under the rule of Joseph in Egypt, and in the exodus of the Israelites from thence.

Ver. 17. *Turn not away.*—In this prohibition, likewise, we see altogether Moses' time before us, in which the seduction of the Israelites to idolatry by means of the Midianitish and Moabitish women was still kept in lively remembrance. It is notorious how Solomon's violation of this law led him into the same error: 1 Kings xi. 1. Polygamy was not, indeed, forbidden by the law; and a distinction must be made between the usual practice of it—the having two or three wives—and the outrageous luxury of the great in Eastern countries, who multiplied their wives to an immoderate degree, partly for ostentation, partly from a refinement of lust and desire. Such excesses, which could not be supported on any mistaken natural wants, necessarily led in ancient times to idolatry.

Ver. 18. *In a book;* i.e., he shall cause a copy to be taken of the book of the law from the original in the hands of the priests. No king of Israel was to regard himself as lawgiver of the people of God; he was rather to place the law of the Lord before his eyes, and to make it his rule and guide.

CHAPTER XVIII.

Ver. 2. *Said unto them.*—Cf. Num. xviii. 8.

Ver. 8. *His patrimony.*—When a priest settles in the place of the sanctuary, in order there to live for the service of God, he shall receive his share in all the sacrifice-gifts, and need not reckon what has been paid him from the sale of his patrimony.

Ver. 9. *Those nations.*—Israel is the people of the living God, Who will not leave nor forget His possession. Therefore the people of God are forbidden all those arts by which the heathen, after their own notions, endeavoured to divert the anger of their gods or to learn their will. On the other hand, a continual and sufficient revelation is promised them by the Spirit and word of God. But as every imperfect fulfilment of a prophecy points to a perfect one, so do we find here the prophecy points to the greatest Prophet, the Mediator of the New Testament.

Ver. 10. *Pass through the fire.*—In which, likewise, human sacrifices offered to the true God are forbidden: cf. Num. xviii. 21.

Useth divination.—Lit., "a divider," as a certain kind of soothsayer was called, probably because certain subjects were separated in soothsaying, and in these departments the signs were observed.

Observer of times.—Heb., "an interpreter of clouds," augur: Lev. xix. 26.

Enchanter.—Heb., "an interpreter of snakes," who predicts according to the movements of these creatures.

Witch.—One who pronounces forms of charming over anything.

Ver. 11. *Charmer.*—Lit., "one who binds the land;" *i.e.*, by a charm lays anything under a ban.

Necromancer.—Heb.: "And he who inquires of a conjurer of the dead, or who has a soothsaying spirit, and he who seeks of the dead." By the first of these three cognate words (Oob) is a man understood, whose calling it was to be able to summon up departed spirits to declare the future, or one in whom himself such a spirit dwelt; therefore, the woman of whom Saul inquired, is said to be, literally, "a woman who possesses an Oob (1 Sam xxviii. 7). And so the old translations explain it by an engastrimythus—a ventriloquist, with which indeed the Hebrew word well agrees, which properly means "a pipe." The second word signifies a "soothsaying spirit," such as the damsel at Philippi had: Acts xvi. 16. This is a kind of soothsaying by means of a strange spirit personally dwelling in the speaker. The third kind is that where access is not sought with persons dealing in these arts, but where possession of such arts is attempted by themselves.

Ver. 12. *From before thee.*—All these things are in themselves an abomination, even independently of the exact idolatry connected with them; since by natural means, by arts which would employ or assure the assistance of the hidden powers of nature, or the higher spirits of nature, men purposed to know God's will. The offering up of children in sacrifice so far resembled these practices, inasmuch as it was a self-appointed offering, not commanded by God, in order to bind Him, to compel Him, as it were, to grant something.

Ver. 13. *Perfect; i e.,* not serve half God, half other powers and spirits.

Ver. 15. *Ye shall hearken.*—God will reveal Himself in sufficient fulness and clearness to His people through the prophets; so that there shall be no need of any additional arts. His word is enough for all, and He will never suffer it to fail His people: cf. Num. xxiii. 23. This is a prediction of Christ as the true Prophet, altogether resembling that of the seed of the woman (Gen. iii. 15). In this prophecy, wherein compensation is promised to the people of God for all the heathen arts forbidden them, there are two points more especially to be observed: First, that the revelation of God through Moses was yet imperfect, and needed the completion of it through the prophets, *i.e.,* through fresh similar revelations; and insomuch as this revelation embraces *all* the prophets who have ever risen in Israel, Christ, the highest of all, is comprehended among them. Secondly, that this Prophet should be *like Moses;* and here the point of resemblance comes into consideration. To this it belongs, that the promised Prophet should not depend on Moses, but should prophesy independently out of the abundance of the Spirit immediately given Him. This is confirmed by the whole of the O. T. afterwards. Its prophets but rarely appeal to the law or interpret it, but supplement the revelation. This is much more the case with Christ and His apostles. Moreover, it is a part of this resemblance, that only then this promise is entirely fulfilled, when a prophet appears who completes that which the law has left unfinished. All the prophets carry forward the revelation; but they themselves point to a time when the revelation and knowledge of the Lord shall be perfect (*e.g.*, Isa. liv. 13; Jer. xxxi. 34). The prophet who completes *all* which Moses left unfinished, is a prophet like Moses. A prophet like Christ can no more come after Him; yet the part of this prediction which promises that a revelation shall never fail the people of God, is fully verified, since the word is all-sufficient; and by this word "the Spirit is poured out on all flesh, that the sons and the daughters of the people of God prophesy" (Joel iii. 1; Acts ii. 17). By a continued inward revelation, though dependent on the word and Spirit of Christ, is that afforded to the people of God in the New Testament, which no heathen people possesses—a continuous stream of enlightening out of the fulness of the grace of God.

Ver. 19. *Require it of him.*—The connection in which, as Moses here announces, that promise was first given, opens to us from another point of view a still further insight into its meaning. There is a progress in the revelation made by prophecy so far as this, that in it the outward terrors are no longer prominent, as in the case of the giving of the law on Mount Sinai; that God will speak to His people no more immediately, but through the mediation of human instruments; and that, therefore, in distinction from the law which raises up an insurmountable barrier betwixt the Creator and the creature, betwixt the Holy One and the sinner, in this revelation the gracious condescension of God to the man, in whom He dwells, and through whom He speaks, is to be eminently conspicuous,—which condescension appears in its completeness in the incarnation of Christ.

Ver. 22. *Not be afraid of him.*—Although, according to ch. xiii. 1, the miracles of a prophet were designed to draw men's attention to him, still they could not be in themselves a sufficient guarantee: on the other hand, a true prophet will never make a false prediction; while every false prophet, in imitating the true, will often miss the truth in his announcements respecting the future. As Israel was pre-eminently a people of the future, the declaration of the future benefits and judgments of the Lord always continued to be an important part of the duty of the prophets.

CHAPTER XIX.

The law respecting the cities of refuge, which was given Num. xxxv. 6, and, in regard to those on the east side of Jordan, carried into execution (Deut. iv. 41), is here (like many of the most important laws) again enjoined, and then the express command given to add three more to those already determined.

Ver. 3. *Prepare thee a way;* i.e., make good, firm ways thither.

Ver. 7. *Command thee.*—This refers to ch. iv. 41, etc.

Ver. 13. *Go well with thee.*—For all this, cf. Num. xxxv. 6. The regulations of the law are only here made more clear.

Ver. 14. *To possess it.*—This great offence is perhaps mentioned here in particular, because the landmarks were of much consequence, especially in reference to the cities of refuge. In Israel, moreover, they had a still higher degree of sanctity, as having been settled by God.

Ver. 15. *Three witnesses.*—Cf. Num. xxxv. 30, ch. xxii. 16; St Matt. xviii. 16.

Ver. 21. *Foot for foot.*—The general law of retaliation, the foundation of the whole law of judicial punishment (cf. Exod. xxi. 25, note), is here expressly repeated in reference to false witnesses, that they shall suffer that which they had purposed to inflict.

CHAPTER XX.

The following laws, which relate to wars, rest on two main principles. The first is, that Israel is the people of the Lord, and carries on war only in His name; therefore, ought not to rely on fleshly might, but to allow freedom from warlike service to all who have either entered on some new relation of life, or who, through fearfulness of heart, are wanting in that courage of faith which should be the strength of the Lord's host. The second is, that God's people ought to love peace rather than war, and may never give way to a savage desire of extermination: and therefore are bound, except in the execution of the judicial punishment commanded by God, always to offer peace, and so to spare the fruit-trees even, which were planted before a besieged place.

Ver. 1. *Is with thee.*—By this one word Israel is reminded of the wonderful fact, that a small, poor, oppressed people were saved out of the hands of enemies mightier than themselves, but at the same time are admonished only to carry on the wars of the Lord.

Ver. 2. *Priest.*—According to Jewish tradition, a priest was especially consecrated to this business, and bore the name of "the anointed of war."

Ver. 5. *Officers.*—The "Schoterim," or scribes who kept the registers of genealogy and the rolls of the tribes, and so had the charge of the levies, and the appointment of the leaders of the army (ver. 9): cf. Exod. v. 6, note.

Ver. 6. *Eaten of it.*—Lit., "made it common." According to Lev. xix. 23, 24, all fruit-bearing trees remained three years untouched; in the fourth year the fruit belonged to the Lord, and only in the fifth year might it be applied to common use: cf. ch. xxviii. 30.

Ver. 17. *Destroy them.*—Cf. Lev. xxvii. 28, note.

Ver. 19. *Is man's life.*—Heb.: "Since thou eatest thereof, and mayest not hew it down (since man is the tree of the field) to come before thee in the bulwark;" *i.e.*, "thou shalt not hew it down for ramparts or stakes, since thou eatest thereof, and man has his subsistence from the trees of the field." The object of this prohibition is not the present utility only, arising from the preservation of the trees, but by this example to teach men a lesson, and to prevent useless devastation. Cf. the prohibition, Deut. xxv. 4, with the interpretation of Saint Paul, 1 Cor. ix. 9, 10.

CHAPTER XXI.

Of such moment was sin considered to be, and especially the greatest of all sin, murder, as a violation of the Divine order in His people, that, even in the case of an unknown committer of it, a certain degree of guilt was attached to the inhabitants of the city in which the murderer probably dwelt, which guilt must be expiated. Every murder must be compensated for by the punishment of the murderer. If that is not possible, then must the supposed place of his residence confess its part in the guilt; and by the expiatory slaying of a beast, with the confession both of its sin and yet actual innocence in this particular instance, purify itself from the defilement. This is the meaning of an act which was not properly speaking a sacrifice, but a judicial atonement of the nature of a sacrifice.

Ver. 4. *Rough valley.*—Heb., "a continually flowing brook," in distinction from a torrent, which only holds water in the rainy season.

Which.—"To (or in) which." "Nachal," as now the Arabian wady, means a valley through which a stream or brook flows. By breaking the neck of the heifer over such a brook, the removal of the guilt by the water was intended to be signified, since the heifer stood in the place of the actual murderer, who could not be found. The heifer was not to have been used and the ground not yet worked, in order that both, free from man's influence, might be the more suited to take the crime on themselves.

Ver. 6. *In the valley.*—Heb., "in the brook."

Ver. 8. *Forgiven them.*—The heifer was not, properly speaking, a sacrifice, since no atonement might be brought for an intentional murder. For this reason the heifer's neck was "struck off" (or broken). She is executed in the place of the murderer. Therefore the elders do not, in the name of the inhabitants, lay their hands on the heifer with the confession of guilt, and its blood is not sprinkled on the Holy Place; rather they declare, by a solemn symbolical act, their innocence, and, in consequence, the guilt, which objectively clings to the city, is removed by the symbolically atoning punishment

Ver. 14. *Humbled her.*—This law was intended to maintain both the dignity and the purity of marriage. A marriage with a heathen was not to be unallowable; but still only permitted when she passed through the probation of natural grief for her separation from her home, and had had time to accustom herself to the new connection. After this had been done, the man might no longer treat her as a slave of war. She has become a free woman by the very marriage itself. The doctrine of marriage, as of a perfect communion spiritual and bodily, is clear from this.

Ver. 17. *First-born is his.*—The case here supposed had actually taken place in the house of Jacob (Gen. xxix. 30). Yet he recognises Reuben expressly as his first-born with the same words, "the beginning of his strength," which are here used, and deprives him of his privilege for another reason. Moreover, he gives to the son of the more loved wife only half of the privilege of the first-born (1 Chron. v. 2). Yet it may be supposed that the regulations of this law, which appear self-evident, were spoken with reference to the possible misunderstanding of that history, and at the same time were designed to act as a necessary limitation to the paternal authority, which was rated so high.

Ver. 21. *Shall hear and fear.*—There is contained in this law at the same time a great mark of respect towards, yet a limitation of, the paternal authority. Obstinate disobedience, open rebellion against parents, may be avenged in certain circumstances even with the most severe punishment of death. But this was not permitted, as was the case with some heathen nations, to the father himself to carry into execution, but a judicial sentence of the elders was required; but then the whole congregation was to take part in the execution of the judgment, in order that the abhorrence of this sin might be general.

Ver. 22. *On a tree.*—That is to say, after he had first been stoned, or put to death in some other way, he was hanged for greater contumely. So was Achan burnt after being stoned (Joshua vii. 25); Pharaoh's baker was first beheaded and then hanged (Gen. xl. 19); the murderers of Ishbosheth were hanged after their death (2 Sam. iv. 12). The crucifixion of live criminals was a Roman punishment.

Ver. 23. *Accursed of God.*—Lit., "is the curse of the Lord;" to which the Apostle's words allude, that Christ was "a curse" for us, Gal. iii. 13. The Son of God was subjected to the extreme severity of the law, so that He was made a curse for us.

For an inheritance.—According to Jewish tradition, this hanging took place a little before sunsetting. When it was done, the law was satisfied and the criminal was buried in witness thereof, while it would have defiled the land for him to hang on the tree for a longer time. All this likewise was fulfilled in Christ (St John xix. 31, 38, 42), in witness that the law had then received its perfect accomplishment.

CHAPTER XXII.

Ver. 2. *Restore it.*—An amplification of the law, Exod. xviii. 4, where, instead of "brother," "enemy" stands, which latter is comprised in the term brother, since a man does not cease to be a brother by reason of personal hostility.

Ver. 5. *Abomination.*—The reason of this prohibition is primarily no other than that drawn from the law, Lev. xix. 19. A violation of God's creation was thereby committed; a self-willed and shameful trifling with the distinctions which He had ordained was forbidden. But, besides this, among the heathen many abominations were connected with this forbidden one—secret intercourse of the sexes, but especially horrible customs in the idolatrous worship, which were intended to imitate certain natural appearances in man.

Ver. 7. *Prolong thy days.*—A law enjoining gentle treatment of animals, and at the same time one, like the preceding, founded on reverence for the sexes which God created, and which, by means of such brutality, might be violated. It is plain that in this small example are portrayed more important relations—that in pity towards animals is inculcated mercy towards men, as ch. xxv. 4, etc. The promise, "that it may be well with thee," etc., is added, according to the observation of the Rabbins, to this least of all commandments, as to the greatest, "Honour thy father and thy mother," etc., in order to show that the keeping of all the commandments flows from one source.

Ver. 8. *Fall from thence.*—The flat roofs of the East, on which persons were accustomed to walk, from whence addresses were made (nay, where even to this day troops are sometimes exercised), required, according to the Rabbins, a battlement of at least three feet, which was to be strong enough for a person to lean against. The reason which is added points to the awfulness of taking away man's life, independently of all sin in the matter, on which feeling the rule ch. xxi. 1, etc., rests.

Ver. 9. *Vineyard.*—The word stands generally for every kind of fruit-garden.

Lest the fruit.—Heb.: "That thou dost not sanctify the fulness of the seed which thou hast sowed, and the produce of thy vineyard;" *i.e.*, if thou doest it, then as a punishment shall not only the fruit sown by thee, but the whole produce of the garden, be forfeited to the sanctuary. Cf. for this and the following, Lev. xix. 19, note.

Ver. 10. *An ass together.*—The yoking together of animals of different species, especially a clean and unclean animal, is hereby forbidden. Of this, also, the remark made, ver. 7, holds good.

Ver. 19. *All his days.*—Even to the present day a similar practice takes place among many Eastern nations, only that, according to the Divine law, it only occurred in the case of an accusation of this kind.

Ver. 21. *From among you.*—The punishment of adultery (Lev. xx. 10) is here extended also to the betrothed damsel. The severity of this law, by which even an innocent person might suffer through the uncertainty of this kind of proof, was probably softened in practice in case of pertinacious denial on the part of the woman, and was, on the whole, rather intended as a threat to deter from the crime.

Ver. 27. *To save her.*—Rape, therefore, is only then particularly punished when it is committed against a betrothed damsel. The inferior position of the woman is apparent in this regulation, which recognises in an especial manner the rights of the man.

Ver. 29. *All his days.*—He loses, therefore, for ever the right of divorce which, according to ch. xxiv. 1, belongs to him. This is therefore the only punishment attached to unchastity of the ordinary kind, together with that in ch. xxiii. 2.

Ver. 30. *His father's skirt.*—A short allusion to the laws against incest, declared more fully Lev. xviii.

CHAPTER XXIII.

Ver. 1. *Congregation of the Lord.*—The meaning of this prohibition is mainly a symbolical one. What was mature and perfect only was to be used for sacrifice; and in like manner no one might belong to the people of the Lord on whose person the Divine creation had been disfigured by man's wilful act Accordingly, the prohibition is parallel with that given Lev. xix. 19. Mutilation, which was so frequent in the East, was therefore on the Israelites in particular prevented by this law. That the literal, and so symbolical, meaning of this law only held good in times of nonage, is clear from Isa. lvi. 3-6.

Ver. 2. *A bastard;* i e., not every child begotten out of the marriage-state, since with such an one the case of ch. xxii. 29 could come into practice, and the child thereby become legitimate, but a child is meant begotten in adultery, or whose father was not known.

Tenth generation.—The number "ten" here and in the following verse is the number of perfection, and it signifies, as is afterwards explained, "shall not come in at all;" literally, it would be after about 300 years.

Ver. 6. *Their peace.*—Cf. St Matt. v. 43, note.

Ver. 7. *Edomite.*—The Moabites and Edomites stand in one respect equal, ch. ii. 29; but in the case of the first there was added the heavy sin in the transaction with Balaam. Moreover, the possession of the children of Lot was also to be spared, ch. ii. 19. The reasons for this distinction were not the mere natural relation of nearer or more distant kinship and old long-passed events; but, as the kingdom of God in the O. T. was very closely connected and bound up with natural relations, and as the whole history of Israel, in all its more salient points, is a holy, significant history, therefore the nations stand in a nearer or more distant connection with the kingdom of God according to these relations, and the danger of intercourse with them was, in proportion, greater or less. The people descended from Abraham over and above the Israelites (the Edomites, a part of the Arabians, the Midianites) remained free from the grosser kinds of idolatry, while Lot's descendants, from that impure connection, sank into the more horrible idolatrous abominations. And that which happened in such important epochs of the sacred history, as, for instance, the march out of Egypt into the Promised Land was, might be regarded as a sample of the whole corrupt disposition of these tribes.

A stranger in his land.—It is worthy of observation how hereby the Israelites are forbidden to requite evil with evil, and are told only to remember the good received in their sojourn in Egypt.

Ver. 9. *Goest forth.*—Heb., "as a camp marchest out"—as an armed host which breaks up its camp.

Ver. 14. *Turn away from thee.*—It is not here spoken of the camp then formed in the wilderness, but of the camp of an army (ver. 9) This was always to be regarded as a holy dwelling-place of the Lord; and the law of separation on account of sexual uncleanness (Lev. xv. 16, 17) was to be applied there, as well as another which in its relation to a natural bodily impurity was an emblem of moral uncleanness.

Ver. 16. *Not oppress him.*—Not Israelitish, but heathen servants, are here spoken of. The people of Israel were not at that time allowed arbitrarily to make war upon heathen nations, far less to seek to free their slaves; but if a heathen servant took refuge with them, seeing so much sin was attached to servitude among all heathen nations, he was not to be delivered up, but to enjoy the blessing of a sojourn with the people of God.

Ver. 17. *No whore.*—Heb., "no devoted woman or man." Among the neighbouring Aramæan and Phœnician people there were everywhere persons of both sexes who prostituted themselves in the temples in honour of the Nature-deities—a horrible abomination, which with that idolatry often was practised even in Israel: 1 Kings xiv. 24, ch. xv. 12, ch. xxii. 47; cf. Num. xxv.

Ver. 18. *Of a dog.*—"Dog," as the name of a very unclean animal, was the designation of men who prostituted themselves So perhaps, also, Rev. xxii. 15.

Abomination.—This prohibition stood also in connection with the practice of such vices to the honour of heathen deities.

Ver. 20. *To possess it.*—Cf. Exod. xxii. 25, note.

Ver. 23. *With thy mouth.*—Upon vows: cf. Gen. xxviii. 20, note.

Ver. 25. *Pluck the ears.*—St Matt. xii. 1.

CHAPTER XXIV.

Ver. 4. *For an inheritance.*—In the Hebrew these four verses form but one period, the first part of which extends to the end of verse 3. A right of divorce is not here introduced, but only mentioned what was the custom as Moses found it. He let the practice continue, and suffered divorce by reason of the hardness of their hearts, while in the history of the creation he had taught the indissolubility of the bond (Gen. ii. 24). In Egypt, where the art of writing was applied at that time in so many matters of daily life, the practice of giving a writing of divorcement might probably have its origin. In ver. 1, it is literally, " And it happens, when she does not find favour in his sight, that he finds in her the shame of a word ;" *i.e.*, a matter of some kind or other which subjects her to shame. For, although the determination on this point was altogether in the husband's hand, yet something actually disgraceful (objectively sinful), and not merely something displeasing to the husband, must be supposed, and the matter left to his conscience to decide on this being so or not. The only peculiarity in the regulation now made is contained in ver. 4 ; viz., that a divorced wife who, after her divorce, has become the wife of another man, might not, in case of her being again free, either by separation or the death of the man, become a second time the wife of the first husband. Such an act is spoken of with a religious horror, no doubt because the second marriage in the lifetime of the first husband had something of the character of adultery, and the re-marrying showed an indifference in respect to such a sin. The prophet (Jer. iii. 1, etc.) points out in a very remarkable way how this was not applicable to the relation of the Lord to His people.

Ver. 6. *Millstone to pledge.*—Heb.: "Thou shalt not take in pledge the two millstones, nor yet the upper millstone." The upper millstone, that is of a handmill, without which it was not useable.

Ver. 11. *Abroad unto thee.*—The debtor was to have the right of choosing the thing which he will give in pledge.

Ver. 13. *Bless thee.*—Exod. xxii. 25, 26.

Shall be righteousness.—A just deed in God's sight—a good work.

Ver. 16. *For his own sin.*—As this horrible law (of putting the children to death for the sins of the fathers) existed, *e.g.*, among the Persians, with whom, in case of an insurrection, whole families were massacred.

CHAPTER XXV.

Ver. 1. *Condemn the wicked.*—Literally, "justify the just, and make the godless godless;" that is to say, by means of a judicial sentence, which in the name of God has such power.

Ver. 2. *Worthy to be beaten.*—Lit., "is a son of beating."

Ver. 3. *Seem vile unto thee.*—Hence the addition of the later tradition, in the genuine rabbinical spirit, that the judge should only command thirty-nine stripes to be given, lest he should by miscounting transgress the law: cf. 2 Cor. xi. 24, note. This trait of humanity in the case of all punishments not capital, is referable to the recognition of the image of God in the very criminal himself.

Ver. 4. *Treadeth out the corn.*—The same tender consideration which in the case of harvest has regard to the poor (ch. xxiii. 24, 25, ch. xxiv. 19-22), is also to be extended to the animals. To this day oxen are used in the East for the treading out of the corn; and a muzzle is not to be put on the animal while toiling for man's benefit, that it may be able to eat some of the corn: cf. 1 Cor. ix. 9, note; 1 Tim. v. 18.

Ver. 10. *His shoe loosed.*—Upon the ancient institution of marriage of the brother's wife, which existed long before Moses' time, see Gen. xxxviii. 1. It is remarkable that there was no compulsion exercised in respect to this law, but merely the punishment of a disgrace inflicted in case of refusal. Hence may be inferred that the exaggerated importance attached to it in patriarchal times was not acknowledged by the Divine law; for it even limits the ancient custom by ruling that the brother was only bound to the marriage when he and the deceased had lived together in the same town. We perceive from Ruth iv. 7, that to stand with his shoe on anything was regarded as a sign of possession (cf. also Ps. lx. 10): to take off the shoe, and give it to any one, was a sign of the transferring of the right. The name constantly given to the refusing brother was therefore meant to signify that his possession was withdrawn from him in a dishonouring fashion.

Ver. 12. *Not pity her.*—When a woman with a good intention, in order to compel another to let go his hold, so violated modesty, she was to be severely punished. Probably this unusual case alludes to some custom which prevailed among the surrounding heathen nations.

Ver. 15. *Just measure.*—Cf. Lev. xix. 35, 36.

Ver. 19. *Not forget it.*—This commandment refers to the history narrated Exod. xvii.; wherein is shown how that powerful people, then in the vigour of their strength, assailed God Himself in His people, and that, as is here added, in a treacherous and cruel manner. Hence the Divine curse upon that people to which 1 Sam. xv. refers.

CHAPTER XXVI.

Moses puts into the mouth of the people prayers in reference to the gifts most closely associated with their temporal domestic life—the first-fruits, and the second tithes—by which a lively consciousness and recognition of the entire relation of Israel to their Lord and King are declared. In the first-fruits is expressed their continuous homage, as regards all earthly possession. While each person acknowledged this by his act, he was at the same time, as member of the united nation, to declare on what gracious favours of God this entire possession rested. The second tithe was designed to change every Israelitish house into a sanctuary, and at the same time to spread a holy, joyful feeling of communion among the whole people, with which the continuance of the Divine blessing on His people was closely connected. Both prayers, becoming not in letter but in spirit a part of the people's customary devotions, would contribute in no slight degree to keep alive outward worship, and to sanctify their whole daily life.

Ver. 5. *A Syrian.*—Every Israelite was to be reminded, on the occasion of making this offering, that Abraham came out of Mesopotamia into Canaan without possession or claim of any kind; as one who was nothing in himself, and had nothing, and received all from God's grace alone. An image of the helplessness by nature of every man.

Ver. 12. *Be filled.*—This tithe was therefore to be eaten not in a holy place, but in every place where they were, as a holy meal, like a sacrificial feast.

Ver. 15. *With milk and honey.*—On this occasion, when the Israelite rejoiced before the Lord by reason of the Divine benefits conferred, he was to feel deeply his own personal obligations to purity and sanctity; and also, that these blessings were conferred on him in consequence of God's general promises, and that he partook of them in virtue of his membership in God's covenant-people.

CHAPTER XXVII.

With the last words of the foregoing chapter closes the reiteration of the law in this book. Thereupon follows the injunction to engrave the law on memorial stones, and to place these on Mount Ebal. These, as well as the stone tables in the ark of the covenant, were designed to bear witness against the apostasy of the people, when in after times they were brought to light and freed from their covering.

Ver. 3. *Hath promised thee.*—The first question which arises is, What was engraven on the stones? "All the words of this law," would, literally taken, mean all the repetition of the law from ch. v.; or, at all events, the whole lawgiving, that on

Sinai inclusive. But it is extremely improbable that so detailed a writing should have been engraven on the stones, especially as in this reiteration of the law so many long exhortations occur, which have not, properly speaking, the character of commandments. And since these stones, as a witness against the disobedience of the people, were clearly similar in their significance to the tables of stone in the ark of the covenant, it is most probable that the "ten words," as they stand ch. v. 6, etc., are intended. A further question is, How was this inscription made? Was it engraven on stone, or on the plaister laid on it? The first is clearly the most likely, since the purpose of the plaister evidently was to preserve the inscription from injury by weather. Such a mode of proceeding in respect to inscriptions on stone was usual in ancient times. This imperishable witness against the sins of the people was to stand on the mountain from whence afterwards the cursings were uttered. The mountain, seen from afar, was itself a memento; but yet much more when, in a time of general disorder and disobedience against God, the stones themselves were brought forth and freed from their covering, and the witness of the Divine Lawgiver testified against the people!

Ver. 4. *Mount Ebal.*—The text here was very early falsified by the Samaritans, and "Gerizim" was put instead of "Ebal." For since, in obedience to a subsequent command, the blessings were spoken from thence, they wished to make out that here the stones were set up, and the altar (ver. 5) built; in which latter act they found a justification of their erection of a temple on the same mountain.

Ver. 5. *Iron tool.*—According to the general injunction, Exod. xx. 25.

Ver. 7. *Rejoice.*—The stones of the law were intended to be a reiteration of the original making of the Divine covenant with the people, and therefore, as a conclusion of the bond, burnt-offerings and thank-offerings were to follow, as Exod. xxiv. 5. Mention is expressly made of the sacrificial meal which followed the thank-offerings (cf. Exod. xxiv. 11) as a part of the rejoicing, by reason of the renewal of communion with the Lord.

Ver. 11. *Moses charged.*—A blessing and a curse, solemnly uttered, follow on the renewal of the covenant. Six tribes are appointed to stand on each of the mountains which rise precipitously out of the valley of Sichem (now Nablus), viz., Ebal and Gerizim. Between the two stood "the Levites," *i. e.*, in this place the priests; since, ver. 12, the tribe of Levi stands among the other tribes. Here, where the point at issue was not the division of the land, but the personal position of the tribes to the Lord, Levi is reckoned among the twelve, and Joseph stands as one tribe. The blessings are not communicated to us—they are not written in this book of the law, as the law still remains true to its prevailing character—to forbid, and to declare the curse consequent on disobedience. The curses bring forward certain main points of the law which comprehend the whole contents thereof. On the curse for secret idolatry follows that against the transgressors of the reverence due to God's representatives, against those guilty of oppression, of cruelty towards the helpless, of incest, of secret murder. Such crimes are mentioned as might escape the eyes even of a watchful judicature, in order to declare that God at all events will find out such sinners, and to impress on the hypocrite a horror of the works of darkness. In the last curse all the rest are included. The number of the curses is twelve, in reference, no doubt, to the number of the tribes, yet without each curse referring to each tribe.

Ver. 26. *To do them.*—In this last declaration, which is a summary of all that has gone before, the office of the law is expressly shown to be that of condemnation. This sentence proves clearly that the preceding separate curses were only uttered in order, by particular examples, to represent in a more vivid manner the nature of *all* transgressions. Each single wilful transgression of the law, therefore (this is the meaning of this solemn declaration), subjects the sinner to the curse of God, from which He alone can free us who has been made a curse for us. Thus is this passage applied by St Paul, Gal. iii. 10, 13.

CHAPTER XXVIII.

This chapter is a further declaration and explanation of that which the tribes were to proclaim on the two mountains. The promises and the threatenings pronounce a blessing and a curse on the smallest relations of life. Every blessing was to be regarded by the Israelite as a *gift* of Divine Providence,—every misfortune as His punishment. This is the main drift; but it would be a perversion of its meaning to look for the literal fulfilment of each particular in every case.

Ver. 5. *Thy store.*—Heb., "thy kneading-trough," in which the meal was made ready for baking, and leavened.

Ver. 7. *Seven ways.*—Shall flee before thee in wild flight on all sides.

Ver. 9. *A holy people.*—A people set apart for Himself.

Ver. 22. *Mildew.*—The first four plagues are sicknesses befalling man, the three last affect the seeds of the earth. "Burning" may mean the hot wind—the simoom, which burns up the plants (cf. Gen. xli. 6, Heb.), or even an internal burning. The "mildew" is also a disease of the corn, which withers and dries it up.

Ver. 52. *Hath given thee.*—After this the plagues especially of a besieged town are described. Cf. the words of Christ, which refer to this description.

Ver. 67. *Shalt see.*—The misery which is here described in such powerful, fearful images, has at all times visited Israel in his banishment. There have been many exceptions indeed, as during the Babylonish captivity; but all these passed away, and were succeeded by times in which many of the features here portrayed were actually realised. Every Israelite, so long as he remains faithful to his law and to his traditions, feels himself miserable among the people of the earth.

Ver. 68. *Shall buy you.*—Or perhaps more correctly, "And there shall be no one to buy you free;" though certainly the other would express a deeper degree of contempt: "If ye shall desire to sell yourselves into slavery, there shall be no one willing to have you." In a certain sense, this was literally fulfilled after the destruction of Jerusalem, when multitudes of Jews were thrown to the wild beasts because no buyers of so many slaves could be found. This, however, is, like many similar sayings in the prophets, not to be taken literally, but in the sense, that Israel would return again into the same condition from which it had been delivered.—"This chapter is both the longest and also the easiest, since it contains nothing but a heap of blessings and curses, and so is an expansion of the preceding. There is nothing which we have to interpret in the case of this history, more than merely to say, we ought to consider and lay to heart how terrible it is to be under the law."—Luther.

CHAPTER XXIX.

The covenant which the Lord had made with Israel in Horeb, is now here solemnly renewed or confirmed; and thereby the new generation, now about to enter Canaan, placed altogether in a similar position with the old, to whom that duty had first been committed. But inasmuch as the words of Moses refer entirely to the covenant already made, there is no need of any further sacrifices, or of any renewal of promises on the part of the people, but only a solemn confirmation of the Lord's blessing on the obedient, and His curse on the disobedient.

Ver. 3. *Those great miracles.*—As among that generation none, with the exception of Joshua and Caleb, had seen the events in the passage out of Egypt, we perceive from these words how the people of the past and present are treated as one, and how they are made responsible both for the sins and the covenanted promises of their fathers.

Ver. 4. *To hear.*—An understanding heart, seeing eyes, hearing ears, are the gifts of the Lord: they are His gifts of grace, though man is not excused for his sins if he has them not.

Ver. 5. *Thy foot.*—Cf. ch. viii. 4, note.

Ver. 6. *The Lord thy God.*—Who can maintain and support you, even without the ordinary means of nourishment: cf. ch. viii. 3.

Ver. 11. *Drawer of thy water.*—All, down to the meanest: cf. Joshua xi. 21, 27.

Ver. 15. *Not here this day.*—The future generations.

Ver. 18. *Gall and wormwood.*—Heb., "poison and wormwood." Cf. Heb. xii. 15.

Ver. 19. *To thirst.*—The last words, which seem like a proverbial mode of speaking and are somewhat obscure, mean, literally, "in order that he may take away" (or, "that the watered may be taken away") "with the thirsty;" and the words "earth," or "land," seem necessary to be supplied. When any one therefore speaks thus in his heart, the immediate consequence is, that the Lord must lay waste the blessed, richly-watered land, like the barren.—The word in the Heb. (sephoth) which is rendered in our version "to add," signifies also, "to destroy, take away;" and the meaning of the expression may be, that this supposed wicked person boasts that the drunken will put away the sober, *i.e.*, that careless, godless living will abolish conscientious scruples.

Ver. 23. *In His wrath.*—With brimstone which fell from heaven the land was burnt up, and salt came in the stead of the fruitful land when the beautiful region of the Jordan was destroyed. So shall Canaan be destroyed on account of the apostasy of the people. From this example we may clearly gather the meaning of all these curses; since, just as at that time the Promised Land is contrasted with the neighbourhood of the Dead Sea, so is the present state of Palestine in striking contrast with its ancient fruitfulness. This curse has been fulfilled to the utmost.

Ver. 29. *To our children for ever.*—We are not to search after God's secret will and counsel. He has given us His law that we should do it; this is the province of duty apportioned us. In the knowledge of that which God has revealed, and in obedience to His will, lies the way to communion with God; but there is no knowledge of Him here on earth so close and entire, but that mysteries and secret things will still continue.

CHAPTER XXX.

Ver. 3. *Turn thy captivity.*—Heb., "So will the Lord return to thy captivity." Literally the passage is, "When all these words come upon thee, the blessing and the curse, and thou returnest to the Lord thy God, then the Lord thy God returns to thy captivity and has compassion on thee, and turns back and gathers thee out of all nations." The expression, "the Lord returns to the captivity of His people" (which from early times have been incorrectly translated "He turns the captivity," or

"He brings back the captivity"), occurs afterwards in almost all the writings of the O. T. which are parallel with this passage,—often in the proper sense of the people scattered among the heathen (so, *e.g.*, Jer. xxx. 3; Amos ix. 14),—often generally of the visitation of grace after terrible punishments (so, *e.g.*, Ps. xiv. 7; Job xlii. 10; Ezek. xvi. 53). In the passage before us the explanation is clear and simple from the context. When Israel in his banishment brings back the word of the Lord to his heart, and thus returns to the Lord, then the Lord returns to His mercy, *i.e.*, to His people languishing in trouble; and this return is shown by His collecting them again.

Ver. 5. *Above thy fathers.*—This is the first of the many prophecies which represents the restoration of the people of Israel as a return unto their land, while Lev. xxvi. 45 only speaks of the continuance of the covenant. But it by no means follows, that because their expulsion from their land is to be understood literally, therefore the return must be taken literally likewise. Rather, it is an essential characteristic of the whole work of redemption, that it not merely restores what was forfeited, but gives in its place something higher and more glorious. The redemption through Christ does not put man in the position of Adam's innocence, and reinstate him in paradise, but the earthly paradise is a type of the heavenly (St. Luke xxiii. 44), to which Christ admits His redeemed. He who for Christ's sake leaves all that he has, does not receive a literal, but a far more glorious compensation, in this world; and so the restitution of earthly losses is a type of the reward of believers (cf. St Matt. xix. 29, note). Christ was raised from the dead by the glory of the Father, but not to the same life which He had till then lived in the flesh. Just as little were the promises of seeing Christ again (St John xiv. 19, xvi. 16) fulfilled in what took place after the resurrection; and in like manner this and similar predictions were not fulfilled in Israel's return after the Babylonish captivity. A literal restoration of the people of Israel would have renewed the old mode of life with all its deficiencies, and would have been of no moment to the kingdom of God under the New Covenant. St Paul explains the true sense of this prophecy (Rom. xi.), and refers its fulfilment partly to the going forth of the elect into the new Church, partly to the conversion of the whole people still to come, which shall pour fresh life into the whole kingdom of God on earth, the precursor of their entrance into the heavenly Canaan.

Ver. 6. *Mayest live.*—The meaning of circumcision as a putting away of natural uncleanness, is here applied to the heart: cf. Gen. xvii. 13, note.

Ver. 13. *And do it.*—The word which commands and the deed which fulfils it are taken together in these expressions. To understand the word and to fulfil it, requires no exertion beyond the limits of man's power (incapability of doing good is not a physical but a moral feebleness—a feebleness of the will); and as a word from God, a revelation of His grace, it brings with it the power of fulfilment. The law which commands is not in this passage severed from the word of the covenant which promises grace; and so St Paul makes such noble use of the passage in his discussion on justification, Rom. x. 6, etc.

CHAPTER XXXI.

Moses' office is now at an end. The whole law concludes with the last solemn declaration of the choice laid before the people, of life and death. Moses' sayings are concluded. He withdraws, and writes down all the repetitions of the law and the additions to it, which he had made in this book. But, besides this, he is commanded to compose and write down a song as God's witness; and this last command gave him the opportunity of inserting in his work his own testimony, that he wrote down the whole law in the book so often mentioned in this history.

Ver. 3. *As the Lord hath said.*—It is promised in the same expressions that the Lord and that Joshua shall go before the people—no doubt, because, in the significant, triumphant name of Joshua, and in his Divine appointment to his office, was given the pledge that the Lord Himself would lead His people: Num. xiii. 17, note.

Ver. 11. *In their hearing.*—According to Jewish tradition, by "this law" was meant the reiteration of it in this book of Deuteronomy. Joshua complied with this command, and in after-times the king recited the law in the court of the temple. It is certainly very improbable that the whole five books of Moses were read, while the character of this fifth book makes it peculiarly suitable for the purpose of being rehearsed in the ears of the people.

Ver. 16. *Sleep with thy fathers.*—Cf. Num. xx. 24, note.

Ver. 19. *Teach it.*—The command applied to Moses and to Joshua. With the writing of all the preceding as far as ch. xxx., or, what is more likely, of this chap. also, the part of Moses terminated, and Joshua wrote down the rest of this book at Moses' request.

Ver. 22. *This song.*—Because this song, as a witness to future generations, was of great moment, it would seem as though Moses first wrote it out, and then solemnly sang it in the ears of the children of Israel (ch. xxxii. 44),—a precedent for many of the predictions of the prophets, which we must suppose to have been published in the same manner.

Ver. 26. *In the side.*—By the side of the ark. In the ark itself were only the two tables with the ten commandments.

CHAPTER XXXII.

Moses concludes his mission to the ancient covenant-people with two songs, replete with the highest prophetic inspiration. The hymn,—soaring aloft, full of deep views of the future and the present; composed in a curt, compressed, yet highly metaphorical style; pungent, keen, piercing, at the same time abounding in holy earnestness; a witness against the disobedience of the people, a lauding of the God of covenant,—gives us once more a brief sketch of the whole life and doings of the great man of God, who especially had the office assigned him to announce condemnation. After the introduction he begins with the praise of the unalterably holy, faithful God of the covenant (vers. 3, 4), who had shown to His unthankful people such an abundance of blessings (vers. 5–14). In spirit he beholds Israel puffed up with this abundance, become arrogant, disobedient (vers. 16–18). The anger of the Lord is kindled; His judgments overtake them; He turns His covenant of grace to the heathen (vers. 19–35).

But these judgments of the Lord sift His people. Among Israel itself, the people of God are separated from His enemies. His servants, on whom He has mercy, celebrate at last a triumph together with the heathen, and, freed from their oppressors, again rejoice in the favour of God. With this simple line of thought, this song is the foundation of all after-prophecies, in which we find the same range of ideas, because in fact they represent the history of the ancient covenant of God. Although, then, the greater part of the song is a stern threatening, a solemn declaration of condemnation, yet we may understand from the main idea and end of the whole, viz., the glorifying of the grace and truth of the eternal, faithful covenant-God, how these His words could appear in the eyes of Moses under the image, so especially delectable in the wilderness, of a rain trickling down on the tender grass. We here see the man of God with the awful brightness of the Divine holiness on his countenance, in whom the glory of the Lord was mirrored with unveiled face, and who is thereby glorified into the same image (2 Cor. iii. 18). Refreshed and strengthened by His grace, he is still more firmly built upon the rock of his salvation.

Ver. 1. *The words of my mouth.*—As Moses before had called heaven and earth to witness, and as, after him, the other prophets do the same (Isa. i. 3; Jer. xi. 12; Micah vi. 1, 2), so does he begin here, in the consciousness of being enlightened and inspired by God, with the address to all His creatures. It is a moment of great importance to the whole of creation. Heaven and earth shall be witnesses of the guilt of the people, and, when they go wrong, shall be their accusers.

Ver. 2. *Upon the grass.*—This image, in the East especially, includes all that is refreshing and strengthening. The riches and fulness expressed thereby can only be the fulness of victory. In this it is signified, how even the most severe chastisement of the law works life and strength to the true servant of the God of covenant, because he is conscious of the grace of his God, who supports him even in His judgments, and by means of them frees him from his enemies within and without.

Ver. 5. *Of His children.*—Lit.: "He has corrupted (his ways) to Him; they, not His children, their (own) spot of shame, the perverse and deceitful (entwined in themselves) generation." God has revealed His truth and grace to the people; all means of grace and holiness are offered them: if they now perish before Him, that is the fault of their own perverseness. The first word, "perverse," means a wandering from the way; the second, "crafty," means one who, as he cannot go the right way, finds out for himself wrong ways.

Ver. 6. *Established thee*; *i.e.*, "Is He not thy Father, who has prepared thee? is it not He who has made and settled thee?"—established, arranged. The name of father is more fully explained by these three words, "prepared, made, established." The first expresses the general creation; the second, the further bringing up and forming; the third, the maintaining and preserving. The people are here spoken of as a whole. God's name as Father stands here more particularly in the sense of producer, as the epithets show. But even in this degree of the revelation of Himself there is much more contained than in the heathen expression, "Father of gods and men," since the relation to God the Father is altogether a moral relation, and the paternal authority in the Mosaic law derives its sanctity from God. It is the holy, tender Father who pitieth His children, that is here set before the eyes of His people (ver. 11; Ps. ciii. 13).

Ver. 8. *Of the children of Israel.*—The care of God for His people did not begin with Abraham and Jacob, but on the first division of the earth after the flood. Then were the boundaries of the nations placed with reference to the number of Israel,—to the greatness of the people, and its subsequent importance in the history of the world and the kingdom of God. A proof of this care, which began in those early times, and to which the words of Moses point, is Noah's prophecy (Gen. ix. 25), in which Canaan's future subjection, as well as Japhet's dependence on Shem, are predicted. This is the high honour of the election of Israel to be God's people (which is now transferred to the spiritual Israel), that the history of all other nations is viewed in distinct reference to theirs; all exist for the sake of the kingdom of God, as Gen. xii. 3, and Acts xvii. 26, 27 express it.

Ver. 9. *Lot of His inheritance.*—Because the divisions of the earth are marked out as with a line: Ps. xvi. 6, cf. Exod. xix. 5.

Ver. 10. *As the apple of His eye.*—Moses begins the subject of Israel's election and merciful guidance by the hand of the Lord with the finding of the people in the desert. The reason that the wilderness and not the exodus from Egypt is selected as the point from which to commence, is because the former offers a more lively contrast than the latter to the fulness of blessing in the Promised Land, which is afterwards described. Israel, freed from his bondage and become an independent people, begins its course without any help or protection in the wilderness. There the Lord finds it as a wandering sheep in the desert, full of howling wild beasts. He undertakes its guidance, gives it by means of the law a regular constitution, and takes it under His care as the apple of an eye. Cf. Ps. xvii. 8; Zech. xi. 8. This latter expression especially refers to the protection afforded the unwarlike, defenceless people against the Amalekites (Exod. xvii. 8, etc.) and the other inhabitants of the wilderness.

Ver. 12. *No strange god with Him.*—The words of ver. 11 are most correctly regarded as the antecedent member of the sentence, and ver. 12 as the answering portion. The passage is differently interpreted;—most closely thus: "As the eagle warms his nest, broods over his young, spreads out his wings and takes them, bears them up in his soaring; even so the Lord alone, etc." Two different acts of the eagle are described: in the first two sentences, his warming, nourishing, and protecting care, when he spreads his wings over the nest; in the last two, his care when he takes the young abroad, teaches them to fly, and guards them against every mischance. The words, "spreads himself over his young," are the same as those used, Gen. i. 2, of the Spirit of God which brooded over the water. It expresses the communication of life-imparting heat. That the eagle, in case of danger, and when he teaches his young to fly, makes them sit on his back or on his powerful wings, is well-proved, and alluded to also, Exod. xix. 4. The first part of the figure refers to the protection of the still weak, helpless people which was afforded to it by the cloudy pillar, which covered and guided it; the second part, to the awakening and strengthening of the people in the wilderness, until it attained some degree of self-reliance and dependence on God's care amid the dangers and privations of the desert. That "He alone" did it, was meant to remind the unthankful people that God's help had always been found all-sufficient, and every trial of the strange help of self-made gods always fraught with mischief. The Angel who went before them was God Himself: Exod. iii. 2, etc., ch. xix. 18, ch. xx. 2.

Ver. 14. *Blood of the grape.*—The whole description translates us now from the wilderness into the riches of the Promised Land. Moses beholds the future as present—Israel in the fullest enjoyment of good things. "He made him go over the high places of the earth," *i.e.*, take possession of the highest mountain regions of Canaan. "Honey" is the so-called wild honey—a juice which is distilled from many trees (1 Sam. xiv. 26, 27; St Matt. iii. 4). That this should come of itself out of the rocks, oil from the hard stones, shows the fruitfulness of the land which produces trees even on the rocky heights. Cf. the passage taken from this description, Ps. lxxxi. 17. The rest means, literally, "Thick milk from cows (the Orientals do not like butter, and only use it for medicinal purposes); and milk from the sheep, with the fat of lambs and of rams, the children of Basan and of goats, and with the kidney fat of wheat: and thou makest them drink of the blood of grapes as pure wine." In the description of the gifts we must supply, "He gave them," from the preceding verse. Basan is the rich pasture country of the east of Jordan, which had been lately taken from Og the king, and which, because suitable to cattle, had been chosen by the Reubenites, Gadites, and half-tribe of Manasseh (Num. xxxii. 1-4); and even to this day is distinguished by its beautiful wood and rich grass lands." The bold expression, "kidney fat of wheat," represents the peculiar beauty of this grain, since the kidney is regarded as the best fat (Lev. iii. 4, 10). Of course, the eating of the fat is not to be taken literally, as that would contradict Lev. iii. 17, but is to be understood of the eating of fat cattle.

Ver. 15. *Art grown thick.*—With these words Moses again returns more in detail to the rebukes which he had begun, ver. 5. Jeshurun is only a somewhat unusual appellation of the people of Israel from "Jaschar," upright, righteous. As it is said, ver. 4, of God, that He is "Jaschar," righteous, so does the name imply that His people are meant to be as He is. This Balaam, in prophetic spirit, acknowledged them to be (Num. xxiii. 21). Israel is the righteous, holy nation. Moses clearly uses this name here purposely, when the reality stood in such sad contrast with the character of the people. Cf. ch. xxxiii. 5, 26; Isa xliv. 2. Israel's pride in the full enjoyment of the blessings of Canaan, and his apostasy resulting therefrom, are here most graphically described as belonging to the past.

Ver. 16. *To anger.*—The jealousy of Israel's Husband is excited by its adulterous intercourse with strange gods.

Ver. 17. *Unto devils.*—Heb., "to the Schedim;" *i.e.*, the bad spirits (from Schad, Schadad, to waste, destroy). Except here, this name occurs only Ps. cvi. For the word "devils," see Lev. xvii. 7, note. How far idolatry is a service of evil spirits, see 1 Cor. x. 19, 20, note.

Came newly up.—Heb., "which came from near;" *i.e.*, to the worship which they received from the neighbouring nations, the Moabites and Ammonites, afterwards more especially from the Canaanites in Phœnicia.

Ver. 19. *His daughters.*—Heb.: "He was displeased with anger upon His sons and His daughters." Here begins the denunciation of the judgments upon God's disobedient people.

Ver. 20. *No faith.*—Lit.: "Since they are a generation of perversities (a lying, deceitful generation), sons no true (firm, trustworthy) among them."

Ver. 21. *With a foolish nation.*—A very remarkable prediction, the foundation of a number of those which follow. It is here declared that God will cast off Israel after the flesh, and choose in his stead the heathen to be His people, as St Paul, Rom. x. 19, quoting these words, explains them. Israel has provoked the jealousy of God by his adulterous service to other gods: now the offended Husband takes to Himself another wife of less note, and thereby arouses on His part the jealousy of His former wife. These heathen "are not a people;" because only the people under the True, Eternal, Almighty King, are in full sense of the word a people. They are "a foolish nation;" since, while they esteemed themselves wise, they became fools, they have given themselves up to a foolish idolatry, Rom. i. 22, etc. This refers both to the might, the success, and the triumph over Israel which God grants to the heathen, and more particularly to the spreading of the kingdom of God, the contracting of the covenant of grace with the heathen. Cf. the jealousy of the Jews, St Luke xv. 28; Acts xi. 1, etc., ch. xiii. 45.

Ver. 22. *Unto the lowest hell.*—God will bring upon them not only temporary, earthly punishments, but utter destruction.

Ver. 26. *From among men.*—The same threatenings which

had already been uttered by Moses, Lev. xxvi. 14, etc.; Deut. xxvii. 28, 29.

Ver. 27. *Wrath of the enemy.*—The meaning of this passage, in which so strong a human mode of expression is used, is this: The highest object in the guidance of nations is the honour of God. Even in the just punishment of His apostate children, He takes care that the ungodly shall not have occasion to boast of His judgments as though it were their doing. Cf. the similar passages, Exod. xxxii. 12; more particularly Isa. x. 5–19; Ezek. xx. 9, ch. xxxvi. 21, etc.

Ver. 28. *Understanding in them.*—Here the holy singer begins to give the reasons why such judgments befall Israel: because they apostatise to unbelief by reason of self-blinding—because God Himself has given them over—because it is His purpose ever more to sever His true servants from the corrupt people—and because the purpose of all His providences is His own glory and the preservation of His true people. Henceforth it is not God but His prophet who speaks, in the name of the true people of God (see ver. 31). And therefore by this change of person a resting-point occurs here; and so the greater care must be taken not to connect ver. 28 too closely with ver. 27, nor to refer what follows to the heathen, for in that way the whole meaning and object of the song would be missed. The "for" rather connects the verse with the main sentence, ver. 26: therefore must God put out the remembrance of them, because they, through their own sinful self-blinding, will not take counsel.

Ver. 30. *Ten thousand.*—An allusion to the promises given, Lev. xxvi. 7, 8; Deut. xxviii. 7, 25.

Had shut them up.—This had not been possible unless the covenant-God, who is the foundation of their very existence, had sold them as something valueless to Himself, and had delivered them over to the enemy.

Ver. 31. *Being judges.*—This remarkable passage points out the transition from the condition of the old to that of the new covenant. Moses and all true servants of God continued to rest all their hope and confidence on the ancient Rock of their salvation, and left the apostates to choose another rock (ver. 37). Henceforth all the promises of blessing and protection appertain to the spiritual Israel, which has grown up as the genuine fruit from the shell of the old carnal Israel. And even the enemies of the old covenant-people recognise the difference betwixt the superstitious worship of the disobedient ancient people of God, and that of the faithful believing servants of the Lord. This recognition will prove to themselves to be the way to their conversion. This is a sublime view from ancient times into the most distant future of the unsearchable judgments and ways of God.

Ver. 33. *Venom of asps.*—Their richest fruits are poisonous. The comparison with Sodom and Gomorrah is repeated by the prophets: Isa. i. 10, ch. iii. 9; Ezek. xvi. 45, 46; Amos iv. 11.

Ver. 35. *Make haste.*—All these things are long since determined: their coming is certain.

Ver. 36. *Repent Himself.*—Even among His people will He make a great difference. He will never give up His true servants for a prey to the enemy. When the chaff is winnowed from the wheat, the latter shall be brought into a safe place.

Ver. 36. *Shut up or left.*—Heb., "is nothing," is annihilated; spoken proverbially, as 1 Kings xiv. 10, ch. xxi. 21; 2 Kings ix. 8: as well the shut up, defended, as "the undefended, abandoned," or "the bound captive, the unbound free;" *i.e.*, all kinds of men, all degrees and relations, are subject to the general calamity.

Ver. 37. *He shall say.*—Which may mean "it is said," and then would express the scorn of the delivered over those who have fallen under punishment through their trust in idols. But as a little before and afterwards the Lord speaks, it is more obvious to take these words as His, representing to the people how they are brought to shame through their idols.

Ver. 38. *Drink-offerings.*—The false gods enjoyed the savour of their offerings, and drank the wine poured out to them; but now they show themselves so thankless in their weakness that they cannot help their worshippers. A similar mockery on the part of the prophets, or of the Lord Himself, is often to be met with in the O. T.: Judges x. 14; Jer. ii. 28; Isa. xli. 22.

Ver. 39. *Deliver out of My hand.*—This is the solemn confirmation of what precedes. Literally it is, "See now that I, I am it." By this express assurance He arouses the people from their dulness, and declares that all depends on Him. God conceals Himself from the generality behind the dealings of His providence, so much so that they can no longer find Him or see Him.

To these He appeals, that they may understand that He is ever the same, whether He kill or make alive; and then alone does He enjoy His full honour when His presence is recognised in all.

Ver. 42. *Upon the enemy.*—After the actual course of God's judgments have been represented in an historical form, at the end they are confirmed with an oath. The words, ver. 40, "I lift up," are to be taken as an act of God's proceeding through all time, as a prophetic oath which continues until the day of its accomplishment. The words, "If I," are to be taken as the form of the oath; for "as truly as I live I will," etc. Heb.: "I lift up My hand to the heaven, and say, I live for ever. I will whet the lightning of My sword, and will seize My hand for judgment; I will recompense revenge to My enemies, and will pay My haters. I will make My arrows drunk with blood, and My sword shall eat flesh, from the blood of the slain and the captives, from the head of the princes of the enemy." This declaration is in striking contradiction to the idea of the apathy, indifference, and disregard which many ascribe to God, and shows His holy zeal, and the reality of His judgments.

Ver. 43. *Rejoice.*—The words literally are, "Shout for joy, ye nations, His people;" and might mean, "Ye heathen, rejoice with the people of the Lord," or, "Rejoice, ye people, who are now His people." The latter is the more likely meaning, as afterwards "His people" merely are addressed. In any case, it is a call on the people of the Lord who have emerged safely from His judgments to raise their last triumphal song. The Lord turns, as the foregoing shows us, from His ancient people to the heathen. Full of compassion, He draws forth His true servants from the mass of His fallen, chastised people, and shows Himself even by these judgments as the true God. By these means the reception of the heathen among His people is prepared. At the conclusion of the song the object of all the dealings of God is shown—the final preservation of the true Israel and of the heathen nations from the destruction of the world.

To His people.—Heb., "and reconcile or atone for His land, His people"—even by the vengeance on His enemies. The sins of His people and of the land have hitherto called down vengeance; now the Divine judgments have overcome the opposition which these unremitted sins raised against the holiness and righteousness of God. Now all transgression is covered, and the

Lord can again turn His full grace to the people. Thus the prophetic witness, which embraces the whole future of the kingdom of God, concludes with the glorification of His deeds in the judgment and redemption, by which are declared those Divine attributes spoken of at the beginning, ver. 4.

Ver. 44. *Son of Nun.*—As Aaron had been before, so was Joshua now, the prophet of the aged man of God—of the man " slow of speech, of a slow tongue." See Exod. iv. 10, 16.

Ver. 47. *Prolong your days.*—The same promise which occurs in the case of many commandments, as Exod. xx. 12. It is the Old Testament form of all promises of blessing, the typical shadowing forth of the promise of eternal life.

Ver. 49. *Against Jericho.*—Cf. Num. xxii. 1, note.

Ver. 52. *Before thee;* i.e., opposite to thee.

CHAPTER XXXIII.

As Moses has received notice of his approaching death, and is about, in compliance with the command of the Lord, to ascend the hill on which he is to die, he once more pronounces a blessing upon the tribes, just as Jacob, before his death, assembled his twelve sons round his bed. The blessing of Moses stands in close connection with Jacob's, partly supplying and softening, partly repeating and enlarging it. It is especially worthy of remark for the understanding of the chapter, how Moses proceeds from the present time, how the immediate view of what either has happened or should happen forms the main foundation from which the promises soar upwards. We may well suppose that this blessing was uttered in a similar way with the song. After the severe witness borne against the sins of the people, this blessing has something soothing about it. Here the revelation of God on Sinai appears majestic indeed, but bringing salvation, and Israel is invited to communion with Him by the most glorious promises of blessing. In the predictions to the different tribes there is nothing threatening. They, as well as the whole people, appear as what they can and ought to be according to God's purpose. The people is assembled before the ark of the covenant. Joshua stood by the side of the stammering man of God as his mouthpiece, and spake loud and distinctly the words of Moses in the presence of all, being himself a participator in the prophetic inspiration. The blessing opens, like the song, with an introduction. Before pronouncing the blessings on the individual tribes, Moses mentions the great and abiding privilege and advantage belonging to them all—the law which the Lord had given them with mighty signs. In a similar tone, the blessing concludes (ver. 26) with the promise of salvation to the whole people.

Ver. 2. *With ten thousands of saints.*—Heb., "and is come out of the innumerable saints;" lit., "the thousands (myriads) of holiness." The lawgiving on Sinai appears under the figure of a rising of the sun. From the east, out of Seir, over the mountains of Paran, from the Promised Land, comes the Lord like the sun. He comes forth from the assembly of His many thousand saints, the angels, to give Israel its law. The Jews of old understood these words as though the angels did not remain behind in heaven, but were really present in all the wonders which accompanied the giving of the law—the thunderings, and smoke, and earthquake. Out of the midst of this His heavenly host, assembled around Him, came forth the Lord as Lawgiver. And with this agrees the representation given by the apostle, that "the law was given by the disposition of angels" (Acts vii. 53; Gal. iii. 19; Heb. ii. 2);—an explanation which at all events is agreeable to the passage before us, and gains force by the probable explanation of what follows, though it is not necessarily drawn from it.

A fiery law for them.—So, as it stands in the text, many old interpreters explain it; though to be preferred is the version, "To His right hand fire is hurled at them"—fearful lightnings, to inspire them (the Israelites) with terror. Here, as already in what precedes, the prophet beholds the scene as present in such sort that he says "them" of the people, without having before named them.

Ver. 3. *He loved the people.*—Lit., "the nations;" *i.e.*, in this place, the assembled tribes of Israel, which is explained by "*all His saints.*" It was important to declare first the general love of the Lord to all His people, as there is an apparent preference of one tribe to another in the blessing which follows.

Are in Thy hand.—The frequent change of person, and immediately afterwards of number, is very remarkable in prophetic language. Moses has just spoken of the Lord: in the midst of the sentence, "*His* saints," he turns round and addresses the Lord, "are in *Thy* hand." This mode of speaking of holy inspiration supplies a pliable instrument for expressing every emotion and feeling.

Of Thy words.—In all this the graphic image of the lawgiving on Mount Sinai, begun at ver. 2, is continued. Even in the fearful apparition of His majesty was the giving of the law a revelation of His love. He embraced all tribes of the people,—all whom He had sanctified He covered amid the signs and wonders with the protection of His hand, and placed them in quiet at His feet to learn from Him.

Ver. 5. *Were gathered together.*—Suddenly the address changes into that of the people who hear and learn. As a narrative, it would be remarkable that Moses should speak thus in his own blessing. But it is altogether in agreement with the spirit of prophetic language, which delights in sudden, rapid transitions, thus to put itself in the position of the people receiving the law; somewhat as if it were said, "Then Moses gave us the law (in Thy name), the inheritance of the congregation of Jacob." The law is also called "my heritage" in Ps. cxix. 111. Immediately upon this, God is spoken of in the third person: literally, "And He was King in Jeshurun, when the heads of the people were assembled, the tribes of Israel with one another." It is very significant that the people here bears the name "Jeshurun." cf. ch. xxxii. 15, note. The King here is God, in whose name Moses gave the law. The day when the Lord, by the solemn giving of the law, formed the tribes of Israel to be His people, was the moment of His assuming His kingly office.

Ver. 6. *Reuben live.*—Lit.: "Let Reuben live, and not die; he and his people be a number,"—*i.e.*, this tribe shall not perish: those of his tribe shall not be able to be counted, *i.e.*, shall be not a few. In the blessing of Jacob, Reuben is deprived of the dignity of his being the first-born. Here continuance and numbers are promised him, to his comfort. This tribe extended a long way in the south of the eastern side of Jordan, as far as the mouths of the Euphrates.—Simeon is not here mentioned (cf. Gen. xlix. 5). The tribe was not to have any independence, but to dwell scattered among the others. But the curse is not here repeated, but rather softened by his being passed over in silence.

Ver. 7. *Bring him unto his people.*—Judah was the leading tribe, out of which the kings were ordained to proceed (Gen. xlix. 8, etc.; Num. ii. 3; Judges i. 2). Moses in spirit sees him march before the other tribes to the holy war, and prays the Lord to grant him victory, and a happy return to his people.

From his enemies.—Lit.: "His hands fight for him, and Thou wilt be a help from his enemies." It is the most warlike tribe, to which the Lord grants victorious strength and defence in its time of trial.

Ver. 10. *Upon Thine altar.*—The blessing upon Levi removes the curse which Jacob had uttered concerning him, Gen. xlix. 7; and, indeed, everything here is viewed as centering in the priesthood and its head, Aaron. The language here is very bold and powerful. The address is to Jehovah, and therefore the words "of Levi" are to be taken in a wider sense, "in respect of Levi." Literally: "Thy right and thy light (the highest marks of the priesthood, the pledges of blessing [Exod. xxviii. 30]) to thy pious one (to him dedicated to Thee in holiness), whom Thou hast tried at Massa, with whom Thou didst strive at Meribah." Moses prays that the Lord would support the high-priestly dignity with the pledge of Divine illumination to the tribe, and therefore to the people. This dignity appears to him as embodied in the person of Aaron. He speaks of the dangerous time which befell to him in the temptation at Massa and Meribah (Exod. xvii. 7), and he calls this a trial of Aaron by God, a proof to which the Lord put him. The mention of it, therefore, on this occasion will mean—"Acknowledge as Thine own, still further, and continually, the consecrated person whom Thou hast proved by so severe temptations."—The address still continues to refer to Aaron, and is literally, "Who (namely, the man consecrated to Thee [ver. 8]) speaks to his father and his mother, I see him not! and beholds not his brother, and knows not his son." Aaron, and in him the priesthood, appears here as the representative of the whole tribe of Levi, since to it is ascribed what the Levites did in the case of the people's apostasy to idolatry (Exod. xxxii. 26–28), when they themselves spared not their nearest kinsmen, when they were taken in the act of idolatry. This is the denying of father and mother, brother and sister, which the Lord requires of His disciples (St Matt. x. 37).—The sacred writer proceeds to speak of the priesthood in general, and thereby explains the preceding. "Since they hold Thy words, and keep Thy covenant, they teach Jacob Thy precepts, and Israel Thy laws: they put incense before Thee, and whole sacrifices on Thy altar." They spread the knowledge of Thy will, and reconcile Thy people to Thee. The sense of the whole is, "Preserve to Levi the pledge of Thy revelation and guidance, since this tribe keeps Thy word, spreads the knowledge of Thee abroad, and preserves Thy favour to Thy people."

Ver. 11. *Rise not again.*—A notification (many similar ones are given, especially in this book [ch. xiv. 27, 29, ch. xvi. 11, 14, ch. xxvi. 12]) that the Levites would often have much difficulty with this perverse and capricious people, who in the times of their apostasy refused the Levites their due.

Ver. 12. *Shall dwell in safety.*—Lit.: "The beloved of the Lord shall dwell safely on Him,"—*i.e.*, on the Lord, as the rock on which he is built. The most beloved son of Jacob will stand in closest communion with the Lord, on whom his own being rests.

Between His shoulders.—"He (the Lord) holds over him (covers him) the whole day, and he dwells between His shoulders." He defends him, and dwells near him. The shoulders are the mountain heights of his country. The temple was in aftertimes built on Moria, the higher peaks of Sion, and the Mount of Olives, in the tribe of Benjamin. The brief expressions of Jacob (Gen. xlix. 27) concerning Benjamin, which promised no peculiar blessings, are here supplied.

Ver. 16. *Separated from his brethren.*—A repetition and more extended description of the blessing of Jacob on Joseph (Gen. xlix. 22), from whom not only two tribes were derived, but those more particularly powerful and extensive, and dwelling in the most fruitful parts of Canaan. This passage literally is thus: "Blessed from the Lord is his land"—now follow the particular parts of this blessing—"with the most precious things of heaven, with the dew and with the deep which lies beneath (*i.e.*, the waters under the earth from which the springs flow), and with the most precious things of the productions of the sun, and the most precious of the fruits of the moon (the fruits which every month brings forth), and with the top of the mountains of ancient times, and with the precious things of the everlasting hills, and with the precious things of the earth and its fulness; and the goodwill of Him who dwells in the bush, let it come on the head of Joseph, and the shoulders of the Nasir of his brethren."

Ver. 17. *Thousands of Manasseh.*—" The glory of a first-born bull (strength, power) is to him, and buffalo-horns are his horns: with them he strikes the people together even to the end of the land."—As before the whole tribe of Levi had been represented by Aaron, so here the whole tribe of Joseph by Joshua the Ephraimite, the conqueror of the Promised Land, who is without doubt the main subject of this promise.

Ver. 18. *In thy tents.*—A short forcible reiteration of the promises of Jacob made to the tribes delighting in trade and in agriculture (Gen. xlix. 13-15).

Ver. 19. *Treasures hid in the sand.*—Here is depicted the wealth which these tribes shall obtain by trading. The most costly sacrifices for the holy mountain will proceed from this tribe: the people, *i.e.*, the tribes of Israel, will take care to provide them, and so serve God acceptably. Perhaps there is an intimation that great riches flowed to Jerusalem from the Israelites dispersed in neighbouring countries, and that also, in spiritual things, through them the good things of other people were imparted to Israel.

Ver. 20. *Enlargeth Gad.*—Gives him the beautiful land of Gilead for a possession. Crown of the head and the arm, as the chief parts, signify the might of his conquests.

Ver. 21. *His judgments with Israel.*—Heb.: " And he provided for him the first-fruits, since there is the inheritance of the hidden Lawgiver: and he came to the heads of the people; he executes the righteousness of the Lord and His judgments with Israel." Gad, with the tribe and a half, chose for himself first the beautiful land on the other side Jordan, which was distinguished as the portion of the master or lawgiver in Israel, Moses, who was there buried in profound secrecy. This circumstance, which could not enter into the mind of Gad when it requested that land, Moses now includes in the blessing, as though an especial mark of God's goodwill towards the tribe. At the conclusion Gad's open way of treating with the chiefs for the land, and his honourable keeping of his word to help Israel in the conquest of Canaan, are brought forward.

Ver. 22. *Leap from Basan.*—Like a bold and wild lion springing forth from the land of Basan, with its woods and rich meadows, shall this tribe go forth to its valiant exploits.

Ver. 23. *The west and the south.*—These obscure words are explained by some to mean, that Naphthali dwelt in the south and west of the new settlements which Dan conquered in the time of the Judges in the north of Canaan (Judges xviii.); by others, that the land of the Philistines in the south-west of Palestine was intended for this tribe, which, however, was never conquered: Joshua xiii. 3.

Ver. 24. *Dip his foot in oil.*—Be rich in posterity and possessions: cf. Gen. xlix. 20.

Ver. 25. *So shall thy strength be.*—Heb.: "Iron and brass be thy bars, and as thy days so be thy rest." Outward security and enduring rest are promised to this tribe.

Ver. 26. *On the sky.*—With these concluding words, Moses again turns to the whole people. Lit.: "There is none like God, O Jeshurun (see ver. 5), who rideth through the heavens to thy help, and in His majesty through the clouds."

Ver. 27. *Everlasting arms.*—The first words remind us of the beginning of Psalm xc. The "ancient God" is He who is from everlasting, always the same; the eternal arms are they which are never weary of holding and supporting.

Ver. 28. *Corn and wine.*—Heb.: "Israel shall dwell securely, the fountain of Jacob, in the land of corn and new wine." The fountain of Jacob is the inexhaustible stream of the people which flows from him—an epithet full of promise to Israel.

Drop down dew.—Not needing perpetual irrigation like Egypt: ch. xi. 10.

Ver. 29. *Saved by the Lord.*—To whom the Lord is a continual helper and defender.

Thy excellency.—Properly, "thy exaltation," thy fame, thy triumph. He, as thy sword, continually gains for thee new triumphs.

Found liars.—Will cringe before thee out of fear, as Ps. xviii. 45, lxvi. 3, lxxxi. 16.

High places.—"Thou wilt take in possession and tread down even their highest mountains." With this promise of the unparalleled friendship, the continual shelter, the unceasing stream of wealth, the defence of God, the final triumph over all enemies, does Moses conclude his blessing. This blessing will only be rightly understood by connecting it with the foregoing prophetic song; and we draw the conclusion, that the people of Israel, which has these eternal promises, is the new covenant-people which comes forth from the old.

CHAPTER XXXIV.

It has been already remarked that this chapter, together with the song and blessing, as the book itself clearly intimates, was added to the rest, most probably by Joshua in his old age. Moses took his last farewell of him, communicated to him God's call to him to die, and the promise of his burial. From this communication is the narrative before us drawn.

Ver. 1. *Against Jericho.*—It has been already remarked, Num. xxi., that the mountain district of Jericho has not been investigated in modern times. We only know this one thing, that the heights there are very considerable, and afford a wide prospect on every side. But at the same time we must suppose a supernatural extension of vision, so that a view is laid before him, in which the natural eyesight is assisted by something beyond nature.

Unto Dan.—Cf. Gen. xiv. 14, note.

Ver. 3. *Unto Zoar.*—All the places here bear the names which they had after the division by Joshua, and not without a significance, because with this destination they had already been shown to Moses.

Ver. 5. *Word of the Lord.*—Lit.: "On the mouth of the Lord," which word often means the same as "at His command:" Gen. xlv. 21. The Rabbins pretend from this that he died by a kiss of the Lord, and this was the easiest kind of death.

Ver. 6. *Unto this day.*—Although Moses really died, and, indeed—as he might have lived still longer (ver. 7)—underwent death as a punishment, for a memorable example of the holy severity of God against sin even in His faithful servant,—still was he after his death to be held in especial honour, as no other man has been honoured. Moses' death was similar to Aaron's (Num. xx. 23), but distinguished by the mysterious burial, the mark of the all-forgiving grace of God towards His severely chastised servant;—hence the narrative Jude 9. The ancient Christians saw in this burial a representation of the burial of the law through Christ, and of the utter absence of all signs of its working. As a distinguishing memorial of this last crowning act of God, the grave of Moses could nowhere be found—perhaps also to prevent any superstitious honour being paid to it.

Ver. 8. *Were ended.*—Cf. Num. xx. 29.

Ver. 12. *In the sight of all Israel.*—These words might well be annexed to this book by Joshua at the conclusion of his own life, in which he at the same time confessed his own inferiority to Moses. Moses was the greatest servant of the Lord in the O. T., both in respect to his nearer intercourse with the Lord, to his clear and comprehensive revelation, and the greatness of the acts performed by him. The Founder of the new and eternal covenant (of whom Moses was a type) is alone worthy of greater honour than he: Heb. iii. 3.

THE END.

BIBLIOLIFE

Old Books Deserve a New Life
www.bibliolife.com

Did you know that you can get most of our titles in our trademark **EasyScript**™ print format? **EasyScript**™ provides readers with a larger than average typeface, for a reading experience that's easier on the eyes.

Did you know that we have an ever-growing collection of books in many languages?

Order online:
www.bibliolife.com/store

Or to exclusively browse our **EasyScript**™ collection:
www.bibliogrande.com

At BiblioLife, we aim to make knowledge more accessible by making thousands of titles available to you – quickly and affordably.

Contact us:
BiblioLife
PO Box 21206
Charleston, SC 29413

Printed in Great Britain
by Amazon